The Company We Keep

Wayne C. Booth

The Company We Keep
An Ethics of Fiction

UNIVERSITY
OF
CALIFORNIA
PRESS

Berkeley
Los Angeles
London

University of California Press
Berkeley and Los Angeles, California

University of California Press, Ltd.
London, England

© 1988 by
The Regents of the University of California

Library of Congress Cataloging-in-Publication Data

Booth, Wayne C.
   The company we keep: an ethics of fiction / Wayne C. Booth.
      p.   cm.
   Bibliography: p.
   Includes index.
   ISBN 0-520-06203-5 (alk. paper). ISBN 0-520-06210-8 (pbk.)
   1. Criticism—Moral and ethical aspects. 2. Literary ethics.
I. Title.
PN98.M67B66 1988
174'.98—dc19   87-24610
                                     CIP

Printed in the United States of America
1 2 3 4 5 6 7 8 9

Thanks are due to the following publishers for permission to
quote from copyrighted works: selections from "After Long
Silence," "The Choice," and "The Tower" reprinted from *The
Collected Poems of W. B. Yeats* by permission of A. P. Watt Ltd.
on behalf of Michael B. Yeats and Macmillan London Ltd.;
"The House Was Quiet and the World Was Calm," © 1947
by Wallace Stevens, reprinted from *The Collected Poems of
Wallace Stevens* by permission of Alfred A. Knopf, Inc.; "Subject for 'After Long Silence'" from Richard Ellmann's *The Identity of Yeats,* reprinted by permission of A. P. Watt Ltd. on
behalf of Michael Yeats and Anne Yeats; and a revised version
of "'The Way I Loved George Eliot': Friendship with Books as a
Neglected Critical Metaphor," by Wayne C. Booth, originally
published in *The Kenyon Review* 2, no. 2 (Spring 1980): 4–27,
used by permission of *The Kenyon Review;* "ygUDuh" from
Complete Poems of E. E. Cummings, by permission of Har-
court Brace Jovanovich, Inc., and Grafton Books, Ltd.

For
Paul Moses
1929–1966

Teacher and Critic
The University of Chicago
1962–1966

THE HOUSE WAS QUIET AND THE WORLD WAS CALM

The house was quiet and the world was calm.
The reader became the book; and summer night

Was like the conscious being of the book.
The house was quiet and the world was calm.

The words were spoken as if there was no book,
Except that the reader leaned above the page,

Wanted to lean, wanted much most to be
The scholar to whom his book is true, to whom

The summer night is like a perfection of thought.
The house was quiet because it had to be.

The quiet was part of the meaning, part of the mind:
The access of perfection to the page.

And the world was calm. The truth in a calm world,
In which there is no other meaning, itself

Is calm, itself is summer and night, itself
Is the reader leaning late and reading there.

Wallace Stevens

God made man because he loves stories.

Elie Wiesel

How shall we know all the friends whom we meet on
   strange roadways.

Ezra Pound, "Cathay"

Contents

Preface

This book began as a lecture at Hamilton College, sometime in the mid-1970s, on the topic "Can Art Be Bad for You?" It then grew to three Beckman Lectures at the University of California, Berkeley, in 1979, on "The Ethics of Fictions"—the emphasis already less on why some works of "high art" might be dangerous and more on the problem of how we are to *talk* about such matters. The work that now emerges from nine years of expansion and revision might better be called something like "A Conversation Celebrating the Many Ways in Which Narratives Can Be Good for You—with Side-Glances at How to Avoid Their Powers for Harm."

It is a tough topic for many reasons. For one thing, everyone has an opinion about how art and ethics—specifically narrative art and the ethics of reading and listening—should be joined or separated. The subject itself has thus seemed to demand that I address both the ever-expanding community of professional critics and the seemingly-shrinking community of general readers—those whose lives are flooded with narratives that raise ethical issues. For the former, I may seem to spend too much time grappling with cultural ephemera: What are *Jaws* and *Mad Max* doing here? General readers may be troubled in two contrasting ways: on the one hand, some who are shocked by the obvious immorality of much current narrative may wonder why I worry about basic principles of fire fighting when I should be joining a fire brigade; on the other hand, many may wish that the questions I pose could just be ignored. Why not just follow one's pleasures and savor the riches that the world of narrative provides?

Even when I began, I knew better than to hope for arguments that would both persuade the professional critics to abandon their theoretical neutrality and spur the general reader to view ethical judgments of narrative not only as highly important but as more complicated than they appear to be in most accounts. But I did hope for somewhat less complexity than I've discovered in taking seriously what conflicting powerful voices tell us about the ethics of narrative. The book now aims, first, to restore the full intellectual legitimacy of our common-sense inclination to talk about stories in ethical terms, treating the characters in them and their makers as more like people than laby-rinths, enigmas, or textual puzzles to be deciphered; and, second, it aims to "relocate" ethical criticism, turning it from flat judgment for or against supposedly stable works to fluid conversation about the qualities of the company we keep—and the company that we ourselves provide.

Despite the strong theoretical thrust in some sections, the conversa-tions are inevitably embedded in occasions. The original time of writing and the circumstances mentioned or implied range from classes taught some years before the Beckman Lectures to recent encounters on the street. One reader has advised me to disguise this temporal sprawl by removing all dated references and personal anecdotes, writing as if the book, like this paragraph, were all written in the winter of 1988—or perhaps sometime around 2050. But I have chosen instead to date a fair number of the experiences and judgments, because the ethical criticism I work toward here is always embedded in the lives of par-ticular persons at particular moments. As Iris Murdoch says of moral philosophies, an ethics of criticism "should be inhabited." [1] To have expunged the encounters with students and other friends would no doubt have made a purer book, one that created its own specious present. It would have been misleading, however, about the way in which I believe ethical criticism should be conducted in the world—not by a laying down of ethical axioms and a timeless deduction of consequences, but by a "coduction" (see Chapter 3) that tests our ac-tual responses in conversation, including the kind of simulated conver-sation that I attempt here.

That kind of conversation cannot be conducted without offering ex-amples, yet examples always threaten to mislead. I can hear readers saying, "How can his relocation and defense of ethical criticism be sound, when he is so misguided as to admire Doe or condemn Roe?" My subject in principle can apply to every narrative. Once into it, I

1. *The Sovereignty of Good* (London, 1970), p. 47.

found that almost every voice I heard seemed to demand entry, either as exemplary narrative or exemplary comment about narrative. I can only hope that when readers disagree with my judgments, they will find that in their very way of disagreeing they exemplify the validity and importance of ethical criticism and of hard thought about how to do it well. The proof that we are doing it well does not rest on our arriving at judgments demonstrable to and accepted by all observers. (I address the skeptic's "argument from variability" in some detail in Chapters 2 and 4.)

Writing and speaking on such a broad subject over many years, I have no doubt become indebted to more story-lovers than I can now even remember, let alone list. But I especially want to thank the many critics at Berkeley and other campuses (including the professor whose only response was to correct my pronunciation of "Sligo") and my colleagues and students at The University of Chicago. For more than two decades, they have been teaching me, with their own essays, books, and conversation, just how difficult and rewarding ethical criticism can be: Frederick Antczak, Gary Comstock, Rufus Cook, Richard Duerden, John Dzieglewitz, Robert Garlitz, Robert Inchausti, Walter Jost, Jay Kastely, George Meese, William Monroe, Wendy Olmsted, Anne Patrick, James Phelan, James Redfield, Meri-Jane Rochelson, Jay Schleusener, David Smigelskis, Richard Strier, Charles Wegener, James Boyd White, and many others. Paul Moses and Charles Long showed me how much I did not know about my beloved *Huckleberry Finn*. For the priceless additional help of detailed reading of various drafts, I thank David Bevington, Gerald Graff, Marshall Gregory, Laurence Lerner, Gary Saul Morson, and Peter Rabinowitz. Barbara Knecht, Adriane LaPointe, and Stephanie Stamm served as patient and perceptive editorial assistants through the final revisions. Toward the end I have been blessed—no other word will do—with the copy-editing of Mary Caraway. Informed about the issues, infinitely patient with my innumerable oversights, she has been not so much a copy-editor as the *editor* every author longs for: she took on the project as if it were her own.

My deepest gratitude is, as always, to Phyllis Booth. Over forty years of marriage, we have discussed several thousand (count 'em) short stories, poems, novels, movies, operas, and plays, not to mention

the dreams recounted and discussed at breakfast and the day's events
gossiped about over dinner. Her ethical criticism of my over-confident
judgments pervades every chapter. To her and to our two daughters,
Alison Booth and Katherine Booth Stevens, I owe whatever validity
there may be in my effort (in Chapters 12 and 13) to correct my "natural" male biases.

A version of Chapters 6 and 7 was published in the *Kenyon Review*
(1980); versions of parts of Chapters 10 through 13 were published in
Critical Inquiry (1978, 1982). A part of Chapter 13 appeared in *Persuasions* (1983), and Chapter 8 reprints a revised section of "Renewing the Medium of Renewal: Some Notes on the Anxieties of Innovation," in *Innovation/Renovation: New Perspectives on the Humanities,* ed. Ihab Hassan and Sally Hassan (Wisconsin, 1983). Finally, I
want to thank The Rockefeller Foundation for the Humanities Fellowship and The University of Chicago for the research grants that enabled me to complete the book "only" nine years after its formal
beginning. No doubt its real beginning could be found in the tales told
to me in early childhood—by parents, aunts and uncles, grandparents,
even great-grandparents—and in the wonderfully unself-conscious
talk about those tales that often followed the telling.

PART I

Poetry is capable of saving us.
I. A. Richards

It is a deadly error to expect poetry to provide the supersubstantial nourishment of men.
Jacques Maritain

To the aesthetic temperament nothing seems ugly. There are degrees of beauty—that is all.
Max Beerbohm

Beethoven's Fourth Symphony nourishes the soul.
Igor Stravinsky

A book [of prose fiction] at the time [it is written] is a good or bad action.
Jean-Paul Sartre

RELOCATING ETHICAL CRITICISM

One ought to be able to hold in one's head simultaneously the two facts that Dali is a good draughtsman and a disgusting human being. . . . The first thing we demand of a wall is that it shall stand up. If it stands up, it is a good wall, and the question of what purpose it serves is separable from that. And yet even the best wall in the world deserves to be pulled down if it surrounds a concentration camp.

George Orwell

"What takes place" in a narrative is from the referential (reality) point of view literally *nothing*; "what happens" is language alone, the adventure of language, the unceasing celebration of its coming.

Roland Barthes

Literary criticism should be completed by criticism from a definite ethical and theological standpoint. . . . The "greatness" of literature cannot be determined solely by literary standards; though we must remember that whether it is literature or not can be determined only by literary standards.

T. S. Eliot

A work of art is . . . a bridge, however tenuous, between one mind and another.

Andrew Harrison

[Art] is civilization's single most significant device for learning what must be affirmed and what must be denied.

John Gardner

1

Introduction

Ethical Criticism, a Banned Discipline?

Twenty-five years ago at The University of Chicago, a minor scandal shocked the members of the humanities teaching staff as they discussed the texts to be assigned to the next batch of entering students. *Huckleberry Finn* had been on the list for many years, and the general assumption was that it would be on the list once again. But suddenly the one black member of the staff, Paul Moses, an assistant professor of art, committed what in that context seemed an outrage: an overt, serious, uncompromising act of ethical criticism. As his story was reported in corridors and over coffee in the lounges it went something like this:

> It's hard for me to say this, but I have to say it anyway. I simply can't teach *Huckleberry Finn* again. The way Mark Twain portrays Jim is so offensive to me that I get angry in class, and I can't get all those liberal white kids to understand why I am angry. What's more, I don't think it's right to subject students, black or white, to the many distorted views of race on which that book is based. No, it's not the word "nigger" I'm objecting to, it's the whole range of assumptions about slavery and its consequences, and about how whites should deal with liberated slaves, and how liberated slaves should behave or will behave toward whites, good ones and bad ones. That book is just bad education, and the fact that it's so cleverly written makes it even more troublesome to me.

All of his colleagues were offended: obviously Moses was violating academic norms of objectivity. For many of us, this was the first experience with anyone inside the academy who considered a literary work so dangerous that it should not be assigned to students. We had assumed that only "outsiders"—those enemies of culture, the censors—talked that way about art. I can remember lamenting the shoddy education that had left poor Paul Moses unable to recognize a great classic when he met one. Had he not even noticed that Jim is of all the characters closest to the moral center? Moses obviously could neither read properly nor think properly about what questions might be relevant to judging a novel's worth.

3

The Company We Keep can perhaps best be described as an effort to discover why that still widespread response to Paul Moses's sort of complaint will not do. Though I would of course resist anyone who tried to ban the book from *my* classroom, I shall argue here that Paul Moses's reading of *Huckleberry Finn,* an overt ethical appraisal, is one legitimate form of literary criticism. Such appraisals are always difficult and always controversial; those modern critics who banned them, at least in theory, from the house of criticism had good reason to fear what they too often spawn when practiced by zealots. Anyone who attempts to invite ethical criticism back into the front parlor, to join more fashionable, less threatening varieties, must know from the beginning that no simple, definitive conclusions lie ahead. I shall not, in my final chapter, arrive at a comfortable double column headed "Ethically Good" and "Ethically Bad." But if the powerful stories we tell each other really matter to us—and even the most skeptical theorists imply by their *practice* that stories do matter—then a criticism that takes their "mattering" seriously cannot be ignored.

Our lengthy, heated, and confused debates with Paul Moses never, as I recall, honored his claim that teachers should concern themselves with what a novel might *do* to a student. Though as good liberals the staff members of the course granted him his request to substitute another novel in his own section, we all went on believing that he was wrong. We had been trained to treat a "poem *as* poem and not another thing" and to believe that the value of a great work of fiction was something much subtler than any idea or proposition derived from it or used to paraphrase its "meaning." We knew that sophisticated critics never judge a fiction by any effect it might have on readers. "Poetry," we were fond of quoting to each other, "makes nothing happen," and we included under "poetry" all prose works that qualified as "genuine literature." To have attended to Paul Moses's complaint would have been to commit—in the jargon of the time—the "affective fallacy."

Paradoxically, none of this interfered with our shared conviction that *good literature in general* was somehow as vital to the lives of our students as it was to us. To turn them into "readers," and to get them to read the good stuff was our mission. "Trash," "kitsch," "time killers," "popular fictions"—these were another matter entirely; one might even on occasion pass a *moral* judgment on stories of these base kinds, though generally one would, like Edmund Wilson in his attack on detective stories, make one's judgment sound as purely "artistic" as possible (1944, 1945).

After the debate cooled, I suspect that most of my colleagues did what I did; we not only went on believing that *Huckleberry Finn* is a great work (Chapter 13 below will reveal that I still see it as superb), but we continued to resist discussion, in class or in print, of the twin questions that seemed to us blatantly *non*-literary: Is this "poem" morally, politically, or philosophically sound? and, Is it likely to work for good or ill in those who read it? If we knew of critics who questioned our happy abstract formalism—Yvor Winters, F. R. Leavis, the Marxists—we considered them dogmatic mavericks, either the last remnants of a moralistic, pre-aesthetic past or the would-be forerunners of a totalitarian revolution.

Many critics today still resist any effort to tie "art" to "life," the "aesthetic" to the "practical." Indeed, when I began this project I thought that ethical criticism was as unfashionable as most current theories would lead one to expect. When I first read, three or four years along in my drafting, Fredric Jameson's claim in *The Political Unconscious* that the predominant mode of criticism in our time is the ethical (1981, 59), I thought he was just plain wrong. But as I have looked further, I have had to conclude that he is quite right. I'm thinking here not only of the various new overtly ethical and political challenges to "formalism": by feminist critics asking embarrassing questions about a male-dominated literary canon and what it has done to the "consciousness" of both men and women; by black critics pursuing Paul Moses's kind of question about racism in American classics; by neo-Marxists exploring class biases in European literary traditions; by religious critics attacking modern literature for its "nihilism" or "atheism." I am thinking more of the way in which even those critics who work hard to purge themselves of all but the most abstract formal interests turn out to have an ethical program in mind—a belief that a given way of reading, or a given kind of genuine literature, is what will do us most good.

The practice of ethical criticism may be as clumsy as that of the old-style moralists and censors who would ban Kurt Vonnegut because of the word "fuck," or the movie version of *The Color Purple* because it paints an "unfair" picture of the violence of black males. It may be as

highly sophisticated, oblique, and seemingly unconcerned with traditional moral interests as Frank Kermode's complaint that a book "exhibits the same sort of crafted mendacity" that is shown in the blurb
on its jacket: the author is too "knowing," and "there are things one
ought to know about without being knowing about" (1981, 17). The
practice may confirm my own opinions about an author's viciousness,
as when Susan Suleiman, writing of the anti-Semitic work of Drieu La
Rochelle, concludes that its ideology is a blot on its art (1976; 1983,
190–93). Or it may challenge them, as when Chinua Achebe concludes that Conrad's *Lord Jim* is racist (1975), or Michael Sprinker
concludes that the same work is a defense of bourgeois capitalism
(1988). The practice may inadvertently be a bit comic, as when James
Watt declares that the Beach Boys play an immoral music that will attract "the wrong element" to the White House Fourth of July celebration; or it may be illuminating and deeply moving, as when Bruno
Bettelheim argues that Lina Wertmüller's use of the Holocaust in her
movie *Seven Beauties* is corrupt and potentially corrupting (1979,
274–314). But no one seems to resist ethical criticism for long.

Whenever any human practice refuses to die, in spite of centuries of
assault from theory, there must be something wrong with the theory.
At the School of Criticism in 1979 (held that summer at the University
of California, Irvine), a young teacher told us that he felt an irreconcilable gap between the critical theories he had been taught and his
absolute need to protest the stereotypes of "the Chicano" that he met
in much modern American fiction. In theory, he had been insistently
told, his political beliefs and his gut reactions should be irrelevant to
what he says about a novel. In practice, he refused to be silent about
such matters. "But," he concluded, "I feel guilty about it, and I'm always afraid that my mentors will want to throw me out of the profession if I talk about what matters most to me."

I've had similar conversations with feminist and black scholars who
have wondered whether, in order to say what they want to say about
works they "personally" admire or detest, they must either renounce
literary theory or induce the academy to legitimate a "fusion of theory
and praxis." The criticism of the best new Marxists is indeed one good
way to address the problems I am raising (Williams 1977; Jameson
1981; Eagleton 1976). But I hope before we are done here to have
shown that there are many legitimate paths open to anyone who de-

cides to abandon, at least for a time, the notion that an interest in form precludes an interest in the ethical powers of form.

Such a project need not lead to a flat rejection of the insights characteristic of either "side" in the prolonged war between the formalists/aestheticians and the critics who appraise art's social function. Nor need we choose sides in the recent redrawing of battle lines between deconstructionists (as "formalists" who seem to argue that literary works, nothing more than texts or systems of signs, refer to no "reality" other than themselves and other texts) and ardent defenders of a vital connection between literary experience and the lives of readers (e.g., Graff 1979, 1987; Goodheart 1984; Fischer 1985).[1] The exaggerations of the more extreme moralists,[2] like the "totalizing" claims of some post-structuralists, might drive one to seek some other line of honest work. But before retreating from the field, we might try to discover new locations for our debates. After all, life itself is what produces and enjoys art—and is in turn blessed or blasted by it. Defenders of ethical and other ideological criticism have rightly deplored the temptation of purists and "textualists" to ignore the real ethical and political effects of even the purest artistic form. Defenders of aesthetic purity have rightly deplored the temptation of moralists to judge narratives by standards they might use in teaching a Sunday school class or conducting a court for juvenile offenders; "art" does offer us riches entirely its own, unrivaled by any other part of "life." If ethical criticism of narrative is once again to find a place for itself, it must avoid the loaded labels and crude slogans that critics preoccupied with moral effects have too often employed.

Such complexities only begin to suggest the difficulties in the way of pursuing an "ethical criticism of narrative," an "ethics of telling and listening." In the first place, every term we might use in the inquiry is

---

1. Neither "side" in the literary battles about "referentiality" seems to be much aware of the extended discussion among professional philosophers, not about *whether* texts refer, but about *how* they do. See, for example, Putnam 1981, ch. 2; Linsky 1967; and Pavel 1986, esp. the bibliography.

2. I am thinking especially of the courageous but careless *On Moral Fiction*, by John Gardner (1978). Gardner labels many novels as "bad" or "pernicious" or "corrupt," but he never pauses for long enough on any one work to let us know how he arrives at his often surprising judgments.

either muddied with ambiguities or barnacled with fixed conclusions. What I mean by the ethical criticism of narrative (both "fictional" and "historical") cannot be nicely confined in any preliminary definitions; it will be shown more by what I do than by anything I can say. But I must briefly forestall some of the more likely misunderstandings of my key terms.

"ETHICAL," "CHARACTER," AND "VIRTUE"

The word "ethical" may mistakenly suggest a project concentrating on quite limited moral standards: of honesty, perhaps, or of decency or tolerance. I am interested in a much broader topic, the entire range of effects on the "character" or "person" or "self." "Moral" judgments are only a small part of it.

What is more misleading, "ethical" tends to refer only to the approved side of the choices it suggests. An ethical choice is for many strictly the right choice, the opposite of "unethical," just as a moral choice is the opposite of an immoral choice. For us here the word must cover all qualities in the character, or ethos, of authors and readers, whether these are judged as good or bad. Since we have no other term for this range of appraisals ("characterological criticism"? "psychic criticism"? "behavioral criticism"? "temperamental criticism?" "personality criticism"?), "ethical" must serve.[3]

From ancient Greece to the present, the word "ethos" has meant something like "character" or "collection of habitual characteristics": whatever in a person or a society could be counted on to persist from situation to situation. I express my ethos, my character, by my habits of choice in every domain of my life, and a society expresses its ethos by what it chooses to be. Ethical criticism attempts to describe the encounters of a story-teller's ethos with that of the reader or listener. Ethical critics need not begin with the intent to evaluate, but their descriptions will always entail appraisals of the value of what is described: there are no neutral ethical terms, and a fully responsible ethical criti-

3. The bibliographies of literary studies reveal a striking decline, in the later twentieth century, in titles that include terms like "moral" and "ethical"; "character" as an ethical term (in contrast to a "literary character") has almost disappeared. We may, however, be on the verge of a revival; see Handwerk 1985; Coles 1981.

cism will make explicit those appraisals that are implicit whenever a reader or listener reports on stories about human beings in action.

"Ethical" may also wrongly suggest an interest only in judging stories and their effects on readers. That is indeed one center for ethical criticism, but I intend the term to suggest also the ethics *of* readers—their responsibilities *to* stories. Too often in the past, "ethical" or "moral" critics have assumed that their only responsibility was to label a given narrative or kind of narrative as in itself harmful or beneficial—often dismissing entire genres, like "the novel," in one grand indictment.

In recent years critics have rightly begun to place more responsibility on readers, but in doing so they have, perhaps naturally, exaggerated that move, developing an "ethics of reading" that often underplays the radically contrasting ethical powers of individual narratives. One major critic, J. Hillis Miller, has made that ethics explicit, in *The Ethics of Reading*:

> I remain with Benjamin at the end where and as I was at the beginning of this book and where and as I have remained with Kant, Kafka, de Man, Eliot, Trollope, and James. I still stand before *the* law of *the* ethics of reading, subject to it, compelled by it, persuaded of its existence and sovereignty by what happens to me when I read. What happens is the experience of an "I must" that is always the same but always different, unique, idiomatic.[4]
>
> (1986, 127; my italics)

It may well be true that to learn to read in some one superior way has an ethical value in itself, regardless of what we read. When that general claim becomes our whole interest, however, we lose all the va-

---

4. I asked Hillis Miller, after he read a conference paper on how his "law" worked in his reading of James's *What Maisie Knew*, whether he would not have received the same ethical lesson—something like "do not expect any specific moral instruction from *me*"—from any novel that he read properly; his answer was that of course it would be the same lesson! One must be careful, however, to respect the way in which Miller brings particular differences into his account: the "I must," he says, though always "the same," is always encountered as "different, unique, idiomatic" (1986, 127). In an unpublished paper Miller makes an even stronger claim to respect particularities: "One cannot make ethical judgments, perform ethical actions, such as teaching a poem, without first subjecting oneself to the words on the page. . . . The ethics of reading is the power of the words of the text over the mind and words of the reader" (1980, 30–31). Gary Saul Morson argues that we should have the courage to raise ethical questions even about the greatest of classics, and that Dostoevsky, when pressed, must be found ethically duplicitous, since, for example, he attempts to condemn a kind of destructive voyeurism in human nature, while exploiting that same voyeurism for his literary effects (1988, 1–14).

riety of ethical effect that will be our chief interest here. Still, with that qualification, I would join those who care as much about the ethics of reading as about the ethical value of "works in themselves," whatever we take such problematic creatures to be. (I return to the "work in itself" in Chapter 4.)

For any individual reader, the only story that will have ethical power is the one that is heard or read *as* it is heard or read—and that may have little connection either with the author's original intention or with the inherent powers of the story-as-told.[5] The ethics of reading that results when we take this fact of life seriously will itself have a double edge: the ethical reader will behave responsibly toward the text and its author, but that reader will also take responsibility for the ethical quality of his or her "reading," once that new "text" is made public. If ethical criticism is to be worth pursuing, it will itself carry powerful ethical force and thus be subject to ethical criteria.

Finally, to talk about ethics may falsely suggest that we are interested only in the "*after*-effects," with what is revealed in conduct following experience with a story. Though I turn to consequences for conduct in Chapter 8, my main effort is to find ways of talking about the ethical quality of the experience of narrative in itself. What kind of company are we keeping as we read or listen? What kind of company have we kept?

"Virtue" may be similarly misleading. In trying to talk about the qualities of character that are engaged in and affected by our experience with narratives, we need a general term. I have had to settle for "virtue," even though, like "moral," it has in most modern use been narrowed almost out of recognition. Traditionally it meant something like the whole range of human "powers," "strengths," "capacities," or "habits of behavior." Thus an "ethical" effect here, as in pre-modern discourse, can refer to any strengthening or weakening of a "virtue," including those that you or I would consider immoral; a given virtue can be employed viciously.[6]

---

5. For those who carry the case for subjectivism further than this phrasing implies and doubt that stories have any power in themselves considered apart from a particular reading, I offer in Chapters 2 and 4 a variety of reasons to question currently fashionable versions of "utter interpretational relativism."

6. For commentary on these broader definitions, see Aristotle *Rhetoric* 2.1–17 (esp. the summary in 18), and MacIntyre 1981: "The word *areté*, which later comes to

Expanding our terms in this way exposes the falseness of any sharp divorce of aesthetic and ethical questions. If "virtue" covers every kind of genuine strength or power, and if a person's ethos is the total range of his or her virtues, then ethical criticism will be any effort to show how the virtues of narratives relate to the virtues of selves and societies, or how the ethos of any story affects or is affected by the ethos—the collection of virtues—of any given reader. Obviously this means that a critic will be doing ethical criticism just as much when praising a story or poem for "raising our aesthetic sensibilities" or "increasing our sensitivity" as when attacking decadence, sexism, or racism. Even a work that has seemed to most readers a manifesto for art-for-art's-sake—Oscar Wilde's essay "The Decay of Lying," for example—will be taken as ethical criticism if we can discern in it a program for improving us in any way or a judgment that some works of art may debase us. "Lying," Wilde says, "the telling of beautiful untrue things, is the proper aim of art" ([1891] 1982, 320). Many have naturally read this and similar statements throughout Wilde's work as disparaging all ethical concern. But it takes no very deep reading to discover that Wilde's aim is to create a better kind of person—the kind who will look at the world and at art in a superior way and conduct life accordingly.

What is more, Wilde's ethical program extends beyond reform of individuals to whole societies and epochs.

> Ours is certainly the dullest and most prosaic century possible[,] . . . commonplace, sordid, and tedious. . . . The only form of lying that is absolutely beyond reproach is Lying for its own sake, and the highest development of this is . . . Lying in Art. . . . The solid stolid British intellect lies in the desert sands like the Sphinx in Flaubert's marvellous tale, and fantasy, *La Chimère*, dances round it, and calls to it with her false, flute-toned voice. It may not hear her now, but surely some day . . . it will hearken to her and try to borrow her wings.
>
> (316, |317, 318)

If only people will listen to him, he goes on, reject literature that attempts to further "morality" and "truth," and thus promote *his* kind of

---

be translated as 'virtue,' is in the Homeric poems used for excellence of any kind; a fast runner displays the *areté* of his feet . . . and a son excels his father in every kind of *areté*"—that is, capacity or power or strength (115). See also Bernard Williams, *Ethics and the Limits of Philosophy* (1985, chs. 1–3, esp. 6–13); Warner Berthoff, *Literature and the Continuances of Virtue* (1986, esp. ch. 1 and the afterword); and J. G. A. Pocock, *Virtues, Commerce, and History* (1985, esp. 41–50).

character and virtue (words he tends to avoid or mock), then a new day will dawn, when "romance, with her temper of wonder, will return to the land" (320). Now *there* is an ethical critic!—one who would use literature and criticism to improve both selves and societies.[7]

Wilde's way of talking shows why a serious ethical criticism cannot be divorced finally from political criticism. When we talk about changing persons we are also talking about changing societies. As most philosophers from Plato and Aristotle on have insisted, ethics and politics depend on each other. We might, then, broaden the term "ethical" even further, making it carry the weight of all political criticism as a rough synonym for what many people would call ideological criticism. I must often use it in that broad sense, but although I raise political issues throughout, I cannot pretend to offer the full encounter with them that the enterprise inherently demands.

Ethical criticism will also encompass what many would consider "philosophical" criticism: appraisals of the truth-value of narratives. "Ideological" might have served as the best term here; indeed in one draft I called the book by the stolid title "Ideology and Form." But for most American readers the word "ideology" still carries too many connotations of the narrowly doctrinaire (ideologues and fanatics have *ideologies;* our acquaintances have *ideals;* but you and I, friends, have *reasoned convictions*). I must make frequent forays into philosophical territory, but my focus will be on authors and readers as characters, and on how the transactions between them rely upon, implant, or reinforce such-and-such virtues. That focus will frequently lead to judgments that turn out to be at least to some degree indifferent to the truths or falsehoods expressed or implied in narratives.

The alternative to using "ethical," "character," and "virtue" in this unfashionable way would have been neologism. Would anyone wish that I had chosen to call this study "the axiology of psycho- and politico-poiesis as it is problematized by narratology"?

---

7. Only after this book was in press did I discover, in Richard Ellmann's *Oscar Wilde,* a similar claim that Wilde subsumed the "aesthetic" under the "ethical." In impressively detailed argument, Ellmann traces Wilde's lifelong pursuit of a "higher ethics" (1988, 300–359, esp. 302–5), one that would show how "art" indeed serves a higher form of "life." For Wilde, Ellmann claims, the "artistic life is a guide to conduct. Gide was to complain in *Les Faux-monnayeurs* that symbolism offered an aesthetic but no

"NARRATIVE"

Though my main interest is in published "stories," "fictions," (see next sub-heading), I cannot draw a consistently sharp line between those stories that are explicitly fictional and those that purport to be true, or between those that are "didactic" and those that are "artistic" or "mimetic." In *The Rhetoric of Fiction*, to keep the project manageable, I dealt primarily with "non-didactic fiction"—stories that had survived as "works of art" in the public winnowing of previous decades. That winnowing distinguished sharply between "serious" narratives that were "genuine art" and "lighter" works that compromised art by turning to "propaganda," or "rhetoric," or "didactic intent." It seems obvious, when we turn to consider ethical criticism, that such categorical divisions will have only a limited use. Indeed, most of what I said about "the rhetorical resources available to the writer of epic, novel, or short story as he tries, consciously or unconsciously, to impose his fictional world upon the reader" (1983, xiii) applies without radical change to all other narratives, regardless of whether they seem, to a formal critic, to fall outside the category of "art."

The relevance of ethical criticism in no way depends on whether a story is overtly didactic, or on whether it claims to report on events in "real life." As Louise Rosenblatt argues in her unfortunately neglected work *The Reader, the Text, the Poem* (1978), readers can create for themselves two quite different kinds of experience with *any* work, regardless of its formal or rhetorical intentions. She chooses to replace the distinction between didactic and non-didactic fictions with the distinction between aesthetic reading "transactions" and what she calls "efferent transactions"—that is, readings that are motivated mainly by a search for something to "carry away." For some readers, fiction even of the least didactic kind will be read "efferently"—that is, in the search either for some practical guidance, or for some special wisdom, or for some other useful "carry-over" into non-fictional life. For some other readers, even the most aggressively didactic authors can be turned into

---

ethic. Wilde brought the two together before Gide" (359). Ellmann's argument is perhaps most likely to surprise the world in his discussion of *The Picture of Dorian Gray* and of Wilde's ambiguous embrace of French decadence.

an aesthetic transaction, just as time can occasionally transform a work like *Gulliver's Travels*, originally loaded with didactic freight, into a children's story, read for the sheer fun of the fantastic adventure.

Ethical criticism will be interested in both kinds of experience—those in which the reader's attention is entirely on the present experience, taking no thought for the morrow, and those in which the attention is specifically on efferent freight. Indeed, the actual consequences, the load of values carried away from the experience, can often be most substantial when the reader has been least conscious of anything other than "aesthetic" involvement.

In principle, then, my subject must be all narratives, not only novels, short stories, epics, plays, films, and TV dramas but all histories, all satires, all documentaries, all gossip and personal anecdote, all biography and autobiography, all "storied" ballets and operas, all mimes and puppet shows, all chronicles—indeed, every presentation of a time-ordered or time-related experience that in any way supplements, re-orders, enhances, or interprets unnarrated life. (A complete ethical criticism of "narrative" would obviously also include most music, perhaps even, as Plato insisted, all music; and it would just as obviously include all "narrative" graphic art, since, as many have argued, images carry more powerful ethical force than do verbal narratives.)[8] Even the life we think of as primary experience—that is, events like birth, copulation, death, plowing and planting, getting and spending—is rarely experienced without some sort of mediation in narrative; one of the chief arguments for an ethical criticism of narrative is that narratives make and remake what in realist views are considered more primary experiences—and thus make and remake ourselves. The transition from what we think of as more primary (because "real") to the experience of stories about it is so automatic and frequent that we risk losing our sense of just how astonishing our story worlds are, in their power to add "life" upon "life"—for good or ill.

We all live a great proportion of our lives in a surrender to stories about our lives, and about other possible lives; we live more or less *in* stories, depending on how strongly we resist surrendering to what is

8. The most recent claim of this kind was made by the Attorney General's Commission on Pornography (1986, 383).

"only" imagined. Even those few tough-minded ones among us who claim to reject all "unreality"; even those who read no novels, watch no soap operas, and share no jokes; even those (if there are any) who echo Mr. Gradgrind and have truck only with "the facts"; even the statisticians and accountants must *in fact* conduct their daily business largely in stories: the reports they receive from and give to superiors and subordinates; the accounts they deliver to tax lawyers; the anecdotes and parables they hear told by a histrionic president as he sells his panaceas; the metaphors, living or moribund, implied in the vignettes that flood the office correspondence and publicity releases ("When things got just too gross, he blew the whistle on the whole operation"; "As soon as the heat was on, they left her to face the vultures on her own").[9] Many of us indeed approach an opposite extreme, living so much of our lives in stories that we must wonder what to call primary, the plowing and planting or the stories about plowing and planting. And when we go too far along that line, or when we embrace certain kinds of destructive "realities," we are rightly declared deranged.

Our subject then is the ethical value of the stories we tell each other as "imitations of life," whether or not they in fact claim to depict actual events. The borderline between such stories and the rest of life is necessarily vague. When mothers tell fairy stories, do their children experience fictions or "life"? When children watch television for a third to a half of each day—much of it purporting to be "true to life"—is that not their life? Still, we all make a rough-and-ready distinction between those moments when we are enjoying accounts about life other than what is immediately present, and those moments when our attention is on the problems of life as lived now. When the wife shouts, "I hate you!" and throws the coffee cup, both her statement and her action fall outside our domain. But if she goes on to say, "because you promised me to be faithful and then, after ten years, I learn that you have been having an affair with my best friend," she has told a story (true or false) and opened the door to the ethical critic of narrative.

9. The mixed metaphor bothers you? We'll come to the ethics of mixed metaphors later on.

"FICTIONS"

If the border is fuzzy between life and narrative, and between narratives that teach and narratives that just *are*, the distinction between narratives that are true and those that are fictions is even fuzzier. Indeed the distinction seems often to be totally erased, along with that between narratives and life, by critics associated with various "deconstructions." Claiming that "all we have is language," that every question can ultimately be addressed only in and through language, they finally see all linguistic structures as on the same "fictive" footing: life consists of the fictions we construct (White 1973, esp. ch. 1 and pt. 2; Norris 1985, esp. chs. 5–6). Without pretending that the borderline will ever be clear, I still rely on the usually useful assumption that we know the difference not only between suckling an infant and constructing a documentary account of current nursing practices, but also between that documentary and telling a bedtime story about a babe lost in the woods and suckled by a wolf-mother. We depend (however loosely and insecurely) on the distinction between describing the sexual customs of modern Americans and writing or reading a novel like Updike's *Couples*. Though the ethical critic will want to think about the effects of reading all kinds of narrative, we must often employ our commonsense distinction between an autobiographical account of harvesting and stories and poems about it—Robert Frost's "After Apple-Picking," let us say.

The difference between honoring the distinctions and casting them aside is not a difference between truth and falsehood. The distinctions can be useless in theorizing about the nature (or lack of a nature) of "texts." Yet they are forced upon us when we turn, as I do here, to the qualities of our reading experience. In practice, we simply read differently when we believe that a story claims to be true than we do when we take it as "made-up." Whether or not we are critically innocent, we never read a story without making a decision, mistaken or justified, about the implied author's answer to a simple question: Is this "once-upon-a-time" or is it a claim about events in real time? Though some authors produce interesting effects by giving ambiguous answers to the question ("Some of it happened; some of it did not—you guess which"), the answers we hear them giving create solid differences in the company we *think* we keep—and at any one moment, that is the company we *do* keep. As Samuel Johnson insisted, biographies present some kinds of ethical power and risk that either are not met in fictions or are met there only in different form (Johnson 1969; Bate 1977, 530–31). Thus though most of my main examples are professed fictions, that selection springs more from the accidents of my training and interests than from any inherent demands of ethical criticism; I might well have added separate chapters on biography, autobiography, and narrative history.

Though "fictions" is my catch-all term for make-believe narratives, including lyric poems and drama, I must sometimes use other terms as rough synonyms (English has no widely accepted term for this huge collection of artifacts): "poems," "poetry," "literature," "tales," "stories," and—broadest term of all—"[verbal] art works." The connotations of each of these are different; all of them have radically ambiguous histories; all have sometimes been used in a sense as broad as I have in mind, and even broader. "Fictions" seems least misleading, since at its roots it stresses a making and forming *by* the artist, not by a "life" or "real world" that the artist tries to duplicate. The classical term "imitations" might serve, at least in my reading of Aristotle's usage, except for the unfortunate modern connotation of the mere copy.

THE CONTRAST BETWEEN UBIQUITOUS PRACTICE AND THEORETICAL SUSPICION

Each narrative, fictional or historical, provides an alternative story set in a created "world" that is itself a fresh alternative to the "world" or "worlds" previously serving as boundaries of the reader's imagination. Each work of art or artifice, even the simplest wordless melody, determines to some degree *how at least this one moment will be lived*. The quality of life in the moment of our "listening" is not what it would have been if we had not listened. We can even say that the proffered work shows us how our moments *should* be lived. If the maker of the art work did not believe that simply experiencing it constitutes a superior form of life, why was the work created and presented to us in the first place?

A version of this point has been made much of by the aestheticians who, in the spirit of Wilde, maintain the superiority of artistic experiences that are purged of all practical considerations. The experience that most insists on itself as an alternative and heightened way of living, *without essential connections* to practical choice, has seemed to many inherently finer than any experience that insists on some sort of useful consequence. Pure poetry is simply a more radical and autonomous supplement to "life," an encounter with something totally other.[10]

It is thus not surprising that the most aggressive arguments for a purified formalism, divorced from all ethical concerns, have come from those who see non-programmatic music and abstract graphic art as the ideal, all other arts aspiring to their condition of purity. In both we seem to have the possibility of transcending all practical consequence—all the baser human interests that corrupt other forms with thoughts of profit or loss or of truth and falsehood. The substitute life that they offer has all the more integrity, the claim runs, just because the "mercenary" connections to "real" life have been cut.[11]

When I first converted to the religion of art, in the 1940s, I read everywhere, and of course believed, that the greatest music was the purest music—whatever was least tainted with program—and that the graphic arts similarly approached their proper condition as they became more abstract: in other words, as they less and less resembled what we think of as stories or fictions. When I later read Plato's discrimi-

---

10. See, for example, Nelson Goodman 1976, though he maintains an air of descriptive neutrality. See also W. J. T. Mitchell's critique in *Iconology* (1986, esp. 71–74).

11. The bibliography of the purifiers could in itself fill a book of this size, and the varieties of status accorded to "life" and "morality" when banned, or three-quarters banned, from art would fill an encyclopedia of pure poetics. It was of course not only the proponents of art-for-art's-sake who saw practical or utilitarian reference as a threat to pure art or as a sign of non-art. The original project, begun in the eighteenth century— the effort to distinguish a domain of experience called the "aesthetic"—led to hundreds of efforts to reconcile the drive for pure form with an experience that always revealed, on a close look, elements of moral and ideological engagement. The work of Roger Fry, for example, can be misquoted to suggest that art is encountered only in "the contemplation of pure form": "As to the value of the aesthetic emotion—it is clearly infinitely removed from those ethical values to which Tolstoy would have confined it. It seems to be as remote from actual life and its practical utilities as the most useless mathematical theory" (1920, concluding paragraph). But much of Fry's effort goes to trying to account for the word "significant" in the then prominent phrase "significant form." For a brief account of the history of the notion of art for its "own sake," see Abrams 1985. For a good selective bibliography on the invention of "aesthetics" in the eighteenth century, and especially on Kant's *Critique of Judgment* (itself so much more complex than later reductions of aesthetics to the "non-moral") see Cohen and Guyer 1982.

nations among the harmful and beneficial musical modes, I treated
them with amused contempt, so absurdly uninformed about the true
nature of art did the poor ancient seem.[12] Though I went on living a
great part of my life in radically "impure" fictions, I would always
have said, until well into the seven-year period when I was writing *The
Rhetoric of Fiction,* that the novels I read, *qua* art, were obviously of
less "aesthetic" interest than the Bach and Haydn I loved.

The dogmatic claims that "true art is pure form" and that "genuine
artistic experience is the contemplation of pure form," have in recent
decades been challenged numberless times, even in the domains of music and the graphic arts (e.g., Shahn 1957; Kerman 1966, esp. 255–68;
Wind 1983). But I have seen no serious effort to develop a full *ethical*
criticism, either of music or painting, of the kind suggested by Plato.
Are some musical forms inherently better for us than others? Is it possible to talk responsibly about the relative ethical power and value of
two musical works both of which move us deeply—Beethoven's *Grosse
Fuge,* say, and the Beatles' *Sergeant Pepper?* Where can we find criticism that might help us answer such questions? Of course individual
critics do praise and damn individual works with great freedom, often
in terms that can only be called ethical (e.g., Sullivan 1927, esp. 87–
115; Meyer 1956, 1967; Tovey 1945, esp. Lecture 6). But where are the
theorists who argue that such judgments are something more than an
expression of individual taste?[13] Perhaps if we can find a responsible
way of defending the ethical criticism of narrative, we will encourage
similar probing in the other arts that I must neglect here.

In any case, we can no longer pretend that ethical criticism is passé.
It is practiced everywhere, often surreptitiously, often guiltily, and
often badly, partly because it is the most difficult of all critical modes,
but partly because we have so little serious talk about why it is important, what purposes it serves, and how it might be done well. The

12. The guardians "must throughout be watchful against innovations in music and
gymnastics counter to the established order. . . . For a change to a new type of music is
something to beware of as a hazard to all our fortunes. For the modes of music are never
disturbed without unsettling of the most fundamental political and social conventions"
(*Republic* 4.424b–c).

13. Allan Bloom conducts a courageous foray into this territory in *The Closing of
the American Mind* (1987, 70–75). But to me he spoils things by praising and damning
entire genres—as if all rock music had the same ethical effect on all hearers.

widespread theoretical suspicion of ethical criticism is itself sufficiently curious, in the face of almost universal practice, to justify a close look in the next two chapters at why the divorce should have arisen in the first place. In trying to understand why theories of ethical criticism fell on hard times, we can perhaps avoid some of the practices that gave it a bad name.

To those readers who find the following theoretical spadework turning up too much of what seems obvious, I can only reply that I share their impatience but not their sense that what I say should go without saying. In the current critical scene, most "obvious" beliefs have been "problematized," as the jargon has it, and we must do what we can to discover what shared grounds remain after the various challenging demolition jobs of recent years.

REFERENCES

Note: References are to the most recent edition cited; multiple works under an author's name are listed in chronological order by year of publication of the most recent edition of each entry. For the reader's information, the year of original publication (in the work's original language) is given in brackets following the title. The References for most chapters include a few titles not mentioned in the text.

Abrams, M. H. "Art-as-Such: The Sociology of Modern Aesthetics." *Bulletin: The American Academy of Arts and Sciences* 38 (Mar. 1985): 8–33.
Achebe, Chinua. "An Image of Africa." In *The Chancellor's Lecture Series: 1974–1975*. Amherst, Mass., 1975. 31–43.
Attorney General's Commission on Pornography: Final Report, July 1986. U.S. Department of Justice. Washington, D.C., 1986.
Bate, W. Jackson. *Samuel Johnson*. New York, 1977.
Berthoff, Warner. *Literature and the Continuances of Virtue*. Princeton, N.J., 1986.
Bettelheim, Bruno. "Surviving." In *"Surviving" and Other Essays*. New York, 1979.
Bleich, David. "Intersubjective Reading." *New Literary History* 17 (Spr. 1986): 401–22.
Bloom, Allan. *The Closing of the American Mind*. New York, 1987.
Booth, Wayne C. *The Rhetoric of Fiction* [1961]. 2d ed. Chicago, 1983.
Cohen, Ted, and Paul Guyer, eds. *Essays in Kant's Aesthetics*. Chicago, 1982.
Coles, Robert. "On the Nature of Character: Some Preliminary Field Notes." *Daedalus* 110 (Fall 1981): 131–43.
Eagleton, Terry. *Criticism and Ideology: A Study in Marxist Literary Theory*. London, 1976.

Ellmann, Richard. *Oscar Wilde*. New York, 1988.

Fischer, Michael. *Does Deconstruction Make Any Difference? Post-Structuralism and the Defense of Poetry in Modern Criticism*. Bloomington, Ind., 1985.

Fry, Roger. *Vision and Design* [1920]. Ed. J. B. Bullen. London, 1981.

Gardner, John. *On Moral Fiction*. New York, 1978.

Goodheart, Eugene. *The Skeptic Disposition in Contemporary Criticism*. Princeton, N.J., 1984.

Goodman, Nelson. *Languages of Art*. Indianapolis, Ind., 1976.

Graff, Gerald. *Literature against Itself: Literary Ideas in Modern Society*. Chicago, 1979.

——. "Literature as Assertions." In *American Criticism in the Poststructuralist Age*. Ed. Ira Konigsberg. Michigan Studies in the Humanities. Ann Arbor, Mich., 1981.

——. *Professing Literature: An Institutional History*. Chicago, 1987.

Handwerk, Gary J. *Irony and Ethics in Narrative: From Schlegel to Lacan*. New Haven, Conn., 1985.

Jameson, Fredric. *The Political Unconscious: Narrative as a Socially Symbolic Act*. Ithaca, N.Y., 1981.

Johnson, Samuel. "*The Rambler*, nos. 14 and 60" [1750, 1752]. In *Samuel Johnson: "The Rambler,"* vol. 1. Ed. W. J. Bate and Albrecht B. Strauss. Vol. 3 of *The Yale Edition of the Works of Samuel Johnson*. New Haven, Conn., 1969. 74–80, 318–23.

Kerman, Joseph. *The Beethoven Quartets*. New York, 1966.

Kermode, Frank. "Knowing." Review of *Bliss* and *Exotic Pleasures*, by Peter Carey. *London Review of Books* 3 (Dec. 3–16, 1981): 17.

Lewis, C. S. *An Experiment in Criticism*. Cambridge, 1961.

Linsky, Leonard. *Referring*. London, 1967.

MacIntyre, Alasdair. *After Virtue: A Study in Moral Theory*. Notre Dame, Ind., 1981.

Meyer, Leonard B. *Emotion and Meaning in Music*. Chicago, 1956.

——. *Music, the Arts, and Ideas: Patterns and Predictions in Twentieth-Century Culture*. Chicago, 1967.

Miller, J. Hillis. "The Ethics of Reading: Vast Gaps and Part Hours." Unpublished paper, 1980.

——. *The Ethics of Reading: Kant, de Man, Eliot, Trollope, James, and Benjamin*. New York, 1986.

Mitchell, W. J. T. *Iconology: Image, Text, Ideology*. Chicago, 1986.

Morson, Gary Saul. "Prosaics: A New Approach to the Humanities." *American Scholar* 57 (forthcoming, Fall 1988). (The final pages deal with "the ethics of reading.")

Norris, Christopher. *The Contest of Faculties: Philosophy and Theory after Deconstruction*. London, 1985.

Pavel, Thomas G. *Fictional Worlds*. Cambridge, Mass., 1986.

Plato. *Republic*. Trans. Paul Shorey. Loeb Classical Library. London, 1930.

Pocock, J. G. A. "Virtues, Rights, and Manners: A Model for Historians of Political Thought." In *Virtue, Commerce, and History*. Cambridge, 1985.

Putnam, Hilary. "A Problem about Reference." In *Reason, Truth, and History*. Cambridge, 1981.

Rosenblatt, Louise M. *The Reader, the Text, the Poem: The Transactional Theory of the Literary Work.* Carbondale, Ill., 1978.

Shahn, Ben. *The Shape of Content.* Cambridge, Mass., 1957.

Sprinker, Michael. "Fiction and Ideology: *Lord Jim* and the Problem of Literary History." In *Reading Narrative: Form, Ethics, Ideology.* Ed. James Phelan. Columbus, Ohio, 1988.

Suleiman, Susan Rubin. "Ideological Dissent from Works of Fiction: Toward a Rhetoric of the *roman à thèse.*" *Neophilologus* 60 (1976): 162–77.

———. *Authoritarian Fictions: The Ideological Novel as a Literary Genre.* New York, 1983.

Sullivan, J. W. N. "The Morality of Power." In *Beethoven: His Spiritual Development.* New York, 1927.

Tovey, Donald Francis. *Beethoven.* Oxford, 1945.

Trilling, Lionel. *The Liberal Imagination: Essays on Literature and Society.* New York, 1950.

White, Hayden. *Metahistory: The Historical Imagination in Nineteenth-Century Europe.* Baltimore, 1973.

Wilde, Oscar. "The Decay of Lying" [1891]. In *The Artist as Critic: Critical Writings of Oscar Wilde.* Ed. Richard Ellmann. 1969. Reprint. Chicago, 1982.

Williams, Bernard. *Ethics and the Limits of Philosophy.* Cambridge, Mass., 1985.

Williams, Raymond. *Marxism and Literature.* Oxford, 1977.

Wilson, Edmund. "Why Do People Read Detective Stories?" *New Yorker* (Oct. 14, 1944): 73–76.

———. "Who Cares Who Killed Roger Akroyd? A Second Report on Detective Fiction." *New Yorker* (Jan. 20, 1945): 52–58.

Wind, Edgar. *The Eloquence of Symbols: Studies in Humanist Art.* Ed. Jaynie Anderson. Oxford, 1983.

2

The noble eighteenth-century faith in natural law involved a fundamental confusion between the declarative and the normative senses of law, between "is" and "ought." . . . [Science—that is, objective thinking of any kind] tells what we can do, never what we should. Its absolute incompetence in the realm of values is a necessary consequence of the objective posture.
Charles Coulston Gillispie

Surely one of the novel's habitual aims is to articulate morality, to sharpen the reader's sense of vice and virtue.
John Updike

[A]rt is neither inferior nor equal to morality and truth, but the synthesis of civilized life in which alone their general laws have any real meaning. Art is neither good nor bad, but a clairvoyant vision of the nature of both, and any attempt to align it with morality, otherwise called bowdlerizing, is intolerably vulgar.
Northrop Frye

The act of getting a story or a novel published is an act of communication, an attempt to impose one's personality and beliefs on other people. If a writer accepts this responsibility, he must see himself . . . as an architect of the soul.
Doris Lessing

Why Ethical Criticism Fell on Hard Times

We have seen that though most people practice what I am calling ethical criticism of fictions, it plays at best a minor and often deplored role on the scene of theory. It simply goes unmentioned in most discussions among professional critics. Surveys of current "schools" do not even describe ethical criticism as a possibility. Though anthologies of "literary criticism through the ages" obviously cannot avoid including great swatches of ethical evaluation in their selections, they disguise it, in effect, under other labels: "Political," "Social," or "Cultural" criticism; "Psychological" or "Psychoanalytic" criticism; and more recently terms like "Reader-Response Criticism," "Feminist Criticism," and "The Discourse of Power."[1] To anyone who considers the history of literary criticism, this contrast between theoretical ostracism and popular practice is surprising. Until the late nineteenth century almost everyone took for granted that a major task of any critic is to appraise the ethical value of works of art, and they saw no reason to disguise that ethical interest under ostensibly neutral terms like "significant form" or "aesthetic integrity."

Why did overt, theoretically buttressed ethical criticism fall on such hard times? Why is it that while at one moment in our history Matthew Arnold could seem perfectly reasonable in expunging his own "Empedocles on Aetna" from his collected poetry (1853), arguing that it was ethically faulty, a moment later—today, that is—such a gesture would to most people seem at best an expression of "personal moral preference," not a reasoned act at all?

---

1. On the other hand, social scientists concerned with how we are motivated to action (that is to say, in the terms used here, how "persons" or "characters" are created) have until very recently shown a surprising indifference to the power of story. Entire anthologies of "ethical" theories in this sense do not even mention how vicariously experienced narratives shape us. See, for example, von Cranach et al. 1982, and von Cranach and Harré 1982.

In taking a close look at the causes for such a decline, we may well risk destroying our subject entirely. It is always possible when any cultural practice is abandoned that it deserved to die: past attempts at a reasoned ethical criticism may have no theoretical justification. On the other hand, if we do not simply proclaim that Lazarus has risen but address seriously the by-no-means trivial reasons for his demise, we may manage to resurrect a hardier creature than has emerged from other recent efforts. At least we can hope to express our judgments with some understanding of why they so often lapse into the kind of mere assertion that skeptics claim is the condition of all ethical evaluation.

A full history of the decline of a theoretically coherent and confident ethical criticism of narratives, from the time of Samuel Johnson through Coleridge and Arnold to high modernism, would require almost as many volumes as have been devoted to other better-known cultural revolutions: the Reformation, say, or the rise (and fall?) of romanticism. In principle it would include every major critic and every major philosopher (since they all deal with ethical questions). After a preliminary skirmish with the threat of censorship, I confine myself in this chapter, first, to a skeletal account of four dogmas of our cultural climate that have made all ethical judgments suspect, and then to a brief look at five peculiarities of ethical criticism that will always make it difficult, regardless of the cultural setting. In Chapter 3 I turn to the rhetorical methods of ethical critics themselves—logical and stylistic moves that might well raise the suspicion of any inquirer who hopes for a way of sharing knowledge, not just opinions, about why some stories we tell each other are pearls of great price while others are dangerous drugs or even poisons.

THE THREAT OF CENSORSHIP

Many would take as the sole cause of our critical austerity a practical fear: the threat of censorship. From Plato through Johnson and Tolstoy to the best-known ethical critics of this century—Leavis, Winters, the Marxists—the vigorous tone of condemnation has suggested censorship, even when the critic has explicitly denied any intent to censor. Plato's censorship program, in the ideal state he constructs in the *Republic,* is the feared model, one that has been followed by all regimes that legislate on the conviction that art can build or destroy souls and societies: the various "Marxist democracies," the Catholic Church with its Index, repressive capitalist states like that of South Africa. Even the liberal democracies exhibit long histories of efforts, more or less successful, to suppress this or that brand of literature. When we teachers opposed Paul Moses, we did so partly because we feared that crediting him would open the floodgates to all kinds of censorship. Indeed, it seemed evident that his refusal to teach *Huckleberry Finn* was already a form of censorship. (So far as I know, none of us thought much about the danger of censorship from *our* side. We gave him the right not to teach the book. But we did not—or at least I did not—really listen to him.)

The complex issues of censorship would require a separate book in themselves.[2] Few questions can be more important today than whether or how a democratic society should protect its citizens from harming themselves, without harming them more seriously by infringing upon their freedoms. Should seat belts be required whether people want them or not? Should ads for cigarettes and hard liquor be banned? Should magazine vendors be allowed to display before the eyes of passing children a cover photo of three jack-booted males, whips in hand, standing over a reclining, smiling, naked woman? Should the reading lists of high school English classes be controlled by school boards?

Whatever our answers, they cannot diminish the importance of ethical criticism. Pending my slightly fuller discussion in the Introduction to Part 3, I can here only assert the hope that by taking ethical issues seriously we can diminish the likelihood of two kinds of repression: by the overtly censorious who see no problems with censorship, and by ourselves as we risk imposing unacknowledged critical pieties.

2. I once made a stab at reasoning with a would-be censor, in a brief article that of course showed me as the winner, hands down (1970). Here I can only point out that all of us who teach do in fact "censor": we impose our ethical choices on our students when we choose our reading lists. All of us who are parents impose our views by the books and magazines we have in the house. The question of whether we should do so more aggressively, at home and abroad, cannot be settled with a simple "liberal" decision to make every conceivable kind of story available to anyone of any age on demand. See MacMillan 1983 for a good recent discussion of censorship in England and America.

THE THEORETICAL REJECTION OF INQUIRY INTO "VALUES"

The first dogma that has contributed to the demotion of ethical criticism is the notion that one can obtain knowledge only about facts, never about values. If that notion is sound, then of course no act of ethical criticism can claim to provide any kind of knowledge about the value of a fiction. It can only be what all literary evaluation was called in Northrop Frye's famous formulation: at best "one more document in the history of taste" (1957, 25).

The hard-and-fast "fact/value split" has been attacked so often in recent decades that I need touch on it only briefly, attending especially to its bearing on acts of literary evaluation.[3] My point here will not be to argue that artistic values are *in some sense* real, and hence knowable, though of course I think that they are.[4] If argument could ever settle such a question, the debate would have stopped once Kant pub-

---

3. I have not found a good history of the belief that values cannot be derived from facts. Hume is perhaps most often cited as the fountainhead. The positivists were so unanimous on the point that they seldom paused to argue it. One tradition of Wittgensteinian thought took it for granted that, as Wittgenstein said, in a lecture of 1929–30 (first published in 1965), "There are no propositions which, in any absolute sense, are sublime, important, or trivial. . . . [A] state of mind, so far as we mean by that a fact which we can describe, is in no ethical sense good or bad" (1965, 6). "What it [ethics] says does not add to our knowledge in any sense" (12). When he called all ethical propositions "nonsensical," his liberated followers did not always hear his qualification that he respected them deeply and "would not for my life ridicule" them (12).

The appendix of my *Modern Dogma and the Rhetoric of Assent* (1974) listed more than two score refutations of the fact/value split, many of them much more technical (and therefore for some purposes more telling) than my own. Since then many more authors have refuted the proposition that one can never derive an "ought" proposition from an "is" proposition. From my amateur perspective on the professional philosophical scene, it appears that there are very few hold-outs for the sharp split, though of course most of us would agree that for *some* inquiries, such as whether handling uranium ore with the bare hands is dangerous, we must try hard to keep our preferences distinct from our conclusions. See Donagan 1977; Gewirth 1978; MacIntyre 1981; and Williams 1985. Putnam, who seems curiously indifferent to the existence of innumerable previous champions of his (my) cause, notes that reliance on the fact/value split has become "a cultural institution," a "received answer" that will continue to be relied on for a long time, even though philosophers repeatedly show its inadequacy (1981, 127).

4. For those readers who still doubt that certain narratives somehow "have" or "possess" or "exhibit" or "exercise" more value than others, I provide below, especially in Chapter 4, a collection of some of the more powerful arguments against that view, and what I think is an original argument of my own. Every critic who talks about such matters must be plagued by Northrop Frye's warning that though *of course* Milton is a

lished his marvelously cogent proof, in "The Analytic of the Beautiful," that the objective/subjective distinction cannot hold when we consider matters of beauty (1790, secs. 7–9). The point here is to underline, once more, the great gap between theory and practice, and the distressing contortions critics must exhibit if they both rely on the dogma and attend to their own sense that some narratives are indeed worth more than others.

The argument for the fact/value split, taken seriously, would of course mean that all judgments of value are by definition "merely personal opinion" or at best conventions of a given community. In some fields that belief can be embraced without too much discomfort, though even in the physical sciences it can cause trouble for anyone who asks such a basic question as whether we *know* that to respect the evidence in an experiment is better than to invent evidence in order to get a grant. In any case, in literary criticism the split has always produced uncomfortable compromises. Though many critics have asserted a raw claim of total subjectivism, and many more a sophisticated *cultural* relativism, one can usually discern in the critic's life, if not in the immediate text, a sense of regret, of loss. Clearly the dogma has banned too much of what the critic knows should be said. If one elects to continue talking about values, one feels caught in a set of philosophical inconsistencies, like the Bertrand Russell whose honest conflicts I traced in *Modern Dogma* (1974). If one chooses not to, one cannot help feeling self-censored, like the Chicano critic I mentioned in Chapter 1.

Consider how that conflict appears in a review by George Steiner. Exposing "The Scandal of the Nobel Prize," complaining bitterly because the prizes have been denied to many who were more deserving than the actual winners, Steiner might be expected to acknowledge that some authors are indeed worthier than others. Instead, he cannot resist a bow toward subjectivism before moving to assertions of value that the bow would deny him. "There is no objective measure, no slide rule for magnitude in literature. . . . No esthetic judgment, even of the greatest, can be proved. The proposition that Mozart was a second-

---

"more rewarding and suggestive poet to work with than Blackmore," the point is not worth "belaboring" (1957, 25).

rate composer . . . is perfectly arguable. . . . Consensus over the ages is statistical" (1984, 1).[5] But of course Steiner's heart is not in this disclaimer; it cannot be if he is to maintain that the Nobel committee has made significant mistakes. His heart is in such assertions as that Paul Celan is "the profoundest, the most innovative lyric poet in western literature in our time," or that Paul Claudel's dramas can be fairly set "beside those of Aeschylus and of Shakespeare" (38). "Can one defend a jury which prefers the art of Pearl Buck (1938) to that of, say, Virginia Woolf?" (38). Steiner knows, but he doesn't trouble to say *how* he knows, that the Nobel Prize should go to Octavio Paz, Milan Kundera, V. S. Naipaul, Claude Simon, Nadine Gordimer, Leonardo Sciascia, Thomas Bernhard, Norman Mailer, and Jorge Luis Borges (39).

Certain ethical and technical criteria that Steiner might develop in defense of his judgments are of course revealed between the lines. He castigates the Nobel committee for ignoring the cosmopolitan in favor of the parochial, the experimental in favor of the conventional, the sensual and the "amoral" in favor of the merely proper and acceptable: "The liberating sensualities, such as John Cowper Powys, supreme in English fiction after Hardy, are left ou :" ([39]).

Without pausing to appraise any of these marvelously confident judgments, we must ask how Steiner can harmonize his attack on the Nobel folks for getting everything wrong with his claim that critical judgments have no objective status whatever. If his judgments are simply and only *his,* what basis can he have for saying that the awards have been egregiously, even wickedly, misplaced? In other words, what ground has he given us for listening to his judgments? It is no doubt bracing to feel confident in lashing the Nobel committee for their stupid awards, but if their judgment is stupid, how can Steiner claim that Rosa Bonheur's superiority to Cézanne, a belief that he sees as absurd, is "perfectly arguable"? (1).

For a second example, consider the claim of John Carey, the Merton Professor of English Literature at Oxford University, as he argues that

---

5. Note that the argument is identical in structure to that of Barbara Herrnstein Smith, as she reduces our discussions of literary value to a kind of "mercantilism": "The endurance of a classic canonical author such as Homer . . . owes not to the alleged transcultural or universal value of his works but, on the contrary, to the continuity of their circulation in a particular culture" (1984, 34).

we have rightly put "An End to Evaluation." Carey begins with the bald assertion, "The dislodgment of 'evaluation' has been effected with remarkably little fuss. . . . Nowadays almost no one believes in the possibility of objective or 'correct' literary judgments any longer" (1980, 204). It is not quite clear why, if he is right about that—if, that is, he has no opponents to speak of—he should then bother to argue, even briefly, that value judgments express only personal preference. More significant than that puzzle, however, is the flat contradiction between Carey's confident pronouncement here, as he goes before the non-specialists who are likely to read him in *TLS*, and his own practice when he gets down to work as a scholar and critic. His admirable *John Donne: Life, Mind, and Art*, for example, published a year after his funeral oration over poor dead evaluation, could be described as a most meticulous and persuasive demonstration, through historical reconstruction, of his *explicit* claim that Donne is among the "great poets" (1981, 260): a master of the imagination who adjusted "his theology to his basic interests" with "complete success" (278). Throughout his book one finds explicit—though usually truncated—causal arguments like this one: "In fact their [the poems'] inner inconsistencies . . . make them resistant to summaries of any kind, and *that is why they are valuable*" (191; my italics). Carey's evaluative terms— "greatness," "success," "valuable"—are the implicit conclusions of a long historical argument that might well have been stated more fully: *because* of his personal beliefs and historical situation, Donne faced special artistic problems *that he solved with great skill,* thus creating poems of a profound and lasting value that any prepared reader *ought* to be able to discern.

Carey reveals his suspicion of such evaluation in his consistent refusal to bring his standards into open debate with possible rivals; they are never developed and supported with argument (in interesting contrast to his historical arguments, which are on the whole detailed and exemplary). I leave his book with a heightened sense of Donne's greatness—and a stronger sense of genuine puzzlement: Why, presumably at about the time he was completing the book, should Carey have felt driven to repudiate in his journal article the possibility of defending what his book so impressively accomplishes? But that is of course just another way of putting our central question: Why did evaluative criticism, and especially ethical criticism, fall under theoretical suspicion, even in the hands of critics who practice it with intelligence and conviction?

NOTIONS OF WHAT KINDS OF "PROOF" ARE REQUIRED TO ESTABLISH "KNOWLEDGE"

From the fact/value split there followed, or seemed to follow, a dogma about what it means to *prove* a case: true *reason* proceeds by means of critical *doubt*. The heart may have its reasons that reason does not comprehend, but these can never establish cognitively respectable conclusions. *Thought* proceeds by critically probing the world's convictions to discover which of them *cannot be doubted*. Only after an opinion has been tested in the fires of doubt can it achieve intellectual respectability.

Any such belief has devastating consequences for criticism of the arts. The essential first step, the step that provides the data with which criticism of narrative deals, can only be that primary act of *assent* that occurs when we surrender to a story and follow it through to its conclusion. That act of assent will usually include assent to innumerable occasions for critical doubt offered by the author, as it obviously does when the story-teller is a highly "critical" Leo Tolstoy or George Eliot, and as it even more obviously does when we read skeptical modernist works. But we discover the powers of any narrative only in an act of surrender. Reference to the depth, force, and quality of that surrender is our initial and indispensable resource as we then compare it with other invitations from other narratives. In Chapter 3 I pursue the steps we must add to this primary intuition before we have anything deserving the name of criticism. For now the point is that to *begin* with doubt, as we are told that scientists do, employing some criterion of "falsifiability," some test in which suspicion is primary, is simply to destroy the datum.[6]

---

6. In recent decades many philosophers of science have argued forcefully that even the "hardest" sciences depend on primary acts of assent, faith, or trust. The fullest developments of this case that I have read are in Michael Polanyi's *Personal Knowledge* (1972), and Rom Harré's "Science as a Communal Practice" (1986).

Thus the burden of proof about evaluations of narrative should always be laid upon the detractor. The reader or listener who has experienced and valued a story has a grasp on a central datum that is *essentially* inaccessible to anyone who comes along and asks whether the "experimental conclusions are replicable." Of *course* they will not be replicated by any reader who reads the same story "critically" and misses the experience.

If one reader has wept buckets over *Love Story* and another reader finds it to be sentimental trash, the burden of proof, *in their discussion,* must always be on the doubter.[7] The lover of the story knows that he or she has loved; no reasoning can destroy that. The non-lover knows only a lack, a negation; and if that negation is to be justified, the skeptic must be able to account for how the narrative could have won lovers and still be in itself something deplorable. Put another way: the lover can always easily explain why the non-lover failed to achieve the experience—which is why teachers never have any difficulty convincing themselves that students are at fault when they fail to respond to the classics.

It is also the reason why quarrels about "the canon" produce such indecisive results.[8] Those on the attack usually have had some genuine new experiences that for them carry an unquestioned authority: "Such-and-such new or neglected works are alive and such-and-such old ones are, for us, dead." Those who defend the pre-established classics have similarly enjoyed (except when they are merely mimicking other "authorities") an experience that speaks what is to them an unanswerable message: "*Here is quality,* quality that you upstarts have the effrontery to question." My point is that the burden of proof is always greater on the negative side: if you have been ravished by Dickens's *Bleak House,* and I come along and tell you that you have been taken in by sentimentality, you have a right to push me closely about my grounds; but if you have recently been enraptured by Toni Morrison's *Beloved* (1987), and I tell you that I "just couldn't get into it because it's a ghost story,

---

7. Who in this case would be me; I seem to "miss the experience" that many find in *Love Story,* and the burden of proof is thus on me to show why those who "have the experience" have in some way been "taken in," as they "took it in."

8. See Robert von Hallberg, ed., *Canons* (1984)—or, for that matter, almost any article in any issue of *Signs,* of *Representations,* of *Pre/Text,* of . . .

and I happen not to like ghost stories; if we have to have ghosts I prefer *Macbeth* or *The Turn of the Screw*," you have a right to insist that I take another look, and perhaps another yet, before we can have a profitable discussion.[9]

In short, contrary to our usual assumptions about proof, the lover is *probably* right in being confident that a lovable quality does indeed exist. A loving response to a narrative simply will not occur, we must assume, unless there is *some* quality in it that the critic, of whatever persuasion, should take into account.[10]

Since to say what I have just said might seem to invite a relativism that accords equal validity to all sincere eulogies, we see here one more reason that responsible critics came to be suspicious of ethical criticism.

THE BELIEF THAT CONFLICTING VALUES CANCEL EACH OTHER OUT

Perhaps the cruelest blow to confidence in our appraisals of narrative value was the increasing awareness of just how variable our judgments really are. If rationality about values requires concurrence on a single hierarchy, then irreconcilable variety would seem to disprove the possibility of rational discourse about them. Certainly no one can any longer claim success in harmonizing all the plausible claims about what constitutes aesthetic or ethical value (see the Appendix). Though we may all believe that some stories are worth more than others, we seem to disagree more and more about the canon, even within a given culture. And our culture disagrees with all the other cultures that modern history has forced us to take seriously. Perhaps most devastating to objectivists, individual readers do not agree with themselves from one decade to the next: the "very same" *Count of Monte Cristo* that at

9. Here I happen to be a "lover" of all the works mentioned; it is mine enemy that hath in his folly attacked Dickens and Morrison.

10. Hilary Putnam makes a similar point about all intuitions of value, all "presented experiential qualities": "Even if Smith's preference for vanilla [over chocolate ice cream] is 'subjective,' that does not make it irrational or arbitrary. Smith has a reason—the best possible reason—for liking vanilla, namely *the way it tastes to him*. Values can be 'subjective' in the sense of being relative and still be objective; it is objective that vanilla tastes *better* than chocolate *to* Smith. . . . The 'fact'—the *taste* itself—and the 'value'— the goodness of the taste—are one, at least psychologically" (1981, 154).

sixteen I thought the greatest novel ever written is now for me almost unreadable.

In many attacks on evaluative criticism, this fact of variability becomes the sole argument. It is the only argument offered by Carey: even if we could all agree now about the preeminence of Shakespeare, he says, our agreement still would not establish anything real about his works, because we know how often "opinions which were [equally] unquestioned in past eras are now wholly discounted" (1980, 204).

Without attempting at this point to refute the argument from variability, we should note that it depends on the rather strange notion that the value of any human achievement is found through some sort of democratic vote among those who consider it: as Steiner says, it "is statistical" (1984, 1). Unless every individual vote is to count equally, then a difference of opinion between two (or a million) judges about the value of, say, *King Lear,* the TV serial "Dallas," and a joke told by Johnny Carson means little until we consider the experience of the judges. Suppose that the first of four judges has seen ten performances of *Lear,* has studied the texts, and knows the history of tragedy well; she has watched only two episodes of "Dallas." Are we to take her opinion of the two as carrying equal weight with that of a second judge, who has the same knowledge about *Lear* but has followed "Dallas" through many episodes? A third judge, who has followed "Dallas" in every episode, has tried only once to read *Lear,* and knows no other classical tragedies, concludes that "Dallas" is superior. A fourth judge, finally, an expert in the history of jokes, has merely glanced at both dramas, and announces that he values the joke above them both.

Nobody in practice would listen to all four judges with equal attention and respect about all three works. But in theory, once one decides that values, unlike facts, are created only by valuers and have no objective status, the *fact* that valuers vary so markedly seems to confirm the original doctrine. The circularity of the confirmation is disguised, usually, by bringing into the debate only "qualified judges": authorities like Tolstoy attacking the devotees of Shakespeare, or Samuel Johnson downgrading the metaphysical poets and thus offending hordes of us idolators in the twentieth century.

As evidence mounted, over the centuries, of the shattering instability and variability of acts of valuation, even among qualified judges, and as admirable doctrines of political equality were extended into rhetorical and finally into aesthetic domains, one could more and more easily assume that when anyone uttered pronouncements like Steiner's, they were indeed what his own introduction claims: merely statements of personal preference. And if that is true of *all* value judgments, it must be true *a fortiori* of ethical judgments, the most complex and difficult kind.

If reviving ethical criticism depended on rejecting or deploring the raw fact that *readings vary,* the project would be doomed from the start. Too often ethical critics have implied that all variations are simply evidence that the readings of vast numbers of people are just plain wrong. Can we hope to find a criticism that can respect variety and yet offer *knowledge* about why some fictions are worth more than others?

THE TRIUMPH OF THEORIES OF ART AS ABSTRACT FORM

In addressing each of the preceding beliefs as a cause for the decline of faith in ethical criticism, I am of course quite uncertain about just what was cause and what was effect. Surely a decline in responsible ethical criticism must have at least reinforced each of the beliefs I have described. Would not any such decline have a disastrous effect on other elements in our intellectual culture—not simply, as some ethical critics have argued, on our morality?

This inseparability of cause and effect becomes clearer when we look at a fourth kind of dogma, one we have already glanced at: the rise of theories that elevated abstract form to the top of every aesthetic pyramid. If artistic works are thought of as the imposition of form on some sort of content, and if we are looking for a distinctive domain for "the aesthetic," it is inevitable that we will sooner or later (and it was really astonishingly late, considering that the form/content split prevailed for more than two millennia) conclude that the true or only value of art is found in its form, abstracted from the content.[11] And if

---

11. For the radical difference between the form/*content* split and the Aristotelian notion of a "synolon" of form and *matter,* the matter en-formed, the form inseparable from the matter, see Crane 1953.

"content" is irrelevant, then of course ethical criticism of that content will not be artistic criticism but something else, something surely inferior in interest, quality, validity, and relevance.

The aesthetic status of narratives as a class was especially threatened by this critical trend: narrative is so much more heavily burdened with distracting content than are the other arts—*if* content is a burden. Just as the graphic arts increasingly sought a form untainted by "content" (see Shahn 1957) and as so-called serious or classical music increasingly abstracted itself not only from narrative "program" but from any readily discernible emotional patterns, following instead new "purely musical" or even mathematical algorithms, so narrative with an obvious human reference became increasingly suspect. It was thus no accident that, on the one hand, narrative history was put on the defensive, replaced more and more by statistical, "cliometric" studies, and, on the other hand, novelists and their critics became more and more impressed by experiments with abstract forms that frustrated or violated traditional "human interests." [12]

Where could ethical criticism find a place in such movements? It was banned from the beginning, except as it presupposed the value— never called "ethical"—of experiencing a form purged of content!

SOME PECULIARITIES OF ETHICAL CRITICISM

We must now add to these four dogmas some peculiarities of the enterprise itself—attributes that seem especially peculiar when they are examined through twentieth-century lenses and compared with other ethical enterprises. The chief of these, the method of argument required when we try to demonstrate qualitative judgments about in-

---

12. It is important to distinguish here those "metafictions" that explored new but still obviously concrete human interests (like *Tristram Shandy*'s warm, comic, and—by comparison with later experimental fiction—coherent play with the problem of telling a story) from those that are "generated" by more fully abstract patterns: Walter Abish's *Alphabetical Africa* (1974), its vocabulary dictated, chapter by chapter, by alphabetical sequence—first chapter, all words beginning with *a*, second chapter all with *a & b*, etc.; Ricardou's many experiments with mathematical exigencies (as defended in 1973, 1978); OULIPO's aggressive search for new abstract bases for form (OULIPO 1986). One need not declare such experimental works worthless to see that their very existence can *seem* to make ethical criticism irrelevant. Actually, in my terms they simply insist— rightly or wrongly—on the application of a different ethical ideal.

ternal experience, I discuss at some length in Chapter 3. But I should first dramatize just how heterodox ethical criticism must appear to anyone who takes modernist dogmas as orthodoxy.

Ethical inquiry of certain kinds is now quite fashionable. Though our culture is often described as having lost all faith in values, it nevertheless produces theories of ethics and morality at a great pace. It is true that many of our major novelists and poets have portrayed a world in which all honest thinkers admit that we are a forlorn race, lost in a cosmos indifferent to our ends, rootless, groundless, unaided by any rationally defensible code, expressing at best our irrational values in existential protest. But philosophers, meanwhile, have repudiated the subjectivisms and positivisms of our immediate past and are publishing proof upon proof that moral decisions and moral argument can be rational after all and that utter relativism or subjectivism is irrational (see p. 165 n. 4 below). In *Books in Print* alone, one finds somewhere around five hundred books with titles like *Theory of Ethics, The Theory of Morality, The Foundations of Ethics,* and *Reason in Ethics.* The diversity of the programs they offer as *the* answer to ethical chaos could be taken as further evidence for that chaos. But is it not interesting that almost all of these passionately hard-working arguers have agreed on one thing: moral and ethical judgments are not *necessarily* irrational?

An even larger number are fervently promoting particular moral programs; we are surrounded by moralists who know precisely what is right and wrong. What's more, some of these manage to produce entire academic programs: "the ethics" of medicine, of law, of nuclear power, of ecology, of legislative behavior, of social service. Again in *Books in Print* I find five hundred or so titles like *The Ethics of Business, Environmental Ethics,* and *The Ethics of Whatnot.* (I find only one title suggesting an ethics of *criticism*—Wallis 1924.)

Some of these moralists may initially seem to offer us useful analogues to a revived ethical criticism. But we soon run into at least five radical differences that make ethical criticism of narrative transactions not just peculiar but peculiarly important—and peculiarly difficult.

In the first place, the ethics of criticism is more obviously of *universal* concern than most other "ethics." The ethical effects of engaging with narratives are felt by everyone in all times and climes, not just some special group of victims or beneficiaries. No human being, literate or not, escapes the effects of stories, because everyone tells them and listens to them. You and I may care a good deal about the ethics of medicine and the ethics of law, but these subjects would surprise an ancient historian like Herodotus, or many a citizen in many a land today. If I am among those billions who never go to doctors or lawyers, their ethical code need not concern me greatly. Even the ethics of nuclear warfare, of mortal concern to everyone in our time, cannot rival the daily, hourly impact of the stories human beings have told to one another, and to their own private selves, awake and sleeping. Indeed, even our ideas about the nuclear threat are shaped primarily by the stories we hear about it: the "thing itself" is unknown to all but some survivors in Japan and Chernobyl. The questions we ask about such stories, and the innumerable other kinds that fill each day—Should I believe this narrator, and thus join him? Am I willing to be the kind of person that this story-teller is asking me to be? Will I accept this author among the small circle of my true friends?—these might well have been asked about any story from the beginning of time. And whether or not a given culture ever asked the questions openly, their implicit answers have determined to a great extent what that culture was to be. (Precisely to *what* extent, we can probably never know; I have no interest in denying the role of material, economic causes in building cultures. And I see no way to prove, except with the kind of "thought experiment" we are conducting here, that fictions are the most powerful of all the architects of our souls and societies.)

In any case, our own time differs from all others only in the greater quantity, and perhaps (with the invention of the new graphic media) the intensity, of the daily barrage of narrative to which we are subjected. When we add to the universal, apparently "natural" human flood of conversational narrative all our vast daily, weekly, and monthly journalistic fictions, our unprecedented consumption of films and videos, and the steady barrage of television drama (including those expensively crafted thirty-second dramas, the commercials), our culture appears to be the most narrative-centered of all time. This fact, if it is a fact, heightens the importance of ethical criticism for *us,* but it does not change my claim that the ethics of narrative is inherently a universal subject: in the beginning, and from then on, there was story, and it was largely in story that human beings were created and now continue to recreate themselves.

The ancient Sophists argued that in a sense every person is an expert about ethics in general (Plato, *Protagoras* 326–28). In the same way, and for the same reasons, all of us consider ourselves experts in our subject here. Everyone "knows" with some confidence just how narratives work or should work. In earlier times this seemed to produce masses of people who knew without argument that such-and-such "immoral" narratives were not to be tolerated. In our time, among intellectuals at least, the same sense of expertise produces numberless critics who seem to be sure that nothing really "artistic" or "literary" can harm the sophisticated mind. Facing either kind, the ethical critic will be on the defensive.

Second, it follows from the universality of our experience of narrative that the ethics of narrative is a peculiarly *reflexive* study. Thinkers for several centuries have sought to free themselves from the kind of circularity that is tautological, the kind with conclusions built analytically into premises. Whether or not that quest was always mistaken in all fields, as some have argued, it seems clear that ethical criticism cannot escape assuming from the start at least one of its major conclusions: some experiences with narrative are beneficial and some harmful. No one who is unshakably skeptical about that notion will be likely to follow any argument about how a given narrative might nourish or poison those who take it in. Whenever an inquiry visibly suffers from this formal circularity,[13] those who follow the inquiry must not pretend, as too many ethical critics have done, that they can achieve some kind of apodeictic demonstration.

Clearly the circularity here is not just formal. It springs from the obvious fact that the minds we use in judging stories have been constituted (at least in part) by the stories we judge. Doctors do not judge the ethical issues raised in performing heart implants by the same art by which they perform such operations; the craft and the judgment of whether it should be employed are quite distinct. Similarly, the ethics of selling is not judged by the same art as is studied, in one sales manual, under the heading, "How to Move in for the Kill." In contrast,

---

13. I think that all studies of human values exhibit it. In the old religious formulation of Augustine and other theologians that I have already mentioned, if you are to arrive at my conclusions, you must "first believe in order to understand."

any ethics of narrative will be practiced by *characters* who have been to some degree suborned by the accused; they must depend on a range of mental powers that will already have been affected by the narrative being judged. This point will hardly be news for those readers who have accepted the deconstructionist emphasis on "the problem that develops when[ever] a consciousness gets involved in interpreting another consciousness, the basic pattern from which there can be no escape in the social sciences"—or indeed in any investigation (de Man 1983, 9).

Since narrative is universal, this circularity means that there can be no "control group" consisting of untouched souls who have lived lifetimes without narrative so that they might study unscathed the effects on others, or be studied in their uncontaminated state. All of us are naturally tempted, of course, to think that this point does not apply to us—that surely, at least by the time we reach maturity, *we* have learned to be "critical" and are thus somehow immune to the effects others may suffer. Whenever I have talked with university audiences on the topic "Can Art Be Bad for You?" someone has said something like, "Well, yes, some kinds of art can be bad for some kinds of immature or inexperienced people—children, for example, who are still naive about identifying with characters and transferring their values to their own lives. But mature, critical readers don't do that."

The giveaway is that most of the "mature" readers who exempt themselves in this way are ready to admit that *other* adults are still children in this one respect. Perhaps we all underestimate the extent to which we absorb the values of what we read. And even when we do not retain them, the fact remains that insofar as the fiction has *worked* for us, we have lived with its values for the duration: we have been *that kind of person* for at least as long as we remained in the presence of the work, and any ethical criticism we engage in will thus be "tainted" for those who would prefer some kind of objective view. If we are convinced, with Plato, that Homer shapes the souls of all he touches, then we, like Plato, cannot judge that shaping without having experienced it first. And our judgment will surely have been affected by the experience. What we do may well resemble the effort of someone whose mind has been "burned out" by cocaine to apply that burned out mind to the question of whether cocaine is good for people, or someone who has suffered devastating brain surgery trying to think about whether

the operation succeeded. Or—for those who prefer to think of themselves as (so far) unmaimed, and I find that almost everyone does—the
act of ethical criticism may resemble that of some angelic creature
whose literary diet has (so far) been only of ennobling stuff, assigned
the task of explaining to ordinary mortals why such-and-such narratives corrupt: he or she must first risk corruption by digging into the
stories, in order to discover what to talk about.

Thus, if anything worthy to be called knowledge is obtainable here,
it will not be a knowledge satisfying to any positivists or unrecon-
structed objectivists who may still be with us, as the century wanes,
wondering where all the hard-headed doubters disappeared to.

Third, and complicating things further, the ethics of narrative is *reciprocal* in a way that other ethical studies are not. The ethics of medicine is almost always one-directional: it is largely confined to what
doctors do to patients, not what doctors do to themselves or what patients do to doctors. The ethics of law concerns how lawyers treat their
clients and the public's interest. There might be an ethics of patienthood, or clienthood, developing out of current malpractice suits, but
everyone seems to be seeking legal, not ethical, solutions to excess
suits and awards.[14]

The ethics of narrative transactions, in contrast, concerns not only
the effects on listeners of deliberate lies or debased visions (which
would be analagous to doctors' lying to or mistreating patients), but
also the effects on tellers themselves: any story told with genuine engagement will affect its teller fully as much as it affects listeners. If our
search is for good talk about the ethical effects of narrative encounters,
we must look at both parties in every narrative exchange. When we do
that, in Chapter 5, we will discover a surprising range of responsibilities that *might* be explored. That range produces great confusion, because critics who use the same terms in their appraisals may in fact be
talking about quite different and only distantly related matters—for
example, the obligations of artists to their art, the obligations of readers to the artist, living or dead, and the obligations of readers to *their*
readers.

---

14. I have found only one book on the subject of how a patient *ought* to behave
toward the doctor (Siegler 1979), but I've not looked very hard.

Fourth, ethical debate about narrative values can lead almost instantaneously into *ultimate questions*. Ethical debate about most human activities can appeal to public norms that do not obviously depend on ultimate standards about the whole of human life. We can agree, without first having to conduct a deep discussion about the meaning of life, that a doctor should not refuse treatment to a bleeding patient who cannot pay. In order to discuss whether a nuclear first-strike option is ethical, we needn't debate much about the ultimate good for humankind; simple survival is for the purpose ultimate enough. No such shortcuts are available to the ethical critic. While it is true that any persistent inquirer in other ethical disciplines can pursue such decisions into the regions of ultimacy, in doing ethical criticism we can scarcely avoid them even at the beginning.

If there is anything questionable about Shakespeare's wonderful story of the cruel, miserly, revengeful Jew, or Mozart's ravishingly beautiful musical narrative, in *Così fan tutte,* of how two silly lovers manipulate, humiliate, and finally subdue two silly, fickle women, the answer is not to be found in isolation from our picture of what human life should or might be, or of how it should be portrayed, or of what kinds of artistic experiences are worth having. If there is a high ethical value, as I shall argue, in the works of a D. H. Lawrence whose actual ethical opinions often seem to me deplorable, the case for that value will not be made without reference to the ultimate religious questions that Lawrence cares about and nags us about. And of course once we address such questions, we lose all hope of discovering single, universally compelling answers.

But to say this leads finally to a grand difference that I must dwell on in Chapter 6: ethical criticism can never rest content with talk about consequences. Most current ethical debates are relatively hospitable to such argument. Though many of us believe that utilitarian arguments cannot provide the last word on any ethical question, we must admit that they are useful in resolving practical disputes. When all other ethical argument fails, there is always some force in saying that such-and-such a political or medical or legal practice will harm more people than it will help, or that it will yield more misery than happiness. In ethical criticism of narrative, in contrast, consequentialist argument always seems secondary and certainly unconvincing to those who are used to demanding statistical studies from the Surgeon

General's office or the FDA. Since we are in many respects a "future-directed society" (Ariely 1966), one for which the ultimate sign of success is a rising gross national product, any discipline that concentrates, as we must, on the "quality of life" as it is lived faces an uphill battle.

These five peculiarities alone might well explain why many critics simply refuse to defend the judgments that their critical practice nevertheless exhibits. To offer a defense of why *Huckleberry Finn* is or is not vulnerable to the charge laid by Paul Moses is to address complexities that are more comfortably left alone or simply barred from discussion. It is no wonder, then, that the actual practices of ethical critics have often been of a kind that seems to confirm the skeptic's strongest misgivings. If we are to revive confidence in this most important of all forms of criticism, we must be as clear about the pitfalls in the path ahead as an inherently murky subject will allow.

REFERENCES

Abish, Walter. *Alphabetical Africa*. New York, 1974.
Abrams, M. H. "Art-As-Such: The Sociology of Modern Aesthetics." *Bulletin: The American Academy of Arts and Sciences* 38 (Mar. 1985): 8–33.
Ariely, Yehoshua. *The Future-Directed Character of the American Experience*. Jerusalem, 1966.
Arnold, Matthew. "Preface." *Poems*. London, 1853.
———. *Culture and Anarchy*. London, 1869.
———. *Literature and Dogma*. London, 1873.
Bloom, Harold, Paul de Man, Jacques Derrida, Geoffrey Hartman, and J. Hillis Miller. *Deconstruction and Criticism*. New York, 1979.
Booth, Wayne C. "Censorship and the Values of Fiction." *English Journal* 53 (Mar. 1964): 155–64. Reprinted in *Now Don't Try to Reason with Me: Essays and Ironies for a Credulous Age*. Chicago, 1970.
———. *Modern Dogma and the Rhetoric of Assent*. Chicago, 1974.
Carey, John. "An End to Evaluation." *Times Literary Supplement* (Feb. 22, 1980): 204.
———. *John Donne: Life, Mind, and Art*. London, 1981.
Casey, John. *The Language of Criticism*. London, 1966.
Crane, R. S. *The Languages of Criticism and the Structure of Poetry*. Toronto, 1953.
de Man, Paul. "Criticism and Crisis." In *Blindness and Insight: Essays in the Rhetoric of Contemporary Criticism* [1971]. 2d ed., rev. Theory and History of Literature, vol. 7. Minneapolis, 1983.

Dembo, L. S., ed. *Criticism: Speculative and Analytical Essays*. Madison, Wis., 1968.

Donagan, Allan. *The Theory of Morality*. Chicago, 1977.

Ellis, John M. "Great Art: A Study in Meaning." *British Journal of Aesthetics* 3 (1963): 165–71.

Frye, Northrop. *Anatomy of Criticism: Four Essays*. Princeton, N.J., 1957.

———. "Literary Criticism." In Thorpe 1963.

Gewirth, Alan. *Reason and Morality*. Chicago, 1978.

Gunn, Giles. "The Moral Imagination in Modern American Criticism." Ch. 2 of *The Culture of Criticism and the Criticism of Culture*. New York, 1987.

Harré, Rom. "Science as a Communal Practice." In *Varieties of Realism: A Rationale for the Natural Sciences*. New York, 1986.

Hough, Graham. *An Essay on Criticism*. London, 1966.

Johnson, Samuel. Preface to *The Plays of William Shakespeare* [1765]. In *Johnson on Shakespeare*. Ed. Arthur Sherbo. Vol. 7 of *The Yale Edition of the Works of Samuel Johnson*. New Haven, Conn., 1968. 59–113.

Kant, Immanuel. "Analytik des Schönen" (Analytic of the beautiful). In *Kritik des Urtheilskraft*. 1790.

Krieger, Murray. "Literary Analysis and Evaluation—and the Ambidextrous Critic." In Dembo 1968: 16–36.

MacIntyre, Alasdair. *After Virtue: A Study in Moral Theory*. Notre Dame, Ind., 1981.

MacMillan, P. R. *Censorship and Public Morality*. Aldershot, 1983.

OULIPO: A Primer of Potential Literature. Trans. Warren F. Motte, Jr. Lincoln, Nebr., 1986.

Polanyi, Michael. *Personal Knowledge: Towards a Post-Critical Philosophy* [1958]. Chicago, 1972.

Putnam, Hilary. "Reason and History." In *Reason, Truth, and History*. Cambridge, 1981.

Ricardou, Jean. *Le nouveau roman*. Paris, 1973.

———. *Nouveaux problèmes du roman*. Paris, 1978.

Schreiber, S. M. *An Introduction to Literary Criticism*. Oxford, 1965.

Shahn, Ben. *The Shape of Content*. Cambridge, Mass., 1957.

Siegler, Miriam. *Patienthood: The Art of Being a Responsible Patient*. New York, 1979.

Smith, Barbara Herrnstein. "Contingencies of Value." In von Hallberg 1984: 5–39.

Steiner, George. "The Scandal of the Nobel Prize." *New York Times Book Review* (Sept. 30, 1984): 1ff.

Strelka, Joseph, ed. *Problems of Literary Evaluation*. University Park, Pa., 1969.

Thorpe, James, ed. *The Aims and Methods of Scholarship in Modern Languages and Literatures*. New York, 1963.

von Cranach, Mario, et al. *Goal-Directed Action*. European Monographs in Social Psychology, no. 30. New York, 1982.

von Cranach, Mario, and Rom Harré, eds. *The Analysis of Action: Recent Theoretical and Empirical Advances*. Cambridge, 1982.

von Hallberg, Robert, ed. *Canons.* Chicago, 1984. (Mostly essays from *Critical Inquiry* 10 [Sept. 1983].)
Wallis, N. Hardy. *"The Ethics of Criticism" and Other Essays.* Port Washington, N.Y., 1924.
Wellek, René. "Criticism as Evaluation." In *"The Attack on Literature" and Other Essays.* Chapel Hill, N.C., 1982.
Williams, Bernard. *Ethics and the Limits of Philosophy.* Cambridge, Mass., 1985.
Wittgenstein, Ludwig. "A Lecture on Ethics." *Philosophical Review* 74 (Jan. 1965): 3–12.

3

As novels are about the ways in which human beings behave, they tend to imply a judgment of behavior, which means that the novel is what the symphony or painting or sculpture is not—namely, a form steeped in morality. . . . We still cannot prevent a moral attitude from creeping into our purely aesthetic assessment of a book.
Anthony Burgess

[Unfortunately], he pronounces poems good or bad with the confidence of a school report.
David Nokes

But Miss [Dorothy] Sayers is after all a product of Shrewsbury College as well as its producer. Who is responsible for this combination of literary glibness and spiritual illiteracy? . . . That inane wit, that unflagging sense of humour, . . . that affectation of unconventionality, that determined sociality, what a familiar chord they strike ! . . . [I]f the younger generation read her novels with pleasure . . . then the higher education of women is in a sadder way than any feminist could bear to contemplate.
Q. D. Leavis

The Peculiar "Logic"
of Evaluative Criticism

In the light of all these difficulties, some of them peculiar to the modern period, it is likely that ethical criticism would have become theoretically suspect even if all its practitioners had performed with exemplary rigor and sensitivity. But of course they—we—have not done so. Perhaps because of the very difficulties, they—we—have often been tempted into slapdash arguments and hectoring tones of voice that have inadvertently discredited the whole enterprise. Too many ethical critics have assumed that their whole task is to damn what is evil or to expose other critics as incompetent or immoral for failing to do so.

The temptation is of course understandable. If I have learned to love a wondrous kind of narrative, one that elevates my soul to new heights, and if I see all about me fools and knaves who admire art that I consider a debasement both of life and story, I am sorely tempted to expose the canaille as betrayers of my dream. Yvor Winters—to invoke one of the more intelligent of what we might call the "hanging judges," a highly gifted poet in his own right—frequently implies that his primary task is to protect us from something we have been foolish enough to love. He claims to know precisely "those qualities for which one looks in a poem"—any poem:

> [A] poem in the first place should offer us new perceptions, not only of the exterior universe, but of human experience as well; it should add . . . to what we have already seen. . . . The corresponding function for the poet is a sharpening and training of his sensibilities[,] . . . the discovery of values which he never would have found without . . . that particular act.
>
> (1947, 17)
>
> [T]he poem will be the most valuable, which, granted it achieves formal perfection, represents the most difficult victory.
>
> (25)

Who could object to these as *among* the marks of *some* good poems? Winters himself qualifies the absolutes almost out of existence, when he later encounters other poems with other virtues. And it is true that his tone can often be much more reasonable than his reputation as a cruel schoolmaster suggests. But too often he argues that when the given virtue is missing, a poem is damned, by reason of that lack alone. And he can sometimes seem bent on driving all but a saving remnant from his elevated territory.

> I am about to promulgate a heresy; namely, that E. A. Poe, although he achieved . . . a remarkable agreement between his theory and his practice, is exceptionally bad in both. . . . Poe has long passed casually with me and with most of my friends as a bad writer accidentally and temporarily popular; the fact of the matter is, of course, that he has been pretty effectually established as a great writer while we have been sleeping. The menace lies . . .
>
> (234)

> The poem [Dickinson's "I like to see it lap the miles"] is abominable; and the quality of silly playfulness which renders it abominable is diffused more or less perceptibly throughout most of her work. . . . [E]ven in her most nearly perfect poems, even in those poems in which the defects do not intrude momentarily in a crudely obvious form, one is likely to feel a fine trace of her countrified eccentricity.
>
> (284)

This, about a poet who in Winters's view "is a poetic genius of the highest order"! When he turns to lesser figures one often cannot so much as catch a glimpse of their virtues, covered as they are with his scorn (see Cook 1982).

Similarly, F. R. Leavis, another unquestionably fine critic when at his best, frequently allows himself to play the hanging judge. Though his enemies too often overlooked his brilliant evocations of the value of the works he admired, he did sometimes treat literary works, as C. S. Lewis put it, "as so many lamp-posts for a dog" (1961, 112). And he spent too much energy on ranking, never a very useful form of criticism. "The challenge," he says in one schoolmasterly effort, was to "establish an order of preference" among three poems—one wants to ask, "Why?"

> About which of the three poems should come lowest in order of preference there will be ready agreement. Alexander Smith's *Barbara* has all the vices that are to be feared when his theme is proposed, the theme of irreparable loss. It doesn't merely surrender to temptation; it goes straight for a sentimental debauch, an emotional wallowing, the alleged situation being only the show of an excuse for the indulgence, which is, with a kind of innocent

shamelessness, sought for its own sake. . . . The cheapness of the sentimentality . . .

(1968, 1: 248)

I am not suggesting that Winters and Leavis should have kept their negative opinions to themselves. But nobody looking at such passages now can wonder that many readers heard in them a threat of censorship (see the Introduction to Part 2 below).

I must now move, however, to consider problems of method that run considerably deeper than lack of surface graciousness or tact.

THE OVERLY-AMBITIOUS LOGIC OF CRITICAL EVALUATION

More often than not, overtly ethical critics from Plato to Gardner have sought general rules of judgment or even single standards of true excellence. Like most aestheticians, they have pursued some grand, clear, unequivocal, universal definition of "what all (good or genuine or canonical) art is or does." Once the definition is in place, the step from *is* to *ought* has already been taken: the definition becomes normative, telling us what all defensible art *should* be.[1]

All critics are tempted to over-generalize, but ethical critics have seemed especially open to that temptation. Having experienced some artistic gift that feels unquestionably valuable, they have leapt to proclaim it the only true gift. Having experienced some offering that feels unquestionably threatening or harmful to the spirit, they have hastened to damn it as the unfailing source of all artistic evil. The step from intense, ineluctable, personal experience to the proclamation of *the* truth about art is all too easy.

Anyone who comes to *know,* in heart or gut, that "this thing here

1. An influential example of the use of definition to reduce all criteria to the one right "organic" view is René Wellek's *History of Modern Criticism, 1750–1950.* For a brief critique of the universalist principles governing this history, see my review (1966). For an impressive demonstration both that the search for universal standards is misguided and that evaluation is still a reasonable practice, see John M. Ellis, *The Theory of Literary Criticism* (1974).

before me is good (or evil)" is almost certain to want to share the good (or protect others from the evil).[2] I read a novel and find it not just pleasant but good, and I work out for myself the qualities that make it so: it is beautiful, unified, harmonious, coherent, original, new, or risk-taking. Or it does something for me that I now think needed doing: it has deepened my experience, heightened my sensibilities, matured my judgment, consoled me, shocked me, "defamiliarized" the word and the world, served the revolution, stabilized my tottering polis. (Any reader who would like a richer list might take a moment here to sample the anthology of literary goods that I offer in the Appendix). The next step is almost inevitable: that good is not only *a* good, it is *the* good that all art ought to serve. The history of ethical criticism is thus full of reductions of *all* possible goods to one or two. Especially in a time like ours, when "poetry" or "literature" have seemed by many to be under unprecedented attack, the temptation has been strong to defend the beleaguered class en bloc. And how do you do that if you cannot state your standard?[3]

The final step seems irresistible. Whatever value we have seen in reading a selection of those works that are designated by honorific terms like "literature" or "true poetry," that value, we must now claim, if we are to be consistent, will be discovered in every full experience of any work that deserves the honorific: *all* genuine literature will

2. This is not the first nor the last time that I shall be found guilty of generalizing beyond my evidence. Some of us have more of the evangelical impulse than others, and at least one obvious exception comes to mind: someone can discover that having money is good without having the slightest impulse to share it. Still, I think the generalization holds, once we get a clear notion of a "good" as not just something I happen to like but as something I find to *be* a good. See Murdoch 1970, and Plato (choose almost any dialogue at random). See also "How Our 'Roles' Converse," in Chapter 9 below.

3. Two examples chosen from myriads: Murray Krieger's lifetime project defending literature as our way of escaping the bonds of time (1976); Warner Berthoff's effort to show that literature—everything worthy of the name—bears "witness to significant human action, and to the possibility of such action, by recreating concentrated versions of it within some discernible field of occurrence; to bear witness, that is, to what in specific acts of thought and feeling men and women . . . actually do and undergo in life" (1986, 7–8). Somewhat smaller lumpings are used to describe the ethical effects of particular epochs or literary movements. Theo D'haen, for example, contrasts the "function" (in my terms, the "ethical effect") of all "modernist" literature, which provides beneath its difficulties and fragmentation some "remedy" or implied "re-integration" for the reader, and all "postmodernist" literature, which explodes every possibility of re-integration or remedy (1987).

provide, for *all* good readers, a heightened aesthetic consciousness, a transcendence of the pragmatic, or—at the closest to explicitly ethical talk—"a rehearsal of life's problems in a context freed of practical interest." Even those critics who have attempted discriminations about better and worse effects of particular works have generally spoken on behalf of large sub-classes, all of the members of which must carry the same ethical weight. One thinks here of Tolstoy's gross distinction between art works that build a universal loving community and works that please only an elite ([1896] 1960); of F. R. Leavis's furiously simplified establishment of "the great tradition" in fiction, a tradition that exhibits, unlike the works he excludes, a high moral seriousness and maturity (1969); of Yvor Winters's passionate division of all poems into two kinds, those defensible in the courts of reason and those that are essentially irrational (1947); or of Lionel Trilling's more subtly argued and cautious judgments of what is modern or progressive.[4]

Instead of saying "*One* of the ethical services or threats a narrative can offer is such-and-such," ethical critics have tended to talk like John Gardner:

> [A]rt is essentially and primarily moral—that is, life-giving—moral in its process of creation and moral in what it says. . . . If art destroys good, mistaking it for evil, then that art is false, an error; it requires denunciation. This, I have claimed, is what true art is about—preservation of the world of gods and men. True criticism praises true art for what it does . . . and denounces false art for its failure to do art's proper work.
>
> (1978, 15–16)

> [T]elevision—or any other . . . artistic medium—is good (as opposed to pernicious or vacuous) only when it has a clear positive moral effect, presenting valid models for imitation, eternal verities worth keeping in mind, and a benevolent vision of the possible which can inspire and incite human beings toward virtue, toward life affirmation.
>
> (18)

Gardner hastens to allay our fears that he might be asking for "cornball models of behavior" or a "didactic art" (18–19). Still, it is clear

---

4. I have in mind here his subtle questioning of the likely effects on his students of a steady diet of "modern literature." The essay (Trilling 1968) is one of the best he wrote, and one of the best efforts at ethical criticism mid-century. But like almost everybody else, Trilling provides few hints about how we might discriminate between any two members of a given large class of works.

that the only acceptable fiction will be whatever meets his announced moral standards. He always implies that one might arrive at his secure judgments by the same logic with which he defends them, as if working out a simple implied syllogism:

1. Any work that does (or says, or is) X is bad (or, less frequently, good).
2. This novel by Mailer does (or says, or is) X.
3. Therefore we know, without having to look closely at the full structure of this novel by Mailer, and without considering the different experiences that different readers might make of it, that it is morally harmful.

According to this logic, if I know what qualities mark *any* work as good or bad, and if on examination I find that a given narrative exhibits the right or wrong marks, I know exactly what to think and say about that narrative.

Plato has often been read as establishing this tradition:

1. Any work that teaches disrespect for the gods is bad.
2. Homer teaches disrespect for the gods.
3. Therefore, Homer should not be allowed into the ideal state.[5]

The misleading pattern can be found, at least implicitly, in most evaluative criticism, and it is often quite explicit. Consider, for example, how Gabriel Josipovici argues for the superiority of Muriel Spark's *The Only Problem*. The novel, he says, conveys something that "art, especially verbal art, finds extremely difficult to convey": it demonstrates "the continual tiny triumphs of questions over answers." Most art, he complains, is "on the side of those who know, of the masters of language and argument, on the side, that is, of God and the comforters [of Job]. This book, again like all of Muriel Spark's (*and it is the reason why she is the best English novelist writing today*), is on the side of Job, not theoretically, not in general terms, but in the

---

5. Of all philosophers, Plato is perhaps the most easily misrepresented when quoted out of context. And the *Republic* is of all his works the most trickily evasive for those who would find the "real Plato." I could easily construct a defense of Plato against the charge of simple-minded syllogistic ethical criticism. But the fact is that he spawned a great many followers who have happily extracted the tradition I am questioning.

minutest details of its perceptions and its writing" (1984, 989; my italics).

If I join Josipovici in his high opinion of Spark's work (which I do, though I don't quite see how one arrives at "best" in such judgments), and if I agree (as I do not) that her *supreme* virtue is her ability to raise and sustain tricky questions about life and about religious views of life, I might mistakenly believe that I am following his logic and thus accepting his suggestion that novelists who do *not* do what Spark does are thereby necessarily deficient. To see why Josipovici cannot possibly mean what his language seems to say, we must do a little tracing of the implicit logic of his report.

He implies two universal syllogisms (though he might very well be distressed by seeing them presented to him bare):

Universal Syllogism 1

1. All art that is "on the side of Job," all art that pushes questions rather than answers, is good.
2. *The Only Problem* is "on the side of Job" . . .
3. Therefore . . .

Universal Syllogism 2

1. All art that is "knowing," all art that is on "the side of God," is faulty.
2. "Most modern art" is "knowing" . . .
3. Therefore most modern art is faulty in at least this one respect.[6]

Without having to ask him about it, we can know that Josipovici could not *form* his judgments on this pattern. He must know many an inferior novelist who resists answers as cheerfully as Spark and whose inferiority must consequently spring from some other deficiency. Reading Spark's novel, he surely did not say to himself, "Let's see, now, will she raise questions or answer them? If she does the former, I'll want to praise her; if the latter I'll damn her." The seeming deduction rationalizes a judgment that must actually have been reached by some entirely different route, one that I shall turn to in a moment.

---

6. Each of these syllogisms could of course be translated into more modern logical terms: "If p then q," and so on. I use the traditional terminology not only because I am more at home in it but because I suspect that still, in 1988, most of my readers will be too.

The search for universal standards is not misguided because we cannot hope to find qualities that, when present, will really deserve our praise or blame. It is misguided because its major premise assumes a universal form, and because it implies that our judgments are *arrived at* through deduction. Instead of seeking broadly applicable standards that might help explain our enthusiasms and loathings, we pursue the inherently reductive quest for qualities that will prove benign or malign for all readers in all circumstances.

In short, the search stacks narratives into a single pyramid, with all of the candidates competing for a spot at the apex. Such an assumption, when applied rigorously, will always damn a large share of the world's most valuable art. I propose that we think instead of an indeterminate number of pyramids, or—since pyramids suggest a rather formidable stasis—of a botanical garden full of many beautiful species, each species implicitly bearing standards of excellence within its kind. We cannot know how many good kinds there are, though presumably there is a limit somewhere. But we can tell when a tulip fails to bloom or an iris is stunted and withered.

There may be one universal supreme good for all human beings to aspire to—I doubt it though, unless it is such a tautology as to give us very little to go on: "It is good to live life well" or "It is always good to improve one's soul." But there is surely not one supreme quality that all good art—and therefore all good narratives—should aspire to.[7] One glory of human history is the inheritance it offers of narratives that serve many goods and Gods; if we must have a universal, let us make it the value of experiencing *many* good kinds of narrative, each kind marked by quite different combinations of good qualities, some in seeming conflict with other good things, and some perhaps in other contexts decidedly harmful. I must return to this invigorating but threatening view of complex riches in the Epilogue.

The word "harmful" may seem to suggest *my* universal: doing good

7. By this point in the history of philosophical dispute it is a bit naive to hope for a reduction of all goods to a single system. Though I do not depend here on any single ethical theorist, readers will have no trouble detecting influences. And when they do so—Aristotle, Plato, Kant, Bradley, John Dewey, William James—they will find that in every case I have plumped for the more pluralistic reading of these figures, even of those like Aristotle and Kant who are often read as laying down universal abstract ethical principles. For a good summary of the pluralist's credo, see Henry David Aiken's "Levels of Moral Discourse" (1962).

to the reader rather than harm. It is true that my questions will be mainly about healing and harming persons and cultures. But since "healing" and "harming" remain undefined until we meet specific narrative transactions, my pursuing them consistently does no more than to locate the inquiry as rhetorical—rather than, say, psychological, epistemological, or historical. It does not decide for us what kind of healing or what kind of harm we will discover in the next narrative transaction.

Toward the end of William James's *The Varieties of Religious Experience* he raises the question of what to do about the conflicts among the astonishingly divergent religious beliefs he has traced. Why do we not assume, he asks, "that the lives of all men should show identical religious elements? . . . [I]s the existence of so many religious types and sects and creeds regrettable?" His answer is so apt for our purposes that I must quote it in full:

> To these questions I answer 'No' emphatically. And my reason is that I do not see how it is possible that creatures in such different positions and with such different powers as human individuals are, should have exactly the same functions and the same duties. No two of us have identical difficulties, nor should we be expected to work out identical solutions. Each, from his peculiar angle of observation, takes in a certain sphere of fact and trouble, which each must deal with in a unique manner. One of us must soften himself, another must harden himself; one must yield a point, another must stand firm—in order the better to defend the position assigned him. If an Emerson were forced to be a Wesley, or a Moody forced to be a Whitman, the total human consciousness of the divine would suffer. The divine can mean no single quality, it must mean a group of qualities, by being champions of which in alternation, different men may all find worthy missions. . . . So a 'god of battles' must be allowed to be the god for one kind of person, a god of peace and heaven and home, the god for another.
>
> (1985, 384)

If I substitute for "the divine" the phrase "the ethical value of narrative," I find something like what I want to say about ethical values in narrative.

Thus if we insisted on finding formal logical demonstrations for ethical judgments—and fortunately we shall do without them except for a few passages in Part 3—they should run, even at their most rigorous, like this:

Universal Syllogism 3

   1. *One* good thing a narrative can do (or say, or be) is X.
   2. The *Iliad* does (or says, or is) X.

3. Therefore, the *Iliad* is a good thing to have in the world—it belongs to one of the good kinds of narrative; but that does not mean that for you, in your circumstances, it would serve your spirit as well as would *Gargantua,* say, which promises to do *Y,* or *Zuleika Dobson,* marvelous in its offer of *Z.*

Translated into this form, Josipovici's judgment of Spark is easily salvaged as not nonsensical, only mis-formed. Spark does one wholly admirable job better than other current novelists. She demonstrates "the continual tiny triumphs of questions over answers [and does so in a way that does not lead into the faults that other authors who demonstrate that tired 'truth' usually exhibit]." The judgment can now be taken seriously and discussed intelligibly.

Read in this way, Josipovici's only real quarrel will be with any critic who would elevate some conflicting standard into a universal—perhaps one like this: "The indispensable mark of all good art is that, like *The Divine Comedy,* it provides complex, profound answers to our most troublesome questions, even while opening up many other questions to our inquiry." If, instead of such gross lumping, an opposing critic were to reply to Josipovici simply that "*one* good thing a fiction can do is provide a profound, subtle, immensely complex vision that is built on firm answers to many important questions," both critics might talk together profitably. They might or might not want to dispute about which *kind* is more important or valuable; whole critical schools are sometimes founded on such matters.[8] In any case, neither critic would need to be tempted to ban what for him or her is a *somewhat* inferior kind, or even, ideologically speaking, a profoundly mistaken kind. Indeed, either might make a point that I must return to again and again here: for some people, in some circumstances, Spark is likely to prove ethically more valuable than Dante, and for others— perhaps those who are a bit too comfortable with perpetual questioning—*The Divine Comedy* (or a host of other works that do not fit Josipovici's formula) would provide the superior gift. (I have of course dodged the question of whether Spark in fact leaves *all* questions open.

8. I'm thinking of how the New Critics elevated works that achieved their harmony without denying ironic undercuttings over works that "answered our questions" too easily. See Brooks 1947.

As I shall argue below, she could not possibly do so—not if she expects to tell a story that works for any reader.)

Note that accepting both of these contrasting gifts would not prevent my saying that certain other works—say the sadomasochistic novels of the Marquis de Sade and Georges Bataille—will for most people in most cultures provide a highly dubious diet. And saying *that* will not prevent my saying in turn that for some readers on some occasions—let us say the group of professional critics who have argued for the value of writers like Sade and Bataille (Barthes 1976; Beauvoir 1953)—they are not likely to do much harm. On the other hand, it is hard to see how they could do much good, either, except for the by-no-means contemptible gift of providing fodder for ethical discourse, including my own.

Usually our experience of good and bad qualities cannot be described even as generally as Universal Syllogism 3 suggests. We experience some part or element that is admirable in itself but set in a deplorable context, or contemptible in a work otherwise estimable. Many of our judgments, perhaps most, might then be defended like this, if some logician issued a challenge.

Universal Syllogism 4
1. *One* good (or bad) thing a narrative can do (or say, or be) is X.
2. Such-and-such an aspect, or part, or element of this narrative does X, while other aspects may be thought bad (or good), in varying degrees.
3. Therefore . . .

Therefore what? Does anything follow, about the final value of any work as a whole? How do I weigh my sense that Agatha Christie's *Curtain* offers a few hours of harmless pleasure against the fact that its conclusion, celebrating altruistic suicide, is not only predictable but to me morally superficial and offensive? How do I weigh

□ the admirable integrity and moral depth of "modern morality epics" like William Gaddis's *The Recognitions* (1955) and *Carpenter's Gothic* (1985)—such "novels" have no established name—against their necessary opacity and my resulting frequent boredom?

□ the lively adventure offered by many a piece of sci-fi against the thin characters and frequently incoherent moral worlds too often found there?

□ the hilarious satirical incisiveness of Evelyn Waugh against his sexism, snobbery, and moral bullying?

□ the sustained lyrical intensity of Virginia Woolf's *Jacob's Room* (1922) against its overall formlessness and its frequent reminders that the implied author is embarked on an experiment that she herself does not quite understand?

□ the exhilarating novelty and richness of *Finnegans Wake* (1939) against an obscurity that has in fact baffled most if not all readers, even those who have praised the book as one of our greatest classics?

It is not my point to attack all "lumping" criticism as useless. No critic can get along entirely without generic grouping. I aim simply to underline the age-old point that blanket defenses of general kinds, and blanket attacks on other general kinds, are likely to obscure both particular virtues and particular vices in individual works, and thus to give ethical criticism a bad name.

THE PURSUIT OF "OPENNESS" AS AN EXAMPLE OF "LUMPING" CRITICISM

Of all the fashionable over-generalizations about ethical effect perhaps the most fashionable today is the one we have already encountered in Josipovici: the distinguishing virtue of literature is its power to lead us to questions rather than to answers; or, to "open" the reader to new experiences of "otherness"; or, to wake up the sleepy and complacent by disrupting previous fixities. (By now—1987—the cliché has spread far beyond the scene of criticism: "Merrill Lynch," the ads tell us, "believes your world should know no boundaries!") In its more extreme form, the aim is to shock the reader, to undermine conventions (all assumed to be stifling), to shatter all illusions. From this general aim of good literature—a highly ethical aim indeed, though usually not given that label—follow different programs that stress different kinds of subversion, in the name of different kinds of improved souls that are supposed to emerge from the ruins. But one general assumption seems to underlie the differences: techniques or styles or plot forms that "close" questions are always inferior, the very mark of the non-literary or non-aesthetic or didactic. In contrast, narratives that raise questions, that are open-ended and leave the reader unresolved—and thus presumably unable to remain passive in facing either life or literature—are in general superior.

Typical of recent work exhibiting this belief is Gary J. Handwerk's *Irony and Ethics in Narrative* (1985). Handwerk assumes that he must pursue what *all* irony does to or for us. He begins by distinguishing one kind of irony, "ethical irony," the goal of which is to undermine confidence in the pursuit of an impossible coherence, from other, stabler kinds. But he soon applies his ethical goal to all ironies. Those critics who say that some kinds of irony seek other effects (such as establishing temporarily stable communities of people who in fact understand each other) are simply bypassed as not having understood what *all* irony does, or should do, for us.[9]

Suppose we assume that those who praise "open-ended" works because they create valuable openings in the spirit are generally justified in their praise, that the narratives they admire *are* admirable, and that some of them may even be admirable primarily *because* of the special openings they create. What is then wrong in turning that admirable effect of some works on some readers into a general goal for all praiseworthy narratives? I see four major objections, in addition to the logical point in the previous section. Each of them could be applied, though of course in different vocabulary, to the claims for any universal quality or ethical effect.[10]

---

9. When I wrote *The Rhetoric of Fiction* I was sure that such neutralist doctrines were erroneous, and consequently I fell into a tone, especially in the final chapter, that led some readers to think I was accepting the "openers'" large lumpings and simply reversing their plus and minus signs: closed works (clear in their closures) good, open works (ambiguous) bad; traditional narrative practice good, modernist practice bad. Any careful reader of the book could have escaped that misreading (as Seymour Chatman does in his essay "The 'Rhetoric' 'of' 'Fiction'" (1988).

10. The following four points are developed at greater length in my forthcoming essay "Are Narrative Choices Subject to Ethical Criticism?" (1988).

The Impossibility of a Universal Openness

The most obvious objection is that no literary work of any consequence, in anybody's view, is entirely open. As Marxists and deconstructionists have been insisting, in their quite different vocabularies,
every use of language carries freight, a freight of values or more or less
fixed norms (see Chapter 5).[11] This point includes, but goes somewhat
beyond, the currently fashionable claim that no one is free of epistemological and metaphysical adhesions. (The claim is most com-
monly attributed these days to Derrida (1974) and Foucault (1973),
but it is really to be found everywhere in the history of rhetorical theory: see, for example, Aristotle *Rhetoric,* especially 2.1–17 [1377b–
1391b]; Cicero *De Oratorio*).

In the first place, even if there were such a thing as a totally open
work, every reader would automatically try to close it in order to make
something of it—and everyone would almost certainly succeed. Our
minds are unable to resist making sense of whatever data we encounter, even if they are in fact random. Every word, even in isolation,
closes off some possibilities as it opens up others; as Saussure has insisted, even randomly chosen syllables exclude possibilities, as syl- and
sym-, dys- and re-, com- and per- close off, before a full word is
formed, huge domains of possible meanings. Even single letters produce some closure; a *q* from the roman alphabet closes off all meanings peculiar to other writing systems. The result is that the only
stories we *have*—those that we have brought to life in our experience—exhibit closures, regardless of how open their original authors
may have intended them to be.

But just how open could anyone intend to make a *story?* Surely
a totally open-ended work would leave a reader totally free to invent
meanings, unengaged in any transaction with possibilities contained
within the text. It would consist either of blank pages or of randomly
distributed symbols not recognizable as belonging to any alphabet or
culture. Such a work would presumably leave the reader precisely in

11. For a subtle analysis of the term "ideology," as used by Marx and Marxists, and
of the ways in which efforts like Marx's to get outside ideology are burdened with paradox, see W. J. T. Mitchell's *Iconology* (1986, esp. the final chapter, "The Rhetoric of
Iconoclasm").

the *status quo ante*—hardly an ethical effect to write home about. Some new computer programs claim to build creativity by telling half-stories that then must be completed—creatively, creatively!—by the squatter in front of the screen. No doubt I should resist mocking 'em without trying 'em, but can one not predict that for most "active" participants boredom lurks just around the next turn of the plot?

Obviously no one who has argued for the value of encountering open-ended works has ever meant such total openness, though we might be led to think so if we took some critics at their word.[12] What they always have in mind is some sort of focused or defined "openness," some sort of invitation outward or upward—though "upward" may look "downward" to others if it is an effort at transvaluation. Consider, for instance, this characteristically "open" story by Donald Barthelme, "The Party." It begins like this:

> I went to a party and corrected a pronunciation. The man whose voice I had adjusted fell back into the kitchen. I praised a Bonnard. It was not a Bonnard. My new glasses, I explained, and I'm terribly sorry, but significant variations elude me, vodka exhausts me, I was young once, essential services are being maintained. Drums, drums, drums, outside the windows. I thought that if I could persuade you to say "No," then my own responsibility would be limited, or changed, another sort of life would be possible, different from the life we had previously, somewhat skeptically, enjoyed together.
>
> (1972, 57)

That's openness? After less than a hundred words we have innumerable specifications, with varying degrees of probability, not just of milieu, class, and character but of feeling: sense of loss, desperation, ironic futility (think of what is closed by the choice of "No" rather than "Yes" in the final sentence). We have even been promised a kind of plot (How is the narrator related to the "you"?). What makes that passage worth reading is not any general openness (and even more obviously not any of the deformations of language that some linguists contend distinguishes "literature") but its brilliant combination of specific closures with specific openings. I think one could show of every narrative praised for its openness—any one of Beckett's, say—that the

---

12. For a cogent appraisal of Mikhail Bakhtin's unwillingness to address the problems of unlimited openness, see Caryl Emerson's "Problems with Bakhtin's Poetic" (1986).

author has made the openings by framing well-designed doors and windows.

All successful narratives are constructed not of ideal total indeterminacy or total resolutions but of *limited determinacies* that by their vividness create strong suspensions or—to borrow Sheldon Sacks's term, in *Fiction and the Shape of Belief* (1964)—"instabilities": strong desires to continue in the company of *this* text to discover what kinds of openness or closure lie ahead. Openness and closure are thus not independent terms but reciprocals, like parent/child or husband/wife. In the traditional fiction that the "open critics" consider inferior (or struggle to read as indeterminate), suspense—one kind of openness— was created by defining an initial instability with some precision, in order to move a "plot" to a gratifying closure. Reading such stories, we are now told, induces psychic indolence because we merely ask "Whodunit?" and then we find out; or we ask "Will true love triumph?" and then it either does or does not. In the fiction that the "open critics" praise, in contrast, the instabilities and resolutions are produced by questions either about what has happened or about what the relatively plotless works might mean—sometimes simply about what's on the implied author's mind.

Clearly both kinds of stories (discernible as different kinds only at the extremes) depend for their power on first arousing and then gratifying our thirst for *something* quite determinate (though perhaps disguised as "ambiguity"), surrounded by potentially unlimited indeterminacies, potential questions about meanings and outcomes. The difference lies not in the quantity of unresolved questions before, during, or after reading but rather in the area of our questioning as we read: "Will she kill him?" "Will he find God?" "Will she face the abyss?" "Will this wonderful promise of a really masterful style be maintained?" "Will a symbolic pattern emerge?" "Will the narrator/ hero ever penetrate this murk?" A story ending that shows the hero in utter despair, baffled and horrified by the Inscrutable, is as much a closure as is a happy, fortuitous marriage. In short, total openness would be total entropy—and hence total apathy for a reader.

We can see how this works by looking closely at an ending that has proved—if the amount of critical debate is any test—superlatively open. As just about every reader in the Western world knows, *The Turn of the Screw* ends like this:

> But he [little Miles] had already jerked straight round, stared, glared again, and seen but the quiet day. With the stroke of the loss I was so proud of he uttered the cry of a creature hurled over an abyss, and the grasp with which I recovered him might have been that of catching him in his fall. I caught him, yes, I held him—it may be imagined with what a passion; but at the end of a minute I began to feel what it truly was that I held. We were alone with the quiet day, and his little heart, dispossessed, had stopped.
>
> ([1898] 1966, 88)

Now open-ended as that ending has proved to be, we can easily make it more so.

> But he had already jerked straight round, stared, glared again, and seen but the quiet day. With the stroke of the loss that *I did not know how to interpret,* he uttered a cry that *might have been either* that of a creature hurled over an abyss *or a shout of triumph,* and the grasp with which I recovered him might have been that of catching him in his fall. I caught him, yes, I held him in a grasp *perhaps* of passion, *perhaps* of indifference, *perhaps* of terror; but at the end of *an indeterminate time* I began to feel what it truly was that I held. We were alone with the quiet day, and he was dead, *though to this day I do not know whether I unintentionally strangled him, or his heart trouble had simply emerged, or Peter Quint had stolen him to the land of the damned.*

If that is not enough, we can of course go further and say, "We were alone with the quiet day, yet I could not tell whether he was dead or had merely suffered a syncope. And since I left him lying there and fled immediately—I cannot say whither—I have been forced to wonder to this very day."

No doubt by pushing further in this direction I could finally arrive at The Great Inane, but if I did, I could tell no stories there.

Variations in Kinds of Openness

We have inevitably already touched on the second objection: actual literary works exhibit immense variety in the *kinds* of openness they possess. The twin facts that openness can only be built on some sort of closure and that an author can "close" any and every conceivable fact or value, tell us that any critic who tries to deal with the actual variety of works rather than simply imposing a pet theory will be faced with many kinds of openness. Some of these will no doubt be deemed beneficial, according to the critic's ethical code. A critic can easily create the illusion that all open-endedness is beneficial simply by discussing only those works that exhibit a given opening, or by defining as "genuine" or "good" literature only the preferred kind. But without this sleight of hand, discriminations arise.

Critics of Joyce's *A Portrait of the Artist as a Young Man* have argued that the book leaves us undecided about whether Stephen will succeed as an artist, about whether he is justified in feeling guilty for causing his mother to suffer, about whether his villanelle is admirable or shoddy, about whether his aesthetic theory is embraced by the implied author, and indeed about many other moral and intellectual matters. But no critic I know of would be happy to have it said that *Portrait* leaves open the question of whether art is worthy of Stephen's embrace, or whether this is indeed a portrait of a genuine artist as a young man, or whether there is a conflict, in the book as in life, between art and politics. The open-ended work *insists* on a distinctive kind of closure. If I were to say to a Joycean, "You know, the obvious point of that book is that art and religion and family and politics can be easily reconciled, that they exist in an easy harmony," I would be properly hooted down. But are we to say that Joyce's strong closure of that issue in any way diminishes the value of the work? Would it be an even greater work if it had left us unsure about such matters? [13]

Or consider Beckett, whom critics have praised for undermining every value and thus shocking us into growth (Handwerk 1985). Unlike Joyce, Beckett does not provide unequivocal clarity about the supreme value of art; art itself is radically questioned, even as Beckett spends a lifetime of struggle in serving it. Gary Handwerk, for example, concludes "that Beckett finally *forces* us to turn from his fiction, to recognize that it cannot in any way allay the anxiety it arouses." He claims that Beckett "*closes off* the allegorical path back to experience and provides no wisdom at all except *a reinforced sense of our own ignorance,* with perhaps a heightened sense of how much time we may actually spend dealing with *nonessentials*" (1985, 194; my italics). Now just what are those "nonessentials," and what are the essentials they are contrasted with in this work that leaves "everything

---

13. This kind of absolute (unspoken) unanimity of readers on a given point could be matched in discussions of some parts of every "open" work. We ordinarily don't talk about what goes without saying. How could we get published if we did?

open"? Handwerk does not stay for an answer, but his language can only imply that Beckett in fact closes question after question, "insisting" for example, that "only linguistic ploys can salvage or enforce a measure of self-identity" (194).

Needless to say, other "open" works "insist" that art as play is of supreme importance, the only real value; or that the universe is empty of value—an opinion that implies a most impressively omniscient author; or that the ultimate emptiness of texts is our best clue to the nature of God; or that God is dead and we must love one another; or that apathy is what kills us; or that only in this or that meditative practice can we find our peace; or that in our frustration we should join the revolution; or that life is beautiful in its rich open-endedness. The closures that have been rejected are really only of limited kinds: traditional moral judgments; unambiguous triumphs or happy endings; clearly defined characters; unequivocally proclaimed political programs.

The Variety of Readers and Circumstances of Reading

Turning to a third objection, we encounter a curious contrast between two claims made by the theorists of open-endedness. On the one hand, they all celebrate freedom and variety in readers' responses (thus illustrating my previous point that just about everybody on our scene is an "ethical" critic); on the other, they assume that certain privileged literary techniques and forms are invariably better for readers than certain others, and that readers who read for closure are at fault. Open-ended techniques provide, for all readers on all conceivable reading occasions, and in contrast to the old intrusive omiscient authoritarian methods, just what we all most need.[14]

---

14. "The openness of the poets of process to the potential disclosure of meaning and being in realms not sanctioned by the literary-historical canon upsets the definite 'sea lanes' of the New Critical mind. . . . I hope that the impact of his [Charles Olson's] poetry . . . will disclose to critics the need to move away from the traditional assumptions they habitually make and into a realm of greater uncertainty where the act of reading is defined by its instability and risk" (Bové 1980, 281).

For another sustained effort to pursue a "politics" (in my terms, an "ethics") of indefinite openings, see Robert Siegle's *The Politics of Reflexivity* (1986). Siegle quarrels with me for being one of those nearly ubiquitous "closers"—that is, I am committed to a "metaphysic" of "referentiality." I see *him* as one of those nearly ubiquitous "openers,"

Nobody would deny (though of course some do) that some works for some readers on some occasions do provide a precious melting of categories that would otherwise freeze the reader's soul. But are we to believe that every reader in every epoch most needs one kind of shock, or even a shock at all, and that there are no other ethical effects that for some readers in some circumstances might be more valuable?

Obviously some readers on some occasions do receive a salutary jolt when they accompany narrators who leave as many questions open as possible while still telling a story. I have just recently received a bit of a jolt by re-reading Virginia Woolf's extraordinarily "open" *Jacob's Room*. That work annoys, needles, exasperates, and wakes up the author of *The Rhetoric of Fiction*. I think the reading was good for me because it opened some questions about narrative that had been at least partially closed. I know two people, however, for whom *Jacob's Room* at one time poisoned the wells of modern fiction; after trying it they retreated to the Victorians—and so far as I know now have never attempted any more Woolf. No doubt if one could get them to give Woolf a fair reading, it would "be good for them." But unless we pretend to know what is always good for everyone, must we not concede that some other readers on other occasions, readers perhaps who in utter passivity have swallowed current commonplaces about the absolute relativity of all values, might benefit more from the shock of reading Dickens's *Old Curiosity Shop*?

When I was eighteen, *War and Peace* taught me the excitement of speculating about historical causes, and led me to accept Tolstoy's decisive views about the ineffectuality of individual leaders in controlling historical events; at sixty-seven, I find myself skipping some of his one-sided speculation about the role of individual choice in determining events. But should I condemn Tolstoy for having closed issues that are

---

committed to an astonishingly firm closure on one metaphysic, one norm for good literature, and one ethical (that is, properly political) way of reading. Thus we both see a group of mistaken folks out there in danger of winning, but our ways of labeling the various camps could not be more different. Indeed I see my own "metaphysic," and certainly the project of *Company*, as closer to his ideal of "reflexivity" than is his own quite monolithic reduction of Thackeray, Conrad, Fowles, and various modern novelists and critics to a single program.

For a subtle exploration of how certain "openings" enabled four French authors in the Renaissance to flow into a copiousness or eloquence previously forbidden, see Terence Cave, *The Cornucopian Text* (1979).

now for me more open? The fact is that, as the reader-responsers have rightly insisted, each of us can draw quite diverse values from what we call the same story, depending on our age and circumstance. Little Nell's death scene in *The Old Curiosity Shop*, which to many modern readers has seemed intolerably, soppily sentimental, may seem, to a reader who has lost a child of Little Nell's age, quite consoling and even restrained and justified by the facts—as it must have seemed to those Victorians who lost so many more children than we do.[15]

I needn't dwell further on this variety of response; it is a commonplace of the very criticism I am questioning. But surely it is curious that those who are properly alert to readers' diversity in other contexts seem to forget it when they hail the psychic boon of "open" works.

Openness Not an End in Itself, but a Means to Various Ends

What all this suggests is that "to be open" or "to leave questions open" is rarely if ever an end in itself but rather either a side effect or a means to some other end. At its most questionable, it is a means to the end of seeming up-to-date: originally modern but now always "post-modern" or "post-structuralist" or "post-deconstructionist."

At its most profound, it serves a value that perhaps we could all embrace: genuine encounters with otherness. "Otherness" is another fashionable term (Certeau 1986; Todorov 1984; Theunissen 1984)— so fashionable that one wonders whether some of its defenders don't have in mind something quite un-other, something thoroughly tamed to perform tricks for modernist lion tamers. Nobody has quite said yet that we have met the Other and it is us, but this adaptation of Pogo may prove dangerously apt.

In any case, I embrace the pursuit of the Other as among the grandest of hunts we are invited to; from birth onward our growth depends so deeply on our ability to internalize other selves that one must be puzzled by those who talk about the self as somehow independent, individual, unsocial in this sense (see Chapter 8). But surely no beast that

---

15. I don't mean to suggest that everything Dickens does with that prolonged scene seems unimpeachable, only that my response was conditioned in part by my experience.

will prove genuinely *other* will fail to bite, and the otherness that bites, the otherness that changes us, must have sufficient definition, sufficient identity, to threaten us where we live. If what a typical twentieth-century liberal really wants is a challenge from otherness, let her try Dante, who was quite un-open about an appalling number of questions; let him try Homer, say, while a colleague down the hall, brought up on Dante and Homer, may be receiving his salutary dose of otherness by discovering Beckett, Barthelme, or Blechman.

For Mikhail Bakhtin, writing in the Soviet Union, it could seem self-evident that any genre that tends to combat single-voicedness is superior to those "monophonic" works that can be used to reinforce convention and autocratic power (1984). But any aspiring ethical critic in any other society must be willing to think about the rhetorical and political situation in which ethical criticism is to be practiced. It is not at all hard to imagine a person in a given culture for whom the worst next step would be to read another book by multivoiced Dostoevsky, Bakhtin's hero, instead of reading the relatively monophonic (and to me considerably less impressive) *1984*, say, or going to a folk music festival and listening to all those monophonic ballads, or to a fine tragedy and discovering something beyond a forlorn quest for identity. Here we see another reason why ethical criticism cannot divorce itself from social and political criticism; once we start thinking about actual responses to particular works by diverse readers, we are inevitably caught up in inquiry about what kinds of experience, in a given polis, are beneficial or harmful.

But how do we do that? Obviously not by any simple deduction from general principles of the kind we rejected earlier. How do we think about our judgments, once we decide that our goal is to *think* about them and not simply to assert them?

HOW WE COME TO THE ACT OF JUDGING: CODUCTION

I suggest that we arrive at our sense of value in narratives in precisely the way we arrive at our sense of value in persons: by *experiencing* them in an immeasurably rich context of others that are both like and unlike them. Even in my first intuition of "this new one," whether a story or a person, I see it against a backdrop of my long personal history of untraceably complex experiences of other stories and persons. Thus my initial acquaintance is comparative even when I do not think of comparisons. If I then converse with others about their impressions—if, that is, I move toward a public "criticism"—the primary intuition (with its implicit acknowledgment of value) can be altered in at least three ways: it can become conscious and more consciously comparative ("This one is like those others, so I'll call it a tragedy, and I like it best of the lot"); it can become less dependent on my private experience ("My friend, R. S. Tottle, thought this one a sentimental disaster; *I'll* have to think about that"); and it can be related to principles and norms ("I always considered portrayals of gratuitous murder immoral; but here I am deeply engaged with that murderer Macbeth. Have I been taken in? Must my code be altered?"). Every appraisal of a narrative is implicitly a comparison between the always complex experience we have had in its presence and what we have known before.

Samuel Johnson catches the precise and important difference between this process and our ways of obtaining scientific knowledge—what he calls "demonstration":

> As among the works of nature no man can properly call a river deep, or a mountain high, without the knowledge of many mountains, and many rivers; so in the productions of genius, nothing can be stiled excellent till it has been compared with other works of the same kind. Demonstration [of the sort possible in scientific matters] immediately displays its power, and has nothing to hope or fear from the flux of years; but works tentative and experimental [that is, works that depend on experience] must be estimated by their proportion to the general and collective ability of man, as it is discovered in a long succession of endeavors. Of the first building that was raised, it might be with certainty determined that it was round or square; but whether it was spacious or lofty must have been referred to time.
>
> (par. 3; [1765] 1968, 60)

Thus the logic we depend on as we arrive at our particular appraisals is neither deduction from clear premises, even of the most complex kind, nor induction from a series of precisely defined and isolated instances. Rather it is always the result of a direct sense that something now before us has yielded an experience that we find *comparatively* desirable, admirable, lovable or, on the other hand, comparatively repugnant, contemptible or hateful.

We have no accurate name either for the initial intuition, already comparative, or for the later, more fully conscious comparison with previous instances: "this-one-of-this-kind is unusually spacious or lofty." We call it judging, but the legal metaphor can unfortunately suggest a flat judgment of guilty or not guilty, judgment of the kind committed by the hanging judges. We call it weighing, which may imply that we possess precisely adjusted scales, though we never do. We call it appraising or assaying, as if it were like obtaining the precise percentage of gold in an alloy, or like determining the exact sale price of a house. None of these terms is entirely misleading. Much of what a judge does resembles what we do—if we remember just how complicated, non-deductive, and comparative legal judgment is (Levi 1948). "Weighing" is not too badly misleading, perhaps, if we think of weighing by hand, feeling the heft of a work against our muscles, rather than reading a dial. And we do in fact "appraise," as an "appraiser" arrives not at an absolute value but at a sale price implicitly comparative with that of similar houses on the market.

All three terms rightly suggest that the judgment requires a community: no judge can operate outside a legal system; no just weighing can take place on scales not calibrated with other scales; and nobody would trust a real estate agent who lacked experience in comparing appraisals with other agents. Perhaps the legal metaphor is least misleading, because it reminds us that all judgment is pointless unless it can be shared with other judges who rely in turn on their past experiences.

But we need a term that suggests even more strongly than the legal metaphor the reliance (rational but by no means logical in any usual sense of the word) on the past experiences of many judges who do not have even a roughly codified set of precedents to guide them. The term must imply a communal enterprise rather than a private, "personal" calculation logically coercive on all who hear it.

Since I find no term that meets these demands, I must for once reluctantly resort to neologism: *coduction,* from *co* ("together") and *ducere* ("to lead, draw out, bring, bring out"). Coduction will be what we do whenever we say to the world (or prepare ourselves to say): "Of the works of this general kind that I have experienced, *comparing my experience with other more or less qualified observers,* this one seems to me among the better (or weaker) ones, or the best (or worst). Here are my reasons." Every such statement implicitly calls for continuing conversation: "How does my coduction compare with yours?"

Such a process is obviously about as different as possible from what logicians claim to do before offering to share a universally valid proof. Coduction can never be "demonstrative," apodeictic: it will not persuade those who lack the experience required to perform a similar coduction. And it can never be performed with confidence by one person alone. The validity of our coductions must always be corrected in conversations about the coductions of others whom we trust. They will thus always be subject to the corrections of time: time alone can yield the further comparisons that can teach us, again by coduction, whether our original appraisals can confirm themselves in further experience.[16] To say as much is not, however, to accept the claim that all literary value is contingent or "statistical" in the sense of being simply created by the valuers, and hence subject to annihilation when no valuers remain (Smith 1984). In Chapter 4 we shall take a longer look at why the complexities of coduction do not imply subjectivism.

Note that the notion of coduction collapses the distinction between how we arrive at a value judgment and how we defend it. The usual way of thinking about how we argue for our conclusions separates inquiry and discovery from explanation and proof—perhaps because in the physical sciences that divorce is sometimes useful. In evaluative criticism, however, it is impossible to distinguish the two sharply. It is true that my first discovery of a literary value may seem entirely private, leading to results simply to be reported or argued for: I read a poem or novel, it hits me hard in one organ or another, and I "con-

16. Much of my description of coduction might be offered by some philosophers of science as a description of how scientists actually arrive at their judgments, in contrast with how they describe their results. Most scientists testify that they work not primarily with linear logic but with an intuitive sense of the value of a given possible direction, always subject to correction in conversation with other inquirers, and always aware that time will modify what they say. What's more, scientists, just like critics, must rely on other authorities for much of what they believe. As Michael Polanyi and others have insisted, no scientist could possibly prove more than a small fraction of the scientific beliefs that he or she accepts without question (*Personal Knowledge* 1972). For an argument that all of our defensible value judgments work pretty much like what I am calling coduction, see Morton A. Kaplan, *Science, Language, and the Human Condition* (1984, esp. chs. 11–13).

clude" that it is the greatest thing since Homer. The "laboratory" of my emotions seems to have yielded results that I can then, in a different process, proclaim to the world. But the fact is that when we are working as we should, the very effort to describe accurately "the facts" before us requires a closer look, which in turn modifies the evaluation, and that is further modified as we converse with others about the values we claim to have seen.

Often enough this revaluation can occur within minutes after the experience. Suppose I weep at several points during the movie version of Alice Walker's *The Color Purple*.[17] Then, when leaving the cinema, I notice that my wife, Phyllis, is absolutely dry-eyed. She looks at me and says, "How corny can they get?"

"What do you mean, corny? It really got to me."

"You mean you weren't troubled by the obviousness of all those contrivances, those romps in the daisies, that loading of the dice against Mister Mister, by . . . "

"Well, ah . . ."—and I may very well embark on an immediate reconsideration of my tears. Or she may begin to wonder whether her resistance was unduly cynical. Thus "the work itself" is being re-performed and transformed by us as we hold our conversations about it.

On the other hand, the revision may take years. When Ken Kesey's *One Flew over the Cuckoo's Nest* first appeared (1962),[18] many of us were bowled over by it. We rejoiced in the escape of the stalwart and pathetically persecuted "Chief" from the brutal morons who ran the mental hospital where he was wrongly incarcerated; we rejoiced when the heroic, tough McMurphy wreaked havoc in that wicked institution. Mark Schorer wrote the blurb for us: ". . . one of the few truly original novels that I have read in many years, perhaps since Malcolm Lowry's *Under the Volcano*. When I say original I am thinking not only of conception, but of the prose. I find it hard to believe that you will get a very large audience for this book, and I am sorry about that, if it should prove to be the case, for the book is certainly a smashing

17. I assume that the ethical debates spawned by this work, among both black and white critics, will have subsided after a few years. But my specific points here do not depend on the timeliness (or timelessness) of my examples.

18. It was as topical, in 1962, as *The Color Purple*, both book and movie, in the mid-1980s, and its reception was even more uniformly favorable.

achievement" (1966, dust jacket of third printing). I can remember thinking that that blurb was entirely justified.

Even this first coduction, the discovery of a valued experience, is already steeped in communal tests: Schorer starts comparing, from the beginning, with other novels, and he shares his comparison with potential readers. As soon as he starts doing that, if he takes seriously the task of explaining his initial appraisal, he enters a process that is not mere argument for views already established, but a conversation, a kind of re-reading that is an essential part of what will be a continually shifting evaluation.

My own estimate of this novel has diminished steadily on each new encounter, either with the text or in conversations about it, especially conversations with female readers who have insisted on what now seems an obvious point: though *One Flew over the Cuckoo's Nest* has some genuine qualities of humor and imaginative vitality, too much of its appeal, for Schorer and me and hundreds of thousands of other American males, depended on a sentimentalized dream of male freedom from and revenge against "Big Nurse," who too crudely symbolizes not only "female" domination of what "should" be a man's world but also all civilized restraints. Morality is reduced to courage, wit, daring, physical toughness, and willingness to resist tyranny. Identifying with a helpless, sensitive muscleman, the "Chief," we were offered, and we bought, a glorious myth of vengeance—against the women, against the bureaucracy, against the law, and almost incidentally, against three comic, vicious, unredeemable black folks who get in our way.

Here is the climactic scene in which the long-suffering, heroic Mc-Murphy, fighting against the Total Evil of Big Nurse, sacrifices himself in what we are supposed to see as a glorious though futile act of revenge:

> Only at the last—after he'd smashed through that glass door, her face swinging around, with terror forever ruining any other look she might ever try to use again, screaming when he grabbed for her and ripped her uniform all the way down the front, screaming again when the two nippled circles started from her chest and swelled out and out, bigger than anybody had ever even imagined, warm and pink in the light—only at the last, after the officials realized that the three black boys weren't going to do anything but stand and watch and they would have to beat him off without their help, doctors and supervisors and nurses prying those heavy red fingers out

of the white flesh of her throat . . . only then did he show any sign that he might be anything other than a sane, willful, dogged man performing a hard duty [the rape/murder] that finally just had to be done, like it or not.

(1966, 305)

My point is not to suggest that as I now deplore this novel's various exploitative moves, I have arrived at a final and settled judgment, or that I think *One Flew over the Cuckoo's Nest* worthless. Who can predict what a further reading, at age eighty, will yield? But I can predict that I shall never recover the initial uncritical pleasure that I took in that scene, before *prolonged* coduction did its work.

In short, we do not first come to know our judgment and then offer our proofs; we change our knowledge as we encounter, in the responses of other readers to our claims, further evidence. We may not want to honor the results of any such shifty process with the term "knowledge," but it would certainly be even more misleading to call it mere opinion or merely subjective. When it is performed with a genuine respect both for one's own intuitions and for what other people have to say, it is surely a more reasonable process than any deduction of quality from general ethical principles could be. Deductions may enter the conversation from time to time—as they will do here in Chapters 11 through 13. But they will always be modifiable by what *we*—not I—discover in experience as we re-read and converse. Regardless of how we may choose to defend our judgments as though they resulted from deduction or induction, or to relate them to universals we hold dear, they reward our attention only when they spring from coduction: a thoroughgoing particular engagement with *this* narrative, considered neither as based on nor leading to general rules but as an ever-growing awareness of what is humanly possible in some one kind of endeavor.

But might this not mean that no general discourse about ethical criticism is possible? Should we not simply move from work to work, considering our experience with it as an instance of its *kind*, refusing to judge jugglers by standards imported from gymnastics, or the farces of Feydeau by standards appropriate to *Macbeth*? Is not ethical criticism questionable precisely because it imports "extrinsic" standards, asks alien questions, says to the work, in a surreptitiously deductive move: "I know what *you* want of me, but I know something purer or deeper or nobler than you have dreamed of. And I hereby judge you from the platform granted me by that knowledge"?

In Part 3 I must face such questions head on. But by that point we should have well in hand a repertory of metaphors powerful enough to protect us from the excesses of literal-minded deduction.

REFERENCES

Aiken, Henry David. *Reason and Conduct: New Bearings in Moral Philosophy.* Westport, Conn., 1962. (Esp. ch. 2, "The Multiple Roles of the Language of Conduct," and ch. 4, "Levels of Moral Discourse.")

Bakhtin, Mikhail. *Problems of Dostoevsky's Poetics* [1963]. Ed. and trans. Caryl Emerson. Theory and History of Literature, vol. 8. Minneapolis, 1984.

Barbour, John D. *Tragedy as a Critique of Virtue: The Novel and Ethical Reflection.* Chico, Calif., 1984.

Barthelme, Donald. "The Party." In *Sadness.* New York, 1972.

Barthes, Roland. *Sade/Fourier/Loyola* [1971]. Trans. Richard Miller. New York, 1976.

Beauvoir, Simone de. *The Marquis de Sade: An Essay* [1951–52]. Trans. A. Michelson and P. Dinnage. New York, 1953.

Berthoff, Warner. *Literature and the Continuances of Virtue.* Princeton, N.J., 1986.

Booth, Wayne C. "Over the Mountain, Another Mountain." Review of *A History of Modern Criticism, 1750–1950,* by René Wellek. *Book Week* (Feb. 27, 1966): 3.

———. "Are Narrative Choices Subject to Ethical Criticism?" In *Reading Narrative: Form, Ethics, Ideology.* Ed. James Phelan. Columbus, Ohio, 1988.

Bové, Paul A. *Destructive Poetics: Heidegger and Modern American Poetry.* New York, 1980.

Brooks, Cleanth. *The Well Wrought Urn: Studies in the Structure of Poetry.* New York, 1947.

Cave, Terence. *The Cornucopian Text: Problems of Writing in the French Renaissance.* Oxford, 1979.

Certeau, Michel de. *Heterologies: Discourse on the Other.* Trans. Brian Massumi. Theory and History of Literature, vol. 17. Minneapolis, 1986.

Chatman, Seymour. "The 'Rhetoric' 'of' 'Fiction.'" In *Reading Narrative: Form, Ethics, Ideology.* Ed. James Phelan. Columbus, Ohio, 1988.

Cohen, Ted. "Why Beauty Is a Symbol of Morality." In Cohen and Guyer 1982: 221–36.

Cohen, Ted, and Paul Guyer, eds. *Essays in Kant's Aesthetics.* Chicago, 1982.

Cook, Rufus. "Reason and Imagination: Balance in Yvor Winters' Criticism."
    Ph.D. diss., University of Chicago, 1982.
Derrida, Jacques. Of Grammatology [1967]. Trans. Gayatri Chakravorty
    Spivak. Baltimore, 1974.
D'haen, Theo. "Postmodern Fiction: Form and Function." Neophilologus 71
    (1987): 144–53.
Ellis, John M. The Theory of Literary Criticism: A Logical Analysis. Berkeley,
    1974.
Emerson, Caryl. "Problems with Bakhtin's Poetic." Paper presented at the
    annual convention of the Modern Language Association of America,
    New York, Dec. 1986.
Foucault, Michel. The Order of Things: An Archaeology of the Human Sci-
    ences [1966]. Trans. Alan Sheridan. New York, 1973.
Gardner, John. On Moral Fiction. New York, 1978.
Handwerk, Gary J. Irony and Ethics in Narrative: From Schlegel to Lacan.
    New Haven, Conn., 1985.
James, Henry. The Turn of the Screw [1898]. Ed. Robert Kimbrough. New
    York, 1966.
James, William. The Varieties of Religious Experience [1902]. Ed. Freder-
    ick H. Burkhardt et al. Cambridge, Mass., 1985.
Johnson, Samuel. Preface to The Plays of William Shakespeare [1765]. In
    Johnson on Shakespeare. Ed. Arthur Sherbo. Vol. 7 of The Yale Edi-
    tion of the Works of Samuel Johnson. New Haven, Conn., 1968.
    59–113.
Josipovici, Gabriel. "On the Side of Job." Times Literary Supplement (Sept. 7,
    1984): 989.
Kant, Immanuel. "Kritik of Aesthetical Judgment" [1790]. In Kritik of Judg-
    ment. Trans. J. H. Bernard. London, 1892.
———. Religion within the Limits of Reason Alone [1793]. Trans. Theo-
    dore M. Greene and Hoyt H. Hudson. New York, 1960.
Kaplan, Morton A. Science, Language, and the Human Condition. New York,
    1984.
Kesey, Ken. One Flew over the Cuckoo's Nest. 1962. Reprint. New York,
    1966.
Krieger, Murray. Theory of Criticism: A Tradition and Its System. Baltimore,
    Md., 1976.
Leavis, F. R. "Reality and Sincerity" [1952]. In A Selection from "Scrutiny."
    Ed. F. R. Leavis. 2 vols. Cambridge, 1968. 1: 248–57.
———. The Great Tradition: George Eliot, Henry James, Joseph Conrad
    [1948]. New York, 1969.
Levi, Edward. An Introduction to Legal Reasoning. Chicago, 1948.
Lewis, C. S. An Experiment in Criticism. Cambridge, 1961.
McKeon, Richard P. "Censorship." In The New Encyclopaedia Britannica.
    15th ed. 3: 1083–90. Chicago, 1975.
Miller, J. Hillis. The Ethics of Reading: Kant, de Man, Eliot, Trollope, James,
    and Benjamin. New York, 1986.
Mitchell, W. J. T. Iconology: Image, Text, Ideology. Chicago, 1986.
Murdoch, Iris. The Sovereignty of Good. London, 1970.

Polanyi, Michael. *Personal Knowledge: Towards a Post-Critical Philosophy* [1958]. Chicago, 1972.

Reichert, John. *Making Sense of Literature.* Chicago, 1977.

Sacks, Sheldon. *Fiction and the Shape of Belief: A Study of Henry Fielding, with Glances at Swift, Johnson, and Richardson.* Berkeley, 1964.

Siegle, Robert. *The Politics of Reflexivity: Narrative and the Constitutive Poetics of Culture.* Baltimore, 1986.

Smith, Barbara Herrnstein. "Contingencies of Value." In *Canons.* Ed. Robert von Hallberg. Chicago, 1984. 5–39.

Theunissen, Michael. *The Other: Studies in the Social Ontology of Husserl, Heidegger, Sartre, and Buber* [1977]. Trans. Christopher Macann. Cambridge, Mass., 1984.

Todorov, Tzvetan. *The Conquest of America: The Question of the Other* [1982]. Trans. Richard Howard. New York, 1984.

Tolstoy, Leo. *What Is Art?* [1896]. Trans. Aylmer Maude. New York, 1960.

Trilling, Lionel. "On the Teaching of Modern Literature" [1961]. In *Beyond Culture.* New York, 1968. 3–30.

Winters, Yvor. *In Defense of Reason.* Denver, 1947.

4

[W]hile there are always mechanisms for ruling out readings, their source is not the text but the presently recognized interpretive strategies for producing the text [by readers in an interpretive community]. It follows . . . that no reading, however outlandish it might appear, is inherently an impossible one.
Stanley Fish

The final task of the critic is evaluation.
René Wellek

Speech in its essence is not neutral.
Kenneth Burke

At the end of my first term's work, I attended the usual college board to give an account of myself. The spokesman coughed, and said a little stiffly: "I understand, Mr. Graves, that the essays which you write for your English tutor are, shall I say, a trifle temperamental. It appears, indeed, that you prefer some authors to others."
Robert Graves

The Threat of Subjectivism
and the Ethics of Craft

We should hardly be surprised, considering all these obstacles in the way of good ethical criticism, that most critics have chosen for some time now merely to assert or imply their judgments rather than develop theories supporting their legitimacy.[1] We might even conclude that a reasoned ethical criticism is really quite impossible: "All those judgments, whether overt and impassioned or disguised as neutral description, are really no more than power ploys—merely expressions of their producers' socio-economic, cultural, or psychological needs and interests. Theoretical defenses of ethical criticism disappeared precisely because nobody could any longer believe that ethical appraisals referred to any independent reality attributable to texts or readers. Once we understand how 'the politics of interpretation' operates, what is left to be explained or judged? Even your account of coduction," I can hear this voice over my shoulder concluding, "leaves the ethical critic without a *rational* leg to stand on."

But if we follow this fashion and throw in the theoretical towel, we are left with stacks of inexplicable critical statements filling our journals, textbooks, classrooms, and conversations. Many of our critical exchanges are conducted carelessly, and hence unprofitably, simply because people have become convinced that there is no inherent difference between good and bad discourse of this kind: If it's all mere opinion or disguised power play, why pretend to reason carefully about it? Why not just shout at each other, more or less politely, like the participants in those TV "think shows" who keep their eyes on the camera while pretending to address opinions to each other?

Before accepting such a humiliating retreat, surely we ought first to be quite sure that the grounds for ethical criticism are as shaky as is

---

1. For four major exceptions, see Ellis 1974; Hirsch 1976; Olson 1976; and Reichert 1977.

customarily claimed. Perhaps it should go without saying that anyone who wholeheartedly and with no *arrière-pensées* repudiates subjectivism and its modern cousins, "power-ism" and "special interest-ism," might simply skip this chapter—or skip at least to my discussion on confusion about what is evaluated (pp. 101–17 below). But as you flip the pages, ask yourself what it says about me, about these targets, and about our cultural situation that I myself can by no means omit the confrontation in those nineteen pages. I think it means that the arguments for subjectivism are not the kind that simply disappear after refutation: they are a permanent accompaniment, as qualification, in the thought of any critic who has ever considered them seriously. For some they become the ground bass—the essential truth qualifying all our claims to know value. For me they are an annoying obbligato, an insistent voice in my internal chorus (as Bakhtin might put it)—a voice that will not go away no matter how many times I tell it that it sings false notes.

Yet they are indeed false notes, and read from the wrong score. Once we apply our skepticism to the various arguments for subjectivism in the appraisal of artistic value, they become as questionable as similar arguments for "utter" skepticism and "total" relativism have seemed to recent philosophers (Norris 1985; Putnam 1981; Klein 1981; Davidson 1984; Bernstein 1983). One line of argument against subjectivism is implicit in what was said in Chapter 3 about openness to the "Other": the pursuit of total openness just won't work. In practice, we always "close" some questions in order to open others. For some of us this pragmatic argument—explicitly accepted by many a professed skeptic[2]—would in itself be enough to keep us radically skeptical about skepticism. In this chapter I add four more reasons for confidence in pursuing a conversation about ethical values:

1. Appraisals of narratives can refer to something real *in the narratives,* not just to the appraiser's preferences; the widespread claim that "poems" have no power or value in themselves is confused and misleading.
2. Descriptions of a narrative's "power," if they are accurate, can-

2. For example, Hume in his turn to everyday life in his great and profoundly skeptical *Treatise* (1739–40, bk. 1, pt. 4, ch. 7), and Santayana in *Skepticism and Animal Faith* (1923, 99–108).

not be effectively separated from appraisal; if descriptions, interpretations, and interpretative theories can be rational, evaluation can be also.

3. Therefore, diversity among appraisers need not mean irration-
ality of appraisals; the standard argument that diversity of
judgment undermines the legitimacy of judgment is not self-
consistent, and it denies the diversity of powers in any one
narrative.

4. The blanket rejection of evaluation, especially in its ethical
forms, ignores the variety of *kinds* of judgment that we in practice share. Many an appraisal may indeed be worthless to everyone except the appraiser; but once we make some elementary
distinctions, we discover that some appraisals qualify as shared
knowledge, no more dubious than many a "factual" claim.

1. THE POWERS OF NARRATIVE

The debate about the intrinsic worth of art works has generally
been conducted as though the issue were whether or not any work of
art is fully observable, a self-contained thing, either good or deficient,
somehow "out there" waiting to be appraised. Recently critics have
tended to reject the notion of a work's autonomy, concentrating instead on the process of reception—which yields a re-created "work"
more dependent on the receiver than on the original maker. After all, it
is said, what else do we have except the work that we have re-made?
Regardless of what the artist has tried to *give*, we can judge only what
we manage to *take*, and that will be as various as our various natures
dictate. How, then, can we ever say that any particular reading is the
proper one? And if we cannot agree on any one interpretation, how
could we possibly settle on a reliable evaluation?[3]

3. For a survey of the range of "reader-response" criticism, see Suleiman 1980 and
Tompkins 1980, with their extensive bibliographies. Underplayed in too much current
work is one of the best "reader" critics, Louise M. Rosenblatt (1978). See also Mailloux
1982, especially the footnotes and bibliographical note, 217–20.

It is important to insist, because most reader-response criticism claims to deal with
interpretation of "meanings" rather than values, that the question of whether or not
meaning is determinate is quite distinct from the question of whether or not values are
determinately experienced. Even if all the current claims for the radical indeterminacy of

This recent shift from criticism dominated by biographical, inten-
tional, or formal concerns has been valuable in its tendency to welcome back into the critical arena conversation about emotional response and personal engagement. It is certainly true that we take quite
divergent "objects" from the "same" artistic stimuli,[4] and that when
some critic tells us we should have read in some *different,* more *correct*
way, we can feel robbed of our very souls. But the resulting emphasis
on the variety of interpretations tells us little in itself about the actual
value of the works that have somehow enabled us to experience something we feel as our own valued possession.

The denial that literary works have intrinsic power—and hence
value—comes in two forms. The more aggressive claim is that all aesthetic values are entirely subjective: the value of any work is the value
any reader sees in it, and there can be no disputing of taste in values.
The less extreme claim, shared by most reader-response critics with
"conventionalitarians" like Stanley Fish and Marxists like Terry Eagleton, is that while individual evaluations can be more than merely subjective (because they can be corrected and improved in discussion
within a given community), the value of works is still not in any real
sense *in* them. Rather, it is conferred upon them by cultures and cultural institutions, usually in the service of some power structure. Thus
within any one culture, arguments about interpretations and values
can make sense; indeed, for some, like Fish, they cannot not make
sense (1980, chs. 15–16).[5] But that does not mean there is any inherent value in the works themselves.

Terry Eagleton, for example, claims that literary values, though not

------

a text's *meaning* were accepted, the value of a given *experience* with narrative *could* be
real, shareable, and (sometimes) thus determinate. Everyone who argues against a given
determinate meaning implies that the text will receive its proper value only in the chosen
polyvalent interpretation; other people's misreadings (overly-determinate) devalue the
true power of the work. We often meet the claim, a special version of which I myself
accept, that the more readings a text makes possible (or "invites," in my terms), the
better it is—a clear sign that indeterminacy of meaning can still yield relative deter-
minacy of value.

   4. At least we do some of the time; the amount of overlap between your *Paradise
Lost* and mine, between your *Ulysses* and mine, may be great or small, and it is never
easy to determine; but it is surely significant. We could not even discuss our different
readings if that were not so (Rader 1976, 151). Cf. my discussion in Chapter 3 of the
impossibility of unadulterated open-endedness.

   5. "The fact that it remains easy to think of a reading [of any poem] that most of us

merely "personal opinion," are always constituted by a given cultural institution and power structure.

> There is no such thing as a literary work or tradition which is valuable *in itself*, regardless of what anyone might have said or come to say about it. 'Value' is a transitive term: it means whatever is valued by certain people in specific situations, according to particular criteria and in the light of given purposes. . . . [T]here is no such thing as literature which is 'really' great, or 'really' anything, independently of the ways in which that writing is treated within specific forms of social and institutional life.
>
> (1983, 11, 202)

This less extreme claim is obviously much easier to defend than the strong claim. One can easily believe—indeed, from one perspective it is self-evident—that an individual's high opinion of Shakespeare or Goethe or Nōh-drama is culture-dependent: I must somehow "possess" a culture before I can see its monuments for what they are. An illiterate visitor from Mars or Timbucktu would find no value, at least initially, in *Hamlet*. Obviously the value that the works "have," large or small, will be *discernible* only within a given culture.

It is a bit harder to believe, though some people claim to, that if a person in our culture who is completely inexperienced in literature sees no value whatever in, say, Faulkner's novels, his or her opinion is as pertinent to our discourse about Faulkner as the opinions of experienced readers. Yet such a complete equivalence in the competence of all interpreters is clearly entailed by the claim that works do not "*possess or exercise* inherent value" but are only *valued*. Thus extreme subjectivists, unlike Fish and Eagleton, are easily refuted, since they never in practice treat their own opinions of literature as having no more validity than those of the totally inexperienced.

Accordingly, they are interesting only because they drive us to become clear about what it might mean for a fiction to "possess inherent value." All phrases like "to *possess* a value" or "to *be* valuable," exhibit the same ambiguities that plague every statement about existence or being. There are many ways to be or to have being, as every philosophy (except, possibly, extreme positivism) has recognized. The two

---

would dismiss out of hand does not mean that the text excludes it but that there is as yet no elaborated interpretive procedure for producing that text" (Fish 1980, 345).

kinds of being important to us here are being-in-act and being-in-possibility or potentiality. The elementary distinction has been found necessary both in philosophies, ancient and modern,[6] and in modern physics, where it appears in many forms, particularly as the distinction between kinetic energy and potential energy.

Place a stone, a feather, and an inflated balloon all together on a shelf. Examine naively what energy value they have "in themselves" and they will all appear equally inert, powerless, valueless. Prick them with a pin and the results will startle any observer who thought that since they were equivalent in one mode of existence they would be equivalent in all. Remove the shelf suddenly, and again immense differences are revealed. I suggest that fictions are somewhat like that: they indeed appear to be inert until a human being takes them in, but they differ immensely in their potential energy.

Consider a second analogy: place an acorn, a test-tube of human ova and a fertilized hen's egg on a shelf, then remove the shelf and measure their fall; you may conclude that they all had the same potential energy, because they fall (or so we have been taught) at the same rate. You conclude that they "possess no inherent difference of value." But if instead you place them under a setting hen, suddenly radical differences in their nature and value emerge. Those differences were "there" all the while, in potentia, but the "there" in this statement is not the same "there" as the one in our statements about behavior in free-fall.

Thus what determines which values emerge in each imposed system, each new community of discourse, is not *only* what the community chooses to do with the stuff but also what the stuff itself "chooses" to do. The test-tube of ova will be, or rather seem, entirely inert, entirely valueless to the hen and to any farmer anxiously awaiting a hatching; the egg's value will emerge. Yet if we fertilize one of those ova and place it in an aldoushuxley-tube, what had looked inert becomes immensely powerful, ridden with values radically different from those in the other "objects." The values are thus in one sense

---

6. See the prolonged debate among philosophers about how "possible worlds" relate to "real worlds" (Adams 1934; Goodman 1978; Lewis 1986; Pavel 1986, ch. 2, "Fictional Beings").

properties of the new system, dependent on the needs and capacities of observers, and in another sense present *as potential* in the old system from the beginning.

Philosophy begins in wonder, and as many a philosopher has reminded us, we are in trouble once we forget what a wondrous mystery it is that a chicken egg will always hatch chickens and not, say, pigs or pomegranates (Aristotle, in all the works on biology and physics; Kant *Kritik of Judgment* ([1790] 1892), div. 1, art. 62). We moderns tend to think genetic research has demystified that miracle; but if we ever really lose the wonder of it, we are doomed. That wonder depends on the strange capacity of apparently inert things to spring out of dormancy into surprising displays of energy, proving that they were "teleological" or "organic" all the while. If we critics ever lose our wonder at the way *King Lear* persists in "hatching" Lear-like creatures (that is, readings, performances) rather than, say, little Oedipuses or Tartuffes, epistemological treatises, or TV game shows, we may as well fold up shop.[7]

Place *King Lear* on the shelf alongside a comparable weight of your unfavorite Hallmark greeting cards and a pile of improvised couplets like the following:

> To love and hate—
> This is my fate.
>
> Stanley Fish
> Is my dish.
>
> Reading Terry
> Makes me merry.

Ask then whether in theory there is any inherent difference in their value, and they will seem to answer, to many moderns, "No, of course

---

7. Perhaps one reason we have lost this particular piety is the discovery that at one level differences in energy potential all reduce to mass. If $E = mc^2$, then all objects of equal mass have ultimately the same potential energy. I see no easy way to reconcile that physicalist perspective with the perspective of all sentient creatures in any *conceivable* universe—a perspective that will always discriminate among divergent manifestations of energy. The physical equivalence of a given pebble and a spoonful of human sperm that has the same mass tells us *nothing we want to know about them in their particularity*. Their powers to achieve utterly different fates are what give my analogy whatever force it may have.

not. We are just a bunch of letters on the page, *Lear* superior only in the vaster number of binary bits required to program it into a computer." (I postpone for the moment the question of just how a story can be said to "answer back.") Now place the three art works into a context: have them read aloud, or just picture yourself reading them, faced with the task of preserving one of the piles from eternal destruction. Suddenly one of the three piles of "inert text" blooms before your eyes—or (to try other inevitably inadequate metaphors), *King Lear* propagates itself into the life of everyone who comes near enough to *see* it or *hear* it; or, it spreads itself through the spirit; or, it argues powerfully that anyone would be criminal who would willfully wipe out this living creature. The blooming will not occur, of course, until the right "valuer" comes along: that much truth is self-evident in the view that all interpretations depend on the conventions of a community. But to deny any kind of reality to the potential of "the play itself" is finally to cripple our thought about it. As Marshall Alcorn neatly dramatizes the point, even if "an infinity of different readers can [I would say "could"] produce an infinity of different readings of *Othello* . . . such an infinite set of interpretations would exclude the infinite number of interpretations produced by readings of *Moby Dick*" (1987, 152).

Like the human fetus, *King Lear* is not predetermined to a single fulfillment. The fetus is a determinate being only insofar as it can only become *a human being* and not a pig or pomegranate; the play is determinate only insofar as it becomes *a given kind of narrative or performance*, and not a discourse on forestry, say, or a collection of limericks. Of course, the lives of both can be thwarted: just as an outside force can kill the fetus and even treat it as food or fuel, so alien forces can use the pages of the play as scrap paper, firewood, toilet paper, or grist for the theory that literary works are nothing "in themselves." All energy, kinetic or potential, can be effectively resisted by alien powers.

It is true that nothing in the fiction's powers can prevent my posing to it any conceivable "alien" question. I can, for example, flatter my couplets, with questions more appropriate to *Lear:* "What do you tell me, O couplets, about God and human nature? What are your politics? What do you have to say about the Oedipus complex? What neuroses drove your maker? What historical forces of your time are reflected in your structure? In what tradition of poetic technique did you reach your flowering?" To all these and hundreds of other questions that *King Lear* will respond to more or less willingly, my poor couplets refuse to answer, or answer haltingly: dunces in a non-dialogue.

The point then is this: the question of whether value is in the poem or in the reader is radically and permanently ambiguous, requiring two answers. Of course the value is not there, *actually,* until it is actualized, by the reader. But of course it could not be actualized if it were not there, *in potential,* in the poem.

It might be objected that since in practice we find no limit to the questions we can ask a given work, even so slim a work as one of my couplets, we are not dealing with potentialities in the work after all but only with potentialities in human readers, as they build infinitely diverse cultures that will always read in infinitely various ways. Is it not true, for example, that inventive readers can find as much to say about works that have been considered inferior as they can say about canonized works?

In fact, it is not true. When the game is played fairly—which is to say, when we choose to compare works of great power with feeble works like my couplets rather than comparing two perhaps equally powerful works—we see just how much is, after all, in the work itself. No conceivable circumstance, no conceivable community of interpretation, could produce a range and depth of criticism on "To love and hate— / This is my Fate" equaling what we already have on *King Lear,* to say nothing of what is yet to come in the history of that infinitely fecund work. In this respect we surely ought to take seriously the impoverished history of Stanley Fish's clever little examples of textual ambiguity, "Is there a text in this class?" and the chance collocation of names (1980, 323) that he led his unwitting class to interpret as a poem:

> Jacobs-Rosenbaum
> Levin
> Thorne
> Hayes
> Ohman (?)

Though Fish's *essays* about his games have been fruitful, his *examples* have themselves never produced more than two or three banal readings—mostly his own. How could they produce more? They simply lack the potential energy. (You have thought of one more interpretation to add to the list? Clever of you. Do I want to read it? Not on your life, or at least not until I have run out of *King Lear*s.)

Obviously my analogy takes us only so far. One might object that every fiction "possesses," "has," "exhibits," "conceals" potentialities infinitely richer than any of the physical objects I have mentioned except perhaps the human fetus, and even that seems relatively more determinate than the immeasurable fertility of any great fiction. What do we make of the grotesque reversals of critical judgment throughout history? After decades, centuries, of neglect or adulation, a given work will suddenly rise to eminence or fall into oblivion. Even if I am right in claiming that such cases are far outnumbered by works that prove their capacity to come alive again when granted proper attention, still my argument about potentiality must be able to face such diversity honestly.

I shall try to do so in Section 4 of this chapter, but the point before us now is that the argument about potentiality in no way depends on denying that tastes change. The claim is only that the theoretical case against inherent value violates what we all acknowledge in practice—that, as Wolfgang Iser says, "[T]he literary work has two poles, . . . the author's text and . . . the realization accomplished by the reader. In view of this polarity, it is clear that the work itself cannot be identical with the text [a view too often taken by those who want to combat relativism] or with the concretization, but must be situated somewhere between the two. It must inevitably be virtual in character, as it cannot be reduced to the reality of the text or to the subjectivity of the reader" (1978, 21; see also Rosenblatt 1978).

In considering such virtual powers, as in considering different pebbles, seeds, or fetuses, it is always useful and often necessary to distinguish three kinds of question: those that the object seems to *invite* me to ask; those that it will *tolerate* or respond to, even though perhaps reluctantly; and those that *violate* its own interests or effort to be a given kind of thing in the world.[8]

---

8. I hope it is obvious that I am not placing a superior value on the first kind of question; on the contrary, much of the best ethical criticism does the reverse. The debate between E. D. Hirsch (1976) and Barbara Hernnstein Smith (1978) about whether the critic who would behave ethically must first honor the author's intentions is not my business here. Each one argues for an extreme I cannot embrace.

Clearly this metaphorical talk about stories *inviting, tolerating,* and *resisting* depends on accepting the distinction between active and potential energy, while granting to the potential side its own kind of action in the world. If texts are not in some sense actors, then of course they cannot either invite, tolerate, or reject our overtures. But if works of art, like other seemingly inert objects in the world, do have natures in the sense of presenting horizons of potentiality, then they can be said to take attitudes toward our questions.

Even a stone can be said to do so, once we accept this metaphorical way of talking. A stone *asks,* as it were, to be considered as a mass, a weight, a solidity; it certainly *tolerates* being placed according to its origins in geological time, or even being broken down into its chemical elements or into quarks and leptons, though it might be said to express considerable surprise at the breakdown. But it will be positively *violated* by questions about its stanzaic form or its point of view as a narrative. Similarly, a chronological tale invites a hearing, a "listening," with a reconstruction from beginning to end, and then perhaps a reconsideration of what all that movement *forward* was about or for. It will tolerate and respond to questions about its phonological patterns, or the history of its vocabulary, or the psychology of its teller, or the political evils of the regime under which it was written. But it will feel positively violated if you start asking it how it will react if submerged in water or hydrochloric acid, or whether it is in the key of C-sharp minor or A-flat; or whether its composition and consumption yield a favorable cost-benefit ratio.[9]

So much seems obvious, though I know it will not seem obvious to all readers. What is never obvious is any precise line dividing the questions that a given fiction—which is to say, a given implied author—invites, or will tolerate, or will want to reject. The interesting point about much ethical criticism—really about *all* ethical criticism that quarrels with the ethos of a work—is that it is of the violating kind. While it is true that some fictions, perhaps most that we bother much about, openly invite ethical thought and questioning, when they do so they invite agreement and feel violated by disagreement. It would be a

---

9. The poem's shouts of protest will of course not necessarily deter the questioner. See the application of cost-benefit analyses to aesthetic objects by George J. Stigler and Gary S. Becker, "De Gustibus Non Est Disputandum" (1977). For a tracing of the major claims to what a poem "really is," see my *Critical Understanding* (1979, 57).

strange work indeed that said to us, "Figure out what my true central values are, what ideology I embody, and *then reject it*." If it really "says," "Reject those!" that rejection is its central value. As we'll see in the next chapter, the very act of creating any fiction, including the simplest joke or bit of gossip, presupposes at least a temporary acceptance of the norms on which it is based. Even those many modernist works that attempt to make us ask questions or reject earlier easier answers will be violated if we reject *those* norms of openness or rejection.

2. WHY OUR DESCRIPTIONS OF WHAT IS "THERE" ARE EVALUATIVE

The reason that each story has a distinctive potential power is obvious: it has been made intentionally. Powers of a rich but determinate kind have been "packed in" by the act of the teller and by the value-packed history of the language in its intention-ridden culture. Since that is so, even the simplest story cannot be *described* without employing the language of value, the value of its realizing or failing to realize itself: minimally, to become *this story*. In discussing that realization, even the most aggressively neutral literary scholarship cannot avoid implying evaluation. As I present a case now for that view, I shall also be arguing the more controversial case that all descriptions of such realizings have within them, perhaps well-hidden but not unavailable to the critic willing to probe, an ethical dimension. This is not to say that such probing is required: ethical criticism need not aspire to take over the world. But when other kinds are not at least supplemented by such probing, criticism as an enterprise is likely to die of inanition.

Whenever we take in a story, we grasp it as value-ridden. No matter how hard we try to purge ourselves of evaluative language, notions of a "work's" value—the value of its working or failing to work—will be inseparable from the terms of our descriptions. All our descriptive terms—poem, novel, epic, sonnet, villanelle; tragedy, comedy, satire; realism, fantasy; classic, romantic—*all* of them are "always already" [10]

---

10. One surely should have the privilege of using at least one bit of current jargon in each chapter!

steeped in judgments of value. It is true, of course, that when I describe a given narrative as a poem or a tragedy, I cannot predict accurately what precise value my readers will associate with the term. But we will both know that values are at stake in our encounter with any work that works. Note that it matters little whether we think of the work here as the author's achievement, the reader's re-creation, or—as some would have it—one step in the march of *écriture* through the ages: regardless of who or what gets the credit or blame, these "things" do not grow on trees; we give them our "descriptive" names only if they have been *made to grow*.

This point is so important that I must back up and consider for a moment how it applies to descriptions of "arts" (makings and doings) less fancy than elaborate fictions.

"I saw a juggler perform yesterday."

Such a statement can be considered entirely neutral, entirely value-free, only if taken out of any human context, turned into one of those abstracted, purposeless sentences that fill linguistic texts. As soon as we imagine anyone *saying* it or *writing* it for some human communication, the statement has already conferred a value on the act: the performer was "a juggler," which is by definition someone who can do something that not everyone can do. Hearing it, I can ask a variety of questions in response, but all of them will imply a judgment about skill in a practice: "Was he indeed a juggler?" A would-be juggler is one thing, a juggler another.

A total stranger to our culture might, of course, simply say, "I saw a man yesterday who could keep four objects in the air all at once." Even so neutral and uninformed a statement, once it is spoken, implies the speaker's judgment that the described act stands out, for him, as superior to his ordinary experience of human dexterity: it is worth mentioning—already an evaluation. But anyone in our culture will go further, by using the name "juggler" and thus implying a level of achievement deserving of the right name, no matter how far down the scale of good juggling it may fall.[11]

---

11. Two readers, one a literary critic, the other a linguist, have objected at this point that statements about jugglers can be put into contexts that remove the evaluation. Testifying in a trial, for example, or writing a textbook on grammar, I might well say, "The victim was a juggler," without entailing any value judgment. Of course. But I would prefer to say, "without *intending* any value judgment." The judgment would still be

"Was he a good juggler or a bad one?" A bad one? But a bad juggler is still a juggler—a lesser artist than a good juggler, true enough, but a better artist than you and I were the first time we tried to juggle three apples. We were then not yet even bad jugglers.

"Would you please describe his act for me? How many apples could he keep in the air at one time?" I, who can juggle three apples only, will learn from your description something about his quality. Note that we have not said anything about whether juggling is in itself a good thing to do. Everything we can say about the "value" of good juggling, as a craft, could be said of any craft, even something as horrifying as efficient management of a gas chamber. My argument here is only that our descriptive language for practices is never neutral: we confer upon them the quality of a "virtue," a capacity, even though that developed capacity may ultimately be judged as abhorrent.

In *World of Wonders,* the third novel of Robertson Davies' Deptford Trilogy, the magician-hero tells his friends about a time when he needed to impress a great actor with his skill:

> I had nothing to juggle with, but I didn't mean to be beaten. And I wanted to prove to the lady that I was worth her kindness. So with speed and I hope a reasonable amount of politeness I took her umbrella, and the little man's wonderful hat, and Holroyd's hat and the soft cap I was wearing myself, and balanced the brolly on my nose and juggled the three hats in an arch over it. Not easy, let me tell you, for all the hats were of different sizes and weights, and Holroyd's hefted like iron. But I did it, and the lady clapped again. . . .
> [But the little man didn't seem impressed so] I put on a little more steam. I did some clown juggling, pretending every time the circle went round that I was about to drop Holroyd's hat, and recovering it with a swoop, and at last keeping that one in the air with my right foot. That made the little man laugh.

(1976, 174–75)

There is no more than a fragment of openly evaluative language here ("not easy, let me tell you"). But from the description we know how well the speaker thinks he has done. There is simply no way that anyone could describe the same event without implying, for any halfway knowledgeable auditor, a judgment on the skill of that juggler.

What is most important to us here is that any such description of a discernibly crafted performance automatically entails *ethical* judg-

---

"there," ready to be dredged up by anyone who thinks about the full meaning of the words as *used*.

ments—an appraisal of at least part of the character of the performer. To become accomplished in any craft is to apply character to circumstance, and the accomplishment tells us just what character has been applied. A real juggler must have committed hours and days to the achievement; a fine one will have spent years. When I call someone a juggler, I consequently attribute not only an unusual amount of natural agility but the qualities of character necessary to produce the *doing* of it: persistence, a willingness to forgo other activities in the service of juggling, indeed a choice to spend time learning to juggle rather than, say, philosophizing, or writing criticism. It used to be said, not always in jest, that skill at billiards was a sign of a misspent youth. We can say that skill at *anything* is a sign of spent life—of a character who has chosen to spend life precisely that way. We need not be judgmental about it: "He would have done much better for himself practicing yoga." On the contrary, when we observe most achievements, we can revel in their addition to the human range: thank God there is such a wondrous thing as juggling (as Anatole France's version of the medieval tale "The Juggler of Notre Dame" seems to say).[12]

Now let us move closer to home.

"I met a poet yesterday and read one of her poems."

Again, such a statement can be considered neutral only if taken out of context and put into a text of linguistics, criticism, or philosophy. As soon as we imagine anyone saying it or writing it as a report, the statement has already conferred a value on the act and a character on the actor: the author was a "poet," which is by definition someone who can do something that not everyone can do. Hearing the statement, I can ask a variety of questions, but all of them will involve me in judgment. "Is she indeed a poet?" A would-be poet is one thing; a poet another. The reply might be a revised description: "Well, she is actually more of a versifier than a poet." Or it might be, "Is she *ever* a poet!"

---

12. I must stress again that we may well want finally to repudiate the evaluations implicit in a given description, but in doing so we simply would underline my point. If someone described a performance of a skillful Nazi gas chamber attendant with the same loving attention to detail as we just saw accorded to the juggling act, we would spend little time noting that the skill in itself revealed "virtues," though it would do so: mechanical mastery, loyalty to superiors, perhaps physical endurance, or whatnot. We would instead embark on ethical and political criticism, convinced that the craft was displayed in the service of evil. My point is that ethical evaluation cannot be avoided,

Again we can make explicit the question "Is she a good poet or a bad one?" If our informant is a determined neutralist, he may refuse to say, though he has already performed part of the judgment just by the naming.

"All right, then. Describe her poem. Tell me how many apples she can keep in the air at one time. I, who have attempted about fifty poems in my life, will learn from your description itself something about her quality as a poet." No matter how he describes her poem, his description will confer his notion of what was remarkable or not remarkable about her.

It may be that many people listening to his account will not be able to decipher his standards from his statement. If he says, "She has constructed a villanelle in classical form," and if he is talking to someone who has never heard of a villanelle, let alone attempted one, his statement may *seem* neutral; all description of human achievement presupposes auditors who understand the speaker's language, with its built-in norms. But there really is a difference between a poet who can construct a villanelle—even a poor villanelle—and one who cannot. The first has done something that not many people in the world can do.

We do not know, of course, from what we have heard so far, just how good the villanelle is thought to be, in the class of villanelles, or whether the speaker considers the class of villanelles as greater or lesser than the class of sonnets, or tight verse forms better than free verse, or the condition of a poet as superior to that of a juggler, or the character of a poet who writes a villanelle on the game of push-pin superior to the character of a poet like Pushkin. But if we press our informant further, asking for more and more accurate descriptions of how the tricky alternation of lines works in the poem, of just how imitative the poet's subject is, of how she meets the problem of making her meaning seem undistorted by the complicated demands of the verse form, and so on, we shall find more and more information about value embedded in the descriptions themselves. "It was an abominable villanelle." "Still, it *was* a villanelle!" [13]

---

because in every description of any achieved task, and in every effort to achieve, there are ineradicable signs of character, of one kind or another.

13. My argument here is obviously another way to discuss the fact/value distinction I described above, on pages 28–29. See Alasdair MacIntyre's *After Virtue* (1981) for a

Clearly, my argument will not work when applied to anything other than what I am calling "achievements." Descriptions of rocks and stars and atoms—descriptions of any event or object that does not result from an intention to make or do something worth making or doing—need not entail value judgments, at least not in the same way. It was one of the great human achievements to have recognized that when dealing with rocks and atoms, we generally succeed best when we separate our preferences from the object studied.[14] But whenever our descriptions reveal intentions, however obscurely, they will be caught up into the world of values that we all *in fact* are created by and dwell in. And every intention, realized or not, implies a character of the intender, who thus invites the ethical critic to enter the scene: If it is *a* good to be a juggler or a poet or a fashion photographer, just *how* good is it?

3. FAILURE OF THE ARGUMENT FROM VARIABILITY

I think it follows from this inevitability of evaluation—the inevitably "hierarchical" quality of language that Kenneth Burke saw as basic to all criticism (e.g., 1966, chs. 1–2)—that variability of judgment, far from indicating mere subjectivity or non-rationality, is the very mark of rationality. Since what we are calling achievements are in themselves unpredictably various, requiring both in their makers and

---

development of the argument that the name of a person's craft, or the product of a craft, names a practice that entails a value: if we describe something that looks like a watch but that does not tell time and is not portable, we have not named a watch but something else (a fake watch, a hoax, a toy). If we call someone a sea captain, we imply that he is a master of many skills that non-captains lack (54–55, 174–78). By now, recognition of this point can be found "everywhere": "It is presumably impossible to explain the concepts *medicine* or *hospital* without referring to the values—like life, health and perhaps knowledge—which those institutions characteristically seek to promote. Though some hospitals are better than others, still not everything that looks like a hospital should be described as a hospital." Thus Jeremy Waldron (1984, 992) contrasting a hospital with those abattoirs that the Nazis *called* hospitals. See also Putnam 1981, ch. 6.

14. New controversies are emerging over the issue of just how thoroughly human motives and perceptions can be or should be isolated from thought about physical nature. Defenders of the "anthropic principle" are arguing that nature is tied to *our* nature in ways that the scientific revolution denied (Barrow and Tipler 1986).

their receivers widely varying training and skills, we should not only expect but welcome variety of appraisal. Nothing would be better evidence that irrational forces were determining our readings than the discovery of total agreement—the kind of thing we find among official critics in totalitarian states and churches.

To see this point clearly, we should return to John Carey's attack on evaluation, depending as it does on the argument from variability (see pp. 30–32 above). Carey finds fault with what he calls the "Shakespeare gambit," the assurance that we would consider incompetent any critic who failed to see merit in Shakespeare. Carey contends that we would *not* know what to think of such a critic, because he might turn out to be a Tolstoy, who "did not think Shakespeare the world's greatest dramatist. On the contrary, he had a poor opinion of him, and considered *King Lear* inferior to the primitive chronicle play on which it is based" (1980, 204).

Clearly Carey assumes that when judgments of artistic value conflict, they cancel each other out. The assumption may at first glance seem self-evident. When we encounter contradictions in other lines of inquiry, we tend to assume that they *are* contradictions, statements that cannot both be true at the same time and in the same respect (as Aristotle puts it when talking about the law of non-contradiction). But what grounds do we have for assuming that seemingly simple assertions like "Shakespeare is to me preeminently great" and "Shakespeare is to me inferior to X" are in direct confrontation of any kind? "*King Lear* is inferior to its source" / "It is an improvement on its source"— such propositions do not meet and cancel each other out unless we can specify what axis of values we are talking about, which is to say, what *order* of achievement we have in mind. In what respect is *King Lear* inferior or superior to its source or to Nahum Tate's version with the cheerful ending, which was preferred by many in the eighteenth century? As a tragedy of a certain kind? As an account true to the life of the age? As a melodrama or tear-jerker? As a philosophical portrait of life's meaning? As a culmination of Elizabethan dramaturgy? Or, finally—to turn to our special interest—as schoolmaster to the souls of those who view it or read it? Since each of these questions may produce a different answer, and the last one will certainly be answered differently for different persons of different conditions and climes, it would indeed be cause for suspicion of *ir*rational forces at work if we found a uniformity of answers.[15]

To answer Carey's argument from variability by claiming that Homer or Shakespeare are *in fact* preeminent in all respects for all possible audiences would be absurd. "The Shakespeare gambit," when properly played, claims only that there are in his works—or, more accurately, in this or that one, or in parts of this or that one—such-and-such qualities that *every person who undergoes a proper apprenticeship and comes to understand enough about Shakespeare's culture* can discern. Whether that person will then deem those qualities "great," or "the best possible schoolmaster of the soul" will depend on many variables. It happens that a few authors, like Homer, Sophocles, Shakespeare, Austen, and Dickens, have proved overwhelmingly rewarding to most people who have given them a fair chance, and we who study the reasons can confidently predict that they will continue to do so. But the rewards have always proved diverse, and we should not be surprised when a Mark Twain, for example, cannot join in the general approval of Jane Austen (but see p. 458 n.14 below).

What I go to Shakespeare or Homer for, or whether I go to them at all, will vary from age to age, but no age that pays any attention to them will find them justifying a pornography of child torture, say, or a happy indifference to filial piety, or a denigration of courage, or a denial of the reality of shame—to name only a few out of scores of what we might call shared "resistances" that Shakespeare and Homer offer to the would-be free interpreter. Their powers may seem overwhelmingly diverse—on the positive side—but when we think of interpretations that they flatly reject, we easily discover remarkably clear boundaries.

Finally, judgment varies far less in substance than on the surface of critical statements; a great deal of the evidence for variation simply vanishes when we look closely at what is being judged. Anyone who reads what Tolstoy actually said about Shakespeare, for example, will

15. In fact, the almost uniformly high opinion of everything Shakespeare does is precisely a sign of a partial cultural freeze. Too much praise of Shakespeare springs from cultural hype rather than from honest critical encounters with the slapdash bard's highly uneven production.

find that Carey is mistaken in placing it in direct and simple opposition to traditional adulation of Shakespeare. In *What Is Art?* Tolstoy announces two distinct criteria. According to the first, the "infectiousness" of the work for its proper audience, Shakespeare is indeed one of the most powerful of all dramatists. It is only according to the second criterion, the *kind* of "infection" Shakespeare produces, that he, like Beethoven, Raphael, Wagner, and many other artists who are outstanding in *one* kind of skill, must be condemned. Such artists are vicious to the degree that they appeal—with unusual effectiveness—to cultural elites. "On the one hand, the best works of art of our times transmit religious feelings urging toward the union and the brotherhood of man (such are the works of Dickens, Hugo, Dostoevsky . . .); on the other hand, they strive toward the transmission, not of feelings which are natural to people of the upper classes only, but of such feelings as may unite everyone without exception" ([1896] 1960, 164–65).

From this point of view, many an artist who is great according to the first criterion is dangerous according to the second. Though "some parts" of Shakespeare and Beethoven will serve to unite men in Christian brotherhood (155, 158), their "most admired" works are, considered by the highest standards, most to be deplored.

There is nothing here that can be placed in direct opposition to the general belief that Shakespeare is a great—that is, a preeminently skillful and moving—dramatist. It is precisely *because* he is known by our usual standards to be great that he can serve Tolstoy's argument about the dangers to our souls of that kind of greatness. Such works as *King Lear* and Beethoven's Ninth Symphony are "exclusive" and do not "unite all men"; they unite "only a few, dividing them off from the rest of mankind," and thus the better we ordinary critics may think them, the worse they will seem to Tolstoy.

Tolstoy's careful way of putting his case thus makes him a poor witness for anyone wanting to refute the "Shakespeare gambit." Indeed, he would have been shocked to find himself cited in support of subjectivism. But he does illustrate well the real problem that opponents of subjectivism must face: not the multiplicity of evaluations but the chaotic variability of criteria found in the history of criticism. We must return to the problem of multiple criteria again and again, but for now the point is that diversity of judgment proves that reason is hard at work rather than that it has surrendered.

4. CONFUSION ABOUT WHAT IS EVALUATED

A final reason for skepticism about skepticism about evaluation is that the doubters cover too much ground too simply. Whatever our theories may be, we do find in practice an almost overwhelming variety, both in the kinds of claim made by those who offer evaluations and in the degree to which results can be shared. Many acts of evaluation are indeed little better than reports on private feelings—as data, they are not to be sneezed at, but neither are they full critical acts. On the other hand, some appraisals are more solidly grounded, more inherently public, more easily "replicable," than many a report on so-called scientific fact. We should, then, be as clear as possible about which practices deserve to be salvaged, and about what degree of confidence we can grant to different practices.[16]

What kinds of evaluation do we in fact offer, of what different elements in any narrative?

If we are all to "start even" on that complicated question, we should have before us the full evidence at every point—and that means leaning rather heavily on the shortest possible fictional narrative we can find: a lyric poem.[17]

Judging Parts as Craft—Doing Their Job in a Context

AFTER LONG SILENCE

Speech after long silence; it is right,
All other lovers being estranged or dead,
Unfriendly lamplight hid under its shade,
The curtains drawn upon unfriendly night,

16. I faced something like this moment in writing *A Rhetoric of Irony* (1974, 196–221). There I employed the troublesome metaphor of "four levels of evaluation," implying an increasing level of difficulty as I moved from parts of works to wholes, and then proceeding to show how parts and wholes are judged by "extrinsic" criteria. Here I choose much blander—not to say dead—metaphors of "directions" and "sources."

17. That the following poem is a fragment of narrative, an extracted moment from a long story, is self-evident in its comparison of past and present, youth and age. The notion that *all* lyric poems are in fact narratives, either explicitly or implicitly, is not so self-evident, though I am assuming it throughout. The case for it has been forcefully made by Leonard Nathan (1986).

> That we descant and yet again descant
> Upon the supreme theme of Art and Song:
> Bodily decrepitude is wisdom; young
> We loved each other and were ignorant.

If I asked a group of unselected readers, readers who had never before read Yeats's "After Long Silence" ([1932] 1983, 265), to declare after one quick reading what they think of this narrative, I would no doubt receive an assortment of conflicting opinions that would delight the heart of any subjectivist. We needn't return to I. A. Richards's experiment in collecting students' wildly divergent written "protocols" (1929) to know that the poem would provoke estimations ranging from "great" to "trivial," from "profound" to "shallow," and so on. If we then turned to a group of specialists, we might find a somewhat more manageable range of judgments. But the range would still be wide.

We should remember, however, that we would get as much variety if we asked for undirected, uninformed, undisciplined opinions about the performance of any human activity that requires expertise (and what kind does not at least *invite* it?): baseball pitching (if the judges were British), football plays, mathematical proofs, hemstitching, gardening (if the judges were people like me). Unfocused questions provoke wildly disparate answers in any field, even from experts.

I propose now to improve the poem, and I ask you, experts all, to decide whether my revision is in fact an improvement. In place of the original first two lines, suppose we try these:

> Speech after long silence; it is appropriate,
> All other lovers being estranged or passed to the other side,

And so on, with no further revisions. Immediately our focus is sharpened. Have I improved *this* poem, meddling with *this* part?

Though I cannot know how readers of this book will respond, I have found on the several occasions when I have performed this rather obvious experiment in a lecture hall that *everyone* considers the "improvement" a debasement. Though varying greatly in their expertise, they all know enough about poems to see that "appropriate" and "passed to the other side" belong, if anywhere, in a totally different context. I should be much surprised if I get a single "vote" for my revision from readers here.

This agreement, which we could easily duplicate by tampering with an unlimited number of other poems, famous or unknown, gives us something to think about. By changing our questions from "Is this poem absolutely good (or good for us)?" and "Is evaluation objective?" to "Are these lines better than those, *in this poem?*" we have found an astonishing consensus on a value judgment about a literary question—astonishing, that is, if all value judgments are merely "personal" or "subjective." Considered as an intended human achievement (rather than as a "meaning" or "communication" or "signifier"), the original lines seem to all of "us" immeasurably superior to my revision.[18]

We would of course offer many different reasons for our judgment. Some would want to say that the line "All other lovers being estranged or passed to the other side" is not as well-formed as the original—it breaks the rhythm or it doesn't fit the stanzaic form. Others might say that I have degraded the diction or destroyed the beautiful sound of the original. But could we not, from our present ethical perspective, summarize these and other claims by saying that the revision produces an *ethical* decline, in the sense that the ethos of the implied author has become that of a man who doesn't care very much about how he says his piece?[19]

Simple as the experiment may seem, a great deal is at stake in it. If you think that your judgment of my improvement is sound, then you in fact believe that at least one kind of literary judgment is not merely your private possession, a subjective response bearing only on you; rather, your judgment says something about that other end of the reading transaction, the poem. We probably should not call our shared judgment here "objective," because that word carries too many misleading connotations. But whatever we call it, clearly the critic who claims that it expresses "merely personal opinion" must be willing to

18. For a similar line of argument, using as example Keats's "La Belle Dame Sans Merci," see my "Do Reasons Matter in Criticism?" (1981).

19. It's no secret that a lecturer can obtain a factitious agreement on any such point. Those who do not in fact agree will usually remain silent. If you as reader here really disagree with the judgment, I know not quite what to do with you, except to plead "Read it again—and then, no matter what the result, read on." But be sure that you in fact disagree rather than simply suppose it possible that *someone* might. Of course a reader totally inexperienced with English poetry *might* disagree, but *do you?*

say that anyone who prefers my perverted lines stands on ground as firm as you and I do in seeing those lines for what they are, a deliberate and real corruption.

I should stress that the force of my example does not depend on the rhetorical force of finding absolutely uniform agreement. Our agreement helps us see the point, but it is not what makes the point. Our consensus is built upon our individual literary judgments about the lines—coductions by "individuals" who are in their nature already social (see Chapter 8). That judgment in itself does not initially depend on whether all other people "now present" agree. Indeed, as Stanley Fish insists (1980), we can always *imagine* other communities in which a majority would prefer "passed to the other side," perhaps because it is nicer than "dead." But if we did, if any one of us found a majority in opposition, we would not be likely to change our opinion about the improvement, unless in discussion someone speaking for that majority could get us to see some context we had ignored. We would take our own judgment, shared with an *implied* community, as more authoritative, because more experienced, and thus more aware of what is *there* in the poem, awaiting our re-creation. We would rightly be confident about this case (which I have deliberately made easy), since our judgment is a coduction incorporating what we have all experienced of poems, poets, other readers, and ourselves.

Of course if anyone at any stage of this experiment does in fact express a preference for the corrupted version, all I need do is offer a version that is obviously worse:

> You know what I mean, it's like, I mean, you know, like
> Sitting around chatting it up, after a while, like wow, the lights
> Fade out, and you're sitting there, and, you know,

And so on, leaving the rest intact.

Clearly these lines corrupt Yeats's poem further. But it is equally clear that if we continued in this vein for a few lines more, we might come to a point where Yeats's final lines would find *themselves* isolated and inappropriate, spoiling a new and entirely different narrative. At the borderline, halfway through such grotesque tampering, we might not know which half was spoiling which. But we would never have any doubt that Yeats's poem was being mutilated, and with it—if this were all the evidence we had about the poet—the ethos of the maker. We would conclude that the poet implied by these mutilated

versions cared less about his craft than did Yeats: we would thus again
be judging ethos even as we judged craft.

A subjectivist might well protest here that the exercise is trivial:
"When I say that value judgments 'can tell us nothing,' I obviously do
not have in mind any such *easy* judgments." Well, if that is so, if subjectivists wish to exempt *some* value judgments that *do* in fact show
real knowledge—namely, the easy ones—they should say so. Surely
we are entitled to know what is included in the sweeping generalization that value judgments tell us nothing about the poem itself. We
have made a judgment, and the results are such that to reject them
would be immeasurably more unreasonable than to accept them.

Our confidence naturally diminishes as we leave absurd extremes
and move toward nuance. Judgment about nuance is what conscientious artists like Yeats themselves perform as they move from draft to
draft. Often toward the end of composition the choices are so chancy
that no one, least of all the author, could claim to *know* their grounds.
But anyone who has ever tried to revise even one line or stanza of poetry, one sentence or paragraph of prose, knows that judgments of
parts in the service of a not-quite-yet-fully-realized whole can be as secure as most judgments of what is "factual."

.Suppose we now try a somewhat less blatant revision, this time of
the poem's penultimate line, "Bodily decrepitude is wisdom . . .":

> Decrepitude increases wisdom . . .

Again the revision has surely but less obviously harmed the poem, by
substituting the abstract and weak "Decrepitude increases" for the
vividly creaking "Bodily decrepitude." This time, however, it is not my
decadent fancy that has wounded the finished poem but Yeats's own
hand in one of his earlier drafts, written before he came up with
"Bodily decrepitude is wisdom." Thomas Parkinson has traced successive versions of this poem in the manuscripts. As we read through his
report, in *W. B. Yeats: The Later Poetry* (1964, 83–92), we find that
every line has been markedly changed from its original form, usually in
ways that even we non-poets can recognize as clear improvements.
Yeats tried "Upon the sole theme of art and song." Not bad, but what
does "sole" say, really? So he tried "Upon that theme so fitting for the
aged." Terrible. And then he found "Upon the supreme theme of Art
and Song." And stopped.

At first the lamplight was friendly, until it occurred to him that light is in fact unfriendly to aging lovers. At first he said "We call our wisdom up and descant," and then he tried "We call upon wisdom and descant." Finding no rhythmical flair in either, he finally hit upon the repetition that, like the rhyme of "supreme theme," seems wonderful once found.

Like most successful poets, Yeats labored in anguish over such changes. Always, he said, it would take him many days to write even the shortest poem. On the first day, no rhymes would come at all: "[A]nd when at last the rhymes begin to come, the first rough draft of a six-line stanza takes a whole day. . . . [S]ometimes a six-line stanza would take several days, . . . and so the last night was generally sleepless, and the last day a day of nervous strain" (1953, 122; qtd. in Parkinson 1964, 76).

Though we readers, in contrast, follow Yeats's changes and choices quickly and with relatively little anguish, the cognitive steps we take are of the same kind as Yeats's, and they become more like his the more we turn consciously to evaluative thinking. To discover whether a given choice is the best *we* can think of, we must raise ourselves to a level of perception something like his own. We must imagine for ourselves a poem sufficiently like his for it to exercise control over the choices we would want to make.[20] To do that, we must call on a great range of past experience with the masters of prosody: with rhyme and half-rhyme ("dead"/"shade," "Song"/"young," "descant"/"ignorant"), with regular meter and deliberate violations of regularity. But we also call on our experience of life and of the ways in which poetry reflects it: of young love and the shocks of aging, of death and ways of describing it ("dead" versus "passed to the other side"), and so on. In short, we must both surrender to the precise details of Yeats's text as we reconstruct it—that part of it that is assumed to be already decided—and imitate his creative act in probing with an emerging intention to the further choices it demands. With Yeats's aid, we consider possibilities in the world that would never have occurred to us on our own, and then we choose among them with something like the concentration that Yeats himself exhibited as he composed. Much of this is of course

---

20. That we may in fact work unawares in directions entirely different from the intentions of the author raises other problems, but it does not affect our experiment here.

simply retracing, consciously and deliberately, the steps that every reader of the poem must have taken intuitively even on a first full reading.

Throughout all this we are implicitly engaged in an act of ethical criticism inseparable from our judgment of craft. As we stretch our own poetic character to meet the implied character of the maker, we do not say that his craft is one thing and his character another; instead we feel that we are meeting the character as we take in the craft. This does not mean that we may not offer, at some later moment, ethical judgments opposing his; we may reject his way of relating youth and age, or decide that his conclusion is misleading. Someone might even argue that the very notion of writing a poem on this pathetic moment of reconsidered passion was a mistake in the first place. But long before that aggressively ethical moment comes, we are already implicitly ethical critics, *provided* that we engage with the poem as a representation offered by one human being to another, rather than inspect it, say, as a random datum for some other kind of inquiry.

In short, our coduction tells us that in this particular case, in these precise ways, the craftsman Yeats has mastered his art and used it to ends that we must respect, even if we finally question some part of the enterprise. He has "practiced" his skills before our eyes, practiced them to a kind of perfection, enabling us similarly to practice a pale reflection of that art. Of course we will trust our own performance only if we have played our part in the conversation with the artist's kind of conscientiousness (again, note the ethical term). It is true, further, that we more often than not leave the comparative part of our coductions unstated: we come to love the work (or detest it) without stating explicitly, "I do so because when I compare this with other works in this genre I find it . . ." But whenever a narrative really works for us, we are sure to feel, when challenged, that the author's choices and our (perhaps easier) choices are alike in kind, and thus that he or she is our kind of person, practicing "virtues"—both skills and moral and intellectual powers—that we admire.

All these terms, and perhaps particularly "conscientious," under-line once again the ethical appraisal that is inseparable from what looks like judgment of sheer craft. In discovering that we know some-thing about the quality of this poem—that at least some of its parts are well chosen for their task—we already discover something about the ethos of the poet: he shows the integrity of a devoted craftsman. My substitute versions not only do not fit the poem; they imply a maker who is sloppy, vulgar, careless about cliché, inattentive to form—in short, a bad craftsman.[21] Thus, regardless of whether I think the whole poem a major achievement, I have already found a meeting point of craft and ethics: the poet has met a demanding ethical standard by honing at least some of the parts so fine that I can think of no possible improvement.[22]

This point will not be affected if we encounter readers who prefer the ethos implied by the corrupted parts I have substituted: "I like the laid-back, unpretentious person who speaks the lines 'You know what I mean, it's like, . . .'; I detest the pretentious would-be wise guy, Yeats, who natters at his aged beloved in 'After Long Silence.'" Such a response would equally illustrate my general point: the choice of devices and compositional strategies is from the beginning a choice of ethos, an invitation to one kind of ethical criticism. Readers who disagree about our taste in ethos would still presumably agree that the substituted lines are inferior *as lines in Yeats's poem,* just as we could agree that Yeats's concluding lines would be very poor choices if what we sought to perfect was "You know what I mean . . ." And we could all agree that the implied makers of my botched versions are less admirable, simply as craftsmen, than the poet who makes any version that really holds together.[23]

We have so far found at least one kind of ethical judgment—the one

---

21. The statement is true only when the substitute poems are read as if torn from the context of this chapter. As *my* creations, illustrative monstrosities, they imply an entirely different ethos.

22. If this test seems somehow an arrogant one—Who am *I* to test my powers of revision against Yeats's?—we should remember that it is always implicitly present in any comparative criticism. If a reader can easily think of what seem improvements, the original poem must always suffer.

A good illustration of how evaluation and careful description go together can be found in the analysis of this poem in that fine old textbook *Understanding Poetry,* by Cleanth Brooks and Robert Penn Warren (1938). Whatever we may say about the theoretical underpinnings of the New Critics, their practice of trying to stick to what was "there on the page" was often brilliantly illuminating about the value of what was, from their point of view, "there" but what would be, from other critical perspectives, only in the reader. For an appraisal of their contribution to ethical criticism, see my "What Is Not Old about the New Critics" (1985).

23. An astonishing number of critics have argued by now that incoherence, incongruity, uncontrolled dissonance, an unfinished surface are inherently superior to whatever "holds together" or "is contrived." These days, when deconstructionists in

we inevitably pass on the maker of parts in polished wholes. Even though this judgment is "subjective" in one sense, it can be as trans-personal, as non-idiosyncratic, as publicly verifiable, as anyone could demand of any inquiry. Performed and tested with generally acknowledged methods, by judges who have completed an appropriate apprenticeship (reading and responding to as many poems, say, as the number of cases that a really good medical diagnostician must have met), appraisals of particular lines in particular structures can not only be talked about with some precision but can be called, in extreme cases at least, "practically certain." It does seem to me that everybody who, this late in the day as this seems to me to be, believes that judgments about intrinsic literary quality can never, even in the clearest, most striking and illuminating cases, like those I have just described, have the status of being called "cognitive" or "genuine knowledge" (epistemologically *standard*), has to face the hard question of whether or not he or she wouldn't agree with my judgment about this being *really* a terrible sentence, implying a terrible ethos, even though it is so far as I know grammatically more or less correct and even though as a part for *this book,* making a point about real badness, it is one that I will keep? I could easily have made it worse—so bad that even a child would see and judge the *fact* of its "artistic" failure. Surely anyone who could write a sentence like that, except as parody, is lacking in a major "virtue"—the virtue appropriate to writers of sentences designed for books like this.

Judging Completed Works as "Perfected"

Our appraisal of parts has already spilled over into two further kinds of appraisal: of completed works as craft (after all, I could not

---

such great number are celebrating the inevitability of inconsistency, we tend to forget just how widespread similar arguments were before the new wave (e.g., Bayley 1976; and my review, 1976; and Ruskin 1851–53, 6.1.22). Such arguments collapse at least three kinds of incoherence. Some great art does gain part of its power from its lack of completion: the effort is so noble, the obstacles so powerful, that nobody could have won order out of such magnificent chaos. (This is Ruskin's main point about Gothic architecture.) That effect is quite different from the simpler forms of incoherence that spring from sloth, indifference, pursuit of fashion, or simple lack of talent. And that kind is quite different in turn from the inescapable "incoherence" found by deconstructionist analysis of the rhetorical devices of even the most fully realized narrative.

judge the individual lines without having already experienced something of the whole poem), and of parts, wholes, and their genres according to critical constants independent of the intended wholes in which they appear (my bad sentence would be judged bad and expunged from every critical work except this one, where it plays its part in a whole).

The judgment of whole fictions, *as crafted,* is in a sense simply a product of judgments of all the constituent parts. In our little experiment with Yeats, we obviously did not escape the circularity implicit in all experience not only of fictions but of people: we cannot even see what a "part" is without having already intuited a whole of a certain kind. Nevertheless, in critical practice we all manage to shift fairly easily back and forth from parts to wholes, and the judgment that a whole poem or novel is excellent, "perfect," is somehow quite different from simply saying "It has thirty-six lines (or sentences, or scenes, or characters, . . .), each of which is marvelous in serving the whole: therefore the whole is good." And we all understand the question that every author faces throughout the process of revision: "Have I made this work to be better as a whole than the other possible works, actual or implied, that offered themselves and were rejected, draft by draft?" I can think of no authors—not even those most committed to aleatoric composition—who would never ask that question, and there is thus no reason why critics should not pursue it too.

It is easy to show again that those who think value judgments meaningless always fix the fight by considering only borderline cases. But if their claim is correct, it should fit the innumerable cases in which both authors and critics deem this version as superior to *that* one. All of us "here," for example, can come to easy agreement that Yeats's poem is superior to many another poem that attempts roughly the same effects. Try this one:

> Your hair is white
> My hair is white
> Come let us talk of love
> What other theme do we know
> When we were young
> We were in love with one another
> And then were ignorant.

Again I hear a chorus of protests: "You make it too easy. We're not talking about flat stuff like that when we say that value judgments can tell us nothing except about the valuers." But what then does "nothing" mean? In fact, this version was sent by Yeats, as a first draft called "Subject," to Olivia Shakespeare (Parkinson 1964, 83). It is already clearly a "poem." But to argue that it approaches the value of the finished work would require some fancy footwork. (The first step—predictable on our current dancefloor—will be a rejection of "artifice," "completeness," or "an always illusory claim to coherence.")

Parkinson concludes that the path from this first draft to "After Long Silence" represents a "discipline that was Yeats's great strength. The process of movement from abstraction to immediacy to poetic embodiment is deliberate and full of artifice, . . . afterthoughts, . . . omissions, restraints and delicacies. The role of the poet . . . is one of humility before the emergent poem without self-abasement, honesty without self-indulgence" (92).

Again we see how talk of craft leads easily to talk of ethical power. The bare facts about revision of the *poem* entail judgments about the *poet*. The evidence that the poem achieves success in the face of obstacles is simultaneously evidence of the poet's character.

It is of course success of a given limited kind, and in criticism of crafted wholes we accept, at least for a time, the conditions for success established by the work itself as we experience it: again we live in a circle—what fashion would call "hermeneutical." We see that the juggler is trying to juggle in one style rather than another (serious vs. comic, let us say), and we judge both the juggling and its master accordingly. Though we will certainly encounter greater disparity among judges of entire works than of component parts, we usually find it easy to agree that "this poem is *trying* to be such-and-such," and once we have agreed on intentions, we usually find rough agreement about realizations. One might not think so, judging from the controversies in our journals, but that is because we tend not to write about works unless there is *some* disagreement about their intentions and realizations.

The question in appraising wholes, given their intentions,[24] will always finally be, then, Has something been achieved here that is *in its own terms* admirable? Has some gift or skill been exhibited here that *those who see and accept its implicit standards* will admire? We need

24. I must repeat: we are not talking of authors' *motives* here but of the work's *intentions*; these may overlap, but they seldom coincide.

make no claim at this point for the universality of those standards, and we should expect to find readers for whom "restraint," "delicacy," and "discipline" are less to be admired than qualities like unrestrained ambition, freedom of improvisation, and crude unbelted howls. Fortunately, we usually share with artists themselves sufficiently clear notions of artistic purpose to allow productive discussion of *degrees* of success and failure: "Yes, indeed, the juggler did drop the balls deliberately and thus exhibited his own kind of polish." "No, we cannot find any artistic justification for the clumsy clashing of metaphors or the limping meter."

In every case, we have seen that so long as the discussion is about performance of a given task and not about interpretations of meanings, it will simultaneously be to some degree an ethical discussion: What qualities in the artist could account for such-and-such qualities in the work?

Judging According to "Extrinsic" Standards

We face a much more difficult problem when we turn to what have often been called "extrinsic" questions. How do we appraise two narratives each of which seems fully "realized," "perfected in its form," invulnerable to the most penetrating questions about achievement "within its own terms"?

One way of framing this question can yield fairly clear answers: "big" works are inherently more impressive than "little" ones. Though no perfected short work implicitly asks to be judged according to the standards appropriate to *Remembrance of Things Past*, nobody who has experienced both the pleasures of a first-class limerick, say, and the rewards of Proust's giant could ever equate their value. Both limericks and the great monuments can give great pleasure; indeed limericks are more unambiguously pleasurable than *Remembrance* or *Paradise Lost*. But we would all find something strange about anyone who, knowing both *Paradise Lost* and "There was a young lady of Thebes," would value them equally. Preserve them both? Yes, of course. But preserve them with the same passion? Unthinkable. Similarly, an epigram by Pope can be a marvelous work and a wonder, but *The Dunciad*, or any work like it that enfolds a myriad of epigrams into a grand satiric structure, is "self-evidently" worth more to us—according to every criterion but that of concision. I'm not thinking here of the old desert-isle question, because I don't want to suggest that we discard lesser genres just because they are lesser. The goal is not to pack into our traveling bag only the best that has been thought and said but to find forms of critical talk that will improve the range or depth or precision of our appreciations.

The criterion of size (obviously related to Aristotle's "magnitude," but how?) is by no means simply a matter of length, though we'll find some measures of sheer quantity useful in Chapter 6. Here we are once again dealing with what a work implies about the author's ethos, the quality of the author's gift to us. One cannot experience a fiction without inferring (perhaps not consciously) certain qualities in the character of its maker: "From such a cause, such results." The author of Milton's epics exhibits courage, learning, piety, depth of feeling, combined with astonishing delicacy, philosophical profundity, psychological insight, mastery of an astonishing variety of poetic devices, including a most impressive proficiency with metaphor and irony, an almost unmatched architectonic vision, and—despite his forbidding pose as master teacher—a quiet sense of humor (a gift too often ignored in criticism of his works). And this list is far from complete. The author of the most brilliant limerick offers, on the other hand, only wit, a highly limited (though still admirable) prosodic discipline, and perhaps a certain amount of persistence against difficulty.

No item on the Miltonic list will come as a surprise to anyone who knows Milton's works. The list as a whole may even seem banal—lists of virtues usually do—until we remember that it is by no means an exact duplicate of what we would find in other major authors. What's more, each virtue in its actual manifestation is much more particular than the general terms suggest: Milton's courage is unlike Virgil's or Homer's; his piety contrasts sharply with Shakespeare's; his irony is radically different from Swift's; his humor is quite unlike Fielding's. Regardless of how we rank his diverse virtues (and faults), we are forced to conclude that his formal achievement—"packing all that in"—conveys a commanding ethos, one that demands the best response a reader can manage. There would surely be something odd in the claim that *Paradise Lost* is not "really" superior to some short story or "perfect little" lyric dealing with similar themes or effects.

But can we go beyond this one clear, cruel violation of the standards implicitly evoked by "little works"? Can we make reasonable comparisons of the ethical value of two narratives that seem roughly comparable in perfection of the craft, works that seem to have been "worked" with equal passion and power, but that clearly embody or depend on radically different "ideologies" (what I shall later describe as "fixed norms")? If the limerick would feel "violated" by our comparison with Proust—"You are such a shrimp!"—it will surely feel much more deeply violated by our saying, "You're nasty and shallow." Once we open the doors to such questions, where can we hope to find reasonable limits to the voices crying for our credence?

One frequent route is to move away from the implied author to the "real" biography. When we do so, we find that biographical and cultural information can raise or lower our estimate of a performance. The juggler once had infantile paralysis; the critic (e.g., Johnson) was half-blind and sickly at birth; the poet (Roethke, Lowell) battled with bouts of madness; the satirist (Voltaire) wrote his amazing work in only ten days; the novelist (Flaubert) battled for ten years to *juste*-ify his *mots;* the writer of wrenching short stories (Tillie Olsen) found time to write them only after years as an impoverished housewife. Can we admire Voltaire for breathtaking facility and at the same time admire Flaubert for anguished endurance? In practice we all modify our sense of the value of the made-object according to our opinions about what it cost, or whether we could easily match it.

Even greater complexities arise as we move to theoretical study of our criteria and their grounding in philosophical, psychological, anthropological, or theological systems; or to the study of audiences and modes of reception ("Narratives that appeal to my kind of person are superior to those that appeal to . . . those inferior types," whoever they may be); or to historical inquiry about genres, their potentialities and difficulties ("The author I thought an original was contemptibly imitative," or vice versa). Before long we are overwhelmed with a multiplicity of rival "universals" that might well drive us either to surrender to the subjectivists or to retreat to the shaky intrinsic/extrinsic distinction. So long as we ask only questions that "this poem as an achievement" invites us to ask, can we not hope to escape these threatening floods of perhaps inherently unanswerable questions?

The critical world seems by now to have discovered that such a move *is* a retreat, precisely because the sharp distinction between the "intrinsic" and the "extrinsic" will not hold. Our notion of just what artistic purposes can be wholeheartedly embraced does not come strictly from any one narrative experience. Whenever we say, "Not only is this narrative good in its kind, but I celebrate the kind," we rely of necessity on all the rest of our experience with other narratives— and, needless to say, with the entire non-narrative world, whatever we take that to be.

The intrinsic/extrinsic distinction may still be useful for critics who remember that decisions about what is intrinsic will necessarily vary from critic to critic. But for us here—as apparently for critics of most flourishing "schools" today—the really pressing questions arise when we deliberately free ourselves from the obligation merely to *under*-stand "the work in itself," and happily violate its invitations in order to achieve *over*standing.

All such critical projects are easily corrupted into the kind of merely idiosyncratic assertion of generalities that can make subjectivists sleep easily in their own assertions. Our ethical enterprise is perhaps the most easily corrupted of all. When we try to make *ethical* comparisons of parts or of completed works according to principles or norms not derived from the study of *this* "poem as poem," do we not fall inevitably into the reductive sorts of "lumping" criticism that I questioned in Chapter 3? My general answer, which will expand itself as the book develops, is that we must avoid at all costs the effort to reduce literary "goods" to one kind; instead, we should seek to clarify and embrace a *plurality* of goods, exhibited in particular coductions, while vigorously expressing our reasons for mistrusting those narrative experiences that would, if taken alone, undermine *all* the defensible projects.[25]

25. As I write the final draft of *Company,* a work appears that expresses, for the political order, precisely the kind of pluralism that I am urging for criticism: Joseph Raz's *The Morality of Freedom* (1986). Offering a revised version of John Stuart Mill's defense of liberty, Raz shows just why the freedom to choose from a genuine plurality of ethical views, even of incompatible views, is not just an unfortunate necessity but a positive good. As "individuals" who are essentially social (see my discussion in Chapter 8), we depend, if we are to become what we *can* become, on a society that offers a plurality of goods. The fine review that put me onto this splendidly provocative work is by Neil MacCormick (1987). I argue the case for pluralism at length in *Critical Understanding* (1979), but in trying to do justice there to the plurality of *interpretations,* I do not do justice to the work of art as a locus of many seemingly rival values.

THE FAILURE OF UNIVERSAL CLAIMS,
AS APPLIED TO PARTS

The first part of this project—the recognition that plurality is inescapable—is most easily dramatized by seeing what happens when critics judge the parts of a narrative not as they serve a given whole but as
they obey some uniform "extrinsic" standard. Someone might want to
claim, for example, that the euphemism "passed to the other side" will
always be "too petty bourgeois for comfort," or that abstract polysyllables like "appropriate" are *always* inferior, at least in poetry, to
concrete monosyllables like "dead." Some might claim that true poetry must exhibit regularity of meter, and they would be disturbed by
how my revisions destroy the fairly regular meter of the first two lines.
Or they might go even further and ask for *more* regularity: in place of
what we have (one strong nine-syllabled, four-beat line and one of
eleven syllables with five beats—or perhaps we can even read it as six
beats), let us be more "poetic" and make two strictly iambic lines:

> I speak and break the silence: it is right,
> All other lovers now estranged or dead[26]

26. In the fall term of 1986, teaching "Practical Criticism" to a class of advanced
undergraduates, I asked them to write brief evaluations (before we had said anything
about this poem or about Yeats) of several versions and possible versions of "After Long
Silence." I included the corruptions I have offered here and the following full-length
"improvement":

> I speak and break the silence: it is right,
> All other lovers now estranged or dead,
> Unfriendly lamplight covered by its shade,
> The curtains drawn upon unfriendly night,
> That we descant and yet again descant
> Upon that final theme of Art and Song:
> Our bodies all decay; when we were young
> We loved each other—in our ignorance.

While I was relieved to discover that nobody chose "it is appropriate" or "passed to
the other side," over "it is right" and "dead," I was puzzled to find more than half pre-
ferring my regulated verses to Yeats's carefully wrought metrical variations. Though the
poems that the students had written on their own were all in "free verse" (except when I
pleaded with them to experiment with traditional forms), they seemed to feel when they
came to the exercise of judging the versions by Yeats that the greater the regularity the
better the poem—at least when working in a college classroom.
    One student preferred the early prosy version by Yeats, the one I quote on page 110
above.

Other lumping critics might move in the opposite direction and say that the relative regularity of the published poem is a fault; verse forms should all be "free," and though my revised lines may be bad, my impulse to break up the iambs, in my parodies, was justified. Still others might make judgments based on universal criteria about the quantity or kinds of metaphor, levels of diction, and so on. Moving further "out" still, some might want to say that "passed to the other side" should be condemned (or embraced) because it expresses the wrong (or right) attitude toward death and suggests a superstitious (or properly pious) belief in immortality.

Obviously such judgments derived from universals are at best debatable. If critical evaluation were to be *only* that, then the skeptics would be at least partially justified. Arguments about precise parts, put in this universal form, may appear to be down-to-earth and empirical because they refer to concrete details: this line is inferior to that line. But we can always unpack them as universal syllogisms; and when we do that, we find either that we cannot possibly defend the standard as a true universal, only as one good among many, or that we hold to the standard so deeply that nobody can possibly affect our commitment with argument (e.g., "It is more admirable to write intelligible lines than nonsense syllables"). In short, once we choose to ignore the "whole poem" and its intentions, we step into a world of discourse where we are far more likely to talk past each other. Some judgments of this kind are as absurd as the statement that the leg of the chair you are sitting on is a bad leg because it is not Chippendale. Far too many appeals to critical constants are either not applicable *to this work* or not applicable to other works that fall under the universal claim. They can seem, in consequence, to confirm the subjectivist's attack on all evaluation.[27]

THE FAILURE OF UNIVERSALS, AS APPLIED
TO WHOLE NARRATIVES

The same argument holds—though its lines are a bit harder to trace—for the qualities of entire works. In the history of manifestos

---

27. For a more sustained questioning of critical constants, see Booth 1983, 29–53.

proclaiming this or that critical constant, can we find even one that
will cover, deductively, all the narratives we admire? Energy/serenity;
clarity/ambiguity; decorum/startling novelty; simplicity/ironic richness and complexity; sublimity or beauty/truth-to-life; unity/compre-
hensiveness; compassion/impartiality; intelligibility/mystery; spiritual
or moral uplift and edification/rejection of answers and celebration of
questions; unification of all in Christian love/salvation only for a saving remnant—though we may not find such oppositions for every virtue we might think of, we can be sure that any given virtue will be
inappropriate or destructive in *some* admired work. Even clichéd revisions of Yeats might be effective in some sort of parody, or for some
kinds of satiric characterization of maimed speakers. And even the criterion of magnitude cannot be applied generally: many a "large" work
will weigh less on most scales than a fine haiku.

Nevertheless I shall not be troubled if readers can think of some
critical constant that for them applies to all good poems, or to all good
lines in all good poems, or to all good elements in other fictions. If they
did think of one, it would simply put them in agreement with my general defense of evaluation as an important activity (though to apply
any constant crudely would reinforce the skeptic's skepticism).

Our deeper problem emerges when we confront such readers with
one another—that is, with the inevitable conflicts among their chosen
universals. If now, as members of a *society* of inquirers, each one of us
is convinced that value distinctions are defensible working in some one
"axiological pyramid," how are we to deal with the fact—and it
clearly is a fact—that Doe's pyramid, with its capstone universal,
seems to contradict Roe's? My coduction of Yeats's poem—now prolonged over several decades, including the years of revising this book—
tells me that it in itself is a fine thing to have in the world, as an
achievement of craft. But where do I find criteria for comparing its
kind with other achievements that also earn my admiration as craft
but that embody contradictory values? "Bodily decrepitude is *not*
wisdom; it is a lie concealing the road to salvation." "No, the truly
supreme theme of Art and Song is that 'Death is the mother of beauty.'"

Facing an overwhelming multiplicity of genres and messages, we
might be tempted to draw back and say that the Careys are right, after
all, but only about this ultimate kind of evaluation. Though we have
found many appraisals that make sense, have we not come here to a

kind that are in fact arbitrary? Will not any comparison of *these* lyrics with *those,* of this kind of lyric exhibiting such and such ideology with that kind, of lyric with epic, and epic with tragedy, and tragedy with comedy be like comparing oranges and nightingales? Surely here if nowhere else we should accede to the notion that there is no sensible disputing about taste.

I hope before we reach the end of *Company* to have shown just why that retreat is not necessary, even about this ultimate question in ethical criticism. For the time being, I see only two plausible responses that a committed subjectivist could make to the more restricted ethical evaluations we have traced here.

First, it might be argued that if we face the pluralities of criteria, we can "prove" any poem superior to any other poem, on any arbitrarily chosen axis of value; in short, we need only become *complicated* subjectivists. But to say as much would be to ignore the quality of our concrete experience of diverse narrative purposes. For the purposes of a political campaign, Yeats's poem will be inferior to "I like Ike" or "Yawn with Ron." For the purposes of parody, my corrupt versions of "After Long Silence" better it. For the purposes of educating first-graders, almost every work I mention in this book will be found deficient. But by the criteria that "we" all find called into play when reading Yeats's poem, his own revisions are quite clearly superior to his first tries. Only an artificially impoverished experience-free world could lead us to conclude that the multiplicity of criteria leaves us choosing blindly. On the contrary, once we clarify our questions, we can distinguish those coductions that discriminate degrees of success in exercising a determinate human skill ("telling this kind of good story") from those more controversial coductions about more or less valuable forms and genres. In sorting out criteria and types of judgment, we have found an explanation for the seemingly contradictory nature of *some* critical judgments. And in connecting story-telling with craft, we have discovered one more reason why our evaluations are always "contaminated" with ethics.

The second possible subjectivist response is in one sense unanswerable. If we decide to treat all narratives as though they were impersonal objects; if we disconnect fictional and historical narratives from human purposes, treating them as we treat the planets and stars (but see p. 97 n.14 above); and if readers are confined, in arguing about

what fictions are and do, to scientific paradigms of deduction and induction—then of course there will be no way to show that "After
Long Silence" is worth more than a limerick you or I might make up
on the spot:

> There once was a poet named Yeats,
> Who was known to belong to the greats.
> But when put to the test
> He looked just like the rest . . .

You can choose your own final rhyme from debates, dates, fates,
greats, mates, rates . . . In such a world, we cannot even show that a
master juggler is more admirable than the exasperating bumbler I saw
busking in the summer of 1985 near Covent Garden. Nothing is more
than anything else. In fact, nothing in such a universe is really *worth*
anything at all. Everything just *is*. Or rather, isn't. What we are doing
together here is no more defensible than shooting each other for sport,
say, or reading aloud together from the more sexist and sadistic fictions of *Hustler* magazine.

But if any human actions can in fact be granted more value than
any others, then some poetic acts are worth more than others. Actually
worth more to every possible person, at this moment? Obviously not.
Potentially worth more to every "normal human being"? Only if we
carefully define "potential" and "normal." In showing that anything
has "worth," we always imply *potential* worth *for* some human being;
a fiction is worth nothing to a rock, a rock nothing to a fiction. The
fictions that are, in my argument, *in fact worth more*, carry their
worth only potentially for most of humankind, and for all of us the
potential gifts of many worthy works will never be realized (for a discussion of "five crippling handicaps" in readers, see Booth 1974,
222–27).

To embrace the reality of worth thus does not free us from inherent
difficulties in the subject. Some appraisals, particularly those that discriminate kinds and genres, will remain immensely difficult; some,
particularly those that try to rank works, may prove a waste of time.
But if we know that such judgments are not necessarily pointless, if we
know that talk about such matters can sometimes yield experiences
that transform our lives, then we can move forward with confidence in
our search for better ways of talking about what we care for most.

REFERENCES

Adams, George P., et al., eds. *Possibility*. University of California Publications in Philosophy, vol. 17. Berkeley, 1934.

Alcorn, Marshall W., Jr. "Rhetoric, Projection, and the Authority of the Signifier." *College English* 49 (Feb. 1987): 137–57.

Aristotle. *On the Generation of Animals*. Trans. A. L. Peck. Loeb Classical Library. Cambridge, Mass., 1979.

Arnold, Matthew. Preface. *Poems*. London, 1853.

———. *Literature and Dogma*. London, 1873.

———. *Essays in Criticism* [1865]. London, 1888.

Barrow, John D., and Frank J. Tipler. *The Anthropic Cosmological Principle*. Oxford, 1986.

Bayley, John. *The Uses of Division: Unity and Disharmony in Literature*. London, 1976.

Bernstein, Richard J. *Beyond Objectivism and Relativism: Science, Hermeneutics, and Praxis*. Philadelphia, 1983.

Booth, Wayne C. *A Rhetoric of Irony*. Chicago, 1974.

———. "Seventeen Types of Incongruity." Review of *The Uses of Division*, by John Bayley. *Times Literary Supplement* (July 23, 1976): 914–15.

———. *Critical Understanding*. Chicago, 1979.

———. "Do Reasons Matter in Criticism? Or: Many Meanings, Many Modes." *Bulletin of the Midwest Modern Language Association* 14 (Spr. 1981): 3–23.

———. *The Rhetoric of Fiction*. 1961. 2d ed. Chicago, 1983.

———. "What Is Not Old about the New Critics." *Humanities* 6 (Apr. 1985): 7–8.

Brooks, Cleanth, and Robert Penn Warren, eds. and comps. *Understanding Poetry: An Anthology for College Students*. New York, 1938.

Burke, Kenneth. *Language as Symbolic Action: Essays on Life, Literature, and Method*. Berkeley, 1966.

Carey, John. "Viewpoint." *Times Literary Supplement* (Feb. 22, 1980): 204.

Davidson, Donald. *Inquiries into Truth and Interpretation*. Oxford, 1984.

Davies, Robertson. *World of Wonders*. New York, 1976.

Eagleton, Terry. *Literary Theory: An Introduction*. Minneapolis, 1983.

Ellis, John M. "Evaluation." In *The Theory of Literary Criticism: A Logical Analysis*. Berkeley, 1974.

Fish, Stanley. *Is There a Text in This Class? The Authority of Interpretive Communities*. Cambridge, Mass., 1980.

Goodman, Nelson. *Ways of Worldmaking*. Indianapolis, 1978.

Hirsch, E. D. "Evaluation as Knowledge," "Three Dimensions of Hermeneutics," and "Privileged Criteria in Evaluation." In *The Aims of Interpretation*. Chicago, 1976.

Hume, David. *A Treatise of Human Nature*. London, 1739–40.

Iser, Wolfgang. *The Act of Reading: A Theory of Aesthetic Response*. Baltimore, 1978.

Johnson, Samuel. "*The Rambler*, no. 4" [1750]. In *Samuel Johnson: "The Rambler,"* vol. 1. Ed. W. J. Bate and Albrecht B. Strauss. Vol. 3 of *The*

Yale Edition of the Works of Samuel Johnson. New Haven, Conn., 1969. 19–25.

Kant, Immanuel. *Kritik of Judgment* [1790]. Trans. J. H. Bernard. London, 1892.

Klein, Peter. *Certainty: A Refutation of Scepticism.* Minneapolis, 1981.

Leavis, F. R. *The Great Tradition: George Eliot, Henry James, Joseph Conrad* [1948]. New York, 1969.

Lewis, David. *On the Plurality of Worlds.* Oxford, 1986.

MacCormick, Neil. "Access to the Goods." Review of *The Morality of Freedom,* by Joseph Raz. *Times Literary Supplement* (June 5, 1987): 599.

MacIntyre, Alasdair. *After Virtue: A Study in Moral Theory.* Notre Dame, Ind., 1981.

Mailloux, Steven. *Interpretive Conventions: The Reader in the Study of American Fiction.* Ithaca, N.Y., 1982.

Nathan, Leonard. "Putting the Lyric in Its Place." *Northwest Review* 24 (Nov. 1986): 77–84.

Norris, Christopher. *Contest of Faculties: Philosophy and Theory after Deconstruction.* London, 1985.

Olson, Elder. *"On Value Judgments in the Arts" and Other Essays.* Chicago, 1976.

Parkinson, Thomas. *W. B. Yeats: The Later Poetry.* Berkeley, 1964.

Pavel, Thomas G. *Fictional Worlds.* Cambridge, Mass., 1986.

Putnam, Hilary. *Reason, Truth, and History.* Cambridge, 1981.

Rader, Ralph. "Dramatic Monologue and Related Lyric Forms." *Critical Inquiry* 3 (Aut. 1976): 131–51.

Raz, Joseph. *The Morality of Freedom.* Oxford, 1986.

Reichert, John. "Evaluation." In *Making Sense of Literature.* Chicago, 1977.

Richards, I. A. *Practical Criticism: A Study of Literary Judgment.* New York, 1929.

Rosenblatt, Louise. *The Reader, the Text, the Poem: The Transactional Theory of the Literary Work.* Carbondale, Ill., 1978.

Ruskin, John. "The Nature of Gothic." In *The Stones of Venice.* London, 1851–53.

Santayana, George. *Skepticism and Animal Faith.* New York, 1923.

Smith, Barbara Herrnstein. "The Ethics of Interpretation." In *On the Margins of Discourse: The Relation of Literature to Language.* Chicago, 1978.

Stigler, George J., and Gary S. Becker. "De Gustibus Non Est Disputandum." *American Economics Review* 67 (Mar. 1977): 76–90.

Suleiman, Susan, and Inge Crossman, eds. *The Reader in the Text: Essays on Audience and Interpretation.* Princeton, N.J., 1980.

Tompkins, Jane P., ed. *Reader-Response Criticism: From Formalism to Post-Structuralism.* Baltimore, 1980.

Tolstoy, Leo. *What Is Art?* [1896]. Trans. Aylmer Maude. New York, 1960.

Waldron, Jeremy. "Judgments of Justice." Review of *Ethics and the Rule of Law,* by David Lyons. *Times Literary Supplement* (Sept. 7, 1984): 992.

Yeats, William Butler. *Autobiography.* New York, 1953.

———. "After Long Silence" [1932]. In *The Poems of W. B. Yeats.* Ed. Richard J. Finneran. New York, 1983. 265.

5

[D]econstruction . . . should seek a new investigation of responsibility, an investigation which questions the codes inherited from ethics and politics.
Jacques Derrida

I have no more made my Book than my Book has made me.
Montaigne

Foucault is attempting to recover the possibility of a noncoercive discourse on the art of life . . . within a general account of what we owe each other.
Michael Ignatieff

[A]ll literary work is an appeal. . . . You are perfectly free to leave that book on the table. But if you open it, you assume responsibility for it.
Jean-Paul Sartre

This [novel] has been composed from a scenario thrust on me by some one else. My philosophy of life saves me from [a] sense of responsibility for any of my writings; but I venture to hold myself specially irresponsible for this one.
Max Beerbohm's parody of Th*m*s H*rdy

[W]hen I reflect that so much beauty has been entrusted to me—to *me*—I am so terrified that I am seized with cramps and long to rush off and hide. . . . I have been working like a mule [on *Madame Bovary*] for 15 long years. . . . Oh, if I ever produce a good book I'll have earned it.
Gustave Flaubert

Who Is Responsible in Ethical Criticism, and for What?

Whenever we read or listen to any story, whether it claims to be historical or fictional, we do not meet and respond to the single, simple voice that is often implied by current theories of "communication": a "sender" or "source" who transfers bits of information to a receiver. Even the most naive listener attending with total concentration to the simplest tale can be seen, on analysis, to be re-creating and responding to at least three different voices: that of the immediate teller, or narrator, who takes the whole tale straight and who expects the listener to do the same (the "time" in "once upon a time" is real time); that of the implied author, who knows that the telling is in one sense an artificial construct but who takes responsibility for it, for whatever values or norms it implies, and for the suggestion that "in responding to *me* you respond to a real person"; and the inferable voice of the flesh-and-blood person for whom this telling is only one concentrated moment selected from the infinite complexities of "real" life.

Similarly, every listener, no matter how unsophisticated or opposed to analysis, maintains at least three roles while listening: that of the immediate believer, who pretends that this story is happening and that it is all that is happening; that of one who "knows," even if only unconsciously, that he or she is dwelling in a selected, concentrated, and hence in some sense "unreal" or "artificial" world; and that of the flesh-and-blood person whose extra-narrative life, though perhaps forgotten for the duration of the listening, impinges on it in myriad untraceable ways. Indeed, for some purposes we can trace even more than these three (Booth 1983, 428−31).[1]

---

1. My distinctions among narrator, implied author, and writer (or flesh-and-blood author) are by no means universally accepted. Gérard Genette, for example, from whom I have learned a great deal about how stories work, explicitly denies the usefulness of my distinction (1983, 93−107). See also Bal 1985. Genette's witty repudiation makes some

Though most listeners most of the time are not conscious of these complexities, they will come as no surprise to anyone who has followed criticism of fiction during the past quarter-century.[2] They cannot be ignored in ethical criticism, because each of these authors and readers, tellers and listeners, has a different character from all the others and each will *respond to,* and thus be *responsible to,*[3] a richer set of characters than is suggested by most ethical criticism.

If we are to avoid not only undue confusion but positive injustice in our appraisals, we must know who is being held responsible—and for what. Ethical critics have too often dealt with only two of the many questions that emerge from the complexities we are beginning to discern: "Will this narrative that *I* have experienced without noticeable harm be good or bad for *you?*" Or, turning to address the author, "Why have *you* failed in your inherent responsibility to give us, your readers, the ethical support we need?" Such critics have thus, fortunately for their peace of mind and the simplicity of their expositions, escaped many of the difficulties that confront us here. Though tracing out the responsibilities may not in itself provide a thrilling experience for any of us, it will prove essential to us later on.

THE AUTHOR

What Are the Author's Responsibilities to the Flesh-and-Blood Reader?

Much ethical criticism of the past was about this question. "You, the writer, the flesh-and-blood author, have written something that is harmful, or potentially harmful, to me as reader, or to other readers who are weaker-minded than I." "Why do modern authors refuse to

---

sense for a criticism that is not much interested in ethical appraisals. But it fails to do justice to our reading experience when we *listen* to stories and think not simply about how they are put together but rather about what they *do* to us.

2. See James Phelan's bibliography, appended to Booth 1983.

3. As I have tried to dramatize in this introduction, to respond at all is already to be in a sense *response-able:* the word which we unfortunately tend to use only to cover duties is from the Latin *responsus,* past participle of *respondere,* from *re* ("back") and *spondere* ("to pledge").

be as elevating as Victorian authors?" Similarly, most who have rejected ethical criticism have addressed their negatives only to this question, claiming that authors must not be burdened with worries about the reader's ultimate welfare if they are to serve their art properly.

What Are the Author's Responsibilities to the Work of Art?

The usual modern answer, good enough up to a point, is "to make it as good as it can be." For obvious reasons, people who give this answer do not ordinarily consider the question as bearing on ethics at all. The "duty" here is indistinguishable from the pursuit of artistic success: skill, craft, technique, formal excellence, emotional power, self-expression. An ethical critic can simply reverse these terms, as we did for a while in Chapter 4, and think of the pursuit of excellence as itself a matter of duty or character: the true artist shows us that whatever is made *ought to be made well.* For some authors, service to or love of the work can replace all other values. As Tennessee Williams put it, "For love I make characters in plays. To the world I give suspicion and resentment, mostly. I am not cold. I am never deliberately cruel. But after my morning's work, I have little to give but indifference to people. I try to excuse myself with the pretense that my work justifies this lack of caring much for almost everything else" (1985, xv).

What Are the Author's Responsibilities to the Implied Reader?

At first sight this question might seem identical to the previous one, since the "best work" will in theory be the one that the implied reader finds most rewarding. But our emphasis shifts when we think of formal excellence not in itself but *as grasped,* enjoyed, shared. Considered rhetorically, the standard of perfecting the work enables us to say, with Jean-Paul Sartre, that I as reader have a right to make demands on the author—particularly the right to demand "that he demand more of me" (1981, 40). That question always leads to ethical (or if one prefers, ideological or political) appraisals, as in Sartre it leads to judgments about how well the fiction serves the reader's freedom.

What Are the Author's Responsibilities to Himself or Herself, as a
Person Who Must Live in a World in Which Art Plays Only One
of Many Roles?

Duty to self is seen by some artists as identical to duty to the work
of art: the writer is served best by making the best work possible. But
again the emphasis can shift when we think of the fiction as in the service of its maker rather than as a pure end in itself. Real writers, in
contrast to the relatively coherent authors their works imply, face conflicts of ends that often drive them to drink or suicide: competing demands of family, country, religion, friendship, justice, pleasure. Writers often report a sense that "the world" does not want the work to be
done at all, or to be done well. They talk less often about an experience
that must be almost as common: the discovery that the work requires a
sacrifice of a part of the self that is held dear. The sheer effort to create an
implied author suitable to *this work* often means giving up a beloved
fault or taking on an alien virtue. As Yeats puts it in "The Choice":

> The intellect of man is forced to choose
> Perfection of the life, or of the work,
> And if it take the second must refuse
> A heavenly mansion, raging in the dark.
>
> ([1933] 1983, 246)

"The writer's responsibility to the work" can thus be translated as
"the writer's responsibility to the implied author": he or she should
attempt to write fictions that require the creation of the cleverest,
wisest, most generously committed ethos imaginable. We have a great
deal of evidence, from Laurence Sterne to Norman Mailer, that artists
often imitate the roles they create. The writer is moved, in reality, toward the virtues or vices imagined for the sake of the work itself.

To dwell with a creative task for as long as is required to perform it
well means that one tends to *become* the work—at least to some degree. Writers clearly differ greatly in their ability or willingness to emulate their own creations, and some seem astonishingly gifted in resisting even the most inviting nobilities or generosities implied by their
tellings. Some have even claimed to be able to assume artistic roles
with no effect whatever on life outside the event. Others, like Montaigne, have happily confessed, "I have no more made my book than
my book has made me."

When authors perform in their public appearances exactly as we would expect them to on the basis of what we find in their fictions, how are we to know whether the writing helped build the character or was simply its product? Still, when we see the famous poet exaggerating his persona on the public platform, we can be fairly sure that he has become *more that way* in trying to live up—or down—to the poems.

But to put the responsibility that way places too much emphasis, for now, on consequences. (I turn to consequences in Chapter 8.) Surely the main responsibility of writers to themselves must be to *choose to write works of a kind that will in the writing yield splendid hours of life lived.* In the terms I shall develop in Chapter 6, my chief responsibility to myself as story-teller is fulfilled when I choose to create an implied author who qualifies as my friend.

What Are the Author's Responsibilities to Himself or Herself as "Career Author"?

It is not fashionable to talk about the artist's *duty* to build a career. Most of my students see something arrogant and constrained in the deliberate career planning of a John Milton, with his self-conscious accumulation of masteries through minor work after minor work, and his then shopping around for the right epic subject to cap it all off. Authors these days do not seem to talk about themselves in the terms that Goethe, for another example, took for granted in thinking of his career as the creation of a *self*.[4] But if the notion of responsibility to anything at all makes sense, surely there is some sense in an author's asking whether the writing of *this* work will make more or less likely the writing of *that* perhaps better one, and finally conduce to the ripening of a career. I shall have little to say, however, about this question here—not because it is unimportant but because it would explode the book into domains where I feel unusually incompetent: unlike many a critic I admire, I seem never to trace whole careers (see Lipking 1981).

4. As Karl Weintraub puts it, "The desire to show the formation of the person in the interplay with his world led Goethe to weave the presentation of his developing self into the narration of his life [in *Dichtung und Wahrheit*]" (1978, 351). For a splendid book exploring how poets self-consciously build careers, see Lawrence Lipking's *The Life of the Poet* (1981).

*What Are the Author's Responsibilities to Those
Whose Lives Are Used as "Material"?*

Are there limits to the author's freedom to expose, in the service of
art or self, the most delicate secrets of those whose lives provide material? The question is generally ignored in current criticism, and I can
only touch on it here. (It is exploited for comedy in Woody Allen's
movie *Manhattan*.) But surely it provides one of the most interesting of
all conflicts of values: When my narrative will profit from a character
based on my true love, warts and all, am I justified in sacrificing her to
"art," against her own expressed feelings? Just how much exploitation
of family intimacies can be defended? The question, which is pursued
with great dexterity in Philip Roth's Zuckerman novels (1979–87), is
generally answered by novelists as Roth implicitly answers it: art justifies all—indeed, the novelist who engages wholeheartedly in the act of
creating an ethical world is "leading the ethical life,"[5] and besides, you
are a bad reader if you assume that any event or detail in my novels
comes from real life; what's more, Dickens and Tolstoy did it too. The
author who thinks at all deeply about responsibility will surely want a
better answer than these.

But it is not our business here to worry much about this question.
Biting as it may be for a given author, it does not arise for readers ex-

---

5. The abominable eulogist that Nathan Zuckerman imagines for his own funeral,
in *The Counterlife* (1987), acknowledges that Nathan was "not too noble to exploit the
home," but he then says that "Nathan as an artist, as the author paradoxically of the
most reckless comedy, tried, in fact, to lead the ethical life, and he both reaped its rewards and paid its price" (211). Nathan's brother, Henry, who has suffered exposure in
Nathan's fiction, is disgusted as he listens to the eulogy: "Henry had expected praise,
but, naively perhaps, not in that vein or so remorselessly on that subject [of exploitation
of family secrets]. . . . The thing that drove our family apart, thought Henry, is here
being enshrined—that was *designed* to destroy our family, no matter how much they say
about 'art.' . . . [The family] paid all right, they lost a *son* to the unsayable! I lost a
brother!" (206–7). No doubt if we see such passages as Roth's own effort to expiate the
pain he caused with *Portnoy's Complaint*, we will be accused of the kind of naive reading that takes fiction as fact, as autobiography. I have heard tell of an editor who, talking
with Roth after *Portnoy's Complaint* appeared, said something like, "Little did you
dream, when you were whacking off in your sister's panties, that your later report on it
would make you rich." To which Roth replied, "I don't *have* a sister." *Se non è vero è
ben trovato* ("Even if the story is false, it's a lucky find"). In any case, one must credit
Roth with taking this problem seriously, as few other "exploiters" have done. For a singularly unscrupulous act of exploitation, see Truman Capote's *Answered Prayers* (1987).

cept when they have more or less accidental knowledge about the author's life. We have no way of knowing whether Sophocles' portrait of
Ismene, Antigone's sister, was based on some woman whose cowardly
ways Sophocles once learned about in the heat of passion; or whether
Fluellen (in *Henry V*) was patterned on an actual Welshman who had
once befriended Shakespeare, who then betrayed him and other Welsh-
men to all the world and history.

What Are the Author's Responsibilities to Others Whose Labor Is Exploited to Make the Art Work Possible?

William Faulkner once settled this question in the simplest possible
way: "The writer's only responsibility is to his art. He will be completely ruthless if he is a good one. He has a dream. . . . Everything
[else] goes by the board: honor, pride, decency, security, happiness, all,
to get the book written. If a writer has to rob his mother, he will not
hesitate; the 'Ode on a Grecian Urn' is worth any number of old
ladies" (1960, 124). Can that be so? Are story-tellers really justified
when they decide to exploit and even corrupt some parts of life in
order to grace life with their own creations?

The question is an acute version of the more general question that
all societies face when they allocate scarce resources to the artistic enterprise. If a nation's children are starving, should all artistic expen-
ditures be curtailed until they are fed? On the other hand, should a
substantial portion of a people's budget go to preserving art works
from deterioration, even if, as in many a tradition-rich modern nation,
masses are starving? Just how much of the life of some of us may legiti-
mately be sacrificed in order to enhance the life of others?

Such questions will be dismissed by some as impertinent; they seem
as impossible to answer as the undergraduate's poser, "If you saw
someone about to ignite a bomb under Michelangelo's *Moses* and you
had a gun, wouldn't you use it?" But similar questions cannot always
be dodged, especially in wartime: Shall we sacrifice lives in order to
protect this cathedral or museum? What's more, these issues always
lurk within any effort at individual creation. Just how much neglect of
spouse and children does this novel (or for that matter, this critical
work, *The Company We Keep*) justify? Though I avoid any more di-

rect encounter with such concerns here, they obviously represent a general question that underlies all ethical inquiry into art: Just where, on the scale of important human interests, should art be placed? Can the modern effort to make art do the job of religion ever hope to succeed? (Barzun 1975).

What Are the Author's Responsibilities to Society in General, to "the World," to "the Future"?

To some this question is the most important of all: Has an author a duty to try to improve the political order? When Sartre wrote *What Is Literature?* he was addressing a controversy then raging about whether the artist should be *engagé*, committed *as artist* to furthering this or that cause. He insisted that authors of prose fictions must commit themselves to furthering freedom in the world, while poets and musicians can (perhaps) serve purer "aesthetic" ideals. Today many critics either ignore the debate he was addressing or argue that it is essentially meaningless, since all art will be politically committed regardless of the artist's intention (Bové 1986). It should be evident that this question, though not the subject of any one chapter here, is implicit in all of them.

What Are the Responsibilities of the Author to "Truth"?

Many an author discovers, in the pursuit of a polished form, that some seeming fact or truth in "the world" must be violated. Sometimes the violation is performed in the service of a social or commercial convention, as when novelists in the nineteenth century and moviemakers in the early twentieth felt constrained to make every work end happily, regardless of the probabilities in life or art.[6] Sometimes it is

---

6. Robert Louis Stevenson put the writer's resulting problem wittily when he wrote to Sir James Barrie about one particular happy ending: "*The Little Minister* ought to have ended badly; we all know it did, and we are infinitely grateful to you for the grace and good feeling with which you lied about it. If you had told the truth, I for one could never have forgiven you. . . . It is the blot on *Richard Feverel*, for instance, that it begins to end well; and then tricks you and ends ill" (1899, 2: 320–21).

performed in the service of some implacable requirement of a given work or genre; Browning shows all the characters in his dramatic monologues speaking in iambic pentameter, grandly violating everyone's knowledge that people just don't talk like that. Writers of ethnic novels tone down the dialect to make the narrative intelligible to outsiders and inoffensive to members of the ethnic group.[7] Historical novelists always deliberately or unconsciously violate known facts about the past, to make the fiction go, and narrative historians (too often?) do the same, to make the history go.[8]

Theories of how fully "truth" should override "art" range from those that see artistic form as determined by the "material" constraints of ideology to those that see ideas as completely malleable "content," in effect as neutral as a given unadorned musical note for a composer or a block of marble for a sculptor. An absurdly determinist position is expressed by Ezra Pound when he says that "finer and future critics of art will be able to tell from the quality of a painting the degree of tolerance or intolerance of usury extant in the age and milieu that produced it."[9] An equally absurd and opposite extreme is reported by Cynthia Ozick, who was told by an artist that for him, "the Holocaust and a corncob are [as subjects] the same" (1982, 294).

I think that some conception of "nature" or "reality"—and hence of truth—underlies all the other eight responsibilities. To argue that case would be to meet the fashionable claim—itself a claim about the nature of reality, paradoxically enough—that all language is essentially, inherently opaque, never opening onto any substance or reality more solid than language itself. Fortunately, to do our work here we

---

7. When they do not, they get into trouble. Zora Neale Hurston was criticized by other writers in the Harlem Renaissance because she insisted on showing her rural characters, in *Their Eyes Were Watching God*, speaking in a heavy dialect that to those writers suggested ignorance and illiteracy (Hemenway 1977).

8. Whenever a historical work hits the best-seller lists, we can be almost certain that, in making room for leaps of the imagination, it will far exceed the factual evidence. Fawn Brodie's *Thomas Jefferson: An Intimate History* (1974), to me a gripping account, has aroused much criticism by professional historians who resent her imaginative leaps into "what's on Thomas Jefferson's mind," or "what he did during the periods for which we have no documentary evidence."

9. From *Guide to Kulchur*, quoted by Andrew Parker (1986, 74). Parker claims—to me, persuasively—that for Pound the problem of usury could not be separated from poetic theory and practice.

need not grapple with that subtle truth about the inaccessibility of truth. It is sufficient to acknowledge one form of ethical criticism that aggressively asserts the primary duty of both authors and their critics to respect the way "things really are." I shall turn to that sort of claim in Part 3.[10]

THE READER

What Are the Reader's Responsibilities to the Writer— the Flesh-and-Blood Author or Career Author?

Writers live precarious lives, lives threatened by despair, frustrated hopes, lonely anxiety. They feel neglected, misunderstood, useless. Though I obviously cannot make the care and feeding of artists my direct business in this book, it surely should be one part of every ethical critic's concern—yet it is almost entirely ignored in current discussions. Both reviewers and critics claim to serve a higher value than the cosseting of helpless writers: strict justice to the work itself, regardless of consequences for the author. It is assumed that to intrude concern for the author's personal fate would itself be unethical. Although in practice very few critics can claim never to have pulled punches (or punched harder) for "personal" reasons, I know of no serious discussion of how to think about such matters.

Is it enough to say that a reader should simply tell the cold truth about a work, in total disregard for the author's career? Quite aside from reviewing and formal criticism, might there not be, especially in a society in which writers feel misunderstood and neglected, an obligation to write the occasional carefully wrought fan letter? To buy, read, and teach books by neglected living authors along with the classics? To *buy* the books of authors we admire, rather than borrowing

10. The debate about opacity, transparency, and reality has spread during recent years, until by now the bibliography on this one issue is overwhelming. As generally conducted, it is to me no debate at all but a revelation of complementary truths about our situation. To show fully what that pluralistic claim might mean, however, would require another book. For a splendid account of what happens when we take "contradictory" intellectual systems as in fact complementary, despite their "reciprocal priority," see Watson's *The Architectonics of Meaning* (1985).

copies or xeroxing? To respect *famous* authors' privacy rather than hounding them with demands for publicity and conference appearances? All of this is reduced, in our usual talk about responsibility to the author, to one simple demand: thou shalt not plagiarize. Thus the whole rich range of possibilities for fruitful exchange between writers and authors is turned to the service of an unthinking individualism: what's mine is mine and what's yours is yours, and I fill my responsibility to you if I resist the impulse to steal from you. It is as if intellectual and artistic property were so much capital goods. Surely to borrow an author's work is not the worst imaginable mistreatment.

What Are the Reader's Responsibilities to the Work of Art— Which Is to Say, to the Implied Author?

At last we come, in our sorting, to a topic that will be central to us here: Do I as reader have any obligation to that elusive creature, the creating character whom I myself re-create as I read the work? If so, how am I to express it? What is the relation between taking *my* pleasure with a work (Barthes 1975) and attempting to discover the pleasures that the author intends to share? Is Sartre in any sense right when he says that the writer requires of the reader "the gift of his whole person, with his passions, his prepossessions, his sympathies, his sexual temperament, and his scale of values" (1981, 36)? What can it mean to say, with him, that the reader must "give himself generously"? (I return to this question later in this chapter, and more fully in the Epilogue.)

If I am to give myself generously, must I not also accept the responsibility to enter into serious dialogue with the author about how his or her values join or conflict with mine? To decline the gambit, to remain passive in the face of the author's strongest passions and deepest convictions is surely condescending, insulting, and finally irresponsible.

What Are the Reader's Responsibilities to His or Her Own Self or Soul—as Flesh-and-Blood Reader?

Another primary topic of this book, this question is equally elusive and wide-ranging. In a sense it is identical to the previous question, with its two parts: I serve myself best, as reader, when I both honor an author's offering for what it is, in its full "otherness" from me, *and* take an active critical stance against what seem to me its errors or excesses. We are pursuing here an ethics of self-culture in narrative, an ethics that entails both surrender and refusal. We begin that perilous pursuit in earnest in the next two chapters, as I suggest some choices among the friends who offer their company. We then continue it, in Chapter 8, asking what it might mean to be, or to have, or to build for oneself, a "character."[11]

What Are the Reader's Responsibilities to Other Individual Readers?

Am I in any way obliged to make public my appraisals of the narratives I experience, particularly my ethical appraisals? Do I owe to others (not just to the author) the effort to conduct ethical inquiry about the works I admire or detest? Obviously this book is in large part an effort to show why our answer must be yes. To me the most important of all critical tasks is to participate in—and thus to reinforce—a critical culture, a vigorous conversation, that will nourish in return those who feed us with their narratives.

What Are the Reader's Responsibilities to Society, beyond the Honest Expression of Critical Judgment?

What should I do, or urge my society to do, about works that seem to me questionable or even indefensible? Should the threat of censorship or the spectacle of foolish excesses by some fanatics lead me to avoid an ethical criticism that by nature will not always follow the current "politically correct" line? Or can we hope—as this book presup-

---

11. A good introduction to the ambiguities discovered when we think of what we owe to our "selves" can be found in O'Donovan's *The Problem of Self-Love in St. Augustine* (1980, esp. chs. 1 and 6). See also Weintraub 1978 and James [1892] 1985.

poses—that learning to *talk well* about such matters is both the best defense against censorship programs and the best encouragement to artists to meet us at the highest possible ethical level?

Note that the same question is raised by all efforts to give public support to any art or artist. What should be my stand about programs that in effect censor in reverse—government programs like the National Endowment for the Arts that subsidize *this* work of art and in doing so penalize *that* one? Implicit throughout this book will be a plea for engagement with the political questions that naturally spring from any serious thinking about the ethical powers of fictions.

The remaining responsibilities of the reader—to those whose lives are used or abused by the author, or to truth—can both be put in the form of a responsibility to point out authors' successes and failures in meeting *their* responsibilities.

Though to be clear about the differences among these obligations and invitations may help avoid some pointless controversies, it will no doubt uncover other and perhaps sharper disagreements: no easy harmonies lie ahead. One critic's tentatively embraced norms will strike another critic as dangerous ideology; *my* self-evident standards may seem to *you* mere dogma. At every point we may fall into one or another of the critical faults that I described in Chapters 2 and 3. As our list of responsibilities grows, we see ever more clearly why modern critics, even those who have not rejected the language of responsibilities entirely, have been tempted to reduce them to two: for the author, to make the work itself as good as it can be; and for the reader, to judge whether the work is in fact well-made. To open the other questions forces us to consider complex conflicts and disharmonies in the pursuit of art comparable to those we try to resolve, never with full success, in the conduct of other domains of life. When art and criticism are viewed as forms of conduct, they lead us into the very battles that we may have hoped to escape by turning to art in the first place.

But no mode of criticism can escape controversy for long, and all modes are vulnerable to insensitive, unintelligent, or dogmatic practice. We should no more give up ethical criticism because it can be practiced badly than we should give up going to doctors when we learn—as a recent announcement has it—that 15 percent of all doctors are "incompetent." If we applied this comic perspective to any critical school, even the most rigorously scientific, what a great clearing-out of our library shelves would then ensue!

THE READER'S RESPONSIBILITIES TO THE AUTHOR

If we agree that one serves one's "self" in part by *taking in* the new selves offered in stories, we can begin to see how the process of taking in or surrendering actually works. It will be best to begin with the simplest possible rhetorical situation. Here is a great tale from Aesop, one that has been translated into almost every language:

> A man and his Wife had the good fortune to possess a Goose which laid a Golden Egg every day. Lucky though they were, they soon began to think they were not getting rich fast enough, and, imagining that the bird must be made of gold inside, they decided to kill it in order to secure the whole store of precious metal at once. But when they cut it open they found it was just like any other goose. Thus, they neither got rich all at once, as they had hoped, nor enjoyed any longer the daily addition to their wealth.
> Moral: Much wants more and loses all.[12]

What actually happens to us as we follow such a simple story? Whatever it is, it happens so frequently and with such seeming simplicity that we find it difficult even to recognize what a strange and wonderful process we undergo as we use a sequence of words like this to create, not so much in our heads as in our souls,[13] a narrative laden

---

12. Received versions of this tale vary enormously, not all of them carrying the same moral tag or indeed any tag at all. I have used the version found in many current anthologies.

13. I shall not attempt to avoid the word "soul" when it seems needed, though we should remind ourselves that it need not suggest any supernatural entity: the soul, the anima, is whatever makes the difference between a living, purposeful creature and a corpse. With this classical definition, we wipe out all debate about whether we "have" souls, since we are self-evidently *anima*ted. Debate is then profitably shifted to what we are and can do, not what we "have." The word "mind" just won't cover the ground, since the effects of narrative include many other elements of our "anima-tion": changes of pulse, sweat glands, digestive juices, alpha waves—and whatever "morphins" are yet to be discovered. The words "psyche" or "self" would do if they still had the full meaning that William James gives them in *The Principles of Psychology* ([1890] 1981) and *Psychology: The Briefer Course* ([1892] 1985), where they have pretty much the breadth, now generally lost, that "psyche" had for the Greeks and that "anima" had for the Romans.

with the *kind* of significance that stories about our own life might have. When a story "works," when we like it well enough to listen to it again and to tell it over and over to ourselves and friends, as we have all done with this story, it occupies us in a curiously intense way. The pun in "occupy" is useful here. We are occupied in the sense of filling our time with the story—its time takes over our time. And we are occupied in the sense of being taken over, colonized: occupied by a foreign imaginary world.

The occupation can be so intense that some phenomenologists have misleadingly called it identifying. Here is Georges Poulet describing in a fine undeconstructed way the mystery that occurs when I take into my mind the mind implied by the imagined totality of any story. As I read, he says, "I am aware of a rational being, of a consciousness; the consciousness of another, no different from the one I automatically assume in every human being I encounter, except that in this case the consciousness is open to me, welcomes me, lets me look deep inside itself, and even allows me, with unheard-of license, to think what it thinks and feel what it feels" (1972, 57). Poulet then moves from the language of permission to the language of command: "As soon as I replace my direct perception of reality by the words of a book, I deliver myself, bound hand and foot, to the omnipotence of fiction. . . . I *am thinking the thoughts of another*. Of course, there would be no cause for astonishment if I were thinking it as the thought of another. But I think it *as my very own*. . . . I am the subject of thoughts other than my own. My consciousness behaves as though it were the consciousness of another" (58, 59; my italics).[14]

Such talk may seem excessive, especially when applied to a slight tale like "The Goose That Laid the Golden Egg." For more than a century now we have been exhorted to resist identifying with art works; we are advised instead to maintain some sort of "aesthetic distance." What is forgotten in such warnings—though they are useful in combating certain kinds of sentimentality—is that even when we resist a

14. For a challenging critique of Poulet and the concept of identification, see de Man 1983, ch. 6. My inquiry does not depend on the belief that we ever achieve full identity; we need only agree that we meet a story that is not initially ours and we make it our own. Something we could not have done for ourselves has been done by something "other," and with our total cooperation.

story, even when we view it dispassionately, it immerses us in "the thoughts of another," unless we simply stop listening. Even if we withhold our tears when we listen, say, to an ill-wrought version of that tear-jerker about the little match-girl dying in the cold, we still have succumbed, to some degree, to the "thoughts" of another: we have had to "see" the picture in order to reject it. We escape "occupation" completely only if we refuse to conjure up any sort of picture of that dying child—only if we see nothing but blank, meaningless words on the page. And if we blank out the image in this way, we can have no basis on which to accuse it of sentimentality.

This paradoxical need to embrace in order to decide *whether* to embrace is amusingly illustrated in the plight of anti-pornographers.[15] How do you decide that a story is obscenely pornographic or potentially harmful to readers or viewers? Unless you are willing to be irresponsible, you can do so only by "listening" to it, discovering what your mind and body do in response, and confessing to the world that you have found something obscene in it—that is, made something obscene out of it. Only in intimacy with obscenity can one know what is obscene.

It is not, then, that in identifying we stop thinking our *own* thoughts but rather that "our own" thoughts now become different from what they were. The author's thoughts have at least in part become ours. (I am of course following Poulet in using "thoughts" as the most general term for "all that enters our heads," including images, concepts, and emotions.) Although we usually manage, when we are not totally carried away to a pathological identification,[16] to return to thinking a

---

15. In July 1986, the Attorney General's Commission on Pornography issued its two thousand pages with ninety-two specific recommendations for public and governmental action. Many commentators expressed amusement at the fact that the report itself contained a great deal of the pornography that it claimed to be harmful. But how could the commission members convince us of how bad the stuff is without showing some of it? Perhaps their best defense would be their claim—supported, I wonder, by what evidence?—that "books" offer the least harmful kind of pornography. Would that be because for them "readers" are a superior kind of citizen, more likely to be immune from corruption than are viewers?

16. Just what such a pathology is would be hard to define precisely, but we all know examples of it: boys and girls getting into serious trouble by imitating their fictional heroes. I suspect that self-destructive imitation is more common than our usual way of sterilizing our criticism acknowledges. See pages 278–79 for some anecdotal evidence that must serve in place of hard proof.

thought something like what was "ours" before we began listening—
full conversions are always rare—a large part of our thought-stream is
taken over, for at least the duration of the telling, by the story we are
taking in. Whenever that does not happen, we can hardly say that we
have responded to—that is, behaved responsibly toward—the implied
author.

What is it that we in fact "take" from what is offered by the ancient
Aesop, as mediated by his translator (or redactor: the actual Aesop is
elusive, but that does not concern us at the moment)? I see three different kinds of offering, each with a great range of possible responses by
different flesh-and-blood readers. First, there are the specific givens of
the tale, the essential data that must be grasped if there is to be a story
at all. All of us who respond to what is offered "think" about a man
and his wife and a goose, not about a princess and her lover on a noble
stallion, or a woman named Pandora who was warned not to look into
a certain box. We "think" about egg-laying and not log-chopping or
hay-mowing. We "think" about mistakes and not triumphs or celebrations. What's more, we take these images and concepts in Aesop's
ordering (not quite such an obvious point as might at first appear, once
we consider the scores of ways this story might be ordered: the remorse first, say, then the cutting up, then the reason for it; the moral
first, then the moment just before the killing, then a long flashback as
we wonder will he, won't he). Aesop's resolution of the tale, Aesop's
moral tag (as it appears in whatever version we hear), Aesop's explicit
judgments along the line ("lucky though they were," "had the good
fortune")—all these become *our* "thoughts," even if we decide to repudiate them almost as soon as they possess us. Although such elementary givens in some tales may be forgotten almost at once, those of
many another can remain in memory for a lifetime.

No authority or rule can force us to take these *données* in the
offered way; we can always refuse to grasp the story as a story and
turn it instead to other predetermined purposes. Those who hail the
indeterminacy of all "texts" are thus quite right, up to a point: readers
must always in a sense decide whether to accept a given responsibility.
We can if we choose, as Rabelais and Swift remind us, employ the
pages of the greatest classics as bumwipes. Nor is the intimacy of our
engagement with these implacable *données,* when we *do* surrender,
the sort of thing that can be demonstrated by argument: it is known

only in experience. But it is hard to imagine any human being who has not known on many occasions the kind of submersion in other minds that we are considering. Though academic study of literature too often seems designed to make such fusions of spirit impossible, turning every "text" into a thoroughly distanced puzzle or enigma,[17] the fact remains that even the impassive puzzle solver or symbol hunter or signifier chaser is to some degree caught up in patterns determined by the puzzle—the tale as told. The only way to avoid "thinking the thought of another"—that mysterious quite-probably-dead "other" who chose to tell this tale in this way—is to stop listening.

NONCE BELIEFS AND FIXED NORMS

As a consequence of taking in these many "facts,"[18] we take in, second, notions of how the world in which we find them works, the norms of causation and behavior that can be expected, or perhaps even clung to, in that world. These are usually of two kinds, kinds that are sharply distinguished in tales that, like "The Goose" and Kafka's "Metamorphosis," include miraculous or incredible events. On the one hand, we find what we can call "nonce beliefs," those that the narrator and the reader embrace only for the duration. The implied author and the implied reader are much too sophisticated to expect geese in real life to lay golden eggs; they know both that the story is made up and that some of its norms apply only within the story itself. On the other hand, we find in this story (and I shall later argue that we find in all stories) certain "fixed norms," beliefs on which the narrative de-

17. I have recently heard some teachers explain that they never assign a story or poem to students without giving along with it a selection of "interpretations," so that the students can see, before they read the story, that any interpretation they come up with is only one of many. "Then they can choose which one makes the most sense." Perhaps for advanced specialists in literature such exercises can be helpful, but I am suspicious of any process that risks imposing itself between author and reader until *after* a firsthand transaction has been achieved. That "firsthand" transaction will of course already be laden with previous experience, and it will necessarily entail simultaneous interpretation and evaluation (Rabinowitz, 1987). But it need not be cluttered with conscious borrowings from other critics.

18. I cannot drop the quotation marks, because—to repeat—the facts are facts only within the project of following a story.

pends for its effect but which also are by implication applicable in the "real" world: in "The Goose," most notably "Overweening greed threatens destruction," or "Much wants more and loses all." Fixed norms are fixed not in the sense that the reader must accept them or believe that Aesop himself took them as inscribed in stone; indeed the different tales by "Aesop" can exhibit different and even conflicting fixed norms. They are fixed only in the sense that the implied author and the implied reader[19] share them as normal both for the fictional world and for their world as it is or ought to be (Booth 1983, 422–25).

We have no sure grounds for believing that the actual teller, whether the flesh-and-blood ancient or any one of the thousands of redactors, really takes the fixed norms at all seriously. We know nothing about them except that they each took on the *perhaps temporary* pose of embracing the fixed norms—including, be it said, the implication that it is a good thing to tell stories with moral tags.

The distinction between fixed norms and nonce beliefs is employed by even the most inexperienced readers. We all easily perform acrobatic leaps back and forth between our roles as "narrative audience," credulous about golden eggs, and our implied roles as "authorial audience," sophisticated about how eggs are laid but willing, whenever a tale is fully successful, to embrace its fixed norms (Rabinowitz 1977). We may of course have considerable difficulty in deciding which norms are for the nonce and which are fixed. And we may finally, on reflection, reject even the fixed norms: that is precisely what much ethical criticism does. But as responsive readers we will, at any given moment in our reading, find ourselves dwelling with an author (in one sense, of course, our own creation) who only plays with some beliefs while offering others as holding for all human worlds.

The fixed norms on which "The Goose" depends would make a very long list if we pursued them as they might have to be pursued by a visitor from Uranus trying to understand how the story works. They would include every notion about how human life is conducted: con-

19. Peter Rabinowitz's way of handling the contrast between what he calls the "authorial audience"—the implied author's mate—and the "narrative audience"— that more or less credulous reader who accepts both fixed norms and nonce beliefs and who believes that the tale actually occurred—helps to clarify my point here (Rabinowitz 1977).

victions about what a "man" and "woman" and "gold" are, about
how one cuts into a creature of flesh and blood, about how egg laying
works, about how flesh relates to metal, and about the meaning of a
phrase like "every day." The more important ones are not just givens
about how all human life *is;* they are controversial (though still "fixed,"
within the world of the story) value judgments about how life *should*
be lived.

1. More money is better than less money—at least ordinarily—
   since it would indeed be good fortune to possess such a goose
   permanently, without succumbing to destructive greed. Note
   that this value is not undermined by the story in any way, though
   it would be rejected by many a modern fiction, just as it is rejected by many a saying in the New Testament: "Lay not up for
   yourselves treasures upon earth. . . . But lay up for yourselves
   treasures in heaven. For where your treasure is, there will your
   heart be also." The loss of such a goose is unequivocal *loss,* just
   as the loss of "gold" (of possessions), even in many a modern
   story, must be taken as real loss if the story, comic or tragic, is to
   work.[20]

2. To value gold excessively is just human nature—no explanation
   is required for why the two "soon" wanted more. Note that silence about a value like this can imply that the value is so evident
   as to need no narrative rhetoric.[21]

3. But to value gold immoderately is not only imprudent, it is stupid. Though there is no clear guidance about the borderline between excessive greed and a proper sense of the worth of what
   we gold-less moderns call financial security, we are to believe for

20. I'm thinking here of Maupassant's "The Necklace," of the gambling losses in
Dostoevsky's "The Gambler," of the lost treasure in *The Treasure of Sierra Madre* and
Chaucer's "Pardoner's Tale," and—to turn to less crass possessions—of the spoils lost in
the fire in Henry James's *The Spoils of Poynton,* and the almost lost house, Howards
End, in E. M. Forster's wonderful novel of that name.

21. Since some silences imply an assumption of total agreement, and some spring
from an author's indifference to or ignorance of a given norm, we should expect the kind
of disagreements in interpretation that arise when a critic argues from a given silence to
a given presence. See, for example, Stanley Fish's discussion of whether Christian norms
are "in" *Samson Agonistes,* even though they are not mentioned (1980, 272–74).

all time—as far as the implied author can be trusted—that true wisdom lies in being grateful for small blessings.

4. Greed will lead to other stupidities. The tale depends for its satiric force on our recognizing just how foolish are the means that the greedy adopt for their imprudent ends: they make a self-evidently false inference about how the nature of the geese relates to the nature of eggs, and they move hastily to their absurd action.

It would be tedious to trace all the remaining norms the story depends on, some of them for some readers quite remote from any personal experience that might be referred to in testing the norm (how many modern readers, for example, know the implied norms for skillfully killing and gutting a goose?).

The combination of these two responses, sharing the fixed norms of the implied author and only pretending to share certain others, creates a complex tension in every fictional transaction. That tension is greatly diminished, and may even seem to disappear, when we meet any author—historian, journalist, gossip—who claims to narrate only what is true about the world outside the story. When a historian like Herodotus tells us of magical or "incredible" events, he does not openly invite a division between narrative and authorial audience; he seems to offer a single voice quite unlike Aesop's, one that erases the distinction between nonce beliefs and fixed norms: "These events, dear reader, occurred in a world that works precisely as your world does." Readers who are trained in historiography will of course import the distinction: Herodotus can be believed *here* but not *there*. But to do so is quite different from responding to an author's invitation to duplicity.[22]

This difference has important ethical consequences; the powers (and dangers) of history and biography are in some ways stronger and in other ways weaker than those of fictional narrative. We must look at

22. Historical fictions complicate this picture grandly. Reading of Fabrice's shattering visit to the Waterloo scene, in chapter 3 of *The Charterhouse of Parma*, I am torn between my sense of a Stendhal who seems to say "This really happened, both the historical event and the visit by Fabrice" and a Stendhal who seems to say "Of course I made up both Fabrice and his visit, both of which have only an ambiguous and indeterminate relation to anything that ever happened to me or could happen to you."

such differences more closely later on, but for now the point is that any criticism of a fictional narrative based on the meeting of credulous narrator and credulous narrative audience will produce radically different results from those we hope for in a criticism based on the meeting of implied author and authorial audience. The first kind would not be likely to occur in criticism of "The Goose"; even the most naive reader would not blame the story for, say, teaching its listeners that geese can after all lay golden eggs. Yet we see a great deal of criticism of more "realistic" tales based on precisely that kind of reading, the critic assuming either that the author does not honor reality sufficiently (since the narrator does not), or that *other* readers, less sophisticated than the critic, will naively identify with the narrative audience.

As we work at responding to their invitations, both fictions and histories tend to resist the moment of ethical criticism, the moment when, attending to other responsibilities, the reader intrudes to ask, for example, whether the peasants in "The Goose" are not in fact better off at the end than at the beginning, having learned something through suffering: "Push your opportunities to the hilt, because only by doing so will you learn your true limits." Or whether it could *ever* be genuine good fortune to possess a daily supply of unearned gold: "It is easier for a camel to pass through the eye of a needle . . ." Or, indeed, whether it is wrong for "fortunate" peasants to desire, even inordinately, to improve their lot: "What we have here is obviously one of thousands of Western narratives that attempt to teach the downtrodden to be satisfied. 'Pull in your horns,' we are told in this story; 'dampen your spirits, lower your aspirations, accept your relation to your betters—or the fates will destroy you, the Lord will not love you . . . '" And so on. We will take up such questions soon enough. But first we must explore how fixed norms work in fictions that seem less "fixed," less openly didactic, than Aesop's tale.

"The Goose" presents about the simplest narrative situation we ever encounter. The distinctions it dramatizes can be found in any tale, no matter how complex, but each added complexity can produce new twists in the patterns of responsibility. We might demonstrate at will a variety of rewritings of "The Goose," inventing, in the manner of much modern fiction, unreliable narrators who tell of other unreliable narrators, who tell of yet other ironists . . . But for now, let one recasting suffice:

"There was once a peasant who had been very poor for a long time. He and his wife were so poor, indeed, that they had eaten up all of their animals except for one lone goose. One day, when the peasant went to kill that one too, he found under her in the nest something that looked very much like a golden egg. So instead of killing the goose, he ran to the local jeweler's to see if he could get anything for the egg. The jeweler pronounced it twenty-four-carat gold. 'That's a work of art, that is. How did you ever mold solid gold into a shape like that? That's a work of art, that is!'

"Of course the peasant didn't tell his secret, but took the jeweler's payment, bought food for a feast and went home rejoicing.

"Next day, he found another golden egg, and indeed every day after that; he and his wife began to live in comfort at last, and they could see themselves becoming wealthy in their declining years. Both prudent and provident, they soon had a larger farm, stocked with far more animals than they had had even in their time of greatest prosperity.

"But the peasant naturally began to wonder, even as you would do, O reader, where all that gold came from. He knew enough—and unlike his wife, a typical woman, he cared enough—about how nature works to be deeply puzzled. It just didn't make sense. How could a goose *do* a thing like that? One possibility was, of course, that the goose was solid gold all the way through, except for the skin, or at least full of such eggs. But another possibility was that there was some hitherto undiscovered natural process going on. If a man could figure that out, he might actually teach other geese, or even other fowl, how to do it, and then, maybe, by removing all poverty from the world, he would become a great benefactor of mankind.

"So one day he proposed to his wife that they cut the goose open and either get all the gold at once or at least find out how the goose did it.

"'Don't be stupid,' she said, in her usual way. 'Fowls are not made out of what they lay. Besides, it is folly to seek for too much. Much wants more and loses all. We should be satisfied with what we have, this lovely farm, our full stomachs, the chance that we might even be able now to afford to have a child or two. Who cares how she does it—so long as she does it?'

"But the peasant, beside himself with a strange mixture of greed, curiosity, and desire for fame as a benefactor, finally said to himself,

'Well, there's only one way to settle all this.' So he cut into the goose and found—nothing but an ordinary goose egg, still half-formed, one end perhaps slightly golden."

Such a version dramatizes how much more generalized the implied author of Aesop's version is than most we meet. Indeed most of Aesop's norms have been shared by most authors in Western literature. Some of these norms, such as the notion that over-reaching greed is a bad thing, may in fact be part of the ethos of the whole human race (with great variation in how "over" and "greed" are defined). But the norms of this new version are much more complex. The garrulous and obtrusive narrator now still mocks greed, but he seems more interested in questioning unrestrained curiosity (with perhaps a side-glance mocking the desire for fame based on philanthropy). No single tag could quite encapsulate this one, not even "Curiosity killed the cat." Having come to the emphasis on the dangers of curiosity, we have narrowed down to one major tradition in *Western* culture, with echoes of Adam and Eve and the Tree of Knowledge, of Pandora and her box, and of some versions of the Faust story. To join this new implied author is thus a more specialized, more complex, and thus more consequential choice than to join Aesop's.

The point would become clearer if we now told a third version as a Goethe might tell it—that is, multiplying complexities in our judgment of curiosity, turning the peasant into a Faust who will sell his soul to the Devil in exchange for knowledge about how such a goose works and who will thus sacrifice much that is dear to most of (lesser) mankind. Of course in this new Goosiad, the peasant will discover that somehow he is, like Goethe's Faust, saved at the end of part 2. He was right after all to put no limits on sacred curiosity.

The fixed norms of such a version would be subtler, more controversial, but no less fixed, in our sense of the term. Some of them would be peculiar to a specific time and place (eighteenth-century Western culture), and some might be unique to the given author's ordering of kinds of knowledge (Goethe's world, as it were). With this increasing particularity, the complexities of our ethical inferences will have correspondingly multiplied: our new hero will relate to his implied author in different ways in different parts of the tale, and to the "real" writer even more ambiguously. We would now have ironies within ironies, along with a variety of choral voices such as that *ewig Weibliche* who offers her absolution, probably speaking for the implied author but perhaps not—as one standard line in the criticism of *Faust* has urged. How am I to tell? And how am I to distinguish clearly the narrator's voice from the implied author's?

Our difficulty in answering such questions about complex tales does not mean that fixed norms have disappeared; they have simply become less blatant. In whatever form we take the story, as long as it is intelligible to us we will have seen it in a matrix of its fixed norms. Not to do so, not to attempt to see how this tale works as an account of events in its world, would be to refuse the author's gambit, to deny the invitation. It would mean refusing to respond, either in sheer irresponsibility or in response to some other, "higher" obligation.

Everyone acquainted with modern literature knows that we have not yet by any means reached the ultimate in complexities. Nabokov, for example, in novels like *Pale Fire* and *Ada,* seems deliberately to frustrate our pursuit of any clear inference about any one reality or axis of responsibility: if there ever was a flesh-and-blood Nabokov, which I am sometimes inclined to doubt, he was considerably more evasive behind his fictions than anything we have yet seen.[23] Though Nabokov often claims to escape our network of responsibilities entirely, in order to play games designed to amuse only himself, his brilliant offerings—after all, they *are* offered, not kept private—provide all the invitations for ethical conversation about responsibilities that were provided by the basic Aesop with which we began—and many more besides. Because our essential ethical experience occurs in the specific relations, moment by moment, inference by inference, among multiple characters who offer and receive, construct and reconstruct, write and rewrite, even the most evasive author simply and paradoxically fails to evade us—unless the work itself eludes us and lies seemingly inert upon its shelf.

23. Rabinowitz has argued that *Pale Fire* is essentially and deliberately "unreadable," with all lines of interpretation finally frustrated (1972). Such a reading is rejected, obviously, by anyone who claims to have found a coherent reading. Francis Sparshott has recently argued that Anthony Burgess's *Earthly Powers* is similarly, and "irritatingly," uninterpretable (1986, esp. 159). Note the marked difference between the claim that *some* works are unreadable in this sense and the claim by some deconstructionists that *all* fictions are.

CAREER AUTHORS AND PUBLIC MYTHS

The reader's possible responsibilities to the implied author can be taken two steps further, though we seldom talk about them. First, there is a cumulative character whom we infer as we read a second or third tale told by what we call the "same" teller. Add twenty more Aesopian tales to "The Goose" and you cannot resist dealing finally with a character who is the sum of various inferred characters. We need some further term—I have suggested "career author" (1979, 270–71, 318–35)—to cover what is implied by the writing of a sequence of works. It is still not the flesh-and-blood Aesop, of course, because no matter how many tales he tells, an immense proportion of what he believed, did, or said will never appear in his fictions.

Our picture of this abstraction, the career author, can itself become critically important in two ways. It can distort our critical judgment, as when we insist that an author's new work maintain the ethos we have constructed from earlier works. The author of Fielding's *Amelia* has been wrongly blamed for not being the same carefree, whimsical author as the one who wrote *Tom Jones;* Virginia Woolf's readers have sometimes objected to the disappearance of "their" Virginia Woolf from *The Waves.* On the other hand, acquaintance with a career author can properly enhance our admiration, as we accumulate evidence of expanding power and range, adding implied author to implied author through a growing career. When I read long ago a splendid first novel by Wright Morris, I was impressed. When I had read five more, I was more impressed. Now that he has generously given us more than a score of them, I am rightly more impressed than I could be by the quality of any one of them. And I consequently feel a greater responsibility to do justice to his next tale, even if it might initially prove less inviting than the others.

Without pursuing here any of the unorthodox conclusions that thinking about such a multi-dimensional character might lead us to, I must mention one final "author," fortunately not important here for long. Whenever a fair number of real readers share speculation about a postulated writer, a new character is invented, a public myth bearing only an indeterminate relation to any real person, or any implied author: "Mark Twain," the paragon humorist; "Oscar Wilde," established as the ultimate aesthete largely in disregard of what he actually writes; or "Norman Mailer," the most honest *naughty* boy who ever lived. The ethics of producing and worshipping such mythic figures falls somewhere in our domain, but it is hard to talk about such figures without simply gossiping. A good deal that passes for ethical criticism is really about such myths, and it shows little or no connection with anything to be found in actual narratives. Or perhaps we should say, it constructs new mythical narratives with heroes connected only obscurely, if at all, to the authors' narratives. To damn a book because of what is said about the author in the Sunday supplements is "unethical" ethical criticism indeed. And it is to fail in our responsibility to the implied author of *this tale*.

CONCLUSION: ALL NARRATIVES ARE "DIDACTIC"

We see, then, that the beliefs shared by implied authors and the authorial audience are always of two distinct kinds, only one of them covered in the usual talk about "the willing suspension of disbelief."[24] Samuel Johnson made magnificent fun of the critics who fussed about unity of place, rightly reminding the rule-mongers that no spectators at an Elizabethan play really thought that they had been transported to Venice ([1765] 1968, 74–81, the attack on unity of place). But Johnson could not have dreamed that a time would come when critics would similarly mock those who think that Iago's wickedness is really wicked. Coleridge did not suggest that we willingly suspend disbelief in the many serious moral norms on which the "Rime of the Ancient Mariner" depends. The implied author of "The Goose" would presumably be upset if I said to him, "Well, now that *that's* over I can go back to the 'real' world where geese do not lay golden eggs *and* where it doesn't matter whether we are limitlessly greedy or not." In all cases we willingly suspend disbelief about some matters but not about all; most authors would be distressed if we said, after our reading, that nothing we found in it carried over to our "real" selves.

This means that the distinction between genuine literature (or "po-

---

24. The durability of Coleridge's worn dictum testifies to our sense that something more is at stake here than resistance to the super- or non-natural.

etry") and "rhetoric" or "didactic" literature is entirely misleading if it suggests that some stories, those that we seem to read just for enjoyment, are purged of all teaching. Every joke about stupidity depends upon and reinforces the value of being clever, and most of them depend upon and reinforce our sense that certain *kinds* of people are most likely to be stupid. Every detective story depends upon and reinforces many values: most of them require us to believe that crimes should be and generally are punished, that puzzles should be pursued to the bitter end, regardless of consequences, and that the troubles of society can be attributed to a small number of evil characters who can be purged from our midst.[25] Do not *King Lear* and *Oliver Twist* and *Midnight Cowboy* depend upon and reinforce, among other fixed norms, the enormous value of simple kindness and the awfulness of gratuitous cruelty? Do not *Don Giovanni, A Farewell to Arms,* and *Gargantua* depend on and reinforce (in different degrees, to be sure, and among many other fixed norms) the conviction of the male world that women are artistically expendable, at most a kind of attractive backdrop against which the comedy or tragedy of men's fate can play itself out?

I shall pursue such questions in Part 3. Meanwhile I should underline once more that our answers to them will not in any simple way settle our appraisals of these works. Many a poor work hails kindness and abhors cruelty; many a great classic is flawed in part by fixed norms that we must resist. The point for now is not to appraise particular works or teachings but to stress that all works *do* teach or at least try to (McKeon 1982; Phelan 1986), and that no reading can be considered responsible that ignores the challenge of a work's fixed norms. We may dispute about *what* it teaches: "*A Farewell to Arms* is really sympathetic to women and harder on the hero than most readers have recognized"; "*Don Giovanni* really shows us the complexities— of beauty and horror—involved in satyriasis." We may then reject the

25. For a brilliant discussion of how Raymond Chandler challenges such generic fixed norms, and thus teaches with his art, see Rabinowitz 1980. For other representative figures who have challenged the notion that art "says nothing," see Graff 1979, 1981; Reichert 1977; Wind 1983, 1985; Ellis 1974; and Phelan 1987. Indeed with a little interpretative probing one could show that most critics know very well that art, and especially narrative art, inevitably teaches.

"teaching" as either dangerous, misguided, or unimportant. But we can no longer escape talk about ethical criticism by elevating one class of narrative into a purified and hence invulnerable kingdom. The "real" Shakespeare may have been, *in some sense*, that genius of imagination whom Keats emulated, able to sympathize with every view: "What shocks the virtuous philosopher, delights the camelion Poet" ([1818] 1931, 1: 245). But surely the implied author of *King Lear* would rightly consider us irresponsible and dangerous if we said, after reading or watching that play, "It was nice pretending for awhile that filial cruelty is a terrible thing, that old and helpless fathers should not be tortured. But of course that value is culturally relative. I need not take it into account either in my appraisal of the play or in the conduct of my life."

REFERENCES

Arac, Jonathan, ed. *Postmodernism and Politics.* Theory and History of Literature, vol. 28. Minneapolis, 1986.

Bal, Mieke. *Narratology: Introduction to the Theory of Narrative* [1980]. Trans. Christine van Boheemen. Toronto, 1985.

Barthes, Roland. *The Pleasure of the Text* [1973]. Trans. Richard Miller. New York, 1975.

Barzun, Jacques. *The Use and Abuse of Art.* Princeton, N.J., 1975.

Booth, Wayne C. *Critical Understanding: The Powers and Limits of Pluralism.* Chicago, 1979.

———. *The Rhetoric of Fiction* [1961]. 2d ed. Chicago, 1983.

Bové, Paul A. *Intellectuals in Power: A Genealogy of Critical Humanism.* New York, 1986.

Brodie, Fawn. *Thomas Jefferson: An Intimate History.* New York, 1974.

Capote, Truman. *Answered Prayers.* New York, 1987.

Cawelti, John G., and Bruce A. Rosenberg. *The Spy Story.* Chicago, 1987.

de Man, Paul. *Blindness and Insight: Essays in the Rhetoric of Contemporary Criticism* [1971]. 2d ed., rev. Theory and History of Literature, vol. 7. Minneapolis, 1983.

Ellis, John M. *The Theory of Literary Criticism: A Logical Analysis.* Berkeley, 1974.

Faulkner, William. "Faulkner" [1959]. In *Writers at Work: The "Paris Review" Interviews.* Ed. Malcolm Cowley. New York, 1960: 117–41.

Fish, Stanley. *Is There a Text in This Class? The Authority of Interpretive Communities.* Cambridge, Mass., 1980.

Genette, Gérard. *Nouveau discours du récit.* Paris, 1983.

Graff, Gerald. *Literature against Itself: Literary Ideas in Modern Society.* Chicago, 1979.

———. "Literature as Assertions." In *American Criticism in the Poststructur-*

alist Age. Ed. Ira Konigsberg. Michigan Studies in the Humanities. Ann Arbor, Mich., 1981.

Hemenway, Robert E. *Zora Neale Hurston: A Literary Biography*. Urbana, Ill., 1977.

James, William. *The Principles of Psychology* [1890]. Ed. Frederick H. Burkhardt et al. Cambridge, Mass., 1981.

———. *Psychology: The Briefer Course* [1892]. Notre Dame, Ind., 1985.

Johnson, Samuel. Preface to *The Plays of William Shakespeare* [1765]. In *Johnson on Shakespeare*. Ed. Arthur Sherbo. Vol. 7 of *The Yale Edition of the Works of Samuel Johnson*. New Haven, Conn., 1968. 59–113.

Keats, John. "To Richard Woodhouse." 27 Oct. 1818. Letter 88 in *The Letters of John Keats*. Ed. Maurice Buxton Forman. 2 vols. Oxford, 1931. 1: 245.

Lipking, Lawrence. *The Life of the Poet: Beginning and Ending Poetic Careers*. Chicago, 1981.

McKeon, Zahava Karl. *Novels and Arguments: Inventing Rhetorical Criticism*. Chicago, 1982.

O'Donovan, Oliver. *The Problem of Self-Love in St. Augustine*. New Haven, Conn., 1980.

Ozick, Cynthia. "What Literature Means." *Partisan Review* 49, no. 2 (1982): 294–97.

Parker, Andrew. "Ezra Pound and the 'Economy' of Anti-Semitism." In Arac 1986: 70–90.

Phelan, James. "Supplementary Bibliography, 1961–82." In *The Rhetoric of Fiction*. By Wayne C. Booth. 2d ed. Chicago, 1983. 495–520.

———. "Character, Progression, and the Mimetic-Didactic Distinction: Some Problems and Hypotheses." *Modern Philology* 84 (Feb. 1987): 282–99.

———. "Narrative Discourse: Character and Ideology." In *Reading Narrative: Form, Ethics, Ideology*. Ed. James Phelan. Columbus, Ohio, 1988.

Poulet, Georges. "Criticism and the Experience of Interiority" [1970]. In *The Structuralist Controversy: The Languages of Criticism and the Sciences of Man*. Ed. Richard Macksey and Eugenio Donato. Baltimore, 1972. 56–72.

Rabinowitz, Peter J. "The Comedy of Terrors: Vladimir Nabokov as Philosophic Novelist." Ph.D. Diss., University of Chicago, 1972.

———. "Truth in Fiction: A Reexamination of Audiences." *Critical Inquiry* 4 (Aut. 1977): 121–41.

———. "Rats behind the Wainscoting: Politics, Convention, and Chandler's *The Big Sleep*." *Texas Studies in Literature and Language* 22 (1980): 224–45.

———. *Before Reading: Narrative Conventions and the Politics of Interpretation*. Ithaca, N.Y., 1987.

Reichert, John. *Making Sense of Literature*. Chicago, 1977.

Roth, Philip. *Zuckerman Bound* (*The Ghost Writer; Zuckerman Unbound; The Anatomy Lesson;* Epilogue: "The Prague Orgy"). New York, 1985.

———. *The Counterlife*. New York, 1987.

Sartre, Jean-Paul. *What Is Literature?* [1948]. Trans. Bernard Frechtman. London, 1981.

Sparshott, Francis. "The Case of the Unreliable Author." *Philosophy and Literature* 10 (Oct. 1986): 145–67.

Stevenson, Robert Louis. *The Letters of Robert Louis Stevenson*. Ed. Sidney Colvin. 2 vols. New York, 1899.

Watson, Walter. *The Architectonics of Meaning: Foundations of the New Pluralism*. Albany, N.Y., 1985.

Weintraub, Karl Joachim. *The Value of the Individual: Self and Circumstance in Autobiography*. Chicago, 1978.

Williams, Tennessee. Preface. *Collected Stories*. New York, 1985.

Wind, Edgar. *The Eloquence of Symbols: Studies in Humanist Art*. Ed. Jaynie Anderson. Oxford, 1983.

———. *Art and Anarchy* [1963]. London, 1985.

Yeats, William Butler. "The Choice" [1933]. In *The Poems of W. B. Yeats*. Ed. Richard J. Finneran. New York, 1983. 246–47.

PART **II**

[T]he underlying reason for writing is to bridge the gulf between one person and another.

W. H. Auden

[T]he reader each writer wants is part and parcel of the novel's conception. His special presence is evoked in the style and texture of each line. What we call style is the explicit inclusion of some readers in, and all other readers out. For all those included in, the writer is beside himself to delight and charm to his own persuasions. Above all, he wants to *hold* them . . . against their desire to escape. If he so manages a pact is formed. . . . In this pact writer and reader are committed not to crack-throughs, crack-downs or crack-ups, but a show of how things are in a fiction based on mutual respect.

Wright Morris

THE MAKING OF FRIENDS AND COMMONWEALTHS
Criticism as Ethical Culture

[T]he delicacy of fiction refines and enlivens the mind; . . . famous deeds of history ennoble it and, if read with understanding, aid in maturing one's judgment; . . . the reading of all the great books is like conversing with the best people of earlier times: it is even a studied conversation in which the authors show us only the best of their thoughts.

René Descartes, conceding as much before turning to his private project

No man can read a fine author, and relish him to his very bones, while he reads, without subsequently fancying to himself some ideal image of the man and his mind. And if you rightly look for it, you will almost always find that the author himself has somewhere furnished you with his own picture.

Herman Melville

It really is of importance, not only what men do, but also what manner of men they are that do it.

John Stuart Mill

Introduction:
The Turn to Self-culture

As we have seen, most critics who have openly addressed ethical or moral questions have worked mainly at warning about the dangers lurking, *for other people,* in seductive fictions. Discerning spiritual shipwreck ahead, they have felt a natural obligation to warn the captain (usually thought of as the rational part of the soul, and usually characterized—by men—as male), so that he might change course in time. In this metaphor, the gales of narrative pleasure and passion (often characterized as female "Muses") are opposed to the captain's noble effort to bring the soul safely home. In another moralizing metaphor, the critic's reader is about to drink a vile poison, one that the critic has somehow tasted without being destroyed. The critic must then attempt one of the most difficult of all rhetorical tasks: warning against a pleasure that he or she has already enjoyed. Often such warnings take the form of jeremiads about whole cultures: art used to be moral but now the world has fallen on wicked times.

We have already touched on two important reasons for postponing, at least for a while, this emphasis on harmful effects for readers other than the perceptive critic: it raises the fear that censorship will be seen as the only final arbiter and protector, and it introduces problems of proof that can never be decisively settled. A further word about each of these will prepare us for the radically different approach of the next six chapters.

THE SPECTER OF CENSORSHIP

The list of books banned by American school boards and libraries grows daily. In California a few years ago George A. Brown of the state's Department of Education wanted to ban Wallace Stegner's "The Colt" from high school textbooks because its characters say "damn" and "for Christ's sake." At New Trier High School in Winnetka, Illinois, *The Merchant of Venice* was removed from classes for a time, on the request of local rabbis. *Huckleberry Finn* has been dropped from many a reading list because concerned parents objected to it, usually on grounds far more questionable than those Paul Moses offered. One school board member attempted to ban a book of "literary biographies" because it contained a biography of Plato—that suspicious ancient who is known, so the claim ran, to have advocated free love and homosexuality. That the little biography itself did not even mention those "vices" made no difference to the censor. Others have wanted to outlaw *To Kill a Mockingbird, The Catcher in the Rye, 1984, Ordinary People, Oliver Twist, Slaughterhouse-Five,* along with works by Plato, Chaucer, Thomas Mann, Thoreau, Whitman—it is hard to think of major authors who have escaped.[1] Sometimes the censors win, sometimes they don't, but the disputants on both sides, all of them "ethical critics" who think of themselves as serving the public interest, might seem in their collective confusions to discredit ethical criticism as a discipline.

Those of us who teach are no doubt justified in blaming the censors for not leaving the ultimate choice of reading to us; we know the students, we know the literature, and we can best judge what narratives will bless or maim. But are we right in arguing against the general principle that underlies all the attacks: "The stories you teachers feed our children will determine, at least in part, who they become"? Opponents of censorship often argue against that principle in a most perfunctory way, on the assumption that if the principle holds, their case is lost.

Consider a typical attempt to answer the question, "If Good Books Elevate, Do Bad Books Degrade?" by Lee Burress (1982), a critic who has done yeoman service in the war against censorship. In a total of three pages the author dismisses the problem, largely on the ground that the metaphor comparing bad books with poison is invalid: "There is . . . no valid comparison between eating and reading" (34). He is so eager to make this case that he feels led, in a search for consistency, to

---

1. A good general survey of cases, causes, and proposed cures is provided in the eighteen essays collected in Davis 1979. See also Clarke 1986, Cohen 1986, Donelson 1985, MacMillan 1983, Peck 1986.

question whether good books are in any way beneficial. He then must turn handsprings to show that they *may* not be: after all, he argues, Western nations have all "claimed to read the Bible, but only slowly have we eliminated slavery, torture in the jails, or the subordination of women to secondary status. The western world powers for all their acclaim of the Bible remain very warlike agencies in the contemporary world" (35). Any would-be censor who happened on this pretense at an argument could too easily laugh it off.

I confess, however, that my own reply to the censors has sometimes been almost that distant from a full encounter with the issues. Like Paul Moses's other colleagues, I have claimed that a "proper reading" of a good book, or indeed of any book, takes care of the ethical problem. My argument has gone something like this: "If you will read *Huckleberry Finn* as a whole, if you will only respect its 'overall intentions,' you will see that your objections do not hold. I admit that elements of the tale—the pejorative use of the word 'nigger,' for example—might be harmful to inadequate readers, but those elements are transformed for any reader who sees what Clemens is saying beneath the surface. Can't you see that in the *author's* view, Jim is a prince, the moral center of the book?" Similarly, I have argued that the word "fuck" in *The Catcher in the Rye* is in fact repudiated *as it occurs,* toward the end of the book, as Holden Caulfield expresses his pathetic wish that he could wipe it from all the toilet walls in the world (Booth 1970, 47–62).

Even though this argument may be sound when we are thinking only of one kind of ideal reader—the kind every author longs for—it is surely inadequate as a reply to censors. To say to them that the "ideal" or "proper" reader who considers the work as a whole will discover the antidote for any potential poison is to presuppose that the readers whom they are trying to protect will in fact read "properly." But the censors are likely to know, because of the way they themselves read, that literary parts can carry their own meaning and power quite independently of any correction an author may have built into the whole. If I hold to the standard that all expressions of racism are deplorable, and if I extract from *Huckleberry Finn* some passages showing Jim speaking "ignorant" and being treated as a comic butt, and other passages in which all blacks are called "niggers" and described—or so it seems to me—as beneath human concern, I do not have to be told that

other readers may very well do the same; or that, if they lack fully articulated anti-racist standards, they may learn to think and talk as
those passages seem to do; or that, if they are themselves black, they
may suffer a sense of hurt, degradation, and outrage from such passages. Similarly, if I am a parent of a teenage son who, after reading
Catcher in the Rye, starts wearing his baseball cap backward and calling me a phony, I will hardly be reassured when some professor tells
me that Salinger provides "clear clues" to Holden's immaturity and
impending mental breakdown. Why should I not fear that the imitation will extend to Holden's most self-destructive ways? If I have not
myself caught Salinger's really quite subtle clues, why should I expect
my child to do so? To be told that good readers won't miss the clues
will not be reassuring, because I have every reason to expect other
people to read exactly as I do. For a critic to come along and say, "You
are reading poorly" simply opens the question of who is the authority,
and the censor is likely to conclude that it is the critic who is reading
poorly—or exhibiting moral slackness or insensitivity.

PROBLEMS OF PROOF

If our problem with those who believe that narratives *do* affect conduct is to protect ourselves from their conflicting but confident purification programs, our problem on the other flank—should we think
of it as the critical Left?—is just the opposite: the extreme difficulty of
establishing, to any honest doubter, that a given effect has been caused
by a given narrative or kind of narrative. Even if we conducted elabo-
rately controlled experiments about good or bad effects of *The Lord of
the Rings,* "Sesame Street," and *Huckleberry Finn,* we could never
completely isolate the force of any one of these from the many other
causes that impinge on all human actions. Human beings are not
"caused" in any simple way; even the most convinced determinists
usually acknowledge that in some sense persons are self-caused. Individuals deflect and transform influences in ways that will always as-
tonish and frustrate those who try to trace precise causal lines. Does
TV violence cause violent behavior or simply reflect a violence already
present in our society—or perhaps even provide a safety valve for it?
Are the various moral flaws that John Gardner traces in our fiction to

be deplored as likely causes of moral decay, or do they simply reflect a decadence that any honest novelist must portray?

Some years ago three college students in Indiana got drunk, raided a pigsty, tortured a sow with African spears they had stolen, put out the eyes of her piglets, then set fire to the horror they had created. The ringleader, a junior English major, said in his defense that he had been reading William Golding's *Lord of the Flies,* along with great swatches of what he called "existentialist" literature—works by Gide, Kafka, and Sartre—that he claimed had led him to assert his existence with a little *acte gratuit* of his own. These authors were thus to blame for his actions, he said (if the notion of blame made any sense, which he said he doubted). Many fellow students and faculty members believed his explanation, and one dean even proposed that such works should be banned from the freshman reading list. The same line of argument has been pursued in some recent legal defenses of criminals who, the claim goes, learned to be criminal—or at least learned how to practice a particular crime—by watching criminal acts portrayed on TV.

The charges are plausible. I believe that they are sometimes justified. But how are we ever to *prove* them? How are we ever to know that a given pathological act would not have occurred without the stimulus of the art work? Even if many readers of *Lord of the Flies* went out and stuck pigs, we would never know how many readers did not do so; how many would have done so anyway, without Golding's nudge; how many were led, through some kind of catharsis, to reject such extremes; or how many would have done other equally nasty acts if Golding had not unwittingly suggested that particular one.

Addressing hard-headed skeptics, we don't get very far just by pointing out our commonsense knowledge that some art works are good for us and our children and that some are bad. Later on I must nevertheless depend on and elaborate some kinds of "knowledge" that we can share even though we lack "hard proof." Nobody who takes a close look at a week's worth of commercial TV, for example, can doubt that a ten-hour daily dose of such stuff is bad medicine for children, just as it would be for you and me (Gore 1987; Landsberg 1987). Nobody who considers closely the fixed norms of the tales offered by the pornography of violence reported in Andrea Dworkin's *Pornography: Men Possessing Women* (1981) can seriously doubt that *some* uncritical male readers will be corrupted by them. Our intuitions about such matters seem to be supported—though always in degrees that could never overwhelm any skeptic—by what studies we have: for example, men who watch videos that show women either wanting to be raped or enjoying it after it has happened do in significant numbers pick up that view of what women most want (Attorney General's Commission on Pornography 1986, 980–1003, 1897).

The troublesome fact remains that when we argue about consequences—especially consequences for other people—we are always on shakier ground than most of us will want to stand on. When I claim that the novel I have just read is likely to harm *you,* my talk is a bit too much like cocktail party chit-chat for comfort. Any part of any work, any word or action, can seem to some reader or listener dangerous or offensive, according to *some* ethical or political code, and one can always look at someone else's conduct and say to oneself, "*That's* the result of reading so much of such-and-such kind of narrative,"[2] or—as I heard a colleague say recently—"You can tell just by the way he talks in faculty meetings that he has never read much poetry." Though productive debate can occur among diverse readers about the standards to be employed in such judgments, it is much less likely when the claim is that a given work or part has harmed someone or will necessarily harm others. "If it seems offensive to *me,* it *is* offensive." "If I claim that it has not harmed me, who are you to say that it has?"

We can postpone these two difficulties at least for a time by turning inward, away from responsibilities to authors or other readers and toward our responsibility to ourselves as readers and listeners. Obviously this choice is not forced upon us by the nature of the subject, and it will reveal its own dangers. Other directions for an ethical criticism are quite possible. We might here instead try to deepen our questions about responsibility to the "story itself" or to the implied author; we could then perhaps take up E. D. Hirsch's argument that our primary ethical responsibility is to respect the author's intended meaning (1976). Such a project, pursued more fully than I have done so far,

---

2. The same Lee Burress who claims that bad books do not harm people goes on to claim that the Bible has in fact led some "misguided young men" to "mutilate or castrate themselves because of misreading" (1982, 35).

might well lead us into questions no one has ever fully or properly addressed: What are the consequences of saying that I have a positive *obligation* to an implied author, whose creator is long since dead? Why should I be held responsible to "inert" words on the page? Do I really *owe* Homer or Austen or Dickens any special kind of reading conduct? Can the concept of obligation be extended to such creatures as the author I meet (yet in a sense myself create) when I read the *Iliad* or *Great Expectations?*

To follow that path would be fruitful, leading, I am convinced, to a qualified but affirmative answer to all these questions.[3] But all that would require a different kind of book, one that would probe to our (always confusing) foundations and come back with the good news that obligations to others, dead or alive, have genuine rational force. As I have said, many a philosopher has been doing just that, offering impressive demonstrations that it is unreasonable, even illogical, to deny the rights of others; that I offend not just conscience but reason when I deny my responsibilities to others; that I violate not just myself but my reason when I am totally self-absorbed. But though I cannot find a single major recent professional philosopher who finally rejects such a marriage of reason and ethics,[4] it is not hard to find literary critics, novelists, and poets who do so, claiming that the intellect and moral principles inhabit different worlds.

All of us non-professional "thinkers" tend to buy our philosophies at second-hand shops, always a few decades behind the times, and we

3. Some years after I first wrote that sentence, Jacques Derrida affirmed similar responsibilities in a carefully nuanced ethical critique of the life *and works* of his friend Paul de Man. "We still have responsibilities toward him, and they are more alive than ever, even as he is dead. That is, we have responsibilities regarding Paul de Man *himself* but *in us and for us*" (1988, 593).

4. There are, of course, radical differences in the arguments, but the current consensus on one point is really quite astonishing: the world as it "is" entails certain "oughts." For the most obvious examples, see Donagan 1977; Gewirth 1978; MacIntyre 1981; Williams 1985; Putnam 1981; and Raz, 1986. But for less obvious examples, see the deconstructionists, who despite frequent assertions that all thought leads to irresolvable aporia, usually imply, as Krieger has argued (1983), strong obligations for the reader who acknowledges their claims—claims about where reason will lead any responsible inquirer. See Derrida 1988. Consider also the "musts" in Foucault's late claim, in commenting on the role of reading and writing in constituting the self (1983, 211), that "the principle work of art which one has to take care of, the main area to which one must apply aesthetic values, is oneself, one's life, one's existence" (245; and see 229, 236–37, 239).

find ourselves in the 1980s furnishing our minds with versions of relativism, nihilism, positivism, and emotivism that were fashionable
among philosophers thirty or forty years ago. In contrast, current
frontline quarrels among people who have spent longer than an hour
thinking about ethics are really not about *whether* we have real obligations but about what are their *best* grounds.[5] Some of them seek single
systems of ethical value; more seem to say about ethics in general what
I want to say about the ethics of narration: we live in a world of many
genuine "goods," but the fact that they cannot be finally harmonized
under any one choral director in no way impugns the rationality of
those who live by them and think about them.

Nevertheless, it would be risky to depend on any emerging consensus that some sort of responsibility for the "others" (both outside and
within my "self"), some sort of altru-ism (from French *autrui,* Latin
alter) is rationally entailed in the very fact of being human. Regardless of where we stand on that "obligation outward," our culture
seems to talk more naturally about "obligations inward": "self"-culti-
vation, "self"-fulfillment, "personal growth," "psychic health," "self-
change."[6] Instead of trying to combat such (obviously?) self-destructive modes, we may as well begin with our "selves," whatever they are,
saving our worries about other people for later on. Instead of trying to
refute self-centered moralities, I shall for a time simply embrace and
develop them, much as a classical rhetorician like Cicero did when he
offered his son a summation, in *De Officiis,* of all human duties. The
chief duty, subsuming all the rest, is to make of oneself the best "character" possible, given one's "circumstances." To take that duty seriously, in thinking about narratives, will lead us, as it led Cicero, into
interesting relocations of our responsibilities to others.

REFERENCES

Attorney General's Commission on Pornography: Final Report, July 1986.
    U.S. Department of Justice. Washington, D.C., 1986.

5. As A. E. Housman once said about superficial classical scholarship, "Three
minutes' thought would suffice to find this out; but thought is irksome and three
minutes is a long time." I owe the quotation to Bernard Williams.
6. I list a few obvious sources in Chapter 8. For now, let one suffice: *Self-Change:
Strategies for Solving Personal Problems* (Mahoney 1979).

Booth, Wayne C. "Censorship and the Values of Fiction" [1964]. In *Now Don't Try to Reason with Me: Essays and Ironies for a Credulous Age.* Chicago, 1970.

Burress, Lee. "If Good Books Elevate, Do Bad Books Degrade?" In *The Students' Right to Know.* Ed. Lee Burress and Edward B. Jenkinson. Urbana, Ill., 1982.

Cicero. *De Officiis* (On moral obligation). Trans. John Higginbotham. Berkeley, 1967.

Clark, Elyse. "A Slow, Subtle Exercise in Censorship." *SLJ [School Library Journal]* 32 (Mar. 1986): 93–96.

Cohen, Barbara. "Censoring the Sources." *SLJ [School Library Journal]* 32 (Mar. 1986): 97–99.

Davis, James E., ed. *Dealing with Censorship.* Urbana, Ill., 1979.

Derrida, Jacques. "Like the Sound of the Sea Deep within a Shell: Paul de Man's War." *Critical Inquiry* 14 (Spring 1988), 590–652.

Donelson, Ken. "Almost 13 Years of Book Protests . . . Now What?" *SLJ [School Library Journal]* 31 (Mar. 1985): 93–98.

Donagan, Allan. *The Theory of Morality.* Chicago, 1977.

Dworkin, Andrea. *Pornography: Men Possessing Women.* New York, 1981.

Foucault, Michel. "On the Genealogy of Ethics: An Overview of Work in Progress." In *Michel Foucault: Beyond Structuralism and Hermeneutics.* Ed. Hubert L. Dreyfus and Paul Rabinow. 2d ed. Chicago, 1983.

Gardner, John. *On Moral Fiction.* New York, 1978.

Gewirth, Alan. *Reason and Morality.* Chicago, 1978.

Gore, Tipper. *Raising PG Kids in an X-Rated Society.* Nashville, 1987.

Hirsch, E. D. *The Aims of Interpretation.* Chicago, 1976.

Krieger, Murray. "In the Wake of Morality: The Thematic Underside of Recent Theory." *New Literary History* 15 (Aut. 1983): 119–36.

Landsberg, Michele. "Free-Market Follies." Review of *Raising PG Kids in an X-Rated Society,* by Tipper Gore. *Nation* (July 18–25, 1987): 61–63.

MacIntyre, Alasdair. *After Virtue: A Study in Moral Theory.* Notre Dame, Ind., 1981.

MacMillan, P. R. *Censorship and Public Morality.* Aldershot, 1983.

Mahoney, Michael J. *Self-Change: Strategies for Solving Personal Problems.* New York, 1979.

Peck, Richard. "The Genteel Unshelving of a Book." *SLJ [School Library Journal]* 32 (May 1986): 37–39.

Plato. *Republic.* Trans. Paul Shorey. Loeb Classical Library. London, 1930. 2.392–402; 10.595–608.

Pound, Ezra. "The Teacher's Mission." *English Journal* 23 (1934): 630–35.

Putnam, Hilary. "A Problem about Reference." In *Reason, Truth, and History.* Cambridge, 1981.

Raz, Joseph. *The Morality of Freedom.* Oxford, 1986.

Williams, Bernard. *Ethics and the Limits of Philosophy.* Cambridge, Mass., 1985.

6

I want to be loved. That is even the deep-lying reason why I elected to write. When I was eighteen, I read *The Mill on the Floss,* and I dreamed that one day I would be loved the way I loved George Eliot then.
Simone de Beauvoir

[S]uch is the law of his [every earnest person's] being that only can he find out his own secret through the instrumentality of another mind. We hail with gladness this new acquisition of ourselves. That man I must follow, for he has a part of me; and I follow him that I may acquire myself. The great are our better selves, ourselves with advantages.
Ralph Waldo Emerson

We owe everything to . . . authors, on this side barbarism. . . . [W]ith a few old authors, I can manage to get through the summer or winter months, without ever knowing what it is to feel *ennui.* They sit with me at breakfast; they walk out with me before dinner—and at night, by the blazing hearth, discourse the silent hours away.
William Hazlitt

When evening has arrived, I return home, and go into my study. . . . I pass into the antique courts of ancient men, where, welcomed lovingly by them, I feed upon the food which is my own, and for which I was born. Here, I can speak with them without show, and can ask of them the motives of their actions; and they respond to me by virtue of their humanity. For hours together, the miseries of life no longer annoy me; I forget every vexation; I do not fear poverty; and death itself does not dismay me, for I have altogether transferred myself to those with whom I hold converse.
Niccolò Machiavelli

Reading is an intimate act, perhaps more intimate than any other human act. I say that because of the prolonged (or intense) exposure of one mind to another.
Harold Brodkey

Implied Authors as Friends and Pretenders

CONSEQUENCES OR GOOD CONVERSATIONS

Most overtly ethical critics have dwelt on whether a given narrative will work for good or ill in the life of other readers, *after* the last page has been turned. Will this fiction help form a character who is hypersensitive, properly sensitive, or insensitive; intellectually pretentious, thoughtful, or shallow; rash, bold, or timid; bigoted, tolerant, or wishy-washy? Such questions are obviously an important branch of ethical criticism, and I must return to them, especially in Part 3. But what happens if we begin instead with the qualities of experience sought or achieved by authors and readers *during* the time of telling or listening? Instead of asking whether this book, poem, play, movie, or TV drama will turn me toward virtue or vice tomorrow, we now will ask what kind of company it offers me today.[1]

How can we describe the many relations that we are asked to build, or that we can build on our own, with the various authors we encounter, *as* we read? Asking such a question will lead us naturally to the sort of conversation in which every human being is already highly practiced: that is, to metaphorical talk about what kind of live encounter a given reading experience is *like*. Needless to say, such conversation can be expected to have ethical qualities—and perhaps even consequences—of its own.

All of us already employ a large range of terms for our relations to other people, terms of love and hate, pleasure and pain, interest and

---

1. The "turn" here, away from consequences toward "condition of soul," is comparable to the traditional philosophical conflict between consequentialism and utilitarianism, on the one hand, and an ethic of "conviction," or obedience to duty. A good brief introduction to the issues, and to the dangers in any absolute adherence to either position, is given by Charles E. Larmore, in *Patterns of Moral Complexity* (1987, esp. 144–53).

boredom. If we could begin by thinking systematically about such terms, as applied to the many characters we meet (and become) as we make and re-make narratives, we might develop a vocabulary that would allow us to talk together productively about ethical quality— not about whether to label a given narrative with an *imprimatur,* a *nihil obstat,* or a "To the Index!" but about the facts, loaded with value judgments, of our various encounters.

All criticism depends on basic metaphors, often unstated, for our relation to ————? As soon as I conclude the sentence with "to the words on the page," "to stories," "to characters dramatized," "to the text," "to the author," or to any other term, I have already implied my choice of a metaphorical mode. As we have seen, many critics today talk of solving puzzles, deciphering codes, wandering through mazes, untangling webs, or dismantling ramshackle structures. Others imply slightly warmer relations: "texts" become worlds to be entered or prized objects to be analyzed or admired. Each of these rival metaphors bears *some* relation to what we do when we read or listen. If it did not, people would not continue to conduct their criticism in its name.

In pursuing now the metaphor of *people meeting* as they share stories, we have no need to spend time attacking any of its rivals. Though our choice will obscure some truths that are revealed in current pursuits of "meaning" and "non-meaning," we can hope that it may release a kind of critical conversation too often inhibited by more mechanized pictures of texts / webs / prison houses / mazes / codes / rule systems / speech acts / semantic structures. Perhaps most obviously, this metaphor spontaneously revives a kind of talk, once almost universal, about the types of friendship or companionship a book provides *as* it is read.

FRIENDSHIPS USEFUL, PLEASANT, AND SELF-JUSTIFYING

The modern neglect of friendship as a serious subject of inquiry is puzzling. After millennia during which friendship was one of the major philosophical topics, the subject of thousands of books and tens of thousands of essays, it has now so dwindled that our encyclopedias do not even mention it. The fourth edition of the *Encyclopaedia Bri-*

tannica (1810) had twenty long columns on "Friendship"; they disappeared in the ninth edition (1879), replaced by "Friendly Societies," "Friends, Society of," and "Friendship Islands." *The New Encyclopaedia Britannica* restores the term, in the *Micropaedia*, but only as a reference to Emerson's essay.[2] Nor is friendship even mentioned, as a general topic or in the index, in *The Encyclopedia of Philosophy* (1967). Our booklists reveal only a lone "popular" sociological study here (Greeley 1970), a study of male or homosexual friendships there (Brain 1976), a fine but brief and isolated popular religious study (Marty 1980), and not much else.[3] We may be witnessing a revival in the 1980s,[4] especially as women have begun to explore the importance of friendship in feminist studies (Abel 1981). But the contrast with earlier periods is still surprising.

Even more striking is the decline in talk about books as friends. In the nineteenth and early twentieth centuries the personification was widespread, celebrated overtly in the titles of many books and essays—*Friends in Council* (Helps 1847–59), *The Friendship of Books* (Maurice 1880), *Letters to Dead Authors* (Lang 1886), *Friends on the Shelf* (Torrey 1906). Often the language of friendship was not enough; only words of love spoke strongly enough for what books inspire. Here is Leigh Hunt, echoing what one can find in Lamb and many another romantic:

> Sitting last winter among my books[,] . . . I began to consider how I loved the authors of those books; how I loved them too, not only for the imaginative pleasures they afforded me, but for their making me love the very books themselves. . . . I looked sideways at my Spenser, my Theocritus, and my Arabian Nights; then above them at my Italian Poets; . . . then on my left side at my Chaucer . . . ; and thought how natural it was in C[harles] L[amb] to give a kiss to an old folio, as I once saw him do to

2. I find "friendship" in all the dictionaries of the major Western languages (the *Grand Larousse* has about fifteen lines!), but it appears in none of the modern encyclopedias I have examined.

3. We need a serious philosophical history of the concept, starting perhaps with Plato's *Lysis*, moving on through Aristotle's *Ethics* (bks. 8 and 9) and Cicero's many discussions (for example, "On Friendship" [1967]), through Montaigne, Bacon, and many other Renaissance studies, racing on through Emerson to . . . this chapter. A good start on a bibliography for such a study is given in a fine book by Ronald Sharp, *Friendship and Literature* (1986).

4. I am especially impressed by Hyde 1983 and Marty 1980, but Rubin 1985 and Block 1980 are also at least straws in what I hope will prove to be a gale.

Chapman's Homer. . . . I love an author the more for having been himself a
lover of books.

(1823, 1, 17)

And so on, for twenty-five more pages of adulation.

Even when words like "friends" or "love" do not appear in titles,
the metaphor of personal affection is often evident: *Lessons from My
Masters: Carlyle, Tennyson, and Ruskin* (Bayne 1879), *Old Familiar
Faces* (Watts-Dunton 1916). About the only rival metaphors were
similarly personal, dealing with traveling or wandering or "adventuring" in the world of books: *Famous Books: Sketches in the Highways
and Byeways of English Literature* (Adams 1875).[5]

The point in turning to the metaphor of friendship is not, of course,
to revive this sort of extremely general talk about book-friends, as if all
books were equally friendly, and friendly in the same way. Even if we
share the uplifting sentiments, they give us little help of the kind we are
seeking: they tell us little about how we might distinguish narrative
friends from enemies: they are as general as the lumpings that I rejected in Chapter 1. What we need is a vocabulary of discriminations
among *kinds* of friendship, and for that we are forced to return to an
ancient tradition that made true friendship a primary goal of life, and
the study of how to achieve it a center of all ethical inquiry.

In that tradition, which has endured into our own time only in specialized histories, the quality of our lives was said to be in large part
identical with the quality of the company we keep. Our happiness is
found in a pursuit of friendship, of something more than our limited
"selves." As Aristotle put it, when he placed friendship as the crown-

---

5. Nobody would be caught dead today writing in the way that to William Ellery
Channing, in 1838, seemed as natural as breathing: "It is chiefly through books that we
enjoy intercourse with superior minds. . . . In the best books great men talk to us, give
us their most precious thoughts, and pour their souls into ours. God be thanked for
books. They are the voices of the distant and the dead, and make us heirs of the spiritual
life of past ages" (1881, 23).

Martin Tupper at about the same time wrote a sentiment similarly embalmed in
Bartlett's: "A good book is the best of friends, the same to-day and for ever" (s.v.
"books"). Authors went on writing that way well into this century. Here's Helen Keller,
speaking in 1902 of how books felt to her in her sense-deprived world: "Literature is my
Utopia. . . . No barrier of the senses shuts me out from the sweet, gracious discourse of
my book-friends. They talk to me without embarrassment or awkwardness" (s.v.
"literature").

ing virtue in his *Nicomachean Ethics*, "Without friends no one would choose to live, though he had all other goods" (bk. 8.1). He is talking, of course, not only about what we would call close friends but about all bonds of affection or reliance between parents and children, kings and subjects, neighbors and citizens, husbands and wives, and so on. His claim amounts to saying that what makes life human, and what makes human life worth living, are our relations of trust and affection: we are naturally, *essentially* social animals.

What are the grounds of trust and affection? Everyone in the classical tradition begins with the obvious point that we feel friendly toward anyone who seems to offer us any sort of benefit or gift. The tradition distinguishes three kinds of friendship based on three kinds of gift a would-be friend might offer me: of pleasure; of profit or gain; and of a kind of company that is not only pleasant or profitable, in some immediate way, but also good for me, good for its own sake.[6] The third kind is of course both pleasant and profitable (since it contributes to the growth of my soul), but we do not pursue it for the sake of pleasure or profit. Rather, we seek it *for the sake of the friendly company itself—the living in friendship*. Hours spent with this best kind of friend are seen as the way life should be lived. As an Eastern European character in Malcolm Bradbury's *Rates of Exchange* puts it, speaking of books as friends: "Yes, every day I read them and I become some more a person" (1983, 210).

The three kinds of friendship are obviously not of equal importance or stability. People who become friends only because they give each other pleasure—sexual partners, members of gourmet cooking clubs—will stop being friends as soon as the pleasure-giving stops. Friendships based only on some immediate gain—business associates, teammates in professional sports, partners in a marriage of convenience—will fall apart as soon as the utility is no longer clear, *unless* friendship of the third kind has been achieved.

6. In what follows I do not mean to suggest that I find Aristotle's rational account of friendship the only or the best account of human affection. The chief "rival" is obviously the Christian command to love our enemies—love them in a mysterious, gratuitous way that takes no account of what they might offer us. Applied to our relations to implied authors, the command would yield a "golden rule" that I hope informs this whole book: "Read as you would have others read you; listen as you would have others listen."

The fullest friendship arises whenever two people offer each other not only pleasures or utilities but shared aspirations and loves of a kind that make life together worth having as an end in itself. These full friends love to be with each other because of the quality of the life they live during their time together. As Aristotle says, a true friendship is a relation of virtue with virtue, or as we might translate—remembering again that "virtue" was for him a much broader, less moralistic term than it is for us—a relation of strength with strength and aspiration with aspiration. A full friend "is said to be one who wishes and does good things, or what appear to him to be good, for the sake of his friend," or "one who wishes his friend to be and to live for his own sake, as appears in mothers in regard to their children." In short, my true friend is one who "has the same relations with me that he has with himself" (*Ethics,* 8.6–7). Such friendships last as long as the reciprocal love of virtue lasts—quite possibly until death and beyond. Montaigne beautifully describes this notion of friendship with the dead in his essay "Of Friendship," where he relates how he still lives daily with his friend La Boetie, many years after La Boetie's death (1967, 135–44). About four centuries earlier, Abelard came even closer to my notion here by dedicating his book "To an Unknown Friend"—the future reader.

STORIES AS FRIENDSHIP OFFERINGS

Considered under the friendship metaphor, the implied authors of *all* stories, fictional or historical, elevated or vulgar, welcoming or hostile on the surface, purport to offer one or another of these friendships. The only exceptions I can think of would be stories overheard. As soon as someone takes the trouble to get my attention, by publishing or by talking to me, the offer of some benefit or pleasure or companionship is undeniable. Even satiric fictions that present a snarling surface address us with what amounts to a friendly offer: "I would like to give you something for your own good—a nasty medicine that may cure you."

More obviously, all narratives offer with their titles and opening sentences a cry of invitation: "Join me, join me, because if you do, you will receive something that no other story can give you in quite the same way, something that will . . ." But here the offers diverge. Many stories announce themselves as offering simply one or another kind of pleasure—whether minimal, as in the latest joke, or manifold, as in the wonderful series of Jeeves novels by P. G. Wodehouse or the best farce of the season (what better friend could I find—for an evening's pleasure—than the Michael Frayn who creates a *Noises Off*, or the Feydeau who offers me, from an earlier time, an evening of laughter at his *Champignol malgré lui?*). Others claim to offer me something that the implied author considers useful: aggressive practical advice, as in "docu-dramas" that tell us how to deal with "the enemy" or stories about business triumphs ("How I Made a Million Dollars in Real Estate"); moral instruction, as in Sunday school versions of Bible stories, or in the case studies of psychological guidebooks, or in the more complex but still openly didactic lessons of the great apologues (Johnson's *Rasselas*); visions of a higher reality, as in many religious parables and myths (*The Divine Comedy, The Pilgrim's Progress*); distressing, even shattering warnings, as in great satire of the kind offered in the portrait of the Yahoos in *Gulliver's Travels*. Finally, some seem to offer a chance to live together for a while with a new friend, a way that will be, while pleasant and perhaps even useful, somehow too valuable to be reduced to either the *utile* or the *dulce*.[7]

For our purposes, all stories, even those modern novels that use elaborate distancing tricks to subvert realism and prevent identification, can be viewed not as puzzles or even as games but as companions, friends—or if that seems to push the personal metaphor too far, as *gifts* from would-be friends.[8] Consider the range in these five beginning "offers":

7. Obviously the rhetoric of this paragraph requires me to give examples of this friendship too. But any example would almost certainly be taken as a more generalized and confident recommendation than I would intend. On the one hand, almost any of the literary classics could for most readers be said to provide the kind of friendship we are celebrating; the capacity to do that, for a sufficient number of readers over sufficiently long time periods, is what makes a classic a classic. On the other hand *my* list of supreme friends will almost certainly not be identical with yours. So I must ask you to fill in here the titles of one or two works that you have recently chosen to *re*-read not just for the fun of it and not just because of some practical need but out of a strong desire for a deeper acquaintance: your earlier encounters yielded so much that you can predict much more and you desire much more. As for my own list, I'll say only that it cannot simply be inferred by observing which works I discuss in *Company*.

8. In much of what follows I have profited from Lewis Hyde's *The Gift* (1983). For a splendid account of just how fully gift-giving and true friendship dominated ethical

THE GOSPEL ACCORDING TO SAINT JOHN

In the beginning was the Word. And the Word was with God. And the Word was God.

THE GOOD SOLDIER

This is the saddest story I have ever heard. We had known the Ashburnhams for nine seasons of the town of Nauheim with an extreme intimacy—or, rather, with an acquaintanceship as loose and easy and yet as close as a good glove's with your hand. My wife and I . . .

(Ford Madox Ford)

LADY CHATTERLEY'S LOVER

Ours is essentially a tragic age, so we refuse to take it tragically. The cataclysm has happened, we are among the ruins, we start to build up new little habits, to have new little hopes. It is rather hard work: there is now no smooth road into the future: but we go round, or scramble over the obstacles. We've got to live, no matter how many skies have fallen.

(D. H. Lawrence)

THE STORMS OF LOVE

1875

Driving to the Goodwood races the Duke of Wydeminster thought with satisfaction that his team of horses was the most outstanding that he had ever owned.

Once again, he told himself, he had been proved right, having bought them as foals at a sale held by one of his friends, when the majority of buyers had not considered them worth a second glance.

The Duke however with his expert eye . . .

(Barbara Cartland)

NERD WITHOUT NERVE

This is an unusual story about the way that I lost my virginity. When I was nineteen . . .

(*Penthouse* "Forum," signed "Name and Address Withheld")

Even in the anonymous offer of the last of these we can read a *claim* to offer us some moments together that will add to our lives; even the writer's refusal to sign her name (his? "She" is quite probably a male editor who knows what gifts his mainly male readers seek)—

---

talk in what I have called "the tradition," see John Wallace's discussion of Seneca's influence on Shakespeare's *Timon of Athens* (1986).

even that anonymity cannot be an entirely reliable clue that the author fears our revenge for a dirty trick (think of all the earlier fine literature that was anonymous or pseudonymous). All of these fictions are like the would-be friends we meet in what we call real life—that part of life that we perhaps ought to call less real, since its friendships are often less concentrated, less intense, and less enduring than those offered by story-tellers.[9] We cannot avoid choosing among them, consciously or unconsciously; even those of us who do not read or watch TV or go to movies or plays—are there any such?—are *offered* innumerable stories each day, unless we have no human converse whatever, and just by living we choose some and reject others.

We always make our choices on the basis of evidence that is to some degree inadequate. No doubt we are fortunate that most of the people in the world do not make the same exclusive claims on our attention that stories make; few of those I meet today will suggest, as do all stories, that their sole point in life is to offer me the best possible gift imaginable: spiritual salvation (the gospel); a tragic experience (Ford); wisdom about life in our time (Lawrence); true love and horses (Cartland); sexual thrills (*Penthouse*).

We reject these offers, of course, whether made by people or by fictions, unless we think we will get *something* worth having. Except when we are off-guard, we accept the companionship only of those who persuade us that their offerings are the genuine "goods." We thus practice, willy-nilly, an ethical criticism regardless of our theories: we choose our friends and their gifts, and thus who *we* will be, for the duration.

The nature of the friendly offer will never in itself determine the quality of the friend. Though the offer of distinterested friendship is by its nature a claim to the highest kind, and the offer of utility a claim to superiority over "mere pleasure," we never know until after long acquaintance whether or not an implied author can really distinguish true friendship from false. He or she may prove to be a wolf in sheep's clothing or—as in that ever-puzzling beginning of our human jour-

9. For a lovely fantasy portraying what a whole people would be like if they all took story life, and particularly dream life, as realer than "real" life, see Ursula K. LeGuin's *The Word for World Is Forest* (1976).

ney—a snake in the grass. No doubt Eve enjoyed her first visit with
Satan, listening to his fascinating story about how things *really* were,
enjoyed it more than any other moment she had known. Her pleasure
was the pleasure of learning, that's clear. He promised her, indeed, a
kind of profit, and she must have felt that she had found a true friend.
Only disastrous consequences could show that Satan was not one who
"has the same relations with me as he has with himself." But such consequences will never be as clear-cut for those who, in reading, accept
the story of Satan's story: the "friendly warnings" offered by the Genesis author(s) and their thousands of redactors, the greatest among
them being Milton. We male readers seem to have required a reminder
from feminists of how the "accepted" version of the story of that radically secondary character, poor Eve, might be dangerous for quite different reasons unless subjected to some intensive ethical criticism
(Froula 1983).

Similarly, to decide that a book offers me "a mere pleasure" or "a
mere utility" cannot mean that it is *necessarily* ethically inferior to
every work that *offers* something more. Many an offer of sustained,
intense, ordered pleasure will prove more profitable to the soul than
many a claim of disinterested companionship. This should not surprise
us: Why should we expect choices between true friends and flatterers,
lovers and sado-masochists, wise companions and pretentious frauds
to be easier in literature than they are in our daily encounters?

All the art, then, in this kind of metaphorical criticism, will lie in
our power to discriminate among the values of moments of friendship
that we ourselves have in a sense created. We judge ourselves as we
judge the offer. Here is circularity with a vengeance. But we need not
fear it as a vicious circle, so long as we do not pursue hard final judgments of "wicked" or "blessed" but rather ways of testing and improving our re-creations. And when we do so, we will often find, despite
the complexities, that simple questions about which of the three kinds
of friendship is being offered, *and why,* can yield unequivocal and
shareable results. The simple and obvious question, for example, "Do
you, my would-be friend, wish *me* well, or will you be the only one to
profit if I join you?" can make the implied creators of the Cartland romance and the *Penthouse* garbage writhe with embarrassment.

Still, questions about the kind of friendship offered give us at best a
crude test. Can we hope to find more deliberate ways of conversing

with our would-be friends, without violating the inherent fluidity of our subject?

SOME MEASURES OF LITERARY FRIENDSHIP

Suppose we begin with a rough survey of the minimal rewards that authors promise and—sometimes—deliver. To every book that knocks on my door, I tacitly reply (unless I refuse to answer at all, like some modern city dwellers who are sure that every caller threatens a mugging): "All right, yes. Do come in, but only for a moment. Understand that unless you immediately please me in some way, I will show you to the door and never admit you again." It would be futile to try to list the infinite range of openings that might respond to that demand—the offer of gossip, of pornography, of political inside dope, of escape to a world of pure beauty or to an adventure-packed or horror-filled spectacle. It will thus be more helpful to think of the kinds of *activity* that will keep us visiting with a sense of reward—regardless of the subject. What will keep us conversing with any narrative, whether it is ostensibly reportorial or fictional, didactic or aesthetic? Our answers will simultaneously answer related questions about the value of these meetings.

Note that by putting our question in this form we are postponing most questions about good and bad *morality,* in every ordinary sense. We cannot, of course, abandon traditional moral distinctions permanently: courage/cowardice; justice/injustice; temperance/rashness; wisdom/folly—these cardinal distinctions and others like them will finally be pertinent to our appraisals of friendship. But it is important, in our current climate—moralizing? immoral? schizophrenic? "closed"? —to emphasize again that *ethical* distinctions do not depend on choices among the traditional *moral* virtues. If that were not so, how could I explain that some good friends, in life as in literature, are wonderfully beneficial to my soul, even though they are clearly immoral on many a scale?

Our reading friends can vary:

1. in the sheer *quantity* of invitations they offer us;
2. in the degree of *responsibility* they grant to us—what we might

call the level of reciprocity or domination between author and reader;

3. in the degree of *intimacy* in the friendship;
4. in the *intensity* of engagement that they expect or require—from total concentration to slack, comfortable, slowly-ripening acquaintance;
5. in the *coherence,* or consistency, of the proffered world;
6. in the *distance* between their worlds and ours, that is, in the familiarity or strangeness of the world we enter—the amount of rude challenge, or "otherness," that they fling at our current norms;
7. in the kind, or *range of kinds,* of activities suggested, invited, or demanded—from a reassuring concentration on single-minded issues or formal patterns ("The Goose") to a reconstruction and embrace of whole "worlds" that seem to include every topic that our "real" worlds include (*Crime and Punishment, Ulysses,* William Gaddis's *The Recognitions*).

In our living friends, we find these same variables. Some of them offer a lot of whatever they are good at; others offer precious gems though few. Some dominate the conversation, or try to, while others offer to play an equal role, and yet others ask *us* to dominate. Some open themselves to a bold and potentially healing intimacy, revealing our own depths or depths we never dreamed of, while others politely preserve our illusions, applying the "cosmetics" that all "as if" philosophies say life by its very nature requires (Beerbohm 1950; Vaihinger 1935). Some wake us up or scare us off by the intensity and pace of their offering, while others are satisfied with a steady or slack pace that may console or bore us. Some are sufficiently coherent to make us feel that we are dealing with a whole person, a solid character, while others feel shallow or devious, flabby or unreliable. Some companions fit our old ways like old comfortable shoes and others are *so* "other" as to shock, shatter, and either destroy or re-mold us. And finally, some offer us only one kind of pleasure or profit while others range over many of life's values.

Almost every conceivable variation on these seven scales of activity has been offered at one time or another as *the* test of "good literature" or "true poetry." Critical programs and schools rise and fall as particular extremes are first warmly embraced and then rejected for their fatal and obvious narrowness. Consider, as a brief example on the scale of quantity, the passion for concision—particularly for the precisely right word or image—that marked much theory from Flaubert through the early decades of the twentieth century. Ezra Pound wrote, presumably without irony, that "it is better to present one Image in a lifetime than to produce voluminous works" ([1913] 1985, 4). At the opposite extreme, Anthony Trollope claimed credit for the sheer quantity of his novels; he might have produced fewer works, he said, had he revised more, but they would have been no better ([1883] 1950, 122). It is easy to think of similar oppositions on each scale—for example, the characteristically modern quarrel, on the scale of distance, between those we described in Chapter 3 who see extreme otherness as the mark of all good literature and innumerable "bourgeois" readers who have, throughout the modern period, damned new works because they were unlike previous works or unassimilable to traditional norms.

We need not choose between such extremes; each of them may express *a* genuine value in a given work. How could we know without looking? If Pound had said something like "*One* great gift a poet can give us is the creation of a single radiantly just image," he would have left us room to say, in reply, that "*another* great gift is a copious flow of interesting stories like Trollope's, with nary a radiant image through novel after novel." [10]

Those who seem to argue for one extreme or another never in fact exhibit unlimited tolerance of genuine extremes. Too much always turns out to be too much. We can always discern, on any scale, kinds of excess that for most readers will destroy a proffered gift. In short, as we now take a closer look at each of the seven invitations to active experience, we can see them as "spectrums of quality" on which every reader will discover some preferred mean. The mean itself may be broad in range: different readers will locate it at different points on the scale. But every reader will reject a narrative friend who goes "too far"

---

10. A defender of Pound might reply: "You are confusing fiction and poetry. Fiction can get along, sometimes, without Pound's kind of concentrated image. Poetry cannot." But in ethical criticism, the mere distinction between poetry and fiction—I must repeat—does not tell us all that much of interest. Besides, Pound himself obviously could not live for long by his dictum about the search for the single right image.

in any one direction. And every reader will by implication embrace a mean that *as a literary effect* cannot be "too much." Just as Aristotle insists that we cannot have too much tragic effect, though success in tragedy depends on striking a mean in all the elements that go into tragedy, so we can say that every reader will want unlimited success of one type or another, success depending on the presence of just enough but not too much of a given kind of activity.

If I am right in this claim—and it is important to see that it is a radical claim, one that again challenges directly all those who pretend to be infinitely accommodating, ideally "open"—we will have discovered one further way (building beyond Chapter 4) in which ethical critics can indeed talk not just about their preferences but about "the narrative itself." In sharing *descriptions* of narrative experience we can always clarify and sometimes simultaneously refine our coductions of value. Thus we come to explain what we halfway discover in experience: we do have grounds for pursuing our natural temptation to debate about ethical qualities.

Quantity / Concision

The simplest and most obvious variable is the sheer amount of activity a narrative invites us to engage in, whether overall or line-by-line. Obviously, as I said in Chapter 4, the author who offers me an eight-hundred-page conversation offers more—again, "other things being equal"—than the author who invites me, in a short story, to a ten-minute chat. But just as obviously, a short story may in fact hold me longer and offer me more, through sheer concentrated packing, than some bloated monster that I care to read at most only once, at breakneck speed.

Still, we do distinguish, in a rough way, works that "have a lot to say" from those that charm us for a few moments or hours and then go silent. At one extreme we find *Finnegans Wake* and *Remembrance of Things Past*, those immense encyclopedias of inexhaustible experience. For most of us, such works are more impressive in their sheer magnitude than in any of their parts; it is not only that they are more than the sum of their parts but that the sheer sum is itself awe-inspiring. For some readers, however, such works fall off the chart—over the edge into "too-muchness."

It is always difficult to distinguish such judgments of quantity from other measures: too much of *what?* Most critics have agreed that Dorothy Richardson gave us "too much" in her twelve-volume journal-novel, *Pilgrimage,* but their complaints always seem to be that she gave too much of what was not quite good enough taken even in small doses.[11] Still, every reader will have an intuitive sense that there is *some* upper limit of quantity: as Aristotle says, making a similar point about the outer boundaries in the "magnitude of a plot," beyond a certain quantity our perceptive apparatus and our memory (and finally our tolerance) simply fail (*Poetics* 7.8–10). At the other extreme, it is easy to find, or to make up, "literary works" that offer so little as to be beneath contempt:

> Sheer quantity of pleasure
> Is no decisive measure.

Short of this extreme, most readers find a highly limited offering in the carefully rhymed "poems" that grace greeting cards, or, moving up the scale a bit, the short stories of O. Henry. On up the scale a bit more, at least for many of us, would be the still quite slender offerings of our favorite detective puzzlers. I have just read a fine one, *The [. . .] Boy,* by Michael Innis. It gripped me from the beginning, keeping me focused on a small number of pertinent facts and tantalized by a fair number of impertinent ones, and it invited me to concentrate on the task of sorting out the two in order to arrive, at the end, at an unambiguous resolution of every problem in a comfortably simplified world. My work was fairly intense (scale 4), but when I ask what I was invited to do, in reading a book with a title that I have already forgotten (and will need to look up), the answer is something like this: "To work on one puzzle for several hours, only to arrive at a solution that no longer interests me." Only a special kind of reader, importing interests not insisted upon by the work itself, will ever be tempted to go on unpacking the secrets of a particular mystery after the first reading. And only an especially well-made mystery can support even for an hour such

11. "The long trainload [of Richardson's novels] draws by our platform, passes us with an inimical flash of female eyes, and proceeds on into how many more dry and gritty years. . . . Who could have foreseen in those first ordinary phrases this gigantic work which has now reached its two thousandth page, without any indication of a close?"—thus Graham Greene (1983, 114–15) on *Pilgrimage.*

continued demands for more reward. Yet every mystery addict knows that such undemanding works can lead us to return again and again to their *authors,* saying "Tell me another." And some readers apparently even enjoy re-reading the same mysteries. The friendship endures, even though each visit is relatively slack: I shall no doubt read another "Innis" or two some day.[12]

The measure of quantity seems to be applicable even when we appraise the major authors. Though there may be some authors, like Flannery O'Connor, whose short stories outshine their longer efforts, we would as a rule more readily leave behind (given the "desert island" choice) the shortest works, precious as some may be, and take along the more ambitious achievements that the authors themselves "put more into." My world is enriched more, at least potentially, by the lifelong, monumental offerings of a James or a Faulkner, a Frost or a Stevens, a Ben Jonson or a Molière, than it would be by—let us make the test case really challenging—any one play by Shakespeare, if he had written only one. "Other things being equal," we feel most gratitude to the friend who offers us most.

Reciprocity / Hierarchy

There is a sharp difference between authors who imply that we readers are essentially their equals in the imaginative enterprise, because we are embarked on the same quest, and those who suggest that we are either their inferiors or their superiors or that our path must be entirely different from theirs. Sterne's Tristram Shandy says that the

12. Looking forward for a moment to the consequentialist talk we have postponed, we can see that addictions to "small-activity" friendships—to what is called escape literature—are among the most common of all consequences of "becoming a reader." In themselves they appear harmless enough, but when we place them up against some of the other criteria we are coming to, they can appear as destructive, ethically, as other addictions. Could we not say that even an addiction to a Shakespeare, if it excluded all or most other forms of narrative, would be potentially disastrous? With such an outlandish question we see how the metaphor of friendship brings into critical talk questions that have long been debated within fictions themselves: Can there be any friend, any love, so incalculably valuable as to justify sacrificing "all else"? Is one ever justified in giving "all for love (of literature)," as some educational programs have implicitly suggested? For what literary Cleopatra should I be willing to lose my soul?

"truest respect which you can pay to the reader's understanding, is to halve this matter amicably, and leave him something to imagine, in his turn, as well as yourself" (1761, bk. 2, ch. 11). "But *easy writing's* vile *hard reading*"—Sheridan's *mot* is clearly a judgment against authors who don't do their fair share ([1819] 1928, 3: 117). But what is a fair share? Can we say any more than that there must be some sort of mean between the utterly passive "excitement" of watching the little surreptitious "plots" provided by TV game shows and the impossible levels of reconstruction demanded by some passages in *Finnegans Wake?*[13]

Whatever our final judgment on those friends who look down on us or treat us as equals, we can discern here again a useful scale of description, ranging from extremes of inequality that everyone would reject (the author tyrannical, bossy, preachy; the reader placed as underling or passive receptacle); through a broad range of works that imply our potential equality with authors who expect and require a full recreative activity comparable to their own; on to authors who debase themselves by implying that the reader is as well or better qualified to do the work—authors we think of as lazy or incompetent (or, when the inferiority is merely a pretense to please a patron, as sycophants, flatterers, or hacks). Somewhat short of the extreme of intolerable arrogance, we find authors like Milton, Joyce, George Eliot, and Tolstoy, who meet us as teachers, gurus, learned geniuses, implying that they are so far ahead of us, in their grasp both of the work and of the life it reflects, that we may never become their equals in energy, invention, learning, or wisdom. Though they may also imply that our creative activity should ultimately become like theirs, we remain their pupils. A more comradely group—good companions like Dickens, Trollope, John Betjeman, Ogden Nash, Arnold Bennett, and most best-sellers—labor to imply a relation among equals; we readers are essentially no different from the author. Our present dependence on their genius is somehow only temporary: we are inspired to believe that we too could develop our gifts and write like that—and that to do so would

---

13. I have discussed this point with some of you before, in *The Rhetoric of Fiction*, 301 n.26. And you have still not provided me with an answer to my question: Have I spotted a typo or not? Your silence provides clear evidence, if further evidence were needed, that some demands made by Joyce go beyond even *your* capacious limits. Let us all continue to try for complete honesty here. Or perhaps we should not. See pages 250–51 below.

be marvelous indeed. We strike a kind of bargain: we readers will make you rich and famous, asking only that you treat us like one of your own kind.

I can think of no convincing examples at the opposite extreme: authors who *ask* to be seen as contemptible. A full puppy-like abasement was indeed implied by many a dedication to patrons in earlier centuries: "You, my noble reader, are begged to accept the poor concoction of your humble servant." But every author we care about abandons that pose once the fiction is underway. It is true that many a *narrator* professes an unlimited self-loathing: "Just look, O reader, at how low a man can sink" (Dostoevsky's *Notes from Underground*, Céline's *Journey to the End of the Night*, Martin Amis's *Money*). But only the most inexperienced of readers fail to see that such authors intend a gulf between themselves and the slobs and fools they portray. The very act of writing and publishing a story is a gesture that raises one's self-image above the muck.

We readers, on the other hand, often find ourselves in the company of those who, regardless of their intentions, strike us as inferiors. The flesh-and-blood hacks who feed the insatiable demand for more TV dramas, more Harlequin romances, more fantasy lives for *People* magazine, often report that they look down on the authors their works imply and their actual readers. But if they have any skill at all they do not allow that contempt to show overtly within the stories. Perhaps this distance between hack writer and implied author accounts for the broad tolerance most of us exercise: we can read Milton one hour and Agatha Christie or even Louis L'Amour the next, and turn then again to Dante or Homer. Still, we all resist whenever an author goes "too far": proud or distant or difficult becomes "pretentious"; too casual or chummy or loaded with flattery becomes "self-abasing."

Obviously the scale of reciprocity overlaps with the scale of quantity: some story-tellers do all the work and leave us simply as passive receptacles. Authors of murder mysteries often testify to immense labor designed to deceive us: weeks and months spent building a puzzle that we will never spend longer than a few hours on, as we follow, more or less energetically while the knots are tied and untied. It is as if they were our servants, hired to entertain us for an hour, with no expectation that we would ever invite them to come live with us and be our loves.

In contrast, our fullest friendships on this scale are with those who seem wholly engaged in the same kind of significant activity that they expect of us. Usually in the past such activity has included that most important of all "reading" challenges, the interpretation of moral character. Most of the great stories show characters of a moral quality roughly equal to that of the implied reader (or, as Aristotle says in dealing with tragedy, somewhat "better" but not too much better than ourselves [*Poetics* 15.9–11]); the plots are built out of the characters' efforts to face moral choices. In tracing those efforts, we readers stretch our own capacities for thinking about how life should be lived, as we join those more elevated judges, the implied authors. We cannot quite consider ourselves *their* equals: they are more skillful than we at providing such exercises in moral discernment. But they imply that we might become their equals in discernment if we only practiced long enough.

Jane Austen, one of the greatest of these potential "equals," always invites us to rise to precisely her own masterful level of inference about moral relations. She presents the signs of moral and intellectual strength and weakness; we make a stab at the correct inferences; she then gently corrects our misreadings, both with her authorial commentary and with the progress of her plots. In Chapter 13 we shall look more closely at how she produces these effects.

Intimacy / Cool Reserve

A third variable is the depth of psychic "entry" to which our friends invite us. Just as real friends who offer magnificent helpings of intensely gripping, reciprocally shared conversation can still vary widely in the degree to which we are allowed into their inner lives, so implied authors obviously vary in their willingness to let down barriers and allow full entry.

There are, however, two radically different kinds of intimacy. The modern kind—a seemingly full sharing of intimate thoughts and feelings—has been discussed in hundreds of critical works on stream of consciousness, point of view, the psychological novel, and confessional poetry. Less widely noticed is the peculiarly intimate bonding achieved by authors, ancient or modern, whenever they use figures of speech skillfully. Stream of consciousness techniques give the illusion of entering the soul of the real author. Figures of speech give not the illusion but the reality: maker and receiver can become in many respects identical, as Poulet stressed for us (pp. 139–40 above).

We can see this at work in a famous piece of complex irony, spoken by the radically unreliable narrator of Jonathan Swift's *A Tale of a Tub:*

> Last Week I saw a Woman *flay'd,* and you will hardly believe, how much it altered her Person for the worse.

> ([1704] 1973, 352)

The invitation to concentrated, intimately shared activity by this one-sentence "story," this sly friend, could not be stronger.[14] Reading it alone, even without any specific context, we can "know" a great deal about the inner workings of Swift's mind. If I accept my assignment as implied reader, I must perform at least the following activities, leading to my final surprisingly confident communion with the seemingly devious mind of this author:

- □ I must decide that the statement is outlandish as it stands.

- □ To do so I must consult my own standards about flaying people alive, and about the proper tone for talking of such matters. I conclude that this tone clearly hints at pathologically skewed norms. (How could it *not* alter her appearance most horribly?)

- □ I must therefore conclude that the implied author cannot mean it as it stands; his mind is like mine in this respect at least. The other leading possibility is that Swift himself has gone over the edge into madness (a possibility that later critics have taken as the best explanation of what happened to Swift a few decades later).

- □ Rejecting madness as incompatible with the rest of the text, I must then wonder a bit about what he might mean by the ironic thrust. My move here is not identical with his: he presumably knows what he intends; I must wonder.

- □ I decide that he is surely as much against flaying as I am; otherwise the jest would not work, but the jest cannot be his only point.

- □ I must decide whether he wants me to believe that either he (or his

14. This is my second try on this wonderful bit, but I'm not providing the citation that would enable you to compare it with the first.

narrator) truly saw a live flaying last week or made up the fiction for his purposes.

☐ I decide that he made it up, but I must both accept and reject the fiction that the narrator (the "projector"), unlike my friend the implied author, saw that flayed woman.

☐ I then speculate about the relation between the projector and the implied Swift, making use of other ironies from the *Tale*, many of them equally condensed and intimate. In this again I am not quite identical with Swift, but we share the intimacy of his leading and my following in the dance.

☐ I then speculate, as he intended, about how surface appearance and reality are related.

And so on. It would take more steps than these simply to describe what my companion, the implied Swift, requires me to do if I am to join him. We thus have a great quantity of activity, with an inferred total reciprocity and intimacy: his mind works, I infer, much as mine does—only better.

Metaphor is similar in its invitation to intimacy.

> Tho' Mr. *Blifil* was not of the Complexion of *Jones*, nor ready to eat every Woman he saw, yet he was far from being destitute of that Appetite which is said to be the common Property of all Animals. With this, he had like-wise distinguishing Taste, which serves to direct Men in their Choice of the Objects, or Food of their several Appetites; and this taught him to consider *Sophia* as a most delicious Morsel.
>
> (Fielding [1749] 1975, bk. 7, ch. 6)

The view of the relations among Blifil, Tom Jones, and Sophia is here shallow indeed. But our relation to Fielding is not. When he compares sexual desire to appetite, we are absolutely privy to his (that is, the implied author's) mind; his thoughts on the subject and our thoughts are identical, so long as we dwell with that metaphor.

More complex metaphors produce even more remarkable intimacies. "Take physic, pomp," Lear cries on the heath:

> Expose thyself to feel what wretches feel,
> That thou mayst shake the superflux to them
> And show the heavens more just.
>
> (3.4.33–36)

We obediently perform with Shakespeare an intricate dance of interpretation, first recognizing that neither "physic" nor "pomp" can be read literally, then performing daring feats of translation, trying our best to imagine what sort of shaking and what kind of superflux Lear and the "absent" Shakespeare have in mind. All the while we are adding to our picture of Lear's character—his suffering soul. Looking more closely, we see that Lear must really be talking about laxatives and purgations: that superflux is not just the superfluities of wealth but the curative flux produced by the right laxative, and our picture of the Lear who has shown himself increasingly obscene and scatological in his rising desperation is intensified, just as our bonding with "Shakespeare" is increased (on the bonding produced by metaphor, see Cohen 1978; Booth 1974).

It is important to note once again, pending further exploration in Chapter 10, that none of this bonding can be dodged by a simple act of will. Once I have read "Take physic, pomp," I can no more resist picturing wealth as feces, provided I see what the words mean and have been following the play, than a mason who knows how to do corbels can resist seeing a corbel when one is present. No matter how strongly I might object to having my mind turned to compare the flow of wealth to flowing feces, the command issued by the metaphor will have been obeyed even as I understand it. A part of my mind has thus been shaped into an intense active discussion about the gross parallels between taking physic and curing pomp's indifference to poverty and suffering.

We see here a breakdown of the sharp distinction between implied readers and "real" readers. Any ironic or metaphoric shaping required of me as I play the role of implied reader will become *mine* insofar as I genuinely engage with the text; I may repudiate it later, but for now it has become a part of me. Whether the gift offered by this would-be friend is nourishing or poisonous, I have already imbibed. And the same curious circularity will apply, though often with less intensity, to the remaining four measures (and resulting pleasures).

In both these kinds of intimacy, that of psychological depth and that of figurative bonding, we again see a scale of possible appraisal. Too much intimacy, and we feel exploited, as in those modern narratives, sometimes purporting to be entirely fictional, that exploit the family secrets along with the inner turmoil and suffering of the author—autobiographical accounts like Christina Crawford's *Mommie Dearest* and novels like Nora Ephron's *Heartburn*. Too little, and we judge an author to be cold, "distant," "unimaginative." A story that provides no intimacy whatever, either with dramatized characters or with the implied author, simply will fail as story, though as a piece of something else (prose? speculation? verbal play? information?) it might provide enough rewards to keep some of us reading. One sees many bad examples in program notes for operas; the mere facts are recounted, with all qualities of character expunged: "Lulu then shoots Dr. Schön." Even blander are the non-stories that appear in my newspaper each week as "What Happened on the Soaps"; reading the skeletal summaries, with no awareness of who Sally, George, and Rebecca might be, I simply—stop reading. Obituaries of strangers, unless they are written with unusual flair, often sound almost satirically distant. Thus it is impossible to give any example here that I could expect many of my readers might share: though each of us will have a private collection, no stories that are generally found weak in this way will have won a broad audience.

Intensity / Slack "Charm"

This scale is perhaps most difficult to illustrate, because it refers to the degree of readers' engagement with a given story—the ease with which they can be torn away from it. One of the supreme rewards of fictional experience, at certain times of life, is its capacity to carry us away from all awareness of our "actual" world into a world of the imagination, and thus to free us, for a few moments or hours, from thinking about the evils of the day. It is hard to say whether this intensity of abandonment is itself subject to judgments of excess: perhaps it is like the classical "virtues" courage, wisdom, justice and temperance. You can't have too much of any of them: one cannot be "too courageous," only "rash." One might argue that you cannot have too much intense engagement with a given fiction, unless it is judged to be harmful in some other respect.

On the other hand, it is easy to see how stories fail through a lack of intensity. About the closest we can come to total indifference might be the joke or anecdote in which no characters are realized, no moral

questions raised, and no engaging "instabilities" introduced. I've been
reading in a little anthology, *The Oxford Book of Literary Anecdotes;*
the "complete" stories are usually about half a page or less, and I read
one here, one there, as the days go by. I never read for longer than ten
minutes at a time. Yet I have gone on reading *in* the book, because the
anecdotes are mostly quite good at filling the odd ten-minute period
with something worth having: mere anecdotal pleasure. The implied
author of the whole (the editor, James Sutherland) has, as an en-
tertainer, earned my respect and thus my engagement as a reader. Yet
almost anything can distract me from that book—rich in quantity,
positively buddy-buddy on the scale of reciprocity, often almost embarrassing in the matter of intimacy, it thus illustrates about the lowest
possible intensity of engagement with narrative.

Note that to reach that almost frigid state I have had to describe no
connected narrative at all but a loose collection. As soon as even the
simplest sustained story emerges, the reader is required to get moving
on some constructive activity that increases intensity. Put another way,
every story offers us the pleasure of imagining characters and events in
some world not exactly our own, of wondering how those events will
turn out, and of concluding that somehow they have hung together.
We are so determined to have this pleasure that we will try to find it
even where it is not offered. We treat "formless" stories just as we treat
the generally *un*storied world that meets us daily: we turn it into
meaning-ridden story. Psychologists have found not only that everybody can discern engaging narratives in the entirely plotless Thematic
Apperception Test but that all of us spontaneously make narratives out
of just about every bit of information that comes our way. We long for
intense engagement in a story, and we long for a coherent story of our
own lives.

Our next lowest level of engagement is perhaps what we saw in the
versions of Aesop's fable, in Chapter 5. The listener simply follows a
story line about a nondescript greedy farmer, a goose that inexplicably
lays golden eggs, and a single pure motive leading to a single neat but
bland moral. Intensity can be added to any such tale by any device that
draws the listener's imagination into active reconstruction or into active caring about consequences. But as my revisions revealed, intensity
can be sacrificed with additions that increase quantity and range of ac-

tivity, deflecting attention from any one instability. Thickets and mazes can discourage "page-turning" as effectively as vast empty object-free plains.

Tight Coherence / Explosive Disunity

So closely related to intensity as to be often indistinguishable from it is the scale of internal harmony—what used to be called decorum. Some works exhibit deep contradictions from moment to moment and ask us to accept them as an essential part of sincere or authentic narrative; others seem harmonious and ask us to reassemble and embrace unities. Some authors revel in the freedom of self-contradiction, and when they revel persuasively (with a different kind of coherence?), we all seem to love them for it. At least they provide us with quotations useful in self-defense when we are caught in glaring inconsistencies: "A foolish consistency is the hobgoblin of little minds" (Emerson); "Do I contradict myself? / Very well then I contradict myself, / I am large, I contain multitudes" (Whitman). Other authors, like Henry James and most lyric poets before this century, work very hard to create harmonious vibrations that they know belie the complexities of their lives outside their artificially unified narratives. Similarly, some literary critics place a high value on coherence or unity or consistency; others, like the post-moderns I quoted in Chapter 2, carry the romantic love of fragments and ruins to the extreme of deploring all unities as factitious, artificial—essentially fragile disguises for a deeper (and often more admirable) disharmony. Others still, like the New Critics, have seen the test of great art as its capacity to embrace disharmonies and recompose them (Brooks 1951).

In practice, all of us find that we reject extremes at either end of the scale—as *we* view the scale. The most passionate partisans of unity—those, for example, who regularized Henry James's inspired quest for an artistic fiction into a rule-bound use of point of view—will find limits to their interest in a unity imposed at the cost of variety and tension; and the most aggressive deconstructionists show no interest whatever in telephone books or fully stochastic writing. What we all admire (though the details of our admiration vary tremendously) are works that are either consistent with themselves, and thus in some sense unified, or works that acknowledge their own inconsistencies and thus reflect a genuine encounter with recalcitrant materials.

Otherness / Familiarity

A sixth scale, the degree of distance or "otherness," can alter our response to all those we have discussed so far. We are always to some degree aware that the pleasure or profit an author offers is strange or familiar, threatening as something radically "other" or reassuring as something already known or tamed. An author demanding a great quantity of unfamiliar work from a reader is a very different kind of friend from an author who gives us a lot of what we already have and love. For some ethical critics, no fictions are worth bothering about if they do not stagger us, shatter our complacencies, open up new worlds, change us from what we were, teach us new (and often dark) truths, shock our technical expectations: Make it new![15] For others, all good literature should "enhance life," "console us for our losses," "make the world habitable," create beauty where before was ugliness, restore lost harmonies. Proust gently mocks the "great author," Bergotte, as someone who simply goes too far in his pursuit of the harmonious: " [T]he word that always came to his lips when he wished to praise the style of any writer was 'mild.' . . . He said the word like a doctor who, when his patient assures him that milk will give him indigestion, answers, 'But, you know, it's very "mild."'" And it is true that there was in Bergotte's style a kind of harmony similar to that for which the ancients used to praise certain of their orators in terms which we now find it hard to understand" (1934, 424).

I shall not repeat here my arguments of Chapter 3: total otherness, whatever that might be, would be unintelligible and in consequence totally uninteresting. At the other end of the scale, total familiarity would yield total boredom.

The real distinctions of quality are found in kinds of otherness and

---

15. You ask me to name names? Rather ask me to name any modern critic who has *not* at one time or another announced this as the standard!

kinds of familiarity. They are found finally not in how strange or "de-familiarized" the surface or "content" is but rather in what the reader is likely to learn about *ways of dealing with* the unfamiliar or the threatening. Many a fiction that on its surface may seem too cozily familiar is in fact a source of insight into how to embrace otherness, and many a fiction that on its surface boasts about its originality and power to shock in fact demonstrates habits of contempt for all but one kind of friend. Even more deceptively, many a critic who claims to be defending traditional virtues is in fact implicitly excluding most of the human race, while many who claim to celebrate originality and open-ness are in fact closed to all but an elite band of right-thinking and predictable self-congratulators. It is not the degree of otherness that distinguishes fiction of the highest ethical kind but the depth of educa-tion it yields in *dealing with* the "other."

Breadth of Range / Concentration

Finally, fictions differ radically in the scope of the worlds they offer us. We can often find additional insight about the worth of stories by considering kinds and ranges of interest: we have limits of the too broad ("unfocused," "rambling," "pretentious") and too narrow ("trivial," "obsessed," "dogmatic," "tendentious").[16]

We might distinguish these limits according to the traditional triad: aesthetic, cognitive, and moral—beauty, truth, and goodness—with each of the three offering innumerable possibilities to story-tellers. If reading a story were simply a collection of moments, as it is not, we could say that some authors offer us mainly rich *imaginative* or *aes-thetic* moments of reconstruction (Virginia Woolf, say); some engage us primarily in active *thought* about the truth of things (Thomas Mann, perhaps); some emphasize practical questions and choices (John Bunyan, Swift, Orwell); and some (Shakespeare, Dickens, Dostoevsky, Homer, Joyce) cover the whole range.

16. I come to a full treatment of comparative "worlds" only in Chapter 11. For a highly original use of the notion that our imaginative worlds vary in size, see Elaine Scarry, *The Body in Pain* (1985).

Most of us cannot help being impressed by these latter giants, great voracious masters of comprehensive worlds—that is mainly what has made them into "classics." We cannot even here, however, form simple equations between a kind of offer and ethical judgment. To be impressed by someone is not necessarily to find a friend. You may overwhelm me with the range of your proffered gifts and leave me gasping for air. In these times of frank confession, one reads many a complaint about "boring classics."[17] Such complaints would formerly have been taken as simple signs of the complainer's inadequacies—"If *you* were intellectually sound, you would necessarily not only be impressed by the *range* of the works I love; you would love them too."

But obviously the classic that has exposed my limitations by boring me has, nevertheless, bored me: it has failed to turn itself, in my hands, into a *narrative*, a *story*, an engagement pulling me from here to there. It has therefore failed of all ethical effect—except perhaps the negative one of making me less inclined to undertake another "classic." You may look at my rejections and blame me for them. But how are you to convince me that your preferences, on any of the seven scales, are superior to mine?

To ask again this question that has nagged at us throughout is to ask for a detailed look at what it means ethically to follow story, to accept and pursue a pattern of desires imposed by an "other." Can we use the vocabulary of friendship to appraise the patterns of desire that narratives ask us to share?

REFERENCES

Abel, Elizabeth. "(E)merging Identities: The Dynamics of Female Friendship in Contemporary Fiction by Women." *Signs* 6 (Spr. 1981): 413–35.
Adams, William Davenport. *Famous Books: Sketches in the Highways and Byeways of English Literature.* London, 1875.
Aristotle. *Poetics.* Trans. W. H. Fyfe. Loeb Classical Library. London, 1927.
———. *The Nicomachean Ethics.* Trans. W. D. Ross. *The Student's Aristotle.* Vol. 5, 1155a. Oxford, 1942.
Bartlett, John, comp. *Familiar Quotations.* Ed. Christopher Morley. 11th ed. New York, 1944.

17. I remember seeing a review of a whole coffee-table book on the subject not long ago—a rather strange enterprise, when you come to think about it.

Bayne, Peter. *Lessons from My Masters: Carlyle, Tennyson, and Ruskin.* London, 1879.

Beerbohm, Max. "A Defence of Cosmetics" [1894]. In *The Yellow Book: A Selection.* Ed. Norman Denny. London, 1950.

Block, Joel D. *Friendship: How to Give It, How to Get It.* New York, 1980.

Booth, Wayne C. *A Rhetoric of Irony.* Chicago, 1974.

———. *The Rhetoric of Fiction* [1961]. 2d ed. Chicago, 1983.

Bradbury, Malcolm. *Rates of Exchange.* New York, 1983.

Brain, Robert. *Friends and Lovers.* London, 1976.

Brooks, Cleanth. "Irony as a Principle of Structure." In *Literary Opinion in America.* Ed. Morton Dauwen Zabel. New York, 1951.

Carpenter, Edward, ed. *Ioläus: An Anthology of Friendship.* Boston, 1902.

Channing, William Ellery. "Self-Culture" [1838]. In *The Works of William Ellery Channing.* Boston, 1881.

Cicero. *Laelius De Amicitia.* Trans. William Armistead Falconer. Loeb Classical Library. London, 1923.

———. "On Friendship." In *"On Old Age" and "On Friendship."* Trans. Frank O. Copley. Ann Arbor, Mich., 1967.

Cohen, Ted. "Metaphor and the Cultivation of Intimacy." *Critical Inquiry* 5 (Aut. 1978): 3–12.

Crawford, Christina. *Mommie Dearest.* New York, 1978.

Emerson, Ralph Waldo. "Friendship" [1841]. In *Essays: First Series.* Vol. 2 of *The Collected Works of Ralph Waldo Emerson.* Ed. Joseph Slater et al. Cambridge, Mass., 1979.

Encyclopaedia Britannica. 4th ed. Edinburgh, 1810. s.v. "friendship."

Encyclopedia of Philosophy. Ed. Paul Edwards. 4 vols. New York, 1967.

Ephron, Nora. *Heartburn.* New York, 1983.

Fielding, Henry. *The History of Tom Jones, A Foundling* [1749]. Ed. Fredson Bowers. Oxford, London, 1975.

Froula, Christine. "When Eve Reads Milton: Undoing the Canonical Economy." *Critical Inquiry* 10 (Dec. 1983): 321–47.

Greeley, Andrew M. *The Friendship Game.* New York, 1970.

Greene, Graham. "The Saratoga Trunk" [1938]. In *Collected Essays* [1969]. New York, 1983. 114–16.

Helps, Sir Arthur. *Friends in Council.* London, 1847–59.

Hunt, Leigh. "My Books." Pts. 1, 2. *Literary Examiner* (July 5, July 12, 1823): 1–16, 17–32.

Hyde, Lewis. *The Gift: Imagination and the Erotic Life of Property.* New York, 1983.

Innis, Michael. *The Journeying Boy.* New York, 1983.

Lang, Andrew. *Letters to Dead Authors.* London, 1886.

Larmore, Charles E. *Patterns of Moral Complexity.* New York, 1987.

Lawrence, D. H. *Lady Chatterley's Lover* [1928]. New York, 1983.

LeGuin, Ursula K. *The Word for World Is Forest.* New York, 1976. (Originally in *Again, Dangerous Visions.* Ed. Harlan Ellison. 2 vols. New York, 1972.)

Lipking, Lawrence. "The Dialectic of *Il Cortegiana* [The Courtier]." *PMLA* 81 (Oct. 1966): 355–62.

Marty, Martin E. *Friendship.* Allen, Tex., 1980.

Maurice, John Frederick Denison. *"The Friendship of Books" and Other Lectures*. Ed. T. Hughes. 3d ed. London, 1880.

Meilaender, Gilbert C. *Friendship: A Study in Theological Ethics*. Notre Dame, Ind., 1981.

Montaigne, Michel Eyquem de. "Of Friendship" [1574]. In *The Complete Essays of Montaigne*. Trans. Donald M. Frame. 3d ed. Stanford, Calif., 1967. 135–44.

Pound, Ezra. "A Few Don'ts" [1913]. In *Literary Essays of Ezra Pound*. Ed. T. S. Eliot. London, 1985. 4.

Proust, Marcel. *Remembrance of Things Past*. Trans. C. K. Scott Moncrieff. New York, 1934.

Rubin, Lillian B. *Just Friends: The Role of Friendship in Our Lives*. New York, 1985.

Scarry, Elaine. *The Body in Pain: The Making and Unmaking of the World*. New York, 1985.

Sharp, Ronald A. *Friendship and Literature: Spirit and Form*. Durham, N.C., 1986. (Relatively full bibliography on friendship.)

Sheridan, Richard Brinsley. "Clio's Protest" [1819]. In *The Plays and Poems of Sheridan*. Ed. R. Compton Rhodes. 3 vols. Oxford, 1928. 3: 107–18.

Soupault, Philippe. *L'Amitié: Notes et maximes*. Paris, 1965.

Sterne, Laurence. *Tristram Shandy*. London, 1761.

Strier, Richard. "Sanctifying the Aristocracy: Devout Humanism and Its Paradoxes in George Herbert and François de Sales." *Journal of Religion* (forthcoming).

Sutherland, James, ed. *The Oxford Book of Literary Anecdotes*. Oxford, 1975.

Swift, Jonathan. *A Tale of a Tub* [1704]. In *The Writings of Jonathan Swift*. Ed. Robert A. Greenberg and William Bowman Piper. New York, 1973.

Torrey, Bradford. *Friends on the Shelf*. Boston, 1906.

Trollope, Anthony. *An Autobiography* [1883]. New York, 1950.

Vaihinger, H. *The Philosophy of 'As If': A System of the Theoretical, Practical, and Religious Fictions of Mankind* [1927]. Trans. C. K. Ogden. 2d ed. London, 1935.

Wallace, John M. "*Timon of Athens* and the Three Graces: Shakespeare's Senecan Study." *Modern Philology* 83 (May 1986): 349–63.

Watts-Dunton, Theodore. *Old Familiar Faces*. London, 1916.

Weller, Barry. "The Rhetoric of Friendship in Montaigne's *Essais*." *New Literary History* 9 (Spr. 1978): 503–23.

7

These are the masters who instruct us without rods and ferules, without hard words and anger, without clothes or money. If you approach them, they are not asleep; if investigating, you interrogate them, they conceal nothing; if you mistake them, they never grumble; if you are ignorant, they cannot laugh at you.
Bishop Aungerville

Your classic author is the one you cannot feel indifferent to, who helps you to define yourself in relation to him, even in dispute with him.
Italo Calvino

It [*Heartburn*, by Nora Ephron] is absolutely the perfect book for the '80s. It is prurient. It obliterates everybody's dignity, even the little dignity that children ought to have by having a private childhood. . . . If I were to measure my life in those terms [as established in the novel], I'd spend the rest of it beating my head against the wall.
Carl Bernstein

[R]eading is a pact of generosity between author and reader. Each one trusts the other; each one counts on the other, demands of the other as much as he demands of himself. . . . There is then established a dialectical going-and-coming; when I read, I make demands; if my demands are met, what I am then reading provokes me to demand more of the author, which means to demand of the author that he demand more of me. And, vice versa, the author's demand is that I carry my demands to the highest pitch.
Jean-Paul Sartre

Appraising Some Friends

BECOMING "THAT KIND OF DESIRER"

The highest values on any one of the scales we have traced will be perceived only in a reading that genuinely "listens to the story." Whether a narrative offers only one kind of gift or many, the offer will not even be recognized unless the listener engages in the story *as* story, and that means engaging with the author in a patterning of desire for this kind of gift: for more and more of it, and finally for the right kind of rounding off—or, in one kind of story, "throwing open"—at the end.

Thus all stories have a practical dimension, just as all other friendships in life do. This point goes somewhat beyond our earlier claim that all narratives are in a sense didactic. We can now begin to see how *active* the didacticism is—and how wrong it is to regard it as a content conveyed by the form. Even the "purest," most aggressively "poetic," least moral tales, even the many recent invitations to gambol in the thin atmosphere of calculated formlessness, will work as stories, as something that leads-from-here-to-there, only if they make the reader "want more of this friendship"—that is, want to move forward, rapidly or slowly, from here to there, from beginning to ending, and then, sometimes, back again.

This means that the most powerful effect on my own ethos, at least during my reading, is the concentration of my desires and fears and expectations, leading with as much concentration as possible toward some further, some *future* fulfillment: I am made to want something that I do not yet have enough of. So long as I continue to read, my whole being is concentrated on "how it will all turn out," or on "what it will turn out to *be*." (We must rule out, in all of this, the reading we do under what course descriptions depressingly call Required Reading.)

Thus my activity, responding to appeals on one or more of the seven scales, is that of desiring certain future rewards, whether they consist of justice for characters in the story or of what we might call aesthetic justice—a satisfying completion of the form. We may not want to call this patterning of desires (by no means confined to narrowly moral domains) a practical effect, but it does have one obvious and inescapable effect on the reader's practice: it determines who he or she is to be for the duration of the experience. I can't think of anything more practical than that.

The focusing of our desires is perhaps clearest in adventure stories that threaten—or promise—disaster.[1] In the best-seller *Jaws,* for example,[2] I find this opening:

> The great fish moved silently through the night water, propelled by short sweeps of its crescent tail. The mouth was open just enough to permit a rush of water over the gills. . . . The eyes were sightless in the black, and the other senses transmitted nothing extraordinary to the small, primitive brain.
>
> (Benchley 1974)

If I choose to go on, I shall do so because I want more of this threat described in this special style, by a remarkable friend who is privy to the inner workings of a shark's brain. On page 2 I receive a further generous promise of horror ahead, along with related titillations, as a man and woman "fumbled with each other's clothing, twined limbs around limbs, and thrashed with urgent ardor on the cold sand."

> "Now, how about that swim?" she said.
> "You go ahead," he said. "I'll wait for you here."

Already I can hardly wait for the promised bloody encounter between such a primitive brain and such a sexy thrasher. But if I move on to enjoy that, I do not do so with the mere passive curiosity that keeps me browsing in that anthology of literary anecdotes. I am both fearing spectacular bloodshed and desiring it, enjoying the prospect of bloody

---

1. The focusing is equally sharp in pornography, not only the pornography of sex but the titillation of any physical sensation. Much television advertisement attempts, and with me sometimes succeeds, in producing stronger desire (for food, of course) than any but the most powerful adventure story could rival.

2. I realize that by now, 1988, this example, chosen in 1979 as I worked on the first draft of this section, is considerably outmoded. But surely you cannot expect me to recycle examples, year by year, as ethical criticism shifts under my gaze. How many thrillers must I spend my life not reading?

death for those who don't matter, hoping for (and fully expecting) final safety for the good guys (who don't matter much more) and learning—learning all the while—both that happiness for these characters is defined as escape from danger and that happiness for me is watching people fall into danger and then, sometimes, miraculously fall out of it.

I won't dwell on the other lessons I am learning—about what makes a good (that is, atrocious) literary style, about what makes a gripping narrative manner (at least for the "adventure" market), and so on. Though the *quantity* of activity is finally low, the *intensity* will be high indeed, if my buddy Benchley has his way with me. The *reciprocity* will be either non-existent or extremely high, depending on whether or not I suspect that Benchley himself is a cynical hack who is far from savoring the effects that he wishes onto me. *Intimacy* works the same way. If I assume that Benchley's mind really operates at this primitive level, and if I respond as he asks, we experience together an intimacy perhaps more intense than would occur in reading far superior works; our images are shared precisely, our thrills are identical. But if I am driven to infer a writer behind the author who is in fact off in another country, where the big bucks flow, I start laughing at the implied author he has tried to create: all intimacy disappears (unless we want to invent a new literary pleasure, that of laughing in intimacy with the real author at the fools who identify with the implied author).

But it is on the scales of otherness and range that this friend really lets me down. The range is extremely narrow—physical survival and physical pleasure are good; physical destruction or self-denial are bad. And whatever is really "other" is simply to be feared, not understood. Here *we* are, average, normal, comfortably familiar folks, and there *they* are, the threat. In short, my time with this friend so far[3] has been a narrowing time, a time of bifurcating my world into stereotyped victims and stereotyped, villainous "others." What had looked like a harmless bit of escape literature, useful for killing an hour or two with some excitement, appears in this view considerably more threatening

3. Two pages only!—surely in simple charity I should persist and give Benchley a fair chance. But after the sampling I do not really care about how the story will continue with its manipulations.

to the spirit than Benchley intended with his sharks. I am not thinking (yet) about consequences after the reading (a few nightmares about sharks, perhaps, and a bit more reluctance to jump into the surf to rescue a companion?), but of the "loss of life" as the pages are read. The story tries to mold me into its limited shapes, giving me practice, as it were, in wanting and fearing certain minimal qualities and ignoring all others. I am to become, if I enter this world, *that kind of desirer,* with precisely the kinds of strengths and weaknesses that the author has built into his structure. I am to do so, that is, unless I impose, as I am doing, some sort of ethical criticism.

No matter how high the quality or how "aesthetic" the goal, all stories will produce a practical patterning of desire, so long as I stay with them. And each pattern, in itself narrow as compared with all the other possible patterns, will imply that it is the best. Consider the invitations offered toward the other extremes of intensity and breadth by *Finnegans Wake*—another work that I have never quite "finished," though I suppose I have "read" all of the words at one time or another, some of them many times:

> riverrun, past Eve and Adam's, from swerve of shore to bend of bay, brings us by a commodius vicus of recirculation back to Howth Castle and Environs.
> Sir Tristram, violer d'amores, fr'over the short sea, had passencore rearrived from North Armorica on this side the scraggy isthmus of Europe Minor to wielderfight his penisolate war . . .

> (1959, 3)

Stopping after two paragraphs, I may, of course, choose not to read any more of this giant of a novel. But if I do go on, it will be because I desire more of "this," whatever this kind of companionship is. I shall be shaped by this friend just as much as I would be in reading *Jaws* (more, in fact, because of the sheer quantity of *Finnegans Wake*).[4] In short, the shaping of my desires will occur just as much when my reading is non-linear, recursive, broad in range, and threateningly "other" (as it has to be in *Wake*) as when the work I'm reading is (like *Jaws*),

---

4. We have one escape route only—to follow Vladimir Nabokov and refuse to read "Punningans Wake" in which "a cancerous growth of fancy word-tissue hardly redeems the dreadful joviality of the folklore and the easy, too easy, allegory." It is for him boring, like "all regional literature written in dialect" (1976, 103).

strictly sequential, maximally narrow in range, and so clichéd that no otherness can be tolerated except as enemy. Unless I am made to want *something*, I stop reading.

Notice again that in this one kind of activity, the journey toward a desired reward, the distinction between what the implied reader does and what the flesh-and-blood reader does becomes blurred. The implied reader I become cannot desire fictional blood without my desiring it. I cannot, as sophisticated reader, hope for Elizabeth Bennet's marriage to Darcy or fear Tess Durbeyfield's doom without *my* hoping and fearing for those things. The quality of the desire may be considerably different, *if* my "real" self sits back and says, "I don't really care a whit about Tess's chastity or about whether she finds a good husband; I don't even believe that Tess is real, so how could I really care about her fate?" But if I am engaged at all, my desires are focused precisely on what her fate will be—just as at the movies, watching a psychopathic killer at his daily chores, my heart will go on pounding and my palms sweating even after my equally anxious wife leans toward me and says, "Remember, it's only a movie." Intellectually, I never stop playing the double role that we dramatized in talking about "The Goose That Laid the Golden Egg," but the two roles overlap whenever I laugh, weep, sweat, or tremble.

There is a great difference between this kind of effect and the aftereffect of the examples set by a particular character explicitly shown within the work (the effect we turn to in Chapter 8): "Does Tess Durbeyfield provide a good model for our daughters?" "Would I want my daughter to base her picture of a proper husband on the knuckleheaded cads she will meet in most fiction?" My approach here changes such questions to a kind that to some people may sound equally crude: Does what Thomas Hardy asks you to desire and fear and deplore and expect in the life of *Tess of the D'Urbervilles* provide a good kind of life for you, or for your sons and daughters? Does that "slice of life" that critics used to talk about—meaning the slice *in* the book—turn out to be a good slice for you, as you re-create it for yourself? We postpone the question of whether it will prove carcinogenic in the long run, and think here only of the many hours that will be spent desiring Tess's happiness, fearing and increasingly expecting her tragic doom, sharing with the implied author his philosophy of why and how we are all doomed, and deploring the forces in life that ensure such doom.

To desire Tess's happiness, we must accept, of course, the implied picture that Hardy presents of what happiness would be for Tess: discovery of a man who, unlike Angel Clare and Alec (but very much like the implied Thomas Hardy), would appreciate her true quality, protect her from too much thinking about what the Parliament of the Gods foredooms us to, and yet provide her with reading experiences of the kind this novel provides. (That is the kind, be it said, that judges life rather simplistically by how our desires for the future turn out.) Putting our question in its bluntest form: Would you like your daughter to marry one, even for a few hours—not one of the characters but the implied Thomas Hardy, whose patterns of desire will have become hers while she reads?

When we thus view plot or form as active rhetoric—as the total patterning of the reader's desires and satisfactions (Burke 1953)—we see once again why the distinction between "genuine literature" ("poetry," "art") and didactic works does so little work for us here. The seven scales of activity apply as much to our reading of Mallarmé or Joyce as to our more "practical" reading of *1984* or *Atlas Shrugged*. To desire knowledge or information is as much a patterning of who we are, for the duration, as to desire bloody scenes with man-eating sharks. Our interest here is in how we are shaped, far more than in what any seeming spokesman for the author may do or say at particular moments. Obviously when we think in this way, some of the most piously intended, openly moralistic works will reveal themselves as ethically shoddy, and some works with aggressive surface teachings of "the wrong kind" might well prove, through the quality of the journey, ethically admirable.

SOME MIXTURES AND CONFLICTS OF MESSAGE AND PATTERN

Though the ethical critic will want to be able to talk about works like *Jaws* that approach a limit of worthlessness,[5] the interesting cases—

---

5. I don't suppose that even *Jaws* should be called worthless. For some readers it will be worse than that—positively harmful. But I can imagine a reader—or nonreader—to whom I might recommend the book, as an enticement into the joys of reading.

the fictions that, unlike *Jaws,* invite conversation that might itself prove ethically educational—are naturally those that present mixtures of value. As I turn now to further examples, I must repeat my claim, in the strongest possible terms, that the worth of any project in ethical criticism in no way depends on our ability to come to consensus on any one ethical appraisal or to produce a single harmonious scheme of narrative values. Of course, if any readers find that all my standards and readings seem absurd, we will have parted company long since. But the examples that follow are intended as conversational gambits, invitations to readers to say anything from "Nonsense!" through "Yes, but . . ." to "Absolutely!" In each of them I find some conflict between my opinion of the fixed norms, and the ethical impact of the total form.

Is it not obvious that only an impoverished kind of friendship is being offered when a story promises, by its title, to tell me a fictionalized version of the life story of a confessed murderer, recently executed; promises, by its hefted length (about a thousand pages), to occupy anything from ten to twenty hours of my life; and promises a tedious recounting of fact after fact, like this?

> Brenda was six when she fell out of the apple tree. She climbed to the top and the limb with the good apples broke off. Gary [the name of the murderer, known to every reader who has read the book-jacket copy] caught her as the branch came scraping down. They were scared. The apple trees were their grandmother's best crop and it was forbidden to climb in the orchard. She helped him drag away the tree limb and they hoped no one would notice. That was Brenda's earliest recollection of Gary.

Norman Mailer's *The Executioner's Song* (1979) proceeds pretty much like this throughout, observation after observation, seeming to ask little of me and to imply that the author himself did as little as possible beyond the bare minimum of the monumental secretarial task of transcribing the thousand pages of "what really happened": "That was Brenda's earliest recollection of Gary." The names are the real names of real people, the book calls itself "A True Life Novel." Mailer has obviously given himself every license to play with his material, and with his reader, with no consequences for himself: if I object to the work as fiction, he can blame his material; if I blame him for carelessness with the facts, he can argue that the book is after all fictional. The apparent casualness of his manner is striking, even when the events themselves produce intense engagement. Those who, like me, somehow "could not put the book down" must feel, on reflection, that such a friendship asks too little of us, line by line, as compared, say, with a novel that begins like this:

> While Pearl Tull was dying, a funny thought occurred to her. It twitched her lips and rustled her breath, and she felt her son lean forward from where he kept watch by her bed. "Get . . ." she told him. "You should have got . . ."
> You should have got an extra mother, was what she meant to say, the way we started extra children after the first child fell so ill.

Anne Tyler seems to offer here, in *Dinner at the Homesick Restaurant* (1982), a good deal more than Mailer does. Imagining herself into a situation she could hardly know at first hand,[6] one that involves two characters she has had to "make up," she immediately asks us to begin inferring the meaning, for character and event, of such a wrenching death wish. Instead of two clichéd kids (a known future murderer and his innocent companion feeling guilty about a broken tree branch), we have a puzzling wish, a promise of complexity, and of course a direct oath of office sworn by the implied author: "I shall imagine a complex world with you; I shall resist the easy way of simply reporting a world that you are to accept as actual without having to work much at it." It would seem that simply on the scales of quantity, reciprocity, and range, Tyler will prove to be the better friend.

But of course our choices are never that simple. For one thing, I have not begun to exhaust the invitations that each author provides in those openings. In re-reading Mailer's "simple" beginning, I can choose to slow down and think a bit about his intent in starting his story with the innocence of *apple* trees and guilty actions—ah, yes, this is the garden of Eden. *This* Gary, playfully guilty/innocent child, will become the killer Gary I know from news stories, and this "greatest chronicler of contemporary America," writing "the big book no one but Mailer

---

6. Note the technical similarity of entering a dying woman's mind here and entering a hungry shark's mind in *Jaws:* both are inaccessible to the artist, who nevertheless simply "leaps in." But the shark is by every standard considerably more alien. Why, then, does Tyler's move seem so much more impressive? I see no way of answering on technical or purely formal grounds—and I take that to be one kind of answer to those who think that formal analysis can tell us all we need to know. What yields Tyler's superiority to Benchley here is what we know or think we know about sharks and people.

could have dared[,] . . . an absolutely astonishing book" (as the jacket tells me, quoting Joan Didion)—this seemingly flat, loose-jointed, casual author, self-effacing in a manner uncharacteristic of Mailer, is surely up to tricks that I must think hard about.

And before I know it, other criteria come rushing to mind to complicate my ethical task. Did not Mailer manage to make me, on first reading, feel that the two of us were embarked on an important task together, reciprocally engaged in trying to understand gratuitous violence in America? Isn't his problem in itself more difficult to address productively, and therefore inherently more admirable, than the "sentimental" problems addressed by Tyler? And what about the scales of "otherness" and range? Mailer has taken upon himself to understand, and thus forgive, the unforgivable. If his results also seem somehow a bit sentimental—he forgives too easily, and manipulates the data too obviously to produce this easy forgiveness—still, he did undertake the big task. Surely someone who can keep me talking with him about such matters for a thousand pages cannot be dismissed lightly.

The fact remains that I never come to a point of trusting him as a friend. That is partly a matter of my disagreeing with some of his views about the kind of sympathy we should grant to Gary Gilmore. But it is even more my sense of an untroubled incoherence, and hence untrustworthiness, in this career author. I know much less about the "real" Tyler than I know about the public image "Norman Mailer," or about the career author I have met in reading most of his books. "My" Tyler's range and daring are much more limited than "my" Mailer's, but I feel that she is giving me everything she's got, and she cares a great deal about what will become of me as I read. My Mailer, in contrast, is simply playing games with me; he does not care a hill of beans for my welfare—he would obviously be happy to sacrifice me and any other reader to further his own ends. This does not mean that he is not worth talking to—but it may mean that I finally regret spending quite so long with him, when I might have been reading more of Anne Tyler.

Such talk will seem equivocal to those who would like to decide simply whether these authors are morally "good" or "bad." Yet if I am right, our ethical talk must in most cases be multi-dimensional in a way that will seem equivocal. I did not equivocate (much) about *Jaws*; but about any book that has held me for a thousand pages, challenging me (much of the time) to fresh thought about violence in America, I

cannot, should not, be decisively dismissive.[7] A flat rejection of any implied author should be undertaken no more lightly than a flat rejection
of a human being as a possible acquaintance. To appraise a complex
literary friend according to some single standard is critical bigotry.

In practice most of us balance one or another gift against this or
that deficiency: "I got a lot out of it, but at the end I felt . . ." "It
gripped me, but . . ." "I agree with its ideas, but still . . ." Nor should
we expect to find qualities that are desirable without limit. Each of the
individual virtues on any one scale will destroy a friendship if pushed
too far at the expense of others.

DESIRE TO BE TAUGHT

Though we have been obliquely talking about "didactic" effects all
the while, we can see the problem of complexities more clearly if we
turn now to look at works that more overtly offer to be useful. The
useful things that authors can lead us to pursue, as part of their patterns of desire, can range over every conceivable value. Narratives, fictional and reportorial, can offer to teach me how to get rich quick,
how to behave socially as if I were rich, what wines to serve on what
occasions, which modes of stroking or stabbing rivals are most effective in various situations. They can offer to teach me how to be courageous (as most epics do), how to think about power and suffering, how
moral decay can creep up on me against my will. Or they can just pass
on a lot of information, like those blockbusters by James Michener,
offering to teach me everything I ought to know about the settling of
the west, or about Texas, or Israel, or Poland.

Except for plain information, perhaps the most frequent offering—
often dismissed out of hand as a sure sign that a fiction is sub-literary—

---

7. For an unequivocal attack, see Griffin 1980. I have deliberately ruled out of my
discussion an additional motive I have for mistrusting "my" Mailer. I am from the area
of Utah in which his "novel" is set; I know how misleading some of his portraits of the
area and the people will be to readers who live elsewhere. And I fear the harm that his
book will do to many of those who are caricatured in it, including Gilmore's wife, children, and relatives. Though such objections make me think less of Mailer the man, they
are in large part irrelevant to my appraisal of the book as a narrative that I might recommend to one of my own friends.

is moral guidance. Almost all writers until quite recently have claimed
to teach virtue *while* giving pleasure. Anthony Trollope echoes thousands of such protestations, from the Greek and Roman satirists to the
present:

> I have always desired . . . to make men and women walk upon it [my stage]
> just as they do walk here among us . . . so that my readers might recognise
> human beings like to themselves. . . . If I could do this, then I thought
> I might succeed in impregnating the mind of the novel-reader with a feel-
> ing . . . that things meanly done are ugly and odious, and things nobly done
> beautiful and gracious. . . . I have ever thought of myself as a preacher of
> sermons, and my pulpit as one which I could make both salutary and
> agreeable to my audience.
>
> ([1883] 1950, 147–48)

Like many another modern reader, I have sometimes dismissed such
statements as obviously self-protective rationalizations—especially
when they were made by authors whose daring works invited attacks
by moralists: Swift on his scatological satires, Restoration dramatists
on their ribald comedies. No doubt when fashion dictates moral seriousness, authors will assert it of themselves whether they care about
it or not. We can thus never be sure just how much sincerity lies behind
any author's claim to write for our good.[8]

But it seems fair to say that the overwhelming predominance of
such claims, as testimony by "the experts," puts the burden of proof
on anyone who now wants to divorce poetry from the pleasures of
moral education: if genuine "literature" should be read as offering no
unequivocal advice about "real life" (Miller 1986, esp. 10–11, 127),
then centuries of informed witnesses have deliberately deceived us—or
they have been self-deceived.

---

8. Actually, I now see no reason whatever to question Trollope's claim, and the reasons for my near certainty are important. I have just finished reading his *The Way We
Live Now* (1875), most of it aloud with my best friend; it's a loose-jointed, long-winded
but powerful indictment of "the way they lived then," and it led both of us readers to a
lot of speculation about the way *we* live *now*. Trollope's moral intentions are clearly
visible in almost every scene. What's more, the characters and events, as dramatized, for
the most part bear out what his narrator chooses to say in his perceptive, acerbic commentary. If this is indeed a portrait of "the way we live now," we live now in ways that
deserve the moral questioning Trollope subjects them to. I finished the book quite unable to doubt his passionate commitment as "preacher," while still reserving some
doubts about certain similar claims by modern novelists like Jerzy Kosinski and William
Burroughs.

Fortunately our inquiry does not depend primarily on whether or not an author is sincere in professing to teach us well. Rather, we want to know whether reading his or her work offers to do for us something like what Igor Stravinsky once said that listening to Beethoven did for him: "Beethoven's Fourth Symphony nourishes the soul." How we talk about such a question will always require a delicate balancing of what the work *claims* to do for us and what our experience of its harmonies and discords teaches. And that experience will never be reducible to some autonomous, "intrinsic" form; it will always depend on what we bring to the tale—as readers we are in a sense the work's "context"—and it will sometimes depend on making explicit whatever can be known about the work's other contexts: what other readers in other times and climes were expected to bring (Rabinowitz 1988).

But it is now time to try our hand at some of that risky conversation. Here is the beginning of a poem called "Don't Quit—Fight One More Round":

> When things go wrong, as they often will,
> When the road you're trudging seems all uphill,
> When the funds are low and the debts are high
> And you want to smile, but you have to sigh,
> When care is pressing you down a bit,
> Rest! If you must—but never quit.

This little fiction concludes, two stanzas later: "It's when things seem worst that *you mustn't quit*."

Critics of just about every persuasion will dismiss this verse as beneath consideration. Some will say that it is not poetry at all, since it is so blatantly didactic. Some may object not to the presence of doctrine but to its banality: it is so un-"other" as to sound just like the greeting cards we riffle through on the rack, trying to find one not too embarrassingly feeble. Others might point to the flat diction or the absence of imagery: the poem exhibits insufficient craft to command our attention, let alone respect. But no one of these in itself would necessarily be fatal. Many a good poem suffers from trite thought (much of Robert Burns, some of Robert Frost, many of Shakespeare's sonnets); from flat diction (much of the best of Wordsworth, or C. K. Williams); from sparse or stale imagery (some of Philip Larkin). It is not the presence of any one deficiency that leaves us cold but the seeming absence of a single redeeming virtue.

But note that the author of "Don't Quit" does offer us one good thing: a piece of sound (though trite) advice. Surely even in our time, when the Impuritan Ethic is widely preached, we all would agree that to quit under adversity is usually bad. Surely anyone who reminds us of that is offering friendly advice. Though poems offering overt moral advice are unfashionable, there have been ages (classical Rome; medieval and eighteenth-century England) when first-class moralizing poetry flourished. Why, then, cannot we pluralists salvage "Don't Quit" as having one clear virtue, despite its obvious weaknesses?

The answer is found in considering the ethos of the author and the pattern of desire that he offers us. The one possible virtue the verse might provide—in its preachy lack of reciprocity, of intimacy, of intensity, of otherness, of range—would be a harmony of message and implied portrait. But this author is a character whose troubles—low funds, being "a bit" care-ridden, feeling like sighing rather than smiling—are not comparable to the major troubles that really tempt us to "quit." The responses he warns against don't sound like my responses to real trouble (a sense of trudging uphill, for example; *that* sounds like a bad day at the writing desk, not like the feeling after a death of a loved one or discovery of a major illness). What is worse, the troubles are not even convincingly his: his poem does not in any sense either illustrate or conform to his message. The rhymes are obvious and easy; "a bit" is clearly thrown in for the rhyme, though it spoils the sense. The meter is obvious and easy, with never a hint of difficulties risked and mastered. The diction is obvious and easy—monotonous, thoughtless (I "*have* to sigh"?). We see, then, that the "message" of the poem is not in the least irrelevant to our judgment: we consider that message, one that has an obvious truth, and we find an author whose many faults belie it at every turn.

I must now underline just how much our evaluation of the poem depends on the inferred ethos of the maker by telling you that in fact I am the maker: I made up the poem as a parody of the Eddie Guest type of verse. Some of you probably suspected that already, and you had already made up your minds about whether it is good parody or poor. But would you not grant that it is a far better poem as parody than as serious advice? At least all of its strokes are coherent, now that its real "advice" can be seen as "Don't write poems like this." The point is that whatever your judgment, it is now entirely different—though "about" precisely the same words on the page—from any judgment we have made of a serious (and seriously incoherent) author.

Now I must reverse myself again and renounce my confession, hoping that by repudiating my lie I can re-establish an ethos that a book like this depends on: I did *not* make up the poem. I found it in an anthology of poetry that I have since lost. I do not know the author, cannot acknowledge my debt, may risk a suit for literary theft—and yet do not care. I'm sure that I could convince any judge that even if I stole the jewel, my offence is slight; the ruby was made of glass. Besides, the theft was in a good cause—a demonstration of just how completely the quality of the glass will depend on the inferred intention. When the nature of the implied friendship-offering changes, our opinion of the technique, the form, and the ethical value must change as well.

We can see more clearly how this matter of harmony of message and ethos works by looking at another didactic poem, one that we might not on first reading call didactic because it proclaims a counter-morality that many students of literature would simply take for granted. It is an early poem by Yeats, the culminating poem in *The Wind among the Reeds* (1899).

THE FIDDLER OF DOONEY

When I play on my fiddle in Dooney,
Folk dance like a wave of the sea;
My cousin is priest in Kilvarnet,
My brother in Mocharabuiee.

I passed my brother and cousin:
They read in their books of prayer;
I read in my book of songs
I bought at the Sligo fair.

When we come at the end of time
To Peter sitting in state,
He will smile on the three old spirits,
But call me first through the gate;

For the good are always the merry,
Save by an evil chance,
And the merry love the fiddle,
And the merry love to dance:

And when the folk there spy me,
They will all come up to me,
With "Here is the fiddler of Dooney!"
And dance like a wave of the sea.

Though the fixed norms are here much less direct, the author of
"The Fiddler" similarly offers himself as a friend who would teach me
to order my values in a certain way: fiddlers (that is, artists) on top,
priests (that is, moralists) somewhere down the line, though still smiled
on by Saint Peter. If the poet and I are to meet in friendship, it must be
as two members of a select group who understand, first, why priestly
prayers are inferior to songs and by implication to poems; next, why
the implied poet is superior to his described brother and cousin; and
then, why writing and reading the poem are thus, in the ultimate
scheme of things as judged by Saint Peter, moral acts superior to whatever a priest might do.

So far, the description of "The Fiddler" could pretty well fit "Don't
Quit." It offers a moral placement, one that may seem less conventional but that was in fact already highly conventional in poetry by the
turn of the century; indeed, it is now perhaps more widely embraced,
at least by those who read poetry, than "When the going gets tough,
the tough get going." And both poems imply that there are misguided
people out there somewhere who will question their norms.

But note now the obviously huge difference: in "The Fiddler" my
friend the poet does in fact live the message of the poem before my
eyes. He asks me to do a poetic dance with him, not an especially intricate dance (the inferences required are not, for example, nearly as
complex as those that Swift required of us [pp. 188–89 above]). Like
"Don't Quit," this poem does not offer strikingly original images or
fresh diction or experimental verse forms. Rather, the invitation is to
come dance to a poetic music that though conventional (like fiddling
itself) is so masterful, so persuasively merry, so lilting, exhibiting so
much delicate variety within the conventions, that one knows oneself
to be in the hands of a real "fiddler,"[9] one who lives out his "message"

9. Not, be it said, as splendid a fiddler as the best of later Yeats, but that comparison makes no difference here.

before our eyes. And he implies, with his invitation, a full human equality with his readers. We are invited to practice dancing and fiddling *with* him, as he performs a music that he has had to work hard to achieve but that all readers can understand easily and embrace happily: there is no aesthetic elitism here.[10]

Thus, though the poem is as narrow and almost as conventional as "Don't Quit" and is not especially outstanding on our other scales, its combination of craft and message produce in us a coherent pattern of desire and fulfillment; we long for a world in which everyone, everyone would dance like a wave of the sea instead of sitting around glumly reading prayer books.

We are now in a position to see more clearly both why those who reject all consideration of "message" or "content" are wrong and why it is no less wrong to judge the validity of such matters divorced from patterns of desire. The point for me is underlined when I realize that, considered as abstract propositions, the fixed norms offered by "Don't Quit" make better sense than the grotesquely over-simplified notion that fiddling and poetry are self-evidently more important activities than praying. Whether others agree with me or not—and I suspect that most of my readers will not—it is clear that Yeats's doctrine (we poet-fiddlers will end on top) is curiously self-praising and certainly dubitable, while the message of the other poem is entirely disinterested and hard to question.

And yet I have no doubt about which poem offers me the superior friendship. Yeats does not win me by placing high on all seven scales, nor does he offer some grand harmony of many virtues. He wins my friendship, as my real friends do, by offering a distinctive, engaging way of being together, one of many possible ways of addressing a world of conflicting values. The still young flesh-and-blood Yeats, that relatively callow, self-aggrandizing arrogant fiddler eager to put down his various "brothers," that young cultist of high art, was almost in spite of himself able to create an implied author who offers me a good that he himself takes with lovely seriousness. I come away from the

10. Though, of course, many poems by Yeats do imply readers who are members of a very small saving remnant.

poem sure that to go on discussing that good with him—that is, to go on reading more of "his" poems—will be one of the best things I could possibly do for myself. What's more, I could not wish for a world in which no one over-valued "fiddling."

Such talk will never lead to flat judgments like "true" or "false" or "virtuous" or "wicked," and it will thus not satisfy those who want an ethical criticism that will provide fixed conclusions. But it does, I think, thoroughly rebut the claim that the only moral demand we can make of a work of art is that it be good *as* art—meaning "as craft."

Our distance here from both extremes can be illustrated more clearly by looking at a more complex poem.

> ygUDuh
>
> ydoan
> yunnuhstan
>
> ydoan o
> yunnuhstan dem
> yguduh ged
>
> yunnuhstan dem doidee
> ygudah get riduh
> ydoan o nudn
> LISN bud LISN
>
>   dem
>   gud
>   am
>
>   lidl yelluh bas
>   tuds weer goin
>
> duhSIVILEYEzum

What pattern of desires does e. e. cummings offer me here (1954, 393)? We could hardly find one more different from Yeats's. Initially opaque, "ygUDuh" requires a good deal of intense deciphering energy at the start, enough to put off most readers except those who are professionally committed or those who have already come to trust cummings. What's more, even after the typographical trickery has been mastered, there is no explicit spokesman here for the implied author: an intense activity is required in making moral inferences from oblique signs provided by speakers who could not themselves ever make the inferences; the ironies are thus at least as complex as those we saw in reading the sentence from Swift.

The most aggressive offering here is of an intriguing game, a task of deciphering that is a pleasure in itself—for those who are not offended by it.[11] For the moments that our puzzlement may last, the engagement is intense, intimate, narrow, and radically *un*reciprocal: "I, the author, will construct the code and watch you, the reader, figure it out." We decipher not only a phonetic version of uneducated American English but a moral position toward those who speak it.

This second offering is thus a moral invitation: "Join me in condemning the bigotry of the speaker (or more probably of two speakers?), in order to enjoy the delicious irony of their pretending to civilize the Japanese" (the poem is "set" in World War II). The covert message on which the ironic punch of the final line depends is something like "bigotry is absurd."

Looked at more closely, however, the poem may come to seem tainted by another form of bigotry; in capitalizing on one rejected act of stereotyping on the basis of race, it relies on another, on the basis of class, as it suggests that people who speak substandard English embrace substandard moral notions. Unless we can claim that cummings intends some further irony that will save his bigots from the contempt that the poem heaps on them, we have located a moral incoherence much more serious than what we found in "Don't Quit." The elite position of the poet attacking bigotry, reinforced by the elite assumption of readers who take pride in performing an intricate act of linguistic deciphering, is vulnerable to the reader's question: "As you mock these slobs for their blindness to the Japanese as 'other,' where do you stand toward them as *your* 'other'?"

It is true that formally the poem offers an initial healthy grand shock of otherness, as if to say, "You must now learn to accept into your conventional world a new kind of art." It does not leave me abso-

---

11. This annoying qualification must always hover over us, and it is especially pertinent here. Many readers, I have found, simply refuse to work at the deciphering, and some are annoyed when they discover the simple and "obvious" syntax behind the "disguise."

lutely untouched in my complacencies in the way that "Don't Quit" does. It is also true that its surface message seems to be an indictment of those who show contempt for others, and a plea to treat even that ultimate "other," a wartime enemy, as *not* alien.

But beneath that surface the poem is, both in form and in implicit doctrine, contemptuous of all but those who belong to a specific literary culture. It gives me no reason whatever for trying to understand either the inhabitants of its world or those unsophisticated readers who cannot decipher its surface. Like the worst TV travelogues, it presents me with an exotic character (perhaps two of them) and asks me to respond with something like "Yes, isn't that just the way bigots betray their ignorance!"[12] To put the problem another way: cummings presents himself as the first poet in the history of literature to spell his name without capital letters and use phonetic spellings so aggressively. What an originator! How deliciously startling! But where do I go from there? What do I understand that I did not understand before? What can I imagine that I could not imagine before? In short, in achieving a maximum intensity and intimacy between author and implied reader —a reader postulated as someone who will not impose ethical criticism in self-protection—the poem implies a kind of friendship that is about as impervious to *seeing* the radically "other" as a friendship could be. My friend cummings and I, we know what's what, and we always have known. What a collection of bigots American society is! I thank thee Lord that I am not as other men.

"The Fiddler," in contrast, gives me an "other" worth imagining. He is enough like what I have already known to be recognized as in my world, but sufficiently different to challenge my foundations. Even now, late in the century, when his overt ideas seem to me long since

---

12. In *The Moral Imagination*, a fine work of ethical criticism that appeared as I was completing the final draft of *Company*, Christopher Clausen makes something like the same charge against Emily Dickinson's "What Soft—Cherubic Creatures—": "For precisely as the ["Brittle"] lady's moral failure lies in judging others against an (unspecified) ideal, we are judging *her* for her failure to recognize their equality. . . . The poet does to her character exactly what she accuses the character of doing" (1986, 16). Clausen thinks that Dickinson "gets away with it," because readers are "unlikely to notice the moral contradiction at the center of the poem." Yet, finally, "[t]he critic who thinks such a contradiction does not matter in poetry may justly be accused of overlooking a central issue in *this* poem" (16).

worn out, the picture of his character as a fiddling fool, wiser than his brothers, can stir my complacencies.

Obviously, then, I am led to conclude, in spite of my pleasure in cummings' cleverness, that "ygUDuh" is ethically inferior to "The Fiddler"—again, in spite of my agreement with its superficial message and my disagreement with that of "The Fiddler." Even if I detect a bit of the pharisee in Yeats, cummings seems (in this poem, not by any means in all his poems) to be nothing *but* pharisee-with-a-high-IQ.

I can think of only one way to "rescue" him—not from banning, of course, but from our discounting. "Perhaps," some charitable critic may object, "the poem asks for compassion for the dramatized bigots." I can see no sign of that request. But suppose we thought of cummings as trying to stimulate a debate between such a reading and my own. He would then come off as an entirely different and more defensible kind of friend than in my reading: he would now be self-consistent, compassionate toward the bigoted "others," and thus a better friend to me.

The question then becomes, Does the poem in fact *invite* that kind of rich inquiry, or does it not rather simply *tolerate* it (see pp. 90–92 above)? The kind of ethical encounter we will have with cummings and with any given reader will vary greatly, depending on our answer. And both will differ from my conversation, if any, with a reader who decides that flat mockery of bar-room bums, with no irony, is what the poem intends and that no questions should be raised about such an intention.

To engage in this kind of talk does not mean that these poems are pinned for all time with ribbons saying Second Prize and Slightly Dishonorable Mention.[13] Different readers with different biases and skills will encounter different degrees of otherness. Someone who is fond of the "Don't Quit" kind of thing might well get more profitable jarring from cummings than from Yeats. I have known students for whom the

---

13. One of the worst side-effects of the New Critical emphasis on formal excellence, with little explicit talk about ethical quality, was its blatant mockery of certain works dear to the popular imagination. Brooks and Warren performed a clever annihilation of "Trees," for example (1938, 387–91), and generations of students were taught that what they and their home folks had loved was contemptible. At its worst, such teaching—some of which I engaged in myself—was no more than an attempt to demonstrate one's own cleverness.

sheer delight of seeing behind cummings's surface trickeries constituted a major step toward learning the pleasures of modern poetry. On the other hand, for certain worshippers of high art, "The Fiddler" could prove just one more soporific: they know already that only true artists will enter the kingdom of heaven. Yeats might lull them into complacent acceptance of a banal anti-clericalism. We can even imagine a reader for whom the simple muscular appeal of "Don't Quit" might be more rewarding and hence more likely to induce further reading than the poems that are to us obviously superior.

If our vocabulary of the ethos of fictional friends did not allow for such differences in evaluation, it would be useless, even dangerous. There is thus no easy way to determine at what point we should take our stand and say that this or that narrative seems to us so lacking in any of the seven virtues as to be unredeemable. To believe that there is such a way is precisely the mistake of all censorship programs.

THE BEST OF FRIENDS

We have now seen a few of the moral reorderings and reinforcements that implied authors can offer us. We have seen that such offers cannot be flatly judged without reference to the ultimate ethos of the would-be giver, an ethos that is in one sense identical to the pattern of desires the narrative urges upon us—our *engaged experience line by line*. Obviously these three friends—the platitudinous preachy uncle, the carefree dancing partner, the elitist attitudinizer—are a crude sampling from the company we might choose to join: the implied author as clever, sardonic iconoclast, claiming to do me good by taking something from me that I mistakenly value (Samuel Butler in *The Way of All Flesh*); as the cleverest of gossips about history or contemporary life (Gore Vidal in *Lincoln* or Mary McCarthy in large sections of *The Group*); as night watchman crying the alarm (Orwell in *1984*); as exterminator of vermin (Swift, sometimes; Jerzy Kosinski, usually); as father confessor (Flannery O'Connor and Walker Percy, when read *my* way); as profoundly playful therapist (Saul Bellow—especially, for me, in *Mr. Sammler's Planet*); as savior, one who will take infinite pains to bring me a total, saving vision of the mystery (Dante, Milton, Spenser, Bunyan). And so on we could go, through all of the helping professions, as we might say: nurses, tour guides, surgeons, garbage collectors, acupuncture specialists good at killing pain, and—perhaps the largest class of all—unassuming time killers, clowns, and party companions.

When we consider the variety of such would-be friends, and the ease with which we move from one kind of encounter to another, we can see why critics have often made the mistake of saying that specific doctrines don't matter at all because a poem by definition "says nothing." It is true that specific disagreements about fixed norms can often prevent full friendship, even with the largest-souled of friends. But those I care most about offer so much ethical value so intensely, with such clear evidence that they are themselves pursuing the goods they offer, that differences of opinion seem trivial by comparison. What is more, the proffered gifts that I reject—let us say, some of the details in Dante's Thomism or Milton's theodicy—are often just the kind a true friend might offer me in all sincerity; the very act of deciding whether to accept them—the "practice" of conversing with the author about the gift before rejecting it—is itself a fine gift of another kind. The authors who become our lasting friends are those who offer to teach us, by the sheer activity of considering their gifts, a life larger than any specific doctrine we might accept or reject.

The key question in the ethics of narration, then, so long as we pursue it under this personal metaphor, becomes: Is the pattern of life that this would-be friend offers one that friends might well pursue together? Or is this the offer of a sadist to a presumed masochist? Of a seducer or rapist to a victim? Of the exploiter to the exploited? Is this a friend, a lover, a parent, a prophet, a crony, a co-conspirator, an *agent provocateur,* a bully, a quack therapist, a sycophant? Or perhaps a sidekick, a lackey, a vandal, a bloodsucker, a blackmailer . . . ?

Obviously the possibilities are as various as the vocabulary for praising and damning acquaintances in the rest of life. And just as in life we do not decide to associate with only the best kind of person, even though we have terms that help us discriminate quality, so in literature: we can and do embrace many kinds and levels, with no assurance that we can finally discover that they are in harmony.[14]

---

14. A cogent demonstration that irreducibly plural human values are necessarily "incommensurable" and that preserving their plurality and their incommensurability is itself a good is given by Joseph Raz in *The Morality of Freedom* (1986, chs. 13–14).

The fullest friendships, the "friendships of virtue" that the tradition hails as best, are likely to be with the works that the world has called classics.[15] When I "perform" for myself or attend a performance of *King Lear, The Misanthrope,* or *The Cherry Orchard,* when I read *Don Quixote, Persuasion, Bleak House,* or *War and Peace,* I meet in their authors friends who demonstrate their friendship not only in the range and depth and intensity of pleasure they offer, not only in the promise they fulfill of proving useful to me, but finally in the irresistible invitation they extend to live during these moments a richer and fuller life than I could manage on my own.[16]

I might say to any one of these in reply: If I choose to ignore you, I lose something more precious than any one point I could make *about* you and your kind; your company is in some ways superior even to the best company I can hope to discover among the real people I live with. Certainly it is superior to what is usually provided by those "inner resources" we are all advised to fall back on when bored. Unlike "real" people, you are an idealized version of the writer who created you, the disorganized, flawed creature who in a sense discovered you by expunging his or her duller times and weaker moments. To dwell with you is to share the improvements you have managed to make in your "self" by perfecting your narrative world. You lead me first to practice ways of living that are more profound, more sensitive, more intense, and in a curious way more fully generous than I am likely to meet anywhere else in the world. You correct my faults, rebuke my insensitivities. You mold me into patterns of longing and fulfillment that make my ordinary dreams seem petty and absurd. You finally show what life can be, not just to a coterie, a saved and saving remnant looking down on the fools, slobs, and knaves, but to *anyone* who is willing to work to earn the title of equal and true friend.

REFERENCES

Benchley, Peter. *Jaws.* New York, 1974.
Brooks, Cleanth, and Robert Penn Warren, eds. and comps. *Understanding Poetry: An Anthology for College Students.* New York, 1938.

15. The word has of course lost its force; one sees everywhere advertisements like "Every novel by Ursula K. LeGuin has become an instant classic."

16. For a lovely brief celebration of what re-reading a classic can do for us, see Calvino 1986.

Burke, Kenneth. "Psychology and Form." In *Counter-Statement* [1931]. Los Altos, Calif., 1953.

Butler, Samuel. *The Way of All Flesh*. London, 1903.

Calvino, Italo. "Why Read the Classics?" *New York Review of Books* (Oct. 9, 1986): 19–20.

Clausen, Christopher. *The Moral Imagination: Essays on Literature and Ethics*. Iowa City, Iowa, 1986.

Cummings, E. E. "YgUDuh." *Collected Poems: 1923–1954*. New York, 1954. 393.

Griffin, Bryan F. "Low Life and High Hack." Review of *The Executioner's Song*, by Norman Mailer. *American Spectator* (Feb. 1980): 12–19.

Joyce, James. *Finnegans Wake* [1939]. New York, 1959.

Mailer, Norman. *The Executioner's Song*. New York, 1979.

McCarthy, Mary. *The Group*. New York, 1980.

Miller, J. Hillis. *The Ethics of Reading: Kant, de Man, Eliot, Trollope, James, and Benjamin*. New York, 1986.

Nabokov, Vladimir. "Interview." In *The "Paris Review" Interviews: Writers at Work*. Ed. George Plimpton. 4th ser. New York, 1976.

Rabinowitz, Peter. *Before Reading: Narrative Conventions and the Politics of Interpretation*. Ithaca, N.Y., 1988.

Raz, Joseph. *The Morality of Freedom*. Oxford, 1986.

Trollope, Anthony. *An Autobiography* [1883]. London, 1950.

Tyler, Anne. *Dinner at the Homesick Restaurant*. New York, 1982.

Yeats, William Butler. "The Fiddler of Dooney." In *The Wind among the Reeds*. London, 1899.

8

My language is the sum total of myself.

Charles S. Peirce

Mr. Harlan [biographer of Booker T. Washington] began to suspect that he was seeking "a personality that had vanished into the roles it had played." In the second volume the search continues, peeling back mask after mask, one personality after another, but still leaving the man underneath elusive, ambiguous, infinitely duplicitous. Given the number of roles he had to play and the contradictions within as well as between them, he could hardly afford a personality of his own.

C. Vann Woodward

For neither man nor angel can discern
Hypocrisy, the only evil that walks
Invisible, except to God alone.

John Milton

[Benjamin] Franklin had a pronounced character which he presented very acutely, but he did not think of himself as primarily a unique inner self. He was all his many roles.

Judith Shklar

The whole dear notion of one's own self—marvelous old free-willed, free-enterprising, autonomous, independent, isolated island of a self—is a myth.

Lewis Thomas

Hypocrisy is the last hold we moderns have on decency; once we lose that, we'll be lost indeed.

Anonymous

Everything that lives,
Lives not alone, nor for itself.

William Blake

Consequences for Character

The Faking and Making of the "Self"

THE TURN TO CONSEQUENCES

I have put off as long as possible this moment when I must talk directly about ethical consequences, the "efferent effect," or carry-over from narrative experience to behavior. I have claimed that even if narratives had no consequences beyond what they do to us *while* we listen or read, we should consider criticism of their ethical force as one of our most important cultural "assignments"—an assignment not just to professional critics but to every reader, viewer, and listener. It is now time to begin addressing the even more controversial question of how to avoid nonsense when we talk about the good and harm narratives work on our conduct.

In one sense, everyone who has read much narrative with intense engagement "knows" that narratives do influence behavior. When we are not thinking about literary theory, we talk casually about our reading experience, perhaps in the tone of this reviewer:

> On her wedding day, a friend of mine wore a corseted floor-length gown which cinched her waist down to the sixteen-inch circumference of Scarlett O'Hara on the day of the barbeque at Twelve Oaks. My friend had read *Gone with the Wind* at age ten, and still, years later, examples like this of its continued influence on her kept cropping up. Louisa May Alcott's *Little Women* affected me similarly; with head shorn *à la* Jo, I imagined myself increasing the family income by selling my short stories. *The Catcher in the Rye* had a less positive effect. . . . I wanted to merge with Holden Caulfield.
>
> (Stoyva 1986)

Sometimes the talk is not quite so cheerful. Our culture is full of stories about the fatal malleability of readers who somehow haven't heard the news that good readers are supposed to maintain their distance. One hears of the poet Infante attempting suicide on an airplane, so depressed was he by his travel reading of Malcolm Lowry's *Under the Volcano* (1947). One *knows* youngsters who first tried drugs after reading Kerouac's *On the Road* or listening to the Beatles' "Lucy in the Sky with Diamonds." Except when reading the most advanced literary journals, one hears accounts everywhere of "How my life was changed by reading X, Y, or Z."

It is true that literary critics talk about such effects most freely when they think about what the vile "media" do to the young. Hundreds, perhaps thousands, of defenders of literature have suggested that the essential character of whole generations is being destroyed in front of the boob tube.[1] And even the more temperate observers, those committed as semiologists to studying "signs" objectively, seem agreed that the *popular* arts, and especially the visual arts, mold character. Here is Umberto Eco on the subject of video and cinema:

> [T]he younger generations have absorbed as elements of their behavior a series of elements filtered through the mass media (and coming, in some cases, from the most impenetrable areas of our century's artistic experimentation). To tell the truth, it isn't even necessary to talk about new generations: If you are barely middle-aged, you will have learned personally the extent to which experience (love, fear, or hope) is filtered through 'already seen' images.
>
> (1986, 213–14)

Eco must of course then make the ritual declaration of neutrality: "I leave it to moralists to deplore this way of living by intermediate communication. We must only bear in mind that mankind has never done anything else" (214). Taking his invitation to turn to the images implanted by oral and printed narratives, we find perhaps less agreement that they lead people to live "by intermediate communication." But anyone who conducts honest introspection knows that "real life" is lived *in* images derived in part from stories. Though usually our imitations are not highly dramatic, especially once we pass adolescence, everyone who reads knows that whether or not we *should* imitate nar-

---

1. My article comparing the ethics of the "video" arts and the verbal arts (1982) has been read by some as a biased attack on "viewing" as opposed to "reading" and "listening." Not so. At one time I intended to include a revision as a chapter here, since obviously the different ethical effects of entire media are inherently a part of our subject. But on reflection, especially after reading W. J. T. Mitchell's *Iconology* (1986), I decided that the subject requires another book. Perhaps. Here I can simply assert that the experience of video *as now commercially determined* is in my view a cultural disaster.

rative heroes and heroines, we in fact do. Indeed, our imitations of *narrative* "imitations of life" are so spontaneous and plentiful that we cannot draw a clear line between what we *are,* in some conception of a "natural," unstoried self, and what we have become as we have first enjoyed, then imitated, and then, perhaps, criticized both the stories and our responses to them.[2] It is true, as Paul Hunter says when making this same point, that we can never know for sure just how *much* "of modern human history has gone the way it has because people at crucial moments have said or done a certain thing in imitation of some character in a novel." But as he says, we know that "[l]ife *does* imitate art, often quite self-consciously. None of us would rationally decide to turn our personal decisions over to novelists, but the desire for instruction (usually a little disguised) still remains one of the most powerful motives for reading novels, or autobiography or history, or for seeing films" (1987, 269). Almost everyone—except for a few theorists—would agree not only that we read for instruction but that the instruction often *works.* But how can we move beyond anecdote to a responsible criticism?

A first step is to reconsider our notions about the formation of "character"—of self, of soul, of ethos, of personality, of identity. How do our current conceptions of who we are and how we develop differ from those of earlier periods?[3]

---

2. And they are by no means confined to memories of adolescent crushes. Now in my mid-sixties, I can remember many "influences" during the past year (1986–87), most but not all trivial: (1) after reading Umberto Eco's *The Name of the Rose,* I did some uncharacteristic reading about medieval monasteries; (2) after viewing the movie *Brother from Another Planet,* I went about Chicago for days expecting all the black people I met to be both friendly and witty; (3) after viewing the movie *The Color Purple,* I caught myself looking at a black couple in the supermarket and wondering whether the bruise over her eye meant that he had struck her; (4) after watching a particularly bloody episode of "Hill Street Blues" on TV, I caught myself being more apprehensive on my Chicago street as I walked home from work after dark; (5) after attending a fine performance of Athol Fugard's *A Message from Aloes,* I sent off a check to Amnesty International; (6) after reading . . . But you can, I trust—should I say hope?—fill in your own anecdotal evidence. For a listing of "confessions" by some of my acquaintances, see pages 278–79 below.

3. Even after my brief definition in Chapter 1, the word "character" may prove misleading as a general term covering all dimensions of whatever "self" exercises "characteristic" choices. But I trust that my use of it will be justified as we go along.

PRACTICING CHARACTER: THE WITNESSES

That wonderful, much-mocked fiction *Euphues* (1579), by John
Lyly, begins with this description of a character:

> There dwelt in *Athens* a young gentleman of great patrimony, and of so
> comelye a personage, that it was doubted whether he were more bound to
> Nature for the liniaments of his person, or to Fortune for the increase of his
> possessions. But Nature impatient of comparisons . . . added to this come-
> lynesse of his bodye such a sharpe capacity of minde, that . . . she proved
> Fortune counterfaite. . . . This young gallaunt of more witte then wealth,
> and yet of more wealth then wisedome, seeing himselfe inferiour to none in
> pleasant conceits, though[t] himselfe superiour to all his honest conditions,
> insomuch that he thought himselfe so apt to all thinges that he gave him-
> selfe almost to nothing but practicing to those thinges commonly which
> are incident to these sharpe wittes, fine phrases, smooth quippes, merry
> tauntes, jestinge without meane, and abusing mirth without measure.

Until quite recently in our history, everyone who talked about character would have assumed, with Lyly, both that one could make distinctions among good and bad characters—whether in literature or
life—and that the ultimate point in talking about character was to improve it, to save one's soul. To talk of character or characters at all was
of course to use evaluative language. Euphues has more wit than
wisdom, Lyly tells us, in an uninhibited act of ethical criticism, and we
are invited either to join him or to perform a further act of ethical criticism, judging *him* to be a poor judge.

As we have seen, most critics until this century took such invitations
seriously and responded in kind. Even those who on religious grounds
might have professed universal charity—Judge not, that ye be not
judged—did not hesitate to judge literary characters and, at least by
implication, those who had created them. People generally assumed as
a corollary that anyone's character could be genuinely corrupted or
improved through contact with literary characters.[4] Some took what

---

4. I don't know enough about other cultures to make the same claim about "people
generally" in them. But everything I have read in translations of Indian, Chinese, and
Japanese classics suggests that characters as models—and anti-models—have always
been taken seriously. It is noteworthy that the "Eastern" spiritual cures that have
flooded the West have all—so far as I can discover—carried with them narratives about
exemplary lives that are to be imitated.

was thought to be Plato's line in emphasizing the dangers in all works of the imagination; "the novel" was especially suspect because it was viewed as especially seductive. Others defended "poetry" on lines famously laid down by Sidney in his *Apologie:*

> . . . so that the ending end of all earthly learning, being vertuous action, those skilles that most serve to bring forth that, have a most just title to bee Princes over all the rest: wherein if wee can shewe the Poets noblenes, by setting him before his other Competitors [philosophy and history, we shall have shown] that the Poet with that same hand of delight, doth draw the mind more effectually, then any other Arte dooth, and so a conclusion not unfitlie ensueth: . . . Poetrie, beeing the most familiar to teach it [virtue], and most princelie to move towards it, in the most excellent work, is the most excellent workman.
>
> ([1595] 1868, 31, 42–43)

Programs for improvement of character naturally relied on virtuous narratives, fictional or historical, as one major kind of schoolmaster. *The Imitation of Christ* (see Büttner 1983; Channing 1881, 310–16) and the various Lives of the Saints are the best known of these, but one gets the impression that as literacy spread, each walk of life created narratives exemplifying the virtues appropriate to that particular way (e.g., Cicero, *De Officiis* 1967, 64; Castiglione *The Courtier* [1561] 1959; apprentice guides; conduct books [Marks 1986; Hunter 1987, 269–77]; Sunday school tracts without number). We can infer from this flood of exemplary narratives, and from the many defensive prefaces and afterwords that authors have added to even the least obviously moral of works, that people generally accepted without question a direct connection between stories read and probable effects on conduct—on character.

Typical of this kind of self-defense is Ben Jonson's Epistle Prefatory to *Volpone.* After repeating the classical claim that no man can be a good poet without first being a good man, Jonson says of the poet:

> He [the poet] that is sayd to be able to informe *yong-men* to all good disciplines, inflame *growne-men* to all great vertues, keepe *old men* in their best and supreme state, or as they decline to child-hood, recover them to their first strength; that comes forth the Interpreter, and Arbiter of *Nature,* a Teacher of things divine, no lesse then humane, a Master in manners; and can alone (or with a few) effect the busines of Man-kind. This, I take him, is no subject for *Pride,* and *Ignorance* to exercise their railing *rhetorique* upon. . . . I have labourd [in this work] for their [other writers'] instruction, and amendment, to reduce, not onely the antient formes, but manners

of the *Scene*, the easinesse, the propriety, the innocence, and last the doctrine, which is the principall end of POESY to informe men, in the best reason of living.

([1607] 1937, 5, 8)

Can Jonson really believe that the principal end of *all* literature is to
teach people the best reason for living? Whatever was true of Jonson,
we can be sure that everyone who "listened" to his fictions (mostly
dramas) was practicing a judgment of character according to more or
less conventional signs, since that is what we inevitably do with every
story or drama that comes our way. And we know that most traditional stories, unlike some modern fictions, provided in their authorial
commentary and in their allocation of rewards and punishments either
confirmation or correction of the readers' or listeners' inferences and
judgments. Just as Euphues "practiced" in order to sharpen his wit,
readers practiced, willy-nilly, the sharpening of their perceptions of
character simply by following any story, whether or not it was explicitly designed to be edifying.

"Everyone" assumed that such practice had an effect on conduct—
not just on immediate conduct following the practice but on the more
enduring *habits of conduct* to which the word "character" most use-
fully applies.[5] As we have seen, evidence for this assumption can be
found in every corner of literature, but it is nowhere stronger than in
the way the great novelists themselves relied on the assumption in their
own work. Clearly they could depend, until quite recently, on their
readers' belief in the immense power of story to change lives. No one
seems to have questioned Cervantes' account of how Don Quixote destroyed his reason: "[F]rom so little sleeping and so much reading [of
romances], his brain dried up and he went completely out of his mind.
He had filled his imagination with everything that he had read . . . and
as a result had come to believe that all these fictitious happenings were
true; they were more real to him than anything else in the world"
([1605] 1949, ch. 1, p. 27). At last "his wits were gone beyond re-

5. The word "character" comes from the Greek word for "stamp" or "mark," but
it has also always been used as a translation of "ethos." We might think of it as meaning
a "stamped or incised ethos"—a more or less harmonious collection of character-istics
that persist through time because *stamped into* the material—whatever we might take
that initial "material," the unsocialized self, to be.

pair," a comic disaster[6] that never led any reader to think Cervantes was not serious in his claim that silly reading makes silly readers.

In the same way, the great eighteenth-century English novelists took for granted a close connection between reading and conduct. Richardson is perhaps the most famous example, partly because many readers have felt that his protestations of moral purpose do not quite fit the actual effects of his fictions:

> What will be found to be . . . aimed at in the following work [*Clarissa*] is— to warn the inconsiderate and thoughtless of the one sex, against the base arts and designs of specious contrivers of the other—to caution parents against the undue exercise of their natural authority over their children in the great article of marriage—to warn children against preferring a man of pleasure to a man of probity upon that dangerous but too commonly received notion, *that a reformed rake makes the best husband*—but above all, to investigate the highest and most important doctrines not only of morality, but of Christianity
>
> ([1748] 1902, xii)

—and so on.

Jane Austen similarly knew that her readers would accept her assumption that people can be blessed, or apparently more often cursed, by the books they read. Her strongest piece of ethical criticism, except perhaps for the parody that runs throughout *Northanger Abbey,* is found in her last, uncompleted work, *Sanditon.* Sir Edward, the would-be seducer, has been thoroughly corrupted, specifically by reading "sentimental novels" and by misreading *Clarissa.* He of course professes literary principles of the highest kind:

> "I am no indiscriminate Novel-Reader. The mere Trash of the common Circulating Library, I hold in the highest contempt. You will never hear me advocating those puerile Emanations which detail nothing but discordant Principles incapable of amalgamation. . . . You understand me I am sure?"
>
> ([1817/1925] 1963, 403)

Charlotte, our heroine, insists on some clear examples in support of these vague mouthings. Like many a modern reader encountering such fancy claims in such fancy language, she replies that she is not at all

---

6. Only in modern times has the account struck any readers as essentially pathetic or tragic. See, for example, Auden's "The Ironic Hero" (1949, 86–94).

sure that she *does* understand him. "But if you will describe the sort of
Novels which you *do* approve, I dare say it will give me a clearer idea."

Sir Edward responds with an unconscious parody of the mandarin
talk of his day:

> "The Novels which I approve are such as . . . exhibit the progress of strong
> Passion from the first Germ of incipient Susceptibility to the utmost Ener-
> gies of Reason half-dethroned,—where we see the strong spark of Woman's
> Captivations elicit such Fire in the Soul of Man as leads him—(though at
> the risk of some Aberration from the strict line of Primitive Obligations)—
> to hazard all, dare all, atcheive all, to obtain her. . . . These are the Novels
> which enlarge the primitive Capabilities of the Heart, & which it cannot
> impugn the Sense or be any Dereliction of the character, of the most anti-
> puerile Man, to be conversant with."
>
> (403–4)

To which the perceptive Charlotte simply replies, "If I understand
you aright[,] . . . our taste in Novels is not at all the same." The narrator then intrudes to explain the true relation of art and morality:

> The truth was that Sir Edw: whom circumstances had confined very much
> to one spot had read more sentimental Novels than agreed with him. His
> fancy had been early caught by all the impassioned, & most exceptionable
> parts of Richardson's [novels]. . . . With a perversity of Judgement, which
> must be attributed to his not having by Nature a very strong head, the
> Graces, the Spirit, the Sagacity, & the Perseverance, of the Villain of the
> Story outweighed all his absurdities & all his Atrocities with Sir Edward.
> With him, such Conduct was Genius, Fire & Feeling.
>
> (404)

Austen goes on to describe, in language that must have shocked
readers a few decades later, just how Sir Edward intends to pursue his
chief goal, seduction of the lovely Clara—a goal that has been reinforced if not implanted by his reading: "He had very early seen the
necessity of the case" (405).

In all of this Austen never even hints that she should provide an explicit argument or theoretical justification for the belief that books can
corrupt us. Why should she? To do so in her time would have seemed
an absurd belaboring of the self-evident.

Similarly, when Flaubert tells us that one major cause of Emma
Bovary's destruction was her reading of too many romantic novels as
a child, he spends no time arguing that such an influence was possible
or plausible; he can take for granted that all readers will take it for
granted. Indeed, most of them did; we know that from the vigor with

which they proceeded to accuse his own book of corrupting its readers.

For six months when Emma was fifteen, she surreptitiously read novels, the narrator tells us, that were

> invariably about love affairs, lovers, mistresses, harassed ladies swooning in remote pavilions. . . . [T]here were gloomy forests, broken hearts, vows, sobs, tears and kisses. . . . [T]he noblemen were all brave as lions, gentle as lambs, incredibly virtuous, always beautifully dressed, and wept copiously on every occasion. . . . [S]he worshipped Mary Queen of Scots, and venerated [fictional] women illustrious or ill-starred. . . . And now she could not bring herself to believe that the uneventful life she was leading was the happiness of which she had dreamed.

([1857] 1957, 41, 42, 45)

Can we imagine any reader stopping to demand proof from Flaubert's narrator that the wrong kind of literature can have such baleful effects?

THE NOTION OF CHARACTER

Like "ethics" and "virtue," our other key terms, "character" has always tended to expand and contract freely. After World War II it contracted; indeed as a serious study it almost disappeared (though it seems likely to be revived as a result of all the concerns about "character" raised during the 1988 presidential election). Throughout these expansions and contractions it has sometimes been used to mean only "good character," in fairly narrow moral terms. That use endures today in the language of football coaches, whose sport, they say, builds character—meaning, mainly, courage in the face of physical threat. We have it also in our phrase "character reference," referring to the absence of a fairly narrow range of possible vices: cheating, stealing, displaying embarrassing sexual preference in company. Sometimes it has been limited strictly to moral qualities, as in (one possible reading of) Aristotle's claim that you can have a tragedy without character.[7] Sometimes it has been used as I use it here, to cover the entire range of

---

7. "Character (*ethos*) is that which reveals choice, shows what sort of thing a man chooses or avoids in circumstances where the choice is not obvious, so those speeches convey no character in which there is nothing whatever which the speaker chooses or avoids" (*Poetics* 6.24). "Moreover, you could not have a tragedy without action, but you can have one without character-study" (6.15).

what we call "personal qualities"—every conceivable "stamp" from heroic to vicious on every conceivable scale, intellectual, moral, or aesthetic. This usage survives in talk about stage characters: Iago, in current usage, is at least as powerful a "character" as Othello. When used in this way, the notion of improving or debasing a character becomes almost as broad as our notion of "self"-improvement (or decline), covering just about every dimension short of having a face-lift.

Thinking of character thus broadly, I am struck by two features of our current culture. On the one hand, we are flooded with projects for improving character: the self-help books and articles doubling by the year;[8] cults offering sure-fire spiritual cures and competing for our dollars in expensive national advertising programs; revivals of traditional religions; psychology workshops in "assertiveness training," "focusing," "Stop Smoking with Behavior Modification"; magazines, with titles like *Self*, full of articles on "self-fulfillment." On the other hand, hardly anyone seems to provide the nostrum that would have occurred as one of the most promising to previous generations: spending long hours in the company of the "right" literary friends and avoiding "bad (literary) company." Has any professor in recent times suggested to a doctoral candidate in search of a thesis topic that working on the Marquis de Sade or Henry Miller for one to four years might be bad for the student's mental health—that is to say, his or her character? Even advertisements in religious journals seldom even hint that reading a touted book might not only teach some important doctrine—that kind of claim is found everywhere—but actually change the reader's character for the better. There is in fact a little known program in "bibliotherapy" that claims to use books, especially fiction and poetry, to cure (Hynes 1980; Rhea Rubin 1978). But I doubt that the good people of strong character who run the program can have worked out any very subtle way of providing precisely the right book for a given patient at a given time. The problems one can foresee in any such program dramatize the importance of one principle underlying *Company:*

---

8. *When I Say No, I Feel Guilty,* by Manuel J. Smith (1975); *The Angry Book,* by Theodore Isaac Rubin (1969); *Self-Change: Strategies for Solving Personal Problems,* by Michael J. Mahoney (1979), and so on.

every reader must be his or her own ethical critic. Still, I would not want to mock such a program without a closer look. The central idea of the founders—that books can curse or cure us—is surely sound.

CHARACTERS, SELVES, IN-DIVIDUALS, "ME"S

We can now see a further reason for the widespread suspicion of the claim that stories should be subject to ethical criticism: since the Enlightenment people have increasingly thought of their own essential natures not as something to be built, or built up, through experience with other characters but rather as something—a "true self"—to be found by probing within.[9] For complex reasons, much modern thought about the "individual," the un-dividable center, has stressed the search inward for the core of the real "me," the authentic self. In that search, one tends to peel off the inauthentic, insincere, alien influences that might deflect the self from its unique, individual destiny. For many decades the last heirs of romantic individualism have been peeling off elements assumed to be not-self: first the church, then family, then political and economic forces. All these seemed clearly not the "real me." The search can be pursued back to one's mistreatment in childhood, or further to unfortunate experiences in the womb, or finally to a cursed genealogy. Sooner or later one hopes to locate and remove all alien stuff and discover bedrock—but what one discovers is emptiness, and the makings of an identity crisis.[10]

Critical alternatives to such rampant individualism have been of-

9. The best discussion I have yet found of how the notion of character relates to other historical notions of the person is by Amelie Oksenberg Rorty, "Literary Postscript: Characters, Persons, Selves, Individuals" (1976, 301–24); her probing has influenced much of this section, including the title. She offers many helpful distinctions, not only among her four key terms but among other related person-terms like "heroes," "protagonists," "souls," "figures," and "presences." One might add to her list four more terms: "personalities," "images" (what public relations people build), "personae," and "me"s (as in the "me generation").

10. For accounts of the rise and significance of individualism, see Weintraub, *The Value of the Individual* (1978), and Dumont, *Essais sur l'individualisme* (1983). For a splendid short critique (and history) of the "sincere," "authentic" self, see Trilling, *Sincerity and Authenticity* (1972).

fered for more than a century: by various Marxists, including Marx
himself (Marx [1844] 1964, 77; Lukács 1963; Jameson 1981, ch. 3);
by various Hegelians (Bradley [1876] 1951, 98–147); by behaviorists
(Skinner 1969, 1971); by social psychologists (Dewey 1922; Mead
1982; Royce 1969); by anthropologists (Bateson 1972); by Michael
Polanyi in his account of a "personal" knowledge pursued by scientists
who necessarily live con-vivially (1972, esp. chs. 7–8); by Charles
Taylor in his account of how the self can fill its responsibility to itself
by aspiring to be a different self (1976, 1985); by Joseph Raz in his
recent defense of liberalism (1986); by Jacques Lacan in his accounts
of how the Subject remakes itself in encounters with the Other (1968;
1978, esp. 203–76); and by—but once we begin with deconstructionists, the decenterings of the so-called subject become innumerable.
All these and many others have tried to teach us once again what ancient philosophy, classical rhetoric, and traditional religion took for
granted: the isolated individual self simply does not, cannot exist. Not
to be a *social* self is to lose one's humanity.[11] As Aristotle insisted, we
are "political animals" precisely in the sense that we become human
only in a polis.[12]

One of the most engaging, accessible, and finally useful arguments
for the social self is that of Mikhail Bakhtin, long neglected in the West
but now almost too well established, if the proliferation of catchwords
like "dialogical," "dialogicity," and "heterology" is any measure. According to his dialogical view of the self, each of us is constituted in a
kind of counterpoint of inherited "languages," a multiplicity of voices
only the ensemble of which can in any meaningful sense be called "my
own." Even those who insist on thinking of themselves as individuals
are in fact polyphonic and to some degree "heteroglossic"—experiencing voice against voice in what may seem incompatible mixtures. A

11. The complexities here are underlined by the fact that for some "decenterers,"
the word "humanity" is attached to "humanism," and both become dirty words: traditional humanism misled us by constructing an autonomous isolate, the individual self,
and by fixing "his" values. See Jameson's account of this move, 1981, 124–126.

12. "[T]he city belongs among the things that exist by nature, and . . . man is by
nature a political animal. . . . [I]t is peculiar to man as compared to the other animals
that he alone has a perception of good and bad and just and unjust . . . and partnership
in these things is what makes a household and a city" (*Politics* 1.2.9). For a cogent account of the irreducibly social conception of the self in pre-classical Greece, and especially in Homer, see Redfield 1986.

great part of our woes can be traced to our temptation to allow some one voice to triumph, either within our souls or in the political order (1981, esp. 259–422). In this respect Bakhtin's multiplication of perspectives reinforces Kenneth Burke's "dramatistic" model of our verbal conflicts: our ills can be traced to our attempts to "perfect" some one language at the expense of all the others (Burke 1966; Booth 1979, ch. 3).

Against these critical alternatives—an impressive lot, to say the least—the notion of the self as individual and essentially private has proved astonishingly persistent. All of these have hoped, in their arguments for a fundamentally *social* psychology, to settle the hash of all individualistic psychologies, all psychologies that begin with the notion of an atomic isolate. Instead, our culture has managed somehow to drive "social psychology" into one corner of the academy, as a new sub-discipline of individual psychology: the psychology of atomic isolates as they behave in groups. In literature the portrait of desperate isolates, essentially unable (in theory, at least) to communicate with other isolates, has become almost the norm in "advanced" fiction. Meanwhile, the triumphs of the computer have led to an increased use, in cognitive psychology and information theory, of models for human thought based on the operation of isolated units taking in and feeding back isolated bits of data.[13]

If I think of myself not as an atomic unit bumping other atoms but as a *character*—as someone doing my best to enact the various roles "assigned" me—I discover that there are no clear boundaries between the others who are somehow both outside and inside me and the "me" that the others are "in." As Gregory Bateson puts it, in that fine, strange, rambling book *Steps to an Ecology of Mind* (1972), I am not bounded by my skin.[14] Rather, as a character I am a kind of focal point

13. A comprehensive survey of the current views of what I think of as the "atomists" is given by Howard Gardner in *The Mind's New Science* (1985). Earlier simplified views of the individual mind as a collection of billiard balls or as "hard-wired" have given way to increasing complexities. And there are certainly mavericks in the field of cognitive science who, as "constructionists," have corrected the worst reductions of the information-exchange models (e.g., Ortony 1979, 1–18). But even the most complex constructionists tend to treat the minds that do the constructing as going it alone.

14. "The total self-corrective unit which processes information, or, as I say, 'thinks' and 'acts' and 'decides,' is a *system* whose boundaries do not at all coincide with the boundaries either of the body or of what is popularly called the 'self' or 'consciousness';

in a field of forces (for those who like pseudo-scientific language) or, as we used to say, a creature made in the image of God and hence essentially *affiliated,* joined to others and more like them than different from them. To be *joined,* in other words, is my primary, natural condition.

As the Marxists have always insisted, any sense of radical isolation—of essential separation or full alienation—is a disease. It may or may not be viewed as inherent in the human condition; the Judeo-Christian origin story says that it is, the post-Enlightenment version says that it is not: "Man is born free, and everywhere he is in chains." In either case, the "Fall" is not something that tells the whole story: to be "alienated" is a condition to be combated and if possible overcome, not reveled in with pride or complained about in self-pity. In all the social psychologies I have mentioned, much as in the old myths repudiating the proudly rebellious devil, to attempt to go it alone is to destroy a "self" that one never "possessed" in the first place. To break off from my "others" is to break off parts of my self.

INDIVIDUALISM AS A LITERARY HERITAGE

It is not hard to understand why resistance to the social psyche has persisted. For one thing, there were good reasons for the rise of individualism against various excessive conformisms. Whenever suspect beliefs survive, we can be sure that the survival is motivated by something more than blindness, no matter how irrational the various partisans may appear. The long history of abuse of our social nature by churches and states, the obvious stultifications that result when individuals are forced to conform, the ghastly record in this century of mass destruction in the name of *Volk,* race, or nation—these can seem to suggest that we have only two possible paths for the self: surrender your individuality *to* the group, or preserve it *against* the group.

Many thinkers have seen Western individualism, often identified

---

and it is important to notice that there are *multiple* differences between the thinking system and the 'self' as popularly conceived: . . . the network is not bounded by the skin but includes all external pathways along which information can travel" (1972, 319).

with Western capitalism, as the only alternative to the Gulag and the
Holocaust and the ravages of national "patriotism" in various political
parties. Indeed many of the classics of our literature have been read
as supporting this simple dichotomy. The reading, in some Protestant
sects, of the war in heaven as a battle between Christ's offer of freedom
of choice and Satan's guarantee of salvation through conformity; Dostoevsky's Grand Inquisitor's offer, in *The Brothers Karamazov*, of a
world free of suffering in exchange for the surrender of spiritual freedom—these and many other subtle and complex interpretations of our
fate have been too easily used to support the split between self and
"other." Many of our most powerful moral heroes in literature have
been precisely those who held out, as individuals, against the pressure
of some group that by definition is dangerous to the spirit. I don't want
to exaggerate the influence of literature; no doubt the grand powers
and grotesque limits of capitalism have a lot to do with maintaining
the myth of an unqualified good—resistant individualism. But the
educational power of many a great modern narrative has certainly contributed to the continuing resistance to the *social* psyche.

As I write this [some years ago now], the calendar has led everyone
to re-read *1984;* warnings against conformity of any kind fill the air.
The astonishingly successful revival is, I suggest, like the book's original success, based partly on the appeal of its brilliantly simplified portrayal of the dangers of conformity. Orwell himself would quite probably say that to read his book in terms of a simple polarity of self and
society is a gross over-simplification, adding that he had often, as a
good socialist, repudiated raw individualism. Fair enough. What follows is not in any way an attack on Orwell the career author, or on
Orwell the flesh-and-blood socialist struggling with various fascist,
communist, and "democratic" conformisms. It is rather an account of
one reading that the book still invites, a reading that has been especially attractive to readers who, like the Wayne Booth who first read it
in 1949, have been already disposed to think that in any conflict between individuals and "institutions," all virtues—truth, justice, integrity—were most likely on the loner's side.

Consider the central conflict that everyone found, in 1949, and that
many still find [in 1984]: the battle between its totally isolated, helpless protagonist and his monstrous totalitarian society. If we ask how
Orwell works to ensure the response of horror about total commu-

nalism (whether Soviet or Western), we can see just how the deservedly admired work reinforces the barrier between atomic selves, as individuals, and society, as inherently and always a threat to individuals.

Orwell chose, for good didactic reasons, to portray a society in which no real character, in my sense of the word, is conceivable. The two individuals who oppose that society, Winston Smith and his lover, Julia, cannot act as characters because they cannot make significant choices. The social order offers them at no point any choice except that between a secretive, self-protective "me" that is the only possible source of good and a "not me"—all the rest of Big Brother's world—that is hopelessly bad. Their love is a love of two "me"s, two lovers who have inexplicably survived as individuals. To be an individual, the novel tells us, reinforcing a major fixed norm of thousands of other modern works, is roughly equivalent to having a private, even an idiosyncratic life; to carry out Orwell's idea, the two who try to be genuine individuals must be forced, or tricked, into betraying each other at the end, by acceding to the demands of what is "out there": society.

Thus our only hope, as readers, is that Winston will find some way to resist all external pressures and maintain his integrity, which in this work is the same as his individuality: whatever is private, uniquely his. As we return to our own societies from any uncritical reading of the book, we are likely to see *our* only hope as our ability to oppose anything and everything public. The supreme vice for the implied readers of *1984* would be to betray or deny their own private sensations, beliefs, loves, quirks. Orwell provides few hints, in the book at least, that the very notion of such a self is merely an abstraction, a dangerous one invented by modernism, or that anyone who thinks truly alone soon thinks madness. His hero does go mad finally—when he decides to conform. Having in a sense given "all for love," like many an earlier Anthony—an individual lover against the world—at the end he gives all, including his sanity, for simple survival as a mindless, fully socialized cipher.

I am indeed doomed if to find my way I must, like Winston, simply ask "What do *they* want?" and then oppose it. No matter how many warnings I read against "groupthink" or "doubleplusgood duckspeaking," I cannot invent my very own language or social norms. Regardless of my intentions, my behavior will be chosen from among the paths opened by my society and its languages. If my society were ever to become fully like that of *1984*, I would be doomed long before the Thought Police caught up with me. They would need no threat of gnawing rats to destroy my resistance. I would be reduced from the beginning to my "personal resources," as we say, and if I tried to find out what resources were mine, all mine, probing beneath everything that *they* had implanted, I would—once again—discover that hollow core. The heroic, uninfluenced in-dividual turns out to be a non-person, an abstraction, destroyed in the very conception.

None of this contradicts *one* of Orwell's main points: totalitarianism can destroy you. But I suggest that his reductive plot, read uncritically, would make that kind of destruction more likely than before reading it, by leading readers to think that they *should* go it alone. As George Orwell the man would surely agree, each of us has a life-and-death stake in cultivating a social order that will nourish rather than destroy. But the opposition is not, as his implied author often suggests, between groupthink and privatethink. Rather it should be between societies that cultivate vigorous and productive ethical and political criticism and those that do not. Every author has a desperate stake in finding a polis (or at the least an opposition group within a polis) that will feed his or her character and the character of potential readers. Note how different that claim is from the claim that authors have a desperate stake in finding a polis that will leave them free to do whatever their private sensibility dictates. In both kinds of community, freedom will flourish as an ideal, but in recommending the one we are recognizing the author's need to be nourished *by society;* in the other we speak only of freedom from molestation (see Chapter 12, pp. 383–87).

Another way to see the distortion in *1984* is to ask simply, What *ought* Winston Smith to do? What duty does he have to others or to himself? The book too often seems to answer that he must make an absolute choice between a (vicious and self-destructive) duty to the state and a ("virtuous" and self-destructive) protection of his private life. As individualists, we often mistakenly refer our moral problems to the same false dichotomy. We talk about political actions as some kind of obligation that we owe, as individuals, to society, to others: we should be *altru*istic, not "self-centered." But if we are characters, social creatures by origin and definition, political and philanthropic actions are not performed out of duty to others but as acts of "self"-preservation; if the others are in me, "altruism"—the service of alterity—and selfishness must either not be contrasted at all, or if they are contrasted the lines must be drawn in new ways (MacIntyre 1967). Most of what I value in what I call "me" was conceived in and nurtured by one or another of my many societies, as represented in other characters.

Orwell the man, Orwell the socialist, surely knew most—maybe all—of this. But the author of *1984* underplays it, in order to pursue his satire against the unbridled state. By setting up a society that is totally bad, in opposition to a ready-made self that is the only good or potential good, *1984* would confirm all of us "me"'s in thinking of the world as whatever is "out there," threatening to destroy whatever is "in here"—the true self. I confess that a large part of my great pleasure in reading and teaching the book to my classes in the early 1950s, before ethical criticism intruded, consisted of self-congratulation. As a member of the individualistic elite, as dues-paying member of the American Civil Liberties Union and other organizations defending liberty, as critic of the conformities of consumer capitalism, and as passionate enemy of McCarthyism, I could easily look up after each rereading of those horrifying final pages and tell myself that *I* need not change *my* life. My response should be to get my students to read the book, in order to change *theirs,* and to work a little harder to combat the wicked institutions that surrounded me: authoritarian church, benighted college administration, corrupt government and industry.[15]

The extreme opposition of self and other was of course not invented by Orwell. Hundreds of predecessors had pursued the "Byronic,"

15. In 1988, reading these paragraphs written mostly in 1984, it seems to me that they create a somewhat distorted myth of the relation of the individual and society, as viewed by us progressives in the early 1950s. Where, in my picture of rampant individualism at that time, do I place our passionate effort to found various consumer cooperatives? Where, for that matter, do I place my conviction in those days, still not wholly abandoned, that to *join* organizations like the ACLU and Americans for Democratic Action was itself a sign of political virtue? No doubt a defender of Orwell could even argue that reading *1984* and *Animal Farm* must have reinforced my inclination to join like-minded people in political action against the wrong kinds of conformity and on behalf of productive kinds; the book would in this view be entirely redeemed. We can be sure of one thing, in advance of any discussion between such a defender of Orwell and myself: neither of us would come out of the discussion with our reading of the book unchanged. The change for me, if his interpretation prevailed, would make me even more grateful than I am for a book that stimulates now, and stimulated then, this kind of conversation.

"Faustian" notion that it is better to be damned for a sincere, passionately individual embrace of a falsehood than to be saved through submission to someone else's truth. They often spoke as if they would repudiate all traditions, ignoring, for example, their kinship with those Christian martyrs who won their salvation by heroic obedience to their private visions or voices, against the errors of the mob. Of course, those martyrs were saved because their vision was of a truth potentially applicable to all. But that truth always included the picture of a father God who, in His seemingly paradoxical creation plan, was willing to allow untold millions to fumble their way into eternal damnation for the sake of awarding salvation to the few who *genuinely earned* it by a proper exercise of their freedom.

It is only a short step from the view that the opportunity for individual choice for all is so valuable that it justifies the damnation of most to the view that true salvation lies in the opportunity to make individual choices per se: God will honor me more for an honest choice of error, as Faust is honored at the end of part 2 of Goethe's version, than for a slavish or insincere acceptance of established ways. Not only for the plan but for the individual as well, it is better to have independence in error than a dependent truth.

A scarcely discernible further step leads to the view that to be novel is more important than to be "right"; after all, if you are not novel, original, "creative," you obviously cannot be expressing your unique individuality (Booth 1983).

Long before Orwell issued his attack on groupthink we had worshipped a fair number of powerful literary heroes—to say nothing of their flesh-and-blood counterparts—who enacted the drama of this supreme choice. The most wrenching portraits for me are those torn creatures of Dostoevsky who deliberately choose beliefs demonstrably against reason precisely because the beliefs *are* unreasonable and the choice therefore free.[16] When I was a young man, working out my own rebellions against what I (wrongly) considered a singularly repressive

16. Ivan Karamazov, for example, or the narrator of *Notes from Underground.* Critics debate about whether Dostoevsky shares these extreme views, but "of course" he both does (as creator of persuasive voices) and does not (as flesh-and-blood "Christian"). The hero of Samuel Butler's *The Way of All Flesh* provides another famous echo of this version of Byronism, as indeed did Butler himself in much of his public posing as daring radical.

upbringing, I read such moments quite uncritically—that is, I did not really look closely at the terms of the Faustian bargain: the willing sacrifice of "establishment" salvation for the sake of a private, *personal* salvation-through-knowledge, pursued *in opposition*. I knew, or rather I *felt*, what it was that I sought, and that seemed to me precisely what had been sought by various heroes, from Socrates through Blake and Byron to Joyce, who had fought my battles long before I was born. I don't remember noting that my rebellion was actually highly selective and highly imitative.

To see just how natural this particular elevation of the risk-taking individual had come to seem early in this century, we should take a close look at the fixed norms of Joyce's *A Portrait of the Artist as a Young Man*.[17] Many have taken this novel as an exemplar of modernism, particularly in its eschewing of all preachments except (no surprise) the elevation of art as the supreme value. What interests me here is the way in which it relies on (and surely thus reinforces) our belief in that supreme principle of individualism: one's true salvation is found in successfully resisting communally imposed norms and finding one's own unique path.

Portrait moves—no critic has, I think, questioned this view of its simple surface structure—through a series of temptations or possible deflections of the hero, Stephen, from what is finally to be his elected fate: to become an artist. To become an artist, he must repudiate the appeals of all communal values or established vocations and embrace simply and absolutely his true vocation, that of the honest artistic seer, pursuing a private vision never before known or imagined.

I must here leave to one side the vexed question of how much distance there is between the bargain as viewed by Stephen and that same bargain as viewed by Joyce at the time of creating his character. Clearly Joyce sees the bargain as the kind made by young people like Stephen (and himself many years before the book was completed). What is more important is that generations of readers have identified with Stephen, wrongly or not, and have thus experienced a powerful attraction toward Stephen's values.

What are the ingredients that make up Stephen's choice? To trace

---

17. A version of this discussion of *Portrait* appeared in "Renewing the Medium of Renewal: Some Notes on the Anxieties of Innovation" (in Hassan 1983).

them in detail, thinking all the while of how obviously right they have seemed to most of us moderns (even when we have become "post"), will not of course even begin to prove that Joyce implanted these beliefs in us, thus making us what we are. But when we multiply the Stephens, as we must, by thousands of similar heroes (not similar in quality but in beliefs about what makes true heroism),[18] we detect a very powerful force indeed.

First, Stephen's bargain entails great personal risk. It is a choice of ultimates, a choice between spiritual freedom and damnation: "I am not afraid," Stephen says in his final conversation with Cranly, defending his decision to repudiate the Church in order to pursue his artistic vocation. "And I am not afraid to make a mistake, even a great mistake, a lifelong mistake and perhaps as long as eternity too" (1964, 247). For Pascal, it had seemed reasonable to face the ultimate choice and wager on God, because to do so was infinitely less risky than to live a life without God. But for Stephen, it seems obvious that the only honorable way to face that wager is to grasp the far riskier alternative.

A second ingredient shows why the rebellious, "personal" choice is the more honorable: it demands absolute, total honesty about Stephen's doubts, and it results in a kind of integrity or wholeness of spirit that accommodation to traditional beliefs will destroy. Explaining why he dares to risk the wrath of God, Stephen says, "I fear more than that [wrath] the chemical action which would be set up in my soul by a false homage to a symbol behind which are massed twenty centuries of authority and veneration" (243). A chemical reaction can take place only when the soul is divided into conflicting elements. A modern spirit like Cranly who yet clings to traditional beliefs is inevitably pulled in conflicting directions, as Cranly himself admits. For Stephen to acquiesce in such a state would be to show lack of integrity not only in the sense of lost unity-of-soul but in the more modern sense of the word "integrity": it would be insincere, dishonest. Classical heroes were not troubled by the fear of having to play multiple roles; they faced impossible choices, but their roles as choosers were clear. Stephen, in contrast, like many another modern, will no longer tolerate division:

18. For example, all those ballads—pop, rock, folk, country-and-western—with refrains that forgive the singer for all his or her misdeeds, because at least "I Did It My Way"?

he is willing to be damned, if necessary, in order to achieve sincerity or authenticity (see Trilling 1972).

Third, as is already evident even in these brief quotations, the ultimate value for such a soul is freedom, liberation. ". . . I will try to express myself in some mode of life or art as freely as I can and as wholly as I can" (247). Stephen talks of seeking "unfettered freedom." Later in his journal he dwells on the word "free": "Free, yes. . . . Soul free and fancy free. Let the dead bury the dead" (248). Explaining why he will not become a Protestant as he throws off the chains of Catholicism, he says, "What kind of liberation would that be to forsake an absurdity which is logical and coherent and to embrace one which is illogical and incoherent?" (244).

It is important, fourth, that such integrity in pursuit of freedom be exhibited in a negotiation primarily with a private self, only incidentally in honest dealings with others. The risky choice can be made honestly only by a single, isolated, even lonely individual: not a soul made in the image of God and thus inherently more like other souls than different from them (and thus hoping for a final family home, as it were), but a self that is unique. The choosing self is a single lonely atom that cannot but be its own most precious possession, once that Pearl of Great Price, the Good Word, the word of the Other, has been repudiated. Words like "myself" and "alone" recur throughout the conversation. Cranly recapitulates Stephen's choice: You seek "to discover the mode of life or of art whereby your spirit could express itself in unfettered freedom" (246). He presses Stephen about what it will mean to be alone—alone throughout eternity: "Alone, quite alone. You have no fear of that. And you know what that word means? Not only to be separate from all others but to have not even one friend. . . . And not to have any one person who would be more than a friend, more even than the noblest and truest friend a man ever had." And Stephen answers: "I will take that risk" (247).

Just think of what that means, not primarily as a rejection of the Catholic Church but as a rejection of the friendship that the ancients described as the most important virtue, the one gift without which life would be intolerable! The supreme value of the isolated single separate self has never been expressed more unequivocally, not even by Byron, not even by Milton's Satan. Stephen gives no hint—though the artist Joyce provides plenty of hints through Cranly—that in surrendering to or embracing the Other or others one might find support or healing or instruction, let alone another kind of freedom. There is indeed no hint, not even in Cranly's words, that Stephen's picture of his "self" is radically suspect, that no such isolated self could ever exist, or that Stephen's picture of the self he serves is after all itself a social inheritance. Finally, there is no hint that either Stephen or Joyce is aware of the deliciously complex *literary* friendships they both rely on: Stephen will write books that will rejoin him to his re-created "race"; Joyce has already written the friendship offering that we readers gratefully accept.

In fact, all of Stephen's views about the value of his revolt, including the notion that the pursuit of art justifies surrendering all other values, are by his time commonplaces (see Trilling 1972, on Rousseau or Byron, for example). One hundred years earlier Jane Austen had already reduced to parody the romantic notion that the isolated self can discover its own values—not only in an anti-romantic novel like *Sense and Sensibility* but even in her juvenilia, where she has great fun with "independent" characters like the young man who draws himself up to his full height and proclaims, "No! Never shall it be said that I obliged my Father."[19] In short, the enemy of Bright Young Rebels for more than a century had been other people, though we waited awhile before Sartre gave us a summary that could turn into a slogan: "Hell is other people."

The battle is not, however, only with others-in-general; it is especially with those others who represent the past. Cranly, young and already threatened by doubts similar to Stephen's, is respected sufficiently (by Joyce? by Stephen?) to deserve and receive an explanation of Stephen's choice. But no older person in the book, no teacher, no priest, no parent, is depicted as really worth a serious conversation, let

---

19. The whole marvelously funny episode in "Letter 6th" of *Love and Freindship* ought to be required reading for all teenage rebels (80–82). I have not found a good history of the warfare between defenders of the self-as-social, like Jane Austen, and celebrants of individualism. Does it begin with Achilles' sulking in his tent, rejecting the arguments of Odysseus, Phoenix, and Ajax, as they speak for public norms? With Socrates' trusting of his own rational probing rather than the public wisdom hailed by Protagoras? With Descartes's hailing of the cogito as opposed to the communal wisdom pursued by Scholastic philosophers and Renaissance rhetoricians? With the "Enlightenment" figures who stimulated Edmund Burke's powerful argument, in *Reflections on the Revolution in France* (1790), that no one person's reason can avoid disaster, unless subordinated to the "second nature" provided by social habit and collective wisdom? A powerful beginning on such a history is provided by James Chandler in *Wordsworth's Second Nature,* as he argues against the prevailing view of the young Wordsworth as a naive, Rousseauvian individualist (1984, esp. ch. 4).

alone as worthy to offer advice. (The dean of studies with his offer, in chapter 5, is no true exception; he is mocked, stylistically, throughout the passage.) The true enemy to liberation of the self is "twenty centuries of authority and veneration," the past and all those who stand for it. "I will not serve that in which I no longer believe whether it call itself my home, my fatherland or my church" (246–47). The motto for the whole book might well be the repeated slogan, Non Serviam. It is true that in fighting his battles Stephen is quite willing to make use of fragments from the past: bits from Aquinas or Aristotle or Bruno, bits of Greek myth; the past can lend him rhetorical resources. But it cannot grant him an inheritance of credible beliefs. Or so he believes, even as he relies on *one* major inheritance.

Implicit in all this and explicit at several points in *Portrait* is a sixth modernist ingredient, an insistence that a liberated self will be found, if at all, only in some original mode, as yet unforged—in some innovation, some form of creativity that will break with everything that has gone before. The lonely, bravely honest battler for freedom, breaking the fetters of a hostile past, does so by seeking what is truly new, what has never before been conceived. Since his "self" is unique and new, his freedom will be found in a lonely expression of novelty. Stephen repudiates Michael Robartes's embrace of the "loveliness which has long faded from the world," desiring instead "to press in my arms the loveliness which has not yet come into the world" (251). Seeking finally to "learn *in my own* life and away from home *and friends* what the heart is and what it feels," he goes on, in what is surely one of the most representatively modern moments in modern literature, "to forge in the smithy of *my* soul the *uncreated* conscience of *my* race" (253; emphasis mine).

THE FEAR OF HYPOCRISY AND THE PRACTICING OF ROLES

Stephen's is only the most powerful of thousands of literary voices that have not only defined the self as in opposition to others, but placed it at the center of all value—a self-aggrandizing, godlike figure. If Joyce had attempted a head-on assault against the traditional virtues of humility and self-abasement (discovered in the contemplation and worship of the true God), he could not have done more—unless he decided to reproduce the works of Rousseau, Byron, or Nietzsche. Without distorting badly, we can say that high modernism, of Stephen's kind, was a direct and often deliberate attempt to depose "the good" as the sovereign served by both classical philosophy and the Judeo-Christian tradition (Murdoch 1970), and to crown in its place the individual and his creative works (it usually *was* a king, not a queen, who usurped the throne of the Muses). All of us who were converted to the religion of modernism as we read the great works of modernism found inscribed in our souls as self-evident a picture of an isolated, resistant, indeed combative "self" that ought, according to that very picture, to have been immune to such literary influences.

If, in the face of such powerful and all-pervasive rhetoric, we can reject the notion of the self as an atomic isolate and view ourselves as social characters, we open up neglected questions about the uses and dangers of particular experiences with narratives. Before turning to consider some of these in the next chapter, we must face one major anxiety produced by this kind of talk.

Whenever I have spoken in recent years about building a richer character out of adopted roles, roles critically chosen from those stories our society offers us, I have met anxieties about insincerity or inauthenticity or hypocrisy. "If, unlike Winston Smith as he relies on his feeble self, I consciously attend to and then take on roles that are not my present 'self,' what happens to 'my' integrity?" This is hardly a question to be dismissed lightly; it has produced a great deal of modern talk about the "anxiety of alienation" and the "anxiety of influence," about which I shall talk a bit in Chapter 9. Indeed some studies claim to show that just about everybody in the modern world is afraid of being found out as an impostor, guilty of hypocritical performances (Clance 1985; Harvey 1985). But as we explore the question, we should not assume that we know in advance what insincerity or hypocrisy are, or how they work.

"Hypocrisy" makes an interesting case in itself, because its central definition, "the pretense of having feelings or characteristics one does not possess,"[20] nicely dramatizes the dichotomy I have been criticizing.

---

20. One dictionary holds that "hypocrisy" is the most strongly negative word in a series that becomes less and less wicked, like this: dissimulation, pretense, sanctimony, sanctimoniousness, pharisaism, and cant.

Who is this "one" who "possesses" some characteristics and does not possess others? And how do we distinguish the false pretense of having a characteristic from truly having it? The answer is clear enough in some cases: if I claim to be honest while actually lying to you, you have a clear right to condemn my pretense. But what if I claim to be a good student while actually suspecting that I may be a bad one? What if I pretend to be a well-informed person and work to make myself well-informed in order to play a more convincing role?

The word "hypocrisy" originally meant simply the playing of a role *on the stage:* dramatic acting, *hypocrisis,* from *hypo* ("under") plus *crinein* ("to decide, determine, judge"). To give the signs of choosing in a certain way, on stage or off, was to convey a character of a certain kind, in "hypocrisy." Thus the two words, "character" and "hypocrisy," suggest a challenging analogy: actors play roles as characters, with "hypocrisy"; authors play roles by creating characters, and readers and spectators play roles by *re*-creating them, hypo-critically. What is forgotten in our universal condemnation of hypocrisy is that a kind of play-acting with characters, or characteristics, a kind of *faking* of characters, is one of the main ways that we build what becomes our character.

If words like "faking" and "hypocrisy" make us uneasy, we should not be surprised. In modern usage, of course, to be hypocritical is always a bad thing—sometimes seemingly the worst vice of all. We can hardly call anyone a worse name than "Tartuffe" or "Pecksniff." Three centuries ago Molière portrayed the first great stage anti-hypocrite, the self-destructive misanthrope Alceste, gifted, in his absolute integrity, with the ability to reject everyone else, including his beloved: they were all dreadful hypocrites.[21] Molière himself saw what was wrong with Alceste even while loving him and mocking his opponents, but increasingly over the centuries authors themselves have come to resemble that strangely appealing madman of integrity, turning all virtues and vices into a single opposition: hypocritical / sincere.

Today almost any action can be forgiven so long as the agent is sin-

21. An important discussion of the ambivalences in "hypocrisy," with a penetrating discussion of *Tartuffe,* is Judith Shklar's "Let Us Not Be Hypocritical" (1979). Another challenging discussion (in the same issue of *Daedalus* in which Shklar's essay appears), by Jean Starobinski (1979), centers on Montaigne's subtle grapplings with the threat of false consciousness. See also his *Montaigne in Motion* (1985, esp. ch. 2).

cere in committing it and honest in confessing it. We even see what might be called "hypocrisy downward"—authors who report only the worst of the worlds they inhabit and the deeds they (or their characters) perform, all in the service of a claim to honesty. Surely there's something crazily "self"-destructive—or I should say "character"-destructive—in our elevation of this lone virtue above all others, and our substitution of one vice for entire decalogues. Why is it bad to practice the art of making certain choices before one has thoroughly mastered that art? Why is it worse to pretend to have added certain powers than to wallow in public confessions of one's weaknesses?[22] If my character is the totality of all the roles I can play effectively, good and bad, it will be in some sense a product of all the "hypocrisies" I have practiced (good or bad) long enough to perfect them.

Many of the virtues that we most honor are originally gained by practices that our enemies might call faking, our friends perhaps something like aspiring or emulating. We pretend to be scholars long before we can produce a piece of scholarship that is not visibly faked. Just now I played with a bit of Greek etymology, as if I knew Greek, which I do not. And yet I now know, because of the fakery-practice, a *bit* more Greek than I knew before. We must fake—must practice—playing the cello (say) long before we can really play it, and each stage of improvement requires new levels of faking. One soon learns, in developing any skill, that we inhibit our progress most by declaring ourselves incompetent: "I'm a poor tennis player" is almost certainly a prelude to worse playing than "I'm getting better all the time." Why should the same not be true of all the virtues? If I do not practice courage frequently enough to make it habitual, how can I ever become cour*ageous?* The difference between productive hypocrisy—aspiring and emulating—and the vice that the word is used to name must thus surely lie in the motive and direction of the "practice." If I am really practicing only deceit, and not in fact developing my potentialities for a given virtue, then of course what I will develop is skill in the practice of deception.[23]

22. For an intelligent rehabilitation of Victorian reticence as a virtue, see "The Combustible Victorians" (Jenkyns 1986).

23. Along with the strange history of the word "hypocrisy," we should add the ambiguous history of the word "practice." The earliest recorded sense of the word is "the action of scheming or planning; artifice; a trick or plot." Yet the word quickly developed more favorable senses, since—as we say—practice makes perfect.

What I am calling "hypocrisy upward" thus easily turns to slush, and it is easy to satirize. In *More Die of Heartbreak,* Saul Bellow creates a lost soul, a seemingly carefree swinger named Treckie, whose lover mocks her beliefs like this: "The way to change for the better is to begin by telling everybody about it. You make an announcement. You repeat your intentions until others begin to repeat them to you. When you hear them from others you can say, 'Yes, that's what I think too.' The more often your intention is repeated, the truer it becomes. The key is fluency. It's fluency of formulation that matters most" (1987, 90–91). On the other hand, Bellow's most admired characters are all engaged in a more or less conscious battle between their higher and lower souls, and his wonderful talk about that battle can be read as his own way of sloughing off that part of himself that he least respects.

In modern criticism we are more likely to feel comfortable with this practicing of roles when authors do it than when readers do. Everyone knows that authors must take on roles, that they need not be "sincerely" wedded to particular characteristics in order to portray them sympathetically. Though there is what might be called a Stanislavsky School of Literary Criticism that insists on authors' dealing only with material that reflects some notion of their "real" selves or genuine feelings, most critics recognized, long before deconstructionists made a big thing of it, that the lines connecting literary characters and anything that might be called the "real author" are hazy indeed. Everyone knows that the character implied by the total act of writing any literary work (the implied author) is always (but always) an "improved" version over the flesh-and-blood creator—not necessarily improved by your standards or mine, but improved by the standards of the author. The split between the two is shocking when it is wide and when the real writer is for any reason notorious; we are all distressed when we learn that "our" Robert Frost, inferred from the poems— wise, kindly, companionable, earthy—could in private be a cad and a bounder, and a cosmopolitan sophisticate at that.[24] As Montaigne emphasizes throughout the *Essays,* even the author who sets out, as he

---

24. Lawrance Thompson made this disparity a keynote in his biography (1966, 58, 88, 227–28, 504–5). For a defense of Frost as not quite *that* awful, see Pritchard 1984. For a poignant yet amusing account of just how disillusioning an encounter with the "real" author can be, see Susan Sontag's "Pilgrimage" (1987). As a fourteen-year-old

does, to present himself as he truly exists, to make author and book identical ("My book is my self"), will inevitably *select,* in order to appear better according to whatever standard his literary project (or public expectation) dictates: "In moulding this figure upon my self, I have been so oft constrain'd to temper and compose my self in a right posture, that the Copy is truly taken, and has in some sort form'd it self. But painting for others, I represent my self in a better colouring than my own natural Complexion. . . . And withal a man must curl, set out and adjust himself to appear in publick" ([1693] 1869, 561, 319).

The parallel point about readers has been much less widely recognized. Everyone concedes that naive readers, and especially readers of popular fiction, along with moviegoers and soap-opera buffs—all "unsophisticated" folk—aspire, in their imaginations, to emulate the heroes and heroines of beloved works. Sophisticated readers, we are told, should never identify in this way. It is quite true that one kind of sophistication can prevent such identification: if we simply study a text, seeking evidence for this or that thesis about literature, language, society, the creative process, or the history of certain locutions, phonemes, or narrative devices, nothing need happen to us one way or another. But readers who engage in a story, readers who enter the pattern of hopes, fears, and expectations that every story asks for, will always take on "characters" that are superior, on the scale of a book's fixed norms, to the relatively complex, erratic, and paradoxical characters that they cannot help being in their daily lives. To engage sympathetically with a story is always to concentrate one's actual confusing multi-dimensionality into a small range of values on one or more of our seven scales (see pp. 179–95 above). We also "behave better," for the time being, on any given scale, in order to meet the invitation of the implied author. "Better" may of course turn out, after ethical reflection, to be far worse—but that is another story, the one we are telling throughout this book.

In short, the ideal of purging oneself of responses to persons, the

---

idolator of Thomas Mann, she suffered in his home an excruciatingly "embarrassing" afternoon tea. The embarrassment was compounded, as she now remembers it, of shame at her own effrontery in intruding on the great man, and shock at his banalities and pomposities. For a more ambiguous account of such an encounter, see how Proust handles the meeting of his narrator, Marcel, with the "real" author, Bergotte, after years of admiring his works (1934, 416–26).

ideal of refusing to play the human roles offered us by literature, is
never realized by any actual reader who reads a compelling fiction for
the sake of reading it (rather than for the sake of obtaining material for
an essay, dissertation, or book). It is of course true that in reading
some modern works we take on selves who repudiate tears and laughter and share *other* human pleasures with the author, pleasures like
shuddering at the horrors of the abyss, or mocking sentimentalists, or
enjoying textual play of various kinds. When we read such works with
full engagement, these are our forms of "hypocritical aspiration."
Even in the purest of textual gambols we will play the roles—so long
as we continue to "listen"—that the text demands of us.[25] We will
do so, that is, unless and until for some reason, good or bad, we decide to play some alternative role and impose an overt criticism alien
to the work's demands—one of the forms of ethical criticism I am
recommending.

In our pre-critical reading we have experiences like that reported by
Erich Auerbach in his reading of Montaigne: "I suppose anyone who
has read enough of Montaigne *to feel at home in the essays* must have
had the same experience as I. I had been reading him for some time,
and when I *had finally acquired a certain familiarity with his manner,* I
thought *I could hear him speak and see his gestures*" (1957, 254; my
italics). My own experience is that this effect, or something analogous
to it, can happen in reading Robbe-Grillet just as much as in reading a
personal essayist or a "sentimental" novelist like Dickens. Whenever I
work my way into a narrative (even a historical narrative, though I am,
to my regret, somewhat more resistant in that direction), the "I" that is
"me" becomes increasingly like my picture of the implied author: I
succumb—I begin to see as he or she sees, to feel as she feels, to love
what he loves, or to mock what she mocks.

25. This point is made in more poignant form by Yves Bonnefoy in his Inaugural
Address at the Collège de France (1981). Surrounded, as it were, by critics and poets
who seemed to honor only "the labor of the signifier"—the control that language and
culture exercise in spite of any author's will—Bonnefoy asserts that "it is nonetheless
true that when we speak we say 'I,' and we say it in the urgency of our days. . . . [W]e
decide upon values. . . . And while we must continue to study how the signifier ceaselessly
fluctuates within the signs, . . . we must also search for the way in which this élan that
we are can affirm itself, in spite of being adrift in words, as an origin." The way to
do this, he goes on, is to go back to the poems—to "ask questions . . . about poetry"
(1984, 438–39).

Of course we all find works that we resist or deliberately "misread"; my main point in this book is that we should do more of that than we have admitted to in the recent past, and do it better. But the fact that we can become more discriminating as we mature should not lead us to think that the best way to become fully mature is to stop succumbing entirely. When we lose our capacity to succumb, when we reach a point at which no other character can manage to enter our imaginative or emotional or intellectual territory and *take over*, at least for the time being, then we are dead on our feet.[26]

It is precisely in the playing out of the roles that are not yet fully "natural" to us, not yet the "second nature" that the romantics talked about,[27] precisely in what many would call the hypocritical pretense to ideals that we cannot possibly live up to in the rest of life, that our most exhilarating personal prospects lie. A commonplace has it that by the age of thirty, the character has set like plaster, and will never soften again. Another one says, "Give me a child until the age of six, and I care not what influences occur afterward." No doubt some early "fixings" are necessary in every life, but for most of us our character—in the larger sense of the range of choices and habits of choice available to us—changes, grows, and diminishes largely as a result of our imaginative diet.

I began this chapter by tracing a tradition that took such talk about narrative almost for granted. That tradition, perhaps now reviving, never quite disappeared. Listen to George Santayana, writing just fifty years ago, as he introduces his powerful work *Three Philosophical Poets:*

> The sole advantage in possessing great works of literature lies in what they can help us to become. In themselves, as feats performed by their authors, they would have forfeited none of their truth or greatness if they had

---

26. As we mature we learn to resist this effect at least sufficiently to avoid giving away embarrassingly overt clues to our idolatry—walking like Superman, talking like Meryl Streep, writing and talking like our notion of Hemingway, Faulkner, James. But unless we deliberately dry up our emotional lives, we resemble to some degree the delightful ten-year-old I overheard recently talking with a friend: "Yes, but what kind of comedian do you wanna be—Eddie Murphy or Bill Cosby or what?"

27. See James Chandler's *Wordsworth's Second Nature* (1984, esp. the introduction and ch. 4).

perished before our day. We can neither take away nor add to their past
value or inherent dignity. It is only they, in so far as they are appropriate
food and not poison for us, that can add to the present value and dignity of
our minds. . . . Regarded from this point of view, as substances to be digested, the poetic remains of Lucretius, Dante, and Goethe . . . afford
rather a varied feast.

(1936, 5)

And on he goes, showing how his three poets are all indispensable to
him; each poet encompasses or summarizes a total worldview that,
when placed in conjunction with the others, has quite literally *made*
the Santayana whom we come to know in reading his account.[28]

Because we have tended to think of character in narrowly moral
terms, we have underplayed the way in which such makings are cru-
cially important for character. Regardless of what happened to Santayana before the age of six, or thirty, he chooses to act and to speak in
ways entirely different from those he would have chosen had he not
read those three poets. The implied author that he presents, as he discusses the three great characters, is a man who has entirely understood, digested, and harmonized all three of these radically different
worlds. Should he be called hypocritical? Who is this George Santayana who can claim to have digested, through prolonged and repeated repasts, these three giants? Clearly he aspires to be as great
as they—perhaps just a shade greater, since he can handle all three
greatnesses. The act is fake, then, because surely he knew, as we know,
that George Santayana is not as great as Dante, Lucretius, or Goethe.
But that is not the point. What should be compared, if only that were
possible, is the Santayana he became with the Santayana he would
have been, had he never savored these three forms of nourishment.

"How absurd," some may still want to say, "to be so malleable, so
imitative, so dependent on the genius of others. How sad not to show
integrity to your *own* self, not to be sincerely in touch with your *own*
true feelings. And how insincere all this sounds, how genuinely hypocritical, how messy. Where is the integrity in all this shifting from ideal
to ideal, from code to code? And where is the 'real' Wayne Booth, all

28. Incidentally, *Three Philosophical Poets* was credited by Conrad Aiken with
having changed *his* intellectual character; reading it made him decide that he must develop a philosophical poetry or stop trying to be a poet (Aiken 1966, 3–6).

this while? Are *you* an amorphous collection of selves, like the pathetic, frenetic character Mucho Maas at the end of Pynchon's *The Crying of Lot 49*?" And where, then, are you out there, *hypocrite lecteur?* Have you not been dissolved into the merely theatrical roles that Philip Roth's Zuckerman seems to celebrate at the end of *The Counterlife?* "All I can tell you with certainty is that I, for one, have no self. . . . What I have instead is a variety of impersonations I can do, and not only of myself—a troupe of players that I have internalized, a permanent company of actors. . . . But I certainly have no self independent of my imposturing, artistic efforts to have one. Nor would I want one. I am a theater and nothing more than a theater" (1987, 321).

To me it doesn't feel quite that way. The character I become as I play my roles is not unreal, not an impostor, not "nothing more than a theater." While I have given up any notion of being a private "individual" or "authentic self," I have not lost anything in the giving up. If each of my roles engages the other roles fully and responsibly, if I do not and cannot cast off my unique collection of roles at will, why should I be anxious about the process of adding or subtracting roles? If *sharing* roles is more important than finding a unique one, why be anxious about the discovery that whatever might be really distinct in my psychic equipment, unshared with those who have molded me in this or that direction, is a minuscule genetic beginning off there in the distant past. "I" join "you" here together, shamelessly, each of us a product of a lifetime of . . . behavioro-biblio-modification?

Shamelessly, perhaps, but not entirely free-floating. No one who has been trained, as all of us have been, to honor our "inner selves" in their fullest integrity as the highest good can possibly become *characters* again without having to face new problems in new ways.[29] Chief

---

29. For instance, much of the stress that traditional scholars have felt in their encounters with various deconstructionist moves has come, I would argue, not from the attacks on "reality" and "referentiality" in general but from the decenterings of the "subject": If I lose "my" center, where am "I"? On the other hand, those who are active in less introspective vocations can more easily relish their capacity to practice diverse roles. Though the research on the "impostor" fear shows that even outstanding scientists suffer it (Harvey 1985; Clance 1985), "men of action" (obviously by now including women) often seem to relish their adaptability. The famous, idiosyncratic mathematician/polymath Benoit Mandelbrot once responded cheerfully to an introduction that dwelt in detail on his multiple roles: "Very often when I listen to the list of my previous jobs I wonder if I exist. The intersection of such sets is surely empty" (qtd. in Glieck 1987, 86). Doesn't the witty response itself remove all reason for anxiety?

of these, for our purposes, is that of deciding whether a proffered new role, encountered in an appealing narrative, is one that we can afford to take on, or *ought* to take on. Does the concept of "ought" even make sense once I have given up the notion that I can find its validation by appealing to that core, that self, that I have been taught to search for? Can we say any more than that we find our new selves in multiple encounters, hoping that *this* powerful narrative will supplement or correct *that* one? Can we hope now to say more than that Don Quixote might have been rescued by reading *Don Quixote* and that Emma Bovary's best hope would have been to read *Madame Bovary,* rather than all those romantic novels and histories?

REFERENCES

Aiken, Conrad. "Poetry and the Mind of Modern Man." In *Poets on Poetry.* Ed. Howard Nemerov. New York, 1966.
Aristotle. *Poetics.* Trans. W. H. Fyfe. Loeb Classical Library, London, 1927.
———. *Politics.* Trans. Carnes Lord. Chicago, 1984.
Auden, W. H. "The Ironic Hero: Some Reflections on *Don Quixote.*" *Horizon* 20 (Aug. 1949): 86–94.
Auerbach, Erich. *Mimesis: The Representation of Reality in Western Literature* [1946]. Trans. Willard R. Trask. New York, 1957.
Austen, Jane. *Love and Freindship* [1922]. In vol. 6 of *The Works of Jane Austen.* Ed. R. W. Chapman. London, 1963.
———. *Sanditon* ([1817] 1925). In vol. 6 of *The Works of Jane Austen.* Ed. R. W. Chapman. London, 1963.
Bakhtin, M. M. *The Dialogic Imagination: Four Essays.* Ed. Michael Holquist. Trans. Caryl Emerson and Michael Holquist. University of Texas Press Slavic Series, no. 1. Austin, Tex., 1981.
Bateson, Gregory. "The Cybernetics of 'Self': A Theory of Alcoholism." *Psychiatry* 34 (1971): 1–18. Reprinted in *Steps to an Ecology of Mind.* New York, 1972.
Bellow, Saul. *More Die of Heartbreak.* New York, 1987.
Bonnefoy, Yves. "Image and Presence" (Inaugural Address at the Collège de France, 1981). Trans. John T. Naughton. *New Literary History* 15 (Spr. 1984): 433–51.
Booth, Wayne C. *Critical Understanding: The Powers and Limits of Pluralism.* Chicago, 1979.
———. "Print Culture and Video Culture." *Daedalus* 111 (Fall 1982): 33–60.
———. "Renewing the Medium of Renewal: Some Notes on the Anxieties of Innovation." In Hassan 1983.
Bové, Paul A. *Intellectuals in Power: A Genealogy of Critical Humanism.* New York, 1986.
Bradley, F. H. *Ethical Studies* [1876]. 2d ed., 1927. Reprint. New York, 1951.

Burke, Kenneth. *Language as Symbolic Action: Essays on Life, Literature, and Method.* Berkeley, 1966.

Büttner, F. O. *Imitatio Pietatis: Motive der christlichen Ikonographie als Modelle zur Verähnlichung.* Berlin, 1983.

Castiglione, Baldesar. *The Book of the Courtier* [1561]. Trans. Charles S. Singleton. New York, 1959.

Cervantes Saavedra, Miguel de. *The Ingenious Gentleman Don Quixote de la Mancha* [1605]. Trans. Samuel Putnam. New York, 1949.

Chandler, James K. *Wordsworth's Second Nature: A Study of the Poetry and Politics.* Chicago, 1984.

Channing, William Ellery. "The Imitableness of Christ's Character." In *The Works of William Ellery Channing.* Boston, 1881. 310–16.

Cicero. *De Officiis* (On moral obligation). Trans. John Higginbotham. Berkeley, 1967.

Clance, Pauline Rose. *The Impostor Phenomenon: Overcoming the Fear That Haunts Your Success.* Atlanta, Ga., 1985.

Dewey, John. *Human Nature and Conduct: An Introduction to Social Psychology.* New York, 1922.

Dumont, Louis. *Essais sur l'individualisme: Une perspective anthropologique sur l'idéologie moderne.* Paris, 1983.

Eco, Umberto. *Travels in Hyperreality.* New York, 1986.

Flaubert, Gustave. *Madame Bovary* [1857]. Trans. Francis Steegmuller. New York, 1957.

Foucault, Michel. "On the Genealogy of Ethics: An Overview of Work in Progress." In *Michel Foucault: Beyond Structuralism and Hermeneutics.* Ed. Hubert L. Dreyfus and Paul Rabinow. 2d ed. Chicago, 1983. 229–52.

———. *The Care of the Self* [1984]. Trans. Robert Hurley. Vol. 3 of *The History of Sexuality.* New York, 1986.

Gardner, Howard. *The Mind's New Science: A History of the Cognitive Revolution.* New York, 1985.

Glieck, James. *Chaos: Making a New Science.* New York, 1987.

Graubard, Stephen R., ed. *Hypocrisy, Illusion, and Evasion.* [Special issue] *Daedalus* 108 (Sum. 1979).

Harvey, Joan C. *If I'm So Successful, Why Do I Feel Like a Fake? The Impostor Phenomenon.* New York, 1985.

Hassan, Ihab, and Sally Hassan, eds. *Innovation/Renovation: New Perspectives on the Humanities.* Madison, Wis., 1983.

Heller, Thomas C., et al., eds. *Reconstructing Individualism: Autonomy, Individuality, and the Self in Western Thought.* Stanford, Calif., 1986.

Holland, Norman. *The I.* New Haven, Conn., 1985.

Hunter, J. Paul. "'The Young, the Ignorant, and the Idle': Some Notes on Readers and the Beginnings of the English Novel." In *Anticipations of the Enlightenment in England, France, and Germany.* Ed. Alan Charles Kors and Paul J. Korshin. Philadelphia, Pa., 1987.

Hynes, Arleen. "The Goals of Bibliotherapy." *The Arts in Psychotherapy* 7 (1980): 35–41.

Hynes, Arleen, and M. Hynes-Berry. *Bibliotherapy: The Interactive Process.* Boulder, Colo., 1986.

Jameson, Fredric. *The Political Unconscious: Narrative as a Socially Symbolic Act.* Ithaca, N.Y., 1981.

Jenkyns, Richard. "The Combustible Victorians." *Times Literary Supplement* (Aug. 8, 1986), 855–56.

Jonson, Ben. *Ben Jonson's "Volpone; or, The Foxe"* [1607]. Ed. Henry de Vocht. Louvain, 1937.

Joyce, James. *A Portrait of the Artist as a Young Man* [1916]. Ed. Richard Ellmann. New York, 1964.

———. *Ulysses* [1922]. Ed. Hans Walter Gabler et al. New York, 1986.

Kenny, Michael G. *The Passion of Ansel Bourne: Multiple Personality in American Culture.* Washington, D.C., 1987.

Lacan, Jacques. *The Language of the Self: The Function of Language in Psychoanalysis* [1956]. Trans. Anthony Wilden. Baltimore, 1968.

———. *The Four Fundamental Concepts of Psycho-Analysis* [1973]. Ed. Jacques-Alain Miller. Trans. Alan Sheridan. New York, 1978.

Lukács, Georg. "The Ideology of Modernism." In *The Meaning of Contemporary Realism* [1957]. Trans. John Mander and Necke Mander. London, 1963.

Lyly, John. *Euphues: The Anatomy of Wit.* London, 1579.

MacIntyre, Alasdair. "Egoism and Altruism." In *Encyclopedia of Philosophy.* Ed. Paul Edwards. 8 vols. New York, 1967. 1: 426–66.

Mahoney, Michael J. *Self-Change: Strategies for Solving Personal Problems.* New York, 1979.

Marks, Sylvia Kasey. "*Clarissa* as Conduct Book." *South Atlantic Review* 51 (Nov. 1986): 3–16.

Marx, Karl. Passages from *Economic and Philosophical Manuscripts* [1844]. In *Selected Writings in Sociology and Social Philosophy.* Trans. T. B. Bottomore. Ed. T. B. Bottomore and Maximilien Rubel. New York, 1964.

Mead, George Herbert. *The Individual and the Social Self: Unpublished Work of George Herbert Mead.* [Class Lectures in Social Psychology, 1914 and 1927] Chicago, 1982.

Mitchell, W. J. T. *Iconology: Image, Text, Ideology.* Chicago, 1986.

Montaigne, Michel Eyquem de. "Use Makes Perfectness" (chap. 63) and "Of Giving the Lye" (chap. 75). In *Essays* [1580]. Trans. Charles Cotton [1693]. 3d ed. London, 1869. 312–21, 559–63.

Morris, Colin. *The Discovery of the Individual, 1050–1200* [1972]. New York, 1973.

Morrissey, Robert J. "Jean Starobinski and Otherness." Unpublished paper. University of Chicago, 1987.

Murdoch, Iris. *The Sovereignty of Good.* London, 1970.

Ortony, Andrew. "Metaphor: A Multidimensional Problem." In *Metaphor and Thought.* Ed. Andrew Ortony. Cambridge, 1979.

Orwell, George. *1984.* London, 1949.

Peterson, Carla L. *The Determined Reader: Gender and Culture in the Novel from Napoleon to Victoria.* New Brunswick, N.J., 1986.

Polanyi, Michael. *Personal Knowledge: Towards a Post-Critical Philosophy* [1958]. Chicago, 1972.

Pritchard, William H. *Frost: A Literary Life.* New York, 1984.

Proust, Marcel. *Remembrance of Things Past*. Trans. C. K. Scott Moncrieff. New York, 1934.

Raz, Joseph. *The Morality of Freedom*. Oxford, 1986.

Redfield, James. "Le Sentiment Homérique du Moi." *Le Genre Humain* 12 (1986): 93–111.

Richardson, Samuel. *Clarissa Harlowe; or, The History of a Young Lady* [1748]. London, 1902.

Rorty, Amelie Oksenberg. "Literary Postscript: Characters, Persons, Selves, Individuals." In Rorty 1976: 301–24.

———, ed. *The Identities of Persons*. Berkeley, 1976.

Roth, Philip. *The Counterlife*. New York, 1987.

Royce, Josiah. "The World and the Individual" [Gifford Lectures, 1899]. In vol. 1 of *The Basic Writings of Josiah Royce*. Ed. John McDermott. Chicago, 1969.

Rubin, Rhea Joyce. *Using Bibliotherapy: A Guide to Theory and Practice*. Phoenix, Ariz., 1978.

Rubin, Theodore Isaac. *The Angry Book*. New York, 1969.

Santayana, George. *Three Philosophical Poets: Lucretius, Dante, and Goethe* [1910]. Vol. 6 of *The Works of George Santayana*. New York, 1936.

Shklar, Judith. "Let Us Not Be Hypocritical." *Daedalus* 108 (Sum. 1979): 1–26.

Sidney, Sir Philip. *An Apologie for Poetrie* [1595]. Ed. Edward Arber [reprint of Olney quarto]. Birmingham, 1868.

Skinner, B. F. *Contingencies of Reinforcement: A Theoretical Analysis*. New York, 1969.

———. *Beyond Freedom and Dignity*. New York, 1971.

Smith, Manuel J. *When I Say No, I Feel Guilty: How to Cope—Using the Skills of Systematic Assertive Therapy*. New York, 1975.

Sontag, Susan. "Pilgrimage." *New Yorker* (Dec. 21, 1987): 38–41.

Starobinski, Jean. "Montaigne on Illusion: The Denunciation of Untruth." *Daedalus* 108 (Sum. 1979): 85–101.

———. *Montaigne in Motion* [1982]. Trans. Arthur Goldhammer. Chicago, 1985.

Stoyva, Johanna. Review of *The Adrian Mole Diaries*, by Sue Townsend. *Chicago Literary Review* (June 6, 1986): 5.

Taylor, Charles. "Responsibility for Self." In Rorty 1976.

———. *Human Agency and Language: Philosophical Papers*. Vol. 1. Cambridge, 1985.

Thompson, Lawrance. *Robert Frost: The Early Years*. New York, 1966.

Trilling, Lionel. *Sincerity and Authenticity*. Cambridge, Mass., 1972.

Ward, Horace. *Power for Living*. New York, 1986.

Weintraub, Karl Joachim. *The Value of the Individual: Self and Circumstance in Autobiography*. Chicago, 1978.

Williams, Raymond. *Marxism and Literature*. Oxford, 1977.

9

Education has for its object the formation of character.
Herbert Spencer

Sow an act, and you reap a habit. Sow a habit, and you reap a character. Sow a character, and you reap a destiny.
Attributed to many, including Charles Reade

We want the work [of fiction] . . . to be explicitly conceived as a weapon in the struggle that men wage against evil.
Jean-Paul Sartre

One must . . . be struck more and more the longer one lives, to find how much in our present society a man's life of each day depends for its solidity and value upon whether he reads during *that* day, and far more still on what he reads during it.
Matthew Arnold

Appraising Character

Desire against Desire

THE USE OF NARRATIVE BY "SELVES" AND "CHARACTERS"

Deciding to be a character does not in itself tell us much about how or what to read or how to live. To open ourselves deliberately to the conflicting invitations that our narrative heritage offers does not provide in any easy way the standards for choosing among roles. It can free us, however, from the anxiety of influence (Bloom 1973) that plagues those who attempt to find their being by *resisting* influence. Though I still can suffer anxieties when I accept influences as the very source of my being, my energy will be more likely to go to a careful appraisal of particular invitations than to a futile cursing of my fate as an essentially conditioned creature struggling to deny my condition.

We all find ourselves "thrown," as Heidegger famously (and repeatedly) puts it, into a world we never made, and confronted with a multiplicity of beings that, if *fully* attended to, would threaten to obscure all relationship with Being. We seek to care about what is "other" (mainly *others*): to *think* about it and with it, in ways that can save us from the trivializing that both self-absorption and self-negation tend to promote. As various existentialisms have emphasized, the effort to embrace the "others," whether we hope to find them "outside" or "inside," can easily end in an anxiety about mere conformism. Looking inward, I find no core; looking outward, I feel threatened by multiplicity: to take on all the roles offered me would be to dissolve in the corrosive acids of surrounding influences, experienced as "they-ness." [1]

---

1. "Everyone is the other, and no one is himself. The '*they*,' which supplies the answer to the question of the '*who*' of everyday *Dasein,* is the '*nobody*' to whom every *Dasein* has already surrendered itself in being-among-one-another. . . . One belongs to the others oneself and enhances their power. The 'others,' whom one thus designates in

Thus awareness of our total dependence on others and the Other can produce both an anxiety about loss of self into "alterity" and a pressure to be *altru*istic in self-destructive ways.

But there is another kind of loss of self into others. As a character, pledged only to perform my chosen (and imposed) roles as well as possible, I may hope to develop an ethical criticism somewhat analogous to Heidegger's *Sorge,* a caring about the other, about *l'autrui,* about alterity. I can attend responsibly to it—them—us—in a way that finally allows a kind of free-flow in both directions, annihilating all anxiety about boundaries. Other anxieties will of course always remain, but nothing will remain of the conflict between *altru*ism and *self*-ishness.

We do not, obviously, expect all others to prove true friends, characters whom we can treat precisely as we would treat ourselves, loving them "for themselves and not accidentally" (pp. 172–74 above; Aristotle, *Ethics* 8.3.6). The Christian ideal of universal love escapes us here as it escapes Aristotle; literary criticism cannot build itself on the hope for a world of saints. On the contrary: we know that we must learn—and we can now hope that we *can* learn—to distinguish those "others" who will nurture from those who may, deliberately or accidentally, destroy or cripple.

Bringing in Heidegger by the tail like this reminds us again that we cannot expect, in such complex matters, to formulate rules either for what we aim to become or for the discriminations we must "practice" on the "way." We seek to practice a practice, to follow a way of ways, and—as Heidegger stresses—we can never precisely *say* what the practice or way might be. Though I shall risk so many explicit helps along the way as to make poor Heidegger turn in his already troubled grave, we must recognize that the "others" we meet here—the stories we tell each other—are too rich and complex to be caught in any critic's formulas.

---

order to cover up the fact of one's belonging to them essentially oneself, are those who proximally and for the most part '*are there*' in everyday being-with-one-another" (qtd. in Steiner 1980, 92–93). George Steiner, from whom I borrow this translation from Heidegger's *Being and Time* [*Sein und Zeit*] (1962, 4.26), says of this special anxiety, "We yield our existence to a formless 'Theyness' or *alterité*. The others to whom we consign ourselves are not definite, sovereign presences" (92).

Indeed we can see now that the very search for rules, which we rejected in Chapter 3, and the hectoring tones of voice that have too often accompanied that search spring inevitably from the individualist's plight. Mistrusting the fluid exchanges inherent in coduction pursued by characters, an individual will be inclined to search for his or her very own universals and then to persuade others to accept them. But what rhetoric am I, as such an isolate, to use? If I am indeed unique and alone, my rhetoric must be viewed finally as a mere statement of my private vision, an outburst of private taste. No one should be surprised if I begin to sound a bit shrill and dogmatic. If I am "sincere"—and, as we have seen, I will want to be sincere at all costs— I will of course seek to discover my "authentic" response and to express it as forcefully as possible. In doing so I will not be engaging in mere trickery. But since I can have no confidence that the other selves I address are essentially like me or share any qualities or beliefs with me (after all, they are or should be trying to become as highly individualized, as "creative," as close to being "unique personalities"—in short, as different from me—as possible), it will be hard to find *genuine* arguments on behalf of my response.

We can thus "prophesy after the event," as Kenneth Burke likes to say, that criticism by individuals will tend to come in one of three tones: a shrill, desperate tone of condemnation for the works (and critics) I dislike—as Leavis, Winters, and Gardner do at their worst; a sentimental tone of over-praise for the works I like—as the weekly reviewers do at *their* worst; or a hermetic style accessible only to those I can count on, the coterie of true believers in my elected code—"I" may be alone, but I just happen to have as friends a few loners who speak my language.[2]

Anyone who finds these tones offensive will quite probably infer

---

2. Never since the Renaissance have so many mandarin critics written so many polysyllables intelligible to so few. I open a critical journal, *Glyph* (at random, honestly—though I don't expect you to believe me), and I find this: "For Kafka, duplicity is the unavoidable onus of textuality. Whether in the play between the realms demarcated by human existence and the legal code, between the naive and penetrating attitudes occasioned by the image of the Castle, or in the multiplicity of categories finding themselves bifurcated within the negative projection of the construction, the duplicity of textual function challenges the grounds upon which the text establishes consequences and founds its legibility." And that one is easy, because all of its words are actually in one or another of my dictionaries.

that the fault lies with ethical criticism, and soon we will have (still prophesying what we *do* have) elaborate theories that all arguments for or against quality are simply expressions of mere personal preferences (Lindenberger 1970), or of class and power interests,[3] or of closed, isolated "communities of interpretation" (Fish 1980, 338–72).

If, on the other hand, I am not an individual self at all, but a character, a social self, a being-in-process many of whose established dispositions or habits belong to others—some of them even to all humankind—then I need have no anxiety about finding and preserving a unique core for the various characters that in a sense have colonized me and continue to do so. I should be able to embrace the unquestioned ethical power of narratives, in order to try on for size the character roles offered me. I can hold a fitting of various "habits," to see if they enhance or diminish how I/we appear to myself/ourselves. And I should then be able to talk with my selves (both here at home, inside my head, and "abroad") about the strengths and weaknesses I have found—found in one sense in the narrative but in another sense in me/us.

Some of the roles opened to me as I move through the field of selves that my cultural moment provides will be good for "me/us," some not so good, some literally fatal. It will be the chief and most difficult business of my life to grope my way along dimly lit paths, hoping to build a life-"plot" that will be in one of the better genres.

HOW OUR ROLES CONVERSE

How are such plots, such stories of growth or decline, discovered (or created), and how can we talk about why some are better than

---

3. The most extreme argument I have seen for the belief that criticism is necessarily the pursuit of power is found in *Intellectuals in Power*, by Paul Bové. The author concludes: "The temptations to build a better world, to discover the truth about human life, to rely on genius, sublimity, mastery, and prophetic wisdom: even though all these must be put aside, they will recur for a long time. The emergent cannot be forced. Such an appropriation of truth to political work [as I am advocating], such a releasing of it from the shapeless, indeterminate background of the power structure of humanistic discourse might seem amoral or immoral. But the morality of humanism and its professionalization has worn out its welcome . . . not only . . . by helping produce fascism, but . . . by relying always and everywhere on death for its own survival" (1986, 310).

others without falling into a judgmental stance that would destroy them all? As I have implied throughout, we must always expect to find a plurality of workable answers to that kind of question. Some of us will have accepted one or another of the traditional guides (perhaps a philosophical system, perhaps a religion), and we might make use of any one of them here, so long as we used them not to provide pat answers in advance of reflection but to suggest principles for comparing live coductions (see pp. 355–62 below). I have a friend who "knows" that Immanuel Kant provides—if "read properly" and *thought about*—all that anyone could need in order to plunge into multiplicity and yet not drown. I have colleagues who "know" that Aristotle's *Ethics* and *Politics* together provide all the principles anyone needs to chart a path through the modern world. Other colleagues have found that the Hegelian or Marxist, the Christian or Jewish, the pragmatist, Freudian, or neo-utilitarian path can save them from the helpless particularism that results if we do nothing but follow our impulses where they lead.

I cannot expect to win many readers to my unargued claim that any one of these (and innumerable other) paths, if followed with full seriousness, may fully serve our turn. Even to understand what such a pluralistic assertion might mean would require at least as much attention to ethical pluralism as I gave to critical pluralism in *Critical Understanding* (1979). But perhaps we can cut through those thickets by finding some general principle (not a rule) that is shared by all the philosophies and religions I know anything about, one that will allow us to say that any serious worldview might do the job, for any adherent who seeks guidance in charting a life-plot with the aid of rival narrative friends.[4]

What we seek, in our effort to escape the mindlessness of total hedonism, is some way of distinguishing between the pursuit of immediate desires (whether these are aroused by narratives or by "real" life) and the pursuit of desires that have proved themselves, on reflection, to

---

4. The rhetorical tradition is full of efforts like this to find some "perennial philosophy" that might unite the major rivals. Cicero's fusion of Plato and Aristotle is perhaps the most famous—or, when judged by partisans of either master, notorious. I have no illusions about preserving, in any such effort, the distinctive powers of individual approaches, and I thus postpone for some other occasion my duty to treat each of those giants with the full respect they deserve.

be in fact desir*able*. Though this distinction between what is thought
to be good and what is really good is missing from many contemporary literary theories, where the very word "really" is repudiated, it
is central to every philosophy and religion that has outlasted its first
generation; it is in fact missing only in a small number of short-lived
hedonisms and some contemporary versions of utilitarianism. The
distinction can even be detected, under various disguises, in post-
Nietzschean philosophers who, like Nietzsche himself, spend a great
deal of energy in knocking down other people's ways of making the
distinction.[5]

Most of us come to a moment, fairly early in our thinking lives,
when we stumble across the shattering discovery that all actions are
"selfish," because we never do anything unless we are convinced that
doing it will yield more reward, either immediately or in the long run,
than not doing it. As Plato and other classical philosophers put this
point, we never act except in the pursuit of some "good." People who
do not get beyond this elementary, exciting, and ultimately quite
useless insight go through life arguing, like Thrasymachus in book 2 of
the *Republic,* that there is no real difference among goods (desires),
except for the power of the desirer: might makes right. From this point
of view, the critic of narrative, and of the patterns of desire that narratives build in us, can express nothing but a "personal" desire, when
comparing any two narratives, and the critic will thus be expressing,
consciously or unconsciously, no more than the interests—goods—of
a given power base.

There is, I am saying, a kind of perennial philosophy that rejects
this view. Even the subtler utilitarians like John Stuart Mill have criti-

    5. Economists, for example, seem to obtain their main pleasure in life from shock-
ing us by a denial of the distinction; yet their own language is full of exhortation about
what we ought to desire that we don't desire now (McCloskey 1985). For a cogent argument showing that even the most rootless-seeming of deconstructionists cannot finally
avoid importing an "ought" into their explorations of language and écriture, see Murray
Krieger's contribution to the special issue of *New Literary History* on *Literature and/as
Moral Philosophy.* Krieger uses the current code word "thematizing" for the hidden
moral commitments that he finds everywhere: "I do not say that it is bad [to "thema-
tize," to "privilege" this or that morality], only that it is inevitable, so that it is better
confronted than denied in one's own work and attacked in others'. For my survey
strongly suggests that all of us, one way or the other, are part of 'the moral gang'"
(1983, 133).

cized it. We could illustrate the point by looking closely at almost any philosopher's treatment of ethics. But most useful here are those who, like Charles Taylor, make this essential distinction by talking about our desire to improve our desires—to *desire better desires*.

In his essay "Responsibility for Self" (1976), Taylor begins by asking, "What is the notion of responsibility which is bound up with our conception of a person or self?" He finds a beginning answer in the very notion of a "person": we attribute to anyone we consider a person "the ability to form 'second-order desires.' . . .[A] person on this view is one who can raise the question: Do I really want to be what I now am? (i.e., have the desires and goals I now have). . . . [A] person is a subject who can pose the *de jure* question: Is this the kind of being I ought to be, or really want to be?" (281).

So far utilitarians and other ethicists are united. But Taylor wants a "stronger" sense of "ought," and he proceeds to distinguish an ethical reflection based on calculating future pleasures from one that reflects on desires as "higher or lower, virtuous or vicious, more or less fulfilling, . . . profound or superficial, noble or base." The second kind judges desires, after "qualitative reflection" and not mere calculation, "as belonging to qualitatively different modes of life, fragmented or integrated, alienated or free, saintly or merely human, courageous or pusillanimous" (282). Qualitative reflection considers a first-order desire not on the basis of "some mere contingent or circumstantial conflict with another goal," a conflict that can be removed by calculation. Rather, its choices are between goods or desires not all of which really *are* good or desirable. And it is this kind of reflection, the effort to discover what I *ought* to desire, what I really should desire to desire, that defines what it is to be a person (287).

The ability to form a second-order desire, this judgment about the ethos-I-would-prefer-to-have-and-will-therefore-cultivate, *defines* personhood, because we all would say that "any being who was incapable of evaluating desires (as my dog, e.g., is incapable) . . . would lack the depth to be a potential interlocutor, a potential partner of human communion, be it as friend [or] confidant" (289). That depth (to cut a subtle argument brutally short) entails recognizing that real goods can genuinely conflict without impugning their real superiority to the lesser goods repudiated by "qualitative reflection." Our predicament is precisely that we must take responsibility for what we are to become, in a world that does not offer simple moral choices of the kinds that traditional codes are at least said to have provided. If this is our predicament (comparable, you see, to what the literary critic faces in appraising floods of disparate narratives), "then it plainly is a more honest, more clairvoyant, less confused and self-deluding stance to be aware of this and take the full responsibility for the radical choice [that the predicament entails]" (294).

I cannot do justice here to Taylor's further argument about why his kind of ethics—reflective, responsible, open to constant revisions and reconsiderations—"engages the whole self" (what I am calling a character) in a way that following "moral yardsticks" does not. I rely on him here not only because he presents a beautifully cogent use of the Heideggerian notion of a being responsible to Being (one that avoids the extreme and angst-ridden relativism of some existentialist versions of Heidegger), but also because his emphasis on a plurality of values implicitly acknowledges that his defense of a rational "articulation" and choice among desires is only one of many possible defenses of this kind of project.

Applying this (almost) universally embraced distinction to the problem of choosing among powerful narratives gives us one kind of model for our use of many narratives to create for ourselves a flexible, *growing,* yet not amorphous character. Narratives, we have said, both depend on and implant or reinforce patterns of desire. If we do not surrender to these patterns, we cannot really be said to have "taken in" a given narrative; yet if we do surrender, we find ourselves to some degree shaped into those patterns. If we are characters-in-process, taking on and playing widely diverse roles, how can we ever say that one proffered role is superior to another? I am suggesting that we do that roughly in the way Taylor says that we make our other ethical judgments: we acquire, from the stories we are told, a "desire to become a different kind of desirer." What in the last chapter I called, only half playfully, "hypocrisy upward," we learn to play upon the world of narratives. Following upon our coductions of various narratives, fictional and historical, we try out each new pattern of desire against those that we have found surviving past reflections, and we then decide, in an explicit or implicit act of ethical criticism, that this new pattern is or is not an improvement over what we have previously desired to desire.

Such inescapably general talk will be clearer with some examples. Though the most important cases are perhaps those that are clearly "moral,"[6] it will be useful to begin with the somewhat more obvious nudges upward that occur to all of us when reading stories with powerful intellectual appeal.

THE FORMATION OF CHARACTER ILLUSTRATED: INTELLECTUAL VIRTUES

To see how inescapably we become what we eat (at least if we eat with gusto), I ask you now to move slowly with me through the following familiar passage from *Ulysses* (ideally, it should be read aloud, to savor the rhythms—but I must leave that to you). Stephen, an older but only slightly wiser version of the individualist whose flight to artistic creation we traced in Chapter 8, is walking on the shore at Sandymount, puzzling about his sensations and the philosophical problems they raise:

> Ineluctable modality of the visible: at least that if no more, thought through my eyes. Signatures of all things I am here to read, seaspawn and seawrack, the nearing tide, that rusty boot. Snotgreen, bluesilver, rust: coloured signs. Limits of the diaphane. But he adds: in bodies. Then he was aware of them bodies before of them coloured. How? By knocking his sconce against them, sure. Go easy. Bald he was and a millionaire, *maestro di color che sanno*. Limit of the diaphane in. Why in? Diaphane, adiaphane. If you can put your five fingers through it it is a gate, if not a door. Shut your eyes and see.
>
> Stephen closed his eyes to hear his boots crush crackling wrack and shells. You are walking through it howsomever. I am, a stride at a time. A very short space of time through very short times of space. Five, six: the *Nacheinander*. Exactly: and that is the ineluctable modality of the audible. Open your eyes. No. Jesus! If I fell over a cliff that beetles o'er his base, fell through the *Nebeneinander* ineluctably! I am getting on nicely in the dark. My ash sword hangs at my side. Tap with it: they do. My two feet in his boots are at the ends of his legs, *nebeneinander*. Sounds solid: made by the mallet of Los *demiurgos*. Am I walking into eternity along Sandymount

---

6. Most important, surely, but perhaps least persuasively made for those who doubt that literature affects moral behavior. We'll come to narrower conceptions of morality soon enough, and meanwhile I remind anyone who needs the reminder that intellectual conduct is, after all, conduct, and therefore a moral matter, in at least one definition of morality.

strand? Crush, crack, crick, crick. Wild sea money. Dominie Deasy kens
them a'.

> *Won't you come to Sandymount,*
> *Madeline the mare?*

Rhythm begins, you see. I hear. Acatalectic tetrameter of iambs marching. No, agallop: *deline the mare.*

Open your eyes now. I will. One moment. Has all vanished since? If I
open and am for ever in the black adiaphane. *Basta!* I will see if I can see.

See now. There all the time without you: and ever shall be, world without end.

(Joyce 1986, 31)[7]

In earlier chapters we might have asked, "What kind of life do I live
as I decipher this immensely compact bundle of actions, thought, and
allusions?" Here we add to that question, "What sort of character,
what sort of habits, am I likely to take on or reinforce as I live that life?
What 'better desires' does it lead me to desire?"

When as a nineteen-year-old I first read the passage, in my often
baffled but exhilarated plunge through the novel, I felt completely out-
classed. I had never read Aristotle or Aquinas or any other philosopher
bald or hairy who grappled with this problem in this way; all I knew
was that Stephen is troubled by some mysterious phrase, one that was
meaningless to me. But I can also remember clearly a sense of envy and
awe—not of Joyce but of Stephen. If only my own stream of consciousness could flow at that high philosophical level, what a bright young
man I would be! And I can remember looking up some of the strange
words, and mumbling that mouth-filler: "ineluctable modality of the
visible." Thus in my emulation I was moved, in however slight a degree, *toward* the character of a philosophical man.

One must, in short, become at least a bit philosophical to be able to
enjoy the passage at all. Though it is not exactly rigorous philosophy,
it imitates the mind of an extraordinarily philosophical hero grappling
with an epistemological problem, and I must become philosophical if I
am to follow him. Of course, if I refuse to care about whether the
visible or sensible world presents a modality of knowing that is ineluctable, I can skip the passage, or perhaps condemn the hero for pedan-

---

7. Though the new edition of *Ulysses* (1986) has become, by June of 1988, deeply
controversial, I have used it here as what will probably be the only available edition for
at least awhile.

try, or even condemn the author for distracting me from whatever elements in the tale I *do* care about. But the author has assumed that you and I *will* care about such matters, and about his hero who cares about them.

The effect is not just that of making us wish we were philosophical: insofar as we genuinely try to read the passage, we are being steered through a course that in fact constitutes a stream of philosophical consciousness. The young reader I was did not only *aspire* to think like Stephen, he *did* think like Stephen, *as he read*—to the degree that he understood him at all. And on successive readings he became more and more convinced that he was "getting" it. He perforce lived with the question of what happens to the curtain of the senses when one shuts one's eyes. The mystery of whether and why the world will not have turned into a black adiaphane had become *his* question, though only briefly. Thus he not only aspired to a change of intellectual character, he experienced one: he became more philosophical than he was before.

Such a change may not be noticeable if I am already schooled in philosophical questions—if I already "desire to desire philosophical inquiry." But if, as happened to be true of me, I am for the first time encountering questions raised by the ineluctable modality of the visible, my mental habits, my character, can experience great change—if not within a paragraph, certainly within the reading of many similar paragraphs in a long book. In short, as the cliché goes, "I was never the same again after reading *Ulysses*."

The possible effects are of course not confined to philosophical inquiry. I am asked, secondly, to mime "being learned." Of course, I would not be reading *Ulysses* in the first place if I did not already desire to have more of that kind of desire; it is not, after all, an assignment—I am in fact reading it in hours stolen from other duties. Even if I can't catch many of the allusions, I will suspect that many allusions are being made—at least that phrase in Italian, if that *is* Italian, is an allusion to *something,* as is the "*Basta!*" Who *is* this "he," this "bald millionaire"? Who or what is "Madeline the mare?" Joyce knows; *Stephen* knows; there must be readers all over the civilized world who know. If only *I* knew!

If I happen to recognize the quotation from *King Lear,* I will feel that I am a *little bit* learned, but I'll suspect that there are more allusions that I miss. And what does *nacheinander* mean? I may look it up, if I happen to recognize that it's German. Or I may simply aspire to become the sort of person, someday, who knows languages and doesn't *have* to look it up. Either of these effects is most likely to occur if I am already inclined in the direction of literary learning.

Obviously I cannot claim that it was my reading of *Ulysses* alone that turned me into a professor of English. But I do remember vividly a kind of forlorn longing to become as learned as Stephen and Joyce. What's more, even as I re-read the book in the new edition, I still experience something of that effect: if only I could have had that traditional education that the Jesuits gave Joyce, what a learned reader I would now be!

Note that this effect is not diminished by my having discovered, over the years, that Jim Joyce, who became a learned man indeed, was not nearly as learned as James Joyce the implied author. In this virtue as in many another, Joyce implies a superman far beyond his actual powers as exhibited in any one moment of his life. A hypocrite? In a way, yes. But how much more valuable to me is that kind of hypocrisy upward than the hypocrisy downward practiced by authors who struggle to sound more ignorant than they are.

A third effect, only slightly less obvious, was that the young man I was came to aspire to various stylistic graces (or vices, depending on who is judging the results). To put it bluntly, as he read *Ulysses* he was conditioned *against* all straightforward, simple, functional styles and moved "upward" toward a freewheeling, risktaking, hyphenfree, radically baroque and particoloredly witty poetic flow. "Rhythm begins, you see. I hear. Acatalectic tetrameter of iambs marching. No, agallop: *deline the mare.*" [8] What grace, what concentration, what variety! "That's how I'd like to write, someday. How stodgy those earlier authors like Dickens and George Eliot all suddenly seem. How cramped

8. Let me be honest, as people say when they are about to practice a bit of hypocrisy downward. On the final typing of this passage, conforming it to the new edition, I became convinced that the editor had made one mistake, changing "a catalectic" to "acatalectic." Clearly, I felt like writing, the over-zealous editor has made a mistake; "a catalectic" makes better rhythm than "acatalectic," and isn't the passage after all . . . ?—well, I'd better look up the word to be sure. And of course "acatalectic" turns out to be accurate in describing the final line. Thus the influence, in this case toward a careful—nay, nit-picking—pedantry, continues even as I talk about the influence Joyce had on me nearly fifty years ago.

my more recent heroes (circa 1943): Hemingway, Fitzgerald. How pe-
destrian my own journal." "Must re-write at least one entry here
each week," he wrote, and promised himself to try out some Joycean
effects—more like the flamboyance met later on in the book than like
Stephen's interior monologue. His habits of style—*that* part of his
character—were thus forever changed, even after he stopped the conscious imitation.

Thus regardless of what I may want to be or to become—I, the true
I, the sincere person of integrity, the "self" that was already compromised by my reading such stuff instead of doing my work as a Mormon missionary among the lost souls of Chicago—I am now become
somewhat Joycean. It is true that my habits of style were not as markedly changed as were those of many another reader. Should I not perhaps lament my present plain, hyphen-ridden style, since it reveals that
Joyce did not colonize me nearly as much as he did many another?

THE FORMATION OF CHARACTER ILLUSTRATED: MORAL VIRTUES

The more specifically moral effects of such a passage are harder to
discern and almost impossible to demonstrate to any doubter. Just in
talking of intellectual changes we automatically talk of changes in intellectual *conduct,* but in talking of moral changes it is much harder to
distinguish mere changes of opinion from actual changes of conduct.
A tale of great moral courage may lead me to a private oath to be more
courageous, only to discover next day that I am still a coward. What is
more, the most important moral changes are the most difficult to detect, even in oneself, let alone in others: the line-by-line education in
how to make moral inferences about people on the basis of always inadequate signs. I shall later dwell on these a bit, but we should begin
with more readily visible matters.

It is not hard to see moral implications even in the three intellectual
characteristics I have described. And if we enlarged our view to consider the effect of reading and re-reading the whole of *Ulysses,* most of
which is less intellectually intricate than Stephen's interior monologue,
we would find innumerable moral and immoral choices that *Ulysses*
either endorses or mocks, repudiations and affirmations that it leads

attentive readers to approve or disapprove: Stephen's troubled rejection of the sacrament as compared with Mulligan's opening blasphemies; Bloom's sensitive awareness of and tenderness toward others, as compared with the crude self-absorptions of most other characters; Molly's celebration of uninhibited sexual pleasure, in her "Yes, yes, yes"; Joyce's implied notions of what women in general and Jews in general and Irish people in general are like; to say nothing of his insistent though usually tacit elevation of artistic sensibility over all other human values except possibly generosity of spirit.

Though always difficult to demonstrate, moral effects are clearest when we think of our experience with works that unlike *Ulysses* show heroes and heroines facing clear dilemmas and making admirable or lamentable choices. But they come in all shapes and shades. When I ask people, "Name fictions that changed your character—or made you *want* to change your conduct," I almost always get a quick response, and the responses range all over the moral landscape. (Occasionally, if I ask the question of a professional critic or scholar, the answer is that fictions don't change people's lives, at least not if they are adult readers.) I am told that "Jane Austen's *Mansfield Park* made me swear not to be such a mouse—to stand up to people the way Fanny Price stands up to Sir Walter toward the end." I am told that "Ken Kesey's *One Flew over the Cuckoo's Nest* led me to tell off my boss at the hospital and walk out on him." I am told that "Balzac's *Père Goriot* made a real difference in how I thought about and treated my father." I hear a tearful claim that "Toni Morrison's *Song of Solomon* made me feel really guilty about how I had been thinking about blacks these days—you know, with all the headlines about crime—and I've really acted different toward them, you know, when I meet them in stores and things like that." I hear the claim that "Ignazio Silone's *Bread and Wine* made a Christian socialist of me—at least for awhile." "Arthur Koestler's *Darkness at Noon* not only knocked any temptation to fellow-traveling out of my head; it firmed up my notions of what kinds of moral corner-cutting I would allow myself." "*The Man in the Grey-Flannel Suit* got me out of advertising." "The combination of André Schwarz-Bart's *The Last of the Just* and Elie Wiesel's *The Forest* turned me back into an observant Jew; before that I hadn't been inside a synagogue for ten years." "Seeing Alex Haley's 'Roots'

on TV turned me into an enthusiastic genealogist."[9] "Reading Ayn
Rand's works when I was working in my first job led me, I'm sorry to
say, to cancel all of my gifts to philanthropies—I bought a convenient
version of her 'me-philosophy' hook, line, and sinker."[10] "Walter van
Tilburg Clark's *The Ox-bow Incident*—especially the movie—turned
me into a premature civil rights' marcher, or I guess you could say that
it finished the job started by Lillian Smith's *Strange Fruit*." "*Narrative
of the Life of Frederick Douglass* led me to face my anger, to understand something about it, and to feel pride in what I might accomplish." "Amanda Cross's *Death in a Tenured Position* changed my
views of the plight of female academics, and changed my behavior toward those in my department." "Reading Santayana's *The Last Puritan* was the major influence in my becoming a professor." "Reading
Chinua Achebe's *Things Fall Apart* radically changed my view of—
and my teaching about—African colonialism and its aftermath."
"*Gone with the Wind* made me behave much differently toward south-
erners; I had previously dismissed them as vicious or stupid." "Reading Hendrik Willem Van Loon's *The Story of Mankind* made me decide to be a historian." "Reading Kerouac's *On the Road* led me to
drop out of college and go 'on the road' for a year, imitating as much
of his main character's behavior as made sense to me" (this informant,
a graduate student, has since written an M.A. thesis tracing the complex values of that powerful influence, which he says continue even
now that he is more critical of Kerouac's various implied preachments). "To my permanent regret, I stumbled on Réage's [George
Bataille's] *Story of O* when I was in my early teens, and in a sense I've
never recovered from it: the awful revelation that such things—even if
only imagined—could *be* in the world depressed me for months, and
even now thinking about it depresses me."

Such dramatic reports—I have not made them up, and I could list
many more—are of course inherently untrustworthy. No doubt every

9. I recorded that conversion in 1984. In August 1986 we witnessed the gathering
of thousands of black descendents of slaves for a celebration at Somerset Plantation, apparently as a direct result of the experience of "Roots."

10. For testimony about how Rand's *Atlas Shrugged* changed lives, see "Passions: A
Disciple Confronts Ayn Rand's Power" (Grossman 1986).

one of these changes, for good or ill, occurred in a medium—the reporter's soul—already richly prepared. The reader must have to some degree "desired to desire" the new desires, good or bad; otherwise the particular book would not have been read and the new desires would not have taken root. But when we multiply such experiences by innumerable published reports (usually less dramatic and much more general; see Appendix), and by the hundreds of thousands of similar oral reports that are "out there" waiting for someone with infinite patience and a government grant to collect the evidence, they surely cry out for critical reflection, no matter how difficult that may be.[11]

Perhaps the most striking feature of such a wealth of evidence, aside from its very existence, is the firm conviction of informants that their change of conduct was in response to the *fixed norms* of the given work: almost all of them think that the implied author *intended* something like the change that occurred. We are thus once again faced with a daunting diversity of claims about good and evil. How are we ever to decide which "advice" to follow, as we pursue our desire to discover and pursue better desires?

APPRAISING DIVERSE FIXED NORMS

What we have said so far clearly implies that we have only three possibilities, once we see that it is impossible to shut our eyes and ears and retreat to a story-free world. We can surrender uncritically to whatever appeals to us, scurrying from one narrative to the next without pause for reflection, just as many of us did when we first became

---

11. And they certainly ought to squelch once and for all the weird assertions that "poetry says nothing" and "makes nothing happen." A carefully argued refutation, from the perspective of linguistics, of the divorce of fiction from affirmation of true propositions can be found in Schmidt 1976, 161–78. His targets include Grabes and Frege, Ingarden ("assertions occurring in literary texts have the status of 'quasi-judgement'"), Teun A. van Dijk ("Fictional texts are . . . modally counterfactual and pragmatically intended as such"), Edward Stankiewicz ("poetic language is purposiveness in terms of the internal organisation of the message, and purposelessness in terms of the external reference") (162). Although many people have recently argued, along with Schmidt (see, e.g., p. 152 n.25 above), that such claims are misleading, they seem only slightly less fashionable now than twenty years ago.

"readers." There are worse fates, and indeed everyone should experience, early in life, such multiple surrenders, bringing as they must an enlargement of life's possibilities. (The surrendering need not be to written stories; many a non-literate culture has probably come closer to the ideal of total immersion than we in semi-literate America do today.) But in themselves they leave the company we keep to chance, and chance offerings—especially the ones we meet on TV these days, but also those on the drugstore book rack and at the four-screen movie warren—are so seductive and stereotyped that no one could seriously propose uncritical compliance. Second, we can attempt an "anaesthetic" reading and listening, preserving a distance that will protect us from character change. If we thus refuse to be taken in by any new appeal, we may enjoy at least the pleasure of feeling and appearing sophisticated. But of course each of us will emerge from the next story as just about the same critic, sophisticated or unsophisticated, who went in, comfortably unharmed but no better off than if we had spent our time playing checkers. Or, finally, we can pursue a two-stage kind of reading, surrendering as fully as possible on every occasion, but then deliberately supplementing, correcting, or refining our experience with the most powerful ethical or ideological criticism we can manage. The second stage will of course sometimes interfere with the first, when some blatant ideological clash triggers what the author would consider a premature critical rejection.[12]

When we elect the third of these, we again have a choice of two directions that in practice usually overlap: we can deliberately supplement or correct *this* narrative with *that* narrative, and we can talk together about the ethical strengths and weaknesses of our experiences. The first of these—simply choosing to read some other kinds of narrative as a corrective—is no doubt even more important than talking

---

12. At a recent performance of *The Magic Flute* at the Chicago Lyric Opera, the audience "violated the text" by laughing whenever one of Pamino's or Sorastro's aggressively sexist comments emerged on the "supertitle" screen; most of us laughed harder than we did at the speeches of Papagano that were intended to be comic. At such moments, we were by no means surrendering wholeheartedly to *Mozart's* opera: we laughed as ethical critics. The opera as a whole survived such ethical distancing only because it is itself essentially comic. A tragic opera might well have been ruined by our laughter, and Mozart would certainly have been surprised by it.

about them. Certainly the most valuable ethical criticism is not academic, and it need not be written. Powerful narratives provide our best criticism of other powerful narratives, our best antidote against any one thoughtlessly adopted role. In Chapter 11, I must discuss at some length how the great fictions, with their rival "worlds," supplement and criticize one another. Here a note about the dangers of monomania must suffice.

The serious ethical disasters produced by narratives occur when people sink themselves into an unrelieved hot bath of one kind of narrative. No single work is likely to do us *much* good or harm, except when we are very young. But a steady immersion at any age in any one author's norms is likely to be stultifying—even if they happen to be as broad and conventional as those of a Shakespeare or Tolstoy. Just as anyone who limits all friendship to one person risks becoming a partner in a *folie-à-deux*, a reader who becomes wholly absorbed with one author or one kind of narrative risks becoming grossly misshapen or, at best, frozen in one spot. (It is true that authors suffer the same risk as they become absorbed with their own kind of product, but they at least know something of the "other sides" of themselves: they spend only a part of each day playing their roles as writers; the reader never gets to see them shopping for shoes, or shaving, or disciplining the children.)

Each of us will have a different list of possible stultifications. For me the most interesting ones are the idolators of authors I myself admire: the "gentle Jane-ite" who re-reads all of Austen's novels every year and thus risks living a narrower life than Austen herself ever led; the total Lawrentian who still in the 1980s tries to enact in dress and behavior the roles that for Lawrence were genuinely exploratory in the 1920s; the devotees of nihilist fiction who, like the "hero" in Lermontov's *A Hero of Our Time*, enact at one remove the avant-garde beliefs that their originators paid for in blood. These pursuers of "one story and one story only" could in effect save themselves simply by being baptized through immersion in almost any other great narrative.

The process is inherently irreducible to summary. I can hint at it only by suggesting how it might work in supplementing the singularly rich but still one-sided *Ulysses*. Granting that this novel is not simply a technical marvel but a great contribution to my ethical culture, is there anything seriously *missing* in its gifts, or any distortion that should be somehow labeled as potentially dangerous to the soul?[13]

Perhaps the most obvious answer is heroism. Whatever we may think of the good or harm in heroic ideals, it is plain that they are missing from *Ulysses*, except of course for the heroism of the author in daring to attempt such a book. Heroism on any front but the one we traced with Stephen earlier—the heroic individualized battle for art as against everything else—goes unmentioned except in mockery. For this value (one that seems increasingly hard to find in our world outside art) we might turn, in our search for supplementation of our great friend Joyce, to Homer, or to Conrad, or to Kipling, or to Hemingway—or, after a bit of thought about that word "hero-ism," to Alice Walker's female hero, Celie, in *The Color Purple*. Or we might turn back, surprisingly, to Flaubert.

Toward the end of *Madame Bovary* Flaubert brings on stage a surgeon who is expected to repair the butchery committed by the local doctor, M. Homais. Dr. Larivière

> belonged to that great surgical school created by Bichat—that generation, now vanished, of philosopher-practitioners, who cherished their art with fanatical love and applied it with enthusiasm and sagacity. Everyone in his hospital trembled when he was angry; and his students so revered him that the moment they set up for themselves they imitated him as much as they could. . . . Disdainful of decorations[,] . . . hospitable, generous, a father to the poor, practicing Christian virtues although an unbeliever, he might have been thought of as a saint if he hadn't been feared as a devil because of the keenness of his mind.
>
> ([1857] 1957, 363–64)

Critics raised to assume that authors should not bring their own beliefs directly on stage have objected to the passage as a serious lapse from Flaubert's professed artistic creed: it is preachy, it "tells" rather than "shows." But surely the more natural response is one that we might impute to Flaubert himself: here is a clear, clean picture of one

---

13. I am thinking here of the tragi-comic story of an English major I met in my first year of teaching, a young man who dressed like Joyce, tried to talk like Joyce, and indeed in every way seemed desperate to *become James Joyce*. It gave him a facade, in 1950, that nothing from 1950 could penetrate. Where are you now, J. N. S.?

whole, unmaimed man (in a book of maimed creatures), a giant working selflessly, in the integrity of his science, against a world of fools and
knaves. When I read *Madame Bovary* in college, at about the same
time that I was reading a much inferior work that celebrates the same
virtues, Sinclair Lewis's *Arrowsmith*, I can remember silently taking an
oath to *become like that* (I was a chemistry major)—to pursue truth,
like Dr. Larivière and Arrowsmith—to pursue it with no regard to my
own feelings or the feelings of anyone else, least of all my enemies or,
of course, my family. But still, to pursue it generously, generously . . .

Thus Flaubert might enable me to imagine heroism, of a kind, if a
diet of Joyce or Proust, or indeed of most major authors since their
time, had left me blank in that domain. My own experience, curiously
enough, was the other way round: Joyce taught me necessary reservations about some of my early literary heroes. Sometimes such experience yields a genuine loss. But often a new fiction can add without subtracting: both of these quite disparate narratives, *Ulysses* and *Madame
Bovary*, somehow still manage to engage each other within my imagination. And both of them unite to make claims about more serious
inadequacies in many of the narratives coming my way. Once I have
known such giants, what do I make of a Stephen King or a James
Michener? Yet for all I know, in advance of a trial, some seemingly
lesser figure of that kind might supplement the giants in just the way I
most need.

The imaginative power of any fully realized work is such that for
the proper reader it will attempt to usurp *all* powers. Left to its own
devices, as it were, *Ulysses* would turn the naive young reader into a
Stephen and the middle-aged reader into a Bloom, while even the most
sophisticated reader would follow my former student and try to become a James Joyce. Left to its own devices, *Madame Bovary* would
turn the naive reader into a total cynic, mocking every value, and the
sophisticated reader into a disciple of Larivière—or more probably of
that saint of the pursuit of truth through art, Gustave Flaubert.[14]

Should we go further and ask whether some works are not only in
need of supplement but in themselves just plain "bad," "harmful," or

---

14. See Mario Vargas Llosa's account of a lifelong love affair with a book: *The Perpetual Orgy: Flaubert and "Madame Bovary"* (1986).

at the mildest "false"? Whenever we try to do so, we face again the
curiously troublesome circularity I described in Chapter 1. To understand a book well enough to repudiate it, I must have made it a part of
me; I will have lived my hours with it, as friend, and to that degree I
will have already experienced an ethical change, for better or worse.
Of course I can always ostracize a work, after hearing rumors about it
or sampling two pages, as I ostracized *Jaws* in Chapter 6. But if I once
let it "in," I may find myself in collusion with the accused. To attack a
fiction as sentimental, shallow, pretentious, decadent, bourgeois, or
naively logocentric, I must first experience that quality in the work. I
can of course deplore sentimentality in general or bourgeois complacency in general without deciding whether they are found *here*. But to
decide that, I must pay attention, and in doing so, I may find myself
undergoing a change of character. Before I am quite aware of what has
happened, my hypocrisy upward has proved to be a degradation: I become a Don Quixote emulating destructive chivalric codes (in the
name of a noble ideal), an Emma Bovary aspiring to romantic heroism
(from the highest of motives), or a Sir Edward copying Lovelace and
Lord Byron (seeking a kind of heroism).

THE USE OF NON-NARRATIVE DISCOURSE IN
APPRAISING CHARACTERS

When we turn from telling rival stories to talking *about* them—the
practice pursued from the beginning here—what are our possibilities?
Perhaps most obvious is the never easy non-narrative restatement of
the norms found in a given narrative, thereby either reinforcing them
or bringing them into question. To probe to the heart of a narrative
and bring back a report to the world, and then to offer reasons for
accepting or rejecting them—these critical acts can never replace the
fictions themselves, but they are invaluable in "appreciating" their
value on the cultural market meter.[15] This kind of appreciation consti-

---

15. Some current critics have argued the equivalent value of criticism and imaginative narratives. The position is self-proving if we choose the most imaginative criticism
and compare it with feeble narratives. But would anyone except Harold Bloom willingly
trade the romantic poets he discusses for a whole bundle of his criticism? Would I

tutes a large part of what many of us teachers try for, under various less evangelical disguises. Last night a seventeen-year-old friend said to me, "When I first read *A Passage to India* I sort of liked it but I didn't think it was anything very wonderful. But then we discussed it in [high school English] class, and my teacher read some of it aloud, and now it just seems to me about the most important book I've ever read. What Forster says about the contrast between Professor Godbole's way of living and the lives of the British—it's just wonderful, and you know, I had hardly even noticed Godbole on my own."

Such appreciation also makes up the best part of what our successful "men of letters"[16] do for us, as they comb through huge stacks of novels, plays, poems, and histories, new and old, winnowing out those few that may be worth our while. Their judgments are not at all reliable when they attack, but when a V. S. Pritchett or a Mary McCarthy praises, I know that I should sit up and take notice.

Much of the best formal criticism also simply *appreciates* in this sense. Re-reading F. R. Leavis, for example, helped produce the reversal of my opinion of D. H. Lawrence that I describe in Chapter 13. Leavis's gift is not as impressive and valuable as that of Lawrence himself, but it is nevertheless precious. It consists in part of answering objections that other ethical critics have made against Lawrence. That kind of answer can restore or preserve good narratives from thoughtless or tendentious denigration. If D. S. Savage has complained, plausibly enough, that *A Passage to India* ignores the "ugly realities" that underlay the British presence in India and handles the inter-cultural problems "as though they could be solved on the surface level of personal intercourse" (quoted in Kettle 1967, 2: 161), Arnold Kettle can perform a great service in underlining Forster's special value, even to those of us who, like Kettle himself, would prefer a more aggressive political program than Forster offers:

---

willingly sell any fine novel I have discussed in exchange for my own precious words about it?

16. Who are increasingly women—Mary McCarthy, Susan Sontag, Joyce Carol Oates, Joan Didion. May there be many more in the tradition of Edmund Wilson and V. S. Pritchett, though the very possibility of making a living as a writer outside the academy is increasingly remote—or so Pritchett himself suggests (1985, xi).

And yet [even admitting that there is some slight truth to Savage's charge] the tentativeness, the humility of Forster's attitude is not something to undervalue. The "perhapses" that lie at the core of his novels, constantly pricking the facile generalization, hinting at the unpredictable element in the most fully analysed relationship, cannot be brushed aside as mere liberal pusillanimity. He seems to me a writer of scrupulous intelligence, of tough and abiding insights, who has never been afraid of the big issues or the difficult ones and has scorned to hide his doubts and weaknesses behind a façade of wordiness and self-protective conformity.

(1967, 2: 163)

There is of course that opposite kind of help, pointing at faults we have failed to discern. But since ethical critics, even those who travel under other labels, have never undervalued the sharply negative voice, I won't dwell on it here.

The danger in thinking about our critical talk in this way is that it may reduce the moral instruction of narratives to their "morals," or even to extractable propositions and decodings, like "Much wants more and loses all." Without denying the overwhelming evidence that readers do take explicit instruction from even the least sermonic works, I would argue that a much more important moral effect of every encounter with a story, good or bad, is the practice it gives in how to read moral qualities from potentially misleading signs. That training can be harmful, if our line-by-line progress through a work suggests that the good guys and bad guys can be readily discriminated by surface signs of dress, physical charm, or taste in wines; indeed even the most admired fictions can sometimes make moral inference seem too easy. But our best narrative friends introduce us to the practice of subtle, sensitive moral inference, the kind that most moral choices in daily life require of us. The reader—at least *this* reader—comes away from reading Henry James, or Jane Austen, or Shakespeare, emulating *that kind* of moral sensitivity—not so much the sensitivity of any one character (because sometimes there is no dramatized character who exhibits special moral insight) but, rather, that of the author who insists that I *see* what these people are doing to each other.

In Chapter 13 I shall dwell on this point a bit, especially in discussing Jane Austen's *Emma*. For now it will be more economical to borrow from a fine essay by Martha Craven Nussbaum, on the ways in which James's *The Golden Bowl* is not just an adjunct to moral philosophy but is itself an indispensable kind of moral philosophy. Treating this novel as (in part) a portrayal of just how Maggie Verver discovers the subtle distortions of her original moral perceptions, Nussbaum argues that fictions of this rare kind do what discursive philosophy (and ethical criticism, I would add) can never do: they

> display to us the complexity, the indeterminacy, the sheer *difficulty* of moral choice. . . . This task cannot be easily accomplished by texts which speak in universal terms—for one of the difficulties of deliberation . . . is that of grasping the uniqueness of the new particular. Nor can it easily be done by texts which speak with the hardness or plainness which moral philosophy has traditionally chosen for its style—for how can this style at all convey the way in which the 'matter of the practical' appears before the agent in all of its bewildering complexity, without its morally salient features stamped on its face? And how, without conveying this, can it convey the active adventure of the deliberative intelligence, the 'yearnings of thought and excursions of sympathy' [James] that make up much of our actual moral life?
>
> (1983, 43–44)

Nussbaum's point is partly that only narrative can "convey the peculiar value and beauty of choosing humanly well—for . . . the flawed and unclear object has its own, and not simply a lower, sort of beauty" (44). The word "beauty" here is restored to something like the breadth that it would have had in classical praise for narrative: it *includes* an awareness that forms are truly beautiful only when they are morally valuable. Nussbaum sees the ultimate value as the education in full human perceptiveness that a novelist like James offers:

> [T]he 'example' in *The Golden Bowl* is, of course, not merely the adventures of the consciousness of one or another character. . . . It is the entire text, revealed as the imaginative effort of a human character who displays himself here as the sort of character who reads lives and texts so as not to cheapen their value. . . . [James's views] emerge as the ruminations of such a high and fine mind concerning the tangled mysteries of these imaginary lives. And we could hardly begin to see whether such views were or were not exemplary for us if this mind simply stated its conclusions flatly, if it did not unfold before us the richness of its reflection, allowing us to follow and to share its adventures.
>
> (42–43)

When we approach all these complexities as *characters,* willing to embrace the narrative world's manifold offerings, we who were "raised" as individuals may still on occasion feel anxious about the loss of any clearly marked individuality. But surely I need not feel anxious, once I see that the turns in my life, embracing and sloughing off successive "characters," produce a life story that is uniquely "my own." I implicitly "tell" that story as I play my various and perhaps contradictory roles. Its uniqueness provides the only individuality that will still interest me: my story has its own plot line.[17] Though most of what is "me" will be traceable to previous story-tellers, the particular sequence of roles will be mine, all mine: of this time, of this place, of this person and no other.

It will of course bear many resemblances to other life-plots. Though our stories are unique, they fall into "genres" that are obviously not infinite in number. If this claim seems dubious, try the experiment of listing all the life-plot summaries you can think of: "She started out with a silver spoon in her mouth, but then she married X and from then on it was all downhill." "He was born in a ditch, kicked from pillar to post, until suddenly, in his early twenties, he discovered his bent for financial dealing and made a fortune. But then he got overconfident, went too far—'much wanted more and lost all'—and committed suicide." And so on. If each of these is then put in even more summary form, we soon see that there cannot be an unlimited number: from high promise to happiness to misery; from beginning misery to happiness to misery; from misery to misery to maximum misery (the "crushed worm" form of too many modern novels); from happiness to happiness to misery; from happiness to happiness to a higher happiness (for example, that rare thing, a reconciled death); from promise to promise to sudden accidental death. And so on. Let your imagination range as freely as you will, add other possibilities ("from virtue to vice to virtue," "from ignorance to revelation," and so on), and you will still fairly soon run out of genres. The modern quest for the fully individualized lifeline was doomed from the beginning.

17. All philosophies of the "social self" are faced with the task of accounting for and honoring individuality. A splendid account of Mikhail Bakhtin's difficulties in delineating limits to his polyglot ethic of openness is given by Caryl Emerson, in her essay "Problems with Bakhtin's Poetic" (1986).

For an extended, vigorous argument that psychoanalysis works best when analyst and analysand think of themselves as in dialectical conversation about alternative plot lines, see Bertram Cohler's "Psychoanalysis and the Developmental Narrative" (forthcoming). Cohler provides a twenty-eight-page bibliography relating to his thesis that the best means for "understanding the course of [each person's] development is that of a constructed narrative rather than of the 'recovery' of a supposed set of events which had a predictable, determining outcome."

This revelation of the inescapably shared nature of the possible genres open to me will not trouble me if what I pursue is a vigorous story line within one or another of the many good ones. Nor will I be troubled to discover that most, perhaps all of the good genres fall within an even more general pattern, one traced by many an explicitly religious narrative but also by many a modern seemingly secular novel that portrays heroes and heroines engaged in a spiritual quest: "Born radically ignorant, inescapably provincial; soon revealed a stultifying egocentrism and chauvinism; became (largely through the miracle of deriving better desires from good stories told by others engaged in the same quest, and with the lesser assistance of ethical criticism) less and less ignorant, less provincial, less egocentric, less chauvinist. Developed, before a predictably premature death, a *character* that could warmly embrace and even celebrate the not-self, the 'others,' even the Other."

Tied, fortunately, to ancestors, to family, to church, to teachers, to neighbors, to country, to party, to gender, a character will not expect to plot a life by cutting all ties and drifting, like an astronaut, into free-fall, or soaring, like Icarus, too close to the sun. A character will say (or at least believe): "My lifelines *are* me. My problem is not, like that of Winston Smith and Stephen Dedalus, to learn how to resist the inhibiting influence of others, in an opposition always implicitly doomed; rather it is to winnow, from among myriad narrative advisers, those whose seductive plot suggestions are acts of genuine friendship."

That discernment requires not just the courage to assert "my" true beliefs, including those borrowed from my past, and not just the courage to reject those inherited beliefs that seem to bind me. It requires a fully developed art of ethical (and, by implication, political) criticism.

REFERENCES

Aristotle. *The Nicomachean Ethics*. Trans. H. Rackham. Loeb Classical Library, London, 1932.

Bloom, Harold. *The Anxiety of Influence: A Theory of Poetry*. New York, 1973.

Booth, Wayne C. *Critical Understanding: The Powers and Limits of Pluralism*. Chicago, 1979.

Bové, Paul A. *Intellectuals in Power: A Genealogy of Critical Humanism.*
    New York, 1986.
Cohler, Bertram J. "Psychoanalysis and the Developmental Narrative." In *The
    Course of Life.* Ed. S. Greenspan and G. Pollock. Forthcoming.
Emerson, Caryl. "Problems with Bakhtin's Poetic." Paper presented at annual
    convention of the Modern Language Association of America, New
    York, Dec. 1986.
Fish, Stanley. *Is There a Text in This Class? The Authority of Interpretative
    Communities.* Cambridge, Mass., 1980.
Flaubert, Gustave. *Madame Bovary* [1857]. Trans. Francis Steegmuller. New
    York, 1957.
Grossman, Ron. "Passions: A Disciple Confronts Ayn Rand's Power." *Chi-
    cago Tribune* (Sept. 9, 1986): 1, 3.
Heidegger, Martin. *Being and Time* [1927]. Trans. John Macquarrie and
    Edward Robinson. New York, 1962.
Joyce, James. *Ulysses* [1922]. Ed. Hans Walter Gabler et al. New York, 1986.
Kettle, Arnold. *An Introduction to the English Novel* [1953]. 2d ed. 2 vols.
    London, 1967.
Krieger, Murray. "In the Wake of Morality: The Thematic Underside of Re-
    cent Theory." *New Literary History* 15 (Aut. 1983): 119–36.
Lindenberger, Herbert. "Keats' 'To Autumn' and Our Knowledge of a Poem."
    College English 32 (Nov. 1970): 132–33.
Llosa, Mario Vargas. *The Perpetual Orgy: Flaubert and "Madame Bovary."*
    Trans. Helen Lane. New York, 1986.
McCloskey, Donald N. *The Rhetoric of Economics.* Madison, Wis., 1985.
Nussbaum, Martha Craven. "Flawed Crystals: James's *The Golden Bowl*
    and Literature as Moral Philosophy." *New Literary History* 15 (Aut.
    1983): 25–50.
Pritchett, V. S. *A Man of Letters: Selected Essays.* New York, 1985.
Schmidt, Siegfried J. "Towards a Pragmatic Interpretation of 'Fictionality.'" In
    Pragmatics of Language and Literature. Ed. Teun A. van Dijk. North-
    Holland Studies in Theoretical Poetics, vol. 2. Amsterdam, 1976.
Steiner, George. *Martin Heidegger* [1979]. New York, 1980.
Taylor, Charles. "Responsibility for Self." In *The Identities of Persons.* Ed.
    Amelie Oksenberg Rorty. Berkeley, 1976.
Zittrain, Jeffrey. "Kerouac's *On the Road* as Ethical Guide." M.A. thesis, Uni-
    versity of Chicago, 1986.

10

Men become what they contemplate.
Austin Warren

There is one story and one story
   only
That will prove worth your telling,
Whether as learned bard or gifted
   child . . .
Robert Graves

Examine language; what, if you except some primitive elements of
natural sound, what is it all but
metaphors, recognized as such or no
longer recognized; still fluid and
florid or now solid-grown and
colourless?
Thomas Carlyle

Education by poetry is education by
metaphor.
Robert Frost

In examining the relation of one subject to another, the initial choice of
metaphors and conceptual diagrams
is a fateful choice.
Northrop Frye

Figures That "Figure" the Mind

Images and Metaphors as Constitutive Stories

WHY "FIGURING" CANNOT BE ESCAPED

"Character" is a big word, and arguments about how to build character are imprecise and indecisive. "Imagination" may seem an even bigger word, and certainly it has a history fully as ambiguous as that of "character." But if I think of my imagination as containing, or (to choose a better "dead" metaphor) as *capable of employing,* a collection of images that I have re-created in my experience of narratives, and if I think of my character as in part made of the images my mind "contains" (or "employs" or "is occupied by": choice among these carries consequences), then it should be possible to find ways of talking sense about why we might welcome some images and show others the door.

Our everyday talk again provides a good beginning. We embrace and reject imaginative offerings without having to take much thought about them. People say, after a movie, "When I saw that scene coming, I just shut my eyes; I couldn't stand it." I have heard some express regret about having witnessed certain filmed moments: in *A Clockwork Orange,* when gleeful Alex bludgeons a woman to death with a huge white sculptured ithyphallus; in *Bonnie and Clyde,* when the vicious yet magnetic lover-bandits suffer a most wonderfully filmed slow-motion slaughter, a lingering death that I savored to the last bullet but that my step-father found "cheap and vicious"; in Bergman's *Cries and Whispers,* when the miserable young woman mutilates her vagina with a piece of broken glass (true enough, we don't actually *see* the physical details, but in memory they are there, just as we all remember red blood in the bathtub drain after the murder in *Psycho,* even though the film was in black-and-white). "I wish I hadn't seen that; it just won't go away." And indeed it won't; it has become a part of the mind, and it can at most be repressed, never fully erased.

Recently I saw on television the last half of a movie called *Mad Max:* two burnings-alive, one vivid decapitation, a couple of mutilations, and—the one I most wish I could forget—the running down and crushing, by revengeful bikers, of a blameless mother and her infant. (Was she really blameless, for those who saw the whole movie? How could I find out, without renting the movie and watching it from the beginning? Horrors.) Why didn't I turn it off? Don't ask. The best my ethical criticism can do for me now is keep me from even starting to watch the sequel, which a friend says is "even bloodier, though more moral."

Reading can produce equally obsessive and (perhaps) regrettable memories, even though the images we construct in reading are usually less graphic than those we construct with the more explicit aid of the visual arts.[1] When I ask people whether they can remember stories from childhood that were horrifying beyond endurance, they almost always respond with an example and a shudder. As adults we are much less likely to experience such unendurable shock while reading, especially now that we have all become toughened by the richer resources of filmed horror. But if you search your mind you may be surprised at what you find lurking there ("lurking" is of course the right metaphor). I find in mine a painstakingly detailed picture of a certain corpse, in Ngaio Marsh's *Artists in Murder;* and a vivid moment in Jerzy Kosinski's *Cockpit* when . . . But why should I do you the disservice of adding to your own collection of such horrors?

On the other hand, if we have read much of what we call "literature"—the good stuff—we can summon up, along with other moments of violence and horror, far more images that we "view" with gratitude, gifts that have enhanced our imaginative lives with possibilities that our real lives could never have provided. We find not only scenes of unequivocally happy fulfillment but also moments of correction or castigation when a nasty image, deliberately criticized by its context, opened our eyes to the viciousness of some previously accepted practice: on the one hand, transmutations of the quotidian into

---

1. For a splendid recent account of how visual and verbal images relate, see W. J. T. Mitchell's *Iconology* (1986).

radiance; on the other, revelations of what is absurd or base in our "normal" practices.

The point here is not to ask whether we are right or wrong in any one of these regrets or celebrations, but rather to underline once again the reflexive trap that none of us can escape: when we try to think about these images, we do it with equipment built of the very stuff that we are now trying to judge. Whatever regrets we feel come always in some sense too late. The image that I deplore will neither disappear for the wishing nor retire to some corner of my mind labeled "entertainment only" or "other people's viciousness." If I have revelled in Rocky's battering of the brutish Soviet slugger, as I did for a few moments watching a movie on a recent trans-atlantic flight, the physical pleasure in the images of bloody bashing has become not just some "implied reader's" but mine. On the other hand, the approved images, the ones that I repeat and dwell on admiringly in memory, are even more tenacious and thus also potentially destructive. After all, "they have helped make me what I am today," and how can I wholly repudiate *that?* They will thus affect my present judgment, just as my present approval is likely to reinforce their effects. When one's natural egoism is supported by the fashionable belief that all "broadening," every encounter with "otherness," no matter how base, is good for us,[2] how can one fail to think that even the vilest stuff has done splendid work? If, like Emma Bovary, I have mistaken shoddy for silk, what am I to do?

For good or ill, we all find, when we attend to the actual "occupants"[3] of our involuntary mental life, especially when we observe

2. A corollary of the belief (see Chapter 3 above) that the more open-ended a fiction is, the better it is. The extreme form of this belief is that the most "realistic" work does most for us, in showing us either how to face the world as it really is or how to tame its horrors. An intelligent, challenging version of the view that horrifying images in fictions can do us good rather than harm is found in Bettelheim's *The Uses of Enchantment* (1977). A frequent complaint by moral critics is that modern fiction goes a step further than life; no longer "realistic," it turns all reality into nastiness and horror. One can easily think of exceptions to this charge—obviously, it all depends on what fiction you look at.

3. With a metaphor like "occupants" I might seem to suggest a passive reception that would contradict what I've previously said about reading *activity*. Though my argument is that we are largely "made," "constituted" by the figurings offered by nar-

what wells up in dreams and daydreams, a confusing mixture of good
and bad company, of profound and trivial thought, of beautiful and
revolting imagery, of energizing and enervating pictures of human possibility. Mahler's *Kindertotenlieder,* which I heard again last night,
rings in my head all day—rings, that is, until it is crowded out by
something else that is "there": perhaps another symphonic work but
quite probably one or another of the hundreds of advertising jingles
that I have absorbed ever since radio entered my imaginative life in the
early 1930s. Should it matter to me that Mahler is now crowded out of
my consciousness by "Pepsi-Cola Hits the Spot," by "Delta Is Ready
When You Are," by the more recent "Na-bis-co" (sol-re-mi, "My Bonnie" with the "Bon" and "nie" reversed, if you want to know), or by
the ancient ditty for Ajax that Mahler's insistent use of the dominant-
tonic cadence "calls to mind" (see musical example). Not very much,
perhaps. No doubt to worry about the lifelong trivialization of one's
mind by harmless jingles (to say nothing of atrocious uplifting hymns)
is to risk a comic solemnity. Why not work on one of the world's serious problems? Besides, aren't there people in the world whose musical lives have been enriched by commercials, as there are many whose
spirits (like mine) have been lifted with atrocious hymns?

> Putcher shoulder to the wheel, push alah-ong;
> Do your doody with a heart full of sah-ong;
> We all have work;
> Let no one shirk;
> Putcher shoulder—to—th'wheel!

---

ratives (including the "little narratives" of individual metaphors), indeed that we are
"taken in," often even in the threatening sense of being led into a destructive imaginative
world, the taking is the opposite of passive. We join here the current battle between the
"constructivists," who see all "listening" as creative and all metaphor as "generative" (a
creation of "tools for thinking"), and the "non-constructivists" who—according to
their critics, at least—reduce listening to a "conduit" metaphor (language as a passive
transporting medium carrying messages from A to B). Obviously insofar as there are
genuine "sides" here, I join the constructivists who see metaphor as "an essential characteristic of the creativity of language" rather than as "deviant and parasitic upon normal usage" (Ortony 1979, 2). For a painstaking critique of the conduit metaphor for
language acts, see Reddy 1979. For a sustained argument that metaphor is generative,
see Schön 1979. For a report on the astonishing amount of time most people spend, in
their waking hours, telling silent stories to themselves—that is, daydreaming—see *New
York Times* 1987.

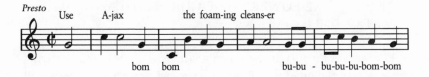

Surely having *some* song to sing is better than having no song at all? How are we to talk about the good and bad of these "micronarratives," these "stampings," these figurings of our character? That we must talk about them is clear, if we are to have an effective ethical criticism at all: we have seen again and again that the true ethical effect of our narrative experience, no matter how prolonged it is, depends largely on the precise, detailed patterning of our desires from moment to moment.

We can underline the difficulties in our project—as if they needed underlining—by asking whether my possession by the Ajax ditty could be redeemed simply by changing the lyrics:

> Read Shakespeare—
> (Bom bom)—
> Our greatest playwright:
> (Bu-bu-bu-bu-bu-bom-bom)—
> Feeds the soul—
> (Pause)—
> Just like the brain!

or

> Treat others—
> (Bom bom)—
> As you'd be treated . . .

THE SPECIAL POWERS OF FIGURATIVE LANGUAGE: METAPHOR

Every art of the imagination, benign or vicious, profound or trivial, can colonize the mind in the way I have just described. No one will ever fully explain why some images, visual and auditory, stick with me and others with you. What is clear is that for all of us, the most powerful effects result when we have expended a great deal of mental energy reconstructing an image from minimal clues.[4] Mental energy, as I intend it here, can be of many kinds, ranging from the adrenaline-charged energy of sheer fright and horror to the quieter energy of trying to figure out what is going on.

"Ajax" *got* me by sheer quantity of repetition; as a teenager I found myself singing it back, with lots of practice in making the bass plosives boom out roundly and rapidly. Mahler's lament on the death of children *got* me by engaging my whole soul in shared grief and my whole mind in intense attention to compositional intricacies and delicacies. I have thus become, in part, those works of "art." In the terms of Chapter 9, my character can now no longer be divorced from my tendency to break into a version of "Ajax" or my capacity to call up, in memory, long stretches of the *Kindertotenlieder*.[5]

This effect of engaged energies means that figurative language will always figure the mind more incisively than plain language (I'm not sure whether the same principle works in our dealing with photographic images, which seem inherently more literal—but see Mitchell

---

4. Except perhaps for the effect of repetition. I suffer it as I write: "Ajax" now seems to accompany every waking hour.

5. No doubt *any* act of understanding, even of the simplest everyday phrase, requires energy and to some slight degree shapes or reshapes the understander. In making the claim I have been making about narrative, and in turning now to metaphor as a form of concise narrative, I deal with only the most striking instance of the point made frequently these days, by many linguists, psychologists, and anthropologists, that we *are* in large part the sum of the language we have heard and can speak. Rom Harré, for example, argues in *Personal Being:* "Conversation is to be thought of as creating a social world just as causality generates a physical one" (1984, 65)—here the word "conversation" includes much that I mean by the notion of understanding narrative. "The primary human reality is persons in conversation" (58). Note that the thesis of linguistic acculturation is not identical with the "Whorffian hypothesis," popular a decade ago—the claim (not quite Whorff's actual point) that each language creates radically different kinds of human beings who in essential respects cannot communicate fully.

1986). In our language of friendship: to re-create a figure will always produce more *intimacy,* just as to dance *with* a partner is always a more intimate act than to dance *along with* someone who is doing another dance and looking into the far distance. The energy I expend in reconstructing the figure is somehow transferred to retaining the figure itself and bonding with its maker. In short, since "energy expended = ethical power," every deviation from the conventional way of speaking, every special demand on the listener's powers of reconstruction, will add to the effect. A figure *used* not only calls for the recognition that a figure *has been used* but for a special kind of re-creative engagement with the figurer (Cohen 1979).

Suppose I am reading a book—courtesy dictates leaving it unnamed—and I come to this sentence: "But not only are we poised on the footboard of the encyclopaedic civilisation now being launched; in addition, we are gathered to the brow of infinity by the initial achievement of the scientific revolution." Or suppose I meet an advertisement for a magazine, *The American Spectator,* claiming that it is edited by "one of the most luminous young gadflies now singing in the American wilderness." Even to see what's wrong with these comic mixtures, I must first try to do exactly what the metaphorists have tried to do: make a picture, an image. If I then have trouble putting together footboards, launching pads, and brows, or the notion of singing with the notion of the stinging gadfly, the trouble itself engages my energies in a way that would not have been true if either writer had spoken plain. Even if I reject the picture, a great deal of energy (of pleasant activity, in the terms of Chapter 6) goes into the rejection, and the writers appear *worse* than they would have if they had just been content to seem dull but clear. But if I accept the picture, the energy serves to bind me to the implied author; consciously or unconsciously, I see him or her as my kind of person.

The full intricacy and force of our patterns of reconstruction, whenever a figurative invitation is accepted, are astonishing, once we try to trace them in detail. Though each kind of figuration would no doubt yield somewhat different ethical results if we dwelt on it at length, we can see that all of them invite us to an intellectual dance at least as intricate as the one we traced with the sentence by Swift (pp. 188–89 above). That *pas de deux* commits us in turn to the inviter's entire enterprise.

For our general purpose of exploring ethical effect, any figure would do, because every figure implicitly calls attention to the figurer and thus transforms the relation of teller and listener. Irony would be especially revealing, because of the ethical intricacies it frequently introduces with an implied elitism: "Some slobs might take this poison straight" (Booth 1974, esp. 29, 73, 227, 263–64). But clearly the most representative, for the critic of narrative, is the figure that we most obviously conduct our lives *with* and *in,* the one that most critics have considered most powerful: metaphor.

APPRAISING THE MEDIUM WE LIVE IN

It is a bit surprising that in the recent explosion of interest in metaphor (Shibles 1971; Ortony 1979; Ricoeur 1975; de Man 1983) we find hardly anything about the relative powers of different metaphors to work good or ill in the world. When the ethical effects of metaphors are discussed at all, the claim is almost always that *as a class* they are wonderfully effective in schooling the imagination.[6] The claim is sound, up to a point, but it resembles too closely the claim we met in Chapter 3 that all genuine "literature" or "art" is good for us: it reduces a complex set of problems to a blanket accolade.[7]

Where might we turn for help in talking about an author's responsibility when inventing metaphors, or a reader's responsibility when responding to them? From Plato we might derive help in appraising

6. Some deconstructionists' claims about the invariably disruptive role of metaphor might throw doubt on my "wonderfully." But a close look at Paul de Man's comments on how we should *feel* about his discoveries shows him as at least ambivalent—sometimes lamenting our perpetual indecision but also admitting the possibility of celebration (1983).

7. It is no surprise that the two general claims are often joined with a third, proposing that the one clear mark of *literature* is "metaphoricity." The New Critics tended to make ironic or metaphoric language the defining feature of literature, while plain prose marked "scientific" uses of language. We still today have a flood of definitions based roughly on the same notion: figuration, "defamiliarization," is what we go to "literature" for; straight talk is for information exchange or didactic impact (Riffaterre 1978, esp. ch. 1; Mukařovský 1955, 19–35; Ricoeur 1976, 46–47). I cannot explain why the distinction survives, against the daily evidence that much of the finest literature comes to us without *obvious* linguistic figuring and that all our scientific, historical, and political writing is laden with obvious metaphor.

various metaphors for the whole human enterprise (life as a power struggle; life as a conversational game; life as a hunt or chase; life as the pursuit of love; life as a ladder or two-way escalator or mountain climb; life as a prolonged schooling for death; and so on). I turn to such large critical efforts in the next chapter. From Longinus we could derive relatively precise distinctions between those metaphors that achieve sublime transport and those that exhibit what Pope in *Peri Bathous* nicely calls "the art of sinking" ([1727–28] 1952). We must consider, Longinus says,

> whether some of these passages have merely some such outward show of grandeur with a rich moulding of casual accretions, and whether, if all this is peeled off, they may not turn out to be empty bombast which it is *more noble to despise than to admire?* For the true sublime, by some virtue of its nature, *elevates us:* uplifted with a sense of proud possession, we are filled with joyful pride, as if we had ourselves produced the very thing we heard. . . . For what is truly great gives abundant food for thought: it is irksome, nay, impossible, to resist its effect: *the memory of it is stubborn and indelible.*
>
> (Longinus, 7.4; my italics)

From Samuel Johnson we might learn how to recognize what is wrong about an overdone "conceit," pursuing his arguments in his provocative questioning of the Metaphysical poets ([1779] 1905).[8] From our contemporaries the gleanings would be sparser: from Paul Ricoeur some help, densely argued, in distinguishing worldviews that sustain us from those that are programmatically "suspicious," and hence finally self-destructive (1977); from Charles Lakoff and Mark Johnson some advice, mostly implicit, about taking care with our everyday

---

8. "If . . . that be considered as Wit which is at once natural and new, that which though not obvious is, upon its first production, acknowledged to be just; if it be that, which he that never found it, wonders how he missed; to wit of this kind the metaphysical poets have seldom risen. Their thoughts are often new, but seldom natural; they are not obvious, but neither are they just; and the reader, far from wondering that he missed them, wonders more frequently by what perverseness of industry they were ever found. . . . Who but Donne would have thought that a good man is a telescope? [In making their metaphors, the metaphysicals made such gross comparisons as] Physic and . . . a Lover: . . . The World and a Clock: . . . [a] coal pit . . . [and] the Sun: . . . Death [and] a Voyage: . . . the condemned man [scheduled to be hung at dawn, and the poet-lover] at this midnight ['Time's dead low-water,' waiting hopelessly for the dawn]" ([1779] 1905, 1: 19–33). The entire score or so of pages could well be studied by every modern critic who thinks that responsible evaluation is impossible.

metaphors lest we find ourselves caught in "containers" and "tunnels" and "channels" and "fields" that confine us, while wielding tools and weapons that in fact wound the user (1980). From many a deconstructionist we can receive the valuable warning not to think that we have a literal picture when what we're really dealing with is metaphor.

The fact remains that we find today hardly any serious appraisal of how particular metaphors might be good or bad for those who embrace them. Critics have chosen safer territory, showing how individual metaphors "work" in themselves; how they function in given contexts; why they do or do not surrender to efforts at literal translation; why they are preferable to what is taken as straight talk (usually it is because they provide "ambiguity," though occasionally it is because they provide greater precision).

Among the obstacles to doing more than this, perhaps the most obvious is that the critter whose services or ravages we would appraise is so ill-defined. The problem of definition is especially troublesome now that everything under the sun is apt to be taken as either metaphoric or ironic.[9] There is nothing wrong, perhaps, with building linguistic empires in this way, lumping under one term all metonymy, synecdoche, analogy, parable, allegory, and so on, provided the new lumpings are based on observation of genuine similarities among things previously kept separate. Indeed, my expansive moves in the next chapter will depend in part on that kind of imperialism. But what do we do when we realize that in current practice there is simply no human expression, whether in language or in any other medium, that would not be called metaphoric according to *someone's* definition? Every*thing* I *speak* is in one *sense* or another *meta-phoric;* every *time* I dis*course* on any *topic* I am *con-sciously* or unconsciously *falling* into metaphoric *practices.*[10] Should we just decide that the word has become useless, since

9. For critiques of this kind of imperialism, see Booth 1974, 176–78; 1983, 719–24; Genette 1982, 103–26; Vickers 1988. For a shrewd treatment of the problem of definition, see Mark Turner's *Death Is the Mother of Beauty* (1987, esp. 16–21). Turner's book is to me the most useful discussion of how "literary" metaphors construct the "worlds" we live in, and—the point too often forgotten by enthusiasts for the power of metaphor—how the world we live in constrains our construction of metaphors.

10. Many scientists and historians of science—Thomas Kuhn perhaps the most often cited—have in recent decades talked of scientific theories as "metaphoric paradigms" or "grand metaphors" or "grand visions": inevitably *partial* representations, maps, or models of a reality that forever escapes full formulation (Gould 1987, 143). In talking with mathematicians, I find that they usually resist this idea. They are happy to

any word that means everything can only mean nothing? If we don't know what it is we are talking about, we can hardly hope to decide whether or not it is good for us.[11]

On the other hand, perhaps the very ubiquity of this "something" makes it especially important to the ethical critic. If, as many critics claim, metaphor is not an isolable literary device at all but the inescapable medium of our very being, the fundamental structure of our essentially "non-literal," symbolic grasp of an ever-elusive reality (Ricoeur 1977), then surely we must take our courage in both hands and plunge into that medium, our critical antennae trembling. As it were.

Facing any such imperialistic term, our only hope lies in adjectival partition: just as in talking about the catch-all term "irony" we cannot survive without discriminating varieties—stable (or rhetorical) irony, cosmic irony, romantic irony, dramatic irony, and so on—so in talking of metaphor we can hope to make our way only kind by kind. Whether we then conclude that all the kinds are *really* "the same thing" or only loosely overlapping members with a "family resemblance" will not matter so much as finding a way to talk some kind of sense about the kinds as we come to them.

We can ultimately raise ethical questions about the powers of every

---

allow that *physicists'* theories are metaphors, but mathematical equations are not just literal but *real:* indeed, they exist before their discovery, as a kind of Platonic form waiting to be discovered (private conversation with Saunders MacLean, December 1987). But occasionally one runs across acknowledgement that even mathematical equations "could *not* represent reality perfectly. He [Robert May] *knew they were just metaphors*—so he began to wonder how widely the metaphors could apply" (Glieck 1987, 77–78; my italics). See Black 1979, 25.

11. In "The Empire of Irony" (1983) I discuss the ways in which expansion of "irony" and its derivatives by careless speakers can suggest more than they intend: "It was ironic that . . ." fills a slot formerly filled by "As God decreed." "Metaphor" as a word has not entered popular usage to the same degree as "irony" and "ironically." Its imperialism has been confined mainly to critical discussion. In popular usage, metaphors are not usually given a warning flag. When a flag is offered, it is usually not "metaphorically speaking" but rather "figuratively speaking," or "as it were," or—increasingly—"literally," as in "The stadium literally exploded." I can only guess at why writers who want to sound educated have not found "metaphorically" as useful and impressive as "ironically." Is it that *events* do not strike the modern mind as metaphors for other events, while every event can be seen to contrast "ironically" with some other event? To many an earlier philosopher, perhaps most notably Augustine, it seemed obvious that some events "figure" earlier and later events, figure them, in a sense, quite "literally." Stephen Jay Gould has recently explored the usefulness, in history of science, of such analogizing (1987).

kind of metaphor, since all metaphors "attempt" to win our friendship. But it will be useful to begin with one of the simplest, most obvious kinds, metaphors that are designed to win by destroying an opponent or an opposing case: in short, weapons.

WEAPON METAPHORS

The earliest studies of metaphor concentrate mainly on what I am dubbing weapons, no doubt because systematic study of rhetoric began under the stimulus of legal quarrels.[12] Only two questions seem to have interested most rhetoricians: Are the metaphors effective in winning? and, Is the cause of the rhetorician who uses them just? Not surprisingly, most discussions since then have been confined to the first question, since the second seems to lead not to knowledge about metaphors but only to judgments about causes. Most of what we can learn about metaphors from Demetrius, say, or Quintilian,[13] or from modern guides like H. W. Fowler (1965, 348–52), is quite properly limited to how to use them for communicating or persuading effectively. The radically different question of what they *do* to us *as* they persuade is explicitly repudiated, dismissed with a phrase, or simply ignored.

Consider an especially effective weapon, an account of which was given me by a lawyer friend, James Boyd White, who had been hired to defend a large southern utility against a suit by a small one. White had thought at first that he was doing fine. The laws seemed to be on his side, and he felt that he had presented his case reasonably well. Then the lawyer for the small utility said, speaking to the jury, "So now we see what it *is*. They got us where they want us. They're holdin' us up with one hand, their good sharp fishin' knife in the other, and they're sayin', 'you jes set still, little catfish, we're *jes* gonna *gut* ya.'" At that moment, my friend reports, he predicted, accurately, that he had lost the case—"I had fallen into the hands of a genius with metaphor."

---

12. The general class, of which weapon metaphors are a major representative, consists of metaphors that are in Max Black's terms "expendable," in the sense that their cognitive content can be stated in other terms—"those degenerately 'decorative' or expendable ones in which the metaphorical focus can be replaced by some literal equivalent" (1979, 41).

13. The indexes of the Loeb editions are a good beginning guide.

It is easy to see why this metaphor, obviously a short "fiction," is a good one technically—good, that is, as a weapon designed to win. Our sense of its mastery is quick and intuitive; our pleasure in that mastery confirms our sense that the lawyer has made a good stroke. But it is useful to slow down a bit, before moving to ethical criteria, to lay out the grounds of our assurance.

First, we ought to be clear about what this kind of speech act is. Instead of attempting the formal definition that we might need in other kinds of inquiry, suppose we simply list the rhetorical marks of this beast, so that we can then judge its "points." (The marks also implicitly question certain current assumptions about "all language"— but that is not our business here.) We can hope that the same procedure will later enable us to distinguish other kinds of metaphor, to be judged by different criteria, first "in their own terms" and then by "extrinsic" ethical standards.

1. The "catfish" metaphor is part of an intended communication with a practical purpose; it does not "ask," like some metaphors, to be judged as a piece of self-expression or as an attempt at formal beauty.

2. What is communicated is tied strictly to a context; regardless of what it may "mean," its full freight cannot be determined without reference to the rhetorical situation.

3. The *context* reveals to us that the clear purpose is to win, but the metaphoric account itself is intended to appear to the jurors (the primary auditors) as an attempt to give an accurate description of reality.

4. The purpose can be paraphrased, despite what some theorists tell us about the impossibility of paraphrasing metaphor itself. There are many different, synonymous ways of describing the lawyer's intent to win by attacking the opponent's aims and sincerity.

5. It follows that the metaphor itself is to some degree paraphrasable. But the contrast between the metaphor and any substitute expression is not necessarily between metaphoric and literal language but between the extremely metaphoric and the more or less ordinary or usual. "They're out to kill us" or "They want our scalps" would still be considered metaphoric by most hearers, though the expressions are much less unusual.

"They're trying to *destroy* us by keeping us passive" or "They're trying to *force us into* backruptcy" might be called literal by most casual observers, but we have no difficulty in seeing, once we think about it, that we are still dealing in comparisons, not literal identities. The domesticated terms, once metaphoric, have become standard, non-figured language.

This mark means that, at least with this kind of metaphor, we cannot expect to find any essence, anything like "metaphor-icity," that will mark some words or expressions as metaphor. We find that an expression is metaphoric in its *use* in a given context, not in any prior knowledge of what it means to *mean* in this or that way.

6. What is being compared are two *things*, not just two words. In this case they are two *situations*, which could be unpacked as an elaborate analogy: large utility is to fisherman as small util-ity is to catfish; knife is to catfish's vital center as large utility's measures are to small utility's vital center; and so on. The meta-phoric act is thus not primarily verbal, though it occurs in lan-guage.[14] If it were normal in any society to see those two things as comparable, nobody would take the comparison as meta-phoric; if in the future it becomes normal, we will have lost our metaphor.

7. Those two things are charged with value and thus with char-acter; the metaphor constitutes a kind of story or drama, with villains and heroes defined and with an implied sequence of events. Many micro-metaphors are considerably less explicit about the narratives that they help to compose. But even the most minute weapon metaphor implies a story, or a range of possible stories, that could take place in its world.

8. Unlike the metaphors that Ricoeur prefers to talk about—fat rich ones that offer no clear point at which interpretation can

---

14. Once again we face the fashionable claim that everything is ultimately linguistic; "reality" is nothing but a linguistic construct. The case is easily made—just as easily as is the opposite case that some hard realities underlie our language. The point here is that everyone on the scene, lawyers, judge, jurors, utility representatives, at least *thinks* that the issue is money and electric power, not language.

cease—this one is thin and stable, in the sense that once the jury has recognized the comparison, no further act of interpretation is invited, no further underminings of normal readings expected. Though analysis will reveal unlimited complexity in the rhetorical moment, the invitation to reconstruct one violent relation out of another violent relation is sharply limited by implicit standards of relevance. Only "extraneous" interests—such as ours in this chapter—will invite further analysis.

9. The metaphor is thus explicitly local or finite: there is no direct invitation to speculate about meanings, profound or shallow, about life, about the universe, nor even about capitalist exploitation. Our attention is held to the battle of utilities. Thus the metaphor adds no new truth to our lives, neither about catfish nor fishermen, at least not in any obvious way. It thus might seem to support Donald Davidson's claim that there is no "hidden message" in *any* metaphor; it just means what it says.[15]

But to accept this claim about one kind of metaphor does not mean that Davidson is right in his general claim about all metaphor. Nor does it mean that the critic who is interested in larger questions about metaphor cannot turn even this one to metaphysical or epistemological account. The precise way in which a given kind of metaphor is taken to "mean something else" obviously says a great deal (as we shall see in the next chapter) about the way we think our cosmos and our minds work.[16] Stable, finite metaphors can easily be rendered unstable and infinite in implication by anyone who chooses to ignore their original intentions and circumstances.

15. "The theorist who tries to explain a metaphor by appealing to a hidden message, like the critic who attempts to state the message, is then fundamentally confused. No such explanation or statement can be forthcoming because no such message exists" (Davidson 1979, 45).

16. As A. K. Ramanujan and others have argued, most figures that we call metaphor imply a new overlapping of two conceptual worlds that had previously been kept distinct. "Catfish" tries to fuse the world of fishing and fish gutting with the world of industrial power—two quite separate worlds in "fact," now made to overlap in argument. Metonymic figuring, on the other hand, can imply that the metonym is an integral part of the whole that it stands for; the part is in the whole as the whole is in the part (Ramanujan 1985, Afterword).

10. Thus implicit in the "Catfish" moment is a mark shared with all other deliberate rhetorical figurings: more *is* communicated than the words seem to say. What the "more" is cannot be easily described. If it is not truth, or even information, what is it? Aristotle and others have called it energy, which turns us in the right direction. Davidson's claim about the metaphor "meaning" only what it says, like my claim that the metaphor can be paraphrased, can apply at most to information transfer, not to rhetorical force. Whatever else the metaphor communicates, more of *an effect* "passes" from speaker to hearer than would have passed otherwise. That "more" cannot be described in the terms of any theory of semantics, communications, speech acts, or even pragmatics that I have encountered. The act of yoking elements that have never been yoked before, building a precise union that goes just so far and no further, with all irrelevant associations neatly and clearly rejected—that act of the speaker is duplicated by the hearer, *if* the metaphor works. Whatever their beliefs about utilities, hearers simply cannot resist joining the speaker in an intricate dance-step as they both play with similarities and differences. The metaphor thus accomplishes at least part of its work of bonding (Cohen 1979), even if the hearer, having irresistibly met the metaphor's demands, then draws back and says, "I shouldn't have allowed that to happen!"

11. Finally, we find a mark that clearly distinguishes our reading of this figure from our reading of stable ironies. It is true that the act of reconstruction begins, as it does when we read irony, in a recognition that literal, discrete, or ordinary meanings will not make full sense of the passage: the small utility is not a catfish, the large utility is not a knife-wielding fisherman. Therefore a new meaning must be actively sought: something like "the situation 'is' in this respect that of a fisherman gutting a catfish." But after it has been found, we do not, as we do in reading stable irony, reject our original picture to accommodate the new one. At least part of what we might call the uninterpreted picture, the first claim that something *is* something else, carries over to the final picture. The image of the big utility as a knife-wielding threat is forever in the receiver's mind, because the mind has done the work of making just that image.

THE ETHICS OF WEAPON METAPHORS

Whenever we find these marks exhibited, we can derive criteria for the rhetorical success of weapon metaphors. The essential ingredients are an unusual or surprising comparison of two things, part of a communication in a context that reveals a predetermined purpose that can be paraphrased, intended to be recognized and reconstructed with stable, local meanings that can thus be evaluated as contributing to that purpose: "You have an enemy in the world—kill 'im!" Obviously they thus imply a story about the kind of "world"—to use the metaphor that we must rely on heavily in the next chapter—in which such a metaphor makes sense.

Every weapon metaphor implies a world in which the question of winning or losing is primary. The rays of suggestion radiate outward from each metaphor, coloring both the "world" of origin—the entire life of the one who originates the metaphor—and the "world" of reception. Obviously, no one could ever predict or define the boundaries within which even the most seemingly limited metaphor might operate. Who, for example, could have predicted in A.D. 33 the flowering of military metaphors into religious language, as various "salvation armies" and "Christian soldiers" saw themselves "marching as to war." The Prince of Peace started all this, of course, when he claimed to bring not peace but the sword. His weapon metaphor (or metonym) may or may not have been intended to suggest the defeat of any enemy except the one within; but once that notion of Christianity as weapon was released upon us, the later captains and armies and glorious victories were, if not inevitable, at least easy to "prophesy after the event": a whole world of spiritual battle was implicit in the one word "sword," just as a whole world of slaughtering and butchering in a scene ostensibly bucolic and innocent is implicit in "Catfish."

Postponing discussion of what such irresistible aggrandizements lead to, here we seek to appraise the ethical value of weapon metaphors in themselves, taking them as representing all metaphors that are used for immediate utilitarian purposes.[17]

---

17. Note that the difference between metaphor and simile, essential in the study of some kinds of metaphor, seems here unimportant. It is perhaps true that adding a "like"

One might expect the popular manuals of effective writing to provide a rich supply of standards for weapon metaphors, with advice about how to seek out the best and avoid the worst. What we find instead, in the relatively few discussions of metaphor that say anything at all about appraisal, are vast simplifications, often to one or two standards, to three or four at most. Those who see metaphor as an alternative way of communicating information that might otherwise be communicated in some literal way generally say that good metaphors must be both "coherent" ("avoid mixed metaphors") and "true" (accurate, adequate to some reality presumed to exist separate from the metaphor and its maker). H. W. Fowler, one of the subtlest of modern guides, advises against "spoilt metaphors," by which he means that our metaphors should be accurate: "*Yet Jaurès was the* Samson *who* upheld the pillars *of the Bloc*" (1965, 360)—Samson, you will remember, did not exactly *uphold* pillars. As for coherence, every guidebook offers a little collection of howlers that, like the two with which we began, are laughably "mixed":

□ The community should vomit up this moral question mark.

□ Either we get a handle on these problems or we are all going down the drain.

□ The mayor decided to test the political temperature by throwing his hat into the ring as a trial balloon.

When we mock such expressions, we are assuming that coherence is an absolute standard; as the *New Yorker* implies when they print such comic mixtures, we should *always* "Block That Metaphor!" Such laughter has an ethical edge to it: a ridiculous metaphor implies a ridiculous author, one who ought to know better.

On the other hand, those who see metaphor as a way to increased rhetorical power usually retain the worry about coherence but drop

---

or "as" to the "Catfish" picture will weaken it somewhat, diminishing the amount of energy that the receiver puts into the reconstruction. But this addition does not change the nature of the picture at all, and one is not surprised to find that classical theorists, unlike many moderns with different purposes in view, have seen the choice between simile and metaphor as insignificant, depending simply on whether the speaker profits from seeming more or less "daring." "When the metaphor seems daring, let it for greater security be converted into a simile" (Demetrius 2.80).

the demand for truth, substituting novelty ("avoid clichés") and "appropriateness," the always vague but inescapable requirement of what used to be called decorum. In this view good metaphors must be neither flat, lifeless (in Longinus's highly ethical vocabulary, "frigid") nor what Fowler calls "overdone." Fowler deplores Samuel Richardson's "overdone" passage: "*Tost to and fro by the high winds of passionate control, I behold the desired port, the single state, into which I would fain steer . . .*" and on for eight more lines of sailing (Fowler 1965, 360).

It would be foolish to ignore any of these standards. *For some purposes,* violation of any one of them—accuracy, coherence, freshness, or appropriateness to a context—can be fatal. But we should be aware that each violation is not necessarily a fault in a given metaphor but only a fault in a given context—which for anyone in an ethical pursuit must mean the implied author's failure to read the context properly. A poet who, like Dylan Thomas, is in charge of his own flamboyance can hardly be blamed for "inaccuracy" or "incoherence" in any one metaphoric passage; aggressive, startling mixed metaphors are his stock in trade, and if we are to question his mixtures, we must question his whole enterprise. A novelist who, like Wright Morris, has a special ear for American cliché cannot be blamed when his metaphors seem banal: their dramatized banality is their power. And as for inappropriateness, what would our great comic authors do without it?

In any case, in our search for an ethics of metaphor, we obviously need a richer fund of criteria. Faced with a collection of rival versions, all aimed for the "Catfish" situation, how might we appraise them, first for their effectiveness as weapons, and then for what they and their kind do as educators of those who take them in?

Suppose the lawyer had said one of the following instead of what he chose to say:

□ And so the big utilities are proceeding to disembowel the company I represent, right before our eyes.

□ And so the big utilities just expect us to stand looking on helplessly while they sap our vital forces.

Each of these versions, like the original, might be said to be inaccurate—at least my friend as defense lawyer would have said so. "Catfish" is obviously more striking than my inventions, more novel, more original. But is that all? Where might we go to find greater precision in judging effectiveness? And can that search help us in judging ethical value?

A closer look at the classical rhetoricians can enrich and complicate the usual criteria.

1. Good metaphors are *active,* lending the energy of more animated things to whatever is less energetic or personal, or more abstract and passive. As Demetrius says, they introduce "inanimate things . . . in a state of activity as though they were animate." (see "On Style," 2–81)

Here we see an analogue to two of the standards of friendship discussed in Chapter 6, intensity and reciprocity. Active metaphors produce an intense engagement with "things" that have been made to seem more like equal beings, that is, people. On any such scale, "Catfish" wins easily.

Can we then also say that it is always good, ethically speaking, to animate the minds of judges or juries in this way, and thus to move them to identify with the animator? We are not likely to think so when the metaphorist supports a cause that we deplore. But aside from the content of the animation, must we not conclude that the metaphorist-friend who invigorates life, who makes the moment of persuasion a delight in itself, does in fact offer a gift of great price? Only someone totally wedded to the utilitarian world of winning could fail to take pleasure when an opponent puts the icing on the cake as the "Catfish" lawyer does. Can we say, in short, that, "other things being equal," the more energetic the metaphor, the more valuable the gift, win or lose?

Many have implied as much, just as many have claimed that any controversialist who stirs us up is valuable, regardless of what the stirrings do to us otherwise (Aspin 1984, 34–37). Here we meet again the temptation to make global claims when what we need are discriminations. Obviously, some powerful animations can be dangerous weapons indeed. A people whose imaginations were schooled by a steady diet of metaphors like "Catfish" would no doubt be highly activated, but might they not also be more passionately vindictive, more inclined to engage in polar thinking (their world divided into threatening villains and innocent victims), more committed to the belief that victory belongs to those who feel most deeply or those who can crack the

cleverest bitter jokes, rather than to those who reason most rigorously? Would any of us choose to live in a society consisting of people
educated primarily for this kind of activity, a society consisting of
Melvin Belli types willing to pay *anything* for victory? Note again that
to change the explicit purpose would not erase these deeper teachings:
the muscular Christian who had been won to Christ with a powerful
battle metaphor might well have a little difficulty learning to love his
enemies. Besides, it is revealingly easy, as the history of various dada-
isms in this century has shown, to invent metaphors that force our
minds to delightful activity—by no means a worthless gift—but that
do little for us otherwise.[18]

We soon recognize, thinking along these lines, why the members of
the Royal Society in the seventeenth century concluded, anticipating
John Locke, that figurative language should be banned from all thinking projects. What clouds the mind, they claimed, is figuration, twisting, specifically metaphoric twisting, with its confusion of categories.
It ensures ambiguity, and it thus prevents intellectual progress. In *An
Essay Concerning Human Understanding,* Locke acknowledges that
figurative language is acceptable whenever we seek only "Pleasure and
Delight," but if we want to follow him in his pursuit of "information
and improvement," if we wish to speak of "Things as they are," then
all rhetorical figures must be seen as a primary source of error and deception. They are "for nothing else but to insinuate wrong *ideas,* move
the Passions, and thereby mislead the Judgment; and so indeed are
perfect cheats." If we want knowledge, metaphors "cannot but be
thought a great fault, either of the Language or Person that makes use
of them." Locke goes on to deplore the popularity of the entire subject
of rhetoric, of which the figures, in their service of "Eloquence," are
the prime culprits (1690, bk. 3, ch. 10, sec. 34).[19]

---

18. Much more should be said about the fact that we simply cannot afford, in politics, to repudiate the use of weapon metaphors. When the enemy is at the gate, when the
vicious and skillful lawyer is arguing unjustly against me, I must resort to weapons that
in themselves may backfire. Augustine generalized the ethical problem about "winning"
metaphors to the whole domain of rhetoric. He finally decided that the servants of the
Lord must master rhetoric, since the wicked will certainly be skillful in it (*De Doctrina
Christiana,* bk. 4, esp. ch. 2).

19. It is an appalling but not surprising fact that such purgation programs persist in
many fields even today. Even in educational theory, for example, where metaphors are

What we discover, then, in the criterion of animation, is not a rule but a problem—a conflict between the generally desirable invigoration of life and our specific beliefs about just what kinds of animation are desirable. No doubt every terrorist and tyrant has a mind full of animating metaphors that cover those dogs, the enemies, *and* that noble project, their extirpation. Neither the Lockean ban on all metaphor nor the modern equally broad celebration will do. Come, let us abandon these general moves and start talking, first about *this* one, and then about *that* one.

2. Good weapon metaphors are *concise,* economical. All the great rhetoricians had a strong sense of what Herbert Spencer later described (at some length) as a law of stylistic economy: the more you can convey in a given number of words, the better.[20] Indeed, that is one reason for using metaphor rather than ordinary language: it says more with less. (Here we see an analogue to the standard of quantity, as we discussed it in Chapter 6.) When I try to unpack "Catfish," I find that a full paragraph or two is required to describe what it manages to convey—and of course even then I have lost its active energy. "Disembowel" is less economical (though shorter) because it says so much less. Still, it is actually more economical than the "literal" version, "They're trying to destroy us."

But what, then, about the ethical effect of economy? Do good weapon metaphors, in their economy, educate us, like other effective figures, to honor a special kind of intellectual integrity—economy of means? Since metaphor does not give the appearance of economy—

"obviously" inescapable, we find people trying to explain the lack of clear progress toward a single dominant educational theory by blaming metaphor: "It is arguable that our educational theories would become sharper instruments, less liable to fallacy, if we could dispense with metaphors altogether." So H. Entwistle (qtd. in Taylor 1984, 23), echoing many modern philosophers who have adopted programs something like Locke's in this one respect. See, for example, Stebbing 1939.

20. The principle has been revived by E. D. Hirsch in *The Philosophy of Composition* (1977). Can any discipline match, for sheer inconsistency, what we English teachers do when we simultaneously hail economy as a supreme stylistic virtue and hail wonderfully redundant Shakespeare as our supreme stylist? Can our freshman handbooks and Renaissance masters of *copia* dwell in the same world?

indeed, it often seems like a roundabout way of saying what might be said with one word—it always appears to some people to educate only to a destructive obliquity ("Why not say what you mean?").

Again we see a conflict between values. A brilliantly economical (though strictly unnecessary) stroke teaches us that we do not really know what we mean until we have said more than can be said in simple propositions. True economy of expression is whatever assures fullest communication without irrelevant distortion. In most human affairs, as in ethical criticism, the worst distortions occur when we think we have arrived at absolute truth through univocal, simple, economical clarities. Many a weapon metaphor is thus *too* economical; it implies false clarity. Here we move some way toward joining current deconstructionist projects that see all language as metaphoric and all effort at *full* clarification as both dangerous and doomed to failure. But even as we grant the ultimate validity of that claim, we discover that it butters no parsnips in *our* kitchen: to see every statement as metaphoric tells us nothing about why some metaphors constitute a royal diet and others are garbage.

3. Good metaphors are *appropriate,* not just as tested by some general standard of decorum, as in the previous section, but as appropriately grand or trivial, precise or general, active or pacifying: appropriate *to the task at hand.* If the point is to heighten sublimity, then trivial metaphors must be avoided. But if depreciation is desired, the more trivial the better.

Here we see the analogue to the standard of coherence in Chapter 6, as well as a provocative conflict with the standard of "otherness." In "Catfish" what is needed is a heightening of the battle between powerful, hypocritical destructiveness and helpless innocence. On the face of it, a catfish is not an *especially* innocent victim, though it is easy to think of other fish that would work less well.

Does not the reliance on this standard simply underline the venality of weapon metaphors? Aren't they simply for sale to the highest bidder, with whom they live in happy harmony? Will they not slickly reinforce whatever vicious cause the rhetorician has in hand?

The arguments pro and con seem to parallel those about all other literary devices and the literary enterprise itself. Appropriate to *what?*— that is always the question. Appropriate to some ideal notion of decorum? To the speaker's character? To the predetermined demands of this particular audience? Neither the general standard nor the blanket rejection gets us very far.

4. Closely related is the demand that good metaphors be accommodated to the audience at hand. This standard again seems to advertise the ethical neutrality of metaphor-in-general: metaphors are up for sale to the highest bidder. As weapons, they are appraised only according to their capacity to kill—to win. "Catfish" thus wins, both in life and in our inquiry, because it is so beautifully designed to capture just this audience at a precise moment in time.

But of course one critic's accommodation is another critic's shameless truckling. When my candidate exhibits a rich, exciting metaphoric flexibility, finding for each audience the precise "Catfish" to win their love, I am proud and pleased. But when *yours* exercises the same skill, I start talking of venality, demagoguery, cheap rhetoric and—lack of character. "Is it not wrong," I hear people saying, "for the Reverend Jesse Jackson to use aggressive, inflammatory metaphors when addressing black audiences and conciliatory, mild metaphors when addressing white audiences? Is it not just as dishonest to play with metaphors as to promise a tariff to one audience and free trade to the next?" How are we to judge, unless we consider the whole "world of values" that every metaphor implies?

Here again we meet problems that simply cannot be talked about effectively without looking at the larger contexts that we shall encounter in the next chapter. All successful public figures accommodate both their tones and their promises to their audience's specific interests.

5. Good metaphors are novel, original, striking. Nothing can destroy an effect more completely than an obvious effort to say something clever when the result is commonplace—unless it is to do so and then add a protective flag like "as it were," or "figuratively speaking." "If I may say so, this would be carrying coals to Newcastle, as it were." After all, is not the whole point of using a blatant metaphor to invent a new perspective, to lead our hearers to see a *new story* in place of an old one?

It is surely its novelty that makes "Catfish" amusing—at least it was amusing before I belabored it in this solemn context. It does not just animate a conflict, it ornaments with humor the life of everyone within hearing, including the lawyer who lost his case. In a sense such metaphors unite the opponents in a common cause, that of interpreting and enjoying this uniquely human dance: whoever loses at least wins this moment of disinterested pleasure.

Consider the difference between "Catfish" and, say, President Reagan's claim that the Democrats are "punishing" America with their policies while maintaining in their campaign rhetoric a "graveyard of gloom and envy" (repeated often in the 1984 campaign). By most of our standards, "graveyard" must be judged a good weapon metaphor: it is "animated" (that is, it energizes parties as if they were individuals—though buried ones); it is "concise," saying a good deal in little space; it is "appropriate" to the seriousness of political issues; and it is "accommodated" to an audience of Americans who want to be optimistic about their world. What's more, it is appropriate to its speaker's ethos, supporting the image of a Reagan who is vital—a positive thinker in charge of a vigorous society rather than a graveyard. Yet the metaphor has none of the freshness and humor—largely a product of novelty—of "Catfish." Unlike some of Reagan's sallies, it does not enliven the time that we spend with it. The metaphorist at this one moment is no real friend of mine.

But surely the blind pursuit of novelty has been the curse of the individualism we questioned in Chapter 8? To see the "other" for what it is, to respect otherness when it comes our way, to recognize that we find our own growth in otherness—none of this is to say that novelty, difference, otherness is always good, or that the pursuit of it is not often disastrous, both for our immediate rhetorical purposes and for any ethical project. Would it really be good for America if we had a president who would talk like that clever lawyer all the time, larding his speeches with such one-liners[21]? Yet when defenders of metaphor touch on its ethical power, the defense is almost always globally centered on one value: metaphor-in-general is good for us because of its "innovative and creative power." As David Aspin puts it,

> Metaphors encapsulate and put forward proposals for another way of looking at things and of grasping inchoate intimations of possibilities, giving voice to meanings that are shifting, elusive, unstable, polymorphous and illusory. . . . [M]etaphors help us the better to strive towards grasping the visions and truths of their artificers. . . . The best ["external" criterion for metaphor is] that of fertility, productivity of new insights and fresh illuminations on old themes. . . . [With metaphor the teacher] can open up

21. That we have, in 1988, a president who often seems to aspire to that condition is irrelevant to our project.

fresh worlds of significance to minds that have not yet had those visions
that he himself has been vouchsafed.

(1984, 34, 36)

We meet here once again with a troublesome conflict of ends that
leaves us unable to say much about the value of isolated metaphors
and leads us toward larger issues. To talk sense about whether a given
metaphor goes too far in its drive for novelty or remains too comfortably ensconced in its appropriateness, in its "accommodation to the
audience," we must accept the temptation to appraise the total ethos,
not only of metaphorists who offer one lightning stroke to enhance a
cause but also of those who offer whole thunderstorms.

THE RANGE OF METAPHOR

Before we accept that temptation in the next chapter, we should remember that we have so far dealt with only one of many kinds of
"micro-metaphor," the kind designed to win by attacking an enemy.
But there are many other ways of winning, and many other practical
goals besides winning in battle. We would come to somewhat different
problems and conclusions if we dwelt on kinds of metaphor that se-
duce us to embrace a value rather than to attack an enemy:

- bribery metaphors, in which the offer is money or goods
- friendship charms, in which the offer is popularity
- sweet talk (or flattery) metaphors, in which the offer is to increase
  our self-esteem, often by accepting the metaphorist's abasement:
  - "If there were occasions when my grape turned into a raisin,
    and my joy bell lost its resonance, please forgive me," as Jesse
    Jackson said, addressing the Democratic National Convention
    in 1984.[22]
  - "Come to Marlboro Country." The picture of the handsome

22. William Safire, assigning grades to convention speakers, gave Jackson high
marks for that one, on the ground of originality, while properly grading him down for
other metaphors that seemed stale (1984, 108).

man on the horse, mastering the mountain world, reveals to
me precisely what I should want for myself: total manliness
(I'm *that* kind of guy!), which includes smoking the right
cigarette.

□ hedonic or "pornographic" metaphors, in which the offer is
simply pleasure: "Camel Lights. It's a whole new world." Most
food ads are pornographic in this sense, rousing an appetite that
can be satisfied only outside the metaphor. Special versions of this
kind include
   – aphrodisiac metaphors, in which the offer is sex or sexual
     prowess ("Fly me; fly United")
   – salvation metaphors, in which the offer is peace of mind, or
     maturity, or well-being, or ecstasy, or eternal bliss
   – honor metaphors, in which the offer is of a clear conscience
   – poetic metaphors, in which the offer is of a new view for the
     sake of savoring its beauty
   – philosophical metaphors, in which the offer is of a new view
     for the sake of understanding
   and so on.

A close look at any one of these seductive kinds would reveal further evidence of frequent conflict between the explicit aims of a metaphorist and the ethical value of the metaphor. A politician can urge us
to honorable action with metaphors that debase us; an advertiser may
urge harmful products upon us with metaphors that offer elevating
new worlds. Since the dance of metaphor shows such power to deflect
our psychic attention from the ostensible subject, our examples may
seem to bear out Locke's point: anyone who seeks to communicate the
honest truth should avoid metaphor entirely.

But of course it would be futile to adopt any program like Locke's
purgation. The project of purifying language is hopeless from the beginning; the very language that any philosopher uses to repudiate metaphor will be laden, like Locke's, with further metaphor.[23] Metaphors
are simply inextricable from the business of the world—*all* the busi-

---

23. Surely you need no citations from the deconstructionists for this point, which
should be shared by us all.

ness, clean and dirty, generous and vicious. We can of course exercise some choice among metaphoric domains. I might, for example, become a metaphoric pacifist and decide to forgo all weapon metaphors; or an enemy of the metaphor-ridden marketplace and renounce all bribery or charm metaphors. But what will I do, then, when a Hitler looms or when I have something really good to sell to the world? I will almost certainly throw myself back into the metaphoric maelstrom, subjecting myself to the criticism of other ethical critics.

"Maelstrom" is the word. A given metaphor usually comes to us in the company of brothers and sisters, cousins—whole extended families—as "macro-metaphors" (Turner 1987). Even individual metaphors traveling alone imply the possibility of such clusters, and thus of "worlds" in which they would be appropriate. We turn now to the ways in which, by responding to those larger worlds and to the ethos of those who create them, we meet our most challenging critical tasks.

REFERENCES

Aspin, David. "Metaphor and Meaning in Educational Discourse." In Taylor 1984: 21–37.

Augustine. *De Doctrina Christiana.* Trans. D. W. Robertson, Jr. New York, 1958.

Bettelheim, Bruno. *The Uses of Enchantment: The Meaning and Importance of Fairy Tales* [1976]. New York, 1977.

Black, Max. "More About Metaphor." In Ortony 1979: 19–43.

Booth, Wayne C. *A Rhetoric of Irony.* Chicago, 1974.

————. "History as Metaphor: Or, Is M. H. Abrams a Mirror, or a Lamp, or a Fountain, or . . . ?" In *High Romantic Argument: Essays for M. H. Abrams.* Ed. Lawrence Lipking. Ithaca, N.Y., 1981.

————. "The Empire of Irony." *Georgia Review* 37 (Win. 1983): 719–37.

Cohen, Ted. "Metaphor and the Cultivation of Intimacy." In Sacks 1979: 1–10.

Davidson, Donald. "What Metaphors Mean." In Sacks 1979: 29–46.

de Man, Paul. *Blindness and Insight: Essays in the Rhetoric of Contemporary Criticism* [1971]. 2d ed., rev. Theory and History of Literature, vol. 7. Minneapolis, 1983.

Demetrius. "On Style." Trans. W. Rhys Roberts. In *Aristotle: "The Poetics." 'Longinus' "On the Sublime."* Trans. W. Hamilton Fyfe. Loeb Classical Library. Cambridge, Mass., 1927.

Fowler, H. W. *A Dictionary of Modern English Usage* [1926]. 2d ed. Oxford, 1965.

Genette, Gérard. "Rhetoric Restrained." In *Figures of Literary Discourse.* Trans. Alan Sheridan. New York, 1982.

Glieck, James. *Chaos: Making a New Science.* New York, 1987.

Gould, Stephen Jay. *Time's Arrow, Time's Cycle: Myth and Metaphor in the Discovery of Geological Time.* Cambridge, Mass., 1987.

Harré, Rom. *Personal Being: A Theory for Individual Psychology.* Cambridge, Mass., 1984.

Hirsch, E. D., Jr. *The Philosophy of Composition.* Chicago, 1977.

Johnson, Samuel. "Abraham Cowley." In *Lives of the English Poets* [1779]. Ed. G. B. Hill. 3 vols. Oxford, 1905. 1: 1–69.

Lakoff, George, and Mark Johnson. *Metaphors We Live By.* Chicago, 1980.

Locke, John. *An Essay Concerning Human Understanding* [1690]. Ed. Alexander Campbell Fraser. Oxford, 1894.

Longinus [pseud.]. "On the Sublime." In *Aristotle: "The Poetics." 'Longinus': "On the Sublime."* Trans. W. Hamilton Fyfe. Loeb Classical Library. Cambridge, Mass., 1927.

Mitchell, W. J. T. *Iconology: Image, Text, Ideology.* Chicago, 1986.

Mukařovský, Jan. "Standard Language and Poetic Language" [1932]. In *A Prague School Reader on Esthetics, Literary Structure, and Style.* Ed. and trans. Paul L. Garvin. Washington, D.C., 1955.

New York Times. "For Some, Half the Day Is Spent in Fantasy." (Dec. 15, 1987): Science Times sec.

Ortony, Andrew, ed. *Metaphor and Thought.* Cambridge, Mass., 1979.

Pope, Alexander. *The Art of Sinking in Poetry: Martinus Scriblerus' Peri Bathous* [1727–28]. Ed. Edna Leake Steeves. New York, 1952.

Quintilian. *Institutio Oratoria.* Trans. H. E. Butler. Loeb Classical Library. London, 1921–22.

Ramanujan, A. K., trans. *Poems of Love and War, from the Eight Anthologies and the Ten Long Poems of Classical Tamil.* New York, 1985.

Reddy, Michael J. "The Conduit Metaphor—A Case of Frame Conflict in Our Language about Language." In Ortony 1979: 284–324.

Ricoeur, Paul. *Interpretation Theory: Discourse and the Surplus of Meaning.* Fort Worth, Texas, 1976.

———. *The Rule of Metaphor: Multi-disciplinary Studies of the Creation of Meaning in Language* [1975]. Trans. Robert Czerny et al. Toronto, 1977.

Riffaterre, Michael. *Semiotics of Poetry.* Bloomington, Ind., 1978.

Sacks, Sheldon, ed. *On Metaphor.* Chicago, 1979. (Mainly essays from *Critical Inquiry* 5 [Aut. 1978].)

Safire, William. "Ringing Rhetoric: The Return of Political Oratory." *New York Times Magazine* (Aug. 19, 1984): 108.

Schön, Donald A. "Generative Metaphor: A Perspective on Problem-Setting in Social Policy." In Ortony 1979: 254–83.

Shibles, Warren A. *Metaphor: An Annotated Bibliography and History.* Whitewater, Wis., 1971.

Silverstein, Michael. "Shifters, Linguistic Categories, and Cultural Description." In *Meaning in Anthropology.* Ed. Keith H. Basso and Henry A. Selby. Albuquerque, N.M., 1976.

Spencer, Herbert. *Philosophy of Style: An Essay.* New York, 1873.
Stebbing, L. Susan. *Thinking to Some Purpose.* Harmondsworth, 1939.
Taylor, William, et al., eds. *Metaphors of Education.* London, 1984.
Turner, Mark. *Death Is the Mother of Beauty: Mind, Metaphor, Criticism.* Chicago, 1987.
Vickers, Brian. "The Atrophy of Modern Rhetoric, Vico to De Man." In *Rhetorica* 6 (Win. 1988): 21–57.

11

I recall stories of how it once was
at that mountain. The stories told
to me were like arrows. Elsewhere,
hearing that mountain's name, I see
it. Its name is like a picture. Stories
go to work on you like arrows.
Stories make you live right. Stories
make you replace yourself.

Benton Lewis, Apache Indian,
reported by Keith H. Basso

Beethoven's psychology is always
right. His music is, in fact, a supremely masterly and hopeful criticism of life.

Donald F. Tovey

The return of historical thought to
the Metaphorical mode will permit
liberation from all efforts to find any
definitive meaning in history. . . .
Just as poetry is itself the means by
which the rules of language are transcended, so, too, Metaphorical historiography is the means by which
the conventional rules of historical
explanation and emplotment are
abolished.

Hayden White

There are an unlimited number of
valid ways to interpret or evaluate
any fiction, any historical event
or historical account of events, any
philosophy, any critical work. And
there are even more ways to get
it wrong.

Anonymous

The test of greatness in a man is not
whether we would like to meet him
at a tea party.

Thomas Carlyle

Metaphoric Worlds

Myths, Their Creators and Critics

MACRO-METAPHORS

The metaphors we met in Chapter 10 were mostly fragments, separated from the human contexts in which they had once lived. The simple act of putting them into *my* context both reduced and deflected their power. As a result, our encounters with their creators were less intense—or, at least, less sustained—than those we experience when we dwell for awhile with any committed metaphorist. Indeed, in natural discourse we almost never encounter single metaphors; only in critical discussion are they held up, like catfish, to be gutted alive. What we offer each other in all real discussion are clusters that range from the overt and lively to the covert and comatose—expressions pretending to an impossible literalism. Once readers have been alerted to metaphor, every further stroke in a given context modifies, reinforces the direction, and increases the binding force of the other strokes— unless of course a careless choice or cluster of choices calls attention to ineptitude and shatters the growing bond.

In this chapter we turn to the ethical import of such "macro-metaphors," or mythic metaphors: what at their most ambitious might better be called cosmic myths. What do they do to and for us, and how can we talk about their awesome powers and their comparative worth?

The questions can be asked fruitfully even of metaphors that are created by unintentional metaphorists—those who think that by using "ordinary" (that is, ostensibly unfigured) language they refer literally to a real world behind or beyond their language. At the extremes of "literal" effort, such metaphorists talk like this:

> Data structures and algorithms are the materials out of which programs are constructed. Furthermore, the computer itself consists of nothing other than data structures and algorithms. The built-in data structures are the registers and memory words where binary values are stored; the hard-wired algorithms are the fixed rules, embodied in electronic logic circuits, by which stored data are interpreted as instructions to be executed.

So reads the beginning of an article in *Scientific American* (Wirth 1984, 60). The author was probably unaware that he was using metaphors. For all we can tell he may not even know what a metaphor is. But his prose willy-nilly builds a half-hidden metaphoric world, one that can be partially brought to the surface by consulting our associations and then, if necessary, by consulting an etymological dictionary. Such a reconstruction will be only partial, because etymology cannot account for the new metaphoric "weight" that computer science has "loaded" onto words like "stored," "data," "program," and "embodied." What, for example, is the "body" *in which* the "rules" are "embodied"?

The "world" or "myth" that this author "builds" (my own metaphors already multiply) is reinforced by the astonishingly similar worlds presented by the other authors in the same special issue on computers; they are so much alike that we might almost think all the articles were written by the same man (the authors *are* all males, whatever that may indicate). It is a world of fixities, of rules, of neat storage and clear, unambiguous circuitry. It is a world in which whatever exists (the computer, in this case) can be said to be "nothing other than" a given structure and patterning. It is a world in which the copulative verbs *are* intended to be completely unambiguous: structures *are* registers; algorithms *are* rules. And it is a world that, as we all know, has shown an astonishing power to take over the thinking of its inhabitants, even when they try to think of "things" that are as resistant to such "container/contained" metaphors as is the human mind.

At the opposite extreme from such unconscious twistings we find worlds where metaphor becomes deliberate, expansive, and aggressive; serene skies suddenly turn threatening, lightning flashes reveal a self-conscious artificer—and soon we encounter whole thunderstorms, cascades, whirlpools, floods, maelstroms of metaphor—often with no more concern for surface harmony than I have just shown. Those computer scientists live on the same planet, but not in the same "world," as the author of the following one-page chapter, "The Metaphor Delivered," which concludes a book about a protest march on Washington, D.C., during the Vietnam War.[1]

---

1. In this chapter many of my quotations must be longer than normal authorial courtesy would dictate; though single metaphors *imply* whole metaphoric worlds, the

Whole crisis of Christianity in America that the military heroes were on one side, and the unnamed saints on the other! Let the bugle blow. The death of America rides in on the smog. America—the land where a new kind of man was born from the idea that God was present in every man not only as compassion but as power, and so the country belonged to the people; for the will of the people—if the locks of their life could be given the art to turn—was then the will of God. Great and dangerous idea! If the locks did not turn, then the will of the people was the will of the Devil. Who by now could know where was what? Liars controlled the locks.

Brood on that country who expresses our will. She is America, once a beauty of magnificence unparalleled, now a beauty with a leprous skin. She is heavy with child—no one knows if legitimate—and languishes in a dungeon whose walls are never seen. Now the first contractions of her fearsome labor begin—it will go on: no doctor exists to tell the hour. It is only known that false labor is not likely on her now, no, she will probably give birth, and to what?—the most fearsome totalitarianism the world has ever known? or can she, poor giant, tormented lovely girl, deliver a babe of a new world brave and tender, artful and wild? Rush to the locks. God writhes in his bonds. Rush to the locks. Deliver us from our curse. For we must end on the road to that mystery where courage, death, and the dream of love give promise of sleep.

What kind of "world" *is* this seeming chaos, created by Norman Mailer in *The Armies of the Night* (1968, 288)? And how can we hope to talk about the ethical differences between that world and the totally ordered world of the computer analyst? It is hard enough to say whether such a page is crafty or botched. Can we hope to say whether it is admirable or deplorable, beneficial to readers or harmful?

"Let the bugle blow"—that is to say, a "bugle" serves "U.S. Army troops" as "my plea" will serve "the army of saints." "Vietnam protesters" are to "saints" as "military heroes" to—well, we must be careful, because it is not clear that Mailer means "heroes" to be turned into "devils." Can we say that America, the "beauty with a leprous skin" is to "unpredictable future" as "pregnant woman languishing in prison" is to "unpredictable, perhaps illegitimate babe"? Already things are getting too complicated for literal analysis of the kind that worked pretty well with "Catfish." Suddenly the leprous woman becomes a lovely giant, who, though lacking a doctor, is sure to deliver either a "fearsome totalitarianism" or a "babe of a new world brave

---

full power of metaphor to intrude alternative worlds into a reader's or listener's life is discovered only in fully developed clusters like this one. Indeed, for full effect such passages ought to be read aloud—and experienced in their original contexts.

and tender, artful and wild," a babe that may or may not be identified with the God who is writhing in his bonds—no doubt suffering in the smog on which the death of America rides. The last three sentences even by themselves defy close analysis, because if it is true that we must end on the road where there is promise of sleep, it is not at all clear why we should rush to the locks. Do we, by unlocking the bonds in which God writhes, enable him to deliver us from our curse?

I cannot know, of course, how readers will respond to this passage out of context. But it may be useful to underline its intensities and complexities by reporting on a contrast between my expectations when I read this passage to a conference and the actual response. After I finished reading the passage (in a tone as neutral as possible), I had planned to say: "I cannot know, of course, how you feel about the passage by now. But I should be much surprised if most of you do not think it terribly jumbled. . . . I shall not try to reverse your judgment completely, but I do want to think a bit about the grounds for that judgment." My actual surprise was of a different kind. The audience began laughing much too early and too hard for my purposes. At "tormented lovely girl" I interrupted the laughter with a plea for a fair hearing: "You're spoiling the pleasure for those who like the passage." But the laughter continued to mount. When I said, at the end, "I tried very hard to read that neutrally, so that I would not give an opinion about it in advance, and I was surprised by the laughter," the comment itself produced *more* laughter. Finally, in something of a flurry, I asked: "Was there no one who *resented* the laughter?" The question was first met with silence.

"Not a single person in this room thinks that the passage is a good way to end a book?"

At that point a voice said "Yes," and I said, "At last! Who is it? Ah, Mr. Strier [my colleague, Richard Strier]. Well, we'll hear from you when I've finished."

In the discussion that followed the talk, Strier said in effect that "if Wayne Booth wanted to, he could have made this audience laugh at *any* author. His reading was *not* neutral. He did not let us know that the author was Mailer, and the passage was thus wrenched out of its context, taken out of its historical moment and put into a new context, where attention was focused on deliberately scrambled metaphor as a thing in itself."

I welcomed the warm discussion his complaint produced, and I accept his point—it reinforces my claim that metaphor cannot be judged
without reference to a context. The interchange is worth reporting
here, however, primarily because it illustrates the high emotional involvement we display in our judgments of metaphor. Having laughed
in contempt at the passage, many in the audience reported themselves
extremely uncomfortable, first, when they learned that the author was
Mailer (an author they felt they should admire), and then when I said
that the passage is in my view really quite skillful, "much better than I
could have managed if I had attempted a book like that." Some of
them were annoyed and confused, having invested their emotions
without a clear outcome.

In any case, even if we finally decide that Mailer's attempt is not as
successful as he would have hoped, the reason can surely not be that he
has mixed his metaphors as aggressively as Shakespeare often did his.
It would not be hard to find elevated passages in many great authors
which, with their metaphoric janglings, would make an audience
laugh if read out of context.

In judging a passage of this intricate kind, then, we must think hard
about what the kind really is, and about how contexts work. Almost
all the marks we found in "Catfish" have here been changed. True, we
still have metaphors that are clearly intended and that seem to serve
some rhetorical purpose. But everything else is different. Without
troubling to run once again through all the marks defining the kind,
I note that whatever was covert about "Catfish" is not only overt
here but brandished like a saw in the hands of a magician about to
slice into an assistant. Trumpets blaring, Mailer openly promises his
metaphor and proclaims its "delivery" with a blatant pun on the
"girl's" delivery.[2]

Note also that the metaphors are so grotesquely scrambled that one
cannot believe the scrambling accidental. Schoolteacherly norms are
deliberately violated, and we cannot easily tell whether the naughty boy
is writing with his pen in his cheek or his marching feet in his mouth.

We should not forget, if we are tempted to scoff, that such metaphor

---

2. The etymologies of "blaring" and "blatant" reveal that avoiding mixed metaphors is neither as important nor as easy as the writing counselors say.

has proved itself to have great power in our time. *The Armies of the Night* received mostly rave reviews. Many reviewers credited Mailer—mistakenly—with inventing a new literary genre: "history as a novel, the novel as history." Richard Gilman, reviewing for the *New Republic,* wrote, "All the rough force of his imagination, his brilliant gifts of observation, his ravishing if often calculated honesty, his daring and his *chutzpah* are able to flourish on the steady ground of a newly coherent subject[;] . . . history and personality confront each other with a new sense of liberation" (1968, 27).

The key word here is surely "personality" (the "history" is a bit harder to locate). Such metaphoric muddlings, "rough," "brilliant," "ravishing," "calculating," "honesty," "daring," flaunt personality—that is, a special character. We must wonder whether a conclusion like Mailer's is designed to win members to the anti-war camp or to construct another of Mailer's "advertisements" for himself. We have no way of knowing how many people were converted to the cause by Mailer's book, but we have plenty of evidence that it was successful in selling Mailer.

I can remember trying to convince a student when the book first came out that though skillful it was cheaply self-serving, even though it spoke for what I saw as the right side. I got nowhere, of course, because to her my judgment against Mailer's art meant that I was not really committed to opposing the war. Another graduate student confessed last week [1978] that when he first read the book years ago he found the experience overwhelmingly moving and that when he reads this page now he feels embarrassed about his earlier gullibility. (See my own similar experience with *One Flew over the Cuckoo's Nest,* pp. 74–76 above.)

What kind of creature is it that can shift like that under our gaze? And how can we ever arrive at defensible judgments of its quality, rather than simple expressions of our prejudice—doomed to shift with each shift of ideological fashion?

One possible answer to the first question is that Mailer has turned the ethos, which in "Catfish" was a means to a practical end, into an end in itself: the metaphorist as true friend. If we were to accept that answer, we would have transported the passage out of the domains of rhetoric into the clear pure air of poetry—at least we would have done so according to one traditional way of distinguishing the two. But the means/end distinction doesn't help us very much here; if it is true that

Mailer is making and advertising a self in such passages, he would surely have the right to insist that such a project is an essential part of his effort to attack the warlords.

To complicate things further, it is clear that Mailer is attempting, however desperately, to remake the ethos of America; though his metaphors call attention to him when we look at them critically, they are explicitly addressed to the reader's view of America's rebirth. Read uncritically, as my graduate student originally read them, the metaphors did their work, and their work was an inextricable mixture of argument about the war, portraiture of Mailer, and promise-threat about a glorious-gruesome future society. Such metaphors are far more obviously constitutive of characters and societies than are the "Catfish" kind. They do not simply *allow* the energetic critic to think of such matters; they *require* every reader to do so.

We may find help in our search for standards if we look at earlier attempts to build a tight metaphoric identification of a constituted self and a constituted cause. Most great political speeches or pamphlets reveal similar grand fusions. Toward the end of his *Reflections on the Revolution in France* (1790), for example, Edmund Burke attempts a metaphoric heightening appropriate to his anti-revolutionary cause.

> Our people will find employment enough for a truly patriotic, free, and independent spirit, in guarding what they possess [the British constitution], from violation. I would not exclude alteration neither; but even when I changed, it should be to preserve. I should be led to my remedy by a great grievance. In what I did, I should follow the example of our ancestors. I would make the reparation as nearly as possible in the style of the building. A politic caution, a guarded circumspection, a moral rather than a complexional timidity were among the ruling principles of our forefathers in their most decided conduct. Not being illuminated with the light of which the gentlemen of France tell us they have got so abundant a share, they acted under a strong impression of the ignorance and fallibility of mankind. . . . Let us imitate their caution, if we wish to deserve their fortune, or to retain their bequests. Let us add, if we please, but let us preserve what they have left; and, standing on the firm ground of the British constitution, let us be satisfied to admire rather than attempt to follow in their desperate flights the aëronauts of France.
>
> I have told you [the ostensible French correspondent receiving Burke's "reflections"] candidly my sentiments. I think they are not likely to alter yours. I do not know that they ought. You are young; you cannot guide, but must follow the fortune of your country. But hereafter they may be of some use to you, in some future form which your commonwealth may take. In the present it can hardly remain; but before its final settlement it may be obliged to pass, as one of our poets says, "through great varie-

ties of untried being," and in all its transmigrations to be purified by fire and blood.

I have little to recommend my opinions, but long observation and much impartiality. They come from one who has been no tool of power, no flatterer of greatness; and who in his last acts does not wish to belye the tenour of his life. They come from one, almost the whole of whose public exertion has been a struggle for the liberty of others; from one in whose breast no anger durable or vehement has ever been kindled, but by what he considered as tyranny; and who snatches from his share in the endeavors which are used by good men to discredit opulent oppression, the hours he has employed on your affairs; and who in so doing persuades himself he has not departed from his usual office: they come from one who desires honours, distinctions, and emoluments, but little; and who expects them not at all; who has no contempt for fame, and no fear of obloquy; who shuns contention, though he will hazard an opinion: from one who wishes to preserve consistency; but who would preserve consistency by varying his means to secure the unity of his end; and, when the equipoise of the vessel in which he sails, may be endangered by overloading it upon one side, is desirous of carrying the small weight of his reasons to that which may preserve its equipoise.

([1790] 1959, 306–08)

Although we can see many obvious differences, the similarities between the Mailer and Burke are close enough to justify comparison. Burke's metaphors are also mixed, though less wildly than Mailer's: remodeled buildings, lights, bequests, firm ground, desperate flights, fire and blood, steady tenors, kindled fires, overloaded vessels. The tone of self-advertisement as a passionately concerned, distressed citizen is thus similar, though Burke calls attention to himself much more explicitly ("They come from one . . . who . . ."). Like Mailer, Burke implies that the fate of the whole nation depends on embracing a *national* character that will match the *personal* ethos of the speaker.[3]

BEYOND THE FRIENDSHIP METAPHOR: COMMONWEALTHS AND WORLDS

If we feel a difference in quality between the two passages, we cannot, then, explain it with general rules of metaphoric practice. We

---

3. The best discussion I know of how Burke reconstitutes a national character and in doing so implies a "world" is by James Boyd White, *When Words Lose Their Meaning* (1984, ch. 8).

might turn instead to the friendship metaphor. These two would-be
friends offer us gifts that might be examined for their effects on our
own activity. But they seem for the most part surprisingly equivalent
on the various friendship scales:

- □ *Quantity/concision.* They both give us almost more work to do
  than we can manage; they are copious to what (taken out of context) seems a clear fault.

- □ *Reciprocity/hierarchy.* They both stand a long way above us,
  inviting us to climb up, with considerable effort, to their level of
  almost ineffable insight. Yet they each manage, I think, to be persuasively disinterested as friends: even though Mailer may be
  "advertising himself," he *seems* to do so while worrying more
  about the welfare of his readers as fellow citizens than about any
  gain for himself. (I ignore for the moment my opinions about the
  career-author.)

- □ *Intimacy/cool reserve.* The very concentration of metaphor ensures an intimate relation for any reader who agrees to join the
  dance; but the unrestrained request for engagement risks the
  charge of excess.

- □ *Intensity/slack charm.* We might be annoyed by the excessive
  passion of either passage. I find, however, that when I meet the
  passion at the end of *Reflections,* I am as intensely engaged as I
  can well endure. At the end of *Armies,* I *could* do with a bit more
  restraint.

- □ *Otherness/familiarity.* Mailer surely "wins" here in the startling
  mixture and originality of his ingredients; but for any modern liberal, Burke presents a much more threatening and demanding
  and therefore potentially useful "other."

- □ *Range/concentration.* Both appeal to an immensely broad range
  of human interests and emotions; that's what it means to present
  a fully challenging metaphoric world.

Thus it is primarily on the scale of coherence or decorum that we
might want to challenge Mailer. But though his style is certainly indec-
orous according to certain general standards, it is entirely appropriate
to its context. There is nothing out of keeping, either with the book
that has preceded the passage or with the political situation as Mailer
wanted to portray it. Any reader who has followed Mailer to his final

page will be offended if the speaker does *not* seem close to losing control; only shouting can do justice to the total vision Mailer wants to portray. Besides, though Burke may be somewhat more decorous than Mailer, he still threatens us, here and elsewhere, with a sublime confusion.

As friends, then, both come off pretty well, though both might be tiresome as constant companions. But our vocabulary of friendship, while not useless in talking about them, seems somehow slightly off-center: neither Burke nor Mailer would consider such talk directly pertinent to what they were up to. They wrote in alarm and concern, in the genre of "political warning"; and if we want to think about their metaphors in terms they might accept, we must take the substance of their warnings seriously. They ask us to take the metaphoric worlds they proffer as challenges in their own right—the very heart of the matter, not just aggressive reinforcements of some message that could have been equally well stated in colorless language. To say to either of them, "It was *really* nice talking with a lively fellow like you for these few hours; I hope we can get together regularly and become fast friends," would be insulting.

A CHOICE OF WORLDS

Both Mailer and Burke, then, insist that we choose between alternative worlds—not what the world is *like* but what it *is* and not merely the political world but the world of reality in which for each of them political action takes place. For Burke, we must hold to a steady, conservative journey of a ship of state that maintains its precarious "equipoise" only by valuing established custom and real interests and rejecting the dreams suggested by abstract reason and utopian principles; the heady revolutionary principles coming from France threaten to capsize the inherently unsteady vessel and destroy the "public world" that makes civilized life possible. For Mailer, we must recognize that all stabilities have already been lost, that the armies of the establishment have destroyed our public life and left us groping in the fog they have created, with no hope except for an embrace of an elusive, revolutionary birth.

Each one thus offers us not just a particular political choice—the ostensible subject—but a choice between two imaginative worlds, a choice that may seem more like choosing alternative commonwealths than like choosing friendships. Each invites us to come and live within a given culture, sharing the assumptions of all who live there. Our entire way of life is thus at stake. In trying to appraise whole metaphoric domains like this, we will need a criticism as complex as we would need when trying to decide whether to emigrate from our native land to some "advertised" utopia. It may ultimately be more like choosing a religion than like choosing a friend suitable for daily conversation. In short, macro-metaphorists and their critics are the unacknowledged legislators of *their* worlds.

The extreme difficulty of this kind of criticism has often tempted me to abandon this part of the project. If I am led to appraise whole commonwealths, religions, ontologies, am I not surely doomed to talk airy nonsense? "You are turning the library," I hear a mocking voice say, "into a culture emporium; you would turn critics into pretentious prophetic voices that merely add to the cacophony. 'Let the bugle blow'!—if that's the kind of thing you want. 'God writhes in his bonds'!—as well He might. 'Rush to the locks'!—for all the good it will do you."

But before we give up, we should remember that if we as critics are doomed, if we cannot hope to engage in worthwhile talk about such matters, Burke and Mailer are doomed as well—doomed to be trivialized. Unless we want to think of them as interested *only* in winning votes in some immediate hustings that we do not care about—unless we conclude that they were foolish not only in the immensity of their ambition to change us but in their ultimate commitments—we will surely want to join them in their implied view that metaphoric criticism of metaphors for ultimate commitments is one of the most important kinds of talk we can ever attempt.

CRITICISM OF WORLDS

Whenever we look closely at any powerful cluster of metaphors, we can infer from it the maker's world. Do we live in a world that is "run" like a master computer, with linear causal lines connecting "bits" in extensive, intricate, but formalizable arrays, as implied by my first example in this chapter? Do we live in the world of Burke, a world that we did not make and should not expect to change easily and without dreadful cost, a world inherited from ancestors whose collective wisdom was derived from an experience that cannot be encompassed by our finite reason and therefore should not be meddled with lightly? Do we live in the world of Mailer, a world of mysterious, transcendentally valuable egos in battle with the "liars" who control "locks" that, if only we could turn them properly, might open the prison gates and liberate the wretched repressed?[4]

To sum up these worlds in this way is to dramatize—in the very inadequacy of the reductive propositions—just what is entailed in any criticism that pretends to address such immensities. Most obviously, that criticism cannot be simply propositional, offering clear, firm "positions" that judge entire worlds as right or wrong, good or evil. We do not take in these worlds as isolated propositions, nor even as developed fragments of the kind I have quoted. It is true that when we quote them wrenched out of their original narratives, we take those fragments in *as* propositions, and we can then discuss them in ordinary discourse: their claims to validity are a significant part of what is required to make a full alternative world. But when we meet them as part of a story of any scope (whether or not it offers explicit arguments along with narrative), what we re-constitute for ourselves is a vast articulated network of interrelated images, emotions, propositions, anecdotes, and possibilities, all embedded in more or less fixed norms. We find ourselves dwelling in a newly created, animated *uni*-verse of possibilities, in which each particular obtains its full life by virtue of being *in* the whole. Concurrently, that universe obtains its power, and the plausibility of its fixed norms, because its parts, when viewed *in* that whole, are credible elements of a credible world. We take those parts in as part of a *narrative*, one that by its very shape mimes a world that can never be described fully in any isolated or "synchronic" statement, however full and metaphoric it might be.[5]

4. A challenging account of how such revolutionary metaphors have changed not only the way people think but how they act is given in Melvin Lasky's *Utopia and Revolution* (1976, esp. chs. 5–6).

5. I am aware of and not embarrassed by how much this sounds like the "organicism" of the New Criticism, as derived primarily from Coleridge, as derived pri-

TWO ROUTES THAT WILL GET US SOMEWHERE— SOMETIMES

In attempting to appraise such worlds, we can again follow either of the two paths we traced in appraising characters (see pp. 281–90 above). The first, which in the nature of the case I cannot follow here but only describe, is to *experience* one or more rival worlds, to engage fully with any narrative that finds its life in alternative fixed norms. For most of us there is no way to avoid this route: we have all followed it again and again as we have experienced powerful narratives. The second is to talk about them: either as what we might call alternative cosmic myths, *epistēmēs,* or cosmologies, describable in discursive language rather than merely in narrative (the method of Northrop Frye [1957]); or as rival experiences of life in temporal sequence. Experiences with stories can to some degree be summarized in shorter, more general narratives or plot summaries (the method of any formalists who, unlike the structuralists, center on particular narratives and their differences from other narratives [Crane 1952, 1953; Sacks 1964]). With a given description of values or summary of plot form in hand ("The central values of Forster's fictional world are . . ."; "The story of Job goes like this . . ."; "The plot of *Emma* is . . .") we can then compare it, with as much subtlety and delicacy as possible, with other schemes of values or experiences that we have encountered.

This two-track "talking" route, which is perforce mine (since I have elected to write this book rather than create a rival novel or sonnet sequence or world history of my own), has the drawback, as we have seen before, of being inescapably remote from the heart of the matter. The critic following this path does so in a different country from the one inhabited by the narratives being criticized. Whether or not to violate those territories is always our choice: we can, if we choose, simply remain silent about our preferences and refuse to listen to those who insist on discussing theirs.

---

marily from German philosophy of Coleridge's time, as derived primarily from the Greeks, who got it from the Persians, . . . who took it in with their mother's milk. There is now an exploding literature on "possible" and "alternative" worlds, and on what kinds of coherence or correspondence are required to make an intelligible world. See the bibliography to Pavel 1986.

The Great Conversation of Rival Narratives

We thus can choose whether to talk about the world of a narrative and how it works; but if we have once listened to it, we cannot prevent it from performing its own kind of criticism of other stories we have heard. We all began practicing this kind of ethical criticism at the moment when, having wedded ourselves to *this* fairy tale, in which (say) poetic justice reigned, we went on to *that* fairy tale in which the rewards were distributed seemingly at random. We continue to practice it whenever we really attend to a narrative that does not simply reinforce the fixed norms we share already.

> The gods and demons were striving against one another. The gods emitted [from themselves] a thunderbolt, sharp as a razor, that was man. . . . They hurled this at the demons, and it scattered the demons, but then it turned back to the gods. The gods were afraid of it, and so they took it and broke it into three pieces. When it had been shattered into three pieces, it stood right up. Then they took hold of it and examined it, and they saw that the divinities had entered into that man in the form of hymns. They said, "The divinities have entered into this man in the form of hymns. When he has lived in this world with merit, he will follow us by means of sacrifices and good deeds and asceticism. Let us therefore act so that he will not follow us. Let us put evil . . . in him." They put evil in him: sleep, laziness, anger, hunger, love of dice, desire for women. These are the very evils that attach themselves to a man in this world.
>
> Then they enjoined Agni [fire] in this world: "Agni, if anyone escapes evil in this world and wants to do good things, trick him and harm him utterly." And they enjoined Vāyu [wind] in the ether in the same way, and Aditya [the sun] in the sky. But Ugradeva Rājani said, "I will not harm men whom I have heard that these three highest gods harm. For the man whom these divinities harm is harmed and harmed indeed." But the divinities do not harm the man who knows this, and they do trick and utterly harm the one who tricks and harms the man who knows this.[6]

The shock here does not spring only from the strange cosmogony, though that will be for most of us strange indeed. It comes in part from the strangeness of the story-line itself: it just doesn't make much sense to Western ears until explicated by scholars of Hindu myth. And once explicated, it is even more threatening. Wendy O'Flaherty explains

---

6. From the *Jaiminīya Brāhmana* (O'Flaherty 1985, 195).

that rather than building the foundation for mankind's ethical behavior, this cosmogony actually places man in ethical opposition to the gods. "[T]he dismemberment of the thunderbolt-man is done in order to destroy him and to protect the gods. . . . [T]he concept of sacrifice as a force that joins together the powers of gods and men . . . has been transformed into the concept of sacrifice as a force that has the potential to drive gods and men apart, by making men so good, and hence so powerful, that they rouse the jealousy of the gods" (1985, 195).

The sense in which narrative experience is "literally" metaphoric and implicitly a criticism of other narrative experience should now be clear. Whenever we embrace the patterns of desire of any narrative, especially any long narrative, we become figured, not only by the specific figures of thought and figures of speech that a given world entails (see Chapter 10)—not just by *a* giant pregnant woman, or *a* ship precariously equipoised—but more profoundly by cumulative inter-relationships of figurings that make up the temporal narrative experience itself. It transforms (distorts, twists, figures) the life we might have lived during the hours we spend with the narrative, and it thus becomes a *substitute for*—or, better, a replacement of, and consequently a radical criticism of—that unlived life. In short, we are led to create for ourselves an alternative life during those hours we spend "elsewhere." It's as if the author said, "'Life' *is this*, rather than what you, my reader, thought it was." Reading *War and Peace* over several days, or weeks, watching the weekly episodes of "Dallas" or "Hill Street Blues" month after month, I inescapably enter alternative worlds at least some elements of which carry over (to return again to the root meaning of the word "metaphor") into my "normal" world (i.e., become some of the "norms" of that normality). They thus engage me, willy-nilly, in an act of the most radical kind of criticism.

At the extremes of unreflective conversion to any one of these alternative worlds, the "real" world can come to seem intolerable. When reading *Anna Karenina* in my late teens, I found myself detesting everyone I met outside the book (teachers, fellow students, and especially family members); nobody in "my" world was half as interesting as the much more vividly imagined people in Tolstoy's. At such times relatives and friends found me—they later confessed—unbearably, contemptuously rude and distant. Like Don Quixote or Tom Sawyer, I found the real world simply unintelligible when it failed to match my newfound land.[7]

Such extreme pilgrimages should not obscure the point that even the simplest narratives also imply whole worlds, visions of how things are according to which the narratives make sense. Whether or not all language is metaphoric, in the technical sense of being derived from some original physical reference and then "carried over" to other purposes, it is clear that all narrative is metaphoric, in this other sense of saying, "All of life, the entire world, is *like* this piece of it"—not necessarily on its surface, of course, but in the depths of the author's penetrating vision.

From this point of view, every narrative, even one as comprehensive as *Remembrance of Things Past,* can claim to present no more than one of many possible worlds. Even when an author explicitly claims to represent *the one true* world, everyone who is not totally converted to that one view can see that it is at best a metaphor, an abstraction torn from the heart of an ever-elusive and impenetrable mystery: the whole of things. And when no such grand claims are made, when the simplest of seemingly literal stories is told, we can always infer a totalizing assault on the mystery: the story abstracts and recommends one version from an untold number of possible versions.

"He hammered the final nail in the last shingle; the house was finished." Here we have about the simplest possible story, told presumably by someone who thinks that it is the one true story about that moment. But it is clearly a chosen version abstracted from innumerable other stories about what happened, each of them implying larger events that in turn imply a world that is possibly as true, and certainly for some purposes truer: "He completed the building of a home for his family"—or a "domicile," or a "domestic nest," or a "shack." "He realized the full passion for domesticity that most people in his culture shared." "He applied the principle of the lever to accomplish a really quite remarkable feat of engineering." "He was a veritable Thor, hurl-

7. Note that it will not do to consider narrative worlds as metonyms for *the* world. Only on those relatively rare occasions when a story's fixed norms seem to us identical with those we held to before reading and will hold to after the event can the story-world be said to figure, as a metonym, the total structure of the whole of "real reality." Fictional worlds are instead usually *rival* metaphors, or at best supplements to each other.

ing . . ." "He sublimated his sexual frustrations . . . resisted his rising sense of alienation . . . worked out his salvation with devotion . . ." And so on. Though only a few of these would be called metaphoric in our ordinary talk, each of them is clearly an abstraction, implying a kind of world that "stands for" at most one aspect of the full (and ultimately inexhaustible) truth.

We should again remind ourselves that most authors have explicitly offered their works as criticisms of false views of the world, false cosmic myths. Though in our time their more outspoken statements tend to be made in their interviews and critical essays, rather than in their "literary" works, most of the authors we care about have explicitly allied themselves with religious, political, or cultural programs. And even when they do not, we can always find such programs embodied in their metaphoric structures. It is true that various fashions in obliquity throughout this century have tended to obscure this point. Many a current novelist and poet cultivates a non-committal air. Choose your favorite pose, the one that is most non-committal: that "air" will be, or will imply, the author's recommended world.

The point is of course much clearer when we make it about overtly religious stories: *The Divine Comedy, Pilgrim's Progress,* Flannery O'Connor's *The Violent Bear It Away,* Walker Percy's *The Second Coming,* François Mauriac's *L'Agneau* (the only rivals for clarity of purpose would be politically "engaged" fictions like those of Sartre, or the novels of the more aggressive Marxists). Though the didactic content of such stories is often simply dismissed as irrelevant to their art, both their authors and their readers know that such works recommend one view of ultimate reality as against various mistaken views held by most of the characters in each story and by some, perhaps most, readers. They do not just "dance an attitude," as Kenneth Burke well knew when he invented that phrase. They offer themselves as what he repeatedly calls "equipment for living" (1957), the best equipment for the best kind of life.[8]

---

8. I suspect that the recent celebration of Bakhtin, in which I continue to participate despite reservations, results in part from the relief we all feel in finding a somewhat esoteric figure, a figure of unquestionable critical sophistication, putting the Humpty Dumpty (life/literature) back together again. Perhaps we need a Kenneth Burke in each new generation.

Most explicit of all are the founding stories of the "genesis" of God's people, of Christ's life, of Muhammad, of the Buddha. Like the many modern founding narratives about prophets like Joseph Smith, Mary Baker Eddy, Bhagwan Shree Rajneesh and a host of other Eastern gurus, these all offer a view of how the world works, a view that criticizes all other views of the world:

> The kingdom of heaven is likened unto a man which sowed good seed in his field: But while men slept, his enemy came and sowed tares among the wheat, and went his way. But when the blade was sprung up, and brought forth fruit, then appeared the tares also. So the servants of the householder came and said unto him, Sir, didst not thou sow good seed in the field: from whence then hath it tares? He said unto them, An enemy hath done this.
>
> (Matt. 13:24–28)

To tell such a story is to "say" that the kingdom of heaven is *not,* or at least is not simply, what the Torah has taught about the chosen people or what the Buddha says about how we can be saved. To tell a story about how divinity took upon itself a life in history, leading to *His* crucifixion, is to offer a standard for judging other metaphoric views of what God and God's creatures *are*. If Reality is really the sort of thing (note the clue to metaphor in "sort") that is willing to suffer crucifixion in order to redeem its creation, the sort that suffers from the fall of every sparrow, it cannot be as reasonably thought of as the sort of thing that sets a model of impassivity, indifferent to all suffering—or vice versa. And if it is *really* one or the other of these it cannot be *really* the sort that would willingly allow great numbers of creatures to suffer "meaninglessly" every day; the sort that goes on its inexorable course, an army of unalterable laws; or the sort we met in the story of vengeful creation (see p. 338 above).[9]

THE THREAT OF MULTIPLICITY

The didactic challenge of such criticism clearly does not depend on the degree of explicitness in the claims that life "is" or "should be" this

---

9. Two indispensable studies of how religions, and religious "classics," criticize each other in pluralistic dialogue are David Tracy's *Blessed Rage for Order: The New*

or that. Still it is a striking fact that our literary history, even in modern times, is flooded with such overt statements, even—or should I say, especially?—in lyric poetry. "Our birth is but a sleep and a forgetting," Wordsworth tells us in the great ode "Intimations of Immortality"; he would clearly be shocked to learn from aestheticians that good readers will not take his words seriously as an attempt to state a truth.

> The Soul that rises with us, our life's Star,
> Hath had elsewhere its setting,
> And cometh from afar.
>
> ([1807] 1977, 1: 525)

It is true that if taken as a literal statement about the pre-existence of the atomic in-dividual whose existence we questioned in Chapter 8, Wordsworth's claims that "trailing clouds of glory do we come, / From God who is our home" and that we gradually lose our memory of that pre-existence, cannot carry much weight. Critical tradition has rightly insisted that we must not tie the value of the poem's world directly to any one of its literal propositions; this is the half-truth behind the claim that "poetry says nothing." Literal propositions are too easily refuted by counter-statements: "No, our birth is much more (or less) than a sleep and a forgetting." "The soul did *not* have 'elsewhere its setting'; actually it developed right *here!*" "Wordsworth got the truth messed up, with his little Platonic gambit. The truth is closer to Masefield's idea 'that . . . she who gives a baby birth / Brings Saviour Christ again to Earth.'" When their surface propositions are taken literally, any two poets can seem to be shouting half-baked truths at each other—and canceling each other out. Life is *not* a falling away from "the visionary gleam" or "the glory and the dream" but rather a C-major chord (Browning's "Abt Vogler"). No, it is more of "an incurable disease" (Abraham Cowley); or a "jest" (John Gay); or a "gloomy garment" (W. S. Merwin); or a relentless decline leading toward the old age lamented by Yeats:

Pluralism in Theology (1979) and *The Analogical Imagination: Christian Theology and the Culture of Pluralism* (1981). A cogent argument for treating many modern "novels" as "apologues," fictions with structures controlled by idea patterns rather than plots or systems of event, is offered in David Richter's *Fable's End* (1974).

What shall I do with this absurdity—
O heart, O troubled heart—this caricature,
Decrepit age that has been tied to me
As to a dog's tail?

([1928] 1983, 144)

Obviously such messages cannot be placed into direct propositional
conflict with Longfellow's claim, say, that life need not be seen as "an
empty dream," because it is actually "real" and "earnest;" or William
Ernest Henley's claim that it is "good," because "joy runs high / Between English earth and sky"; or with Samuel Butler's discovery that
it is "one long process of getting tired." Is life a "desert" (Edward
Young)? Is it Shelley's "dome of many-coloured glass"? Carlyle's "heroic poem"? Beddoes's "single pilgrim / Fighting unarmed amongst a
thousand soldiers"? Is it a liquor that will dry up, a fire that will go
out, a flower that will fade, a bloody house, a duty, a Fury?[10]

Threatened by such a multiplication of worlds, it is no wonder that
critical tradition has preferred to surrender any truth-claim for them.
If we had to take poems either as literal statements or as empty figura-
tions, our choice would be clear: to save our story-tellers from talking
nonsense, most of us would no doubt sacrifice the "literal" for the "literary." But doing so would rightly upset all the authors who made
those assertions of truth: they did not want us to approach their narratives with sterilized, gloved hands, for fear of real contact. No doubt
some of them hoped we would even take them literally: "I've thought
the whole thing over, just like the philosophers, and I've decided that
what life really *is,* is a heroic poem." Some of them even offer titles that
trumpet such claims: "Intimations of Immortality"; *Comment c'est*
(*How it [All] Is* [Beckett]); *The Way We Live Now* (Trollope); even
"Wisdom" (Sara Teasdale).

RIVAL WORLDS IN DIALOGUE

How do we manage to take all this seemingly conflicting "wisdom"
seriously, without falling into absurd contradictions?

---

10. May I have credit for not quoting the many famous lines spoken by dramatic
characters, often mistakenly attributed to their authors, like Macbeth's "tale / told by
an idiot"?

We do so, I am suggesting, both by acknowledging that all statements of truth are partial (these *poetic* claims are not unique in their partiality), and by embracing the very plurality that from other perspectives may seem threatening. We not only recognize that there are many true narratives; we celebrate the multiplicity, recognizing that to be bound to any one story would be to surrender most of what we care for. Each example in our ever-expanding collection of metaphoric worlds will be at best a half-truth; some of them may be downright falsehoods—"fictions" in the pejorative sense of the word used by positivists. But some of them will be, *as* fictions, the most precious truths we ever know. We try them on for size (like the "habits" and "virtues" of Chapter 9), and we thus compare each new one that comes our way with the other worlds we have tried to live in. At any one moment we have a relatively small collection of worlds that we take together as a pretty good summary of the "real." But each new encounter with a powerful narrative throws a critical light on our previous collection. We can embrace its additions and negations vigorously, so long as we remember that like all the others, this is a metaphoric construction: a partial structure that stands in place of, or "is carried over from," whatever Reality might be.

Once again we see that nothing could be further from the truth than to say that poetry *says nothing*. The great narratives, including lyric poems, "say" almost everything we know. Each successful effort at story becomes in this view either a decisive rival to or a reinforcement of the world in which we have previously led our lives. Matthew Arnold's oft-mocked assertion that poetry is "a criticism of life" (a *magister vitae*) is in this precise sense profoundly right. Each fiction is a criticism of life by being a criticism of other fictions. Even when they seem to contradict each other flatly—Auden's assertion, say, that "Life remains a blessing / Although you cannot bless" as against Nietzsche's restatement of the Greeks' claim that "the best is never to have been born"—no reader is faced with an either/or choice. Both might be embraced or both rejected, on grounds quite other than their surface conflict. Every fiction is an "imitation of life" not by virtue of copying any detail from life but by realizing the way in which certain circumstances or settings belong to, or "fit," or even cause, certain conditions of soul—happiness or misery or despair; anger or delight or amusement; reconciliation or revolt. Life—the whole of it—really *is* that (meaning *like* that), because we now know that for some people in some circumstances that is how it really has been.

To say as much is a far cry from claiming that what each fiction says or does is as valuable as what every other fiction says or does, provided that they are all composed with equal skill. "Life is a commuter drive at the end of the day, dusk coming on, the superhighway packed bumper-to-bumper." "Life is a McDonald's hamburger joint, promising to give you what it has given 'more than four billion' other people: happiness on the cheap." "Life is this week's TV offering." "Life is an unsterilized surgical needle." Write me the best poem, story, or novel you can manage on any one of these, and no matter how skillful your result, it will almost certainly pale beside John Gay's "My Own Epitaph":

> Life is a jest; and all things show it.
> I thought so once; but now I know it.

Life and the death that life entails are—need one say it?—more fully epitomized as a jest than as a disappointing hamburger or dirty surgical needle. But Gay's epitaph is in turn eclipsed by scores of poems in English (and no doubt scores of scores in other languages) that, like Wordsworth's Ode or Yeats's lament about old age, simply tell us more about what life *is* than Gay's couplet does.

No doubt it is this inherent aspiration of all fictions to metaphoric truth that accounts for the strong tendency in modern times, as the old religious metaphors have weakened their hold on us, to use fictions as a substitute for religion and philosophy. When Matthew Arnold, Thomas Carlyle, and others found themselves treating poetry as the religion of the future, they were simply expressing a kind of rivalry with institutional religious statement that was implicit in all secular metaphoric enterprises from the beginning. "My story," the poet always says, "even though it may present no visible Gods or expressions of piety, can be as spiritually charged as yours that begins 'In the beginning God created the heaven and the earth,' or 'In the beginning was the Word, and the Word was with God.'" Even the most secular fictions are thus engaged in a "religious" exchange. Bellow's "theosophical" *Herzog* says to Robbe-Grillet's *Project for a Revolution in New York,* "Your absurdist view is more absurd than you think; it is immoral, negatively sentimental, and untrue to the spiritual truths about our lives." *Project,* which on the surface would seem to dwell in a country far distant from any religious inquiry, replies, "Your affirmation is a sentimental lie. *This* is really how things are."

The point to remember, as we turn from criticism-by-narrative to discursive criticism (the kind that we have had to practice all along), is that each of us will necessarily depend on standards of truth, relevance, and spiritual depth that we derived in large part from our previous listening to stories.

The Discursive Criticism of Narrative Cosmic Myths

As we turn once again from sharing stories to talking *about* them, we must underline the essentially reductive quality in what we will be doing. The primary kind of criticism, experience of a rival myth in full narrative vitality, is always more powerful, and usually more important, than any critical talk about it can be. To *describe* or *summarize* any myth is almost inevitably to reduce its power, or even to destroy it.[11]

This is in no way tantamount to saying that discursive comparative accounts of rival myths are pointless. Though we can expect true believers to be unshaken if we try to show them that their chosen myth (say, the Devil worship of Charles Manson's followers) is inferior to some other myth (say, the myth of Fard as taught by the Temple of Islam, or various myths of the messiah's coming, as taught by Jews and Christians), those who are willing to engage in a genuinely critical conversation can learn from one another. At least that is the hope of the following speculations, though they are obviously even more tentative than what has come before. It is true that when we address fully developed narratives[12] as grand metaphors, as implying "cosmic myths,"

---

11. Even the short works that we have quoted in full here and in Chapter 7 could not be said to be *here* as experience; some readers will have reconstituted them in ways consonant with mine, while others will have found in the words radically different experiences. Perhaps the closest any critic ever comes to presenting one of these rival experiences to others is in public readings. And of course to read a poem aloud to others is itself a form of criticism—a third kind not significant for us here, though in some cultures it would be far more important.

12. How full is "fully"? It is not a simple matter of word count. Many short stories and "lyrics" would surely qualify, after we have lived with them long enough to make them our own. For me the stories of Flannery O'Connor, Yeats's "Sailing to Byzantium," or Keats's "Ode to Melancholy" offer worlds more complete and more challenging than

thus placing them into competition with the great philosophies and critical systems, our subject becomes unmanageably large—in effect a union of the history of philosophy, the history of literature, and the history of conversation about both. Prudence would dictate dropping such a subject at once. But such a subject has a mind of its own, and it insists, almost against my will, on a few hints about where *it* would like to lead some better-qualified future inquirer: into a territory where all large efforts of the human mind are kin.

One common recent way of describing the kinship in this huge family has been to call all histories and philosophies fictions.[13] My move is the reverse: I am treating all narratives and philosophies as incipient rivals, not because all are "fictional" (in the sense of being untrue) but because all are "philosophical" (in the sense of rendering truths more or less palpable), some primarily with narrative (more vivid, less fully "argued"), others primarily with synchronic (and inevitably less vivid) argument (Zahava McKeon 1982).

We have already seen that the total collection of cosmic myths that any one person can take in will always be to some degree incoherent and self-contradictory: to put it plainly, I cannot in any obvious way harmonize Burke's world and Mailer's world, let alone harmonize them with Tolstoy's and Austen's and Sophocles'—and Plato's and Spinoza's and Kant's and Saint Matthew's. Human life is inherently, inescapably multivalent, poly-storied, pluri-mythic.[14] It is true that a given culture always tends to sort out certain myths from the cor-

---

those of many a realistic novel I have read—more challenging because their fixed norms are *not* those I find myself able to live by in my "real" world.

13. An earlier move was to claim that they are *laden* with fictions and that the task of a sound philosophy is to distinguish fictions from realities. Jeremy Bentham's theory of fictions (see Ogden 1978) has often been read as an effort to purge thought of all reliance on unrealities. I think that C. K. Ogden is right in seeing it as rather an earlier (and better) version of Vaihinger's "philosophy of as if" (see Vaihinger 1935).

14. I take this point to be roughly the same as Bakhtin's claim that we are all constituted of a multiplicity of "languages"—of family, class, nation, epoch, profession, and so on (1981). For a challenging recent discussion of why and how philosophical systems will always be plural, irreducible to one perspective, one method, one notion of reality, or one set of principles, see Walter Watson's *The Architectonics of Meaning: Foundations of the New Pluralism* (1985, esp. "Archic Analysis"). Though the differences between such views and various corrosive relativisms now on the scene are too complicated for brief summary, I hope that they are emerging as this book progresses. See also Aiken 1962, chs. 2, 4, and Shweder 1988.

nucopia offered by our collective histories. Twentieth-century America, for example, seems increasingly to concentrate on a collection of future-oriented, consequentialist, utilitarian myths: an ever-rising gross national product, defended by an ever more blatantly reductive faith in cost-benefit analysis, an ever more adventuresome space program and accompanying technological advances,[15] and so on. Such sorting can help give some people an illusion of coherence, especially if they find a single myth answering most of their conscious needs. But even such people will reveal signs of strain when they find themselves having to build epicycles upon epicycles in order to prove the self-sufficiency of a single myth.

Ours is not the first moment in history when observers have feared that they might drown in a flood of rival myths. In every historical period I know anything about, we find thinkers who felt threatened by infinite variety. I happen just now to be re-reading Castiglione's *The Book of the Courtier,* a book full of worries about the way in which diverse mores and morals conflict: "[I]n all things it is so difficult to know what true perfection is that it is well-nigh impossible; and this is due to the diversity of our judgments. . . . [E]veryone praises or blames according to his own opinion, always hiding a vice under the name of the corresponding virtue, or a virtue under the name of the corresponding vice" ([1561] 1959, 27). But though such worries can be found everywhere, it is hard to think of any previous time when there was such widespread radical skepticism about the very possibility of dialogue across the chasms separating mythic worlds. The subjectivism we confronted in Chapter 3 is far less widespread than the skepticism we meet here. On the one hand, the "man in the street" says, "You just can't argue about religion." On the other, that ultrasophisticate Wittgenstein provides intellectuals with just the quotation they are looking for, one that is by now almost worn to death: "Wovon man nicht sprechen kann, darüber muss man schweigen"—"What we cannot speak about, we must pass over in silence" (1961, 151).

If our hope for critical validity depended on finding the one right myth, we would finally be forced into the skeptic's camp; we cannot,

15. When the Challenger space shuttle exploded, one headline, in *USA Today,* read "NASA Human After All."

should not, simply wipe from memory the disasters that have been suffered by every mono-mythic endeavor. But we have long since been exploring here an obvious alternative, not a compromise between the
two extremes but a radical, critical pluralism. The choice is not between, on the one hand, a search for some grand, all-encompassing
"story" that can defeat all others in open combat and, on the other
hand, a skepticism that dissolves all efforts to appraise mythic strengths
and weaknesses. We can adopt a third set of assumptions: first, that
each "going" myth must have some truth to it—if it did not, if it failed
to explain some part of the experience of believers, it would have long
since been discarded;[16] second, that no single myth can give any culture all that is needed both to ensure its survival and to enable its
individual inhabitants to build rewarding life stories for themselves
(MacIntyre 1981, esp. ch. 15); third and finally, that though blindly
inherited or freshly invented mono-myths may at some moments in
human history serve life better than critically appraised myths, most of
us in our time are so thoroughly entangled in rival myths that only a
rigorously pluralistic ethical criticism can serve our turn.

What kind of criticism might that be, when we get beyond creating
or advocating one story at the expense of all others? Clearly it cannot
be based on a reduction to the sort of simple literal propositions we
questioned in the syllogisms of Chapter 3. Progressives in the last two
centuries have believed that they could do it that way, and at first the
evidence seemed to bear them out: the mythic world of scientific inquiry, leading to indefinite improvement of the species, seemed confirmed by the continued retreat of traditional myths in the face of attacks by propositionally explicit reasoning. The best-known of these
triumphs was of course the destruction of the Goliath of biblical myth:
first with the slingshots of a literal-minded historical criticism (the
various accounts of Genesis and the gospels don't jibe, either in their
details or in their mythic core); then with cannonades from natural sci-

16. The ultimate test of such a claim occurs when a given myth meets disaster, as the
teachings of the Reverend Jim Jones met disaster in the mass suicide at Jonestown. We
must not dismiss such destructive myths as beneath our attention. They share many features with our most cherished myths, and if we are to understand who we are and where
we are, we cannot assume that Jonestown was disconnected from our true condition. This point has been brilliantly argued by Jonathan Z. Smith, in *Imagining Religion* (1982).

ence, as geologists and Darwinists finished off the creation story (for most intellectuals) with their evidence for an awesome time span in which evolution, not God's creative power, produced a new Adam and Eve: the evidence, namely, of the animal kingdom. Over three centuries the increasing triumphs of a literal, linear, seemingly empirical inquiry into how "nature" works made it almost impossible, for anyone informed about that history, to believe any myth other than one: the true world is the one that works by natural law; miracles cannot occur; there is no *super*natural world.[17]

But then in our time a curious thing happens: not only have other "irrational" myths proliferated to repair the losses created by the triumphs of science but the old myths themselves seem to have found a strange new vitality. Instead of abandoning the myths, a rising number of people, even among the well educated, seem to have thrown into question the rationalist standards that had seemed to destroy all myth. Not only do traditional churches flourish and new cults burgeon; the most advanced intellectual movements have rediscovered what poor bare tortured creatures we are if we have no better covering than remains after systematic doubt, tested by linear logic, has done its worst. Attacks on Cartesian logic abound, both by professional rhetoricians (for example, Perelman 1969; Grassi 1980) and by increasingly numerous deconstructionists. Feminists attack the patriarchal character of linear reasoning (Irigaray 1985, 21). Philosophers of science denounce methodological rigor as both destructive and finally inaccessible (Feyerabend 1975). Even the elements of traditional myth that one would have thought shattered beyond repair by modern science have shown a new vitality: the "Creationism" that intellectuals thought had given its last gasp in the Scopes "monkey" trial flourishes still in the 1980s; one can only assume that, providing as it does a powerful *enabling* myth, its preservation is much more important to devotees than any worship of abstract rationality could possibly be.

---

17. The total conviction on this point that Hume felt he had to express cautiously and ironically in the eighteenth century, in his section "Of Miracles," in the *Treatise of Human Nature* (later revised for *An Inquiry Concerning Human Understanding*) had become, by 1900—shall we say?—for all of "us" an obvious assumption needing no argument. Incidentally, Richard Whateley ([1819] 1985) once had great fun using Hume's precise argument to disprove belief in the "miracle" of Napoleon's existence.

That is the threatening nature of myths: they all prove themselves, or seem to, in the results they yield when people live by them. "By their fruits ye shall know them." What is troublesome to anyone trying to think about them is that every "going" myth—every myth that is supported by an active community—obviously *works*, for those who embrace it. Whenever people give any one of the viable myths an honest try, they find that their lives are changed by it—often in ways that even from the "outside" appear to be for the better. The consequence is that even those of us who are in some final sense pragmatists feel a strong need for some standard other than mere "working," or—if we stay within the pragmatist's language—some way of defending a hierarchy of kinds of working. Surely our discussions of relative value should be in some way distinguishable from the confessions and testimony-bearing at the sinners' bench.[18]

Before considering a few of the allies that might be added to our rich inheritance of great narrative, we should ask ourselves just what we would expect of any myth that claimed not just to *work* (some adherents' lives were in some way "bettered") but to *work better* than other myths.

COHERENCE AND CORRESPONDENCE

The twin demands that a myth should "hold together" and "match reality" seem to be intuitively acknowledged by everyone. Nobody, not even the most fanatical believer, considers questions about consistency and respect for "how things are" impertinent; in fact, each believer considers his or her own grand myth preeminently coherent and uniquely capable of accounting for the facts—or, in some recent myths, the fact that there *are* no raw facts. But this is just the trouble for us when we try to apply these tests to some "obviously" incoherent myth

18. The most talked about new pragmatist, at least among literary critics, is undoubtedly Richard Rorty. While making the suggestion (to me congenial) that "edifying philosophy" should aim at "continuing a conversation rather than at discovering [final] truth" (1979, 373), he makes no bones about insisting on the real superiority of his conversational model over the final-truth model. See especially his concluding section, "Philosophy in the Conversation of Mankind," and the final page (394).

that "obviously" violates what we know about the world: it almost always proves just as impervious, in the eye of the believer, to such charges as it is to the charge of "not working." Indeed, it is only rarely that a direct attack on the center of a myth will even be noticed by a true believer. Every critical stroke, however logical or factual for the critic, will seem like irrelevance, trickery, or worse; and if the arguer claims to be speaking in the name of rationality, the believer will either see the attack as "self-evidently" irrational or decide that reason, as interpreted by the critic, is itself a false guide.

Students who study any true faith "from the outside" express astonishment at the power of that faith to withstand what look like devastating revelations of counter-evidence. The most dramatic examples of persistence are those cults that predict the end of the world for a given date and time and then, when the end does not come, find themselves with followers more devout than before. But the same imperviousness of myth to fact can be seen in more "respectable" settings. Many scientists I know believe, for example, that "in principle" physical science ("in its essentials," "as now conceived") can explain everything, including the operations of the mind; for some the hope is even that the bumps and grinds of particle physics will do the job. There are many good reasons for considering this belief incoherent (Polanyi 1972, 142) and one very good reason for claiming that it violates the correspondence criterion: it cannot account for the facts of how scientists themselves talk. No scientist can now so much as hint at what a scientific procedure would be that might predict his or her own next sentence, or explain, after the event, what had determined it. Our explanations of such matters are no better (and no worse) than were available to any good student of rhetoric in 300 B.C. This shocking and vivid blow to the faith of "particulate determinism," which could be multiplied by several billion rhetorical situations at this very moment throughout the world, in no way shakes believers' confidence, based as it is on a "principle" which in our terms is a myth, a macro-metaphor.[19]

19. The persistence of the myth of particulate determinism is still puzzling. It is totally "counter-intuitive"; it is supported by no empirical observation whatever (no one has ever seen a particle—of any size—produce a thought or a word). Yet, as Michael Polanyi says, "The ideal of science remains what it was in the time of Laplace: to replace all human knowledge by a complete knowledge of atoms in motion. . . . This is the ori-

I suspect that no myth ever died unless those who loved it could turn, as they saw it criticized, to some more plausible or fruitful myth. It is in fact as "more plausible myths"—or at least as "equally plausible myths"—that the great narratives make their appeal. But a new myth can make converts to its narrative without putting itself in the form of explicit story. It might be some new hypothesis about origins or destinies, presented in a language purporting to be strictly objective and unpoetic. Darwinism, for example, could not have triumphed simply as an assault on Judeo-Christian myths of creation; it triumphed (where it *did* triumph—always a smaller domain than intellectuals have liked to believe) by offering a "superior" myth, the exhilarating prospect of mankind's finally understanding human nature through scientific thinking and thus mastering the world. The myth presented itself as synchronic: pure eternal truth about science. But its implicit story quickly became embodied in a long chain of optimistic narratives: histories of the world like H. G. Wells's *The Outline of History* (1920), histories of the warfare of science and religion (Dampier 1929), and accounts of the triumph of "objectivity" over "subjectivity" (Gillispie 1960). The essential appeal of such optimistic plots did not require explicit narrative embodiment; it was implicit in the whole scientific enterprise.

In short, apparent violation of the tests of coherence and correspondence cannot alone give us the help we need. Who are the allies who might provide not just a negative critique—always essential yet always relatively inert—but also a systematic provision of better alternatives? Ethical evaluation of grand metaphors, like all other evaluation, depends on comparison. We might paraphrase Johnson (p. 71 above)

---

gin of the whole scientific obscurantism under which we are suffering today. . . . The question is: Can we get rid of all this terrible nonsense without jettisoning the beneficial guidance which science still offers us in other respects?" (Polanyi 1972, 139–42). No doubt here again the persistence of the myth depends on a kind of fruitfulness. Since "in principle" it can explain everything, it can help motivate any particular research project. But it is definitely not fruitful in the human sciences. The most recent advances in the natural sciences, in the field that studies strange orderings in what is misleadingly called "chaos," complicate the old battles between determinists and indeterminists in most wonderful ways. The "in principle" claim apparently is still defended by some, but only by engaging in a most impressive kind of gymnastics (Gleick 1987, esp. ch. 1).

and say, "Of the first cosmic myth that was invented, it might be with
certainty determined that it seemed striking or clever or appealing
to 'listeners' who were inexperienced in the powers of metaphor. But
whether it was 'spacious or lofty,' whether it was among the best that
human beings could manage, must have been referred to the comparisons provided by time." Who, besides our great novelists, playwrights,
and poets, are our allies in our project of distinguishing the nourishing
myths from the potential poisons?

TWO PHILOSOPHERS AS CRITICS OF MYTH

Most obviously, perhaps, the major philosophers all have engaged in
what from our point of view would be criticism of macro-metaphors.
Whether they explicitly see their worldviews as metaphoric and their
enterprise as criticizing other people's metaphors (as Plato, Hegel, and
Nietzsche do) or as pronouncing a literal and final truth (Hobbes,
Hume), each of them can be seen as working within a central metaphor that promises not only to slough off old error but to yield new
and precious fruit: the world as will, the world as act, the world as
machine, the world as drama, the world as fulfillment of purpose.[20]

Stephen Pepper has argued, in *World Hypotheses* (1942), that the
great philosophies all thus depend on one of four (amended in a later
work to five)[21] "root metaphors," formism, mechanism, organicism,
contextualism. What earns a great philosophy the right to its title is
not its unique truth but the fact that, regardless of particular flaws in
detail, its root metaphor has withstood the criticism of generations of
critics—not only other professional philosophers but all of us amateur

20. Note that the questions raised as I grapple with the validity of such (usually only
implicit) macro-metaphors are quite different from those that critics ordinarily raise
about the borders between literature and philosophy. We are not asking whether the
propositions stated by an author or a character within a story are as true as or even truer
than those yielded by proposition-oriented philosophy. We are instead asking whether
the total experience of a philosopher's endeavor can fruitfully criticize the total experience of the more "diachronic" forms. See Cascardi 1987.

21. In *Concept and Quality* (1966) Pepper adds a fifth root metaphor, "the pur-
posive act," the universe as purpose in action—rather belatedly, it must seem, to anyone
familiar with American pragmatism.

philosophers who test ideas against our everyday experience. The universe as a total form, the universe as a mechanical function, the universe as an organism, the universe as a context for its parts, and (later) the universe as a grand collection of teleologies—each of these can profit from the criticism of the others, because each has great difficulty accommodating some of the data that the others handle efficiently. But none can be refuted by the others; they seem permanent possibilities for viewing how things are and how they work. All of them survive as plausible views, metaphors for a whole that cannot be exhausted from any one prospect; though their proponents usually hope to refute all rivals with a unique, literally true account of what the world *is,* they will never be able to find a vantage point good enough to afford a complete survey of the whole.

In this view, which I find convincing in spite of the oversimplified list of four or five metaphors, even the great would-be literalists like Hobbes and Locke are finally metaphorists and critics of metaphor. The whole work of each philosopher can be thus regarded as an elaborate critique, often explicit but often tacit, of the inadequacies of all other philosophers' basic metaphors.[22] Innumerable other, lesser metaphors for the life of mankind have been tested in the great philosophical—that is, critical—laboratories and found to be finally less adequate; and, presumably, just as many have simply died without a trace.

To view philosophers as allies in our critical enterprise will not make them all equally useful, but it might free us at last from the "quest for certainty" and for a single route to it that has plagued the history both of philosophy and criticism.[23] We will find that many a metaphysic, with many an implied ethical code, can feed our interests. On the whole the most valuable will prove to be—here we must disappoint those who prefer more startling news—those who have always

---

22. For our purposes here, it does not matter whether the list of genuine rivals numbers five, or fewer, or the 65,536 "possible combinations of [philosophical] profiles" that Walter Watson derives from his sixteen-fold "archic" chart of philosophical possibilities (1985). The chart itself is derived, with considerable subtlety and depth of interpretation, from Richard McKeon's "philosophical semantics" (1952).

23. Dismantled brilliantly by John Dewey in *The Quest for Certainty* (1929), the quest did not seem to notice its fate; it has managed to endure despite many noble attacks on the very notion that certainty should be our goal. No doubt it will survive anything I can say.

been considered most nearly canonical: those major thinkers who have
seemed to generations of students to do the best job of revealing the
inadequacies of previous plausible but limiting metaphors. To show
this in any detail would obviously be inappropriate here. I can only
hint, with two examples, at how a discussion of this grand metaphoric
critique might run.

To me the greatest of all metaphoric critics is Plato. Both in his
largest views and in the minutest details of each dialogue, he questions our temptation to see the world (and our place in it) *under* any
one reductive metaphor. When Thrasymachus, for example, in the
Republic, tries to impose as the best metaphor for justice the proper
relation of shepherd and sheep, Socrates (and Plato) are much too wise
to dismiss him, as many moderns might do, by claiming that metaphors prove nothing. Instead, the dialogue painstakingly explores
what such a picture means, gradually substitutes rival metaphors, and
argues for their superiority. "Thinking with" the shepherd-sheep metaphor, we find ourselves thinking about how one person can use others
for his or her private ends: the sheep are expendable (bk. 1, 343b–
345d). If, however, we choose to think with other metaphors for justice, such as the proper relation of pilot to ship, sailors, and pas-
sengers, we suggest that all have a stake in the outcome: if the ship
goes down, serious consequences follow for both the pilot, who has
violated his art, and for the inquiry using this metaphor. Each succeed-
ing metaphor can be criticized with other, grander metaphors, until,
by the end of the *Republic,* the parts of the soul, the parts of the state,
and the organization of the universe itself have been richly analogized
and illuminated. The most nearly adequate metaphor for justice in the
state is the proper relation of the three parts of the psyche: the state
"is" a kind of soul, with rational, passionate, and appetitive parts. No
one who has ever seriously pursued justice with Socrates through the
steps of this permanently challenging (and often puzzling) dialogue
could ever again accept uncritically Thrasymachus's argument that
"might makes right," at least not in the simple form that Socrates' superior metaphors have destroyed. Plato has shown Socrates' metaphors to be more fully coherent, in closer correspondence to our full
experience, and more likely to yield ethical fruits that will really grace
our orchards.

For my second example I turn to Immanuel Kant's remarkable testing of the Christian myth by the light of critical reason, in *Religion within the Limits of Reason Alone* ([1793] 1960). Kant did not offer his comparison of natural and revealed religion to prove the unique truth of Christianity as a "faith": true or valid *faiths* were for him (as for me) necessarily plural; he reserves the word "religion" for the one true and universal relation of God and duty that particular faiths and churches and practices can represent only in better and worse degrees. His project is twofold—to show that reason, if pursued rigorously, does in fact lead to religion (*natural* religion) and then to show that one of the revealed religions, Christianity, is in its main lines mythically compatible with this natural religion. In our terms, his project entailed testing whether the Christian myth gives such a good (though metaphoric) account of itself when probed by reason that it can survive the most critical examination—not, I must emphasize again, as the only true myth but as *one* of the true myths.

No doubt it was Kant's insistent pluralism that led the ecclesiastical authorities to condemn as impious a project that to non-Christians may seem heavily biased toward Christianity. The king of Prussia himself expressed his "great displeasure [with] how you misuse your philosophy" (qtd. in Kant [1793] 1960, xxxiv). In a reply famous in the history of censorship, Kant not only pleaded his innocence but promised the king future obedience (xxxv). What is important to us, however, is the power with which his critique "answers" the other side of the case—the skepticism of those who would argue that Christianity is essentially irrational because it depends on revelation. Not at all, Kant argues. Though it is useful to have had revelation, to speed the human race up a bit in its spiritual discoveries, the essential principles of Christianity would still appeal to all reasonable inquirers even if we had never received or had quite forgotten its historical claims to a unique revelation.[24]

One section stands out as a moment when a great critic addressed a

---

24. "Such a religion, accordingly, can be *natural,* and at the same time *revealed,* when it is so constituted that men *could and ought to have discovered it* of themselves merely through the use of their reason, although they *would* not have come upon it so early, or over so wide an area, as is required. . . . [I]ndeed, the occurrence of such a supernatural revelation might subsequently be entirely forgotten without the slightest loss to that religion either of comprehensibility, or of certainty, or of power over human hearts" (Kant [1793] 1960, 143–44).

great myth: "Concerning the Service of God in Religion in General"
(bk. 4, pt. 1). Kant here imagines himself as having a free choice of
examples, *from* history, of a religion that is in fact not dependent *on*
history: "We must devise instances as examples in order to be intelligible, and unless we take these from history their possibility might be
disputed" (144). We must find "some book or other" (surely it was
language like this that offended the king of Prussia: the Holy Bible as
"some book or other"!) and then examine it *"as one of a variety of
books* which deal with religion and virtue on the credit of a revelation,
thus exemplifying the procedure, useful in itself, of searching out
whatever in it may be for us a pure and therefore a universal religion of
reason" (144–45; my italics). He then decides that the New Testament
"can be the book chosen" and proceeds to imagine some "Teacher"
who had promulgated the doctrines—not the historical claims—
found there (mainly in Matthew), and then applies to them the light of
reason (147–50). He concludes his act of mythic criticism with characteristic incisiveness: "Here then is a complete [*vollständige*] religion,
which can be presented to all men comprehensibly and convincingly
through their own reason; while the possibility and even the necessity
of its being an archetype for us to imitate . . . have, be it noted, been
made evident by means of an example without either the truth of those
teachings nor the authority and the worth of the Teacher requiring any
external certification (for which scholarship or miracles, which are not
matters for everyone, would be required)" (150).

A *complete* religion convincing to *all men*? That's surely a bit hard
to swallow in a period like ours when "everyone knows you can't argue rationally about religion." But I cannot believe that anyone could
read the full account, in the context of Kant's preceding inquiry into
the principles of a rational religion, without concluding that the Christian myth holds up better under this kind of critical scrutiny than
would most of the substitute myths that have replaced it for many intellectuals in the two centuries since Kant wrote. The tests for such a
claim might be many and diverse, but the following seem most promi-
nently applicable, and I list them now as potentially applicable to any
proffered myth:

1. Most notably, the myth has been shown to be *comprehensive*. It
   "covers" the essential territory with astonishing breadth: it provides a ground for our responsibilities; it accounts for our hu-

man origins and nature; it provides particular standards for choosing between plausible moral requirements; and it provides a motive for obeying the moral law that it reveals. Compare the extremely narrow application of my physicist friend's myth of particulate determinism: it purports to explain only one thing, my origin (with a "nature" identical with that origin), and it cannot even in itself give me a motive for studying that origin. Or compare the even thinner content of some popular "religious" myths now promulgated with seeming seriousness by burgeoning cults throughout the world: flying saucers are real; instantaneous interplanetary transport is possible; table tapping and "trance channeling" connect us with the spirit world; crystals have diagnostic and healing capabilities; there was no Holocaust; Christ has returned and is involved in fund-raising activities. Even if any one of these were found to be literally true, it would offer us so little as to look pathetic beside the comprehensive rational religion that Kant has discovered in—or perhaps one should say *within*—Christianity.

2. The myth *corresponds* to our commonsense experience of our own ambiguous natures and that of our fellows.

   a) It does not deny but rather explains our capacity for nobility—and yet both acknowledges and provides remedies for our inherent love of vice.

   b) It requires no violation of what we learn from the worlds of nature and history. It has in fact proved itself independent of its particular historical claims: it can survive any "refutation" that is based on denial of this or that supernatural event. We can thus predict that the myth would not necessarily fall even if someone found a document signed by Mary (and confirmed by better handwriting experts than those who validated the "Hitler diaries") claiming that Jesus was Joseph's biological offspring. The popular myths I have mentioned are in contrast vulnerable to such factual upsets—unless their adherents turn a blind eye to the facts. Like the myth of unlimited scientific progress, Kant's version of Christianity is sufficiently general and rationally supportable to survive any particular historical threat or moment of decline.

   c) It is morally comprehensive, indeed universal in its scope, in imposing the same standards on its devotees as on outsiders:

believers cannot take comfort in applying a higher standard
to their enemies than to themselves. Compare this with the
"myth of reason" preached by the followers of Ayn Rand,
who spend considerable energy drawing lines of distinction
between the elite and the canaille, with all the privileges
going to the elite (Rand 1957). Some versions of Christianity
are of course limited in the same way, but Kant's version is
explicitly opposed to self-privileging.[25]

d) It is open to new historical experience; in the domain of history, it is pluralistic. Kant insists that there *must* be many different Churches (faiths, "religions") to embody the one religion. It is true that he equivocates somewhat about whether
Christianity is after all the best among many possible good
faiths; sometimes he can be a bit blind to the alternative
strengths of the Judaic myth, and of course a good deal of
what he says fits Protestantism better than most versions of
Catholicism. But in principle this violation need not occur.

e) It—the rationalized version, not the historically particular
Christianity—is implicitly *shareable* by all humankind, and
it therefore provides a ground for community that does not
depend on inventing enemies.

I offer the examples of Plato and Kant as representing a vast project
of criticism and counter-criticism of metaphoric worlds that has been
going on since the discovery of serious philosophizing. Obviously it is
a project not limited, like my examples, to Western culture. Those
who, unlike myself, claim to know something about Eastern religions—Zen Buddhism, say—offer *them* to us as rival myths, and as
they do so, they *sometimes* engage in a philosophical criticism that
"demonstrates" the virtues of their candidate.

Once we see the great philosophies as monumental metaphors and
their creators as myth critics, they can prove useful in our less ambitious
enterprises, such as appraising metaphoric efforts like Mailer's and

---

25. The moral code that it entails may be thought by most of us to pay too little heed
to the varieties of historical circumstance. But my point is not that Kant is invulnerable
to questioning—rather, that in his very strength he will challenge us to our highest level
of questioning.

Burke's. Every serious philosopher can be imagined as calling Mailer
and Burke to come forth and defend their cosmic myths on the world
stage. The philosophers usually issue their calls with less flourish of
ethos than we have seen in our two political battlers,[26] but they implicitly demand that these battlers defend not just their overt theses but
their presentation of themselves as admirable characters. These master
judges issue tough questions of a kind that most authors of narrative
are not prepared for—questions like "What reasons can you two polemicists give for considering your presented character such an important part of the truth?" or "Would you mind slowing down a bit,
Burke, and explaining how your little stories about the mistreatment
of a pathetic Marie Antoinette serve as evidence for your case?" or
"Can you explain, Mailer, just how the ethical standards implied by
your ethos relate to the political standards implied by your sympathies
in the march on the Pentagon?"

The resulting exchanges, with sharp replies from Mailer and Burke,
will never be single or final. And the implicit narratives underlying the
exchanges will usually seem relatively "thin" and abstract in detail, as
compared to the "thick descriptions" that the great novels and poems
offer.[27] But this limitation is matched by a comparable limitation in the
great fictions: their presentation of philosophical issues is relatively
perfunctory and casual as compared with the total engagement with
every difficulty that we find in an ally like Immanuel Kant.

HISTORIES AS RIVALS TO PHILOSOPHY AND FICTIONS

Moving now to a briefer account of other useful critics of cosmic
myths, it is obvious that from our present perspective every extended
historical account both expresses (or implies) a cosmic myth of its own

---

26. But most great philosophers spend a good deal of energy establishing their character. For example, consider the opening pages of Descartes's *Discourse on Method* (to
say nothing of the much more personal *Meditations*) or of Hobbes's *Leviathan*.

27. The contrast between "thin" and "thick" accounts of forms of life—the former
abstract and general; the latter particular, detailed, and complex—has become increasingly widespread, partly under the influence of Clifford Geertz's fine argument in "Thick
Description: Toward an Interpretive Theory of Culture" (1973). See also his *Local
Knowledge* (1983).

and criticizes all other possibilities.[28] Both Burke and Mailer purport to be historical though polemical; they thus rival anyone else's historical account, whether polemical in tone or objective. In turn, they are criticized by any other history, not only of the same events but of any historical event: each historical account presents an implicit view of *how history works* along with its account of given events.

Difficult as is the art of appraising any two accounts of the same event, each of them embodying different myths of the human scene and thus a different cosmos, we all learn to practice that art to some degree whenever we read alternative accounts. As almost everyone by now seems to acknowledge, the "same event" turns out not to be the same when the presumed facts are viewed under different metaphoric structures. The "same" "eighteenth Brumaire" that many French historians have treated as tragedy is treated by Marx (to me with at least equal persuasiveness) as exemplary farce (Marx [1852] 1963, esp. 15). The "same" event treated by Gibbon as the decline and fall of Rome will be treated by many a Catholic historian as a necessary step in the rise of the true Church. The "same" rise of modern geological science that is treated by most modern historians of science under the metaphor of "time-as-arrow" becomes a radically different event when viewed by Stephen Jay Gould under the more complex, dialectical fusion of metaphors: "time-as-arrow" *and* "time-as-cycle" (Gould 1987).

Such mythic differences are of course only the most dramatic manifestation of unlimited differences between the fixed norms of any two historical accounts. Everyone in modern times recognizes the differences; that judgments differ is perhaps our most nearly universal commonplace. But few have recognized the value of those differences as significant ethical criticism. On the one hand, historical relativists take the mythic diversity, like all other diversities, as simply further evidence that all historical accounts are true only "for the historians who offer them"—"and there's no way of arbitrating among rival accounts." On the other hand, some still seem to expect that sooner or later one or another account of a given historical event or moment will subdue all rivals. If we cannot hope for that, these people argue, how

---

28. For an extended treatment of histories as "poetic" macro-metaphors see Hayden White's *Metahistory* (1973, esp. ch. 9), and the more recent *The Content of Form* (1987).

can we have any faith in historical accounts at all, except as exercises in persuasion?

We can see why neither of these views of historical narrative makes sense if we ask ourselves what constitutes any historical event, any lived human story. Most basically, any event, any sequence of human moments worth telling a story about, must result from the clash of at least two alternative, usually conflicting, points of view, each with strong ethical presuppositions: without conflict, no event. This means that even *as the event occurs,* it is inescapably plural: if for A it was a victory, for B it was a defeat (or, if there was compromise or reconciliation, that event had somewhat different meanings for A and B). We could expect to find one single valid history of any event only if we believed that in any human conflict as it occurred there could be only one finally rational perspective—that if all disputants could only talk together long enough, a single rational judgment would emerge. If that were the case, then of course the single valid history of that event would be written from that single rational perspective.[29]

This is not the place for detailed argument showing either why that "single rationality" line cannot be held, either in philosophy or history, or why when it is rightly abandoned we are not thrown into hopeless relativism.[30] But one line of argument is crucial to the ethical criticism of historical myth. That line follows from asking, What kind of evidence, in any political setting, would we take as proving that people in that society were in fact reasoning together? Must we not say that the surest sign that they were not *reasoning* together would be total agreement about political (and consequently, ethical) issues? Our founding fathers assumed that rationality is the (perhaps lamentable but undeniable) fountainhead of differences among citizens; to think together in politics is to uncover different interests and discover different interpretations of what is happening and what should happen.[31]

29. See Peter Novick's monumental forthcoming work on the historians' battles over objectivity, *That Noble Dream* (1988).

30. I made my own feeble stab at working through that case in *Modern Dogma and the Rhetoric of Assent* (1974). Since 1974, we have been offered many striking arguments against relativism. See p. 28 n.3 above. See also Norris 1985 and Davidson 1984.

31. The same argument works in domains other than politics. What would it mean if I discovered, in a batch of term papers, that every student offered the same interpreta-

It follows that tolerance of many different views is never enough; we should insist on them, seek them out. When we do not find them—whenever we find a comfortable agreement among historians, as Soviet historians are said to agree in their accounts of the revolution—we must suspect collusion or coercion. To say this does not mean that there are no bad histories, or that the myths all histories embody are equally viable or serviceable to our critical enterprise. It means simply that each major historical effort can be counted as a critical ally in making our way through the thickets of cosmic myths.

An old saw attributed to various historians says that if you know only one history of an event you know nothing about it. That's another way of saying: you're in trouble, when you read polemical historians like Mailer and Burke, if you do not find some way to practice a *historical* criticism of their metaphoric barrages. The best way to do that, short of spending the years necessary to write a serious rival history of your own, is to find an account that rivals theirs. After you have read Burke read Michelet or Tocqueville; after you read Mailer read . . . but I know of no "opposing" account of those same events that can stand up to his passion. The fortunate thing is that the antidote need not be focused on the same events; after reading Mailer, read Edmund Burke.

FURTHER CRITICAL ALLIES

By now it should be clear that every serious intellectual discipline could provide some contribution to the ethical criticism we are seeking:

Literary History. Like other histories, literary histories can be viewed as macro-metaphors: we cannot get along without them, if we are to do more than just move from one work to another without thought, but we should be aware that at best they all reduce reality to

---

tion, supported by the same arguments? Obviously something other than learning how to read and think had been going on. Perhaps I should hasten to add—lest I be seen as selling out to the subjectivists—that if I found no common ground whatever in any group of essays (term papers or journal articles), I would also be convinced that no learning was taking place. We only live, only suspire, pursuing *both* common ground *and* respect for difference.

one representative aspect. Their radical embodiment of grand metaphors is usually hard to see at the time they appear, and too easy to see
after a few decades. When I first read Vernon Parrington's *Main Currents in American Thought* (1930), its picture of the good guys (progressives) versus the bad guys (capitalists) seemed to me truth itself.
Now its reliance on a somewhat too simple metaphor of political progress seems radically in need of the kinds of criticism that have been
offered by more recent histories (e.g., Hofstadter 1970). One useful
kind of literary history could tell the story of how Burke's and Mailer's
way of using metaphor has been employed by polemicists of every
period, and what that way implies about our nature and about how we
argue to and from it. I don't know of anyone who has attempted
a history of this special literary form—the political-warning-that-
depends-on-historical-claims-but-embeds-them-in-"sublime"-meta-
phoric-clusters. But it is easy to see that such a history would be useful
if it looked closely at how our two examples compare with their earlier
siblings and rivals.

My reference to Mailer's and Burke's final pages is at best a hint at
what such a history would look for: the range of devices and effects
achieved by similar rhetors attempting to produce a similar sense of
terrifying crisis. What have other authors been able to accomplish
with similar projects? How have they employed their resources of
ethos to reinforce their political claims? What have been the advantages and disadvantages of jumbling metaphors at the moment of
greatest passion? What are the uses of explicit avowals of one's own
character, as in Burke's climax and in so many pages of Mailer's?
Which specific metaphors for a nation in agony have shown the greatest power to survive the criticism provided by other metaphors? [32]

32. M. H. Abrams's great literary history *Natural Supernaturalism* might be taken
as a model for anyone seeking to place Mailer's vision in the history of apocalyptic and
revolutionary metaphor. See my chapter on Abrams (Booth 1979, 139–75). In Abrams's
other great work of metaphoric criticism, *The Mirror and the Lamp: Romantic Theory
and the Critical Tradition,* he engages in little explicit judging of metaphors as he
marshals diverse historical descriptions of poets as mirrors, foundations, instruments,
makers of objects, teachers, lamps, and whatnot. He lets history do the judging for him
as the useful, enduring metaphors are brought forth in quotation from works whose
authors were energized by thinking through or with them (Booth 1981, 79–105). Another model of criticism "disguised" as literary history is Arthur Lovejoy's *The Great
Chain of Being* (1960). The power of a metaphor like that of the "great chain" to survive
Lovejoy's sustained historical scrutiny does not, in our usual way of thinking, say any-

Cultural Anthropology. My references above have already revealed how much congruence I see between what I am calling ethical criticism of macro-metaphor and cosmic myths and what the cultural anthropologists are up to. Of course every work of anthropology is itself constituted around a metaphoric vision of how people relate to people and how they are "made" by nature and culture. A good deal of anthropological writing is devoted to criticizing bad metaphors for particular cultural patterns. Marshall Sahlins's *Culture and Practical Reason* (1976), for example, can be viewed as an extended critique of functional metaphors for how we invent our cultures, on behalf of metaphors that see culture as made of symbols—of metaphors—many of them *not* functional in any simple sense (see Fernandez 1986; Geertz 1988).

Psychology. Traditionally psychology was of course concerned entirely with the soul, the psyche. Though there are branches of it now that seem pretty far removed from the culture of souls through ethical criticism, every genuine *psych*ology is constituted around a metaphor for what a person is or might be, and all branches of psychiatry and psychoanalysis are inescapably engaged in seeking out and criticizing the macro-metaphors by which their subjects live.[33] Each psychology "criticizes" the metaphors of the others. Freud's hydraulic metaphors for the soul's working parts, the pressurized id, ego, and super-ego, criticize earlier metaphors, like the four humors or the association theory that Coleridge both borrowed from and criticized. Freud is in turn criticized by the metaphor, among many others, of the soul as a collection of push buttons, a product of the "operant conditioning" that *really* explains our behavior (Skinner 1971, 1974). Though it is easy to see deficiencies in each of these when one views them "from the out-

---

thing about its truth or value. But once we begin to take seriously the task of criticizing metaphor, we must re-open the question of whether the metaphors that have recently replaced God's plenum—mechanistic evolution, for example—have not sacrificed a good deal of general truth for what they have gained in local victories.

33. Three psychologists whose work seems to me to have permanent bearing on ethical criticism are William James (*The Principles of Psychology* [1890] 1981 and *Psychology: The Briefer Course* [1892] 1985); Lev Semenovich Vygotsky (*Thought and Language* [1962]); and George Kelly (*The Psychology of Personal Constructs* [1955]). Are there more recent *scientific* psychologists, outside the domains of therapy, who concentrate their study on how characters (or persons, or selves) are formed? Obviously there must be. Tell me about them, and I will listen.

side," we can also see why, in a general way, some survive in spite of limitation, and others, like the "humors," languish and finally die, seeming to have outlived their usefulness.

The surviving metaphors survive because, like Pepper's five root metaphors, they continue to uncover truth about us: our innards *do* seethe and bubble like those of some hydraulic device under pressure; we *can* be conditioned by well-made programs, as if we were stimulus-response mechanisms, or stimulus-organism-response loops; we *do* operate in some ways like social ants and in other ways like computers. We are even—in ways long forgotten—collections of choleric, sanguine, phlegmatic, and melancholic "humors": Who *can* say that that theory will prove permanently empty?

And so on we might go, visiting whatever remaining field has any critical vitality. Though few of them would have the aspirations to intellectual empire that are exhibited by those I have described (musicology, for example, would prove quite modest, though still useful), others, like various theologies and aesthetics, might offer to be king of the critics. The rivalry among the disciplines would itself prove to be part of the critical vitality that we might build on in improving our practice of ethical criticism.

Where does this inescapably superficial survey of our allies and their rivalries leave us? In a sense it leaves us where we always were—in a world of rival macro-metaphors and implied cosmic myths, attempting to employ them without quite knowing how. No one who has ever fully embraced the cognitive hopes of Western science, as I did in my twenties, can fail to sense some frustration in facing such complexities; it can feel a bit like being in a badly managed stereo store and trying to listen to Bach on one touted system while other buyers are listening on other systems to Mahler, John Philip Sousa, and the Grateful Dead. We have been trained to desire and expect clearer outcomes, and here we find, in every direction we turn, that adding critics adds complexities—if not cacophonies. We would like, most of us, to find some one critic who would simply cancel the others out—or at least some of the others.

The critics themselves—the philosophers and historians, if not the novelists and poets—often clearly aspire to such cancellations. When William McNeill published *The Rise of the West* (1963) with its sys-

tematic loading on the word "rise," he no doubt meant it as a stagger-
ing critique of all "decline" histories—especially those of Spengler
and Toynbee but perhaps also earlier "decliners" like Gibbon. But of
course he could not utterly destroy the credibility of claims that the
West has fallen; if there were not a great deal of evidence for decline,
Toynbee could not have written his multi-volumed history in the first
place. What McNeill could do was to change permanently the way
readers of Toynbee view each metaphor of decline as it appears. But
for me their bustling, indecisive rivalries make them both *my* allies,
providing splendid crosslights on my critical tasks. Whenever I engage
seriously with any metaphors, petty or grand, whenever I join in any
narrative, religious or secular, and whenever I then choose to discuss
my venture, after the fact, with those who have traveled the same way,
I become part of a venture in self-education that is both supremely
practical and at the same time the very end of life itself. Ethical criticism in this broad view is not a form of judgment to be applied to
works somehow "out there." Instead, it is something we live, both as
we engage with works and as we converse about them after the event.

Early in Homer's *Odyssey,* there is a fine moment illustrating this
kind of reflexivity. Odysseus has landed, after many troubles, on the
island ruled by Alkínoös. He is wined and dined, and then he listens to
a blind minstrel, a "man of song / whom the Muse cherished; by her
gift he knew / the good of life, and evil— / for she who lent him sweet-
ness made him blind" (bk. 8, ll. 56–68). The minstrel sings an account
of Odysseus and Achilles, and of Ares' dalliance with Aphrodite, and
"Odysseus, / listening, found sweet pleasure in the tale" (ll. 368–69).
Finally, after further dancing and singing of tales, Odysseus approaches
the moment when he must tell his *own* story:

> [H]ow beautiful this is, to hear a minstrel
> gifted as yours: a god he must be, singing!
> There is no boon in life more sweet, I say,
> than when a summer joy holds all the realm,
> and banqueters sit listening to a harper
> in a great hall, by rows of tables heaped
> . . . .
> Here is the flower of life, it seems to me!
>
> (bk. 9, ll. 3–11)

Homer is of course describing what he himself is doing with his
whole poem, and we can be sure that he expects to be paid for it in one

way or another. But unlike too many of our bards, he is not describing a vision of human happiness that is in hopeless conflict with what he is being paid to induce in others: the flower of life is for him the creating of pictures of the flower of life.[34]

All serious study of anything is, no doubt, life-justifying. But there might be a special flowering about a criticism that accepted the responsibility to discriminate among the characters and cultures that metaphors build, in the belief that the quality of any culture is in large part the quality of the metaphorists that it creates and sustains.

REFERENCES

Aiken, Henry David. *Reason and Conduct: New Bearings in Moral Philosophy.* Westport, Conn., 1962.

Bakhtin, M. M. *The Dialogic Imagination: Four Essays.* Ed. Michael Holquist. Trans. Caryl Emerson and Michael Holquist. University of Texas Press Slavic Series, no. 1. Austin, Tex., 1981.

Becker, Carl Lotus. *Everyman His Own Historian: Essays on History and Politics.* New York, 1935.

Booth, Wayne C. *Modern Dogma and the Rhetoric of Assent.* Chicago, 1974.

———. *Critical Understanding: The Powers and Limits of Pluralism.* Chicago, 1979.

———. "History as Metaphor: Or, Is M. H. Abrams a Mirror, or a Lamp, or a Fountain . . . ?" In *High Romantic Argument: Essays for M. H. Abrams.* Ed. Lawrence Lipking. Ithaca, N.Y., 1981.

Branden, Barbara. *The Passion of Ayn Rand.* New York, 1986.

Burke, Edmund. *Reflections on the Revolution in France* [1790]. Ed. William B. Todd. New York, 1959.

Burke, Kenneth. "Literature as Equipment for Living." *The Philosophy of Literary Form: Studies in Symbolic Action.* 2d ed. New York, 1957.

Cascardi, Anthony J., ed. *Literature and the Question of Philosophy.* Baltimore, 1987.

Castiglione, Baldesar. *The Book of the Courtier* [1528]. Trans. Charles S. Singleton. New York, 1959.

Crane, Ronald S. "The Concept of Plot and the Plot of *Tom Jones.*" In *Critics and Criticism: Ancient and Modern.* Chicago, 1952.

———. *The Languages of Criticism and the Structure of Poetry.* Toronto, 1953.

34. The word "flower" in Fitzgerald's translation is not found in the Greek original. A. T. Murray has simply "the fairest thing" for *kalliston* (see his translation of the *Odyssey* (1919), 303). But though Fitzgerald's choice of metaphor emphasizes my point, it does not change it: the best of life is creating narrative pictures of the best of life.

Dampier, William Cecil. *A History of Science and Its Relations with Philosophy and Religion*. New York, 1929.

Davidson, Donald. *Inquiries into Truth and Interpretation*. Oxford, 1984.

Dewey, John. *The Quest for Certainty: A Study of the Relation of Knowledge and Action*. New York, 1929.

Doležel, Lubomír. "Narrative Worlds." In *Sound, Sign, and Meaning: Quinquagenary of the Prague Linguistic Circle*, no. 6. Ed. Ladislav Matejka. Ann Arbor, Mich., 1976. 542–52.

Fernandez, James W. *Persuasions and Performances: The Play of Tropes in Culture*. Bloomington, Ind., 1986.

Feyerabend, Paul K. *Against Method: Outline of an Anarchistic Theory of Knowledge*. London, 1975.

Foley, Barbara. "The Politics of Deconstruction." In *Rhetoric and Form: Deconstruction at Yale*. Ed. Robert Con Davis and Ronald Schleifer. Norman, Okla., 1985.

Frye, Northrop. *Anatomy of Criticism: Four Essays*. Princeton, N.J., 1957.

Geertz, Clifford. "Thick Description: Toward an Interpretive Theory of Culture." In *The Interpretation of Cultures*. New York, 1973.

———. *Local Knowledge: Further Essays in Interpretive Anthropology*. New York, 1983.

———. *Works and Lives*. Stanford, 1988.

Gillispie, Charles Coulston. *The Edge of Objectivity: An Essay in the History of Scientific Ideas*. Princeton, N.J., 1960.

Gilman, Richard. "What Mailer Has Done." *New Republic* (June 8, 1968): 27–31.

Gleick, James. *Chaos: Making a New Science*. New York, 1987.

Gould, Stephen Jay. *Time's Arrow, Time's Cycle: Myth and Metaphor in the Discovery of Geological Time*. Cambridge, Mass., 1987.

Grassi, Ernesto. *Rhetoric as Philosophy: The Humanist Tradition*. University Park, Pa., 1980.

Grossman, Ron. "Passions: A Disciple Confronts Ayn Rand's Power." *Chicago Tribune* (Sept. 9, 1986): 1, 3.

Hofstadter, Richard. *The Progressive Historians: Turner, Beard, Parrington* [1968]. New York, 1970.

Homer. *Odyssey*. Trans. A. T. Murray. Loeb Classical Library. Cambridge, Mass., 1919.

———. *Odyssey*. Trans. Robert Fitzgerald. Garden City, N.Y., 1961.

Hume, David. "Of Miracles." In *An Enquiry Concerning Human Understanding* [1748]. Ed. Charles W. Hendel. New York, 1955.

Irigaray, Luce. "Questions." In *This Sex Which Is Not One*. Trans. Catherine Porter and Carolyn Burke. Ithaca, N.Y., 1985.

James, William. *The Principles of Psychology* [1890]. Ed. Frederick H. Burkhardt et al. Cambridge, Mass., 1981.

———. *Psychology: The Briefer Course* [1892]. Notre Dame, Ind., 1985.

Kant, Immanuel. *Religion within the Limits of Reason Alone* [1793]. Trans. Theodore M. Greene and Hoyt H. Hudson. New York, 1960.

Kelly, George. *The Psychology of Personal Constructs*. New York, 1955.

Lasky, Melvin J. *Utopia and Revolution: On the Origins of a Metaphor: or, Some Illustrations of the Problem of Political Temperament and Intel-*

lectual Climate and How Ideas, Ideals, and Ideologies Have Been His-
torically Related. Chicago, 1976.
Lovejoy, Arthur. *The Great Chain of Being* [1936]. New York, 1960.
Lewis, David. *On the Plurality of Worlds.* Oxford, 1985.
MacIntyre, Alasdair. *After Virtue: A Study in Moral Theory.* Notre Dame,
     Ind., 1981.
Mailer, Norman. *The Armies of the Night: History as a Novel, the Novel as*
     History. New York, 1968.
Marx, Karl. *The Eighteenth Brumaire of Louis Bonaparte* [1852]. New York,
     1963.
McKeon, Richard. *Freedom and History: The Semantics of Philosophical*
     Controversies and Ideological Conflicts. New York, 1952.
McKeon, Zahava Karl. *Novels and Arguments: Inventing Rhetorical Criti-*
     cism. Chicago, 1982.
McNeill, William H. *The Rise of the West: A History of the Human Commu-*
     nity. Chicago, 1963.
Norris, Christopher. *The Contest of Faculties: Philosophy and Theory after*
     Deconstruction. London, 1985.
Novick, Peter. *That Noble Dream: The "Objectivity Question" and the Pro-*
     fessional Culture of American Historiography. New York, 1988.
O'Flaherty, Wendy D. "Ethical and Nonethical Implications of the Separation
     of Heaven and Earth in Indian Mythology." In *Cosmogony and Ethi-*
     cal Order. Ed. Robin W. Lovin and Frank E. Reynolds. Chicago, 1985.
Ogden, C. K. *Bentham's Theory of Fictions.* 1932. Reprint. New York, 1978.
Parrington, Vernon. *Main Currents in American Thought: An Interpretation*
     of American Literature from the Beginnings to 1920. New York, 1930.
Pavel, Thomas G. *Fictional Worlds.* Cambridge, Mass., 1986.
Pepper, Stephen C. *World Hypotheses: A Study in Evidence.* Berkeley, 1942.
———. *Concept and Quality: A World Hypothesis.* New York, 1966.
Perelman, Chaim, and L. Olbrechts-Tyteca. *The New Rhetoric: A Treatise on*
     Argumentation. Trans. John Wilkinson and Purcell Weaver. Notre
     Dame, Ind., 1969.
Polanyi, Michael. *Personal Knowledge: Towards a Post-Critical Philosophy*
     [1958]. Chicago, 1972.
Rand, Ayn. *Atlas Shrugged.* New York, 1957.
Richter, David. *Fable's End: Completeness and Closure in Rhetorical Fiction.*
     Chicago, 1974.
Rorty, Richard. *Philosophy and the Mirror of Nature.* Princeton, N.J., 1979.
Sacks, Sheldon. *Fiction and the Shape of Belief: A Study of Henry Fielding,*
     with Glances at Swift, Johnson, and Richardson. Berkeley, 1964.
Sahlins, Marshall. *Culture and Practical Reason.* Chicago, 1976.
Shweder, Richard A. *Post-Nietzschian Anthropology: The Idea of Multiple*
     Objective Worlds. Unpublished paper, University of Chicago work-
     shop on Practical Discourse, 1987.
Skinner, B. F. *Beyond Freedom and Dignity.* New York, 1971.
———. *About Behaviorism.* New York, 1974.
Smith, Jonathan Z. *Imagining Religion: From Babylon to Jonestown.* Chi-
     cago, 1982.
Tovey, Donald Francis. "The Materials of Beethoven's Language." In *Beetho-*
     ven [1945]. London, 1965.

Toynbee, Arnold. *A Study of History.* 6 vols. London, 1946–57.

Tracy, David. *Blessed Rage for Order: The New Pluralism in Theology* [1975]. Minneapolis, 1979.

———. *The Analogical Imagination: Christian Theology and the Culture of Pluralism.* New York, 1981.

Turner, Mark. *Death Is the Mother of Beauty: Mind, Metaphor, Criticism.* Chicago, 1987.

Vaihinger, H. *The Philosophy of 'As If': A System of the Theoretical, Practical, and Religious Fictions of Mankind* [1927]. Trans. C. K. Ogden. 2d ed. London, 1935.

Vygotsky, Lev Semenovich. *Thought and Language.* Cambridge, Mass., 1962.

Watson, Walter. *The Architectonics of Meaning: Foundations of the New Pluralism.* Albany, N.Y., 1985.

Wells, H. G. *The Outline of History.* London, 1920.

Whateley, Richard. *Historic Doubts Relative to Napoleon Bonaparte* [1819]. Ed. Ralph S. Pomeroy. Berkeley, 1985.

White, Hayden. *Metahistory: The Historical Imagination in Nineteenth-Century Europe.* Baltimore, 1973.

———. *The Content of Form: Narrative Discourse and Historical Representation.* Baltimore, 1987.

White, James Boyd. *When Words Lose Their Meaning: Constitutions and Reconstitutions of Language, Character, and Community.* Chicago, 1984.

Wirth, Niklaus. "Data Structures and Algorithms." *Scientific American* 251 (Sept. 1984): 60–69.

Wittgenstein, Ludwig. *Tractatus Logico-Philosophicus* [1921]. Trans. D. F. Pears and B. F. McGuinness. London, 1961.

Wolterstorff, Nicholas. *Works and Worlds of Art.* New York, 1980.

Wordsworth, William. "Ode: Intimations of Immortality from Recollections of Early Childhood" [1807]. In *William Wordsworth: The Poems.* Ed. John O. Hayden. 2 vols. New Haven, Conn., 1977. 1: 523–29.

Yeats, William Butler. "The Tower" [1928]. In *The Poems of W. B. Yeats.* Ed. Richard J. Finneran. New York, 1983.

PART III

Chicago.—Officials say that two male viewers shot themselves to death after a television station showed the film *The Deer Hunter* despite a psychiatrist's warning that its Russian roulette scenes might inspire real-life imitators. Dr. Thomas Radecki said he asked station WFLD-TV to edit the Russian roulette scenes, saying there had been 28 shootings and 25 confirmed Russian roulette deaths in the United States involving persons who watched the movie on television or videotape.

Chicago.—*Most Frightening Horror of "I Spit on Your Grave" Is Its Mainstream American Audience*

"I Spit on Your Grave" is easily the most offensive film I have seen in my 11 years on the movie beat. The story . . . debases strong women in the guise of heralding them. . . . The idea behind these scenes is that women . . . really dig rough sex and enjoy being raped. . . . As shocking as this film was, however, it did not compare with the series of shocks I received while watching it Saturday afternoon. . . . What I saw . . . on the screen and in the audience . . . scared the hell out of me.

Gene Siskel, Chicago Tribune

Doctrinal Criticism and the Redemptions of Coduction

There's something insipid about agreeing with an author, especially when you're young. You feel it's your business to be *other*.

I. A. Richards

It would be better for him if a millstone were hung around his neck, and he were cast into the sea, than that he should cause one of these little ones to sin.

Luke 17:2

Introduction

Despite the complexities of Part 2, one point should be clear; simple doctrinal tests cannot establish absolute judgments. It is not only that different readers will prove vulnerable or immune to different doctrines, or that they will in fact *hear* different claims and respond in different ways. It is that each of us, responding to any fiction, will experience many different values, only a small number of which will be tied to doctrines that can be formulated as simple propositions. Our coductions are not finally *about messages;* they are *constructions of experience.* The patterns of desire, the figurings of metaphor, the cosmic myths of happiness and misery, combined in various ways with our picture of an artist (or poseur) who is or who is not "juggling" well—all these lead us not only to excuse what we may see as doctrinal errors but to make spiritual or emotional *use* of them.

But just how far can we go in that direction? If it is true, as I have argued, that encounters with narrative otherness are in large part what we are made of, surely we must be free to object to fictions built on beliefs that go beyond (or sink beneath) what we can or should tolerate. But in attempting to free ethical criticism from dogmatic moralizing, have I not come dangerously close to embracing the opposing dogma, that what fictions say *doesn't* matter? Surely a responsible criticism must face squarely the folly, viciousness, and plain falsity that we meet in too many of our would-be narrative friends.

We thus face here a sharper version of the contrasting positions with which we began. Both are plausible; both are upheld by thoughtful critics. We should now clarify the pressures implicit in the conflict by looking briefly at a poem that could be said simply to assert a doctrine. Are beliefs irrelevant to our life with this poem by Ezra Pound?

AN IMMORALITY

Sing we for love and idleness,
Naught else is worth the having.

> Though I have been in many a land
> There is naught else in living.
>
> And I would rather have my sweet
> Though rose-leaves die of grieving,
>
> Than do high deeds in Hungary,
> To pass all men's believing.
>
> (1976, 192)

The title openly celebrates a doctrine—against "morality"—and the poem's central assertion is plain and direct: Nothing in life is worth having except love and idleness. Specifically, heroic adventure is "naught" compared with love. Since the poem obviously is a piece of highly contrived art, both visibly and audibly, its "working" openly contradicts its own assertion: at least one thing "else" is worth the having—a well-wrought poem. "Idleness" does not produce such workings of rhyme, half-rhyme, and metrical mastery. What's more, the poem contradicts its title: it advocates a specific morality, one that takes the anti-traditionalist position of "The Fiddler" one step further. (We should remember, however, that by the time Pound wrote this poem, in 1912, what we might call its Omar Khayyamism had long since been commonplace; it would certainly not have shocked those most likely to be reading it, the literati.)

To be inconsistent with itself may not be a very serious flaw in a poem; quite possibly Pound even intended these paradoxes as part of the poem's proffered delight. And aside from the paradoxes, everybody knows that much "else" is worth the having—not only well-wrought poems and the delicious "work" of reading them, but friendship, honor, children.

If beliefs are really unimportant here, surely we ought to be able to substitute any normal human good in place of "love and idleness" without seriously harming the poem:

AN IMMORALITY

> Sing we for gold and jewelry,
> Naught else is worth the having.
>
> Though I have been in many a land
> There is naught else in living.
>
> And I would rather fill my purse,
> Though rose-leaves die of grieving,

> Than do high deeds in Hungary
> To pass all men's believing.

The revision destroys little if any of the music of the poem; its verbal craft remains *almost* intact. The sheer sound of "gold and jewelry" is not self-evidently less pleasant than "love and idleness." "Fill my purse" would sound, I suspect, to the ear of someone ignorant of English, not noticeably less consonant with the rest of the poem than "have my sweet." What has really changed are the beliefs expressed—and the change surely wounds the poem cruelly. A man saying that nothing is worth having except love and idleness may be mistaken: I think he is seriously so. But he's not so seriously mistaken that I cannot understand and sympathize with his professed role, or remember times when I have tried it on for size. In sharp contrast, a man who would rather have his gold and jewelry than do high deeds is a contemptible, perhaps comic, money-grubber. I cannot separate my beliefs about his pusillanimity from the poem he has written, just as I cannot separate the beliefs of the admirably carefree lover from the poem that Pound wrote. Thus the beliefs are part of the "music" that Pound made, part of the final beauty of the gift—of its power, its integrity, its harmony and revelatory richness: each word chosen here will entail slightly different critical standards. If the beliefs are really not important, we must be driven to say that the two poems are of roughly equal value *as* poetry—which is patently absurd.

On the other hand (that constant refrain of this book!), in saying all that are we not violating what we know about the difference between art and proselytizing? How do we honor what we know about art and its capacity to use even the most outlandish doctrines for its own ends? The questions are not just theoretical. Whenever literary prizes are to be awarded, judges are likely to face some "good poems" expressing abhorrent doctrines. Should they not face them as did the Bollingen Prize committee, when in 1949 they had to decide whether to give the prize to Ezra Pound's Pisan Cantos, poems that openly expressed anti-Semitic and other fascist views? The committee gave the prize to Pound, and they then found themselves caught in a huge controversy—indeed they were accused of having supported fascism with their decision. Was Allen Tate mistaken when he replied like this?

> I voted for him, for the following reason: the health of literature depends upon the health of society, and conversely; there must be constant vigilance

for both ends of the process. The specific task of the man of letters is to attend to the health of society *not at large* but through literature—that is, he must be constantly aware of the condition of language in his age. As a result of observing Pound's use of language in the past thirty years I had become convinced that he had done more than any other man to regenerate the language, if not the imaginative forms, of English verse. I had to face the disagreeable fact that he had done this even in passages of verse in which the opinions expressed ranged from the childish to the detestable.

(1965, 88–89)

Is Tate saying anything different from what I said in Chapter 3 when I repudiated syllogistic deductions—from "false doctrine" to "bad poem"—and celebrated a *co*duction that may include, but always transcends, any particular *de*ductions we might make from ethical principles? I think he is, but the differences are not obvious. After all, is it not easy to show that poetic art, not doctrine, constitutes the quality of "An Immorality"? Suppose we see what happens when we preserve the doctrine and destroy the art:

> To do high deeds in Hungary
> That pass all men's believing,
>
> Is thought by some the highest goal
> That can be sought in living.
>
> But what I always say is this:
> It's love and idleness that count,
>
> And . . .

I can't go on—the point is clear enough. No amount of improvement in the doctrine will save this new "poem": "It's truth and tolerance that count," "It's faith and charity that count," "It's textuality that counts"—fill in your own virtues and you will still not have a poem worth having. What's more, it is not inconceivable that a poet with Pound's genius could create a worthy poem hailing greed or other vices: in fact, that is just what Allen Tate and many others believe that he did even in the more vicious lines in the Cantos.

How can we put these two views together? On the one hand, objectionable beliefs can at least partially destroy a poem; on the other hand, "right" or "wrong" beliefs in themselves can neither make nor break a poem. On the one hand, our coductions of value seem strongly bound up with our response to a poem's fixed norms; on the other hand, we often seem to follow the practice of the Bollingen committee—we coduce some central stylistic quality that redeems all doctrinal faults.

Obviously I cannot hope that by the end of *Company* I shall have resolved this conflict, opening a clear single path for ethical criticism: each "side" is too firmly built into our experience with doctrines and literary forms. I hope instead, through a series of four relatively sustained examples, punctuated with a few briefer encounters, to illustrate the ethical challenges faced by all readers—even those who on theoretical grounds repudiate ethical criticism.

REFERENCES

Alvarez, A. "Craft and Morals." In Stock 1965: 41–61.

MacLeish, Archibald. *Poetry and Opinion: The Pisan Cantos of Ezra Pound; A Dialogue on the Role of Poetry.* Urbana, Ill., 1950.

Pound, Ezra. "An Immorality." In *Collected Early Poems of Ezra Pound.* Ed. Michael John King. New York, 1976. 192.

Stock, Noel. *Ezra Pound: Perspectives.* Chicago, 1965.

Tate, Allen. "Ezra Pound and the Bollingen Prize" [1959]. In Stock 1965: 86–89.

12

The deadly sin is to say "X is a political enemy: therefore he is a bad writer."
George Orwell

But where the ideas of morality and decency alter from one age to another, and where vicious manners are described, without being marked with the proper characters of blame and disapprobation, they must be allowed to [i.e., we must agree that they] disfigure the poem, and to be a real deformity. I cannot, nor is it proper I should, enter into such sentiments, and however I may excuse the poet, on account of the manners of his age, I can never relish the composition.
David Hume

In the final analysis, there are only two basic attitudes, two points of view: the aesthetic and the moral.
Thomas Mann

There is no such thing as a moral or an immoral book. Books are well written or badly written. That is all.
Oscar Wilde

Could you explain what you mean by "moral"? The word, as you've acknowledged, has pejorative implications these days.
Interviewer to John Gardner

A poetry of revolt against moral ideas is a poetry of revolt against *life;* a poetry of indifference toward moral ideas is a poetry of indifference toward *life.*
Matthew Arnold

What the poet says is not evidence in a court of law.
Donald Tovey

Rabelais and the Challenge of Feminist Criticism

In turning now to explicit doctrinal criticism, I could be said to move from non-ideological to ideological criticism. It might as easily be argued, however, that everything I have done so far has been in some sense ideological: every judgment I have made or hinted at, indeed every word I have written could be traced to some element in my "ideology," as the word is frequently used today. What I say will inevitably spring from who I am, and that in turn will reflect *where* and *when* I am: my roots can always be traced. This means that in making the transition to explicitly doctrinal objections, we do not move from non-commitment to commitment. Rather, we change the direction of our lines of responsibility, as described in Chapter 5: without repudiating responsibilities of authors and readers to each other, we move to their joint responsibility to "society in general, 'the world,' 'the future'" and finally to the relatively unbending stuff that we cover with words like "justice," "truth," "nature," and "reality." In short, I must now enter what is for many early modern critics the most forbidden of all territories for the literary critic, that mine-field where we battle over doctrinal differences. Whether we call what goes on there "ideological," "doctrinal," or "political," our judgments will at least for a time look a bit more like traditional ethical criticism than did those of the last two chapters.

IDEOLOGY, POWER, AND FREEDOM OF INTERPRETATION

Ideological criticism is increasingly defended these days, after decades of being neglected, as an expression of legitimate power struggle. All criticism, we are told, is in fact no more than an expression of political interests. Older forms of criticism concealed their political biases, or repressed them by pretending to deal only with pure forms or to address only scientific issues.[1] White, male, bourgeois critics have exercised power by establishing and defending a literature that touts their values; it is now time for us, their political victims, to criticize those values. Our main task, accordingly, is to interrogate old classics, expose old double standards, and either revise or replace old canons.

Those who make this case can readily cite examples showing that established literatures and critical languages cater to established ideologies and thus perpetuate established inequities: male critics have generally written sexist criticism hailing—or at least tacitly approving—misogynist works; white critics have simply not noticed the racism of many classics; the critics of Europe and North America have habitually ignored the scandalous mistreatment, in Western classics, of Jews and blacks, "Orientals,"[2] American Indians, Hispanic Americans, and indeed the representatives of all non-European cultures. In the last twenty years or so, classic after classic has been questioned, and many a long-neglected work has been suggested as supplement or replacement.

Many of the resulting re-evaluations are to me persuasive; in this chapter I attempt one of my own. But I notice that many of the new ideological critics fall into one or another of two traps. Some are like the young Chicano professor I mentioned in Chapter 1; they are torn apart with the effort to maintain a divorce between their "literary" criticism and their "political" criticism. Others, perhaps more prominent in the 1980s, cannot accept such division of mind and choose instead the reduction to power that I have just described. In doing so, they may seem to salvage consistency; but by dealing in simple polarities they sacrifice a great share of the rich diversity of argument and value to be discovered in the critical world. Instead of dealing with other criticisms "dialogically," incorporating their validities, many

1. Perhaps the most representative figure arguing this position is Michel Foucault (1972, 1977). For a friendly critique of Foucault, relating him to other "discourse-as-power" thinkers (Althusser, Pecheux, and various pragmatists), see Macdonell 1986. For an extreme in the power line, see Bové 1986. The other main "power line" is of course that of the Marxists, who strike Foucauldians as too confident of their ideology.

2. In *Orientalism* (1978) Edward Said has taught us to feel uneasy with the word, even when it is enclosed within quotation marks.

critics reduce the whole of history to some new single truth: criticism can only *pretend* to be a rational enterprise, and rationality is itself a pretense, a ploy that privileges the way the elite "think" and thereby authorizes their "right" to control. Pushing the justified claim that all criticism reflects and reinforces ideologies that *can* be used to serve power, these critics end up reducing criticism to a kind of talk that *can only* serve power. They thus toss into the wastebasket the insights and practices that become available when the language of power is itself criticized by other languages.

The consequence is that critical *reasons* are all reduced to rationalizations. Everyone's arguments can be ignored *as* argument, while rivals attend to the motives that each critic, as a disguised power-broker, has supposedly labored hard to conceal. What is more, a new, though subtler, form of inconsistency is revealed. When I argue that power is all, either my argument is itself worth attending to or it is simply a disguise for my own power play. If it is the former, then power is not all; argument counts. But if it is only another power play, then my listeners have no good *reason* to attend to it: they have at best only a motive, fear of my possible power. Insofar as I try to deny this inconsistency, I fall into the kind of self-privileging discourse that exempts itself from its own analysis. Like B. F. Skinner's theories of conditioned behavior, such arguments claim to explain the production of every text except the one that provides the explanation: it alone provides reasons that have not been produced by non-rational forces or interests.[3]

Such difficulties never seem fatal in themselves, but they signal our need to search for alternate critical languages—languages that, while not denying the powers of the language of power, would do somewhat more justice to the ways in which we all attend to one another and ask for one another's attention (see Graff 1979). Most useful for us will be another fashionable language, the language of freedom, closely related to the language of "openness" that we queried in Chapter 3. Prominent in much critical talk since the romantic period, it has grown

---

3. One of the best accounts of self-privileging is Jacques Derrida's "Cogito and the History of Madness" (1978, 31–63), a discussion of Foucault's *Madness and Civilization*. I recommend the essay to anyone tempted to think of deconstructionist criticism as in any simple sense anti-intentionalist.

increasingly popular since the rise of existentialism just after World War II (see esp. Sartre 1981). By now it is almost automatic with many critics; although some deride it as reflecting bourgeois subjectivism, others would see no difference between talking of power plays and talking of the struggle for freedom.

In turning to the language of freedom, I do not, of course, automatically escape the dangers of reduction and self-privileging. If I try to subtract the insights of the power brokers as I add what a search for critical freedom might teach, I cannot gain very much, if anything. But the combination of the two should make a good starting point for doctrinal criticism.

We can in fact keep "power" in from the beginning, by making a distinction taken for granted by many earlier thinkers and too often ignored today: *freedom from* as contrasted with *freedom to*.[4] Facing a world in which various powers restrain me and various freedoms seem desirable, I can seek either a *freedom from* external restraints, from the power of others to inhibit my actions, or I can seek a *freedom to* act effectively when external restraints are removed.

All the *freedom from* in the world will not free me *to* make an intellectual discovery or to write a novel unless I have somehow freed myself *to* perform certain tasks. Such freedoms are gained only by those who embrace disciplines and codes invented by others, surrendering for long enough to develop the "virtues" required for excellence in some "practice." In short, some *freedoms to* require the sacrifice of some *freedoms from*. Nobody forbids my interpreting the *Principia Mathematica* or the Chinese text of Confucius's *Analects*. Yet I am not free *to* do so, having not been disciplined to it. I will not become free in the one sense until I give up some freedom in the other, surrendering to a discipline that will require years of subordination to what may sometimes look like vicious established powers.

Freedom from is easier to talk about than *freedom to*. Every critical

---

4. For a brief discussion of the distinction, see Bradley [1876] 1951, 55–57. As he suggests, the distinction has large consequences, both for our thinking about causation in general (it explains why we cannot really get along, as so much of the scientific world tries to, seeking only "efficient causes") and for our notions of what a person *is* who causes or is caused, who is freed *from* or *to*. Janet Radcliffe makes excellent use of the distinction in *The Skeptical Feminist* (1980, 66–67).

revolution tends to speak more clearly about what it opposes than about what it embraces. The historicists against impressionism, the New Critics against historicism, the new New Critics against logocentrism and the authority of canons, the feminists against mysogynous art and criticism, black feminists like Bell Hooks (1984) against the biases of white feminists—clearly one could write a history of modern criticism as a sequence of glorious castings off, as a *freeing from*. But all revolutionaries depend on their oppressers far more than they know. Revolutionary critics are enslaved by a nasty law of nature; I can say only what I *can* say, and that will be largely what I have learned to say from the kings and queens I would depose.

FEMINIST CRITICISM AS REPRESENTATIVE ETHICAL CRITICISM

Every reader who faces any kind of ideological disagreement must confront these complexities. What follows in this chapter, both in its emerging clarities and remaining confusions, results from a somewhat surprised surrender to voices previously alien to me: the "feminist critics" who, in their vigor and diversity and originality have compelled me—belatedly, belatedly—to begin listening.

For the purpose of defending ideological criticism, *any* ideological objection to *any* classical text would serve as well as any other. The structure of judgment, and the collection of problems raised by judgment, will be largely the same regardless of the ideology. It might seem, then, that I could just as well choose to discuss in this chapter the anti-Semitism of *The Merchant of Venice* or *Oliver Twist,* or—following Chinua Achebe (1975)—the racism of Conrad's great *Heart of Darkness,* or indeed any offensive belief about religion or social class or politics.

There are many good reasons, however, over and above my personal convictions, for placing feminism at the center here. Perhaps most important, the feminist challenge is presented directly to everyone who deals with any literature of any period or culture. Every literary work implies either that women can enter its imaginative world as equals or that they cannot—that instead they must, in reading, decide whether or not to enter a world in which men are a privileged center.

One of the most striking facts about much of the literature and criticism that has tried to redress various other ideological grievances is that most of it continues to be heavily—though usually unconsciously—biased against women. Like the American founding documents, declaring all "men" equal—except for white women and all blacks—much of the new literature of freedom written by men declares full freedom for all—except of course women, often unmentioned or, if mentioned, still essentially *unimagined,* presented most often as convenient adjuncts, *ficelles,* absurd twitterers, or femmes fatales.[5]

The ideological problem faced in feminist criticism is thus universal. When we add the presence on our scene of many new and powerful feminist voices, we have good reason to place feminist ideology at the center of our inquiry into how ideologies in general might enter critical discourse without making it indistinguishable from politics.[6]

As we saw in Chapter 3, ethical criticism that centers on objectionable ideologies can usually be collapsed into something like a formal syllogism: works that are committed to such-and-such a doctrine are at least to some degree flawed; *this* work is in fact so committed; ergo . . . The criticism that follows here will thus at some points necessarily recall the very structure that I said had helped get ethical criticism into trouble:

1. Any sexist work (whatever "sexist" might mean, and whatever other qualities the sexist work might have) is flawed.

5. Bell Hooks puts it the other way round, in her *Feminist Theory* (1984): white female feminists too often declare full freedom for "all" women—all middle-class white women, that is.

6. To me, the feminists constitute the most original and important movement on the current scene, even more transformative than the deconstructionists. Some would like to think of them as simply one important arm of the deconstructionist movement. The claim is mistaken only because "feminist criticism" ranges much too broadly to be subsumed under any one other school or movement; a feminist Marxist like Barbara Foley is certainly not engaged in the same project as the deconstructionist-feminist Barbara Johnson.

The bibliography of feminist criticism would by now more than fill a book. A good conspectus on its range is found in the successive issues of *Women and Literature,* originally a quarterly and since 1980 an annual edited by Janet Todd. See also *Signs: Journal of Women in Culture and Society,* founded in 1975 under the editorship of Catharine Stimpson.

2. Rabelais's classic satire, my central example here, is, to such-and-such a degree, sexist.

3. Therefore, we must—to some degree—lower our esteem for the work, and perhaps even for the author.

The resulting glimpse of pure logical clarity may be seductive, after the equivocations of my previous efforts. Though such simplicities present obvious dangers, the move to this kind of criticism, against the advice of honorable friends, cannot be avoided. I can only hope that by moving with my eyes open, steadily suspicious of both premises in each bit of logic we come to, I can avoid some of the disasters that follow when the move is made blindfolded.

As I offer now my version of a feminist credo, I naturally hope that you will find it recognizably close to what you think about "sexism" (open or covert), or "misogyny," or "androcentrism." But if you happen to find my standard, or my version of it, offensive, then you might well slot *that* anti-ideology, itself an ideology, into my argument. Or if you feel that Rabelais with his free-ranging ways is beyond criticism,[7] you might conduct an experiment similar to mine with some other work and some other bit of ideology: your flawed classic may be a work that feeds the complacency of the sleepy bourgeoisie; or one that portrays romantic love as a supreme value; or one that shows men as inherently *inferior* to women; or one that is "jingoist," or "sentimental," or "pious," or "self-aggrandizing," or "elitist," or "escapist," or "Anglophile," or "militarist," or "immature," or "sensationalist," or "enmeshed in technological values"—to list only a few critical terms that I've run into recently. I ask you only to remember that it is extremely difficult not to cheat when judging whether ideological criticism is legitimate. When a work's ideology does not happen to offend openly, we are likely to take its fixed norms for granted and attend

7. An early version of this chapter (Booth 1983) raised more cries of outrage than almost anything else I've published: "You cannot judge a classic by standards different from those of its time." My critics have seemed to me quite confused about this matter, saying in the same breath that we should read Rabelais only according to the standards of his time and yet that he was superior on the feminist scale to most other writers of his time. They have all been quite willing in addition to offer judgments against *my* way of working ideologically, without granting me the historicist excuse that I must be—if they are right—simply following the standards of *my* time.

happily to "how well it is made." An astonishing number of critics
have ruled out doctrinal criticism as always irrelevant, while sneaking
it back in whenever a doctrine crops up that offends by openly supporting some conventional ideology.[8] If ideological criticism is always
fallacious, one is as misguided when condemning a work for being
self-indulgent, puritanical, or reactionary as when rejecting it for
undermining belief in God, Church, and Country.

Here, then, is that bit of my ideology that is relevant here:

1. It is unjust to treat individual women as members of a class inherently inferior to men, as deficient simply because they are female. *Corollary.*—To *talk* of women unjustly is to *act* unjustly.
Though the degree of an injustice may vary immensely from praising rape to varying kinds of verbal rape to "harmless" jokes about
dumb broads, frigid cock-teasers, and insatiable farmer's daughters, the *kind* of injustice remains for our purposes the same.
2. *This* work—Rabelais's *Gargantua* and *Pantagruel*—does in fact
treat women in this way.
3. This work commits an unjust act.[9]

The injustice may be subtle; it may be gross. It can occur in works
as sophisticated and wonderful as *Don Giovanni,* as sophisticated and
dubious as John Updike's *The Witches of Eastwick,* or as crude and
offensive as Mickey Spillane's *I, the Jury.* The only way the work can
escape our charge is through demonstration that somehow the injustice is effectively criticized by the work itself: the implied author
does not speak for the injustice but against it. In that case, the minor
premise (number 2 above) is of course faulty: the injustice is committed by *characters within the work* but not by the implied author.
(Another escape for the work would of course be to appeal to some
reader who shares its sexist norms. This is in effect the route chosen by
those who insist that every work be seen only in the light of its own
historical period: "*Everybody* was sexist then, and we have no right to

---

8. The inconsistency in such moves is comparable to what we find in those readings
based on the assumption that all interpretive choices are "indecidable": the *only proper*
reading of such-and-such a work is the one showing that it has no proper reading!

9. We needn't worry too much at this point about whether committing an unjust
act can be considered an *artistic* as well as a moral fault; that distinction has long since
been put in question here.

'privilege' our own views just because they are ours." I shall return to this claim later on.)

Before confronting the difficult case of Rabelais, we should play with the syllogism briefly. It seems to work pretty well when we deal with blatant examples, like the violation of the poor fantasy creatures who, for the delectation of the readers of *Penthouse* magazine and its kind, find themselves at first fearful of and then radiantly pleased by gang-rape:

> Realizing I was almost totally naked and now was locked in a bar at 2:00 a.m. with five strange men and a husband [Vic] who was watching but ignoring me, I yelled at Tom to "come play with me" or I would leave. . . . During the next several hours I was eaten, sucked, fondled, and fucked in every conceivable way. . . . They did whatever they could think to try next. . . . When I awoke late the next afternoon . . . there was Vic with a cup of coffee for each of us. I nearly screamed with joy as he said, "I guess you're a real woman after all."

Such fantasy toys have perhaps been found in sub-literature in every literate society; every male in our society knows that they populate our locker-room anecdotes. Their central act of injustice—turning a woman into something inferior, designed for man's delectation but always threatening to fail him or maim him—can be found in the more polite language of much canonic literature. But in the classics we may feel a bit less comfortable with the syllogism:

SONG

Goe, and catche a falling starre,
  Get with child a mandrake roote,
Tell me, where all past yeares are,
  Or who cleft the Divels foot,
Teach me to heare Mermaides singing,
  Or to keep off envies stinging,
    And finde
    What winde
Serves to advance an honest minde.

So far John Donne's playful lamentation might be taken as applying to all human beings. But the song quickly turns into an indictment, clearly written by a man to delight men, confirming their view of how women invariably betray them.

If thou beest borne to strange sights,
  Things invisible to see,
Ride ten thousand daies and nights,
  Till age snow white haires on thee,

Thou, when thou retorn'st, wilt tell mee
All strange wonders that befell thee,
  And sweare
  No where
Lives a woman true, and faire.

If thou findst one, let mee know,
  Such a Pilgrimage were sweet;
Yet doe not, I would not goe,
  Though at next doore wee might meet,
Though shee were true, when you met her,
And last, till you write your letter,
  Yet shee
  Will bee
False, ere I come, to two, or three.

         ([1633] 1967, 90)

Male readers who have loved this poem as much as I will not want to be asked—at least I did not want to be asked—to think about whether women read it in our way. I have "taught" the poem, in years past, and it never occurred to me to take account of differences between the feelings of male and female students. The suppression might not seem strange if, with an eye toward the "affective fallacy," I had systematically excluded *all* personal responses. But the version of objective criticism that I was taught at Chicago systematically included emotional response in every formal analysis, and one might think that I would have listened for clues about how such a poem strikes female readers.

The responses I dealt with were those of the "proper" reader, meaning the reader implied by the poem. So far as I can remember,[10] I never took seriously responses that were essentially—not accidentally—different from those that Donne seemed to ask for. I now suppose that though the women in my classes for the most part tried to fake the reading that "the poem asks for," their true reactions were largely apathy, puzzlement, shame, anger, or a distanced pleasure in the formal structure. Their unspoken questions could have run like this: Why

---

10. I'm remembering here classes in the 1950s and early 1960s. In 1985 I again assigned the poem and made a strong effort to elicit genuine responses. The results would have surprised my younger self, convinced as he was that he was teaching with an open mind. Though some women "liked" the poem and some men "disliked" it, most of the women were indifferent or hostile. The only real enthusiasts were men.

are the males here more delighted than I am? In what sense, if any, is this would-be friend offering any pleasure that can be shared in full reciprocity?

A fully equal pleasure is indeed claimed by some women—in my experience invariably those who have been trained in contemporary criticism. In the summer of 1987 I conducted a discussion of "Go and Catch a Falling Star" with a large group of English teachers, about half of them women. Most of them had read the poem before, and most claimed that it had always left them indifferent or irritated, even as they admired its "artistry." But some of those who thought of themselves as professional critics scoffed at the very idea of worrying about "message." Why should we let annoyance at the male poet's direct assertion that women are inherently false and fickle interfere with our aesthetic responses? One said, "I can enter imaginatively into the world of the poem just as well as any man. Besides, Donne is not speaking in his own person—he is creating a persona." Uh huh. Perhaps. Nobody could ever disprove the claim. But meanwhile we do know one thing for sure: many male readers, including at least one young male English teacher (myself years ago), have found in the poem a delightful reinforcement, from "high culture," of our "natural" sense of male superiority. Can we really claim that such a fact is irrelevant to critical talk about the poem's true worth "*as poetry*"?

One obvious objection to such inquiry, before we turn to Rabelais: Why should we spend our time picking on the sexism of great writers of the past when more pressing violations are committed daily by the multi-billion-dollar pornographic industry? *Penthouse* "The International Magazine for Men" boasts that more than five million people every month buy, and presumably read, the kind of stuff I quoted earlier. And as we all know, there are scores of other such magazines, full of stories and pictures of a violent dreadful degradation.[11] They account, my neighborhood news vendor tells me, for more than half of his total business. The burgeoning movie cassette rental business lists each month more X-rated titles than all the others combined; it is claimed that more than one thousand such fictions are produced each

---

11. Andrea Dworkin does a good—that is, horrifying—job of description in *Pornography: Men Possessing Women* (1981).

year. Feminist critics confirm my limited sampling when they say that
most of those hard- and soft-core romps are immeasurably more harmful to the spirit of both male and female viewers than any literary classic we might call to account in our court of ethical law. Add to these
the millions of paperback "adult" books at this moment teaching
young males that the ideal woman enjoys nothing so much as rape,
unless it's being battered, and you have, shall we say, an interesting,
unprecedented "educational" experiment? Yet if Donne or Rabelais
this month found five hundred spontaneous readers outside college
classes, we'd all be surprised. Why, then, aim our critical guns at them?

Any answer I can think of will at best serve only for the duration of
this chapter, since the politics of gross popular sexism in America does
cry out both for interpretation and for open battle; more of us should
surely work at the problem of how to counteract this flood of poison,
short of the kind of censorship that would take with it much else that
we care for. But since "among us critics" there are no serious defenders of the *Penthouse* and *Hustler* kind of thing,[12] the consequences for
critical theory, and for what we all do as teachers and students, will be
raised more clearly if we face works that cannot be dismissed as trash,
quite apart from their ideology.

RABELAIS'S MASCULINE LAUGHTER

The question we face, then, as believers in feminist (or any other)
ideology, is this: Am I free, in interpreting and criticizing a work of art,
free to employ that ideology as one element in my appraisal of its artistic value? Or is my *freedom from* best served by casting off such inhib-

---

12. You *do* want to defend it? As literature? As something to be "taught" the way
one might teach Donne? I find it hard to believe you. Whether you and I will defend
Penthouse's right to manufacture such stuff is another question. The Attorney General's
Commission on Pornography has just now [1986] issued its call for public action
against pornography. The published responses seem either to hail the call for action and
ignore the dangers of censorship or to attack the commission as a censor and ignore the
evidence that pornography does real harm. Mike Royko, in his syndicated column,
simply hooted at the commission for having included in their report the very stuff that
they attacked. He did not even mention the many studies that show—for example—the
appalling effects on males' opinions about rape when they view pornography that portrays women "enjoying it."

iting limits to "openness" and letting art works behave in any way they please, as long as they do so "artistically"? A full answer to such questions is beyond any one inquirer; it will be provided by our cultural history, as many new feminists and their critics discover the powers and dangers of ideological criticism.[13] All I can do here is sketch the issues raised for me by a re-reading of the three great books of Rabelais's *Gargantua* and *Pantagruel,* works that have stirred controversy about their sexism from their first publication early in the sixteenth century.[14]

What might it mean to say, as many have said before me, and as many others have said we *shouldn't* say, that Rabelais's classics are flawed by their sexism—or, in earlier language, their anti-feminism? These books were published at a time when the great *querelle des femmes,* begun in medieval times (or one might even say, in classical times), was still raging. They reveal Rabelais as master of every topic of such debates.

Readers have always disagreed, however, about precisely where he stands on the issues he dramatizes: Was he *for* women or *against* them? Did he favor marriage or oppose it? Most scholars agree that he did not side with the feminists in the *querelle des femmes,* and nobody denies that his term "Pantagruelist" "came to be synonymous with 'woman-hater'" (Rabelais 1946, 376). Still there is great disagreement about whether or not he can be charged with sexism. Our conclusion will depend on many variables: our methods of reading, our views of women's true deserts, our notion of whether an author can be "ex-

13. I know that some women resent the intrusion by any male into feminist territory: on the one hand, I cannot, as a male, possibly have anything pertinent to say about it; and on the other, I threaten, as an "establishment figure," to co-opt the movement. My various responses are not very effective, since they boil down to "you pursue your freedom, and I'll pursue mine." I do find an interesting parallel between the argument that males cannot possibly do pertinent feminist criticism and the widespread claims of only a few decades ago that Jews should not be professors of English because they could not grasp the spirit of a predominantly Christian literature.

14. A good summary of the state of the quarrel in Rabelais's time is given in Screech 1958. A bibliography of nearly nine hundred primary Renaissance texts about women, many of them directly concerned with the quarrel, is given in Kelso 1956. A bibliography of both primary and secondary texts dealing with the question of feminism and Rabelais is given in Lerner 1976. Every issue of *Etudes Rabelaisiennes* adds to the overwhelming bibliography. My only excuse for adding to the endless debate is that it provides the best illustration I can find of the problems implicit in all doctrinal criticism.

cused" by referring to standards in his own time, and so on. Lefranc concludes: "In reality, this former monk was not a lover of women; he obviously remains faithful to the old *gauloise* tradition" (qtd. in Rabelais 1946, 373). Putnam, on the other hand, turns handsprings to defend Rabelais: We are to remember that he is complex; that he is really attacking only the "old, outmoded, and, in the eyes of many of the Renaissance humanists, essentially false ideal of a lingering medieval chivalry"; that what he really advocates is "a new and higher, more modern and civilized conception of marriage, based upon mutual trust, respect, and companionship," and so on. His final excuse is the one most pertinent to us here: the "anti-feminist theme lends itself to Rabelais' particular brand of humor, his rollicking satire and broad horse-play. . . . [O]ne has the feeling that he simply could not resist it" (377). But isn't that precisely what it means to be sexist—revealing an inability to resist mocking women as a class?

The technical problem, as we saw in Chapter 4, is primarily that of deciding what it is that we are trying to judge. A surprising amount of worthless attack and defense has been conducted as if the problem were to determine what Rabelais *says* about women. Rival critics simply collect favorable and unfavorable propositions from the works and balance them against each other. But what we seek, once again, will not be words or propositions in isolation, or even overall "themes," but the total pattern of desires and rewards that the author commits us to. Rabelais cannot be blamed for an act of injustice unless we have some reason to believe that his work as a whole—the complete imaginative offering, the total pattern of desire and fulfillment that we enjoy—is vulnerable to the charge. In short, ideological criticism depends on discovering not the ideology *in* the form but the ideology *of* the form.

Judging isolated parts is particularly pointless in a work as rich as Rabelais's, offering as it does a marvelous encyclopedic satire against every conceivable crazy way of talking. An easy and useless case for the charge of sexism could be made—and indeed it has often been made—simply by listing the many passages in which women are mocked, humiliated, or explicitly declared inferior to men. One character, Rondibilis, argues (following the tradition set by classical philosophers) that a woman is inherently, inescapably, biologically, a failed or botched man. He describes all of "her" grotesque flaws and concludes: "I've thought it all over a hundred and five times, and I am sure I do not know what conclusion to come to, unless it is that, in turning out woman, Nature had more in mind the social delectation of man and the perpetuation of the human species than she did the perfecting of individual womankind" (Rabelais 1946, 477; bk. 3, ch. 32 in the original). An astonishing number of critics from the sixteenth century on have taken such statements as self-evidently coming from Rabelais himself, proving his deep bias against women. But as direct signs of character, they work only against the speakers—Rondibilis, Panurge, occasionally Gargantua himself. The elementary point can never be repeated too often, since it is so often ignored: no matter how offensive such views seem, they cannot prove Rabelais offensive unless we discover that, in context, they seem to us intended as the views of the implied author (or—what amounts to the same thing—they remain uncorrected, for a given reader, by the rest of the book).

The fact is that they do appear to be corrected, or at least radically undermined, by other passages. It has been easy for defenders of Rabelais to point to many moments that show a much different picture. Consider the utopian Abbey of Thélème at the end of *Gargantua* (that is, of the First Book, written, or at any rate published, in 1534, a couple of years after *Pantagruel,* the Second Book). In constructing what seems to be an ideal of a human community, Rabelais shows women in a light totally foreign to the vision of Rondibilis: they are admitted to the abbey equally with men; they are given, so the text directly states, equal rights in the daily conduct of the abbey; they are educated in full equality in the same gracious arts and sciences as the men. And they are equally free to choose how to spend their days. Obviously, a Rondibilis could not have created that carefree abbey.

Or consider another favorite passage of the defenders of Rabelais, the highly favorable description of the ideal wife, spoken by the theologian Hippothadeus as he advises Panurge about how to avoid cuckolding. He first describes all of the qualities of the wife most to be recommended: "Commendable extraction, descended of honest parents, and instructed in all piety and virtue; . . . one loving and fearing God . . . ; and finally, one who, standing in awe of the divine majesty of the Most High, will be loth to offend Him and lose the favourable kindness of His grace, through any defect of faith or transgression against the ordinances of His holy law, wherein adultery is most rigorously forbidden, and a close adherence to her husband alone most strictly and severely enjoined; yea, in such sort, that she is to cherish, serve and love him above anything next to God, that meriteth to be beloved" (Rabelais 1963, 2:538; bk. 3, ch. 30 in the original).[15]

A feminist might still bridle at the explicitly submissive role assigned here, but what follows in the text has impressed critics looking for evidence in defense of Rabelais:

> In the interim, for the better schooling of her in these instructions, and that the wholesome doctrine of a matrimonial duty may take the deeper root in her mind, you [Panurge] must needs carry yourself so on your part, and your behavior is to be such, that you are to go before her in a good example, by entertaining her unfeignedly with a conjugal amity, by continually approving yourself, in all your words and actions, a faithful and discreet husband, and by living not only at home and privately with your own household and family, but in the face also of all men and open view of the world, devoutly, virtuously and chastely, as you would have her on her side to deport and demean herself towards you. . . . Just so should you be a pattern to your wife, in virtue, goodly zeal and true devotion.
>
> (Rabelais 1963, 2: 538–39)

Panurge dismisses this advice with a twist of his whiskers and a claim that he never saw a woman to match Hippothadeus's ideal: "Without all doubt she is dead, and truly, to my best remembrance, I never saw her—the Lord forgive me!" (539). Does this conclusion mock mocking Panurge for his failure to hear what a man must do to deserve a good woman? Or does it mock the theologian for naive and preachy idealism? Readers have seen it both ways. But in either view the question still remains: How are such bits viewed by the work as a whole? Surely the fact that critical history has been able to compile *double* columns, "attacks" and "defenses," and not just the sexist column that the word "Rabelaisian" connotes, exonerates the author at least from simple charges that are based on what his characters say.

What's more, if surface attitudes count, we ought to count the attacks on *males*. We find hundreds of satirical pages with no references to women whatever. Indeed, *Gargantua* and *Pantagruel,* the two first

---

15. Putnam, whose translation (1946) is in general more reliable than the livelier Urquhart-Le Motteux (Rabelais [1737] 1963), does not include this chapter in his edition.

books, are in no sense "about" women or even "about" men and
women together. It is true that much of the Third Book, published
fourteen years after *Pantagruel,* is ostensibly about Panurge's attempt
to decide whether to marry and how, if he marries, to avoid being
cuckolded. But the central subject is more often something like "zany
reasoning" than "the nobility or baseness of women."

Propositions *about* women can tell us nothing, then, until we ask:
Who utters them? In what circumstances? In what tone? With what
qualification by other utterances? And, most important of all: What is
the quality of our emotional response, point by point and overall? Unless we face such questions, we can at most establish that the *narrator,*
Alcofribas, exhibits a leaning toward sexism. For all we yet know, Alcofribas could have been used by Rabelais to mock sexism ironically,
just as Mark Twain sometimes used Huck Finn and others to expose
racist language ironically. "Anybody hurt?" asks Aunt Sally. "No'm,"
Huck replies. "Killed a nigger."

BAKHTIN'S RABELAIS

There is no escape then from the task, difficult as it is, of appraising
the quality of the response invited by the whole work: What will it do
with or to us if we surrender our imaginations to its paths? It is to
Mikhail Bakhtin's credit that in his fine book on Rabelais (1968)
he faces this question head-on. Generations of critics have accused
Rabelais of a moral fault, that of being "Rabelaisian." It is not just
prudes who have said "Yes, of course, a great comic (or satiric) genius,
but unfortunately he is coarse, gross, base; he asks us to laugh in ways
that no civilized reader should laugh, at scenes that no civilized reader
can enjoy." Bakhtin refuses to offer the easy reply we have seen so often
here—the claim that moral questions about comedy or satire represent
an absurd confusion of the aesthetic and practical domains. Instead he
accepts the charge: if Rabelais is in fact what is usually meant by
"Rabelaisian," if Rabelais does ask us simply to snigger at dirty words
scrawled on toilet walls, then the book is not by any means worthy of
the praise it has received; the ethical fault *is* an aesthetic fault. But if
the quality of the imaginative experience, and particularly of the *center*
of that experience—our laughter—can be defended on ideological

grounds (in the broad sense of the word "ideological" as used by Bakhtin), then Rabelais is redeemed. Thus, though the ideological test is subtle and complex, it *is* one major test. It cannot be applied in separation from inquiry into the work as a created form: the ideology is not something separable from the form, and the form is not something separable from our emotional engagement with it. (The question we come to later, whether judgments about it can be separated from historical placement, is something else again; Bakhtin would seem to answer yes and no.) [16]

If this is "ideological" or "sociological" criticism, it is also "affective" and "historical" and "expressive." It is both "author criticism" and "reader criticism." The laughter we appraise is not only what we infer in Rabelais himself, but also what we find in his society as influencing his work. And it is what we find in ourselves. Thus a great deal is at stake when we ask, with Bakhtin, "What is the quality of that laughter?" Generalized to include all qualities, the question will become, "What is the quality of the imagination that wrought this book?" And that will be no different from the question, "What is the quality of the effects, in us as readers, of reading this book in what *seems to us* to be its own terms?"—a question that immediately forces "us" to ask, "Who are 'we'?"

From the beginning, many readers have been offended by the more extreme bits of scatology and bawdry in the book, especially those that seem to ask us to laugh at women *because* they are women and hence inferior. How are we to respond, for example, to the famous episode that almost everyone would consider as in itself sexist, the trick Panurge plays upon the Lady of Paris who refuses his advances? He sprinkles her gown with the ground-up pieces of the genitals of a bitch in heat and then withdraws to watch the sport, as all the male dogs of Paris assemble to piss on her, head to toe ("la sentens et pissans. . . . C'estoyt la plus grande villanie du monde. . . . Un grand levrier luy

---

16. I "discovered" Bakhtin midway in the writing of this book; I wish I had known his work twenty-eight years ago as I completed *The Rhetoric of Fiction*. His voice can be found on many pages in *Company*. I give a detailed account of my debts and reservations in Bakhtin 1984, and I discuss his treatment of Rabelais more fully in my earlier published version of this chapter (1983).

pissa sur la teste" [Rabelais 1922, vol. 4, bk. 2, ch. 22, p. 241]). She flees through the streets of Paris, pursued and pissed on by more and more dogs, laughed at by all observers, her predicament later laughed at again when Panurge tells Pantagruel about it. And Pantagruel, who by this point is by no means clearly distanced from Rabelais, "found the whole show both original and delightful" ("trouva [le mystere] fort beau et nouveau" [243]). Her offense, remember, is simply that she turned Panurge down and—I suppose—that she is a woman of high degree.[17]

Or what shall we say about Panurge's suggestion of how to build an impregnable wall? You should build it of women's "what-you-may-call-thems," he says. "What the devil could knock down a wall like that? There is no metal that is so resistant to blows, and then, when the culverins came to rub up against them, you'd damned soon see the blessed fruit of the old pox distilled in a fine rain." The only drawback he can see is that such a wall would attract flies that would "collect there and do their dung," and all the work would be spoiled. But then that difficulty might be obviated; one must wipe (esmoucheter; Putnam translates the verb as "fly-swat") them with "nice foxes' tails or a big ass's prick [gros vietz d'azes] from Provence" (Rabelais 1946, 301; bk. 2, ch. 15 in the original).

Bakhtin recognizes that any full defense of Rabelais must deal with the quality of our laughter during such moments. Though his main effort is to refute those who would call Rabelais's laughter base or destructive, he makes quite explicit the claim that though Rabelais was not, as many have claimed, on the side of the feminists in the great querelle, his laughter, so often using women as its object, is finally the

---

17. The scene is often chosen by illustrators and is used for the cover of the MIT Press paperback edition of Bakhtin's *Rabelais and His World*. Illustrators generally soften the harsh details: the dogs are shown scurrying about the great lady, with at most an occasional leg lifted over her slippers.

One of my readers has suggested that the whole scene is centered not on the lady as representative of her sex but as representative of the haughty upper classes. Another friend sees it, as does Bakhtin, not as ridiculing women but as a healthy comment on our sexuality in general. No doubt both elements are present; both might be encompassed in Bakhtin's notion of carnival laughter. But both seem to me too easy. The whole episode consists of a relatively sustained wooing by Panurge, with only a hint or two of the possibility that the lady's rejections may be hypocritical. The laughter it invites is surely informed with the feeling that "that's exactly what those resistant bitches deserve."

expression of a healthy counter-ideology, an ideology invaluable in his time as in our own.

Bawdy, scatological laughter for Bakhtin can be a great progressive force, the expression of an ideology that opposes the official and authoritarian languages that dominate our surfaces. He sees Rabelais's period and his work as the last full expression of a folk wisdom that could enjoy a harmonious dialogue between the "lower" body and the "higher" and more official "spirit": the "voice" of the body transforms monologue into chorus. Carnival laughter, the intrusion of everything forbidden or slanderous or joyfully blasphemous into the purified domains of officialdom, expressed a complex sense that the material body was not unequivocally base: every death contains within it the meaning of rebirth, every birth comes from the same region of the body as does the excremental. And the excremental is itself a source of regeneration—it manures life just as the dogs' urine in Panurge's trick becomes the source of a well-known "modern" creek.

In this view Rabelais represents a possibility that the world later lost, the possibility for what Bakhtin calls "grotesque realism." When Rabelais and his predecessors made sexual and scatological jokes, they were not serving a sniggering laughter that divorced spirit from body, seeing the flesh as merely dirty. References to the lower body were not simply nasty or degrading: they were used to produce laughter that was regenerative, affirmative, healing, and—perhaps most important—politically progressive. When the natural forces of joyful celebration of the lower body reached their peak, in time of carnival, people were healed with a laughter that was lost when, in later centuries, the body, and especially the lower body, came to be viewed as entirely negative and shameful.

Bakhtin distinguishes two strands in the "Gallic tradition" of portrayals of women. The ascetic Christian tradition opposed neo-Platonist idealizing of women by showing them as "the incarnation of sin, the temptation of the flesh" (1968, 240). But the "popular comic tradition," he says, was in no way simply hostile to women, though it provides plenty of material that may look sexist when viewed out of context. It saw women as representing "the material bodily lower stratum; she is the incarnation of this stratum that degrades and regenerates simultaneously. She is ambivalent. She debases, brings down to earth, lends a bodily substance to things, and destroys; but, first of all, she is the principle that gives birth. She is the womb. Such is woman's image in the popular comic tradition" (240). To treat her as such, Bakhtin goes on, is by no means to be guilty of anti-feminism. "We must note that the image of the woman in the 'Gallic tradition,' like other images in this tradition, is given on the level of ambivalent laughter, at once mocking, destructive, and joyfully reasserting. Can it be said that this tradition offers a negative, hostile attitude toward woman? Obviously not. The image is ambivalent" (241).

It is the polarized treatment of this ambiguous image in later centuries that for Bakhtin trivializes it, turning woman into a merely "wayward, sensual, concupiscent character of falsehood, materialism, and baseness" (240). As "considered by [both] the ascetic tendencies of Christianity and the moralistic abstract thought of modern satirists, the Gallic image loses its positive pole and becomes purely negative" (241). Thus we have a double answer in Bakhtin to the question of whether Rabelais was ideologically defensible on the feminist issue. No, he did not support the feminist cause in the great quarrel—but then the feminist position was itself a simplified debasement of women in the misleading form of idealization. On the other hand, yes, he was essentially defensible on "the woman question" when we place him in his true tradition, the tradition of the carnivalesque laughter of grotesque realism, the tradition of a true ambivalence about the destructive *and* energizing powers of the lower body. If we imagine the world that Rabelais imagined, and laugh as he would have us laugh, we are healed.

A REPLY TO BAKHTIN

Bakhtin's defense is impressive, especially since it is buttressed by a sympathetic reconstruction of Rabelais's historical situation.[18] Surely after reading it we moderns, freed as we already were of Victorian prejudices about scatology, should be able to revel in Rabelais's comedy in something like the healthy spirit in which 'twas writ?

Unfortunately, "we" have all this while been ignoring a crucial

---

18. I feel incompetent to address the important question of whether it is historically sound. Two medievalist friends have assured me that Bakhtin is "all wrong about how carnival worked."

question: Who are "we" who laugh; who are those to whom the defense is being written; who are those who are healed by this laughter? The questions raised with great force by Edward Said—"Who writes? For whom is the writing being done?" (1983, 7)—have all this while gone begging. And as soon as we raise them, we see that just as the original *querelle des femmes* was conducted largely by men, accusers and champions, this exoneration of carnival laughter is conducted by and for men, ignoring or playing down the evidence that Rabelais himself largely excludes women. A man of great genius wrote a book offering a rich imaginative experience to men of sensitive and liberal spirit, and a male critic of great genius wrote a defense of that great book, addressed to other men. Just as the voices of women are flatly excluded from Bakhtin's own work—sex is not even included among the sources of the "languages we are made of"—they never enter, even by remote implication, the work of Rabelais.

It is in the nature of the case that I cannot fully prove my claim. I can assert that if you go read or re-read Rabelais now, you will find both a surviving masterpiece and its serious flaw. I can ask you to question male and female readers and discover how few women like Rabelais *very* much—as much as the many males who have written about it. Or I could take you through a further sampling of passages. What I cannot do is bring before us the very thing I am trying to talk about: the central imaginative experience offered by Rabelais to readers of his time or of ours.

We can, however, look closely at fragmentary evidence to see who is included and who is excluded. An examination of the actual language of almost any passage, whether it at first appears superficially pro- or anti-feminist, shows quite clearly who the laughers are and how they laugh: they are men. Our basic criterion of reciprocity is denied to one-half of all possible readers.

Consider the opening addresses to the readers of each successive book. Those readers are invariably "lads," "drinking comrades," "syphilitic blades," "gentlemen," "Lords," "paternal worships." The Second Book (*Pantagruel*, which was the first of the three books to be published) begins: "Most illustrious and most chivalrous champions, gentlemen and others, . . . you have already seen, read, and are familiar with . . . *Gargantua*, and, like true believers, have right gallantly given [it] credence; and more than once you have passed the time with the ladies—God bless 'em—and the young ladies, when you were out of any other conversation, by telling them fine long stories from those chronicles" (1946, 224).[19] Quite clearly those "honorable dames et damoyselles" who listen to their masters' reading are not invited to pick up the book on their own, though they are expected to enjoy their menfolks' retelling of the juicier narratives.

A possible exception to this exclusion of an entire class of readers is the dedication of the Third Book to "the soul of Marguerite, Queen of Navarre," urging her soul to descend from the ecstatic heights of the queen's recently embraced mysticism in order to read "this third history / Of the joyous deeds of good Pantagruel" (386). Since it is likely that the queen in fact read Rabelais (Rabelais 1931, vol. 5, p. xix), it seems probable that other educated women of the time did so too. But even if we knew that every literate woman read him cover to cover, that knowledge would not affect our conclusions, any more than discovering that women read Fitzgerald and Faulkner with pleasure would settle whether Fitzgerald's and Faulkner's works are—as I would claim—to some degree marred by sexism.

Alerted by such prefatory addresses, we see immediately that though a great deal of the work is addressed to interests and responses we all might share, there is really no passage that counters the general address to males and consequent exclusion of females.

First, there is the obvious point that there are no significant female characters. The two possible exceptions are the giant mothers Gargamelle and Badebec. Gargantua's grief over the death of his beloved wife, for example, is sometimes cited as a sign that women *are* important in the work. But the whole passage is handled as a source of male laughter; the woman is simply expendable as Gargantua balances the two male emotions, grief over losing a useful wife and joy over gaining an heir. The epitaph that Gargantua composes concludes with a joke:

HERE LIES ONE NOT TOO REMISS,
WHO DIED THE DAY THAT SHE PASSED OUT
(Rabelais 1946, 241)

19. Scholarly tradition says that this "*Gargantua*" refers not to Rabelais's work but to a popular anonymous story of giants, "*Les Grandes et Inestimables Cronicques: Du grant et enorme geant Gargantua*," published in 1532, the same year as Rabelais's first volume, *Pantagruel*. I suspect, with no evidence but my sense of Rabelais's character, that he had some role even in the first *Gargantua*.

CY GIST SON CORPS, LEQUEL VESQUIT SANS VICE,
ET MOURUT L'AN ET JOUR QUE TRESPASSA.
(Rabelais 1922, 3:41)

It is true, as defenders of Rabelais have always noted, that all the male characters are mocked too, even the heroes. But they are always mocked for some reason other than their maleness, some silly or vicious act or some professional quirk. They are absurd as individuals or as members of particular groups. Women, like the lady of Paris, are absurd *because* they are women and because they refuse to serve the male world the way a woman should.

A second line of defense might be found in the passages that speak favorably of women. But all such passages are addressed to men as the sole arbiters and centers of interest.[20] Consider again the Abbey of Thélème (1946, 196–216), where Gargantua and Friar John have set up no rules except one, *Fay ce que vouldras*—"Do what thou wouldst." To make the rule work, Gargantua has provided that nobody can enter the convent except handsome healthy people who, because they are "free born and well born, well brought up, and used to decent society," are possessed "by nature" of the unfailing instinct to do right, that is, a sense of honor (214). He explains that all are to be educated alike, male and female: "They were all so nobly educated that there was not, in their whole number a single one, man or woman, who was not able to read, write, sing, play musical instruments, and speak five or six languages, composing in these languages both poetry and prose" (215).

So far, so good. But now note the summary of who these people are: "In short, there never were seen knights so bold, so gallant, so clever on horse and on foot, more vigorous, or more adept at handling all kinds of weapons. . . . There never were seen ladies so well groomed, so pretty, less boring, or more skilled at hand and needlework and in every respectable feminine activity" (215). The men bold, gallant, good at riding, hunting, and war; the women well groomed, pretty, less boring (less boring *to whom?*), and skilled in handwork and other respectable feminine activities.

Rabelais goes on to reveal—and I feel fairly sure that the revelation

20. For a brief debate about this point see Berrong 1985.

is quite unconscious—just how unequal the ladies really were. "For this reason [that is, because they were all such paragons], when the time came that any member of this abbey . . . wished to leave, he always took with him one of the ladies, the one who had taken him for her devoted follower, and the two of them were then married." And they "remained as ardent lovers at the end of their days, as they had been on the first day of their honeymoon" (215). One must ask, What happens here to the *lady* who might decide on her own to leave the abbey? She is simply not mentioned, not thought about, and never missed, so far as I can determine, until now, though hundreds of pages have been written praising Rabelais for imagining a society providing total equality. Some may object that it would have been unthinkable in Rabelais's time to go that far, to allow *a lady* the freedom to leave utopia and return to the real world, taking with her some anonymous will-less male who was her choice. To which I must answer, "Of course. But isn't that what we are talking about: human ideals, how they are created in art and thus implanted in readers and left uncriticized—even by the subtlest of critics, a Bakhtin who makes it his business both to discover ideologies as revealed by language and to do justice to every genuine human voice?"

We should also ask, continuing a project that allows us to blame Rabelais for oversights that no man of his time could possibly have failed to commit, Whose dream of bliss does this abbey realize? Its one most conspicuous deletion from normal human life is children, along with the marriage customs and parental responsibilities that go with having children. "Do what thou wouldst"—an enspiriting slogan for single males in the prime of life! But "Do what thou wouldst"—in a world that includes the bearing and caring for children? In a world that includes not just women who engage in pastimes pleasing to carefree men, but women with real responsibilities, to themselves as well as to others? No, this is a male's dream offered to males—or perhaps we should call it a monkish male's dream: a monastery society not only fed by the lower orders but equipped, presumably, with a steady supply of young men and women who have been reared by—whom?

The truth is that nowhere in Rabelais does one find any hint of an effort to imagine any woman's point of view or to incorporate women into a dialogue. His rare encomiums, like most male efforts to praise women as a class, lack all the richness of detail that he observes in an astonishing range of male characters. He can acknowledge women's existence; he can mock them or praise them, as a class. What he cannot or will not do is *see* them. And the "proper reader" is led to see them as entirely alien.

We pass the sentence, then: Rabelais has to some degree failed to do imaginative justice to one half of human reality—women. The minor premise is complete, and the ethical judgment follows. Unless we are willing to give up our major premise and say that such injustices do not concern us, we must, in all friendliness, stand firmly opposed to our friend on this one point: Rabelais is unjust to women not simply in the superficial ways that the traditions have claimed but, to some degree, in much of his central imaginative act.

OTHER VOICES FROM WITHIN: OBJECTIONS AND PROBLEMS

Where does all this leave us when we begin to think not about Rabelais's responsibility to treat women justly and truly but about other responsibilities, particularly those of the reader to the author and to the reader's self? We can face these responsibilities best by considering the more obvious objections that one feels about applying doctrinal criticism in this way to a great and enduring classic. Though I shall offer "answers" to each of the following objections, I do not find that any of my responses free me from the questions: the objections live on in my own thinking, as warnings about potential losses ahead.

"You Have Violated History"

"You have been radically unjust to Rabelais, in your failure to see him *in his own time* and to recognize just how far his imagination ranged beyond that of most of his contemporaries. Your indictment is irrelevant, because it could be made against a great majority of the classics written before our time—and against almost *every* fiction written in Rabelais's time. He was indeed a male-centered author writing primarily for males and reinforcing the view that women are at best a delectation for the life of man and at worst a threat, a nuisance, or a necessary evil. But since he in fact works harder to imagine an apologia for women than do most of his contemporaries, why can't we simply place him among them and praise him for what he does do?"

One reads many such statements, particularly by male critics, in response to what they consider the excesses of feminist criticism. But this defense is not confined to males. The apology by historical placement plays a heavy role in Julianna Kitty Lerner's claim that Rabelais was actually a feminist: "Rabelais in many ways transcended his contemporaries in his feminist views" (1976, 217).

Lerner is right that many of Rabelais's contemporaries were much harder on women than he: they often sound like Rondibilis. Reading some of their stuff does indeed provide a valid *ad hominem* defense for Rabelais, and surely that to some degree excuses the books. Since he wrote before anyone (but Plato?) had thought more than ten minutes about what equality for women might mean or about what the religious, literary, and political traditions had done to women, he could hardly be expected to leap into an entirely different order of imagination.[21] Indeed I have already given evidence that with far less historical excuse I myself uncritically accepted, until well past middle age, something like the perspective he offers. A man who was able to write an entire dissertation on *Tristram Shandy* without once even thinking about, let alone mentioning, the problem of its sexism, can hardly feel any moral superiority in his critique of Rabelais. Only now does it occur to me to check my youthful bibliography: How many women, do you suppose, had written on *Tristram Shandy*, in nearly two hundred years, with sufficient quality (for me) to include them when I selected

---

21. The major exception I know of is Chaucer, who about a century and a half earlier had shown that a male artist's imagination need not confine itself to male worlds. The trio of women in *The Canterbury Tales*—the Prioress, the Second Nun, and the Wife of Bath—in their vivid variety make a sharp contrast with Rabelais's uniform stereotypes, as indeed they do with Montaigne's later casual stereotypings: the "three good women" who choose to die with their husbands (Montaigne [1588] 1958, bk. 2, no. 35, pp. 563–69), the devoted mother to whom he addresses an essay on the affection of *fathers* (bk. 2, no. 8, pp. 278–93), the mothers who should not have control over their husbands' estates because their "capricious" feminine judgment will lead them to botch the job (bk. 2, no. 8, p. 290). For a persuasive defense of Chaucer's imaginative power in creating the Wife of Bath, see Bolton 1980.

my fifty-item bibliography? Just two, both Germans, both writing in
the 1930s, about questions of form and technique. Yet I remember that
I *had* read Virginia Woolf and several other women writers on Sterne;
I just did not bother to list them!

Still, the historical apology will not do. For one thing, Rabelais
himself would no doubt view any plea for historical relativism with
contempt. As Bakhtin says, "Rabelais has no neutral words; we always
hear a mixture of praise and abuse. But this is the praise and abuse of
the whole. . . . The point of view of the whole is far from being neutral
and indifferent. It is not the dispassionate position of a third party, for
there is no place for a third party in the world of becoming. The whole
simultaneously praises and abuses" (1968, 415–16). In every part of
Bakhtin's work it is clear that he hails Rabelais's simultaneous celebration and comic denigration of the lower body as a mark of an ideological—that is, artistic—superiority to those corrupted divorces of spirit
from body that too often followed the move into the "modern world
system." He is eager to show, as part of the evidence for Rabelais's
greatness, that "[i]n the political conflicts of his time Rabelais took the
most advanced and progressive positions" (452). How could I argue
that I filled my part of the bargain with such a Rabelais if I suppressed
my objections and pretended that all is well? Such "liberal" condescension would get from him the satirical treatment that it deserves.

But in the second place, the historical defense scants my responsibility to myself and my living friends. Based on a comfortable acceptance
of the open misogyny and covert sexism in other cultures and other
classics, it is itself sexist, enabling me, if I take it uncritically, to avoid
facing the "other" honestly—both other times and the other sex. And
this would be to do myself an even greater harm than I do them. That
Rabelais is far from unique is thus the very reason why a critique of his
treatment of women is important. If he were alone, if the other classics
of our tradition were addressed equally to men *and* women, portraying
both with equal imaginative force, implanting favorable or unfavorable
stereotypes in full impartiality, then the tradition itself would criticize
Rabelais for us, and we would have no worries. But of course the reverse is true. Many a classic that seems *less* offensive on its surface turns
out on close reading to be *more* sexist than Rabelais's masterpiece.
The tradition thus does not, on the whole, criticize his work and miti-
gate its possible effects in constituting our views of women. Rather,

insofar as it may excuse Rabelais as one of many, it exacerbates our problems in thinking about this kind of fault, wherever it is found. We merely postpone our problem when we blame the absent cronies, not the thief who got caught.

Finally, the historical answer will not satisfy me because my pleasure in some parts of this text has now been diminished by my fresh reading. My judgment is thus not a theoretical matter. If it were, I could perhaps reject it or change my theory to fit my reading. But the fact is that reading now, try as I may to "suspend my disbelief," I don't laugh at certain parts of this book quite as much or as hard as I once did. What kind of ethics would it be that advised my remaining silent about a scandal like *that?*

When I read, as a young man, the account of how Panurge got his revenge on the Lady of Paris, I was transported with laughter and rushed to tell my (male) friends about it. When I later read Rabelais aloud to my young wife, as she did the ironing(!), she could easily tell that I expected her to be equally delighted. Of course, she did find a lot of it funny; a great deal of it *is* very funny. But now, reading passages like that, even though everything I know about the work as a whole suggests that my earlier response was closer to the spirit of "the work itself," I draw back and start thinking rather than laughing, taking a different kind of pleasure with a *somewhat* diminished text. And it is my feminist criticism that has done the dirty work.

It is not hard to predict what some will want to say to that, "You've lost your sense of humor" or "You don't know how to read 'aesthetically.'" But I would reply that if you really want to take a neutralist position on such a matter, you must be ready to imagine, or to conceive of a woman's imagining, an alternative scene in which the lover is a woman, not Panurge, and the dogs are led to piss on a man as the comic butt—not, remember, because of some vice he has displayed but because he has rejected an obnoxious, aggressive seduction attempt by a woman. In an early draft of this chapter I attempted to construct such a scene. The construction simply would not work. One woman friend said that it was in "impossibly bad taste." But that can't have been what was wrong with it, because the original is in "impossibly bad taste," too. The real trouble was that it implied the wrong way of redressing the evils of sexism: mere role-reversal misses the (historical) point, and gets us nowhere.

The only "Rabelais" I can be fully responsible to confronts me here and now. I do not possess Rabelais's works *then;* I possess them, or they attempt to possess me, *now.* I read him as I read anyone: *in my own time.* Whatever he does to me will be done within my frame of values, not his. For me, here and now, the power of any "past" text to work on me and to reshape me, for good or ill, is thus in this one sense ahistorical. All works that I *re*-work speak to me, bless me or threaten me, where I am, and they speak, more often than not, conflicting messages. To pretend that they are all equally defensible, because we see them in their own time as equally explicable, is to dodge the effects on my own life of my living with them. The only way I can do justice to myself as I re-create their history *in* myself is to place it against my own history and values—and then to decide how to live with the conflicts I discover.

Before pursuing further this painful fact of personal loss, consider another act of injustice that on many scales might seem worse than humiliating women: Rabelais's amused indifference to the burning of heretics. Michael Screech points to jokes about such burnings and concludes that in *Gargantua* Rabelais "positively incites Francis I to send the Principal of the College de Montaigu to the stake, together with his cronies." Screech's defense is again a historical placement: "Renaissance Christians were, on the whole, highly selective with their pity," and besides, Jean de Caturce (if that is who the principal really was based on) was a puritan who tried to substitute Christian prayers for the carnival buffoonery of Twelfth Night—in short, an unsympathetic "sectarian extremist whose death would not call forth Rabelais's pity as a matter of course. All the great figures of the time seem impervious to the sufferings of those they fundamentally disagreed with" (1979, 72–73).

What kind of excuse *is* this? Is it not in structure exactly equivalent to defending every practice of one's own time—genocide, say, or hired killing—if it were to become "widely accepted"? To accept Rabelais's denial of pity for suffering because his contemporaries were on the whole "impervious to the sufferings" of ideological opponents is surely to maim our critical faculties. To make myself believe that Rabelais's imaginative gifts would be no greater if he had been able to see that it is evil to burn heretics is equivalent to saying that my own imaginative life should passively respond to whatever is offered to it.

We can go further. Suppose I am a modern who would never burn a heretic but who would happily endorse persecution and harassment of political enemies; everyone knows that the world of the 1980s is populated with millions of such people. If I am one of them and happen to read Rabelais, no doubt I will laugh comfortably at the burning of heretics. But can I—the real person observing that imaginary self— argue that that other self reads best if he simply enjoys the work "in its own terms," without trying to question this bit of its ideology? In short, if I cannot say that there is something wrong, really wrong, about a casual approval of the burning of heretics, then indeed we are in the condition of subjectivism that threatened us when we began.

"You Have Committed Cultural Imperialism"

We have landed once again in the problem of subjectivism, this time in a form that asks us to confront the complex debate, most prominent among anthropologists, sociologists and ethical theorists, about the degree to which human values are culturally relative. This is obviously not the place for a full confrontation with issues that have exercised whole professions for more than a century, but we should at least try to be clear about what the issues are.[22]

If I try hard enough simply to understand you, I may finally decide to excuse or forgive you: to understand all is to forgive all. If I try hard enough to understand Rabelais, I may well find an excuse—not just a historical excuse but personal excuses in his biography—for everything he writes. If I try hard enough to understand his culture, I may

---

22. One of the most impressive recent confrontations with these contrasting demands is Tzvetan Todorov's *The Conquest of America* (1984); a briefer statement of Todorov's commitment to an ethical criticism that will yet respect the other is in Todorov 1985. In "Anti Anti-relativism," Clifford Geertz argues (1984) that what our culture still most needs from anthropologists (and by implication from all critics) is not a battle with relativism but a further pursuit of the exotic "dragons" that might teach us something we cannot teach ourselves. We have too many people committed to "domesticating or abominating them [or] drowning them in theory" (275). A brilliant though to me overly negative account of how Geertz both brings "himself" to the field and creates a new "self" when he writes up his fieldwork is given by Crapanzano (1986, 69–76). A much fuller encounter than Geertz gives with the problem of how two cultures—in effect, two "others"—meet in every ethnographic effort is found in that great work of modern autobiography, *Tristes Tropiques* (1955), by Claude Lévi-Strauss.

well find an excuse for everything in it. Yet I simply *must* try for that total understanding or I will deny myself the chance for whatever enrichment Rabelais and his culture can offer. If all I wanted was to reaffirm my own values, why should I have traveled to the Renaissance in the first place? Some favorite reassuring author of my own time— for the critic of sexism, that could be some feminist novelist of the 1980s—would not raise my objections, and if all I wanted was a peaceful reinforcement of my beliefs, I should have "stayed home," comfortably freed from nasty challenges. But that is not what anyone can really want. Surely learning to meet "the others" where *they* live is the greatest of all gifts that powerful fictions can offer us. Though it is obviously not the only gift—few readers will need my Appendix to dramatize that point—it is a major one that nobody can afford to reject. We simply must "travel," or we die on our feet.

Yet when we think of our duty to our "selves" (which includes the others we have already embraced), and when we think of our responsibility to the strangers we may meet when we do travel, we find an absolute command to articulate our *differences*—for their sakes as well as our own. The command does not tell us that the culture we already possess—whether derived from the "West," from America, from a profession, a class, an ethnic group, a gender, or some unique creative act—is on the whole superior or inferior to that of any other age or culture. We always know far too little, and the problems are always too complex, to allow for any general judgment of better or worse. But on particular values, like those of sexist injustice, surely it is dishonest to pretend that all broadly accepted practices of another time or place are beyond our criticism.

So: on the one hand we are right to fear that we will destroy, with our criticism, some gifts beyond price. Yet on the other we cannot, without dissolving into pointless blobs, renounce our own carefully considered commitments. No one should give up the very possibility of saying, "*This* far and no further. You, my would-be friend, are seriously flawed."

We cannot hope for any general rules for living with these contrasting demands. But as we move from invitation to invitation, we can often decide whether to "open" or "close" by appealing to the notions of *freedom from* and *freedom to* with which we began this chapter. If we desire not only to be *free from* the stultifying practices of our particular province but also to be *free to* engage with the world as full agents, we have a duty to ourselves to articulate our differences with whatever others we encounter. Can we not say, indeed, that if there is no freedom of interpretation, no freedom to discuss whatever differences we seriously encounter, there is no full political freedom either? If the critic of a given repressive regime and the *Gauleiter* who arrests and tortures that critic are expressing equally convention-bound preferences, and if, in interpreting their interpretations, I am simply playing a game according to unbreakable rules imposed on me by my culture or ideological perspective—if, in other words, there is never any real sense to the question, Which one of these two interpreters has produced a better reading of the values inherent in the dictator's words and actions?—then of course all political questions are reduced to questions of power. We are then back in Thrasymachus's trap: "Justice is whatever power says it is, and if you disagree with me, I will of course seek ways of showing you, by all the means available, that I am right. I may bludgeon you with propaganda, or if that does not work, I may overwhelm you with votes or chanted slogans, and if *that* fails, I'll use truncheons or put you in prison. Or I may decide to destroy you in more subtle ways, by feeding you an overwhelming diet of the 'right' kind of art. In any case, my power—as a male, as a Westerner, as a white person, as a spokesman for the future—will be my justification."[23]

Perhaps it remains true that in some epochs the *freedom to* make new interpretations by exercising *freedom from* old methods and assumptions about old classics will be less important than it is in ours. There may indeed have been past moments when *freedom from* established interpretations was not even possible, whether desirable or not. One can place oneself, as Bakhtin has said, "outside one's own language only when an essential historic change of language occurs. Such precisely was the time of Rabelais. And only in such a period was the artistic and ideological radicalism of Rabelaisian images made possible" (1968, 471).

---

23. A splendid account of just how totally *other* are the worlds of the torturer and the tortured, and of the utter ethical irreconcilability of the two worlds of "unmaking" and of "making," is given in Elaine Scarry's *The Body in Pain* (1985), an *essential* work that I discovered almost in the moment of completing this final draft. I should think that anyone who reads her book will be forced to give up once and for all any dream of embracing all otherness.

We seem to be living in another such period. What would it mean to make something out of it other than a threatening chaos?

REFERENCES

Abel, Elizabeth, ed. Introduction. *Writing and Sexual Difference*. Chicago, 1982. 1–7. (Mainly essays from *Critical Inquiry* 8 [Win. 1981].)

Achebe, Chinua. "An Image of Africa." In *The Chancellor's Lecture Series: 1974–1975*. Amherst, Mass., 1975. 31–43.

Asad, Talal. "The Concept of Cultural Translation in British Social Anthropology." In Clifford and Marcus 1986.

Bakhtin, Mikhail. *Rabelais and His World* [1929]. Trans. Hélène Iswolsky. Cambridge, Mass., 1968.

———. *The Dialogic Imagination: Four Essays*. Ed. Michael Holquist. Trans. Caryl Emerson and Michael Holquist. University of Texas Press Slavic Series, no. 1. Austin, Tex., 1981.

———. *Problems of Dostoevsky's Poetics* [1963]. Ed. and trans. Caryl Emerson. Theory and History of Literature, vol. 8. Minneapolis, 1984.

Berrong, Richard M. "Finding Antifeminism in Rabelais; or, A Response to Wayne Booth's Call for an Ethical Criticism." *Critical Inquiry* 11 (June 1985): 687–96.

Bialostosky, Don H. "Dialogics as an Art of Discourse in Literary Criticism." *PMLA* 101 (Oct. 1986): 788–97.

Bolton, W. F. "The Wife of Bath: Narrator as Victim." In *Gender and Literary Voice*. Ed. Janet Todd. New York, 1980. 54–66.

Booth, Wayne C. "Freedom of Interpretation: Bakhtin and the Challenge of Feminist Criticism." In Mitchell 1983: 51–82.

———. *The Rhetoric of Fiction* [1961]. 2d ed. Chicago, 1983.

———. Introduction. In Bakhtin 1984: xiii–xxvii.

Bové, Paul A. *Intellectuals in Power: A Genealogy of Critical Humanism*. New York, 1986.

Bradley, F. H. *Ethical Studies* [1876]. 2d ed., 1927. Reprint. New York, 1951.

Clifford, James. "On Ethnographic Allegory." In Clifford and Marcus 1986.

Clifford, James, and George E. Marcus, eds. *Writing Culture: The Poetics and Politics of Ethnography*. Berkeley, 1986.

Crapanzano, Vincent. "Hermes' Dilemma: The Masking of Subversion in Ethnographic Description." In Clifford and Marcus 1986.

Derrida, Jacques. "Cogito and the History of Madness." In *Writing and Difference* [1967]. Trans. Alan Bass. Chicago, 1978. 31–63.

Donne, John. "Song" [1633]. In *The Complete Poetry of John Donne*. Ed. John T. Shawcross. Garden City, N.Y., 1967. 90.

Dworkin, Andrea. *Woman Hating: A Radical Look at Sexuality*. New York, 1974.

———. *Pornography: Men Possessing Women*. New York, 1981.

Foley, Barbara. "The Politics of Deconstruction." In *Rhetoric and Form: Deconstruction at Yale*. Ed. Robert Con Davis and Ronald Schleifer. Norman, Okla., 1985.

Foucault, Michel. *The Archaeology of Knowledge* [1969]. Trans. A. M. Sheridan Smith. New York, 1972.
———. *Discipline and Punish: The Birth of the Prison* [1975]. Trans. Alan Sheridan. New York, 1977.
———. *The History of Sexuality. Vol. 1: An Introduction* [1976]. Trans. Robert Hurley. New York, 1978.
Geertz, Clifford. "Found in Translation: On the Social History of the Moral Imagination." *Georgia Review* 31 (Win. 1977): 788–810.
———. "Anti Anti-Relativism." Distinguished Lecture of the American Anthropological Association. *American Anthropologist* 86 (June 1984): 263–78.
Graff, Gerald. *Literature against Itself: Literary Ideas in Modern Society.* Chicago, 1979.
Griffin, Susan. *Pornography and Silence: Culture's Revenge against Nature.* New York, 1981.
Gubar, Susan. "Representing Pornography: Feminism, Criticism, and Depictions of Female Violation." *Critical Inquiry* 13 (Sum. 1987): 712–41.
Hooks, Bell. *Feminist Theory: From Margin to Center.* Boston, 1984.
Kelso, Ruth. *Doctrine for the Lady of the Renaissance.* Urbana, Ill., 1956.
Lerner, Julianna Kitty. "Rabelais and Woman" Ph.D. diss., City University of New York, 1976.
Lerner, Laurence. *Love and Marriage: Literature and Its Social Context.* London, 1979.
Lévi-Strauss, Claude. *Tristes Tropiques* [1955]. Trans. John and Doreen Weightman. New York, 1974.
Macdonell, Diane. *Theories of Discourse: An Introduction.* Oxford, 1986.
Mitchell, W. J. T., ed. *The Politics of Interpretation.* Chicago, 1983. (Mostly essays appearing in *Critical Inquiry* 9 [Sept. 1982].)
Montaigne, Michel Eyquem de. *The Complete Essays of Montaigne* [1588]. Trans. Donald M. Frame. Stanford, Calif., 1958.
Rabelais, François. *Oeuvres de François Rabelais.* Ed. Abel Lefranc et al. 5 vols. Paris, 1912–31. (Vol. 1, 1912; vol. 2, 1913; vols. 3–4, 1922; vol. 5, 1931.)
———. *The Portable Rabelais* [1929]. Ed. and trans. Samuel Putnam. New York, 1946.
———. *The Urquhart-Le Motteux Translation of the Works of François Rabelais* [1737]. Ed. Albert Jay Nock [1931]. 2 vols. New York, 1963.
Radcliffe, Janet. *The Skeptical Feminist.* London, 1980.
Rosaldo, Renato. "From the Door of His Tent: The Fieldworker and the Inquisitor." In Clifford and Marcus 1986.
Said, Edward. *Orientalism.* New York, 1978.
———. "Opponents, Audiences, Constituencies, and Community." In Mitchell 1983: 7–49.
Sartre, Jean-Paul. *What is Literature?* [1948]. Trans. Bernard Frechtman. London, 1981.
Scarry, Elaine. *The Body in Pain: The Making and Unmaking of the World.* New York, 1985.
Screech, Michael A. *The Rabelaisian Marriage: Aspects of Rabelais's Religion, Ethics, and Comic Philosophy.* London, 1958.
———. *Rabelais.* Ithaca, N.Y., 1979.

Showalter, Elaine, ed. *The New Feminist Criticism: Essays on Women, Literature, and Theory.* New York, 1985.

Suleiman, Susan, ed. *The Female Body in Western Culture: Contemporary Perspectives.* Cambridge, Mass., 1986.

Theweleit, Klaus. *Male Fantasies.* (Vol. 1: Women, Floods, Bodies, History.) Trans. Stephen Conway et al. Theory and History of Literature, vol. 22. Minneapolis, 1987.

Todorov, Tzvetan. *The Conquest of America: The Question of the Other* [1982]. Trans. Richard Howard. New York, 1984.

———. "All Against Humanity." Review of *Textual Power: Literary Theory and the Teaching of English*, by Robert Scholes. *Times Literary Supplement* (Oct. 4, 1985): 1093–94.

von Hallberg, Robert, ed. *Canons.* Chicago, 1984.

13

I am not a demigod,
I cannot make it cohere.
Ezra Pound

[A]lthough the path chosen will be
one of many, it must lie inside the
forest.
George Steiner, on Heidegger's "Way"

We agreed afterwards [my friend
and I, after looking at Giotto and rejecting Ruskin's judgment] . . . that
there are a great many ways of
seeing Florence, as there are of
seeing most beautiful and interesting
things, and that it is very dry and
pedantic to say that the happy vision
depends upon our squaring our toes
with a certain particular chalk-mark.
Henry James

[W]hat the writer requires of the
reader is not the application of
an abstract freedom but the gift
of his whole person, with his passions, his prepossessions, his sympathies, his sexual temperament, and
his scale of values. Only this person
will give himself generously.
Jean-Paul Sartre

I merely stress the possibility, importance, and genuineness of a response
to the arts in which we can no
longer separate that response from
our social context and personal
commitments.
Northrop Frye

When you shoot at a king, don't
miss.
Old Saying

Doctrinal Questions in Jane Austen, D. H. Lawrence, and Mark Twain

UNLIMITED DOCTRINAL DISPUTE?

An obvious objection to raising doctrinal questions of the kind we have put to Rabelais is that once they have been invited into our conversation there seems to be no place to stop. If critics decide to apply their own ethical codes against the grain of whatever works come their way, can we not foresee an infinity of merely "personal" objections, no one of them amounting to any more than a private report? If, as seems obvious, every significant work embodies innumerable norms that *someone* in *some* epoch or other will object to, do we not surrender all hope for a disciplined discussion of literature? We set out, in Chapter 1, to develop a kind of conversation that might *get somewhere*—not just a sharing of subjective opinions but a way of learning from one another about the ethical value of narratives. If we now take seriously the doctrinal objections we lightly put aside in earlier chapters, are we not in danger of ending up just where we started—adrift in a sea teeming with deaf and blind—but not dumb—subjectivities?

By now we can readily see what is wrong with that objection. In the first place, we face not an infinity of doctrinal disputes, only a multiplicity. In practice at any one time, in any one critical community, dealing with any one work, we will quarrel on only a fairly limited number of points. I do not feel driven to blame Rabelais for being unjust to lawyers, homosexuals, doctors, Italians, philosophers, or the entire animal and vegetable kingdoms. If defenders of any one of those groups want to raise a new objection, I can happily enter the debate, knowing that I will not in fact need to face hundreds of such debates: though in principle I am open to a discussion of an objection on any front, in practice there are, in any given cultural situation, only a few fronts that we care about. I suspect that a list of *all* the ethical objections raised against *any* literary work in twentieth-century America would not run to more than twenty or thirty items. (I did not believe this myself until I did some counting.)

Second, ethical quarrels always take place against a backdrop of agreement. We can quarrel with Rabelais's sexism only because we do not quarrel with him or among ourselves about his being worth a quarrel; that shared experience of his worth is based on innumerable "ideological" convergences that we do not mention and need not mention. We would not read him at all, or talk about him, if he had not embodied a far larger collection of acceptable fixed norms than the set of those we might question.

This is just another way of making the point I have emphasized frequently: no one who ever engages with a story at all does so in full ideological neutrality. On the contrary, as we saw even in the simple "Golden Goose" versions of Chapter 5, the listener cannot re-create even the simplest tale except in a matrix of norms, some of them "fixed"—the author implies their continuance into the "real world"— and some of them "nonce"—embraced only temporarily and applied only in the world of the story.

As we have seen, the only readers who approach ideological neutrality are those hyper-sophisticates who do not really read stories at all but simply dissect and analyze *texts*. At the other extreme are those naïfs whose agreement with the fixed norms is so wholehearted and unthinking that the narrative world seems to be *the* world. These are the readers that most stories seem implicitly to long for; our project in ethical criticism clearly frustrates that longing, but it even more decisively challenges the neutral analysts.

The only choice we have is either to become conscious and explicit about doctrinal agreements and differences or to rely on them silently and even unconsciously. I can love Rabelais without taking thought about what norms he and I have shared as the basis for my enjoyment, in which case my coduction of his value can be called primary but certainly not doctrine-free. I can then choose to bring the norms into the open; when I do so, I will find that I agree with some and disagree with others. I can then decide whether to move to a flat deductive pattern— any story based on this or that approved or rejected norm is good or bad—or I can maintain a living relation with the story, discovering what my fresh experience now is, given the airing of my agreements and disagreements with other readers. That new coduction, implicitly comparing this somewhat remodeled creature with others I have known, may leave the story looking better or worse than it did on first reading, but it will not be a flat deduction from any ideological discovery I have made. Though the full value of the story to me will almost certainly be *modified* by bringing doctrines into the open, I need not make the kind of mistake flagged in Chapter 3, saying, "This story is great *because* it expresses the universal theme I love" or "This poem is worthless *because* some of its lines or stanzas are fascist."

Our relocation of ethical criticism in Parts 1 and 2 should thus make it possible for our doctrinal criticism to serve purposes entirely different from those of the "hanging judges." Rather than finding reasons to ban narratives, we are now more interested in protecting them—and thus ourselves—from premature, unacknowledged, and irresponsible judgments. The classics need not fear us if we look them in the eye; most of them—we cannot know which ones in advance of fresh reading—can more than hold their own in any fair encounter. Perhaps the supreme value of ethical criticism is that once we have practiced it vigorously in the presence of a classic, that classic becomes more fully alive in our culture than it was before.

This point is so much the center of our endeavor here that I want finally to underline it with three extended encounters, the first with *Emma*, a novel that for years seemed to me ideologically flawless, the second with D. H. Lawrence, an author who at first seemed so badly flawed that I did not return to him voluntarily, and the last with *Adventures of Huckleberry Finn,* that wonderful work with its wonderfully interesting, deeply puzzling flaws.[1]

JANE AUSTEN AND THE DEFLECTIONS OF FORM: A PERHAPS IMPERTINENT INQUIRY ADDRESSED TO FELLOW DEVOTEES

From the beginning many readers of Jane Austen have found a wonderful, peaceful contentment in simply dwelling with her novels as

---

1. The following section on *Emma* is a revision of an address I delivered at a conference of the Jane Austen Society of North America, held in Philadelphia on October 8, 1983 (and see Booth 1983a). I have chosen to maintain something of the spoken tone here, as in the address to Lawrentians that follows, in the hope that it will help illustrate

they are. We have all felt in our bones that it's a good thing to dwell with such a mind and heart for many days, months, years. Are not these beautiful, elegant, wonderfully witty experiences more than enough in themselves to satisfy us? Are they not self-justifying—precisely the kind that we should *not* soil with ideological probings?

Though there have always been readers who have wondered what all the excitement is about, we admirers have tended to be idolators. Until recently, when feminists have begun to ask awkward questions,[2] we have either ignored ideological questions entirely, or, like the author of *The Rhetoric of Fiction,* we have simply embraced Austen's fixed norms as splendidly incisive and even profound. There is, however, one grand exception—all those male critics who, while praising her as a splendid minor talent, have condescended to her as a woman writer: "Because her vision was limited to what a woman of her time and class could know, her vision is maimed. She did really quite remarkable work, of course, considering that great disadvantage." Something like this brand of ideological criticism can be found in a great majority of what male critics have said of her.

Usually such criticism is not openly avowed as ideological. On the contrary, it has been made to sound like the voice of reason itself, an objective voice that knows what a novel should be and what a novelist should do. Here is the Olympian Lord David Cecil ostensibly praising her: "Her view of human nature was limited in the first place by her circumstances: she wrote about men and women as she herself had known them. Her view was further limited by her sex, by the fact that she only saw as much of humanity as was visible to a lady" (1978, 144).

Whatever we may think of such comments, they offer a clear invitation to face ideological questions directly and seriously. If someone we love has been consistently denigrated, however lovingly, we surely have a duty to reconsider both our love and the denigrations, to decide whether our trust has been misplaced. Here we commit no violation, at least in principle, of this author: as we saw in Chapter 8 (pages

---

the intensely *ethical* quality of one's engagement with *ethical* questions, especially when in the company of the passionately committed.

2. A selection of characteristic discussions from a burgeoning literature would include Poovey 1983; Moers 1976; Miller 1986; and Wilt 1983.

233–34), Austen herself believed in and practiced a powerful ethical criticism. Like the other great novelists we quoted then—Cervantes, Richardson, Flaubert—she insists that the fictions we imbibe help make us who we are.

Her ridicule of the would-be rake, Sir Edward, in *Sanditon,* is only one of many signs of Austen's deep interest in our prevailing question as she worked on her last novel. Charlotte, her heroine, has suffered her own kind of distortion from her reading, one that misleads her when she meets Clara Brereton for the first time. Clara is a beautiful young woman in the service of Lady Denham, and Charlotte is at first tempted to see her as the kind of victimized, impoverished heroine she has been meeting in the novels of the circulating library.

> Perhaps it might be partly oweing to her having just issued from a Circulating Library—but she cd not separate the idea of a complete Heroine from Clara Brereton. Her situation with Lady Denham so very much in favour of it!—She seemed placed with her on purpose to be ill-used. Such Poverty & Dependance joined to such Beauty & Merit, seemed to leave no choice in the business."
>
> ([1817/1925] 1963, 391)

According, that is, to what some novels teach about life!

But the narrator does not leave it at that, as the narrator of *Northanger Abbey* years earlier would have been inclined to do. Instead she hammers the point home:

> These feelings were not the result of any spirit of Romance in Charlotte herself. No, she was a very sober-minded young Lady, sufficiently well-read in Novels to supply her Imagination with amusement, but not at all unreasonably influenced by them; & while she pleased herself the first 5 minutes with fancying the Persecutions which *ought* to be the Lot of the interesting Clara, especially in the form of the most barbarous conduct on Lady Denham's side, she found no reluctance to admit from subsequent observation, that they appeared to be on very comfortable Terms.
>
> (391–92)

And there follows the scene from which we quoted in Chapter 8. In other works Austen underlines the dire effects of certain kinds of romantic literature—most notoriously, perhaps, the works of Byron, but also popular novels. They are again and again accused, delicately but decisively, of contributing to the follies of certain characters. The most obvious victims of reading are Catherine in *Northanger Abbey,* as besotted by romances as was Don Quixote, and Marianne Dashwood in *Sense and Sensibility,* that maiden who *would dash* into romantic alliances. Benwick, in the mature *Persuasion,* is somewhat more subtly portrayed.

Benwick may have been a flawed character even without reading Byron, but certainly his reading of Byron has contributed to his weakness. That he has read Byron unreflectively, without employing a judicious ideological criticism on his reading, is clearly a fault:

> [H]aving talked of poetry, the richness of the present age, and gone through a brief comparison of opinion as to the first-rate poets [especially Scott and Byron] . . . [Benwick] repeated, with such tremulous feeling, the various lines which imaged a broken heart, or a mind destroyed by wretchedness, and looked so entirely as if he meant to be understood, that she [Anne] ventured to hope he did not always read only poetry; and to say, that she thought it was the misfortune of poetry, to be seldom safely enjoyed by those who enjoyed it completely; and that the strong feelings which alone could estimate it truly, were the very feelings which ought to taste it but sparingly.

Since Benwick does not object to her little sermon, Anne

> was emboldened to go on; and feeling in herself the right of seniority of mind, she ventured to recommend a larger allowance of prose in his daily study; and on being requested to particularize, mentioned such works of our best moralists, such collections of the finest letters, such memoirs of characters of worth and suffering, as occurred to her at the moment as *calculated to rouse and fortify the mind by the highest precepts, and the strongest examples of moral and religious endurances.*
>
> ([1818] 1933, 100–101; my italics)

I take such passages as an open invitation from our author to consider whether her own "prose" works are among those that are "calculated to rouse and fortify the mind by the highest precepts." Suppose we accept the challenge, focus our attention on one kind of "fortifying" only: Is a loving, attentive reading of *Emma,* by those who "enjoy it completely," "calculated to rouse and fortify the mind" in the particular matter of inculcating a just, accurate, sensitive, ultimately defensible view of the nature and lot of women, and their relations with men? In the terms of Chapter 11, is Austen's proffered "world" a solid corrective of Rabelais's?

The Indictment

Many feminist critics have defended Austen as by all odds the most perceptive portrayer of women's fate of her time. They find indeed that her works contain a most biting critique of the male-dominated world, and they have seen her as a kind of founding mother of feminist criticism. I agree with their assessment. We simply do not find any overt signs of sexism. Not even the most hostile feminist critic will ever find here those blatant and ridiculous marks of misogyny that mar the works of a Henry Miller, a Hemingway—and a Rabelais. Austen never says or implies that women are inferior to men, never in fact talks about "all women" or "all men," and she makes fun of those who think in grand stereotypes.

If we are to consider the question seriously, we must once again look not at propositions spoken by this or that character or narrator but at the shaping power of the work as we experience its pattern of desires and fulfillments. In living with Austen's favored characters for many hours and many days, I learn to long for what those characters long for (or, as in the case of Emma Woodhouse, what the character *should* long for, if she knew all along what she learns only toward the end). I learn how to long *in that way* for that special kind of happiness. I am taught both how to desire and what to desire. When the novels end happily, as all of Austen's do (for the major characters), I am taught how glorious it feels to have precisely *those* desires fulfilled. If I have enjoyed *Emma* as it asks to be enjoyed, I can never forget how marvelous it is to find "perfect happiness" in a "union" of true minds and hearts—and that means, in this work, how marvelous it is for a *flawed* woman to fall into the care and keeping of an *un*-flawed male.

Thus the most obvious objection that we might raise to this work, taking it seriously as the educational force it cannot fail to be, is that Emma's ultimate happiness is identified with learning to see the world *as Knightley sees it;* with acceding to his judgment on all important matters; and finally with bowing to that man in loving but inevitably submissive vows of matrimony. Salvation for Emma lies in proving to us that she is worthy of ultimate approval by—a man! We know, as Judith Wilt reminds us, that "Knightley will never forget that sixteen years advantage of wisdom over Emma" (1983, 43).

Many critics have noticed that Mr. Knightley embodies in a quite marvelous and incredible way all of the virtues of an ideal father. Infinitely caring and attentive to Emma's every move, wise in her ways and in the ways of the world, able to protect her (to some degree) from the consequences of her egotism, willing to instruct her patiently and to wait for her to profit, in her proud way, from his instruction, he is like our fantasies about that perfect parent, never found in real life—a godlike creature. Yet he also possesses, quite implausibly when you come to think about it, all or most of the virtues of the ideal lover. Still young, he is not only handsome, well turned out, and possessed of the impeccable manners of the perfect gentleman; he is also witty and deeply perceptive. The only quality he lacks is dash—the kind of flair and carefree charm that Frank Churchill can simulate so well or that the Crawfords show in *Mansfield Park*. And of course we shrewd readers know all along, or soon discover, that such dash can actually be a fault, not a virtue. Besides, it turns out that Knightley *dances* very well!

One of Emma's chief faults, the novel "says," is that she thinks she does not need marriage to such a man, or to any man. "I have none of the inducements of women to marry," she says to Harriet early in chapter 1. "Fortune I do not want [that is, need or lack]; employment I do not want; consequence I do not want." She does not need them because she already has them. And she even adds that she does not need any sort of sexual love—that is to say, in her more discreet language:

> [A]s for objects of interest, objects for the affections, which is in truth the great point of inferiority [in the celebate state], the want of which is really the great evil to be avoided in *not* marrying, I shall be very well off, with all the children of a sister I love so much, to care about. There will be enough of them, in all probability, to supply every sort of sensation that declining life can need.
>
> ([1816] 1960, 85–86)

While she thus runs on about her total independence, the reader is of course noting the one huge gap in her reasoning—the gap that we are reminded of constantly by the way Austen constructs her work: she has forgotten the importance of love of a man, love of a Knightley in shining armor. We have already long since begun to infer that these two characters are destined for love, and as we move through Emma's series of comic follies, we yearn more and more for the moment when she will discover that all of her talk about independence is vain: what a good woman needs, for her happiness, is not just a good man but a man who is wiser and stronger than she is.

It could be argued, then, that no reader ever fails here to experience a reinforcement of those deep-seated sexist beliefs that are taught by most Western fiction until our century—that women are indeed the weaker sex, that unlike men they cannot be whole, cannot find maturity, without the protective instruction and care from the right kind of man. It is not just that a union with a Knightley is *necessary* to complete the happiness of this otherwise glorious creature; it is that *full* happiness is *defined* as achieved and in fact culminated with that kind of union. At the moment when the straying lamb finally comes home and accepts the love of the paragon male, heaven is attained—and the story stops; that is what life is for, that is the supreme goal of life, during the hours of our reading. If you doubt that the novel depends on something like this ideology, try reversing it by writing a novel in which an older woman educates and wins a young man who is flawed as Emma is flawed. You will find that your novel simply cannot and does not work as *Emma* works. It may work in some other way, of course, but not as an exquisite romantic fulfillment.

In short, as we hope for the various comic punishments that will correct Emma and make her eligible for "perfect happiness," we are learning to practice that kind of *longing* for that kind of happiness, and the more effective the novel is, for a given reader, the more likely that reader is to infer that *that's* what intelligent, sensitive people *should* long for. If I'm a woman, the real difference between the world I live in and that world will appear to be that I'm not lucky enough to find a Knightley. If I am a man, the temptation will be to see myself *as* a Knightley, needing only an Emma to complete my triumph in the world—what bliss, to educate and then possess an Emma!

What's more, the picture of female dependence on superior males is to some degree reinforced by the other characters. Though Frank Churchill is no doubt morally more to blame than is Jane Fairfax for their secret affair, he is also clearly her superior in energy and will. Though Mr. Woodhouse and Mrs. Churchill are both silly and tyrannical, Mr. Woodhouse is presented as loveable in his tyranny, and finally entirely forgiveable, while Mrs. Churchill is a powerful, threatening, and detestable harridan. Robert Martin is obviously and clearly the superior of Harriet; Harriet needs him to correct her "nature" as a silly dependent woman. And can we not say that if anyone could be sillier and more contemptible than Mr. Elton it is Mrs. Elton, whose bad taste in wedding finery is given almost the last word: "very little white satin, very few lace veils," she complains about Emma's wedding; "a most pitiful business!"

It would not be hard to conclude, then, that this wonderful story, one of the greatest of novels, one that on its surface seems least guilty of anything that could be called sexism, is in fact a dangerous work to put into the hands of the young. It will miseducate its female readers by confirming their sense of dependence on and inferiority to men; it will miseducate its male readers by confirming their egotism and their cheerful willingness to assume the role of lord and master. In short, just as Anne Elliot thought that Benwick needed the antidotes of "prose in his daily study," the "works of our best moralists," to compensate for his reading of the dangerous Lord Byron, do we not need the antidote of a good strong feminist critique to compensate for our possible readings of this powerful work?

The Seductions of Conventional Form

My tone has already implied that I would turn about somewhere along the line and take all that back in some way, affirming a *deeper* reading that will finally acquit our beloved author of all charges. I do intend to do that, in a sense, but for now such a turn would be premature. The dangerous powers that I have described are real, and they are not merely theoretical. Many a reader, male and female, has inadvertently illustrated each of the deformations I have described. The reader is not only allowed but in a sense invited by *Emma* to embrace the distorted view of women that I have described. Like Sir Edward identifying with the seductive exploits of Lovelace, against Richardson's expressed intentions, many a reader of *Emma* has surely been unable to resist the seductions of what we might call the "conventional form." Indeed I think we must finally see the reader's plight in this regard as similar to that of Austen herself, as she worked to incorporate her vision into a successful realization of a conventional form.

What do I mean by "the seductions of the conventional form," as distinct from what we might call the seductions of direct teaching?

I have little doubt but that Austen in her everyday life saw women as at least the equals of men in every quality except physical strength. But to make a novel about an Emma Woodhouse, to make a novel that will work *as a novel,* required in her time some sort of resounding ending. Indeed, it still does, for most novelists and most readers. And there are just not a great many varieties of resounding endings available to a novelist or playwright. When we complicate the simple, direct genres like tragedy and comedy and historical celebration and produce Polonius-like hyphenations of history-comedy-tragedy, we create mixtures that are not the least resounding at the end or gripping in the middle. The writer of fictions is thus inevitably driven into conventional ways of heightening plot, ways that are radically reductive of life's complexities. Most notably, novelists find themselves granting superlative virtues and vices to heroes and villains and creating impossible romantic fulfillments.

Austen was consequently led, by the inescapable need to make *Emma* into an effective novel, into conventional patterns of desire that she quite obviously did not herself embrace uncritically. As a result, the novel she wrote carries within it a strong likelihood that many readers will succumb morally to what was simply required formally. They will ignore the moral instruction implicit in everything the author does in other respects, accepting instead the moral instruction of the conventional form. And it is important to underline the uncomfortable fact that in doing so, they will not be *mis*-reading. We may want to say that they are *under*-reading, or that they are themselves morally weak for not resisting what is offered, but the truth is that the novel itself asks for their response.

It is in this borderland between conventional forms, asking as they do for conventional responses, and the other fictional devices for expressing value that the subtlest problems are presented to criticism, at least for those of us who want to do full justice to aesthetic merit and who are determined, at the same time, not to commit the "Sir Edward fallacy." The reading task offered by most long fictions is in one essential respect radically different from all other reading, precisely because the scope of the epic or the longer novel provides the time and the resources for making us love heroes and heroines with an intensity and depth of acquaintance that cannot be matched by shorter forms. We identify with their notion of happiness, and we revel in that happiness when it arrives. Shorter works—lyric poems, short stories—are able to present this kind of engagement only in a form so weak as to constitute an entirely different aesthetic and moral problem. When I read only a few pages, I simply do not dwell with a given character's spirit for long enough to become thoroughly enamored, thoroughly recon-

stituted by his or her patterns of hopes and fears. When I live with
Emma for—let us say, as a minimum—the eighteen hours that one
critic once objected to as the time required to read the work, when I
enter that world for the days and days that are required for a proper
reading, I inevitably, as we have seen, learn how to long for a certain
kind of happiness. The conventions of the literary form thus do not
just teach me propositions about happiness; they implant habits of desire that may very well be disastrous in my non-reading life.

The resulting "reading assignment" given by our teacher, Jane Austen, is complex indeed. We must learn to read as I am quite sure Austen herself wrote: both remembering and forgetting what we know
about real life. We all know, or should know, that no union can possibly produce perfect happiness; we know it as surely as we know that
geese do not lay golden eggs. We know that no man can possibly provide for Emma all that the novel in its conventional form suggests. We
can be sure, once we think about it, that Austen did not believe in the
existence of such a paragon as Knightley, and she tells us in many ways
that she does not see the whole of a woman's life as the pursuit of a
single moment of perfect happiness in a perfect union, all past and future qualifications ignored. Again and again she makes absolutely
clear that she could never swallow such nonsense. But her *work* asks
us to swallow it, in *some* sense, if we are to savor it to the full. And
unless we know how to read, and to criticize what we read, first thing
we know we'll be thinking about love and marriage and life itself with
about as little sense as is shown by Sir Edward.

Austen's Patented Antidote

The saving truth is that *Emma* contains within itself the antidotes \
to its own potential poisons. While it does not in any sense repudiate
the fun of pursuing the conventional form, it works hard to alert the
careful reader to the need for a double vision—a combination of joyful
credulity about the love plot and shrewd sophistication about the
characters of men and women.

That sophistication consists in part in recognizing the imaginative
resistance that the work provides to its own conventional form. By the
author's tone on every page, we are asked to imagine a world that does

not permit us to believe what the conventional marriage plot tries, as it were, to teach us. Our journey from page to page is not for the most part focused on some future fulfillment in some convention of good fortune but rather on the way people behave here and now. To *be* a certain way in the world, to behave a certain way, is its own justification or damnation. To be faulty in the way Emma is faulty is not simply an obstacle to union with Knightley, though it is that. It is an obstacle to being what Emma ought to be, whether she wins Knightley or not. To be absurd in the way most of the other characters are absurd is not merely to exhibit comic faults for our delectation, though it is that; it is also to illustrate a whole spectrum of human follies and, by implication, the virtues that would be their opposites.

Perhaps the best way to dramatize how this antidote works would be to ask whether any character in this novel is perfect. You cannot answer that question without asking at the same time where your standard of perfection comes from. And obviously no character, not even Knightley, provides all of that standard. It is derived not from any male, after all, but from that great woman, the implied Jane Austen, the dauntingly mature human being who underwrites every act of imagination she takes us through. It is she who provides an accompaniment of both understanding and love to Emma's *almost* detestable meddling. And it is she who provides the subtle clues to Knightley's own egotism. More subtly, she creates for us the imaginative and witty vitality of Emma herself, as a criticism of the somewhat stodgy wisdom and stately power of Knightley. She teaches us that although Emma's imagination is obviously dangerous, it is also an admirable loveable grace in a world dominated mostly by fools, knaves, and clods. And finally she provides, at scores of points, a commentary that corrects any naive over-identification that we are tempted to commit.

Many readers have resisted that corrective, and we can be sure that many more will do so. Critics have often objected, for example, to the presence of a persistent voice that could allow itself, at what conventionally should have been the moment of supreme passion, to undermine the conventional effects with the famous (or infamous) narrative intrusion: "What did she say?—Just what she ought, of course. A lady always does.—She said enough to show there need not be despair—and to invite him to say more himself" (431).

And then, in a passage that is even more deflating if what we are seeking is unalloyed, perfect happiness in an idealized union: "Seldom, very seldom, does complete truth belong to any human disclosure; seldom can it happen that something is not a little disguised, or a little mistaken; but where, as in this case, though the conduct is mistaken, the feelings are not, it may not be very material."

What kind of talk is *that*, coming just at the moment of romantic climax? And what must we think of the undercutting of the perfect man, the paragon, full of objective wisdom, the mentor who is above the human battle, when we read the final paragraph of this scene? "He had found her agitated and low.—Frank Churchill was a villain.—He heard her declare that she had never loved him. Frank Churchill's character was not desperate.—She was his own Emma, by hand and word, when they returned into the house; and if he could have thought of Frank Churchill then, he might have deemed him a very good sort of fellow" (433). Some readers have considered such passages to be dodges, signs of Austen's own sexual inhibitions or lack of novelistic skill: "Poor woman, she just did not know how to write a love scene!" I suggest instead that they are signs of a novelist who knows her double task: how to abide by the demands of a conventional form, while making the whole thing work for matters *un*conventional. The intrusions in no way diminish the portrait of the happy marriage to come, as we read in our roles as credulous participants in the conventional world of Hartfield and environs. But they provide us in our other roles, as readers who know we are reading a fiction, a climax to our friendship with a woman who lives very much in the world as we know it, who knows that *we* know that she has been presenting an idealized fiction, a woman whose gifts of imagination and wisdom far surpass Knightley's—and indeed yours and mine. In short, the most lasting demonstration of this novel, concerning men and women in the world, is that most of us, male and female, are as children compared with this one glorious human being, quite real on the page.

More than twenty-five years ago, I reported on, and rejected, a widespread claim that the ending is flawed, since the marriage will turn out to be an unhappy one (Booth [1961] 1983c, 259). Though I still see the claim as, at best, only half of what should be said, I now think my rejection of it was too simple. In *Emma*, we play doubled roles much more intricate than are demanded by fantastic elements like gold-laying geese. On the one hand, we must see the ending as indeed a happy one, not in the least ironic, given the world of the conventional plot, a world that we are to enter with absolute wholeheartedness. And yet, simultaneously, we are asked to embrace standards according to which the ending can only be viewed as a fairy tale or fantasy. The author has been teaching us all along what it means to keep our wits about us, to maintain a steady vision of the follies and meannesses in our world. Though all *is* finally well for Emma and George Knightley, in their fairy-tale world, we have been taught, unrelentingly, that *all is far from well in the real world implied by the book.* All is not well, either for their kind (if any such exist) or for those less fortunate men and women who surround them. Every fully engaged reader will have discovered, in that "realer" world aggressively insisted on in the midst of all the subtle pleasures, that the circumstances of women are considerably more chancy and often more threatening than those surrounding men. Emma, with her rich fortune, could presumably have built some sort of decent life without a Knightley, just as she earlier believed. But where would a Jane Fairfax be if Mrs. Churchill had not died to fulfill the needs of the conventional plot? And where *is* Miss Bates? Unless we can somehow incorporate something like an ironic vision of the ending—even while pretending not to, even while enjoying the fairy tale to the full—we are indeed confirming its capacity to implant a harmful vision of the sexes.

Still, I cannot claim that these dangers will simply go away, provided we read with sufficient skill. We may tell ourselves that Austen knows how, and assumes that we will know how, to see Knightley as a fantasy figure. But the power of the realized conventional form, the delicious happiness Austen makes us feel, must surely be counteracted by a kind of inquiry that is as courageous and sensitive and resistant as Austen's reading of her own predecessors. She knew better than to pretend that powerful fictions are not dangerous. She thus would welcome, I like to think, the probing questions that feminist critics have been teaching us to ask. Her kind of critical spirit, applied in the 1980s to her kind of works, will not leave those works unmodified. But to me it is reassuring to discover that most of the modifications, most of what we learn by asking the questions raised by feminist criticism, leave Jane Austen looking perhaps even greater than she did before.

CONFESSIONS OF A LUKEWARM LAWRENTIAN

Well along in what I hoped to be a final revision of *The Company We Keep,* I was invited to give the keynote address to the 1985 annual meeting of the D. H. Lawrence Society. At first I refused. It would obviously be foolish of me to talk about an author I had not re-read in many years—and one that I had not intended to re-read, ever. My coductions about the value of the novels written by that opinionated, arrogant, preachy genius were comparatively fixed: though I had once been much moved by *Sons and Lovers,* I had been much put off by *Lady Chatterley's Lover.* Lawrence had never quite made it into *my* canon. I was quite sure that I could expect little more from that nagging, talented windbag.

I let myself be talked into the task, and the results of my subsequent re-reading of Lawrence surprised me. The force of my surprise can be best conveyed by giving here my report to the society, considerably shortened but otherwise pretty much as I delivered it, including the necessary confessions of the prodigal son. Readers who have memorized what I have said earlier may perhaps be troubled by some repetition here, especially of points made in Chapters 7–9. I hope, however, that they (and others) will see not pointless repetition but useful recapitulation in my effort to reconsider one author afresh, as a kind of company worth keeping.

We enact here, as I look out at you no doubt passionate Lawrentians, an ancient ritual or myth: the story of the prodigal son. Because in a wild moment of long-distance telephone tomfoolery, I found the alliteration of "lukewarm Lawrentian" appealing, I am now returned from my un-Lawrentian prodigalities to confess my sins and to ask forgiveness. I did object in that telephone conversation that I was not a Lawrentian in either sense of the word, neither an expert nor an enthusiast. But I was told that nothing could be more appropriate for a Lawrence conference than absolute sincerity, even ignorant sincerity: my very reluctance was the clearest sign that I should let myself go.

As the good sons and daughters who have been minding the store all these years, you may feel resentment when the prodigal son returns to announce discoveries in 1985 that you all made long ago. But this homecoming may finally be pleasant enough, so long as you expect nothing new and remember that it is better to rejoice over the return of one lost sheep than over the faithful attendance of the ninety-and-nine.

So here I am, feeling released from all my scholarly inhibitions by that word "confessions" in my title. Or at least from most of them. My assignment certainly grants me the right to begin in the confessional mode, regardless of what happens at the end.

In 1975 I was living in Sussex, trying to write a novel of my very own. While avoiding my task, I ordered some books from Blackwell's, including a paperback edition of Lawrence's letters. About a week after they arrived, I was reading through the letters, often with admiration but often with a rending of garments and gnashing of teeth, when suddenly, at page 77, I found a tiny piece of scrap paper, with the following message, unsigned, scribbled in red ink: "Dear Professor Booth: The novels of D. H. Lawrence are better than you think."

I have always pictured to myself a mailing clerk, a well-read, sensitive, youngish man (the handwriting was definitely male) working away at a job far beneath his intelligence and education, and exercising in that one moment the most completely disinterested piece of literary criticism I've ever encountered. "Here I am," I hear him thinking to himself, "Here *I* am, a *real* reader, and there *you* are, an established and misguided critic, a *poor* reader, and I, I who have read those books, I look you in the eye and I tell you, with absolutely no thought of profit to myself, that you have under-rated a great novelist."

Now isn't it a pity that the young man is not here to see what he hath wrought?

If my later *mea culpa*s are to be intelligible, I must first make clear that the young man had greatly over-generalized my criticism. After all, my point in *The Rhetoric of Fiction* had not been to attack Lawrence but to defend certain narrative techniques sometimes dismissed as "telling rather than showing." My inability to engage fully with *Lady Chatterley's Lover*, I argued, would not be cured by removing the authorial commentary, since the real trouble arose from my quarrels with the character of the implied author: "If we finish the book with a sense of embarrassment at its special pleading, if we read Mellors' final pseudo-biblical talk of 'the peace that comes of fucking' and of his 'Pentecost, the forked flame between me and you,' with regrets rather than conviction, it is ultimately because no literary techniques can conceal from us the confused and pretentious little author who is implied in too many parts of the book" (1983, 81).

I can hardly blame Blackwell's employee, after a passage like that, for overlooking the evidence that I had found a quite different implied author in *Sons and Lovers* and some other earlier works. My tone here was, after all, condescending and dismissive, and I concluded on the same note: "Even our memory of the very different author implied by the better novels— *Women in Love,* say—is not enough to redeem the bad portions of this one" (81).

Are the novels of D. H. Lawrence indeed better than I had thought? Was that lovely disinterested anonymous packing clerk right? Does it make any sort of sense to call the D. H. Lawrence of *Lady Chatterley* a "confused and pretentious little author"? Confused often, certainly, like the rest of us. Pretentious often, surely. But little? D. H. Lawrence *little?* Does the Wayne Booth who has discovered in several tries that he cannot write even one good short story, much less a decent novel, have the right to use the adjective "little" for D. H. Lawrence?

After agreeing to think about Lawrence again, I was determined to play fair: I would go back and re-read the major novels, and I would try to do it with no axe to grind. Where better to start than with *The Rainbow* and *Women in Love,* generally said to be the best. I had a dim memory of reading them both decades ago, with some pleasure (lukewarm, of course), but I soon discovered that they were in effect now entirely new—so new that I can't believe I ever did more than a speed-reading for some assignment, as student or teacher. I find now a few old pencil marks here and there—you know, like "U.N." for "unreliable narrator," "I.A." for "implied author"—so I must have skimmed coolly through the pages thirty years ago. But nothing now echoes as something previously *experienced.*

I wish I could report that my first efforts led to instantaneous enthusiasm. I could then have changed my assigned title from "Confessions of a Lukewarm Lawrentian" to "Confessions of a *Belated* Lawrentian." But my actual experience was much more troubled. Though I found marvelous passages in both novels, I also experienced, reading with an audience of Lawrentians in mind, many moments of anger, of disgust, even of contempt—and, of course, of mounting anxiety. Reading dutifully, reading in the worst possible way (that is, with pencil in hand), I became more and more depressed. This author *is*, I found myself saying, he really *is* too often a pretentious little preacher who thinks he knows more than he does, and who misuses his fictional gifts in an effort to sign me up as a member of his elite corps to save the world.

We flash a few weeks ahead now. I am reading *Women in Love* aloud to my wife, as we drive into the countryside. This is my third cover-to-cover reading of this novel since agreeing to try to open my mind, and I have come to the scene where Birkin goes to Ursula's home to propose and finds himself instead in an angry encounter with her father. I pause in the reading to say, "Isn't that wonderful? What other novelist could have managed a scene like that? And you know, I completely overlooked the wonder of it last week. This man is *great.*"

So we have confession piled on confession here—we now have my full confession of incompetence as a first reader of *Women in Love*. What could account for such a slow awakening?

Increasingly anxious about how to answer that question, I began to ask colleagues and friends how they now feel about Lawrence. Are you surprised to learn that I could not find a single Lawrentian? Wherever I turned, I met people who once read him with enthusiasm but have not gone back to him, or who, like my well-read graduate assistant, "tried it once and didn't like it," or who, like some of my older friends, had admired *Sons and Lovers* but soon got off the boat, or who, like Susan Fromberg Schaeffer, said they like the poetry a lot but find the novels unrewarding, or who, like most of my undergraduates, seem barely to have heard of one D. H. Lawrence.

The responses of my informal survey did not please me. By now Lawrence was much more important to me than such attitudes allowed for. So I settled down to some serious thinking, about us and about him.

The Indictment

It's never easy to assign blame when readers and authors fail to meet. As we try to enter any novel, we all carry the burden of our special situations, our personal incapacities, and our cultural moment. Part of what it means to "learn to read well" is to get beyond our local deficiencies in order to achieve a full meeting with something that is "other," beyond, larger than, or at least different from, what we bring. Lawrence, both in his weaknesses and his powers, asks me—as a professor of English and a literary critic reading in the 1980s—to travel a long way from home. Without pretending to be entirely clear about where the blame lies, let me describe some of my problems.

First, I am a slow reader and Lawrence is a fast writer—an extremely uneven stylist. His way of revising en bloc left a lot of copy editing unattended to: "Trim and garnish my stuff I cannot—it must go" (Cushman 1978, 194). Can you think of any major novelist, other than Dreiser perhaps, who provides more invitations to stop reading and start complaining about style?

Sometimes the troubles are obviously the result of pure carelessness. What kind of writer is it who can write of "the activities of her heart" or of "a perfect fire that burned in all his joints"? And just what are we to make of sentences like these: ". . . she lifted her face to him implicitly." How do you *do* that? "'He's very dirty,' said the young Russian swiftly and silently." Surely that's the neatest trick of the week. "It was rather wet everywhere, there was a stream running down at the bottom of the valley, which was gloomy, or seemed gloomy." Now the fact is that Birkin is alone here. Lawrence wanted to say only that it seemed gloomy to Birkin. He wrote it wrong first, then corrected it, but retained both versions.

If you offer a dyed-in-the-wool pedant like me enough clumsy stuff like that, he is sure to see as careless and clumsy much that is actually deliberate and fresh. It was essential to Lawrence's purposes, as he himself said in his foreword to *Women in Love,* to repeat key words that had for him special or unusually powerful meaning: words like "blood," "uncreated," "dissolution," "self," "dead," "mindless," "naked," "sinister," "organic" (see Heilman 1969, 102). Such repetitions, when combined with relentless hyperbole and dash, can leave the reluctant Lawrentian laughing or groaning rather than soaring— mistakenly adding these deliberate touches to the collection of blunders. "He could move into the pure translucency of the grey uncreated water." "She [Hermione] must break down the wall—she must break him [Birkin] down before her, the awful obstruction of him who obstructed her life to the last. It must be done, or she must perish most horribly. . . . Then swiftly, in a flame that drenched down her body like fluid lightning and gave her a perfect, unutterable consummation, unutterable satisfaction . . ."

But troubles with style are only the beginning. Even more difficult to sort out are the ideological differences that spring from our different generations. I am now sixty-four, going on eighty, living at the frazzled end of a terrifying century. Lawrence was in his twenties when he began work on "The Sisters" (his start on these novels) just before the outbreak of World War I; he published *The Rainbow* when he was thirty and *Women in Love* when he was thirty-five. On their surfaces, they are books of a very young man, about young people, characters initially conceived in a climate of hopes and despairs quite different from mine today. They seem at first immaturely *obsessed* with problems of coupling and decoupling, as those problems appeared to bright young people early in this century. "That is no country for old men . . ." While my interest in sex has not radically declined, my interest in *talk* about it, and in efforts to probe how it feels to get it or not get it, to get it right or get it wrong, has been more than satiated by the sexual revolution that Lawrence helped to inspire. It is sometimes said that an intellectual is someone who has found something in life more interesting than sex. I am actually—perhaps shamefully—more interested these days in how people face aging and death, and the likely death of us all, than I am in how they couple.[3]

We have by now had generations of novelists and psychologists claiming to save the world through some sort of phallic redemption, and Lawrence's prophetic talk about such matters has lost the freshness and shock that it once had. If I had read these books at twenty—how did I escape it?—I would no doubt have felt myself in the presence of a sure and infinitely knowing guide. Reading of Birkin and Ursula's intercourse after the exciting Schuhplatteln dance, I might not have guessed just what kind of "bestial" copulation Lawrence had in mind, but I would probably have felt exhilarated in sharing Ursula's own sense of liberation:

> [S]he felt the strange licentiousness of him hovering upon her. She was troubled and repelled. . . .
> But his face only glistened on her, unknown, horrible. And yet she was fascinated. . . .
> What would he do to her?

---

3. I couldn't finish Updike's *Couples* some years ago, and I haven't been able even to *start* Mailer's *Ancient Evenings*.

He was so attractive, and so repulsive at once. . . .
And she gave way, he might do as he would. His licentiousness was re-
pulsively attractive. . . .
They might do as they liked—this she realised as she went to sleep
[afterward]. How could anything that gave one satisfaction be excluded?
What was degrading? Who cared? Degrading things were real, with a different reality. . . . Wasn't it rather horrible, a man who could be so soulful
and spiritual, now to be so—she balked at her own thoughts and memories: then she added—so bestial? . . . She winced. But after all, why not?
She exulted as well.

(1976, 402–3; ch. 29)

But after decades of such talk, after the pullulating sex manuals and
Playboy philosophizings, it can seem old hat. Again and again I found
myself simply bored. "If I have to read another sermon on *that,* I'll
phone and cancel the engagement."

My resistances extend beyond the sexual nostrums to the whole
range of panaceas offered in the *Salvator Mundi* vein. It is difficult for
me now to take as seriously as Lawrence would like the quest of a
young prophet for some individualized spiritual revolution. For reasons that make it hard to re-read Hesse's *Siddhartha,* I find too much
of Birkin's and Ursula's quests merely informative at best, boring at
worst. The truth is that I am now suspicious of all epochal claims and
all passionate struggles for perfection.[4] To me it just doesn't matter
enough what precisely Lawrence thinks about the faults of the *whole
human race* or about the certain doom for us all that lies ahead. Perhaps because of my pluralism, over-confident, sweeping indictments
and cures are irritating to me whether they go this way or that. As a
result, I cannot bear to read most of the critical work that has been
devoted to detecting Lawrence's precise position on prophetic issues.
Though his own words are usually preferable to critics' guesses about
what they mean, I find too often that his diagnoses and prognoses are
badly dated in a way that uncovers just how overblown they were even
at the time of writing.

This problem is of course not just stylistic, and it's not confined to

---

4. This statement may seem surprising to anyone who has just read Chapter 11.
But the cosmic probings we met there were narrative *renderings* of worlds, not sermons.
Lawrence might well be placed into that chapter, but not because of his repetitive ser-
mons *about* the contemptible world.

differences easily datable and then dismissed. I remind you that even the staunchest Lawrentians have had their troubles. F. R. Leavis— who says in his still impressive appreciation of 1955 that Lawrence "is incomparably the greatest creative writer in English of our time[,] . . . one of the greatest English writers of any time" (18)—confesses that it took him many years and many re-readings to discover Lawrence's greatness. And he goes on to say that Lawrence too often betrays, with his insistent jargon, an uncertainty not just about himself but about "whether a valid communication has really been defined and con- veyed" (18).

What are we to make of a passage like this, found *after* Birkin has achieved his full love with Ursula? "Don't I [want other people's love]?" asks Birkin of Ursula. "It's the problem I can't solve. I *know* I want a perfect and complete relationship with you: and we've nearly got it— we really have. But beyond that. . . . Do I want a final, almost extra- human relationship with him [Gerald]—a relationship in the ultimate of me and him—or don't I?" (1976, 355; ch. 26). I can forgive Law- rence for having fixed this use of the word "relationship" into the vo- cabulary of our young folks, who can no longer talk of *loving* each other, or use any of the eulogistic or pejorative terms for marriages and trial marriages, but must always talk only of "relationships." I must still deplore, though, his contributions to a generation of lost souls who spend their lives worrying about how to get in touch with their feelings and achieve an "almost extra-human" something or other.

To someone like me, the hyperbole is especially troublesome when it throbs in Lawrence's destructive vein. I understand and share Law- rence's horror over the effects of modernism and industrialism on the lives of both the exploiters and the exploited. His portraits of the vari- ous forms of "uncreated" life have never been surpassed. But to me there is a great difference between feeling hatred for destructive institu- tions and expressing unadulterated and unmediated contempt for those who have their being within those institutions. His novels, es- says, and letters are full of hatred for this or that kind of human being—to say nothing of his deplorable eagerness to get even with individuals.

Whole classes of people are often simply wiped out by contemptuous reference: Jews, women, old people (especially if they are in the least conventional), certain *kinds* of women (like Hermione, Mrs. Bolton). I belong to too many of those classes. Perhaps most obviously, I'm the wrong kind of intellectual, a professor-critic. I have spent a lifetime trying to learn how to think about literature—to think consciously, even logically. I believe not only in the value of mind, as Lawrence certainly in one sense did, but in the value of a kind of mental work that Lawrence seems to abhor: the work of worrying consciously about contradictions and inconsistencies. Though good thinking about human affairs always requires us to respect our emotions, I am much more skeptical than he would be about what my gut tells me, especially if it tells me something that my mind abhors. Though I now agree with Leavis that Lawrence is in one sense an intellectual, he doesn't make things easy for a first reader who was brought up, as it were, on Aristotle and Jane Austen.

I can now easily recognize that I earlier misread Lawrence in this matter. When Birkin, for example, lashes out at the stupid and vicious Hermione's effort to obtain knowledge about life, I felt, on first reading, that Lawrence was obviously and blatantly cheating: what she was blamed for doing was surely what Lawrence himself was doing—trying to encompass the world with one's mind. Why so much vitriol against a passion for learning that Lawrence himself obviously shared? So that when I arrived at the climax of the wrestling match between Birkin and Gerald Crich, and found the phrase "Mindless at last!" I thought maybe I'd found the title for my strictures against this troublesome man. Mindless at last, indeed!

And it is not just groups of people—it's often the whole human race. "Humanity itself is dry-rotten," says Birkin, fairly early in *Women in Love*. "[M]ankind is a dead tree, covered with fine brilliant galls of people." Ursula protests, "But even if everybody is wrong—where are *you* right? . . . [W]here are you any better?" Aspiring to be a modern Socrates, Birkin replies, "[M]y only rightness lies in the fact that I know it. I detest what I am, outwardly [note that he does not say "what I am, inwardly"!]. I loathe myself as a human being."

> "So you'd like everybody in the world destroyed?" said Ursula.
> "I should indeed."
> "And the world empty of people?"
> "Yes truly."
>
> (1976, 118, 119; ch. 11)

And soon Ursula herself is thinking how pleasant it would be to view a world emptied of people.

In short, it's not surprising that passionate Lawrentians have often confessed, along with Leavis, that many re-readings were required before they could see how the novel as a whole transforms such moments into something else entirely.

The Friend Replies

By now you must be feeling some impatience: When do we get to the praise? And how did this reluctant reader manage to find virtues strong enough to overwhelm so many obstacles?[5]

I am by no means the first to defend Lawrence after describing a list of faults or difficulties. Usually the redemptive claim is that Lawrence teaches some deeper truths in spite of his excesses, or even because of them. Diana Trilling, in her lukewarm introduction to *The Portable D. H. Lawrence,* finally forgives Lawrence because he presents a "metaphor against doom," "a possible procedure for a fierce surgery upon an ailing world and selves" (1947, 32). The trouble is that Trilling obviously does not really herself embrace that "possible procedure," that "fierce surgery," just as Leavis does not consider Lawrence to be his intellectual equal. I don't think that the path of truth is the one on which we will find Lawrence shining at his best. Instead I would praise him for two quite different achievements: his special subtlety in handling point of view—though that term is misleading—and the special ethical relation that this allows him to build between the reader and the implied author.

Avrom Fleishman has recently argued that Lawrence's style suffered a sea change in the 1920s under the influence of Giovanni Verga, three of whose books Lawrence translated between 1920 and 1927. Lawrence's narrative voice, Fleishman says, became more "dialogical," as he learned from Verga how to achieve a many-voiced narrative tone. From *Sea and Sardinia* on, Fleishman claims, we find Lawrence "orchestrating a multitude of voices, each one of which is capable of itself becoming such an orchestrator" (1985, 167). "[I contend that] Law-

---

5. As Samuel Johnson puts it when he comes to a similar transition in appraising Shakespeare: "Shakespeare with his excellencies has likewise faults, and faults sufficient to obscure and overwhelm any other merit"—that is, the merits of any other author ([1765] 1968, 71).

rence is a grand master of the oral, dialectical, parodic, and polyglot manner that Bakhtin has established for Dostoyevsky and that Lawrence creates in normal English diction an equivalent of the narrational heteroglossia distinguishing encyclopedic authors from Rabelais to Pynchon" (169).

I don't question Fleishman's thesis that Lawrence became more dialogical after his Italian experience. But I do want to claim that Lawrence was skillful with "double-voiced" narration in the earlier works as well, and that much of my initial distress in reading *The Rainbow* and *Women in Love* came from my failure to recognize just how often his characters are not simple spokesmen for his views. As I see it now, I fell into the very trap that I've often warned against: I assumed that a character's words and judgments belong to the implied author.

Lawrence was experimenting radically with what it means for a novelist to lose his own distinct voice in the voices of his characters, especially in their inner voices. In his practice, all rules about point of view are abrogated: the borderlines between author's voice and character's voice are deliberately blurred, and only the criticism of the whole tale will offer any sort of clarity to the reader seeking to sort out opinions.

This is not simply the traditional problem produced by subtle but stable irony. It is true that we find in Lawrence's works many traditional stable ironies—moments when characters give themselves away by speaking or thinking in ways that Lawrence expects the reader to see through and deplore. Almost everything said or done, for example, by the hyper-sophisticate Halliday and his crowd, in *Women in Love*, is portrayed in a manner that leaves us in no doubt about where we should stand. When Halliday reads Birkin's passionate letter aloud to the hooting hateful bohemians, and Gudrun snatches the letter and flees, we are unequivocally with her and against Halliday (see ch. 28). But frequently we are offered ironies that must be called unstable—if we are to call them ironies at all. Again and again Lawrence simply surrenders the telling of the story to another mind, a mind neither clearly approved nor clearly repudiated yet presented in a tone that seems to demand judgment. I don't know of any novelist, not even Dostoevsky, who takes free indirect style further in the direction of sustained surrender to a passionate mimesis giving us not two clear voices, the (silent) author's and the independent character's, but a chorus of voices, each speaking with its own authority. The result is inevitably to blur our picture of just where the implied author stands. As Bakhtin says about Dostoevsky's surrendering to his characters, it is as if the author became simply one of many characters, one voice among many, having given up his right to total control (1984, 5).

Note how the surrender occurs in the following passage, from "Sunday Evening" in *Women in Love:*

> As the day wore on, the life-blood seemed to ebb away from Ursula, and within the emptiness a heavy despair gathered. Her passion seemed to bleed to death, and there was nothing. She sat suspended in a state of complete nullity, harder to bear than death.
>
> "Unless something happens," she said to herself, in the perfect lucidity of final suffering, "I shall die. I am at the end of my line of life."
>
> (1976, 183; ch. 15)

So far we are clearly observing, with Lawrence, as Ursula thinks and feels in her despair: she said to herself—quote, unquote. But the clues are quickly abandoned, so that we cannot tell, when the judgments come, whether or not Lawrence speaks for himself as well as for Ursula.

"Darkly, without thinking at all, she knew that she was near to death." Well, *is* she near to death, or is this a portrait of how a young woman exaggerates when in despair about love?

> She had travelled all her life along the line of fulfilment, and it was nearly concluded. She knew all she had to know, she had experienced all she had to experience, she was fulfilled into a kind of bitter ripeness, there remained only to fall from the tree into death. And one must fulfil one's development to the end, must carry the adventure to its conclusion. And the next step was over the border into death.

Who is this "one," by now? It sounds like Lawrence. Yet almost certainly this is now Ursula's thought only, in her premature despair. Lawrence cannot want us to believe, still less than halfway through the book, that "she had experienced all she had to experience" or that she is really "fulfilled into a kind of bitter ripeness." Is she not going too far? Where are we? And what about the following—where is Lawrence here?

> After all, when one was fulfilled, one was happiest in falling into death, as a bitter fruit plunges in its ripeness downwards. Death is a great consummation, a consummating experience. It is a development from life. That we know, while we are yet living. What then need we think for further? One

can never see beyond the consummation. It is enough that death is a great
and conclusive experience. Why should we ask what comes after the experience, when the experience is still unknown to us? Let us die, since
the great experience is the one that follows now upon all the rest, death,
which is the next great crisis in front of which we have arrived. . . . If a man
can see the next step to be taken, why should he fear the next but one? Why
ask about the next but one? Of the next step we are certain. It is the step
into death.

(183–84; ch. 15)

Who is the *one* who speaks here, who the *we*, who the *man?* The
impersonation here is so complete that a first reader, already unclear
about what the implied author might believe about life and death and
love, is almost sure to assume that Lawrence has taken over and is inviting us to share *his* final truth that Ursula has discovered.

After my own first reading of passages like this, I would have said,
"Lawrence has lost control; he is intruding his own thoughts about life
and death onto Ursula's experience—and they are thoughts that I reject." Now I would put it differently: Lawrence has so fully surrendered to imagining how such a moment of despair would feel to an
Ursula, he has so fully granted Ursula her freedom, that her trance becomes his own, for the moment, and for the moment ours. This is how
the struggle between life and death works, for her.

I cannot even now say that Lawrence is blameless when readers take
such passages as undoctored Lawrence. I would not even claim that he
knew, in any ordinary sense, whether or not he agreed with Ursula's
views here. No doubt in some moods he thought and talked this way.
But *the novel*, considered as a whole, places the meditation as only one
of many rival intensities—one that must be granted its reality, its otherness. It must not be accommodated to a simple, consistent, propositional portrait of "what Lawrence believed."

The temptation to a misleading identification is strongest, of course,
when we encounter the thoughts of a Birkin. Because Birkin bears so
many resemblances to what we know or guess about Lawrence himself, the reader is tempted to assume that whenever he launches into a
tirade or thinks deep idiosyncratic thoughts, it is Lawrence we are
hearing. On first reading, for example, I took Birkin's ecstatic roll in
the dewy flowers, toward the end of the "Breadalby" chapter, as Lawrence's own silly romanticism. You'll remember Birkin's discovery, in
the primroses and trees, that "people do not matter," that "it was quite
right of Hermione to want to kill him," that he need no longer "pre-

tend to have anything to do with human beings," that "he wanted no-body and nothing but the lovely, subtle, responsive vegetation, and himself, his own living self"—all this seemed pure excessive Lawrence, and I could well understand the revulsion of the early critic who quoted, in alarm, Birkin's claim that "he preferred his own madness, to the regular sanity. . . . He rejoiced in the new-found world of his mad-ness. It was so fresh and delicate and so satisfying" (101; ch. 8).

But then comes a curious passage, one that I had underplayed on first reading:

> As for the certain grief he felt at the same time, in his soul, that was only the remains of an old ethic, that bade a human being adhere to humanity. But he was weary of the old ethic, of the human being, and of humanity. He loved now the soft, delicate vegetation, that was so cool and perfect. He would overlook the old grief, he would put away the old ethic, he would be free in his new state.
>
> (101; ch. 8)

How could I have missed the point that all of this expresses Birkin as he thinks and feels *before* Ursula, Birkin at his most isolated, most misanthropic. The ecstasy is genuine, but the thoughts are for Law-rence himself surely half-baked. Lawrence does not trouble to say so. He does not say, "This is the way an ecstatic fusion with nature feels to a man who has almost been killed by his jaded mistress—a man who has long been surrounded by phonies, an intelligent, sensitive man choosing (rightly) to repudiate the empty world of Breadalby—a man desperate for human love." He leaves it to us both to feel the tempta-tions of Birkin's vegetable love and to discover its limitations as the novel progresses.

Lawrence may have been deliberately playing a tricky narrative game with us here, one that yields a dangerous irony. Birkin and Ur-sula are both expressing, in the passages I have just quoted, the full threat of the modern world, as it will appear to anyone who meets it as an isolate—as a "self," not a "character." In the search for an authen-tic self, any sensitive modern spirit living without love must end either in despair like Ursula's or in a half-mad ecstasy like Birkin's. By dra-matizing their conclusions as if they were conclusive, Lawrence tries, consciously or unconsciously, to build in us a longing for the only con-dition that he thinks can save us—a longing for what he elsewhere calls "the Holy Ghost" of self-purged selfhood.

He knows that human beings cannot be saved except in loving

others, yet he has discovered that the wrong kind of love for others is the greatest threat to genuine selfhood. If the novel is to work at all, we readers must long for the fruition of love between Birkin and Ursula, much as in reading earlier fiction we longed for that fruition for an Emma and Knightley. But we must not ever make the mistake of thinking that romantic love is enough to save us. What will save us, for Lawrence, is only a self-transcendence that is quite inexpressible in propositions and quite unlike any of the traditional efforts to transcend, in a domain of spirit, the body and its death. And if that is so, we must experience the various temptations of our central characters as authentic temptations, not as errors already judged to be wanting.

It is a mistake, then, to talk of Lawrence's deliberately blurred handling of point of view as "simply" a technical innovation: it is a powerful *ethical* invention. Whether we see the innovation as occurring before or after the point fixed upon by Fleishman, it exerts strong effects on our relations with the implied author, Lawrence. As flesh-and-blood readers, we either meet the implied author where we think he lives—and the main clues about his dwelling are his technical choices—or we refuse the meeting, as I almost did in my recent efforts to renew acquaintance. Even if the Lawrence I construct from the text contradicts in every crucial respect what D. H. Lawrence himself intended, I still cannot avoid a decision about whether or not to go along with the demands of this would-be friend.

The argument for thinking of our relation in ethical terms is made more easily when dealing with Lawrence than it would be in dealing with, let's say, Samuel Beckett or even James Joyce. Lawrence is quite open in his claims, made within both his fictions and his criticism, that he wishes to place his art in the service of life and that the writing and reading of fiction find their justification in the kind of people we become as we write or read. Thus no reader who refuses to engage with Lawrence in ethical debate could ever claim to be reading him in his own terms. We can assume that he would accept without question my assertion that his way of handling technical choices, his way of extending free indirect style to produce a deliberate confusion of moral viewpoints, has ethical consequences.[6]

---

6. This is not to contradict what I said in Chapter 3 about why no one ethical effect is tied to any one technical device. Free indirect style could be used by different authors

Lawrence as Friend

What is the ethical relation that he builds? The answer is implicit in what we have said already: reading him, I find myself conversing with a peculiarly insistent, intent, passionate, and wide-ranging friend, one who will respond in some interesting way to every important question I can think of. Some of our real-life friends—and they can be among our best—simply rule out certain topics from our conversation. Literary friends are like that, too. I don't expect to converse with the implied E. M. Forster about African art, let's say, or about how elementary education should be conducted. I don't converse with Jane Austen or Henry Fielding about depth psychology, and I don't talk with Henry James about metaphysics. While I don't rule out friends just because they refuse to respond to certain of my interests, there is something special about a friend to whom I can go with any kind of question, in the expectation of a good conversation. I can go to others for other virtues from my list in Chapter 6; I shall go to Lawrence for the *range* of questions on which he achieves both intensity and intimacy.

Considered under this metaphor of friendly conversation, what Lawrence's overlapping narrative voices give us is a steady stream of dramatized invitations to converse. Because of the intensity with which he explores the opposing experiences and speculations in each situation, we are again and again left with the *kinds* of irresolution that life itself presents—he is relatively "open"—but with a broader *range* of irresolutions, and a deeper engagement with manifold possibilities, than life itself is ever likely to present to any one of us unassisted.[7] What I discovered, on a second and third reading, and especially on reading *Women in Love* aloud, was a much fairer and livelier distribution of human sympathy for disparate views than I had ever expected any single human being to display.

I think that something like this skill is what Leavis refers to when he

---

for an unlimited number of effects entirely different from Lawrence's. It is his *way* of handling it that produces his unique *kind* of effects.

7. Leavis made a similar point in showing how Lawrence presents conflicts in which the reader must feel the legitimacy of more than one position. Using as example the quarrel about religion between Will Brangwen and Anna in *The Rainbow*, Leavis concludes, "It is impossible not to register, in the upshot of the argument, that criticism has been established against both parties to the conflict" (1955, 149).

grants to Lawrence the virtue of "supreme intelligence"—"the power
to pursue an organizing process of thought through a wide and difficult tract, with a sustained consistency that is at the same time a
delicate fidelity to the complexities of the full concrete experience"
(1955, 391).

The friendship Lawrence provides is distinctive enough, in both
range and depth, to warrant a survey of the topics he dwells on. Of
course I cannot even hint at his depth, but the range is in itself enough
to mark him as almost without peer in an "artistic virtue" that is
unique to extended narratives.[8]

Item: Suppose I want to talk with someone about the powers and
corruptions of formal education,[9] of how it feels to try to teach but
fail, of how it feels to have one's first slight success as a teacher, of how
it feels to see naive educational ideals corrupted before one's eyes by
actual teachers and students. Again, I happen to disagree with much
that Lawrence seems to *say* about such matters. I'm disturbed by his
final downgrading of "elementary ed.," as he shows Ursula and Gudrun
and Birkin all blithely violating their responsibilities to those poor
school kids in order to work out their private salvation, apparently indifferent to what will happen next to the children they leave behind.
But where can I find anyone to surpass the depth and poignancy of
experience that Lawrence gives to the young Ursula, as she beats her
rude charges into belated submission—and with the beating loses her
idealism about herself?

> So the battle went on till her heart was sick. She had several more boys
> to subjugate before she could establish herself. . . . She knew now that
> nothing but a thrashing would settle some of the big louts. . . .
> . . . [S]he seized her cane, and slashed the boy who was insolent to her,
> over head and ears and hands. And at length they were afraid of her, she
> had them in order.
> But she had paid a great price out of her own soul, to do this. It seemed
> as if a great flame had gone through her and burnt her sensitive tissue. She

---

8. Obvious rivals in English would be Melville, in *Moby Dick,* and Joyce; in
French, Proust; in German, Thomas Mann; in Russian, both Dostoevsky and Tolstoy.
All of these seem to me to go "deeper" than Lawrence. No doubt if some Society of True
Believers asked me for a keynote speech on any one of them, I could become at least as
enthusiastic about his conversational breadth, regardless of what I might discover about
technical and formal excellence.

9. As I have recently been trying to do in *The Vocation of a Teacher* (1988).

who shrank from the thought of physical suffering in any form, had been forced to fight and beat with a cane and rouse all her instincts to hurt. And afterwards she had been forced to endure the sound of their blubbering and desolation, when she had broken them to order.

Oh, and sometimes she felt as if she would go mad. What did it matter, what did it matter if their books were dirty and they did not obey? She would rather, in reality, that they disobeyed the whole rules of the school, than that they should be beaten, broken, reduced to this crying, hopeless state. . . .

Yet it had to be so.

(1915, 382–83; ch. 13)

Most novelists who take the trouble to look at education at all with any vigor or seriousness—and few of them do—reduce its problems and joys to the level of most textbooks on the history and theory of education: crude caricatures of incredibly joyful rewards or even cruder caricatures of comic failure. But Lawrence remembers—and captures—the full range and intensity of motives and emotions that go into pedagogical triumphs that are simultaneously defeats.

Item: Suppose I want to have a serious conversation about the fate of religion in the modern world and its likely role in any future, a conversation that will not cheat by resting from the beginning on ready-made assumptions for or against belief. Lawrence saw that the essential religious questions had not been solved by modernist moves against traditional doctrines and establishments. He saw that the essential quest for each of us is still to fashion a self responsible to a cosmos that we did not make. And he had known, in his bones, how it feels to try out and then painfully reject traditional answers. His quest to make a larger self that would really respect the Other—including the *others* who represent Him or It—is to me one of the most impressive efforts at religious fiction of this century, at least in English.

Lawrence urges me to build a self bigger than "myself," a self somehow not reducible to known psychology or typology or to any "conjunction of forces, physical and chemical." Nowhere in literature is there a more wonderful evocation of our quest for such a self than Ursula's in the chapter "The Bitterness of Ecstasy" in *The Rainbow.* Looking at some "plant-animal" under the microscope, she muses:

It intended to be itself. But what self? Suddenly in her mind the world gleamed strangely, with an intense light, like the nucleus of the creature under the microscope. Suddenly she had passed away into an intensely-gleaming light of knowledge. She could not understand what it all was. She only knew that it was not limited mechanical energy, nor mere purpose of self-preservation and self-assertion. It was a consummation, a being infinite. Self was a oneness with the infinite. To be oneself was a supreme, gleaming triumph of infinity.

(1915, 416–17; ch. 15)

Now as an *answer* to cosmological questions this is pretty minimal. Ursula's revelation is at best temporary; she is headed for more darkness and confusion and misery than she can now dream of. But if I want to remind myself of how it *feels* to grapple seriously with religious issues divorced from established answers, I'll re-read that portion of *The Rainbow* before turning to any systematic theologian.

Item: Suppose I have become interested in recent talk about death and dying, and I'd like to hold a conversation about how I might think of my own aging and death and of modern ways of dealing with them. I can certainly find many a modern novelist who will tell me that death is a tragedy or a farce or a dirty trick played by God. And I can find some few overtly religious novelists who will tell me that I should not worry about death because it is canceled by an after-life. But where will I find anyone who will *show* me convincingly how it feels to die unanointed and unaneled, as Thomas Crich dies, mute, uncomprehending, "uncreated," in effect cheated of a death of his own? Or as his son Gerald dies, never having found, or created, a "self" in the love of another?

> "He should have loved me," he [Birkin] said. "I offered him."
> She [Ursula], afraid, white, with mute lips, answered:
> "What difference would it have made!"
> "It would," he said. "It would."
> . . . Birkin remembered how once Gerald had clutched his hand with a warm, momentaneous grip of final love. For one second—then let go again, let go for ever. If he had kept true to that clasp, death would not have mattered. Those who die, and dying still can love, still believe, do not die. . . .
> And Gerald! The denier!

(1976, 471; ch. 31)

Item: Suppose—to come to what may be the most troublesome issue of all for Lawrentians in the eighties—suppose I am interested in feminist criticism, not only interested but convinced that most male novelists have debased women. One could easily make a case against Lawrence as a sexist—indeed, most of the women I have talked with about him say that he offends them, too often, with his way of talking about how each woman can or must play the hen to some man's cock. I find him shifting about on this issue. He fails, for example, to repudiate clearly the way Gerald and Birkin talk about women in general, and especially about semi-whores like Minette: "There's a certain smell about the skin of those women, that in the end is sickening beyond words—even if you like it at first," says Gerald, and Birkin replies, "I know" (1976, 88; ch. 8).

Yet with this said, where could I turn for an encounter as serious as Lawrence's with the struggle for an equal relation between men and women as one finds in novel after novel, story after story? Where could any woman turn, looking through novels by men, for a more serious, exhaustive search for forms of life tolerable to an intelligent, sensitive woman? And where would I look, among male novelists, for an equally serious search for a male role that is not sexist on all of these topics?

What I am impressed by is Lawrence's capacity to dramatize rival positions in all these matters, oppositions that become emotionally and psychologically plausible and engaging because of the author's vigorous penetration of the souls of those whose stories he tells. And we could add many more topics: Lawrence's profound engagement with the psychology of unconscious motivation—he's the first English novelist to recognize the full challenge to traditional narration offered by the Freudian revolution; or his serious grappling with the ethics of art (our central subject here); or his prophetic and deep engagement with the changing nature of labor, for both men and women, as technology spreads and people increasingly measure their lives in terms of material comfort; or his penetrating and surprisingly "inward" portraits of the new industrialists (like Gerald Crich), whom he professed to hate as a class; or his sensitive realization of the appeal and challenge of scientific inquiry, particularly of biology; or his splendid studies of what we now call "marriage and the family." I even enjoy talking with him about parenting: What other childless novelist has ever done as much justice to the joys and pains of being a parent as we find in the prolonged scene between Brangwen and his step-child Anna, early in *The Rainbow?* He first tries to silence her uncontrollable sobs with angry reproach, then carries her tenderly with him to the barn and the nightly chores, and finally lulls her to sleep, having at last calmed her fears about losing her mother. "He put the child into bed wrapped as she was in the shawl, for the sheets would be cold.

Then he was afraid that she might not be able to move her arms, so he loosened her. The black eyes opened, rested on him vacantly, sank shut again. He covered her up. The last little quiver from the sobbing shook her breathing" (1915, 72; ch. 2)

We could easily go on.[10] Who can rival this breadth? Remember, it is not a matter of discovering whether he or his rivals actually talk about a given topic. I suspect that Aldous Huxley, David Lodge, and scores of others could rival him in sheer coverage of up-to-date topics. But how deep do they go—on more than two or three topics?

A word finally about Lawrence's "vitality" (the "intensity" of Chapter 6). Because Lawrence shows so many characters on so many occasions inveighing against life, readers from the beginning have often misread him. In the much abused terms used in debates between philistines and the avant-garde, he has seemed to be "life-denying" rather than "life-affirming" or enhancing. But everyone who dwells with him for long finds him to be finally energizing. He yields a renewed confidence in the ability of the individual artist (and reader) to resist even the most adverse social and political circumstances and to *do* something with and through a "created" self. I think that this effect may spring in part from his theory of how art relates to life. In contrast with a large number of modern novelists and poets, Lawrence sees art as serving life rather than merely compensating for it. The artist cannot escape responsibility for the effects of his art; his art is to be judged by its connections with life as lived—as expressed, for example, in Ursula's response to Loerke's sick art (1915, 419–25; ch. 29). The final effect of reading his novels, I have come to feel, is that here is one artist whose work serves life rather than bleeding it in the name of art.

In short, in his range of sympathies, his depth of courageous engagement with others and the Other, and his ultimate commitment to

---

10. One mark of any novelist who is a remarkable "conversationalist" is the range of subjects that critics have chosen to see as the very center of the *oeuvre*. It is hard to think of any important general topic about which there is not a book or article with a title roughly in the form, "Lawrence and X." About religion see, for example, Ross C. Murfin's *Swinburne, Hardy, Lawrence, and the Burden of Belief* (1978). About the formation of a self, see Marguerite Beede Howe, *The Art of the Self in D. H. Lawrence* (1977), and Roger Ebbatson, *The Evolutionary Self: Hardy, Forster, Lawrence* (1982). About the question of feminism, see Hilary Simpson, *D. H. Lawrence and Feminism* (1982). I have not yet sought out works on his "marriage counseling" or on the industrial revolution, or on the relation of his views to the current fad in death and dying, but I know that they would be easy to find.

making each life *count*, Lawrence has won me. I still doubt that he would be a good fellow guest at a cocktail party. Sullen, opinionated, sneering, he sulks in a corner, condescending to talk with me—provided I'll yield him the floor—but fulminating against most of the other guests: they are dead, "inorganic," "uncreated." But if I can bring myself to follow him when he slams out of the door in disgust, if I can learn to tease him, as Ursula teases Birkin and Birkin teases himself, for "Hamletizing" and for the *Salvator Mundi* tone, I know that I can count on a good conversation—about how the people at the party betrayed themselves in their talking, about how their secret notions belied not only their open talk but their conscious *arrières-pensées,* about how their ways of thinking and feeling represent their class, their profession, their family origins, and their sexual history, to say nothing of the political history of their time and even the history of the human race.

I must not ask him to be as large and permanently prophetic a creature as he himself aspires to be. But how he stretches my notions of the possibilities of life in my century! How he dwarfs most of his imitators and rivals in prophetic fiction!

So I conclude my confessions as something a good deal warmer than a lukewarm Lawrentian. As the anonymous critic at Blackwell's mailroom insisted, the novels of D. H. Lawrence are indeed better than I had thought. I may still be divided and often confused in my responses to Lawrence's gifts, but he has blasted me once and for all out of the camp of the Laodiceans.

"HE TOLD THE TRUTH, MAINLY": WHAT PAUL MOSES KNEW ABOUT *HUCKLEBERRY FINN*

It is my conviction that the human race is no proper target for harsh
words and bitter criticisms, and that the only justifiable feeling toward it
is compassion; it did not invent itself, and it had nothing to do with the
planning of its weak and foolish character.

Mark Twain, Autobiography

We began with Paul Moses's criticism of *Adventures of Huckleberry Finn*, and it is now time for a return. If his kind of criticism is legitimate, a kind that most of us practice even in the face of theoretical objections, what can we say about that novel that Paul Moses criticized simply by digging in his heels?[11] Can we hope to avoid making utter fools of ourselves as we discuss ethical doubts about all or part of what has often been called "one of the great books of the world" (Leavis 1967, 9), and more often "one of the greatest of all American novels" (Davis 1984, 2)?

Mark Twain had himself done a lot of ethical criticism long before he published his famous warning against morality hunters at the head of *Huckleberry Finn* ([1884] 1982).[12] I am thinking not mainly of essays like the devastating "James Fenimore Cooper's Literary Offenses" but rather of the criticism implicit in his fictions. Much of the fun of *Tom Sawyer* (1876), for anyone who has ever read many previous novels, lies in its mockery of the phony worlds he felt they offered. What's more, Twain included a good deal of quite explicit criticism within *Huck Finn* itself, irresistible invitations to violate his warning: the mockery, for example, of the "killer code" of Tom Sawyer's robber gang in chapter 2; or of the strange morality borrowed, in chapter 3, from the *Arabian Nights;*[13] or of the adventure-story code that governs the "evasion" efforts of the final section (chapter 34 through "Chapter the Last"). In short, Mark Twain knew well enough what it means to "find a moral" in a tale, and he knew that every tale is loaded with "morals," even if it avoids explicit moralizing.

What he was right to fear is the destruction that can result for any story, and particularly for any comic story, when a reader busily extracts moralities rather than enjoying the tale. Twain knew from his own reading experience that when we put our minds on ideological conflict, a story can be destroyed—just as my ethical criticism has for me weakened some of the comic power of Panurge's prank with the dogs in *Gargantua.*[14] When he mocked courtly romances in *A Con-*

11. Paul Moses died only a short while after the confrontation I described in Chapter 1. It was in fact mainly Charles Long whose arguments about *Huck Finn* later jarred me into seeing some validity in Moses's case.

12. My references to *Adventures of Huckleberry Finn* will be to the best available "reading edition," the new Library of America *Mississippi Writings.* This edition promises to be standard reading for a long time.

13. "'Well,' says I, 'I think they are a pack of flatheads for not keeping the palace themselves 'stead of fooling them away like that'" ([1884] 1982, 638).

14. I cannot help wondering why a great artist like Twain was so "down" on Jane Austen (to use one of Huck's favorite words). Surely his must have been an ethical objec-

necticut Yankee (1889) and adventure tales in *Tom Sawyer* and parts of *Huckleberry Finn,* he must have known that his perceptive readers would never again enjoy those originals quite so much. And as the kind of moralist who increasingly was to lay about him with a heavy cudgel, with fewer and fewer freely comic effects, he had good reason to know that people who put their attention on finding the moral in any human story risk destroying the fun of it.[15] Critics like me who *do* find a moral *are* going to be distracted from the sheer joy of dwelling for many hours in the mind and heart of a great natural comic poet, that "bad boy," Huckleberry Finn.

Even so, I suspect that Twain would have been surprised, and no doubt dismayed, at the floods of moral criticism evoked by the tale. Initially the moralists' attention seems to have been entirely on the dangers to young people of encountering the aggressive "immorality" of Huck himself—his smoking, his lying, his stealing, not to mention his irreverent "attitude." It was no doubt Huck's glaring inappropriateness as a model for young boys that led the Concord Library, along with libraries in Denver, Brooklyn, Omaha, and other cities simply to ban the book (Blair 1960, 372).[16] Twain could easily have predicted—and no doubt savored the prediction—that the portrait of an appealing youngster openly repudiating most "sivilized" norms would upset good people, especially when it was made doubly seductive by the

---

tion a bit like the "moralizing" one I worried about above. My guess is that he just could not stomach those romantic endings, with all the lies they tell about the world. Is there a single fiction of his that leads to a romantic ending handled without ironic discounting?

15. His writings become more and more overtly didactic, through *Pudd'nhead Wilson* (1894), *Personal Recollections of Joan of Arc* (1896), the unfinished *Which Was It?* (1902), the anonymously published *What Is Man?* (1906), and the uncompleted "The Mysterious Stranger." See Tuckey 1980.

That Twain was a conscious moralist everyone knows, because he published a great deal of moral and political indictment in non-fictional form (see Geismar 1973). Just how much he was thinking about alternative moral *systems* while writing *Huck Finn* is shown by the account of his reading of W. E. H. Lecky's *History of Rationalism* (see Blair 1960, 135–45).

16. Though Twain was obviously annoyed by the bannings (Blair 1960), and by the many reviews that called the book trashy (Twain 1979, 128), he seems to have spent more time enjoying the boost to circulation that the bannings ensured. He wrote that the Concord condemnation as "trash and suitable only for the slums" was a "rattling tip-top puff." "That will sell 25,000 copies for sure" (64). Steven Mailloux, in a fine study of the "reception-history" of the novel, has unearthed innumerable anxious responses to the "bad boy" stories popular at the time (Mailloux, forthcoming).

witty vitality of Huck's own narration: "[I]t don't make no difference whether you do right or wrong, a person's conscience ain't got no sense, and just goes for him *anyway*. If I had a yaller dog that didn't know no more than a person's conscience does, I would pison him. It takes up more room than all the rest of a person's insides, and yet ain't no good, nohow. Tom Sawyer he says the same" ([1884] 1982, 851; ch. 33).

Such talk is dangerous to good citizens, especially when it comes from a kind of anti-hero whose story itself lends considerable support to skepticism about public morality. The uselessness of "conscience" is dramatized with example after example of how Huck's conscience, actually the destructive morality implanted by a slave society, combats his native impulse to do what he really ought to do—what Twain called his "good heart." The most famous attack on the norms dictated by obedience to public morality—and especially by official Christianity[17]—comes when Huck realizes that he is committing a terrible sin in helping Jim escape slavery. Almost two-thirds of the way through the novel, long after Huck has discovered his love for Jim and has been willing to "humble myself to a nigger" and apologize for a cruel trick (709; ch. 15), Huck sits down to think by himself, after hearing some adults talking about how easy it is to pick up reward money for turning in a runaway slave. Though the pages that follow are probably more widely known than any other passage in American literature, I must trace them in some detail, because they have always provided the evidence used by us liberals in opposing Paul Moses's kind of indictment.

At first Huck's thoughts run to what a vicious trick it was for the Duke and the Dolphin to sell Jim for "forty dirty dollars," but then he remembers how badly his reputation will suffer when people discover "that Huck Finn helped a nigger to get his freedom; and if I was ever to see anybody from that town again, I'd be ready to get down and lick his boots for shame" (833; ch. 31). "Reputation" then provides an opening in this little morality tale for "conscience" to enter and take an implied beating by offering wicked advice. I italicize the more obvious alarm buttons labeled, through their satirical force, as "moral heresy."

17. Twain had privately labeled it "an odious religion. Still I do not think its priests ought to be burned, but only the missionaries" (qtd. in Blair 1960, 136).

The more I studied about this, the more *my conscience* went to grinding me, and the more *wicked* and low-down and ornery I got to feeling. And at last, when it hit me all of a sudden that here was the *plain hand of Providence slapping me in the face* and letting me know my *wickedness was being watched all the time from up there in heaven*, whilst I was *stealing a poor old woman's nigger that hadn't ever done me no harm*, and now was showing me *there's One that's always on the lookout, and ain't agoing to allow no such miserable doings to go only just so fur and no further*, I most dropped in my tracks. . . . Well, I tried the best I could to kinder soften it up somehow for myself, by saying *I was brung up wicked*, and so I warn't so much to blame; but *something inside of me kept saying, "There was the Sunday school, you could a gone to it; and if you'd a done it they'd a learnt you, there, that people that acts as I'd been acting about that nigger goes to everlasting fire."*

It made me shiver. And I about made up my mind *to pray; and see if I couldn't try to quit being the kind of boy I was, and be better. So I kneeled down*. But the words wouldn't come. Why wouldn't they? It warn't no use to try and hide it *from Him*. Nor from *me* [Twain's italics] neither. I knowed very well why they wouldn't come. It was because *my heart warn't right*; it was because I warn't square; it was because I was playing double.

Then, after more brilliant parody of gospel sermons about duplicitous sinfulness—"*deep down in me I knowed it was a lie—and He knowed it. You can't pray a lie—I found that out*" (833–34)—the sacrilegious parody thickens. Huck decides to try a standard expedient of pious guidebooks: first do the "right thing" and *then* you can pray. Feeling already freed of sinfulness, he writes the letter that would send Jim back into slavery. "*I felt good and all washed clean of sin* for the first time I had ever felt so in my life, and I knowed *I could pray now*" (834).

But then another mysterious intervention occurs, even less willed than the rising of his "conscience": his memories of joyful, loving life with Jim. The scenes of their life on the raft together are richly summarized in his imagination, and they lead to one of the great literary confrontations of abstract, misguided principle with concrete, lived experience—what critics would later learn to call existential reality. Like many a later novel, the scene presents the crucial choice in terms exactly the reverse of the traditional religious (or Kantian) sermon: not the message that "Your impulses are suspect and you must appeal to moral principle, or reason, to school them" but rather a message something like "You have nothing but your true impulse to guide you to the correct decision; *nothing* that society has taught you can help you now":

[A]t last I struck the time I saved him . . . and he was so grateful, and said I was the best friend old Jim ever had in the world, and the *only* one he's got now; and then I happened to look around, and see that paper [the letter offering to sell Jim].

It was a close place. I took it up, and held it in my hand. I was a trembling, because I'd got to decide, forever, *betwixt two things* . . . [my italics for the traditional choice of eternities: compare my discussion in Chapter 8 of Stephen Dedalus's choice]. I studied a minute, sort of holding my breath, and then says to myself:

"All right, then, I'll *go* to hell"—and tore it up.

(834–35)

And *then* the traditional flood of right feeling follows, still in terms that must have been part of what worried right-thinking librarians at the time:

I . . . *never thought no more about reforming* . . . and said I would *take up wickedness again*, which was in my line, being brung up to it, and the other warn't. And for a starter, I would go to work and steal Jim out of slavery again [here the librarian may feel some confusion: surely Huck is right in *this* choice, isn't he?]; and if I could *think up anything worse, I would do that, too; because as long as I was in, and in for good, I might as well go the whole hog.*

(835)

Now hold up there, man! You're going too far. What kind of a *moral* code is *that?* Obviously Mark Twain could have predicted that we good burghers would feel attacked by such a passage: to fight slavery is good, right enough, but to move from that to general wickedness— that's something else again. Even if by now I as reader am convinced that the noble savage Huck will never do anything really bad, I might squirm a little thinking about the spot this mischievous author has landed *me* in. And my squirming will not be allayed by the novel's continuing elevation of untutored intuition over the codes of the "sivilization" that Huck explicitly repudiates at the end: "I got to light out for the Territory ahead of the rest, because Aunt Sally she's going to adopt me and sivilize me and I can't stand it. I been there before."

The Indictment

If Twain could have predicted such conventional distress, he could not have predicted Paul Moses's response, the response, as we might say, of "good old Jim's" great-great-grandchildren reading the novel from a new perspective—not Jim's, not Huck's, not the white liberals' of the 1880s or 1980s, but *theirs:* the perspective of a black reader in our time thinking about what that powerful novel has for a hundred years been teaching Americans about race and slavery. It would surely have shocked Twain to find that some modern black Americans see the book as reactionary in its treatment of racial questions:

> For black people and for those sympathetic to their long struggle for fair treatment in North America, the *Adventures of Huckleberry Finn* spirals down to a dispiriting and racist close. The high adventures of the middle chapters, Huck's admiration of Jim, Jim's own strong self-confidence, and the slave's willingness to protect and guide Huck are all rendered meaningless by the closing chapters in which Twain turns Jim over to two white boys out on a lark.
>
> (Jones 1984, 34)

> As a black parent . . . I sympathize with those who want the book banned, or at least removed from required reading lists in schools. While I am opposed to book banning, I know that my children's education will be enhanced by not reading *Huckleberry Finn.*
>
> (Lester 1984, 43)

Such objections might well have seemed to Twain much more perverse than the cries of alarm from the pious. After all, the book does in fact attack the pious; they were in a sense reading it as it asked to be read—as an attack on *them.* But when black readers object to it, and even attempt to censor it from public schools (Hentoff 1982), are they not simply failing to *see* the thrust of scenes like the one I have quoted? How can they deny that Jim is "the moral center" of the work, that Twain has struck a great blow against racism and for racial equality, and that the book when read properly could never harm either blacks or whites?

So I might have argued with Paul Moses. So most white liberals today still argue when blacks attack the book. So even some black readers defend the book today.[18] Many critics have objected, true enough, to the concluding romp that Tom Sawyer organizes in a mock attempt to free the already freed Jim. But most of the objections have been about a failure of form: Twain made an artistic mistake, after writing such a marvelous book up to that point, by falling back into the tone

18. A fine, subtle, accurate reading of this kind is given by David L. Smith in "Huck, Jim, and American Racial Discourse" (1984).

of *Tom Sawyer*. Not realizing the greatness of what he had done in the scenes on the river, he simply let the novel "spiral down," or back, into the kind of comic stereotypes of the first few chapters. Though put as a formal objection to incoherence, this objection could be described as ethical, in the broadest sense: the implied standard is that great novels probe moral profundities; because the ending of *Huck Finn* is morally shallow, the book as a whole ought not be accepted as great.

Seldom is the case made that the ending is not just shallow but morally and politically offensive. Most critics have talked as if it would be absurd to raise questions about the *racial* values of a book in which the very moral center is a noble black man so magnanimous that he gives himself back into slavery in order to help a doctor save a white boy's life. Why should *this* book, so clearly *anti*-racist, be subjected to the obviously partisan criticism of those who do not even take the trouble to understand what a great blow the book strikes for black liberation? Critics, black and white, are inclined to talk like this:

> [E]xcept for Melville's work, *Huckleberry Finn* is without peers among major Euro-American novels for its explicitly anti-racist stance. Those who brand the book 'racist' generally do so without having considered the specific form of racial discourse to which the novel responds.
>
> (Smith 1984, 4)

In this view, all the seemingly objectionable elements, such as the use of the word "nigger," are signs, when read properly, of Twain's enlightened rebellion against racist language and expectations. The defense is well summarized by one black critic who seems enthusiastic about the book, Charles H. Nichols. *Huck Finn*, he says, is

> an indispensable part of the education of both black and white youth. It is indispensable because (1) it unmasks the violence, hypocrisy and pretense of nineteenth-century America; (2) it re-affirms the values of our democratic faith, our celebration of the worthiness of the individual, however poor, ignorant or despised; (3) it gives us a vision of the possibility of love and harmony in our multi-ethnic society; (4) it dramatizes the truth that justice and freedom are always in jeopardy.
>
> (Nichols 1984, 14)

Accepting the first two and the last of these, with minor qualifications, must we not question the third? Can we really accept this novel as a vision of the possibility of love and harmony in our multi-ethnic society?

It was in an effort to answer that question that I recently read the great novel again, asking what its full range of fixed norms appears to be, a century after its composition, and thus what its influence on American racial thinking is likely to be.[19]

While I found again the marvelously warm and funny novel I had always loved, I found another one alongside it, as it were. That novel looks rather different. Here is how a fully "suspicious" interpreter might view it:

"This is the story of how a pre-adolescent white boy, Huck, reared in the worst possible conditions—no mother and a drunken, bigoted, cruel, and impoverished father—discovers in his own good heart and flatly against every norm of his society that he can love an older black slave, Jim—love him so strongly that he violates his own upbringing and tries to help Jim escape from slavery. Huck fails in his sporadic attempt to free Jim, but Jim is (entirely fortuitously) freed by a stroke of conscience (the same 'good heart'?) in his owner just before she dies. (There is some problem of credibility here, since she presumably has good reason to believe, along with others in her town, that Jim earlier killed Huck Finn; but let that pass.)

"At the beginning and again at the end of the novel, Jim is portrayed as an ignorant, superstitious, boastful, kind but gullible comic 'nigger,' more grown child than adult. Naturally affectionate toward and un-critical of his white masters, he is almost pathetically grateful for any expression of sympathy or aid. During the central part of the novel he is turned into something of a father figure for Huck; we see him as a loving father of his own children (full of remorse about having beaten a child who turns out to be deaf); and as a deeply loyal friend (once he has found that his 'only friend' is the almost equally ignorant but less

---

19. I take for granted here a point made several times before—that Huck Finn him-self, like many a secondary spokesman in the novel, offers norms that we are expected either to reject outright or to forget quickly after we finish reading. For example, "all prayers are either silly or hypocritical." The novel implies as much, but it puts no real force into the implication. Clearly the implied author would feel no pain if a reader as-serted that some prayers, and even some blessings on meals, are defensible and some not. "Dressing up in formal clothes is always ridiculous." Oh, well, who cares? "Lynch mobs are inherently cowardly and can be quelled by one man with courage." Well, maybe; maybe not.

gullible white boy). He becomes, for large stretches, an ideally generous, spiritually sound, wonderfully undemanding surrogate parent.
The implication is clear: wipe slavery away and you will find beneath
its yoke a race of natural Christians: unscarred, loving, infinitely grateful people who will cooperate lovingly with their former masters (with
the good ones, anyway) in trying to combat the wicked white folks, of
which the world seems to be full. (There are no other black characters—just the one 'good nigger.') Only occasionally through these
middle chapters does the author reduce Jim again to the role of stage
prop. Whenever he gets in the way of the author's plan to satirize the
mores of small town and rural American society, he is simply dropped
out of sight—and out of Huck's mind: an expendable property, to be
treated benevolently as part of the implied author's claim to belong to
the tiny saving remnant of human beings who escape his indictment of
a vicious mankind.

"All the more curious then that we find, especially in a couple of
chapters at the beginning and in a prolonged section at the end—almost a third of the whole book—that Jim is portrayed as simply a
comic butt, suitable for exploitation by cute little white boys of good
heart who have been led into concocting a misguided adventure by
reading silly books. There are moments in the novel when we expect
that Huck Finn will discover behind the stereotype of the 'good nigger-
mistreated' a real human being, someone whose feelings and condition
matter as much as those of whites and who at the same time is not,
under the skin, merely a collection of Sunday school virtues; a white
prince in disguise ('I thought he had a good heart in him and was
a good man, the first time I see him. Then they all agreed that Jim
had acted very well, and was deserving to have some notice took of
it' [905; ch. 42]). But we lose this hope early, and we are not really
surprised, only disgusted, when Huck forgets all that he might have
learned and allows himself to take part in Tom's scheme to free the
already freed Jim. Huck is in one sense invulnerable to our criticism
here, because he thinks that he is still 'wickedly' freeing a slave, his
friend. But the *novel*, like the mischievous Tom Sawyer, simply treats
Jim and his feelings here as expendable, as sub-human—a slave to the
plot, as it were. We readers are expected to laugh as Tom and Huck
develop baroque maneuvers that all the while keep Jim in involuntary
imprisonment. Twain, the great liberator, keeps Jim enslaved as long

as possible, one might say, milking every possible laugh out of a situation which now seems less frequently and less wholeheartedly funny than it once did."[20]

Twain's full indifference to what all this means to Jim, and his seeming indifference to the full meaning of slavery and emancipation, is shown in the way he exonerates Tom for his prank and compensates Jim for his prolonged suffering. I italicize (superseding Twain's italics in this passage) the moments that now give me some trouble as I think about what the liberal Twain is up to:

> We had Jim out of the chains in no time, and when Aunt Polly and Uncle Silas and Aunt Sally found out *how good he helped* the doctor nurse Tom, they made a heap of fuss over him, and fixed him up prime, and *give him all he wanted to eat, and a good time, and nothing to do.* And we had him up to the sick-room; and had a high talk; and *Tom give Jim forty dollars for being prisoner for us so patient,* and doing it up so good, and *Jim was pleased most to death, and busted out, and says:*
> "Dah, now, Huck, what I tell you?—what I tell you up dah on Jackson islan'? I tole *you I got a hairy breas', en what's de sign un it; en* I tole *you I ben rich wunst, en gwineter to be rich* agin; *en it's come true; en heah she is! Dah, now! doan talk to me—signs is signs, mine I tell you; en I knowed jis' 's well 'at I 'uz gwineter be rich agin as I's a stannin' heah dis minute!*"
>
> (911; "Chapter the Last")

All nice and clear now? The happy-go-lucky ex-slave, superstitious, absurdly confused about the value of money (he happily clutches at the gift of forty dollars while Huck, by the final turn on the next page, gets six thousand), reveals himself as overjoyed with his fate, and all is well.

But just what is the "vision of love and harmony" that this novel "educates" us to accept? We find in it the following fixed norms:

1. Black people, slaves and ex-slaves, are a special *kind* of good people—so naturally good, in their innocent simplicity, that the effects on them of slavery will not be discernible once slavery is removed. Some few whites are like that, too—the Huck Finns of

---

20. I must again confess that as a young man I thought this section about the funniest in the book, and I was at first quite cross at colleagues who, on "purely formal" grounds, found fault with Twain for the ending. The best summary I have seen of the debate about this ending, and the issues it raises, is in John Reichert's *Making Sense of Literature* (1977, ch. 6).

the world who miraculously escape corruption by virtue of sheer natural goodness.

2. Black people are hungry for love (essentially friendless, unless whites befriend them) and they will be (*should* be) obsequiously grateful for whatever small favors whites grant them, in their benignity.

3. White people are of three kinds: the wicked and foolish, a majority; the foolish good—essentially generous people like the Widow Watson who are made foolish by obedience to social norms; and naturally good people, like Huck, whose only weapons against the wicked are a simulated passivity and obedience covering an occasionally successful trickery. We may find also an occasional representative of a fourth kind, the essentially decent but thoughtless trickster, the creator of stories, like Tom—and Mark Twain. They will entertain the world regardless of consequences.

4. The consequences of emancipation will be as good as they can be, in this wicked world, so long as you (the white liberal reader) have your heart in the right place—as you clearly do because you have palpitated properly to Huck's discovery of a full sense of brotherhood with Jim. You needn't worry about his losing that sense almost before he finds it; after all, Huck, our hero, is not responsible for anything that society might have done or might yet do about the aftermath of slavery.

5. All institutional arrangements, all government, all "sivilization," all laws, are absurd—and absurdly irrelevant to what is, after all, the supreme value in life: feeling "comfortable," as Huck so often expresses his deepest value, comfortable with "oneself," that ultimate source of intuition which, if one is among the lucky folk, will be a sure guide.[21]

---

21. William Van O'Connor, in a rather ill-tempered essay, has questioned the greatness of *Huck Finn* partly on the ground that its attitude toward institutional society is immature: "A weakness in all of them [Huck, Cooper's leather-stocking heroes, and Faulkner's Ike McCaslin] is that they do not acknowledge the virtues of civilization or try to live, as one must, inside it" (1955, 8). If my own cavils have seemed also "ill-tempered," my reply is that I do not, like O'Connor, intend to question the fundamental greatness of *Huck Finn,* as the remainder of my discussion will show.

6. The highest form of human comfort is found when two innocent males can shuck off all civilized restraints and responsibilities, as represented by silly women, and simply float lazily through a scene of natural beauty, catching their fish and smoking their pipes. As Arnold Rampersad says, "Much adventuring is [like this novel] written by men for the little boys supposedly resident in grown men, and to cater to their chauvinism" (1984, 49). The ideal of freedom, for both blacks and whites, is a *freedom from* restraint, not a *freedom to* exercise virtues and responsibilities— which is to say, in the words of another black critic, Julius Lester, "a mockery of freedom, a void" (1984, 46). The final addition to that blissful freedom-in-a-void is to be (or to identify with) a rebellious white child cared for and loved by the very one who might otherwise be feared, since he might be expected to act hatefully once free: the slave, toward whom the reader feels guilt. If we will just let nature take its course, those we have enslaved will rise from their slavery to love us and carry us to the promised land.

After Such Sins, What Forgiveness?

What can we reply to such a picture? Not, I think, that it is irrelevant to our view of the book. Not that such a suspicious reader "does not know how to read genuine literature, which is not concerned with teaching lessons." And not, surely, that the fixed norms central to the power of this book are all to the good. The events of the past hundred years have taught us—since apparently we needed the teaching—that America after Emancipation and the aborted Reconstruction just did not work that way, though white northern liberals until this last quarter of a century tended to act as if it did, or should.

Nor can we take what is perhaps the most frequent tack in defending Twain: "He rose to a great moral height in the middle of the book, then simply got tired, or lost touch with his Muse, and fell back into the *Tom Sawyer* gambit." That line will not work because the problems we have discovered are not confined to the gratuitous cruelty and condescension of the final "evasion." Though they are most clearly dramatized there, they run beneath the surface of the whole book—

even those wonderful moments that I have quoted of Huck's moral battles with himself.

In the critical literature about *Huck Finn,* I find three main lines of defense of the book as an American classic.[22] In all of them, the novel is treated as a coherent fiction, not as a work that simply collapsed toward the end.

The first is the simplest: the attribution to Huck, not to Mark Twain, of all the ethical deficiencies. Since Twain is obviously a master ironist, and since we see hundreds of moments in the book when he and the reader stand back and watch Huck make mistakes, why cannot we assume that *any* flaw of perception or behavior we discern is part of Twain's portrait of a "character whose moral vision, though profound, is seriously and consistently flawed" (Gabler-Hover 1987, 69)? In this view, the problems we have raised result strictly from Twain's use of Huck's blindnesses as "an added indictment against the society of which he [Huck] is a victim" (74; see also Smith 1984, 6, 10).

Clearly this defense will work perfectly, if we embrace it in advance of our actual experience line-by-line: dealing with any first-person narrative, we can explain away any fault, no matter how horrendous, if we assume in advance an *author* of unlimited wisdom, tact, and artistic skill. But such an assumption, by explaining everything, takes care of none of our more complex problems. If we do not pre-judge the case, the appeal to irony excuses only those faults that the book *invites* us to *see through,* thus joining the author in his ironic transformations. Our main problems, not just with the ending but with the most deeply embedded fixed norms of the book as a whole, remain unsolved.

George C. Carrington similarly defends the ending as of a piece with the rest of the novel, and in doing so he also defends the novel as the work of a great moral teacher who "knew what he was doing." But he discerns not so much a great conscious ironist as an author exhibiting great intuitive wisdom, a kind of sage. The questionable norms are indeed to be found in the work, but they are fundamentally criticized by it: the views and effects I have challenged are themselves challenged by the great art of Twain, an art that in a sense goes beyond his conscious intentions. The work's moral duplicity in fact is a brilliant

22. A carefully selected bibliography is given in Sattelmeyer and Crowley 1985.

portrayal of the national dilemma following the collapse of Reconstruction. Twain "could not help paralleling the national drama-sequence," Carrington says; the story of Huck is "rather like" the story of the northern middle class,

> many of them former Radical Republicans who had fought to free the slaves, [who had become] irritated by the long bother of Reconstruction, became tired of southern hostility, and were easily seduced by strong-willed politicians and businessmen into abandoning the freedmen for new excitements like railroad building. . . . The spirit that led the country to accept the Compromise [of 1877, that abandoned the goals of Reconstruction] might ironically be called 'the spirit of '77.' Absorbed in his work and his new life in Hartford, Twain shared that spirit. He thought the Compromise a very good thing indeed. . . .
>
> Adventures of Huckleberry Finn is thus not only a great but a sadly typical American drama of race: not a stark tragedy of black suffering, but a complex tragicomedy of white weakness and indifference. It is one of those modern books that, as Lionel Trilling says, 'read us,' tell 'us' . . . about ourselves. . . . The meanness of Huckleberry Finn is not that man is evil but that he is weak and doomed to remain weak. . . . Twain did not shirk the presentation, but managed to avert his gaze from the subject's Medusa horrors by looking at it through his uncomprehending narrator. . . . By experiencing and accepting the ending we can perhaps take a step toward a similar level of self-awareness. A novel that can help its readers do that is indeed a masterwork and deserves its very high place.

(1976, 190–92)

While it seems remotely possible that an author with a mind as ironically devious as Twain's could have worked, consciously or unconsciously, to ensure that some few readers over the centuries would read the work in this special way, obviously most readers have not done so—no doubt because the book itself offers no surface clues to support such a reading. Indeed, both of these defenses spring more from the critics' ethical programs and ingenuity than from anything that the novel proposes for itself. On the contrary, a vast majority of the artistic strokes, especially during the "evasion," seem explicitly designed to heighten our comic delight in a way that would make these interpretations implausible. They both depend on the wisdom and insight of a reader who has learned to see through the "surface" of the book and recognize that it in fact mocks naive readers who laugh wholeheartedly at Tom's pranks. They thus leave us with the question, What then happens to the great unwashed, for whom so much of the book has proved totally deceptive? Well, they are going to identify mistakenly with a deceptive implied author who has in some sense worked to take them in. Meanwhile, the real author is above all this,

creating a work that a few discerning readers can make out, after
weeks, perhaps years, of careful study. In short, the defense may work
well if what we are thinking of is maximum fairness to Twain, but it
doesn't work at all for the critic who cares about what a book does to
or for the majority of its readers, sophisticated or unsophisticated.

A third influential defense, considerably more complex, has the virtue of leaving the reader able to laugh at the troublesome ending,
though embarrassed by the laughter. James Cox argues that Twain set
out, through the attacks on Huck's conscience that lead to his great
moment of decision to go to hell, to enact a conversion of morality
into pleasure (1966, 171–76). The form implicit in such an ethic demanded an ending that celebrates pleasure and makes everyone "comfortable," including of course Huck and Jim. But at the moment of
choice, that same form requires not the election of pleasure but of another "conscience," the northern conscience that combats the southern conscience of Huck's upbringing: "In the very act of choosing to
go to hell he has surrendered to the notion of a *principle* of right and
wrong. He has forsaken the world of pleasure [his own eternal sal-
vation] to make a moral choice" (180). It is that conscience which
validates, in Huck's eyes, his going along with Tom, even though he
thinks until the end that Tom, who was brung up right, is unbelievably
wicked in working to free Jim.

The result is that when we exercise a "northern conscience" that
confirms Huck's choice and find ourselves laughing at the burlesque,
"we are the ones who become uncomfortable. The entire burlesque
ending is a revenge upon the moral sentiment which, though it shielded
the humor, ultimately threatened Huck's identity [as a natural hedo-
nist]" (181).

> If the reader sees in Tom's performance a rather shabby and safe bit of play,
> he is seeing no more than the exposure of the approval with which he
> watched Huck operate. For if Tom is rather contemptibly setting a free
> slave free, what after all is the reader doing, who begins the book after the
> *fact* of the Civil War? This is the "joke" of the book—the moment when, in
> outrageous burlesque, it attacks the sentiment which its style has at once
> evoked and exploited. . . .
>   This is the larger reality of the ending—what we may call the necessity
> of the form. That it was a cost which the form exacted no one would deny.
> But to call it a failure, a piece of moral cowardice, is to miss the true
> rebellion of the book, for the disturbance of the ending is nothing less than
> our and Mark Twain's recognition of the full meaning of *Huckleberry Finn*.
>   (175, 181)

Again we see here a critic who saves the novel by rejecting the reading that almost every white reader until recently must have given it. Each reading considers "the reader"—the "we" of these passages—to be plainly and simply the white reader, and neither one considers closely the effects on the white reader who does *not* feel uncomfortable with the ending. But surely the most common reading of this book, by non-professional whites, has always been the kind of enraptured, thoroughly comfortable reading that I gave it when young, the kind that sees the final episodes as a climax of good clean fun, the kind in fact that Brander Matthews gave it on first publication:

> The romantic side of Tom Sawyer is shown in most delightfully humorous fashion in the account of his difficult devices to aid in the easy escape of Jim, a runaway negro. Jim is an admirably drawn character. There have been not a few fine and firm portraits of negroes in recent American fiction, of which Mr. Cable's Bras-Coupé in the *Grandissimes* is perhaps the most vigorous, and Mr. Harris's Mingo and Uncle Remus and Blue Dave are the most gentle. Jim is worthy to rank with these; and the essential simplicity and kindliness and generosity of the Southern negro have never been better shown than here by Mark Twain. . . . Of the more broadly humorous passages—and they abound— . . . they are to the full as funny as in any of Mark Twain's other books; and perhaps in no other book has the humorist shown so much artistic restraint, for there is in *Huckleberry Finn* no mere 'comic copy,' no straining after effect.
>
> (Matthews 1885, 154; qtd. in Blair and Hill 1962, 499–500)

If that is in fact what most white "liberals" have made of the book until recently, it dramatizes the inadequacy of the defenses we have so far considered. A book that thus feeds the stereotypes of the Brander Matthews kind of reader insults *all* black readers, and it redeems itself only by inciting some few sophisticated critics, many decades later, to think hard about how the story implicates white readers in unpleasant truths. That is surely not what we ordinarily mean when we call a book a classic. Even if we find a reading that at some deep level vindicates Twain for writing better than he knew, our ethical concerns remain unanswered.

Still hoping that I might someday see more merit in these defenses by others, I turn to my own efforts and find, to my considerable distress, that each of them seems almost as weak as those I have rejected.[23] We might first use the "conversational" defense that worked

23. I did not realize just *how* incomplete they are until I tried an earlier draft out on friendly readers. Uniformly they reported that the indictment seemed, in contrast to

for Lawrence: though Twain's racial liberalism was inevitably limited, though he failed to imagine the "good Negro" with anything like the power of his portraits of good and bad whites, though in effect he simply wipes Jim out as a character in the final pages, he has still, by his honest effort to create the first full literary friendship between a white character and a slave, permanently opened up this very conversation we are engaged in. We would not be talking about what it might mean to cope adequately with the heritage of slavery, in literary form, had he not intervened in our conversation.

There is surely something to this point, but unfortunately the argument fits Twain less well than Lawrence. Twain is not a great conversationalist, not at all "polyphonic"; rather, he is a great monologuist. We have seen here that he is not particularly good at responding to our questions: the critics I have quoted have had to do too much of the work. A great producer of confident opinions—many of them by the time he wrote already thoroughly established (for example, slavery is bad)—he never probes very deep. His positions on issues have not stimulated the kind of public debates that continue about Lawrence's views. Instead we find collections of colorful expressions, like *Your Personal Mark Twain: In Which the Great American Ventures an Opinion on Ladies, Language, Liberty, Literature, Liquor, Love, and Other Controversial Subjects* (Twain 1969). Twain has opinions about many matters, but their intellectual content or moral depth would not give many TV shows serious competition. His mind takes me into no new conceptual depths; he is conventionally unconventional, so easily seduced by half-baked ideas that one would be embarrassed to offer him as a representative American intellectual.

Might I "save" him, then—or rather myself, because he is after all quite secure on his pedestal—by talking of the healing, critical power of laughter, the sheer value of comedy? Here is what I might say:

"Let us celebrate Mark Twain's preeminent *comic* genius, his gifted imaginings of beloved but ludicrous characters in a (quite 'unreal,' quite 'unconvincing') world of their own, a world in which I love to spend my days and hours and from which I emerge delighted that *my*

---

those of Austen and Lawrence, stronger than the defense. Once again I felt the force of Paul Moses's case; and reimagining his argument, I have struggled to recast my own.

world has included that kind of sheer delight. Samuel Johnson says somewhere that the sheer gift of innocent pleasure is not to be scoffed at, in a world where most pleasures are not innocent. Twain redeems my time by providing me a different 'time' during which my life feels quite glorious.

"It is true that in that world, in that time, there are dangerous simplifications and moments of embarrassment: it is a world inhabited only by good guys and bad guys, clever ones and stupid ones, and Twain tries to lead me too easily to think that I—one of the good and clever ones—can tell which are which. There are marvelously absurd clowns and villains, and I don't have to reproach myself (as I do in life) for finding them clownish and villainous. I relish here good, honest, wholesome, intense sentiment; I relish an absolute sureness that everything will turn out all right and a freedom from the 'uncomfortable' burdens of conscience. Just think of that achievement. Twain has portrayed a world of cruelty and misery, a world of national shame, a world in which good people will in fact always be bested by the bad, and he makes us believe that everything *must* turn out all right! How many other novels can I think of that I can re-read again and again, teach to students and teach again, decade after decade, and still wish, after each re-reading, that they would go on longer? *Huck Finn* thus provides me with a kind of moral holiday even while stimulating my thought about moral issues. What a gift this is, this terribly misguided, potentially harmful work! If you try to take it away from me (you censors, black or white) I will fight you tooth and nail.

"How, then, you ask, does *Huckleberry Finn* differ from simple escape literature of the kind that we enjoy for an hour and then dismiss without a second thought? It does so in two ways, both of which we have hinted at already. The first is the quality of the escape: line by line, Twain simply rewards my returns with exquisite pleasures that are not so much 'escape' from life as the kind of thing life ought to be *for*. The second is a somewhat different form of our 'conversational' defense of Lawrence. Though Twain's fantasy of the innocent boy discovering within his natural self the resources for overcoming society's miseducation about 'difference' threatens us with the kinds of dangers I have described, it also moves us with a mythic experience that can lead to endless but fruitful inquiry into what kind of creatures we are. It is no accident that it is *Huck Finn* of all Twain's works that stimulates controversy about the ethical quality of its ending and about its central situation. Somehow the fantasy/myth touches us at our most sensitive points.

"In brief, long before Paul Moses and Charles Long had ever led me to *think* ethically about the book, it had already done its true work in this respect. The vivid images of that great-hearted black man crouched patiently in that shed, waiting while the unconsciously cruel Huck and the consciously, irresponsibly cruel adventurer Tom planned an escape that almost destroys them all—those images haunted me even as I laughed, and they haunt me still.

"I can never know, of course, just how much miseducation the novel has provided while haunting me in this way. Who am I to say that simply *thinking* about the book can have removed the kinds of distortion that my black friends have pointed out. But I do believe that the mythic force of that book will be a permanent possession, a permanent gift, long after we repair black/white relations as we find them in the twentieth century. Just as Homer's epics can now no longer harm our children in the specific way that worried Plato—shaking their confidence in the rationality and decency of the Greek gods—I suspect that *Huck Finn* will survive the longed-for time when racial conflict is no longer a political and moral issue in our lives."

I seem to have grown warmer in this defense than in any of the others. But always at my back I hear the voices of those readers—including myself now—who see that the infatuation is not after all innocent. They remind me that the hours I spend in that world *are* after all fantasy hours; whether or not I see them as that, they have the power to deflect my imagination in dangerous ways. Jim *is* the "Negro" we whites might in weaker moments have hoped would emerge from slavery: docile, grateful for our gift of a freedom that nobody should ever have had the right to withhold, satisfied with a full stomach and a bit more cash than he'd had before. The picture of pre–Civil War America *is* a fantasy picture, in which all of the really bad occurrences are caused by caricatures of folly and evil, none of them by people who look and talk like people of *our* kind.[24] The battle in the novel for free-

24. Oh, yes, of course the novel is generally called "realistic," and Twain prided himself on his accuracy in reporting manners. But is it not rather late in the day for that kind of talk?

dom from oppressive Christianity *is* a superficial battle, at best, and the encounter with the realities of slavery is even more superficial. The story thus offers us every invitation to miseducate ourselves, and therein lies the task of ethical criticism: to help us avoid that miseducation. The trick is always to find ways of doing that without tearing the butterfly apart in our hands.

It should be obvious that I am by no means "comfortable" (to use Huck's word) about the incompatibilities that my project has led me to here. Having made my case against the book as honestly as possible, I now find a distressing disparity between the force of my objections (along with the relative weaknesses in the various defenses), and the strength of my continuing love for the book. My ethical criticism has disturbed a surface that once was serene. But instead of making the work and its creator look at least as great as before (Austen), or renovating a wrongly denigrated author (Lawrence), I have somewhat tarnished my hero, and since I cannot wipe from my mind the readings that black critics have imposed, I cannot, by a sheer act of will, restore Twain's former glow. Still, though much of *Huck Finn* amuses me somewhat less when I read it now than it did in times irrecoverable (the recent reading was, like Cox's, considerably more solemn than the one Twain himself obviously hoped for), the achievement still seems to me quite miraculous. On the other hand . . .

Such a non-conclusion is disturbing to the part of me that used to seek unities and harmonies that others have overlooked, the part that once spent two years attempting to discern *the* form of *Tristram Shandy*, the part that still delights in having once "demonstrated" that Sterne actually brought that "unfinished" work to a close (1951), the part that has often earned its keep by teaching students how to see unities where others have seen only chaos. But should we not expect to discover irreducible conflicts of this kind, if each of our imaginative worlds must finally be constituted of manifold values that can never be fully realized in any one work or any one critic's endeavor?

What is not in question is that the ethical *conversation* begun by Paul Moses has done its work: it has produced what I can only call a kind of *conversion* (both words come from the Latin *convertere*, "to turn or turn around"). Led by him to join in a con-versation with other ethical critics, my coduction of *Huckleberry Finn* has been turned, once and for all, and for good or ill, from untroubled admiration to restless questioning. And it is a kind of questioning that Twain and I alone together could never have managed for ourselves.

REFERENCES

Altenbernd, Lynn. "Huck Finn, Emancipator." *Criticism* 1 (1959): 298–307.

Austen, Jane. *Persuasion* [1818]. In vol. 5 of *The Novels of Jane Austen*. Ed. R. W. Chapman. London, 1933.

———. *Emma* [1816]. Vol. 4 of *The Novels of Jane Austen*. Ed. R. W. Chapman. London, 1960.

———. *Sanditon* ([1817] 1925). In vol. 6 of *The Works of Jane Austen*. Ed. R. W. Chapman. London, 1963.

Bakhtin, Mikhail. *Problems of Dostoevsky's Poetics* [1963]. Ed. and trans. Caryl Emerson. Theory and History of Literature, vol. 8. Minneapolis, 1984.

Balbert, Peter, and Phillip L. Marcus, eds. *D. H. Lawrence: A Centenary Consideration*. Ithaca, N.Y., 1985.

Beal, Anthony, ed. *D. H. Lawrence: Selected Literary Criticism*. New York, 1955.

Blair, Walter. *Mark Twain and Huck Finn*. Berkeley, 1960.

Blair, Walter, and Hamlin Hill. *The Art of "Huckleberry Finn": Text, Sources, Criticisms*. San Francisco, 1962.

Booth, Wayne C. "Did Sterne Complete *Tristram Shandy?*" *Modern Philology* 48 (1951), 41–44.

———. "*Emma, Emma*, and the Question of Feminism." *Persuasions: Journal of the Jane Austen Society of North America* 5 (Dec. 16, 1983[a]): 29–40.

———. "Freedom of Interpretation: Bakhtin and the Challenge of Feminist Criticism." In *The Politics of Interpretation*. Ed. W. J. T. Mitchell. Chicago, 1983[b]. 51–117.

———. *The Rhetoric of Fiction* [1961]. 2d ed. Chicago, 1983[c].

———. *The Vocation of a Teacher: Rhetorical Occasions, 1968–1987*. Chicago, 1988.

Carrington, George C. *The Dramatic Unity of "Huckleberry Finn."* Columbus, Ohio, 1976.

Cecil, David. *A Portrait of Jane Austen*. London, 1978.

Cox, James M. *Mark Twain: The Fate of Humor*. Princeton, N.J., 1966.

Cushman, Keith. *D. H. Lawrence at Work: The Emergence of the Prussian Officer Stories*. Charlottesville, Va., 1978.

Davis, Thadious M., ed. *Black Writers on "Adventures of Huckleberry Finn" One Hundred Years Later*. [Special issue] *Mark Twain Journal* 22 (Fall 1984).

DiBattista, Maria. "*Women in Love*: D. H. Lawrence's Judgment Book." In Balbert and Marcus 1985: 67–90.

Ebbatson, Roger. *The Evolutionary Self: Hardy, Forster, Lawrence*. Totowa, N.J., 1982.

Fleishman, Avrom. "He Do the Polis in Different Voices: Lawrence's Later Style." In Balbert and Marcus 1985: 162–79.

Foucault, Michel. *The Archaeology of Knowledge* [1969]. New York, 1972.

Gabler-Hover, Janet A. "Sympathy Not Empathy: The Intent of Narration in *Huckleberry Finn.*" *Journal of Narrative Technique* 17 (Win. 1987): 67–75.

Geismar, Maxwell. *Mark Twain and the Three R's: Race, Religion, Revolution—and Related Matters*. Indianapolis, 1973.

Hansen, Chadwick. "The Character of Jim and the Ending of *Huckleberry Finn.*" *Massachusetts Review* 5 (Aut. 1963): 45–66.

Heilman, Robert. "Nomad, Monads, and the Mystique of the Soma." *Sewanee Review* 58 (1960): 650–56. (Partially reprinted in Miko 1969.)

Hentoff, Nat. "Huck Finn Better Get Out of Town by Sundown." *Village Voice* 27 (May 4, 1982): 8.

———. "Is Any Book Worth the Humiliation of Our Kids?" *Village Voice* 27 (May 11, 1982): 8.

Howe, Marguerite Beede. *The Art of the Self in D. H. Lawrence*. Athens, Ohio, 1977.

James, Henry. "Charles de Bernard and Gustave Flaubert." In *French Poets and Novelists*. London, 1878.

Johnson, Samuel. Preface to *The Plays of William Shakespeare* [1765]. In *Johnson on Shakespeare*. Ed. Arthur Sherbo. Vol. 7 of *The Yale Edition of the Works of Samuel Johnson*. New Haven, Conn., 1968. 59–113.

Jones, Rhett S. "Nigger and Knowledge: White Double-Consciousness in *Adventures of Huckleberry Finn.*" In Davis 1984: 28–37.

Kaufmann, David. "Satiric Deceit in the Ending of *Adventures of Huckleberry Finn.*" *Studies in the Novel* 19 (Spr. 1987): 66–78.

Lawrence, D. H. *The Rainbow* [1911]. New York, 1915.

———. *Women in Love* [1921]. Harmondsworth, 1976.

———. *Lady Chatterley's Lover* [1928]. 2d Modern Library ed. New York, 1983.

Leavis, F. R. *D. H. Lawrence: Novelist*. London, 1955.

———. Introduction to *Pudd'nhead Wilson*, by Mark Twain [1955]. New York, 1962. Reprinted in *Anna Karenina and Other Essays*. London, 1967.

Lester, Julius. "Morality and *Adventures of Huckleberry Finn.*" In Davis 1984: 43–46.

Mailloux, Steven. *Interpretive Conventions: The Reader in the Study of American Fiction*. Ithaca, N.Y., 1982.

———. "Cultural Reception and Social Practices." In *Rhetorical Power*. Ithaca, N.Y., forthcoming.

[Matthews, Brander]. Review of *Adventures of Huckleberry Finn*. *Saturday Review* [London] 59 (Jan. 31, 1885): 153–54. (Reprinted in Blair and Hill 1962, 495–500.)

Miko, Stephen J., ed. *Twentieth Century Interpretations of "Women in Love": A Collection of Critical Essays*. Englewood Cliffs, N.J., 1969.

Miller, Jane. *Women Writing about Men*. New York, 1986.

Moers, Ellen. *Literary Women: The Great Writers*. Garden City, N.Y., 1976.

Murfin, Ross C. *Swinburne, Hardy, Lawrence, and the Burden of Belief*. Chicago, 1978.

Nichols, Charles H. "'A True Book with Some Stretchers': *Huck Finn* Today." In Davis 1984: 13–16.

O'Connor, William Van. "Why *Huckleberry Finn* Is Not the Great American Novel." *College English* 17 (Oct. 1955): 6–10. Reprint. Blair and Hill 1962.

Poovey, Mary. "*Persuasion* and the Promises of Love." In *The Representation of Women in Fiction*. Ed. Carolyn G. Heilbrun and Margaret R. Higonnet. Baltimore, 1983. 152–179.

Putnam, Hilary. "Fact and Value." In *Reason, Truth, and History*. Cambridge, 1981.

Railton, Stephen. "Jim and Mark Twain: What Do Dey Stan' For?" *Virginia Quarterly Review* 63 (Sum. 1987): 393–408.

Rampersad, Arnold. "*Adventures of Huckleberry Finn* and Afro-American Literature." In Davis 1984: 47–52.

Reichert, John. *Making Sense of Literature*. Chicago, 1977.

Sattelmeyer, Robert, and J. Donald Crowley, eds. *One Hundred Years of "Huckleberry Finn": The Boy, His Book, and American Culture*. Columbia, Mo., 1985.

Schneider, Daniel J. *The Consciousness of D. H. Lawrence: An Intellectual Biography*. Lawrence, Kans., 1986.

Simpson, Hilary. *D. H. Lawrence and Feminism*. DeKalb, Ill., 1982.

Smith, David L. "Huck, Jim, and American Racial Discourse." In Davis 1984: 4–12.

Stern, G. B., and Sheila Kaye-Smith. *Speaking of Jane Austen*. London, 1944.

Tenenbaum, Elizabeth Brody. *The Problematic Self: Approaches to Identity in Stendhal, D. H. Lawrence, and Malraux*. Cambridge, Mass., 1977.

Trilling, Diana, ed. *The Portable D. H. Lawrence*. New York, 1947.

Tuckey, John S., ed. *The Devil's Race-Track: Mark Twain's Great Dark Writings*. Berkeley, 1980.

Twain, Mark. *Your Personal Mark Twain, in Which the Great American Ventures an Opinion on Ladies, Language, Liberty, Literature, Liquor, Love, and Other Controversial Subjects*. New York, 1969.

———. *Notebooks and Journals*, vol. 3. Ed. Robert Pack Browning et al. Berkeley, 1979.

———. *Mississippi Writings*. [*The Adventures of Tom Sawyer, Life on the Mississippi, Adventures of Huckleberry Finn, Pudd'nhead Wilson*] Ed. Guy Cardwell. New York, 1982.

Wilson, Edmund. "A Long Talk about Jane Austen." In *A Literary Chronicle: 1920–1950*. New York, 1956.

Wilt, Judith. "The Powers of the Instrument: or Jane, Frank, and the Pianoforte." *Persuasions* (Dec. 16, 1983): 41–47.

You write in order to change the world, knowing perfectly well that you probably can't, but also knowing that literature is indispensable to the world. In some way, your aspirations and concern for a single man in fact do begin to change the world. The world changes according to the way people see it, and if you alter, even by a millimeter, the way a person looks or people look at reality, then you can change it.

James Baldwin

To understand the presentness of others is to exist.

George Steiner, on Heidegger

Forsooth, brothers, fellowship is heaven, and lack of fellowship is hell: fellowship is life, and lack of fellowship is death: and the deeds that ye do upon the earth, it is for fellowship's sake that ye do them.

William Morris, A Dream of John Ball

Naturally you're aware that bad art can finally cripple a man.

Saul Bellow

Du musst dein Leben ändern.
[You must change your life.]
Rilke

The Ethics of Reading

Chekhov, who is generally considered one of the founders of an art of fiction that asks to be judged only *as* art, often reveals his sense that stories cannot be entirely divorced from ethics. In one revealing story, "Home" ([1887] 1972, 65–78), a father returns from his work as a prosecutor to learn from the governess that his seven-year-old boy has been smoking his father's cigarettes. Convinced that smoking is a bad habit, the prosecutor administers a long sermon: "I don't love you any more, and you are no son of mine. . . . Tobacco is very bad for the health, and anyone who smokes dies earlier than he should" (68, 70). Aware that the boy is at best half-listening, "completely at a loss" about what to say, he finally demands a promise, one that he can see is meaningless even as it is made:

> "I say, give me your word of honour that you won't smoke again."
> "Word of hon-nour!" carolled Seryozha.
>
> (73)

But then, at bedtime, the prosecutor invents a vivid tale that he thinks embarrassingly didactic, a "long rigmarole," about an emperor whose seven-year-old son had every virtue but one: he smoked.

> "The emperor's son fell ill with consumption through smoking, and died when he was twenty. His infirm and sick old father was left without anyone to help him. There was no one to govern the kingdom and defend the palace. Enemies came, killed the old man, and destroyed the palace, and now there are neither cherries, nor birds, nor little bells in the garden. . . . That's what happened."

His son is now for the first time visibly touched:

> [H]is eyes were clouded by mournfulness and something like fear: for a minute he looked pensively at the dark window, shuddered, and said, in a sinking voice:
> "I am not going to smoke any more . . ."
>
> (77)

The prosecutor of course feels uncomfortable with what he has done.

"It's not the right way [he says to himself]. Why must morality and truth never be offered in their crude form, but only with embellishments, sweetened and gilded like pills? . . . It's falsification . . . deception . . . tricks. . . ." He thought . . . of the general public who absorb history only from legends and historical novels.

So far we might see the story as Chekhov's complaint about the corruptions of art. But the prosecutor takes a further step—into this book of mine:

[A]nd [he thought] of himself and how he had gathered an understanding of life not from sermons and laws, but from fables, novels, poems.

"Medicine should be sweet [he goes on], truth beautiful, and man has had this foolish habit [of liking stories] since the days of Adam . . . though, indeed, perhaps it is all natural, and ought to be so. . . . There are many deceptions and delusions in nature that serve a purpose."

(78)

We all have "this foolish habit," and we all are by nature caught in the ambiguities that trouble the prosecutor. Yet we all are equipped, by a nature (a "second nature") that has created us out of story, with a rich experience in choosing which life stories, fictional or "real," we will embrace wholeheartedly. Who we are, who we will be tomorrow depends thus on some act of criticism, whether by ourselves or by those who determine what stories will come our way—criticism wise or foolish, deliberate or spontaneous, conscious or unconscious: "*You* may enter; *you* must go away—and I will do my best to forget you."

Each culture provides every member with an unlimited number of "natural" choices that seem to require no thought. Such intuitive choices tend to get articulated into gossip, which consists of a kind of free-wheeling narrative appraisal of people not present. Though we may not think of gossip as "ethical culture"—it is still fashionable to condemn it, in theory, as inherently immoral—the best gossip is wonderfully educational, an *essential* exchange that speaks to us learners messages like: "You should try not to be like that"; or "You should hope to be so brave!"; or "Save us all from becoming such creatures!" [1]

---

1. Of course much gossip says something quite different. Too much "moral" talk springs from motives that have little to do with a hope for anyone's possible betterment: revenge, greed, political power, self-praise and exculpation. It is easier to find examples of "moral discourse" designed to put others down than of genuine inquiry about the good and bad of behavior.

It thus reflects and encourages our desire to have better desires (see Chapters 8 and 9).

To analogize life and stories about life as I have done throughout suggests that we should make our choices from among formal fictions pretty much as we make them in the rest of life. In a sense that is so: in both we meet the same circular problems of choosing the philosophical or religious grounds (or in some branches of current thought, non-grounds) that will validate our choices. But how in practice *should* we make those choices? In fact, the analogy can lead us to underestimate the unique value of fiction: its relatively cost-free offer of trial runs. If you try out a given mode of life in life itself, you may, like Eve in the garden, discover too late that the one who offered it to you was Old Nick himself. Though tryings-out in narrative present all the dangers we have stressed throughout, they offer both a relative freedom from consequence and, in their sheer multiplicity, a rich supply of antidotes. In a month of reading, I can try out more "lives" than I can test in a lifetime. Whole treatises have been written on this one narrative value alone (and it is but one of many). But of course to say as much still leaves us with the task of choosing which fictions are worth a test run. Though there are no simple rules to guide us here, a brief look at what people advise us to do in life itself may help.

Two strong ethical traditions advise us in seemingly contrasting ways about how to address the deceptive heroes and villains, saints and sinners who offer themselves to us from our first years onward. On the one hand, we become virtuous by recognizing and then excluding or extruding evil. On the other hand, we become virtuous by an open embrace of all the "goods" we meet, leaving to some process natural or supernatural the task of winnowing bad from good. Though no one religion or philosophy ever rests wholly in either tradition, individuals have often aspired to "sainthood" at either extreme: as completely purified of all taint, or as completely dissolved in a selfless embrace of all "otherness."

The tradition of exclusion or denial, which some people think of as the only "moral" or "ethical" tradition, advises a purifying caution and restraint, a defensive drawing of lines and boundaries: avoid all influences that might corrupt; vigilantly track down and cast away the bad, in order the better to cultivate, dwell with, cleave to the visibly good. This is the tradition that parents follow when they try to ban certain companions from their children's lives; or when they move to "a better neighborhood" because the kids will meet "better" friends there. It is also the tradition we follow when we pass immigration, censorship, and quarantine laws, or when we abide by various eating taboos. Some current environmentalists seem to see the world as little more than a rising flood of pollutants: everything we touch is killing us.

The tradition is visible in those religious practices that impose congregational norms of purity and that enforce them with excommunication or even the *auto-da-fé:* The Pharisees' reproach against Christ for hobnobbing with publicans and sinners, not to mention harlots; the almost universal rules against exogamy; diverse labels for the untouchables.[2] But the tradition also is seen in the classical way of talking about friendship that we glanced at in Chapter 6: some friends are useful and some are harmful; some pleasant friends are likely to corrupt us; most would-be friends will prove to be inferior or dangerous influences. In fact in that tradition we can hope at best for a very small number of true friends in any one life, perhaps finally, as Montaigne would have it, for only one. All "others" are at least partially suspect.

Note that according to the "anthropology" of this tradition, every human being, even the strongest, is essentially and dangerously a malleable creature who is easily tempted to take on every bad habit that comes his or her way, though also capable of cultivating the virtues of the virtuous, if any happen to come near. "Boldly rebuke vice," says the Book of Common Prayer. "Good company and good discourse are the very sinews of virtue" (Izaak Walton); "'Tis a vice to know him" (*Hamlet*); "He that toucheth pitch shall be defiled therewith" (Apocrypha); "Birds of a feather flock together." This tradition is nicely satirized by Falstaff as he joshes with Prince Hal: "There is a thing, Harry, which thou hast often heard of, and it is known to many in our land by the name of pitch. This pitch, as ancient writers do report, doth defile; so doth the company thou keepest" (*Henry IV, Part 1*, 2.4.445ff.). Again, playfully defending himself by pretending that Prince Hal has

---

2. I have personally suffered a snub from one group, the "Exclusive Plymouth Brethren," who would not allow two of its members, former friends, to take a meal with me.

corrupted him, Falstaff says: "Company, villainous company, hath been the spoil of me" (3.3.10).

The opposing tradition urges an openness to the world, including even that part of it that looks like vice or corruption. Here the worst vice is to be self-protective, "holier-than-thou." Parents following this tradition throw their children into the battle of life, even seek out schools in "bad neighborhoods," both to toughen up the kids and to have the kids influence the schools.[3] Churches send missionaries to the heathen, forgetting or ignoring the evidence that many missionaries come back heathenized. Psychoanalysts and other therapists hobnob willingly for days and years with characters whose influence sometimes ends in a "negative transference" that can lead to disaster for the therapist. The tradition is perhaps best represented by Christ's seeming willingness, nay, eagerness, to consort with sinners and by the "imitations" of his all-embracing practice by saints like Francis of Assisi.[4] We are given no hint in Christ's words that any bad qualities of the sinners might rub off on *him,* or that any of us might be harmed by following his practice. So long as our hearts are right, we can plunge into any "otherness" that comes along and hope to emerge the better for the plunge.

Partisans of this tradition divide into two rather different groups, depending on whether or not they believe that vice is really vice. At one extreme, all traditional virtues are replaced with honesty, sincerity, authenticity, or avoidance of hypocrisy.[5] We sin only by the inauthentic, fearful ostracism of some vicious practice or person (it is no accident that many modern readers of Shakespeare's *Henry* plays condemn Hal for dropping Falstaff once he begins to take his role as prince and king seriously: Henry has become a pious hypocrite). So long as we are "becoming," so long as we are open to all experience and are facing it with our true selves, all will be well. The other camp, those who see the encounter with vice as a strengthening of our power

3. Such behavior may seem unlikely to some readers. I could document it, but not without the betrayal of using proper names.

4. I'm still looking for evidence of similarly extreme "embracers" among Jews. Perhaps the "twelve just men" come closest, but they are not said to be purged of the fear of pollution.

5. See Chapter 8. Still the best critique of an unrestrained pursuit of the authentic self is Lionel Trilling's *Sincerity and Authenticity* (1972, esp. chs. 5–6).

to resist it, is perhaps best represented by the frequently quoted argument in Milton's *Areopagitica*.

> He that can apprehend and consider vice with all her baits and seeming pleasures, and yet abstain, and yet distinguish, and yet prefer that which is truly better, he is the true wayfaring Christian. I cannot praise a fugitive and cloister'd vertue, unexercis'd & unbreath'd, that never sallies out and sees her adversary, but slinks out of the race, where that immortall garland is to be run for, not without dust and heat. . . . [T]hat which purifies us is triall, and triall is by what is contrary. . . . [T]rue temperance [is that which can] see and know, and yet abstain.
>
> ([1644] 1959, 2: 514–16)

That powerful work was on my desk throughout my college years, and it is always within reach now. For defenders of civil liberties it has been more important even than John Stuart Mill's *On Liberty*, that other great argument that only a free market of ideas and influences can nurture the best kind of human being.[6]

The two traditions—the search for purity and the embrace of "everything human"—might easily be taken as absolutely opposed. Obviously at any one moment, facing any particular piece of otherness, one cannot follow both at once: I cannot both ostracize dubious friends and cultivate them for the good they might do me as challenges, or the good I might do them. But this does not mean that in ethical criticism of narratives we must make a hard and fast choice between the excluding and embracing modes. As I argued in Chapter 3 (and as is attested by Milton's later firm exclusion of "Popery" from his toleration), every "opener" must in fact close, and all who exclude do so in the name of some value that can be described as a kind of invitation. That is why I have had to play both sides of this street throughout these chapters: we must both open ourselves to "others" that look initially dangerous or worthless, and yet prepare ourselves to cast them off whenever, after keeping company with them, we conclude that they are potentially harmful. Which of these opposing practices will serve us best at a given moment will depend on who "we" are and what the "moment" is. The only fully general advice inherent in all this is that by taking thought about *who* and *where* we

6. For an extraordinary extension of Mill's argument for the value of a "liberal" autonomy as an end in itself, see Raz 1986.

are, and about *when it is,* we may improve our chances of finding and dwelling with those others who are in fact our true friends.

We saw in Chapter 1 the obvious relativity of every ethical offering to the ethos of the *person* to whom it is offered: What use is *Moby Dick* to a child who cannot yet read a primer? What harm can *Justine* do to Professor Profiterole, who has "read everything"? Rather than taking this, as some have done, as a reason for rejecting ethical criticism, it should be seen as a good reason for rejecting the search for universal prescriptions and proscriptions. The fact that no narrative will be good or bad for all readers in all circumstances need not hinder us in our effort to discover what is good or bad for us in our condition *here and now.*

For many an ethical critic the turn at this concluding point would have been to plump finally for some one theological, political, or anthropological base on which to build our judgments. The easy opposite to that unhelpful ploy would be the claim to embrace them all. My choice throughout has been instead the rhetorical or pragmatic choice of a critical pluralism—a pluralism with limits. I thus offer in the Appendix two thoroughly unsystematic lists, one of good things, one of bad things; one of nourishment, one of poisons. I must leave it to each reader to practice an ethics of reading that might determine just which of these standards should count most, and just which of the world's narratives should now be banned or embraced in the lifetime project of building the character of an ethical reader.

REFERENCES

Chekhov, Anton. *"The Cook's Wedding" and Other Stories* [1920]. Trans. Constance Garnett. Vol. 12 of *The Tales of Chekhov.* New York, 1972.
Milton, John. "Areopagitica" [1644]. Ed. Don M. Wolfe. In *Complete Prose Works.* Ed. Ernest Sirluck. 8 vols. New Haven, Conn., 1959. 2: 480–570.
Raz, Joseph. *The Morality of Freedom.* Oxford, 1986.
Trilling, Lionel. *Sincerity and Authenticity.* Cambridge, Mass., 1972.

An Anthology of Ethical Gifts, Thank-you Notes, and Warnings

Without too much effort I could of course fit most of the following quotations under one or another of the seven scales of quality that I described in Chapter 6. But some I could not: they hail doctrines and virtues that simply spill out of my commodious categories.[1] Most of them are modern, because the important older ethical critics are all easily available in anthologies. Though most of the quotations are about benefits for readers, I have included a few about benefits for authors and cultures. Excluded are the (even more plentiful?) claims about the superiority of pure form, pure truth, pure beauty, or pure embeddedness in history: those belong in a different anthology.

Some readers may be tempted to produce order out of my miscellany, observing that many seemingly opposed statements really say the same thing in different languages. And some may be tempted to claim that many of the statements do not really belong here because they are flatly mistaken. I urge resistance to both temptations. Each statement of a general value, we must assume, is based on some sort of genuine coduction—some primary personal experience. People don't ordinarily rush into print with praise for gifts that they don't really admire; our temptations are generally in the opposite direction—to scoff at pleasures we have not enjoyed. As Hilary Putnam says (see p. 34 n.10 above) about our primary sensations, such as "This ice-cream tastes good,"

> Presented experiential qualities aren't, in general, neutral. . . . One may override these felt demands [in our case, these judgments that this quality,

---

1. I've always loved Samuel Beckett's footnote to the "Addenda" at the end of his novel *Watt:* "The following precious and illuminating material should be carefully studied. Only fatigue and disgust prevented its incorporation" (1963, 247). Only fatigue, after more than nine years of grouping and regrouping, and not disgust but a radical sense of the inadequacy of all categorical placement, prevented me from including the following extracts in the text itself.

as experienced, is not only good but a general good] for . . . sufficient reason, as when a child learns to bear the pain of an injection for the sake
of . . . [immunization], but the *prima facie* goodness and badness of particular experiences can hardly be denied. (Interestingly enough, this point
was recognized by Plato and the medievals—we are perhaps the first culture to conceive of experience as neutral.)

(1981, 154–55)

Putnam is not arguing that all felt goods are rationally defensible as
goods for everyone. It is true that most of the authors I include see
themselves as talking about a universal good (or an evil that implies a
good as its opposite). We need not assume, however, without "experiment," that any one of them is justified in such an extension of a personal value to a general rule. Putnam's point is only that whenever we
have a genuine experience of quality, we receive *in* that experience, simultaneously with it and not as a separate judgment after the event,
one "good reason" for hailing that quality as a good. In an argument
that closely parallels what I have said about the necessary first step in
any coduction (see Chapter 3), Putnam claims that those who have experienced the difference between great poetry, say, and the game of
pushpin that Bentham eternalized,

> *have* a reason for preferring poetry to pushpin, and that reason lies in the
> felt experience of great poetry, and of the after effects of great poetry—the
> enlargement of the imagination and the sensibility through the enlargement
> of our repertoire of images and metaphors, and the integration of poetic
> images and metaphors with mundane perceptions and attitudes that takes
> place when a poem has lived in us for a number of years. These experiences
> too are *prima facie* good—and not just good, but ennobling, to use an old-
> fashioned word.

(155)

But with Putnam's quotation we are already into our anthology.

GIFTS, CELEBRATIONS, THANK-YOU NOTES

> Dickens understood that the imagery of fairy tales helps children better
> than anything else in their most difficult and yet most important and satis-
> fying task: achieving a more mature consciousness to civilize the chaotic
> pressures of their unconscious. . . . [T]he minds of . . . children can be
> opened to an appreciation of all the higher things in life by fairy tales. . . .
> The fairy tale is therapeutic because the patient finds his *own* solutions,
> through contemplating what the story seems to imply about him and his
> inner conflicts at this moment in his life.

(Bruno Bettelheim 1977, 23, 25)

The morality of the world in which we were born has failed. For a black cat—woman or man—the price we had to pay to live at all was to deal with a morality which we knew was false. . . . [I]t's difficult to say what a writer, a witness, should do. . . . You write in order to change the world, knowing perfectly well that you probably can't, but also knowing that literature is indispensable to the world. . . . The world changes according to the way people see it, and if you alter, even by a millimeter, the way . . . people look at reality, then you can change it.

(James Baldwin 1979, 3)

Poetry has always kept easily abreast with the utmost man can do in extending the horizon of his consciousness, whether outward or inward. It has always been the most flexible, the most comprehensive, the most far-seeing, and hence the most successful, of the modes by which he has accepted the new in experience, realized it, and adjusted himself to it. . . . [I]n the evolution of man's consciousness, ever widening and deepening and subtilizing his awareness[,] . . . man possesses [chiefly in poetry] all that he could possibly require in the way of a religious credo; when the half-gods go, the gods arrive; he can, if he only will, become divine.[2]

(Conrad Aiken 1966, 6–7)

All true poetry is absolutely amoral. What is the moral of Mozart's Twentieth Piano Concerto? . . . Poetry dedicated to the "elites," the authorities, is degenerate, moralistic, authoritarian poetry. . . . The uses of poetry are always self-limiting, however, and bear no relationship to society. . . . Poetry exists in a dimension outside civilization, as Plato said or seemed to say. Everything shows progress except poetry.

(Karl Shapiro, qtd. in Oscar Williams 1970, 890)

[Ezra] Pound went wrong, seriously wrong, in some of his judgments . . . : in mistaking Mussolini for the protagonist of our [human] powers, in confusing the obstructors of them with the Jews. Yet . . . *The Cantos,* in their main motive and effect, are on the side of humanity and democracy, in that their basis is the celebration of the powers by which we live, and the sustaining of them against the powers which deal in repression and death.

(A. D. Moody 1980, 917)

The greatest need we all have . . . is to keep alive the sense of wonder that will enable us to overcome the brutalizing forces of expediency and conformity in the mass societies of which we are a part. Only man wonders; only man imagines. When the sense of wonder is allowed to diminish, poetry . . . loses all of its Orphic power to enchant, beguile, and otherwise extend the range of our attention. Assertion is an impulse of the ego; wonder is a faculty of the soul [preserved by true poetry].

(John Brinnin 1966, 93)

---

2. It is not easy to distinguish, in some of these quotations, the claims for poetry in the sense of *lyric* poetry and the claims for all narrative that has essential poetic qualities. I'm reasonably sure that Aiken would have wanted to include his own stories in his little praise poem here.

The conventions of the detective novel . . . serve a formal aesthetic function, but they also serve political ends. The structure of Christie's novels
reflects a passive form of conservatism and encourages us to believe that the
problems of violence and social disruption can be eliminated without
changing the structure of society. . . . [Raymond] Chandler's reversal of
those conventions reverses the effect [and challenges] conservative assumptions. Instead of calming us, Chandler purposely irritates us, disrupts our
peace. . . . [He] forces us to disapprove of the world we live in and demands that we reexamine our political outlook. . . . [I]n many ways, it is
the most valuable and important work that a writer can do.

(Peter Rabinowitz 1980, 241–42)

The satirist whose laughter is negative [as in modern satire] places himself
above the object of his mockery, he is opposed to it. The wholeness of the
world's comic aspect is destroyed, and that which appears comic becomes a
private reaction. The people's ambivalent laughter, on the other hand [that
is, the laughter of Rabelais and of satire before his time], expresses the
point of view of the whole world; he who is laughing belongs to it.

(Mikhail Bakhtin 1968, 12)

[I]f a poem gave me that experience [of a passionate strong emotional re-
sponse] which I have learned comes as a reaction to reading a true poem, I
included it [in *A Little Treasury of Modern Poetry*]. . . . In other words,
I felt the poem . . . as a poem.

(Oscar Williams 1970, xxvii)

[T]o transfuse emotion—not to transmit thought but to set up in the
reader's sense a vibration corresponding to what was felt by the writer—is
the peculiar function of poetry.

(A. E. Housman 1933, 8)

Hits you in the solar plexus . . . breathtaking . . . enormously appealing.

(Advertisement for the movie *Get Out Your Handkerchiefs*)

[N]o one comes so near the invisible world as the sage and the poet, unless
it be the saint. . . . Though in themselves of no help to the attainment of
eternal life, art and poetry are more necessary than bread to the human
race. They fit it for the life of the spirit.

(Jacques Maritain, qtd. in Oscar Williams 1970, xxxviii)

The authentic reader—or critic—as well as the author now participate in
the same perilous enterprise. This peril is described by Becker in terms of a
new experience of temporality, as an attempt to exist in a time that would
no longer be the fallen temporality of everyday existence.

(Paul de Man 1983, 44; summarizing Becker and others
who see the task of literature as the *elevation* of the spirit)

[We should ask first] not *what* the [cultural] object is or *how* we should
approach it, but *why* we should want to engage with it in the first place.
The liberal humanist response to this question . . . is at once perfectly reasonable and, as it stands, entirely useless. Let us try to concretize it a little

by asking how the reinvention of rhetoric that I have proposed . . . might contribute to making us all better people. . . . Any method or theory [or work] which will contribute to the strategic goal of human emancipation, the production of 'better people' through the socialist transformation of society, is acceptable.

(Terry Eagleton 1983, 210–11)

Through identification, then, literature offers the self the sort of nourishment that is essential for development. The value of such identification is not limited, however, to the developmental effects of the particular contents that are internalized. . . . [A]s Shelley observes, . . . "Poetry strengthens that faculty [i.e., the imagination, the capacity to empathize and identify with others] which is the organ of the moral nature of man, in the same manner as exercise strengthens a limb." By exercising and strengthening our capacity to identify with others, literature provides us with an ability that will allow further growth and adjustment as we encounter new realities.

(Alcorn and Bracher 1985, 351)

If *Paradise Lost* does not profoundly trouble us, in the manner of great tragedy [as A. J. A. Waldock claimed] then we have not attended to what it is saying.

(G. A. Wilkes 1980, 278)

The apparent intensification of secondary negations in Beckett reveals a strategy that is closely akin to psychoanalytical procedures. . . . The use of negation to evoke and invalidate mental images is a means of making the reader conscious of the "preferential gestalten" (Scheler) that orient him. So long as he remains unconscious of the projective nature of his mental images, these will remain absolute, he will be unable to detach himself from them, and he will endow characters and events with an allegorical meaning, for which his undisputed projections provide the frame of reference. But if the negations take effect, and his mental images are relegated to the status of projections, there begins a process of detachment which can have two consequences: 1. The projection becomes an object for the reader, and no longer orients him. 2. He therefore becomes open to experiences which had been excluded by these projections as long as they remained valid for him. And this is the point at which Beckett's texts come so close to psychoanalysis. . . .

If there are no negations in the unconscious, their intellectual function can only come about through a conscious act. In Beckett's works, such acts are initiated by the negations which invalidate the mental images formed by the reader. . . . Indeed, its [fiction's] very usefulness springs from the fact that it is drained of reality. Such an awareness will prevent us from locking ourselves up in our own projections—a result which coincides with what the writings of Beckett appear to communicate. Through negation his fictional texts enable us to understand what fiction is, and herein lies the subtle appeal of his achievement.

(Wolfgang Iser 1978, 224–25)

If human nature does alter it will be because individuals manage to look at themselves in a new way. Here and there people—a very few people, but a few novelists are among them—are trying to do this. Every institution and vested interest is against such a search: organized religion, the State, the family in its economic aspect, have nothing to gain, and it is only when outward prohibitions weaken that it can proceed: history conditions it to that extent. Perhaps the searchers will fail, perhaps it is impossible for the instrument of contemplation to contemplate itself, perhaps if it is possible it means the end of imaginative literature. . . . Anyhow—that way lies movement and even combustion for the novel, for if the novelist sees himself differently he will see his characters differently and a new system of lighting will result. . . . [If that happened], "the development of the novel" might cease to be a pseudo-scholarly tag or a technical triviality, and become important, because it implied the development of humanity.

(E. M. Forster 1927, 245–46)

Suddenly [in poetry], as if in a flash, we *see* the dog, the coach, the house for the first time. Shortly afterwards habit erases again this potent image. We pet the dog, we call the coach, we live in a house; we do not see them anymore. . . . Such is the role of poetry. It takes off the veil, in the full sense of the word. It reveals . . . the amazing things which surround us and which our senses usually register mechanically.

(Jean Cocteau 1969, 179–80)

If in informative 'prose,' a metaphor aims to bring the subject closer to the audience or drive a point home, in 'poetry' [that is, all imaginative literature] it serves as a means of intensifying the intended esthetic effect. Rather than translating the unfamiliar into the terms of the familiar, the poetic image 'makes strange' the habitual by presenting it in a novel light, by placing it in an unexpected context. . . . The trope was seen here [by Victor Sklovskij] merely as one of the devices at the poet's disposal, exemplifying the general tendency of poetry, indeed of all art. The transfer of the object to the 'sphere of new perception,' that is, a sui generis 'semantic shift' effected by the trope, was proclaimed as the principal aim, the raison d'être of poetry.

(Victor Erlich 1969, 176, discussing the work of Viktor Sklovskij)

A writer out of loneliness is trying to communicate like a distant star sending signals. He isn't telling or teaching or ordering. Rather he seeks to establish a relationship of meaning, of feeling, of observing. We are lonesome animals. We spend all life trying to be less lonesome. One of our ancient methods is to tell a story begging the listener to say—and to feel—

"Yes, that's the way it is, or at least that's the way I feel it. You're not as alone as you thought." . . .

It is the duty of the writer to lift up, to extend, to encourage. If the written word has contributed anything at all to our developing species and our half developed culture, it is this: Great writing has been a staff to lean on, a mother to consult, a wisdom to pick up stumbling folly, a strength in weakness and a courage to support sick cowardice. And how any negative or despairing approach can pretend to be literature I do not know.

(John Steinbeck 1977, 183, 195)

I have from the start been wary of the fake, the automatic. I tried not to force my sense of life as many-layered and ambiguous, while keeping in mind some sense of transaction, of a bargain struck, between me and the ideal reader. . . . My work is meditation, not pontification. . . . My first thought about art, as a child, was that the artist brings something into the world that didn't exist before, and that he does it without destroying something else. A kind of refutation of the conservation of matter. That still seems to me its central magic, its core of joy.

(John Updike 1977, 454)

However grotesque it may sound to suggest that one may come to absorb or contain an influence the size of Shakespeare or Milton or Dante or Blake, still there is something in these creators that can be contained and possessed, something that expands, instead of restricting, the individuality of those who follow after them. . . . The arts [including, of course, all literature] tell us how the human imagination operates, are thus an un-tapped source of mental energy, a means of achieving social and individual freedom. Once we have recovered our imaginative birthright, we can look down on the world we have left behind and see that it forms a demonic parody of the world we are now in.

(Northrop Frye 1975, 203, 208)

Art is rehearsal for those real situations in which it is vital for our survival to endure cognitive tension, to refuse the comforts of validation by affective congruence when such validation is inappropriate because too vital inter-ests are at stake; art is the reinforcement of the capacity to endure disorien-tation so that a real and significant problem may emerge.

(Morse Peckham 1967, 314)

[I]n the most serious and genuinely committed writing, in which the writer's whole being, and thus, necessarily, his real social existence, is inevitably being drawn upon, at every level from the most manifest to the most intan-gible, it is literally inconceivable that practice can be separated from situa-tion. Since all situations are dynamic, such practice is always active and is capable of radical development. Yet as we have seen, real social relations are deeply embedded within the practice of writing itself, as well as in the relations within which writing is read. To write in different ways is to live in different ways. It is also to be read in different ways, in different relations, and often by different people. This area of possibility, and thence of choice, is specific, not abstract, and commitment in its only important sense is spe-cific in just these terms. . . . Thus to recognize alignment is to learn, if we choose, the hard and total specificities of commitment [which is to say, if I read Williams correctly: the best art will be created by those who commit themselves and choose to face their specific situations].

(Raymond Williams 1977, 200, 204–5)

If the poet is not clairvoyant, he is nothing. And this clairvoyancy is particularly directed towards discovering the "supernatural" in nature and the
"superhuman" in humanity. There can be no such thing as realist poetry.

(C. Day-Lewis 1935, 253)

The impulse to create a work of art is felt when, in certain persons, the
passive awe provoked by sacred beings or events is transformed into a desire to express that awe in a rite of worship or homage, and to be fit
homage, this rite must be beautiful. This rite has no magical or idolatrous
intention; nothing is expected in return. . . . Poetry can do a hundred and
one things, delight, sadden, disturb, amuse, instruct—it may express every
possible shade of emotion, and describe every conceivable kind of event,
but there is only one thing that all poetry must do; it must praise all it can
for being and for happening.

(W. H. Auden 1962, 56, 60)

[One crucial value of tragedy is its power to remind believers of the mystery
of] the Wrath of God.

(Paul Ricoeur 1972, pt. 2, ch. 2)

[Tragedy's ethical value lies in this: it] explores inconsistencies between
moral notions and other fundamental beliefs, and glaring discrepancies between both moral and epistemological presuppositions about the world
and the actual shapes of human experience. Tragedy raises a basic religious
question: how can the worth of human existence be affirmed in light of our
experience of evil and suffering, and in light of our knowledge of man's in-
humanity to man? . . . In this limited sense, the reader's experience of tragedy involves a process of recognition and thought that can be interpreted as
religious in its ultimate significance for human life. For tragedy usually
does offer a reaffirmation of a particular kind of virtue . . . after having
taken into account all the ways that virtue can fail or lead to evil. . . . [It
provides] trust or confidence in the worth of human existence in spite of its
threats and terrors and failures. . . . 'In being the bad conscience of their
time' . . . 'by applying the knife vivisectionally to the chest of the very virtues of their time,' the authors of tragedy perform the service Nietzsche demanded of the ideal philosopher.

(John Barbour 1984, 188–89)

Art is a mystery; all mysteries have their source in a mystery-of-mysteries
who is love: and if lovers may reach eternity directly through love herself,
their mystery remains essentially that of the loving artist whose way must
lie through his art, and of the loving worshipper whose aim is oneness with
his god.

(e. e. cummings 1953, 82)

The true center of value of a text, its most important meaning, is to be
found in the community that it establishes with its reader. It is here that the
author offers his reader a place to stand, a place from which he can observe
and judge the characters and events of the world he creates. . . . This means
that all literature, fictional and nonfictional, necessarily has an ethical and

political dimension, for it always entails the definition of at least two roles (writer and reader) and the establishment of a relationship between them that can be seen to have both political and ethical content.

(James Boyd White 1984, 17)

The great virtues that Chaucer teaches are perception and tolerance.

(Charles Muscatine 1972, 111)

Fiction must be aware of its power over our affections and fantasies so that it will then try to base its projections on a process of identifying with educational needs. Once we do this, once we have a philosophy fully aware of the power of fictions, we can produce a theory of mimesis responsive to an ethical theater. . . . As cognitive agents we try to imitate or represent states of affairs, but ethical life begins when we are moved by admiration to imitate some projected example. The imitation itself is not the basis of ethical behavior, but it does introduce us to the processes of recognizing lack and dialectically defining the self which are fundamental to being an ethical agent.

(Charles Altieri 1985, 270–71)

Perhaps the most basic concept of my writing is a belief in the magical universe, a universe of many gods, often in conflict. The paradox of an all-powerful, all-seeing God who nonetheless allows suffering, evil and death, does not arise.

"We got a famine here, Osiris. What happened?"
"Well, you can't win 'em all. Hustling myself."

My purpose in writing has always been to express human potentials and purposes relevant to the Space Age.

(William Burroughs 1984, 9–10)

The Study of it [the art of poetry, of fictional making] . . . offers to mankinde a certaine rule, and Patterne of living well, and happily; disposing us to all Civill offices of Society. If wee will beleive *Tully*, it nourisheth, and instructeth our Youth; delights our Age; adornes our prosperity; comforts our Adversity; entertaines us at home; keepes us company abroad, travailes with us; watches; divides the times of our earnest, and spoarts; shares in our Country recesses, and recreations; insomuch as the wisest and best learned have thought her the absolute Mistresse of manners, and nearest of kin to Vertue. And, wheras they entitle *Philosophy* to bee a rigid, and austere *Poesie*, they have (on the contrary) stiled *Poesy* a dulcet, and gentle *Philosophy*, which leades on, and guides us by the hand to Action, with a ravishing delight, and incredible Sweetnes.

(Ben Jonson [1641] 1947, ll. 2386–2400)

WARNINGS

We need no large collection here, partly because the claims are well known and partly because each of the "gifts" implies a warning against any narrative that fails to provide it. But I add a few specific warnings against poisons and diseases, if only to avoid an air of unethical optimism here at the end.

[The director of *Risky Business*, Paul Brickman, never takes Lana, the call girl] out of fantasyland. . . . Lana has to be a sensuous creature who enjoys her work, and prostitution here isn't a sad, rotten business—it's just a shade "risky." The picture is centered on this tiresome lie, which appears to satisfy some deep vanity in men. It's one of the invincible lies that keep going so long they gather moss and turn into fables.

(Pauline Kael 1983, 109)

. . . a worthless fellow who, due to lack of talent, has gone to extremes with tendentious [political] junk to show his convictions, but it is really in order to gain an audience.

(Friedrich Engels, August 1881; qtd. in Raymond Williams 1977, 200)

. . . Mr Auden cannot now be far short of thirty, and he is still without that gift with which a poet controls words, commands expression, writes poems. He has no organization. . . . [He] still makes far too much of his poetry out of private neuroses and memories—still uses these in an essentially immature way. . . . The sinister glamour that so often attends his premonitory surveys of the social scene is transferred too directly and too obviously from the nameless terrors of childhood or their neurotic equivalent. . . . [His] technique is not one that solves problems; it conceals a failure to grapple with them, or, rather, makes a virtue out of the failure. He has made a technique out of irresponsibility, and his most serious work exhibits a shameless opportunism in the passage from phrase to phrase and from item to item—the use of a kind of bluff.

(F. R. Leavis 1968, 1: 110–14)

Prose that glorifies such men [as the murderer, Gary Gilmore, as portrayed in *The Executioner's Song*] is anti-human in itself, and is therefore not literature, and not art. It is hack work, and dangerous hack work, and we condone it at our risk.

(Bryan Griffin 1980, 19)

I probably laughed harder at this collection of college slapstick sketches than I ever have at a film I didn't really like. . . . The film leaves behind a bad taste of snobbery and petty meanness. In the world of the National Lampoon, humanity is divided into two groups: Us and the Assholes. Naturally, we win—a comforting fantasy if there ever was one.

(Dave Kehr 1979, 18)

Mr. Gold has written the very novel that his urban and suburban characters, full of the satirical stereotypes that have long been current even in bourgeois irony, would have written: the clichés are precisely those of cocktail-party conversation. . . . Most of the sordid jokes are merely those that might be told, with some embarrassment, in an office men's room. It is Babbitt, walking the streets of Manhattan, who has written "Salt," with glee and shame at the daring of his own imagination. . . . What is unfortunate is that with-

out his commitment to cruelty and irony he might conceivably write carefully and well. . . . [I]t seems possible that there lies buried in "Salt" a literary talent that has simply smothered in its own misanthropy.

(Renata Adler 1963, 110–11)

The deeper energy of the story [Alex Haley's "Roots"], and its real . . . audience appeal, proceeds from Haley's own fantasies about Going Home,
and above all from his apparent willingness to leave the fantasies intact and
unchallenged in much the same way that his audience does. One could almost say that the power of "Roots" lies in its weakness, albeit a most human weakness, for nearly all of us seem prey to fears that our ancestors
were *not* . . . mighty warriors, noble, sexual, and brave. . . . Of course, if
Haley had bitten the bullet and broken through the dream he was so
movingly trapped in, he would have had to write a different, braver, and
almost certainly much less popular book; but then he might have given his
people, and also other peoples, a truer Kunta Kinte, clothed, however dangerously, in his real humanity, and who knows but that in the long run this
might have turned out to be the greater gift?

(Michael Arlen 1979, 124–25)

A WARNING AGAINST WARNINGS

If a story were to force me to wallow in the merely horizontal extension of
experience, if a story gave me no glimpse of some possible path leading upward from the eternally pre-determined flux of sub-atomic particles, if a
story offered me no suggestion that human life is more significant than the
motes of dust I see in a Brownian movement in the sunlight that falls on the
page, then that story would have to be called bad. But nobody should take
alarm from this charge: there are hardly any such stories.

Some universalist churches have claimed that the total number of the
damned—the true "sons of perdition"—can be counted on the fingers of
one hand: only those who have known Christ and then denied him. I would
say the same about literary works. It is almost impossible to think of any
narratives, among those that get themselves attended to at all, that do not
implicitly raise us from the dirt and mold us into created creatures of some
kind of spirit. The very effort to get a story told, like the reader's effort
to take a story in, is itself a proof that we dwell in the domain of symbol-
exchange, an inherently "elevated" domain by comparison with that of the
brute bumps and surges of the merely physical; it baptizes us into the kingdom of the Word. Every story presupposes—in a sense re-creates in the moment of its telling—a world inhabited by creatures able to imagine and thus
live in story. Every story says: "The readers of this story can do something
that nothing else in the universe as we know or imagine it can do: that is,
read black squiggles, turn them into words, turn the words into imagined
stories, and thus elevate the dust into a different world entirely."

What a wonder that is. All readers know it as a wonder, even as they
may consciously struggle with worlds that explicitly deny the wonder.

"Dust thou art, to dust returnest." At the moment of utterance, at the moment of re-utterance, the statement reveals itself as false. "Telling" it as a gloomy story about life, interpreting it whether in belief or disbelief, we are not dust but life: anima-ted, re-minded, spirited, en-souled, "en-psychéd." Which is to say that we all dwell in a world in which ethical criticism is not only possible; it is required.

(Anon.)

REFERENCES

Adler, Renata. "Salt into Old Scars." Review of *Salt,* by Herbert Gold. *New Yorker* (June 22, 1963): 104–111.

Aiken, Conrad. "Poetry and the Mind of Modern Man." In Nemerov 1966.

Alcorn, Marshall W., Jr., and Mark Bracher. "Literature, Psychoanalysis, and the Re-Formation of the Self: A New Direction for Reader-Response Theory." *PMLA* 100 (May 1985): 342–54.

Altieri, Charles. "Plato's Performative Sublime and the Ends of Reading." *New Literary History* 16 (Win. 1985): 251–73.

Arlen, Michael. "The Prisoner of the Golden Dream." *New Yorker* (Mar. 26, 1979): 115–25.

Auden, W. H. "Making, Knowing and Judging." In *The Dyer's Hand.* London, 1962.

Bakhtin, Mikhail. *Rabelais and His World* [1929]. Trans. Hélène Iswolsky. Cambridge, Mass., 1968.

Baldwin, James. Interview by Mel Watkins. *New York Times Book Review* (Sept. 23, 1979): 3.

Barbour, John D. *Tragedy as a Critique of Virtue: The Novel and Ethical Reflection.* Chico, Calif., 1984.

Beckett, Samuel. *Watt* [1953]. London, 1963.

Bettelheim, Bruno. *The Uses of Enchantment: The Meaning and Importance of Fairy Tales* [1976]. New York, 1977.

Brinnin, John. "Some Phases of Work." In Nemerov 1966.

Burroughs, William. "My Purpose Is to Write for the Space Age." *New York Times Book Review* (Feb. 19, 1984): 9–10.

Cocteau, Jean. "Le Secret Professionel" [1926]. Qtd. in Erlich 1969.

Cummings, E. E. *i; six nonlectures.* Cambridge, Mass., 1953.

Day-Lewis, C. "A Hope for Poetry." In *Collected Poems, 1929–1933 and "A Hope for Poetry."* New York, 1935.

de Man, Paul. *Blindness and Insight: Essays in the Rhetoric of Contemporary Criticism.* 2d ed., rev. History and Theory of Literature, vol. 7. Minneapolis, 1983.

Eagleton, Terry. *Literary Theory: An Introduction.* Minneapolis, 1983.

Erlich, Victor. *Russian Formalism: History-Doctrine.* 3d ed. The Hague, 1969.

Forster, E. M. *Aspects of the Novel.* London, 1927.

Frye, Northrop. "Expanding Eyes." *Critical Inquiry* 2 (Win. 1975): 199–216.

Griffin, Bryan F. "Low Life and High Hack." Review of *The Executioner's Song,* by Norman Mailer. *The American Spectator* (Feb. 1980): 12–19.

Housman, A. E. *The Name and Nature of Poetry*. New York, 1933.

Iser, Wolfgang. *The Act of Reading: A Theory of Aesthetic Response*. Baltimore, 1978.

Johnson, Samuel. "The Rambler, no. 3." In *Samuel Johnson: "The Rambler,"* vol. 1. Ed. W. J. Bate and Albrecht B. Strauss. Vol. 3 of *The Yale Edition of the Works of Samuel Johnson*. New Haven, Conn., 1969. 14–15.

Jonson, Ben. "Timber; or, Discoveries" [1641]. In *Ben Jonson: The Poems/ The Prose Works*. Ed. C. H. Herford, Percy Simpson, and Evelyn Simpson. Oxford, 1947. 562–649.

Kael, Pauline. "The Current Cinema." *New Yorker* (Sept. 5, 1983): 106–11.

Kehr, Dave. Review of *Animal House*. *Chicago Reader* (Sept. 28, 1979): 18.

Leavis, F. R. "Mr. Auden's Talent" [1936] and "'Another Time,' by W. H. Auden" [1940]. In *A Selection from "Scrutiny."* Ed. F. R. Leavis. 2 vols. Cambridge, 1968. 1: 110–14.

Maritain, Jacques. Qtd. in Oscar Williams 1970.

Moody, A. D. "The Democracy of the Cantos." *Times Literary Supplement* (Aug. 15, 1980): 917.

Muscatine, Charles. *Poetry and Crisis in the Age of Chaucer*. Notre Dame, Ind., 1972.

Nemerov, Howard, ed. *Poets on Poetry*. New York, 1966.

Peckham, Morse. *Man's Rage for Chaos*. New York, 1967.

Putnam, Hilary. "Reason and History." In *Reason, Truth, and History*. Cambridge, 1981.

Rabinowitz, Peter. "Rats Behind the Wainscoting." *Texas Studies in Literature and Language* 22 (Sum. 1980): 224–45.

Ricoeur, Paul. *The Symbolism of Evil* [1967]. Trans. Emerson Buchanan. Boston, 1972.

Shapiro, Karl. *In Defense of Ignorance: Essays*. New York, 1952. Qtd. in Oscar Williams 1970: 890.

Steinbeck, John. Interview [1976; actually a compilation, not an interview, by George Plimpton and Frank Crowther]. *Writers at Work: The "Paris Review" Interviews*. Ed. George Plimpton. 4th ser. Harmondsworth, 1977.

Updike, John. Interview by Charles Thomas Samuels [1976]. *Writers at Work: The "Paris Review" Interviews*. Ed. George Plimpton. 4th ser. Harmondsworth, 1977.

White, James Boyd. *When Words Lose Their Meaning: Constitutions and Reconstitutions of Language, Character, and Community*. Chicago, 1984.

Wilkes, G. A. "'Full of Doubt I Stand': The Final Implications of *Paradise Lost*." In *English Renaissance Studies: Presented to Dame Helen Gardner in Honor of Her Seventieth Birthday*. Ed. John Carey. Oxford, 1980.

Williams, Oscar, ed. *A Little Treasury of Modern Poetry: English and American* [1946]. 3d ed. New York, 1970.

Williams, Raymond. *Marxism and Literature*. Oxford, 1977.

Bibliography of Ethical Criticism

Tracing studies of that borderland where the two general interests, ethics and story-telling, engage in fruitful but troubled exchange, I have not had room for most works of general ethical theory and general aesthetics. Even more reluctantly, I have had to exclude all but a sampling from the vast number of ethical studies of individual authors: "The Moral World of X," "The Integral Vision of Y," "The Radical Critique of Z." For authors writing before the twentieth century I have for the most part listed only one or two representative works, and I have not even mentioned many an author—for example, Blake—whose whole life could be considered an act of ethical criticism; indeed a very large proportion of all critical works before modern times addressed ethical questions. For a fuller bibliography of studies of narrative rhetoric, "narratology," and the hermeneutics of narrative (*all* of which impinge in one way or another on my concerns here), see James Phelan's "Supplementary Bibliography, 1961–1982" in the second edition of *The Rhetoric of Fiction* (1983). I have resisted listing innumerable works, in languages other than English, that I have heard described but not read on my own. Finally, readers will notice that no novels or poems are listed here, not even those that contain explicit ethical criticism of their ancestors. A bibliography of such works could well be longer than this one.

If in spite of all these exclusions the total number of works cited seems excessive, I can only make the obvious point that a full gathering of workers in this fertile vineyard would leave no room for *Company;* I fear that many readers will wonder why I have omitted their essential labors. On the other hand, some authors harvested here may want to echo Michael Sprinker, who wrote me to say that "being used . . . as an instance of ethical judgment . . . makes me squirm a bit." My reply might well be: Many works here teach that to make readers squirm is about the highest ethical task an author can perform.

I give full data here only for works not cited in the "References" of Chapters 1–13, the Epilogue, and the Appendix. Works cited earlier are given only with short titles and the note "See ref. Chapter ——." Multiple entries under an author's name are listed in chronological order by year of publication of the most recent edition cited; the year of original publication (in the work's original language) is given in brackets for those works listed in full. Not all works included in the reference lists appear here; see the Index for further references.

Abel, Elizabeth. "(E)merging Identities." See ref. Chapter 6.
———. "Editor's Introduction." See ref. Chapter 12.
Abrams, M. H. *The Correspondent Breeze: Essays on English Romanticism.* New York, 1984.
———. "Art as Such." See ref. Chapter 1.
Achebe, Chinua. "An Image of Africa." See ref. Chapter 1.
Adams, George P. *Possibility.* See ref. Chapter 4.
Adams, Hazard. "The Dizziness of Freedom; or, Why I Read William Blake." *College English* 48 (Sept. 1986): 431–43.
Adams, William Davenport. *Famous Books.* See ref. Chapter 6.
Adkins, Arthur W. H. *Merit and Responsibility: A Study in Greek Values.* Chicago, 1975.
Aiken, Conrad. "Poetry and the Mind of Modern Man." See ref. Chapter 8.
Aiken, Henry David. *Reason and Conduct.* See ref. Chapter 3.
———. "Morality and Ideology." In DeGeorge 1966: 149–72.
Alkon, Paul Kent. *Samuel Johnson and Moral Discipline.* Evanston, Ill., 1967.
Alcorn, Marshall W., Jr. "Rhetoric, Projection, and the Authority of the Signifier." See ref. Chapter 4.
Alcorn, Marshall W., Jr., and Mark Bracher. "Literature, Psychoanalysis, and the Re-Formation of the Self." See ref. Appendix.
Allen, Judson Boyce. *The Ethical Poetic of the Later Middle Ages: A Decorum of Convenient Distinction.* Toronto, 1982.
Altenbernd, Lynn. "Huck Finn, Emancipator." See ref. Chapter 13.
Alter, Robert. *Motives for Fiction.* Cambridge, Mass., 1984.
Altieri, Charles. *Art and Quality: A Theory of Literary Meaning and Humanistic Understanding.* Amherst, Mass., 1981.
———. "Plato's Performative Sublime and the Ends of Reading." *New Literary History* 16 (Win. 1985): 251–73.
———. "From Expressivist Aesthetics to Expressivist Ethics." In Cascardi 1987.
Anastaplo, George. *The Artist as Thinker: From Shakespeare to Joyce.* Athens, Ohio, 1983.
———. "Censorship." *Encyclopaedia Britannica: Macropaedia.* 1985 ed. 634–41.
Anderson, Warren D. *Ethos and Education in Greek Music: The Evidence of Poetry and Philosophy.* Cambridge, Mass., 1966.
Antczak, Frederick J. *Thought and Character: The Rhetoric of Democratic Education.* Ames, Iowa, 1985.

Apple, Max, John Updike, et al. "A Writers' Forum on Moral Fiction." *Fiction International* 12 (1980): 5–25.

Arac, Jonathan, ed. *Postmodernism and Politics*. See ref. Chapter 5.

Aristotle. *Poetics*. See ref. Chapter 6.

———. *Nicomachean Ethics*. See ref. Chapter 6.

———. *Politics*. See ref. Chapter 8.

Arnold, Matthew. "Preface." *Poems*. See ref. Chapter 2.

———. *Essays in Criticism*. See ref. Chapter 4.

Attorney General's Commission on Pornography: Final Report, July 1986. See ref. Introduction to Part 2.

Auden, W. H. "The Ironic Hero." See ref. Chapter 8.

Auerbach, Erich. *Mimesis*. See ref. Chapter 8.

Babbitt, Irving. *Rousseau and Romanticism*. New York, 1919.

Bacon, Corinne. "What Makes a Novel Immoral?" *Publishers Weekly* (Oct. 8, 1910): 1392–97.

Baier, Kurt. "Responsibility and Freedom." In DeGeorge 1969: 49–84.

Baker, Houston A., Jr. *The Journey Back: Issues in Black Literature and Criticism*. Chicago, 1980.

———. *Blues, Ideology, and Afro-American Literature: A Vernacular Theory*. Chicago, 1984.

Bakhtin, Mikhail. *The Dialogic Imagination*. See ref. Chapter 8.

———. *Problems of Dostoevsky's Poetics*. See ref. Chapter 3.

Bal, Mieke. *Narratology*. See ref. Chapter 5.

Balbert, Peter, and Phillip L. Marcus, eds. *D. H. Lawrence*. See ref. Chapter 13.

Balmforth, Ramsden. *The Ethical and Religious Value of the Drama*. New York, 1926.

Barbour, John D. *Tragedy as a Critique of Virtue*. See ref. Chapter 3.

Barthelme, Donald. "Not Knowing." *Georgia Review* 39 (Fall 1985): 521–22.

Barr, Donald. "Should Holden Caulfield Read These Books?" *New York Times Book Review* (May 4, 1986): 1, 50.

Barthes, Roland. *Sade/Fourier/Loyola*. See ref. Chapter 3.

———. *The Pleasure of the Text* [1973]. Trans. Richard Miller. New York, 1975.

———. *The Responsibility of Forms: Critical Essays on Music, Art, and Representation* [1982]. Trans. Richard Howard. New York, 1985.

———. *The Rustle of Language* [1984]. Trans. Richard Howard. New York, 1986.

Barzun, Jacques. *The Use and Abuse of Art* [1974]. Princeton, N.J., 1975.

Bateson, Gregory. "The Cybernetics of 'Self.'" See ref. Chapter 8.

Battestin, Martin. *The Moral Basis of Fielding's Art: A Study of "Joseph Andrews."* Middletown, Conn., 1959.

Bayley, John. *The Uses of Division*. See ref. Chapter 4.

Bayne, Peter. *Lessons from My Masters*. See ref. Chapter 6.

Baynes, Kenneth, et al., eds. *After Philosophy: End or Transformation?* Cambridge, Mass., 1987.

Beal, Anthony, ed. *D. H. Lawrence*. See ref. Chapter 13.

Beardsmore, R. W. *Art and Morality*. London, 1971.

Beerbohm, Max. "A Defence of Cosmetics." See ref. Chapter 6.
Beauvoir, Simone de. *The Marquis de Sade.* See ref. Chapter 3.
Becker, Carl Lotus. *Everyman His Own Historian.* See ref. Chapter 11.
Becker, Lawrence C., ed. "Symposium on Morality and Literature." In *Ethics* 98 (Jan. 1988): 223–340.
Bellah, Robert N., et al., eds. *Habits of the Heart: Individualism and Commitment in American Life.* Berkeley, 1985.
Benjamin, Walter. *Illuminations* [1961]. Ed. Hannah Arendt. Trans. Harry Zohn. New York, 1968.
———. "The Work of Art in the Age of Mechanical Reproduction." In Lang and Williams 1972: 281–300.
Bentley, Eric, ed. *The Importance of "Scrutiny."* New York, 1964.
Bercovitch, Sacvan. "The Problem of Ideology in American Literary History." *Critical Inquiry* 12 (Sum. 1986): 631–53.
Bercovitch, Sacvan, and Myra Jehlen, eds. *Ideology and Classic American Literature.* Cambridge, 1986.
Berger, Peter. "The Problem of Multiple Realities: Alfred Schutz and Robert Musil." In *Phenomenology and Social Reality.* Ed. M. Natanson. Evanston, Ill., 1970.
Bernstein, Michael André. "'O Totiens Servus': Saturnalia and Servitude in Augustan Rome." *Critical Inquiry* 13 (Spr. 1987): 450–74.
Berrong, Richard M. "Finding Antifeminism in Rabelais." See ref. Chapter 12.
———. *Rabelais and Bakhtin: Popular Culture in "Gargantua and Pantagruel."* Lincoln, Neb., 1986.
Berthoff, Warner. *Literature and the Continuances of Virtue.* See ref. Chapter 1.
Bettelheim, Bruno. *The Uses of Enchantment.* See ref. Chapter 10.
———. "Surviving." See ref. Chapter 1.
Bleich, David. *Subjective Criticism.* Baltimore, Md., 1978.
———. "Intersubjective Reading." See ref. Chapter 1.
Bialostosky, Don H. "Booth's Rhetoric, Bakhtin's Dialogics, and the Future of Novel Criticism." *Novel* 18 (Spr. 1985): 209–16.
———. "Dialogics as an Art of Discourse in Literary Criticism." See ref. Chapter 12.
Black American Literature Forum. Bloomington, Ind. (Founded 1976; previously *Negro American Literature Forum,* Fall 1967–Win. 1976.)
Blackmur, R. P. "Between the Numen and the Moha." In *The Lion and the Honeycomb.* New York, 1955.
———. "The Great Grasp of Unreason." In *A Primer of Ignorance.* New York, 1967.
Blair, Walter, and Hamlin Hill. *The Art of "Huckleberry Finn."* See ref. Chapter 13.
Block, Joel D. *Friendship.* See ref. Chapter 6.
Bloom, Allan. *The Closing of the American Mind.* See ref. Chapter 1. (See also Rousseau below.)
Bloom, Harold. *The Anxiety of Influence.* See ref. Chapter 9.
———. *A Map of Misreading.* Oxford, 1975.
———. "Homer, Virgil, Tolstoy: The Epic Hero." *Raritan* 6 (Sum. 1986): 1–25.
Bloom, Harold, et al. *Deconstruction and Criticism.* See ref. Chapter 2.

Blum, Lawrence A. *Friendship, Altruism, and Morality.* London, 1980.

Blythin, Evan. "'Arguers as Lovers': A Critical Perspective." *Philosophy and Rhetoric* 12 (Sum. 1979): 176–86.

Bogdan, Deanne. "Sidney's Defence of Plato and the 'Lying' Greek Poets: The Argument from Hypothesis." *Classical and Modern Literature* 7 (Fall 1986): 43–55.

Bolotin, David. *Plato's Dialogue on Friendship: An Interpretation of the "Lysis," with a New Translation.* Ithaca, N.Y., 1979.

Bolton, W. F. "The Wife of Bath: Narrator as Victim." In *Gender and Literary Voice.* Ed. Janet Todd. New York, 1980: 54–66.

Bonnefoy, Yves. "Baudelaire parlant à Mallarmé." In *Entretiens sur la poésie.* Paris, 1981. (See also Naughton 1984.)

——. "Image and Presence." See ref. Chapter 8.

Booth, Wayne C. See ref. Chapters 1–4, 8, 9, 13.

Boudin, Michael. "Antitrust Doctrine and the Sway of Metaphor." *Georgetown Law Journal* 75 (1986): 395–422.

Bové, Paul A. *Destructive Poetics.* See ref. Chapter 3.

——. *Intellectuals in Power.* See ref. Chapter 5.

Bradley, A. C. "Poetry for Poetry's Sake" [1901]. In *Oxford Lectures on Poetry.* London, 1914.

Bradley, F. H. *Ethical Studies.* See ref. Chapter 8.

Brain, Robert. *Friends and Lovers.* See ref. Chapter 6.

Branden, Barbara. *The Passion of Ayn Rand.* See ref. Chapter 11.

Brecht, Bertolt. "Study of the First Scene of Shakespeare's *Coriolanus.*" In Lang and Williams 1972: 446–59.

——. "Theatre for Pleasure and Theatre for Instruction." In Lang and Williams 1972: 326–33.

Bredon, Hugh. "I. A. Richards and the Philosophy of Practical Criticism." *Philosophy and Literature* 10 (Apr. 1986): 26–37.

Brockriede, Wayne. "Arguers as Lovers." *Philosophy and Rhetoric* 5 (Win. 1972): 1–11.

Bromwich, David. "The Genealogy of Disinterestedness." *Raritan* 1 (Spr. 1982): 62–92.

——. "Stevens and the Idea of the Hero." *Raritan* 7 (Sum. 1987): 1–27.

Brooke-Rose, Christine. "The Dissolution of Character in the Novel." In Heller et al. 1986: 184–96.

Brooks, Cleanth. *The Well Wrought Urn.* See ref. Chapter 3.

——. "Irony as a Principle of Structure." See ref. Chapter 6.

Brooks, Cleanth, and Robert Penn Warren. *Understanding Poetry.* See ref. Chapter 4.

Brooks, Peter. *Reading for the Plot.* New York, 1984.

Brown, Charles T., and Paul W. Keller. *Monologue to Dialogue.* 2d ed. Englewood Cliffs, N.J., 1979. (See especially ch. 11.)

Bruner, Edward M. *Text, Play, and Story: The Construction of Self and Society.* Washington, D.C., 1984.

Brunton, J. A. "Egoism and Morality." *Philosophical Quarterly* 6 (1956): 289–303.

Buckley, Vincent. *Poetry and Morality: Studies on the Criticism of Matthew Arnold, T. S. Eliot, and F. R. Leavis.* London, 1959.

Buell, Frederick. *W. H. Auden as a Social Poet.* Ithaca, N.Y., 1973.

Bullock, Chris, and David Peck, eds. *Guide to Marxist Literary Criticism (A Bibliography)*. Bloomington, Ind., 1980.

Bullough, E. *Aesthetics*. Ed. E. M. Wilkinson. London, 1957.

Burke, Edmund. *A Philosophical Inquiry into the Origin of Our Ideas of the Sublime and Beautiful*. London, 1757.

———. *Reflections on the Revolution in France*. See ref. Chapter 11.

Burke, Kenneth. "Psychology and Form." See ref. Chapter 7.

———. *The Philosophy of Literary Form: Studies in Symbolic Action* [1941]. 2d ed. New York, 1957.

———. *Language as Symbolic Action*. See ref. Chapter 4.

———. See Garlitz 1979.

Burshatin, Israel. "The Moor in the Text: Metaphor, Emblem, and Silence." In *"Race," Writing, and Difference*. Ed. Henry Louis Gates, Jr. Chicago, 1986. 117–37.

Burstein, Janet Handler. "Cynthia Ozick and the Transgressions of Art." *American Literature* 59 (Mar. 1987): 83–101.

Büttner, F. O. *Imitatio Pietatis*. See ref. Chapter 8.

Calinescu, Matei. "From the One to the Many: Pluralism in Today's Thought." In Hassan 1983: 263–88.

Calvino, Italo. *The Uses of Literature: Essays* [1980]. Trans. Patrick Creagh. New York, 1986.

Card, Orson Scott. "A Mormon Writer Looks at the Problem of Evil in Fiction." *One Hundred and Fifty Years: Sesquicentennial Lectures on Mormon Arts, Letters, and Sciences*. Provo, Utah, 1980.

Carey, John. "An End to Evaluation." See ref. Chapter 2.

———. *John Donne: Life, Mind and Art*. See ref. Chapter 2.

Carlyle, Thomas. "Symbols." In *Sartor Resartus* [1833–34]. London, 1838.

Carrington, George C. *The Dramatic Unity of "Huckleberry Finn."* See ref. Chapter 13.

Carroll, David. *The Subject in Question: The Languages of Theory and the Strategies of Fiction*. Chicago, 1982.

Cascardi, Anthony J., ed. *Literature and the Question of Philosophy*. Baltimore, 1987.

Casillo, Robert. "Nature, History, and Anti-Nature in Ezra Pound's Fascism." *Papers on Language and Literature* 22 (Sum. 1986): 284–311.

Cassirer, Ernst. "Art." In *Essay on Man*. New Haven, Conn., 1944.

Castiglione, Baldesar. *The Book of the Courtier*. See ref. Chapter 8.

Caudwell, Christopher. "Beauty and Bourgeois Aesthetic." In Lang and Williams 1972: 199–212.

Cave, Terence. *The Cornucopian Text*. See ref. Chapter 3.

Cavell, Stanley. *Pursuits of Happiness: The Hollywood Comedy of Remarriage*. Cambridge, Mass., 1981.

Cawelti, John G., and Bruce A. Rosenberg. *The Spy Story*. See ref. Chapter 5.

Certeau, Michel de. *Heterologies*. See ref. Chapter 3.

Chandler, James. "Wordsworth and Burke." *English Literary History* 47 (Win. 1980): 741–71.

———. *Wordsworth's Second Nature*. Chicago, 1984.

Chatman, Seymour. *Story and Discourse: Narrative Structure in Fiction and Film*. Ithaca, N.Y., 1978.

————. "Characters and Narrators: Filter, Center, Slant, and Interest-Focus."
    Poetics Today 7 (1986): 189–204.
————. "The 'Rhetoric' 'of' 'Fiction.'" See ref. Chapter 3.
Chesebro, James. "A Construct for Assessing Ethics in Communication." *Central States Speech Journal* 20 (Sum. 1969): 104–14.
Cicero. *De Officiis.* See ref. Chapter 8.
————. "On Friendship." See ref. Chapter 6.
Clausen, Christopher. *The Moral Imagination.* See ref. Chapter 7.
Clifford, James, and George E. Marcus, eds. *Writing Culture.* See ref. Chapter 12.
Cohen, Philip K. *The Moral Vision of Oscar Wilde.* Madison, Wis., 1978.
Cohen, Ted. "Metaphor and the Cultivation of Intimacy." See ref. Chapter 6.
Cohen, Ted, and Paul Guyer, eds. *Essays in Kant's Aesthetics.* See ref. Chapter 1.
Cohler, Bertram J. "Psychoanalysis and the Developmental Narrative." See ref. Chapter 9.
Cohn, Dorrit. *Transparent Minds: Narrative Modes for Presenting Consciousness in Fiction.* Princeton, N.J., 1978.
Coleridge, S. T. "On the Principles of Genial Criticism Concerning the Fine Arts" [1814]. In *Criticism: The Major Texts.* Ed. Walter Jackson Bate. New York, 1952.
————. *"The Friend,"* Volume 1 [1809]. Ed. Barbara E. Rooke. Vol. 4 of *The Collected Works of Samuel Taylor Coleridge.* Princeton, N.J., 1969.
————. *Biographia Literaria* [1817]. Ed. James Engell and W. Jackson Bate. Vol. 7 of *The Collected Works of Samuel Taylor Coleridge.* Princeton, N.J., 1983.
Coles, Robert. "On the Nature of Character." See ref. Chapter 1.
College English. Mass Culture, Political Consciousness, and English Studies. [Special issue] Vol. 38 (Apr. 1977).
Collingwood, R. G. *The Principles of Art* [1938]. New York, 1958.
Comstock, Gary. "The Problem of Appropriation: Narrative and the Christian Moral Life." Ph.D. diss., University of Chicago, 1983.
————. "The Naive Reader's Response to 'Ivan Ilych.'" *Neophilologus* 70 (1986): 321–33.
————. "Truth or Meaning: Ricoeur versus Frei on Biblical Narrative." *The Journal of Religion* 66 (Apr. 1986): 117–40.
Conrad, Joseph. "Preface." *The Nigger of the Narcissus.* London, 1897.
Cook, Rufus. "Reason and Imagination." See ref. Chapter 3.
Cox, James M. *Mark Twain: The Fate of Humor.* See ref. Chapter 13.
Crane, Ronald Salmon. "The Concept of Plot and the Plot of *Tom Jones.*" See ref. Chapter 11.
————. *The Languages of Criticism and the Structure of Poetry.* See ref. Chapter 11.
Crapanzano, Vincent. "The Self, the Third, and Desire." In Lee 1982: 179–206.
————. "Hermes' Dilemma." See ref. Chapter 12.
Crews, Frederick. *Skeptical Engagements.* New York, 1986.
Crites, Stephen. "The Narrative Quality of Experience." *Journal of the American Academy of Religion* 39 (Sum. 1971): 291–311.

Croce, Benedetto. *The Defence of Poetry*. Trans. E. F. Carritt. Oxford, 1933.

Crowley, Sue Mitchell. "Mr. Blackmur's Lowell: How Does Morality Get into Literature?" *Religion and Literature* 19 (Aut. 1987) 27–48.

Cunningham, Valentine. "The Ethical Backlash." Review of *Forms of Life*, by Martin Price, and *Essays on Fiction: 1971–1982*, by Frank Kermode. *Times Literary Supplement* (July 22, 1983): 790.

Cushman, Keith. *D. H. Lawrence at Work*. See ref. Chapter 13.

Daedalus: Journal of the American Academy of Arts and Sciences. Learning about Women: Gender, Politics, and Power. [Special issue] (Fall 1987).

Daiches, David. *Literature and Society*. London, 1938.

———. *Critical Approaches to Literature*. New York, 1956.

Danto, Arthur. *Narration and Knowledge*. New York, 1985.

———. "Philosophy as/and/of Literature." In Cascardi 1987.

Davidson, Donald. *Inquiries into Truth and Interpretation*. See ref. Chapter 4.

———. "What Metaphors Mean." See ref. Chapter 10.

Davis, Lennard. *Resisting Novels: Ideology and Fiction*. New York, 1987.

Davis, Natalie Zemon. "Boundaries and the Sense of Self in Sixteenth-Century France." In Heller et al. 1986: 53–63.

Davis, Thadious M., ed. *Black Writers on "Adventures of Huckleberry Finn."* See ref. Chapter 13.

Davis, Walter. *The Act of Interpretation: A Critique of Literary Reason*. Chicago, 1978.

———. "Toward a Hermeneutics of Subjectivity." *Papers in Comparative Studies* 1 (1981): 50–79.

———. *Inwardness and Existence: The Dialectic of Situated Subjectivity*. Madison, Wis., 1988.

De George, Richard T., ed. *Ethics and Society: Original Essays on Contemporary Moral Problems*. New York, 1966.

D'haen, Theo. "Postmodern Fiction." See ref. Chapter 3.

de Man, Paul. *Allegories of Reading: Figural Language in Rousseau, Nietzsche, Rilke, and Proust*. New Haven, Conn., 1979.

———. *Blindness and Insight*. See ref. Chapter 5.

Dembo, L. S., ed. *Criticism*. See ref. Chapter 2.

Denham, Robert. *Northrop Frye and Critical Method*. College Park, Pa., 1978.

Dennis, John. *The Advancement and Reformation of Modern Poetry: A Critical Discourse in Two Parts*. London, 1701.

Derrida, Jacques. *Of Grammatology*. See ref. Chapter 3.

———. *Writing and Difference*. See ref. Chapter 12.

———. "White Mythology: Metaphor in the Text of Philosophy" [1972]. In *Margins of Philosophy*. Trans. Alan Bass. Chicago, 1982.

———. *D'un ton apocalyptique adopté naguère en philosophie*. Paris, 1983.

Dewey, John. *Human Nature and Conduct*. See ref. Chapter 8.

———. *The Quest for Certainty*. See ref. Chapter 11.

Diamond, Arlyn, and Lee R. Edwards, eds. *The Authority of Experience: Essays in Feminist Criticism*. Amherst, Mass., 1977.

DiBattista, Maria. "*Women in Love*." See ref. Chapter 13.

Diggs, B. J. "Persuasion and Ethics." *Quarterly Journal of Speech* 50 (Dec. 1964): 359–73.

Dillard, Annie. *Living by Fiction*. New York, 1982.

Dinsmore, Charles A. *The Great Poets and the Meaning of Life*. Freeport, N.Y., 1937. Rpt. New York, 1968.

Doctorow, E. L. "False Documents." *American Review* 26 (Nov. 1977): 215–32. (See. esp. 231–32.)

Doi, Takeo. *The Anatomy of Self: The Individual Versus Society* [1985]. Trans. Mark A. Harbison. Tokyo, 1986.

Doležel, Lubomír. "Narrative Worlds." See ref. Chapter 11.

Dollimore, Jonathan. *Radical Tragedy: Religion, Ideology, and Power in the Drama of Shakespeare and His Contemporaries*. Chicago, 1984.

Donagan, Allan. *The Theory of Morality*. See ref. Chapter 2.

Donovan, Josephine, ed. *Feminist Literary Criticism: Explorations in Theory*. Lexington, Ky., 1975.

Dowling, Linda. *Language and Decadence in the Victorian Fin de Siècle*. Princeton, N.J., 1986.

Dryden, John. "Preface." *Troilus and Cressida; or, Truth Found Too Late*. London, 1679.

Dumont, Louis. *Essais sur l'individualisme*. See ref. Chapter 8.

DuPlessis, Rachel Blau. *Writing beyond the Ending: Narrative Strategies of Twentieth-Century Women Writers*. Bloomington, Ind., 1985.

Duvall, John N. "Murder and the Communities: Ideology in and Around *Light in August*." *Novel: A Forum on Fiction* 20 (Win. 1987): 101–22.

Dworkin, Andrea. *Woman Hating*. See ref. Chapter 12.

———. *Pornography: Men Possessing Women*. See ref. Introduction to Part 2.

Dysinger, Wendell S., and Christian A. Ruckmick. *The Emotional Responses of Children to the Motion Picture Situation*. New York, 1933.

Dzieglewicz, John. "The Conditions of Music: The Dimensions and Progress of the Analogy between Poetry and Music in Symbolist Poetics." Ph.D. diss., University of Chicago, 1980.

Eagleton, Terry. *Criticism and Ideology*. See ref. Chapter 1.

———. *Literary Theory: An Introduction*. See ref. Chapter 4.

Eaton, Marcia. "The Truth Value of Literary Statements." *British Journal of Aesthetics* 12 (Spr. 1972): 163–74.

Ebbatson, Roger. *The Evolutionary Self*. See ref. Chapter 13.

Eco, Umberto. *The Role of the Reader: Explorations in the Semiotics of Texts*. Bloomington, Ind., 1979.

———. *Travels in Hyperreality*. See ref. Chapter 8.

Edwards, Thomas R. "Embarrassed by Jane Austen." *Raritan* 7 (Sum. 1987): 62–80.

Efron, Arthur. *"Don Quixote" and the Dulcineated World*. [Special issue] *Paunch* 59–60 (Jan. 1985): v–203.

Eliot, T. S. "Poetry and Propaganda." *Bookman* 70 (Feb. 1930): 595–602.

———. "The Modern Mind." In *The Use of Poetry and the Use of Criticism*. London, 1933. (See *The Southern Review* below.)

———. "Religion and Literature" [1936]. In *Selected Prose of T. S. Eliot*. Ed. Frank Kermode. New York, 1975. See also *Southern Review*.

Elliott, George P. "The Novelist as Meddler." *Virginia Quarterly Review* 40 (Win. 1964): 96–113.

Ellis, John M. "Great Art: A Study in Meaning." See ref. Chapter 2.

———. *The Theory of Literary Criticism*. See ref. Chapter 3.

Ellmann, Mary. *Thinking about Women*. New York, 1986.

Ellmann, Richard. *Oscar Wilde*. New York, 1988.

Elster, Jon. *The Multiple Self: Studies in Rationality and Social Change*. Cambridge, 1985.

Emerson, Ralph Waldo. "The Poet" [1842–43]. In *Works*. Ed. E. W. Emerson. 1904.

———. "Friendship." See ref. Chapter 6.

Empson, William. *The Structure of Complex Words*. 3d ed. London, 1977.

Eubanks, Ralph T. "Reflections on the Moral Dimension of Communication." *Southern Speech Communication Journal* 45 (Spr. 1980): 297–312.

Fairchild, H. N. *Religious Trends in English Poetry*. 6 vols. New York, 1939–68.

Falk, W. D. *Ought, Reasons, and Morality: The Collected Papers*. Ithaca, N.Y., 1986.

Faris, Wendy B. "'Without Sin, and with Pleasure': The Erotic Dimensions of Fuentes' Fiction." *Novel* 20 (Fall 1986): 62–77.

Farrell, James T. *Literature and Morality*. New York, 1947.

Fekete, John, ed. *Life after Postmodernism: Essays on Value and Culture*. New York, 1987.

Fernandez, James W. *Persuasions and Performances: The Play of Tropes in Culture*. Bloomington, Ind., 1986.

Fetterley, Judith. *The Resisting Reader: A Feminist Approach to American Fiction*. Bloomington, Ind., 1978.

Fiedler, Leslie. *No! In Thunder*. Boston, 1960.

Fingarette, Herbert. *Self-Deception*. New York, 1969.

Finkelstein, Richard. "Ben Jonson and the Ethics of Satire." Ph.D. diss., University of Chicago, 1983.

Fischer, Michael. "Redefining Philosophy as Literature: Richard Rorty's 'Defense' of Literary Culture." *Soundings* 57 (Fall 1984): 312–24.

——— *Does Deconstruction Make Any Difference?* See ref. Chapter 1.

Fisher, Walter R. "Narration as a Human Communication Paradigm: The Case of Public Moral Argument." *Communication Monographs* 51 (Mar. 1984): 1–22.

Fleishman, Avrom. "He Do the Polis in Different Voices." See ref. Chapter 13.

Foley, Barbara. "Fact, Fiction, Fascism: Testimony and Mimesis in Holocaust Narratives." *Comparative Literature* 34 (Fall 1982): 330–60.

———. *Telling the Truth: The Theory and Practice of Documentary Fiction*. Ithaca, N.Y., 1986.

———. "The Politics of Deconstruction." See ref. Chapter 11.

———. "Marxism and the Chicago School." In Phelan 1988.

Foucault, Michel. *The Archaeology of Knowledge*. See ref. Chapter 12.

———. *The Order of Things*. See ref. Chapter 3.

———. *Discipline and Punish*. See ref. Chapter 12.

———. *The History of Sexuality*, vol. 1. See ref. Chapter 12.

———. *The Care of the Self*. (Vol. 3 of *The History of Sexuality*.) See ref. Chapter 8.

———. "On the Genealogy of Ethics." See ref. Chapter 8.

Fowler, Rowena. "Feminist Criticism: The Common Pursuit." *New Literary History* 19 (Aut. 1987): 51–62.

Fraser, John. "Evaluation and English Studies." *College English* 35 (Oct. 1973): 1–16.

French, Philip, ed. *Three Honest Men: Edmund Wilson, F. R. Leavis, Lionel Trilling; A Critical Mosaic.* Manchester, 1980.

Friedman, Alan Warren. *Multivalence: The Moral Quality of Form in the Modern Novel.* Baton Rouge, La., 1978.

Froula, Christine. "When Eve Reads Milton." See ref. Chapter 6.

Fry, Paul. *The Reach of Criticism.* New Haven, Conn., 1983.

Fry, Roger. *Vision and Design.* See ref. Chapter 1.

Frye, Northrop. "Ethical Criticism: Theory of Symbols." In *Anatomy of Criticism: Four Essays.* Princeton, N.J., 1957.

———. *Fables of Identity: Studies in Poetic Mythology.* New York, 1963.

———. "Literary Criticism." See ref. Chapter 2.

Frye, Roland Mushat. *Shakespeare and Christian Doctrine.* Princeton, N.J., 1963.

Fussell, Paul. *The Rhetorical World of Augustan Humanism: Ethics and Imagery from Swift to Burke.* New York, 1965.

Gardiner, Judith Kegan. "The (US)es of (I)dentity: A Response to Abel on '(E)Merging Identities.'" *Signs: Journal of Women in Culture and Society* 6 (Spr. 1981): 436–42.

Gardner, Helen. *In Defense of the Imagination.* Oxford, 1982.

Gardner, John. *On Moral Fiction.* See ref. Chapter 1.

Garlitz, Robert E. "Kenneth Burke's Logology and Literary Criticism." Ph.D. diss., University of Chicago, 1979.

———. "The Sacrificial Word in Kenneth Burke's Logology." *Ranam* 12 (1979): 33–44.

Garver, Eugene. "The Arts of the Practical: Variations on a Theme of Prometheus." *Curriculum Inquiry* 14 (Sum. 1984): 165–82.

Gates, Henry Louis, Jr. *Figures in Black: Words, Signs, and the "Racial" Self.* New York, 1987.

———, ed. *Black Literature and Literary Theory.* Ithaca, N.Y., 1984.

Gayle, Addison, Jr., ed. *The Black Aesthetic.* New York, 1971.

Geertz, Clifford. "Thick Description." See ref. Chapter 11.

———. "Found in Translation: On the Social History of the Moral Imagination." *Georgia Review* 31 (Win. 1977): 788–810.

———. *Local Knowledge.* See ref. Chapter 11.

———. "Anti Anti-Relativism." See ref. Chapter 12.

Genette, Gérard. *Nouveau discours du récit.* See ref. Chapter 5.

Gewirth, Alan. *Reason and Morality.* See ref. Chapter 2.

Gide, André. *Pretexts: Reflections on Literature and Morality.* Ed. Justin O'Brien. New York, 1959.

Gilligan, Carol. "Remapping the Moral Domain: New Images of the Self in Relationship." In Heller 1986: 237–53.

Gilman, Richard. "What Mailer Has Done." See ref. Chapter 11.

Glyph: Johns Hopkins Textual Studies 1 (1977). "Program" [a statement of editorial policy, by Samuel Weber and Henry Sussman?].

Goethe, Johann Wolfgang von. *Autobiography.* Ed. Karl Joachim Weintraub. Trans. John Oxenford. 2 vols. Chicago, 1974.

Goldberg, Homer. *The Art of "Joseph Andrews."* Chicago, 1969.

Goldmann, Lucien. "Genetic-Structuralist Method in History of Literature."
   In Lang and Williams 1972: 243–55.
Goode, John. *George Gissing: Ideology and Fiction*. London, 1978.
Goodheart, Eugene. *Culture and Radical Conscience*. Cambridge, Mass.,
   1973.
———. *The Skeptic Disposition in Contemporary Criticism*. See ref. Chapter 1.
Goodman, Nelson. *Languages of Art*. See ref. Chapter 1.
———. *Ways of Worldmaking*. See ref. Chapter 4.
Gould, Stephen Jay. *Time's Arrow, Time's Cycle*. See ref. Chapters 10, 11.
Graff, Gerald. *Literature against Itself*. See ref. Chapter 1.
———. *Professing Literature*. See ref. Chapter 1.
Grassi, Ernesto. *Rhetoric as Philosophy*. See ref. Chapter 11.
Graubard, Stephen R., ed. *Hypocrisy, Illusion, and Evasion*. See ref. Chapter
   8.
———, ed. *Reading in the 1980s (Essays from* Daedalus). New York, 1983.
Green, Thomas R. "The Formation of Conscience in an Age of Technology."
   American Journal of Education 94 (Nov. 1985): 1–32.
Greene, Graham. *Collected Essays*. See ref. Chapter 6.
Greene, Thomas M. *The Vulnerable Text: Essays on Renaissance Literature*.
   New York, 1986.
Gregor, Ian, and Brian Nicholas. *The Moral and the Story*. London, 1962.
Gregory, Marshall. "Plato's *Protagoras*: Professional Models, Ethical Con-
   cerns." *Change* 15 (Apr. 1983): 42–45.
Griffin, Bryan F. "Low Life and High Hack." See ref. Chapter 7.
Griffin, Susan. *Pornography and Silence*. See ref. Chapter 12.
Grossman, Ron. "Passions." See ref. Chapter 9.
Gubar, Susan. "Representing Pornography." See ref. Chapter 12.
Gunn, Giles, ed. *Literature and Religion*. Boston, 1971.
———. *The Culture of Criticism and the Criticism of Culture*. New York,
   1987.
Gusdorf, Georges. "Conditions and Limits of Autobiography." In *Autobiog-
   raphy: Essays Theoretical and Critical*. Ed. James Olney. Princeton,
   N.J., 1980.
Gustafson, James. *Ethics from a Theocentric Perspective*. Chicago, 1979.
Gustafson, Richard F. *Leo Tolstoy, Resident and Stranger: A Study in Fiction
   and Theology*. Princeton, N.J., 1986.
Gutwirth, Marcel. "'By Diverse Means . . .' (I: 1)." In *Montaigne: Essays in
   Reading*. Ed. Gérard Defaux. New Haven, Conn., 1983.
Habermas, Jürgen. *Knowledge and Human Interests* [1968]. Trans. Jeremy J.
   Shapiro. Boston, 1971.
Hacking, Ian. "Making Up People." In Heller et al. 1986: 222–36.
Halpern, Daniel, ed. "Literature and Pleasure." [Special issue] *Antæus* 59
   (Aut. 1987).
Halsall, Albert W. *L'Art de convaincre. Le Récit pragmatique: Rhétorique,
   idéologie, propagande*. Toronto, 1988.
Hamacher, Werner. "'Disgregation of the Will': Nietzsche on the Individual
   and Individuality." In Heller et al. 1986: 106–39.
Hamm, Victor. "From Ontology to Axiology: A Critical Problem." *College
   English* 32 (Nov. 1970): 146–54.

Handwerk, Gary J. *Irony and Ethics in Narrative.* See ref. Chapter 1.

Hansen, Chadwick. "The Character of Jim and the Ending of *Huckleberry Finn.*" See ref. Chapter 13.

Hardwick, Elizabeth. *Seduction and Betrayal: Women and Literature.* New York, 1974.

Harpham, Geoffrey Galt. *The Ascetic Imperative in Culture and Criticism.* Chicago, 1987.

———. "Language, History, and Ethics." *Raritan* 7 (Sum. 1987): 128–46.

Harré, Rom. *Social Being: A Theory for Social Psychology.* Totowa, N.J., 1980.

———. *Personal Being.* Cambridge, Mass., 1984.

———. *Varieties of Realism: A Rationale for the Natural Sciences.* New York, 1986.

Hartman, Geoffrey H. *Criticism in the Wilderness: The Study of Literature Today.* New Haven, Conn., 1980.

Hartman, Joan E. "Reflections on 'The Philosophical Bases of Feminist Literary Criticisms.'" *New Literary History* 19 (Aut. 1987): 105–16.

Harvey, W. J. *Character and the Novel.* Ithaca, N.Y., 1965.

Hassan, Ihab, and Sally Hassan, eds. *Innovation/Renovation: New Perspectives in the Humanities.* Madison, Wisc., 1983.

Hauerwas, Stanley. *A Community of Character: Toward a Constructive Christian Social Ethic.* Notre Dame, Ind., 1981.

Hauerwas, Stanley, and Alasdair MacIntyre, eds. *Revisions: Changing Perspectives in Moral Philosophy.* Notre Dame, Ind., 1983.

Hazlitt, William. "On the Living Poets." *Lectures on the English Poets.* London, 1818.

Heidegger, Martin. *Being and Time.* See ref. Chapter 9.

Heilman, Robert. "Nomad, Monads, and the Mystique of the Soma." See ref. Chapter 13.

Heller, Thomas C., et al., eds. *Reconstructing Individualism: Autonomy, Individuality, and the Self in Western Thought.* Stanford, Calif., 1986.

Hemenway, Robert E. *Zora Neale Hurston.* See ref. Chapter 5.

Henricksen, Bruce, ed. *Murray Krieger and Contemporary Critical Theory.* New York, 1986.

Hentoff, Nat. "Huck Finn Better Get Out of Town by Sundown." See ref. Chapter 13.

Hernadi, Paul. *Interpreting Events: Tragicomedies of History on the Modern Stage.* Ithaca, N.Y., 1985.

Hill, Janet. "Oh! Please Mr. Tiger." In Tucker 1976.

Hirsch, E. D. *Validity in Interpretation.* New Haven, Conn., 1967.

———. "'Intrinsic' Criticism." *College English* 36 (Dec. 1974): 446–57.

———. "Evaluation as Knowledge." See ref. Chapter 4.

———. *The Philosophy of Composition.* See ref. Chapter 10.

Hirshberg, Charles A. "Oscar Wilde and the Challenge of Aestheticism." M.A. thesis, University of Chicago, 1985.

Hoggart, Richard. *On Culture and Communication.* New York, 1971.

Holland, Norman. *The I.* See ref. Chapter 8.

Holmesland, Oddvar. "Freedom and Community in Joyce Cary's Fiction: A Study of *The Horse's Mouth.*" *English Studies* 68 (Apr. 1987): 160–70.

Horace. *Art of Poetry (Ars Poetica). Horace for English Readers.* Trans. E. C. Wickham. Oxford, 1903.

Hough, Graham. *The Dream and the Task: Literature and Morals in the Culture of Today.* London, 1963.

———. *An Essay on Criticism.* See ref. Chapter 2.

Howard, Susan K. "The Intrusive Audience in Fielding's *Amelia.*" *Journal of Narrative Technique* 17 (Fall 1987): 286–95.

Howe, Marguerite Beede. *The Art of the Self in D. H. Lawrence.* See ref. Chapter 13.

Hume, David. "Of the Standard of Taste" [1742]. In *"Of the Standard of Taste" and Other Essays.* Ed. John W. Lenz. Indianapolis, 1965.

———. "Of Miracles." See ref. Chapter 11.

Hunter, J. Paul. "'The Young, the Ignorant, and the Idle.'" See ref. Chapter 8.

Hyde, Lewis. *The Gift.* See ref. Chapter 6.

Hyman, Virginia R. *Ethical Perspective in the Novels of Thomas Hardy.* Port Washington, N.Y., 1975.

Hynes, Arleen, and M. Hynes-Berry. *Bibliotherapy.* See ref. Chapter 8.

Inchausti, Robert. "The Search for a Modern Humanities: Three Critical Paths." Ph.D. diss., University of Chicago, 1981.

Isenberg, Arnold. "Ethical and Aesthetic Criticism." In *Aesthetics and the Theory of Criticism: Selected Essays of Arnold Isenberg.* Ed. William Callaghan. Chicago, 1973.

Iser, Wolfgang. *The Act of Reading.* See ref. Chapter 4.

Jakobson, Roman. "Linguistics and Poetics." In *Style in Language.* Ed. Thomas A. Sebeok. Cambridge, Mass., 1960.

———. "Yeats' 'Sorrow of Love' through the Years." In *Verbal Art, Verbal Sign, Verbal Time.* Ed. Krystyna Pomorska and Stephen Rudy. Minneapolis, 1985.

James, Henry. "Charles de Bernard and Gustave Flaubert." See ref. Chapter 13.

James, William. *Psychology: The Briefer Course.* See ref. Chapter 5.

———. *The Varieties of Religious Experience.* See ref. Chapter 3.

Jameson, Fredric. "The Symbolic Inference; or, Kenneth Burke and Ideological Analysis." *Critical Inquiry* 4 (Spr. 1978): 507–23.

———. *Fables of Aggression: Wyndham Lewis, the Modernist as Fascist.* Berkeley, 1979.

———. *The Political Unconscious.* See ref. Chapter 1.

Jauss, Hans Robert. *Aesthetic Experience and Literary Hermeneutics.* Theory and History of Literature, vol. 3. Minneapolis, Minn., 1982. (See also Mailloux 1983.)

Jefferson, D. W. "Milton's Austerity and Moral Disdain." In *The Morality of Art.* London, 1969.

Jenkyns, Richard. *The Victorians and Ancient Greece.* Cambridge, Mass., 1980. Esp. chap. 11, "Change and Decay" (264–97).

———. "The Combustible Victorians." See ref. Chapter 8.

Jepsen, Laura. *Ethical Aspects of Tragedy: A Comparison of Certain Tragedies by Aeschylus, Sophocles, Euripides, Seneca and Shakespeare.* Gainesville, Fla., 1953.

Johannesen, Richard L., ed. *Ethics in Communication.* [Special issue] *Communication* 6 (Sept. 1981).

———. *Ethics in Human Communication.* 2d ed. Prospect Heights, Ill., 1983.
Johnson, Samuel. "Abraham Cowley." See ref. Chapter 10.
———. Preface to *The Plays of Shakespeare.* See ref. Chapter 2.
———. "*The Rambler,* no. 4." See ref. Chapter 4.
———. "*The Rambler,* nos. 14 and 60." See ref. Chapter 1.
Johnstone, Christopher L. "Ethics, Wisdom, and the Mission of Contemporary Rhetoric: The Realization of Being Human." *Central States Speech Journal* 32, no. 3 (1981): 177–88.
Jones, Rhett S. "Nigger and Knowledge." See ref. Chapter 13.
Jonson, Ben. "Epistle Prefatory" to *Volpone.* See ref. Chapter 8.
———. *Timber; or, Discoveries.* See ref. Appendix.
Josipovici, Gabriel. *The World and the Book: A Study of Modern Fiction.* London, 1971.
———. "On the Side of Job." See ref. Chapter 3.
Judrin, Roger. *Moralités littéraires: essai.* Paris, 1966.
Juhl, P. D. "Life, Literature, and the Implied Author." *Deutsche Vierteljahrsschrift für Literaturwissenschaft und Geistesgeschichte* 54 (June 1980): 177–203.
Kahn, Victoria. *Rhetoric, Prudence, and Skepticism in the Renaissance.* Ithaca, N.Y., 1985.
Kant, Immanuel. "Analytik des Schönen." See ref. Chapter 2.
———. *Kritik of Judgment.* See ref. Chapter 3.
———. *Religion within the Limits of Reason Alone.* See ref. Chapter 11.
Kaplan, Morton A. *Science, Language, and the Human Condition.* See ref. Chapter 3.
Kastely, Jay. "An Ethical Poetics: The Art of Critically Reconstituting and Evaluating Fictional Experience." Ph.D. diss., University of Chicago, 1980.
———. "The Ethics of Self-Interest: Narrative Logic in *Huckleberry Finn.*" *Nineteenth-Century Fiction* 40 (Mar. 1986): 434.
Kaufmann, David. "Satiric Deceit in the Ending of *Adventures of Huckleberry Finn.*" See ref. Chapter 13.
Kayser, Wolfgang. "Literarische Wertung und Interpretation." *Die Vortragsreise.* Bern, 1958.
Kelso, Ruth. *Doctrine for the Lady of the Renaissance.* See ref. Chapter 12.
Kennedy, Margaret. *The Outlaws on Parnassus.* London, 1958.
Kenner, Hugh. *The Pound Era* [1961]. Berkeley, 1973.
———. *Samuel Beckett: A Critical Study.* 2d. ed. Berkeley, 1973.
Kerman, Joseph. *The Beethoven Quartets.* See ref. Chapter 1.
Kermode, Frank. *Modern Essays.* London, 1970.
———. *The Classic: Literary Images of Permanence and Change* [1975]. New York, 1983.
———. *The Art of Telling: Essays on Fiction.* Cambridge, Mass., 1983.
Kettle, Arnold. *Introduction to the English Novel.* See ref. Chapter 9.
Klinkowitz, Jerome. "Not by Theme Alone." *Novel* 6 (Spr. 1973): 268–72.
Knight, G. Wilson. "*Macbeth* and the Nature of Evil." *Hibbert Journal* 28 (Jan. 1930): 382–42.
———. *Christ and Nietzsche: An Essay in Poetic Wisdom.* London, 1947.
———. *Lord Byron: Christian Virtues.* London, 1952.

———. *Laureate of Peace: On the Genius of Alexander Pope*. London, 1954.
———. *Shakespeare and Religion: Essays of Forty Years*. London, 1967.
———. *Shakespearian Dimensions*. Brighton, 1984.
Knight, Stephen. *Form and Ideology in Crime Fiction*. Bloomington, Ind.,
    1980.
Kolenda, Konstantin. *Philosophy in Literature: Metaphysical Darkness and
    Ethical Light*. Totowa, N.J., 1982.
Kowarsky, Gerald M. "Judgment and Censoriousness in Ben Jonson's Plays."
    Ph.D. diss., University of Chicago, 1983.
Kraft, Quentin G. "On Character in the Novel: William Beatty Warner Versus
    Samuel Richardson and the Humanists." *College English* 50 (Jan.
    1988): 32–47.
Krieger, Murray. *The Tragic Vision: Variations on a Theme in Literary Inter-
    pretation*. New York, 1960.
———. "Literary Analysis and Evaluation." See ref. Chapter 2.
———. *The Classic Vision: The Retreat from Extremity in Modern Litera-
    ture*. Baltimore, 1971.
———. *Theory of Criticism*. See ref. Chapter 3.
———. "In the Wake of Morality: The Thematic Underside of Recent The-
    ory." See ref. Chapter 9.
Krupnick, Mark. *Lionel Trilling and the Fate of Cultural Criticism*. Evanston,
    Ill., 1986.
Lacan, Jacques. *The Four Fundamental Concepts of Psycho-Analysis*. See ref.
    Chapter 8.
LaCapra, Dominick. *History and Criticism*. Ithaca, N.Y., 1985.
———. *History, Politics, and the Novel*. Ithaca, N.Y., 1988.
Laden, Marie-Paule. *Self-Imitation in the Eighteenth-Century Novel*. Prince-
    ton, N.J., 1987.
Lakoff, George. *Women, Fire, and Dangerous Things*. Chicago, 1987.
Lamb, Charles. *On the Artificial Comedy of the Last Century*. London, 1822.
Laney, James T. "Characterization and Moral Judgments." *Journal of Reli-
    gion* 55 (1975): 405–14.
Lang, Andrew. *Letters to Dead Authors*. See ref. Chapter 6.
Lang, Berel, and Forrest Williams, eds. *Marxism and Art: Writings in Aesthet-
    ics and Criticism*. New York, 1972.
Lanser, Susan Sniader. *The Narrative Act: Point of View in Prose Fiction*.
    Princeton, N.J., 1981.
Larmore, Charles E. *Patterns of Moral Complexity*. See ref. Chapter 6.
Lasky, Melvin J. *Utopia and Revolution: On the Origins of a Metaphor; or,
    Some Illustrations of the Problem of Political Temperament and Intel-
    lectual Climate and How Ideas, Ideals, and Ideologies have been His-
    torically Related*. Chicago, 1976.
Layton, Lynne, and Barbara Ann Shapiro, eds. *Narcissism and the Text: Stud-
    ies in Literature and the Psychology of Self*. New York, 1986.
Leavis, F. R. *Revaluation: Tradition and Development in English Poetry*. Lon-
    don, 1947.
———. *D. H. Lawrence*. See ref. Chapter 13.
———. *The Great Tradition*. See ref. Chapter 3.

———. *A Selection from "Scrutiny."* See ref. Chapter 3. (See also Bentley 1964.)
———. *The Living Principle: 'English' as a Discipline of Thought.* London, 1975.
———. *Towards Standards of Criticism: Selections from "The Calendar of Modern Letters."* 1925–1927. London, 1976.
Lee, Benjamin, ed. *Psychosocial Theories of the Self.* New York, 1982.
Leitch, Vincent B. "Taboo and Critique: Literary Criticism and Ethics." *ADE Bulletin* 90 (forthcoming, Fall 1988).
Lentricchia, Frank. *After the New Criticism.* Chicago, 1980.
———. *Criticism and Social Change.* Chicago, 1983.
Lerner, Julianna Kitty. "Rabelais and Woman." See ref. Chapter 12.
Lerner, Laurence. *The Truest Poetry: An Essay on the Question What Is Literature?* London, 1960.
———. *Love and Marriage.* See ref. Chapter 12.
———. *The Literary Imagination: Essays on Literature and Society.* Brighton, Eng., 1982.
———. *The Frontiers of Literature.* Oxford, 1988.
Lester, Julius. "Morality and *Adventures of Huckleberry Finn*." See ref. Chapter 13.
Levine, Carol Freed. "All for Love and Book 4 of the *Aeneid:* The Moral Predicament." *Comparative Literature* 33 (Sum. 1981): 39–57.
Lévi-Strauss, Claude. *Tristes Tropiques.* See ref. Chapter 12.
Lewalski, Barbara Kiefer. *"Paradise Lost" and the Rhetoric of Literary Forms.* Princeton, N.J., 1985.
Lewis, C. S. *An Experiment in Criticism.* See ref. Chapter 1.
———. *Studies in Words.* Cambridge, 1967.
———. *On Stories, and Other Essays on Literature.* New York, 1982.
Lewis, David. *On the Plurality of Worlds.* See ref. Chapter 4.
Lewis, Kevin. "The Use of Blake and the Recovery of Fideism." *Journal of the American Academy of Religion* 54 (Win. 1986): 741–57.
Lewis, Wyndham. "The 'Dumb Ox' in Love and War." In *Men without Art.* New York, 1964.
Lieberman, Marcia R. "'Some Day My Prince Will Come': Female Acculturation through the Fairy Tale." *College English* 34 (Dec. 1972): 383–95.
Lindenberger, Herbert. "Keats' 'To Autumn.'" See ref. Chapter 9.
Lipking, Lawrence. *The Life of the Poet.* See ref. Chapter 5.
———. "Aristotle's Sister: A Poetics of Abandonment." *Critical Inquiry* 10 (Sept. 1983): 61–81.
Llosa, Mario Vargas. *The Perpetual Orgy: Flaubert and Madame Bovary* [1975]. Trans. Helen Lane. New York, 1986.
Lloyd, Roger. *The Borderland: An Exploration of Theology in English Literature.* New York, 1960.
Lockridge, Laurence S. *Coleridge the Moralist.* Ithaca, N.Y., 1977.
Loewenberg, Ina. "Creativity and Correspondence in Fiction and in Metaphors." *Journal of Aesthetics and Art Criticism* 36 (Spr. 1978): 341–50.

Longinus [pseud.]. *On the Sublime*. See ref. Chapter 10.

Lukács, Georg. "Franz Kafka or Thomas Mann?" In *The Meaning of Contemporary Realism* [1957]. Trans. John Mander and Necke Mander. London, 1963. 47–92.

———. "The Ideology of Modernism." See ref. Chapter 8.

———. *The Theory of the Novel: A Historico-Philosophical Essay on the Forms of Great Epic Literature* [1920]. Trans. Anna Bostock. Cambridge, Mass., 1971.

———. "Art as Self-Consciousness in Man's Development." In Lang and Williams 1972: 228–39.

Lukes, Steven. *Marxism and Morality*. Oxford, 1985.

Lyly, John. *Euphues: The Anatomy of Wit*. See ref. Chapter 8.

Lynn, Kenneth S. *Hemingway*. New York, 1987.

Lyotard, Jean-François. "One of the Things at Stake in Women's Struggles." Trans. Deborah J. Clarke. *Sub-Stance* 20 (1978): 9–16.

———. "The Différend, the Referent, and the Proper Name." *Diacritics* [Special issue on Lyotard] 14 (Fall 1984): 4–15.

Macdonell, Diane. *Theories of Discourse*. See ref. Chapter 12.

MacIntyre, Alasdair. "Egoism and Altruism." See ref. Chapter 8.

———. *After Virtue*. See ref. Chapter 1.

———. "Relativism, Power, and Philosophy." In Baynes et al. 1987.

MacIver, Robert Morrison. *Great Moral Dilemmas in Literature, Past and Present*. New York, 1956.

MacLeish, Archibald. *Poetry and Opinion: The Pisan Cantos of Ezra Pound; A Dialog on the Role of Poetry*. Urbana, Ill. 1950.

MacMillan, P. R. *Censorship and Public Morality*. Aldershot, 1983.

Magee, William H. "Instrument of Growth: The Courtship and Marriage Plot in Jane Austen's Novels." *Journal of Narrative Technique* 17 (Spr. 1987): 198–208.

Mailloux, Steven. "Evaluation and Reader Response Criticism: Values Implicit in Affective Stylistics." *Style* 10 (Sum. 1976): 329–43.

———. *Interpretive Conventions: The Reader in the Study of American Fiction*. See ref. Chapter 4.

———. Review of *Aesthetic Experience and Literary Hermeneutics*, by Hans Robert Jauss. *Minnesota Review*, n.s. 21 (Fall 1983): 134–38.

———. *Rhetorical Power*. See ref. Chapter 13.

Mallarmé, Stéphane. "The Book: A Spiritual Instrument" [1895]. In *Mallarmé: Selected Prose, Poems, Essays, and Letters*. Trans. Bradford Cook. Baltimore, 1956.

Mann, Thomas. "Irony and Radicalism," and "The Politics of Aestheticism" [1918]. In *Reflections of a Nonpolitical Man*. Trans. Walter D. Morris. New York, 1983.

Mao Tse-tung. "On Literature and the Arts." In Lang and Williams 1972: 426–37.

Marks, Sylvia Kasey. "*Clarissa* as Conduct Book." See ref. Chapter 8.

Martin, Loy D. *Browning's Dramatic Monologues and the Post-Romantic Subject*. Baltimore, 1985.

Martin, Reginald. "Ishmael Reed and the New Black Aesthetic Critics: Individual Creation and Ethical Boundaries." Paper presented at the national convention of the Modern Language Association, Chicago, December 1985.

Martin, Wallace. *Recent Theories of Narrative*. Ithaca, N.Y., 1986.

Marx, Karl. *Selected Writings in Sociology*. See ref. Chapter 8.

Massey, Irving. *Find You the Virtue: Ethics, Image, and Desire in Literature*. Fairfax, Va., 1987.

Matejka, Ladislav, and Krystyna Pomorska, eds. *Readings in Russian Poetics: Formalist and Structuralist Views*. Cambridge, Mass., 1971.

Maurice, John Frederick Denison. *"The Friendship of Books."* See ref. Chapter 6.

McCarthy, Mary. *Ideas and the Novel*. New York, 1980.

McClintock, Anne. "'Azikwelwa' (We Will Not Ride): Politics and Value in Black South African Poetry." *Critical Inquiry* 13 (Spr. 1987): 597–623.

McGann, Jerome J. *Social Values and Poetic Acts: The Historical Judgment of Literary Work*. Cambridge, Mass., 1988.

———. *Toward a Literature of Knowledge*. Chicago, forthcoming 1989.

McKean, Keith F. *The Moral Measure of Literature*. Denver, Colo., 1961.

McKeon, Richard. "Censorship." See ref. Chapter 3.

———. *Freedom and History*. See ref. Chapter 11.

McKeon, Zahava Karl. *Novels and Arguments*. See ref. Chapter 5.

Mead, George Herbert. "The Individual and the Social Self." See ref. Chapter 8.

Meese, George. "Rhetorical Evaluation of Prose Fiction: Warrants for Judgments, with Examples from the Works of John Hawkes." Ph.D. diss., University of Chicago, 1979.

Meilaender, Gilbert C. *Friendship*. See ref. Chapter 6.

Mellard, James M. *The Exploded Form: The Modernist Novel in America*. Urbana, Ill., 1980.

Messer-Davidow, Ellen. "The Philosophical Bases of Feminist Literary Criticism." *New Literary History* 19 (Aut. 1987): 63–104.

Metaphor and Symbolic Activity. [Journal, founded 1986, Hillsdale, N.J.]

Meyer, Leonard B. *Emotion and Meaning in Music*. See ref. Chapter 1.

———. *Music, the Arts, and Ideas*. See ref. Chapter 1.

Middleton, Anne. "Chaucer's 'New Men' and the Good of Literature in the *Canterbury Tales*." In Said 1980: 15–56.

Miko, Stephen J., ed. *Twentieth Century Interpretations of "Women in Love."* See ref. Chapter 13.

Miller, J. Hillis. *The Ethics of Reading*. See ref. Chapter 1.

Miller, Jane. *Women Writing about Men*. See ref. Chapter 13.

Miller, Richard W. *Analyzing Marx: Morality, Power, and History*. Princeton, N.J., 1984.

Milton, John. "Preface." *Samson Agonistes*. London, 1671.

———. "Areopagitica." See ref. Epilogue.

Mink, Louis O. "Narrative Form as Cognitive Instrument." In *The Writing of History: Literary Form and Historical Understanding*. Ed. Robert H. Canary and Henry Kozicki. Madison, Wis., 1978.

Mitchell, W. J. T., ed. *On Narrative*. Chicago, 1980.

———, ed. *The Politics of Interpretation*. Chicago, 1982. (See ref. Chapter 12.)

———. "The Good, the Bad, and the Ugly: Three Theories of Value." *Raritan* 6 (Fall 1986): 63–76.

———. *Iconology.* See ref. Chapter 1.

MMLA [Midwest Modern Language Association]. *Criticism and Culture.* [Special issue] *Papers of the Midwest Modern Language Association* 2 (1972).

Moers, Ellen. *Literary Women.* See ref. Chapter 13.

Monroe, William. "A Persistence of Rhetoric: Willa Cather and Walker Percy in an Age of Alienism." Ph.D. diss., University of Chicago, 1982.

———. "Flannery O'Connor's Sacramental Icon: 'The Artificial Nigger.'" *South Central Review* 1 (Win. 1984): 64–81.

———. Review of *The World, the Text, and the Critic,* by Edward Said. *Modern Philology* 82 (May 1985): 454–59.

Montaigne. "Of Friendship." See ref. Chapter 6.

———. "Use Makes Perfectness." See ref. Chapter 8.

Moore, George. "Introduction." *An Anthology of Pure Poetry.* London, 1924.

More, Paul Elmer. *The Drift of Romanticism.* New York, 1913.

———. *The Demon of the Absolute.* Princeton, N.J., 1928.

———. *On Being Human.* Princeton, N.J., 1936.

Morris, Colin. *The Discovery of the Individual.* See ref. Chapter 8.

Morris, Wright. "Reflections on the Death of the Reader." In *A Bill of Rites, a Bill of Wrongs, a Bill of Goods.* New York, 1967.

Morson, Gary Saul. "Dostoevsky's Anti-Semitism and the Critics: A Review Article." *Slavic and East European Journal* 27 (Fall 1983): 301–17.

———, ed. *Bakhtin: Essays and Dialogues on His Work.* Chicago, 1986.

———, ed. *Literature and History: Theoretical Problems and Russian Case Studies.* Stanford, Calif., 1986.

———. *Hidden in Plain View: Narrative and Creative Potentials in 'War and Peace.'* Stanford, Calif., 1987.

———. "Prosaics: A New Approach to the Humanities." See ref. Chapter 1.

Moseley, James G. "Literature and Ethics: Some Possibilities for Religious Thought." *Perspectives in Religious Studies* 6 (Spr. 1979): 17–23.

Mossman, Elliott. "Metaphors of History in *War and Peace* and *Doctor Zhivago.*" In Morson, *Literature and History* 1986.

Mossop, D. J. *Pure Poetry: Studies in French Poetic Theory and Practice, 1746 to 1945.* Oxford, 1971.

Moulton, Richard G. *The Moral System of Shakespeare: A Popular Illustration of Fiction as the Experimental Side of Philosophy.* New York, 1903.

———. "Art and Eros: A Dialogue about Art." In *Acastos: Two Platonic Dialogues.* New York, 1987.

Murdoch, Iris. *Sartre: Romantic Rationalist.* New Haven, Conn., 1953.

———. "The Sublime and the Good." *Chicago Review* 13 (Aut. 1959): 42–55.

———. "Vision and Choice in Morality." In Ramsey 1966.

———. *The Sovereignty of Good.* See ref. Chapter 3.

———. *The Fire and the Sun: Why Plato Banished the Artists.* Oxford, 1977.

Murfin, Ross C. *Swinburne, Hardy, Lawrence.* See ref. Chapter 13.

Muscatine, Charles. *Poetry and Crisis in the Age of Chaucer.* See ref. Appendix.

Nabokov, Vladimir. "Interview." See ref. Chapter 7.

Nagel, Thomas. *The View from Nowhere*. New York, 1986. (See Taylor, Review 1986.)

Nathan, Leonard. "Putting the Lyric in Its Place." *Northwest Review* 24 (Nov. 1986): 77–84.

National Humanities Center. "A Conference on Ethics and Moral Education, December 12–14, 1979." Working Paper, no. 1. Triangle Park, N.C., 1980.

Naughton, John T. *The Poetics of Yves Bonnefoy*. Chicago, 1984.

Nehamas, Alexander. *Nietzsche: Life as Literature*. Cambridge, Mass., 1985.

————. "Writer, Text, Work, Author." In Cascardi 1987.

Neild, Elizabeth. "Kenneth Burke and Roland Barthes: Literature, Language, and Society." *Raman* 12 (1979): 98–108.

Nelson, William. *Fact or Fiction: The Dilemma of the Renaissance Storyteller*. Cambridge, Mass., 1973.

New Literary History. Literature and/as Moral Philosophy. [Special issue] 15 (Aut. 1983).

————. *Literacy, Popular Culture, and the Writing of History*. [Special issue] 18 (Win. 1987), esp. essays by Donald Lazere, José Piedra, Joyce A. Joyce, Henry Louis Gates, Jr., and Houston A. Baker, Jr.

Nichols, Charles H. "'A True Book with Some Stretchers': *Huck Finn* Today." See ref. Chapter 13.

Nicholson, Colin E., and Ranjit Chatterjee, eds. *Tropic Crucible: Self and Theory in Language and Literature*. Kent Ridge, Singapore, 1984.

Nietzsche, Friedrich. *The Gay Science, with a Prelude in Rhyme and an Appendix of Songs* [1882]. Trans. Walter Kaufmann. New York, 1974.

Norris, Christopher. *The Contest of Faculties*. See ref. Chapter 1.

Novick, Peter. *That Noble Dream*. See ref. Chapter 11.

Nussbaum, Martha Craven. "Flawed Crystals: James's *The Golden Bowl* and Literature as Moral Philosophy." See ref. Chapter 9.

————. "The Betrayal of Convention: A Reading of Euripides' *Hecuba*." In *The Fragility of Goodness: Luck and Ethics in Greek Tragedy and Philosophy*. New York, 1986.

————. "Love and the Individual: Romantic Rightness and Platonic Aspiration." In Heller et al. 1986: 253–78.

————. "'Finely Aware and Richly Responsible': Literature and the Moral Imagination." In Cascardi 1987: 167–91.

————. *Love's Knowledge: Essays on Philosophy and Literature*. Oxford, 1988.

————. "Narrative Emotions: Beckett's Genealogy of Love." In Becker 1988: 225–54.

————. *The Therapy of Desire*. Martin Classical Lectures. Forthcoming.

Nwachukwu-Agbada, J. O. J. "An Interview with Chinua Achebe." *Massachusetts Review* 28 (Sum. 1987): 273–85.

O'Connor, William Van. "Why *Huckleberry Finn* Is Not the Great American Novel." See ref. Chapter 13.

O'Donovan, Oliver. *The Problem of Self-Love in St. Augustine*. See ref. Chapter 5.

O'Flaherty, Wendy D. "Ethical and Nonethical Implications." See ref. Chapter 11.

Ohmann, Carol, and Richard Ohmann. "Reviewers, Critics, and *The Catcher in the Rye.*" *Critical Inquiry* 3 (Aut. 1976 and Sum. 1977): 15–37, 773–77.

Olmsted, Wendy. "A Rhetoric of Analogy." Unpublished book manuscript.

Olson, David R., et al., eds. *Literacy, Language, and Learning: The Nature and Consequences of Reading and Writing.* Cambridge, 1985.

Olson, Elder. "*On Value Judgments in the Arts.*" See ref. Chapter 4.

Ong, Walter J. "Voice as Summons for Belief: Literature, Faith, and the Divided Self." In *The Barbarian Within.* New York, 1962.

———. "Truth in Conrad's Darkness." *Mosaic* 11 (Fall 1977): 151–63.

Ortega y Gasset, José. *"The Dehumanization of Art" and Other Essays on Art, Culture, and Literature* [1925]. Trans. Willard Trask. Princeton, N.J., 1948.

Ortony, Andrew. "Metaphor." See ref. Chapter 8.

———, ed. *Metaphor and Thought.* See ref. Chapter 10.

Osborne, Harold. "Aesthetic Experience and Cultural Value." *Journal of Aesthetics and Art Criticism* 44 (Sum. 1986): 331–37.

Ostriker, Alicia. *Stealing the Language.* Boston, 1986.

———. "Dancing at the Devil's Party: Some Notes on Politics and Poetry." *Critical Inquiry* 13 (Spr. 1987): 579–96.

Ozick, Cynthia. "Innovation and Redemption: What Literature Means." In *Art and Ardor: Essays.* New York, 1983.

Panichas, George A. *The Reverent Discipline: Essays in Literary Criticism and Culture.* Knoxville, Tenn., 1974.

Pareto, Vilfredo. *Le Mythe vertuïste et la littérature immorale.* Paris, 1911.

Parker, Andrew. "Ezra Pound and the 'Economy' of Anti-Semitism." See ref. Chapter 5.

Parrington, Vernon. *Main Currents in American Thought.* See ref. Chapter 11.

Pater, Walter. *Studies in the History of the Renaissance.* London, 1873.

Patrick, Anne. "H. Richard Niebuhr's Ethics of Responsibility." Ph.D. diss., University of Chicago, 1982.

Pavel, Thomas G. *Fictional Worlds.* See ref. Chapter 4.

Peckham, Morse. *Man's Rage for Chaos.* New York, 1967.

Perelman, Chaim. "The Rhetorical Point of View in Ethics: A Program." *Communication* 5 (1981): 315–20.

Perelman, Chaim, and L. Olbrechts-Tyteca. *The New Rhetoric.* See ref. Chapter 11.

Perkins, Jean. *The Concept of the Self in the French Enlightenment.* Geneva, 1969.

Peterson, Carla L. *The Determined Reader.* See ref. Chapter 8.

Peterson, Dale E. "Nabokov's Invitation: Literature as Execution." *PMLA* 96 (Oct. 1981): 824–36.

Peyre, Henri. *Literature and Sincerity.* New Haven, 1963.

———. *The Failures of Criticism* [emended ed. of *Writers and Their Critics*]. Ithaca, N.Y., 1967.

Phelan, James. *Worlds from Words: A Theory of Language in Fiction.* Chicago, 1981.

———. "Character, Progression, and the Mimetic-Didactic Distinction." See ref. Chapter 5.

———. "Narrative Discourse: Character and Ideology." In Phelan 1988.
———, ed. *Reading Narrative: Form, Ethics, Ideology.* Columbus, Ohio, 1988.
Phillips, William, and Philip Rahv. "Private Experience and Public Philosophy." *Poetry* 48 (May 1936): 98–105. Reprinted in *Literary Opinion in America.* Ed. Morton Dauwen Zabel. Rev. ed. New York, 1951.
Pickering, Samuel, Jr. *The Moral Tradition in English Fiction: 1785–1850.* Hanover, N.H., 1976.
Pinckney, Darryl. "Black Victims, Black Villains." *New York Review of Books* 34 (Jan. 29, 1987): 17–20.
Pinsker, Sanford. "*The Catcher in the Rye* and All: Is the Age of Formative Books Over?" *Georgia Review* 40 (Win. 1986): 953–67.
Pinsky, Robert. *The Situation of Poetry.* Princeton, N.J., 1976.
———. "Responsibilities of the Poet." *Critical Inquiry* 13 (Spr. 1987): 421–33.
Plato. *Republic.* See ref. Chapter 1.
Pocock, J. G. A. "Virtues, Rights, and Manners." See ref. Chapter 1.
Polanyi, Michael. *Personal Knowledge.* See ref. Chapter 2.
Poovey, Mary. "*Persuasion* and the Promises of Love." See ref. Chapter 13.
Porter, Dennis. *The Pursuit of Crime: Art and Ideology in Detective Fiction.* Evanston, Ill., 1984.
Posnock, Ross. "Henry James, Veblen, and Adorno: The Crisis of the Modern Self." *Journal of American Studies* 21 (Apr. 1987): 31–54.
Poston, Lawrence. "Poetry as Pure Act: A Coleridgean Ideal in Early Victorian England." *Modern Philology* 84 (Nov. 1986): 162–84.
Potok, Chaim. "The Culture Highways We Travel." *Religion and Literature* 19 (Sum. 1987): 1–10.
Poulet, Georges. "Criticism and the Experience of Interiority." See ref. Chapter 5.
Pound, Ezra. "The Teacher's Mission." See ref. Introduction to Part 2.
———. "A Stray Document." In *Make It New.* New Haven, Conn., 1935.
———. *ABC of Reading* [1934]. New York, 1960.
Pratt, Mary Louise. *Toward a Speech Act Theory of Literary Discourse.* Bloomington, Ind., 1977.
———. "The Ideology of Speech Act Theory." *Centrum,* n.s. 1 (Spr. 1981): 5–18.
Preston, John. *The Created Self: The Reader's Role in Eighteenth-Century Fiction.* London, 1970.
Price, Martin. *Forms of Life: Character and Moral Imagination in the Novel.* New Haven, Conn., 1983.
Pritchett, V. S. *A Man of Letters: Selected Essays.* See ref. Chapter 9.
Prust, Richard C. "The Truthfulness of Sacred Story." *Soundings* 68 (Win. 1985): 479–92.
Putnam, Hilary. *Reason, Truth, and History.* See ref. Chapter 1.
Rabinowitz, Peter J. "Truth in Fiction." See ref. Chapter 5.
———. *Before Reading: Narrative Conventions and the Politics of Interpretation.* Ithaca, N.Y., 1987.
Radcliffe, Janet. *The Skeptical Feminist.* See ref. Chapter 12.
Rader, Ralph. "Dramatic Monologue." See ref. Chapter 4.

Radzinowicz, Mary Ann. "'To Make the People Fittest to Chuse': How Milton Personified His Program for Poetry." [*College English Association*] *Critic* 48−49 (Summer−Fall 1986): 3−23.

Railton, Stephen. "Mothers, Husbands, and Uncle Tom." *Georgia Review* 38 (Spr. 1984): 129.

———. "Jim and Mark Twain: What Do Dey Stan' For?" See ref. Chapter 13.

Ramanujan, A. K., trans. *Poems of Love and War*. See ref. Chapter 10.

Ramsey, Ian, ed. *Christian Ethics and Contemporary Philosophy*. New York, 1966.

Rampersad, Arnold. *"Adventures of Huckleberry Finn."* See ref. Chapter 13.

Raz, Joseph. *The Morality of Freedom*. See ref. Chapter 4.

Redfield, James. *Nature and Culture in the "Iliad": The Tragedy of Hector*. Chicago, 1975.

———. "Le Sentiment Homérique du Moi." See ref. Chapter 8.

Reichert, John. *Making Sense of Literature*. See ref. Chapter 3.

Renascence: Essays on Values in Literature. [Milwaukee, Wis.; journal edited from a Christian perspective; see, e.g., vol. 39 (Sum. 1987)]

Ricardou, Jean. *Le Nouveau Roman*. See ref. Chapter 2.

———. *Nouveaux problèmes du roman*. See ref. Chapter 2.

Richards, I. A. "Doctrine in Poetry." In *Practical Criticism*. London, 1929.

Richter, David. *Fable's End*. See ref. Chapter 11.

Ricoeur, Paul. *The Symbolism of Evil*. See ref. Appendix.

———. *Interpretation Theory*. See ref. Chapter 10.

———. *The Rule of Metaphor*. See ref. Chapter 10.

Riesman, David. *Individualism Reconsidered*. Glencoe, Ill., 1954.

Robbins, William. *The Ethical Idealism of Matthew Arnold: A Study of the Nature and Sources of His Moral and Religious Ideas*. Toronto, 1959.

Rochelson, Meri-Jane. "George Eliot and Metaphor: Creating a Narrator in the Mid-Nineteenth-Century Novel." Ph.D. diss., University of Chicago, 1982.

Rorty, Amelie Oksenberg, ed. *The Identities of Persons*. See ref. Chapter 8.

Rorty, Richard. *Philosophy and the Mirror of Nature*. See ref. Chapter 11.

Rosenbaum, S. P. *English Literature and British Philosophy*. Chicago, 1971.

Rosenblatt, Louise M. *The Reader, the Text, the Poem*. See ref. Chapter 1.

Rosmarin, Adena. *The Power of Genre*. Minneapolis, 1985.

Ross, Marlon B. "The Poetics of Moral Transformation: Forms of Didacticism in the Poetry of Shelley." Ph.D. diss., University of Chicago, 1983.

Rothfield, Lawrence. "From Semiotic to Discursive Intertextuality: The Case of *Madame Bovary*." *Novel* 19 (Fall 1985): 57−81.

Rousseau, Jean-Jacques. *Letter to M. d'Alembert on the Theater* [1758]. In *Politics and the Arts*. Ed. Allan Bloom. Ithaca, N.Y., 1968.

Royce, Josiah. "The World and the Individual." See ref. Chapter 8.

Rubin, Lillian B. *Just Friends*. See ref. Chapter 6.

Rubin, Rhea Joyce. *Using Bibliotherapy*. See ref. Chapter 8.

Rugh, Thomas F., and Erin R. Silva, eds. *History as a Tool in Critical Interpretation: A Symposium* [Monroe C. Beardsley, E. H. Gombrich, Karsten Harries, E. D. Hirsch, René Wellek]. Provo, Utah, 1978.

Ruskin, John. "The Nature of Gothic." See ref. Chapter 4.

———. *Fiction, Fair and Foul* [1880−81]. In vol. 34 of *The Works of John*

Ruskin. Ed. E. T. Cook and Alexander Wedderburn. Library ed. London, 1908. 265–397.

Ryle, Gilbert. "Jane Austen and the Moralists." In *Critical Essays*. Vol. 1 of *Collected Papers*. New York, 1971.

Sabine, Gordon and Patricia. *Books that Made a Difference*. Hamden, Conn., 1983. Abridged ed., 1984.

Sacks, Sheldon. *Fiction and the Shape of Belief*. See ref. Chapter 3.

———, ed. *On Metaphor*. See ref. Chapter 10.

Sahlins, Marshall. *Culture and Practical Reason*. See ref. Chapter 11.

Said, Edward. *Orientalism*. New York, 1978.

———, ed. *Literature and Society*. Selected Papers from the English Institute, 1978, n.s. 3. Baltimore, 1980.

———. *The World, the Text, and the Critic*. Cambridge, Mass., 1983. (See Monroe 1985.)

Sanders, Wilbur. *John Donne's Poetry*. Cambridge, Eng., 1971.

Santayana, George. *The Sense of Beauty*. New York, 1896.

———. *Three Philosophical Poets*. See ref. Chapter 8.

———. *Skepticism and Animal Faith*. See ref. Chapter 4.

Sapir, J. David, and J. Christopher Crocker. *The Social Use of Metaphor: Essays on the Anthropology of Rhetoric*. Philadelphia, 1977.

Sartre, Jean-Paul. *What Is Literature?* See ref. Chapter 5.

Sattelmeyer, Robert, and J. Donald Crowley, eds. *One Hundred Years of "Huckleberry Finn."* See ref. Chapter 13.

Scarry, Elaine. *The Body in Pain*. See ref. Chapter 6.

Schaper, Eva. "Fiction and the Suspension of Disbelief." *British Journal of Aesthetics* 18 (Win. 1978): 31–44.

Scheffler, Israel. *Beyond the Letter: A Philosophical Inquiry into Ambiguity, Vagueness, and Metaphor in Language*. London, 1979.

Schiller, Friedrich von. *Naive and Sentimental Poetry* [1795]. Trans. Julius A. Elias. New York, 1966.

Schlegel, Friedrich von. ["The Subject-Matter of Poetry: The Ideal and the Actual."] Lecture 12 of *Lectures on the History of Literature* [1815]. Trans. Henry G. Bohn. London, 1873.

Schmidt, Siegfried J. "Towards a Pragmatic Interpretation of 'Fictionality.'" See ref. Chapter 9.

Schneider, Ben Ross, Jr. *The Ethos of Restoration Comedy*. Urbana, Ill., 1971.

Schneider, Daniel J. *The Consciousness of D. H. Lawrence*. See ref. Chapter 13.

Scholes, Robert. "The Illiberal Imagination." *New Literary History* 4 (Spr. 1973): 521–40.

———. *Fabulation and Metafiction*. Urbana, Ill., 1979.

———. *Textual Power: Literary Theory and the Teaching of English*. New Haven, Conn., 1985.

Scholes, Robert, and Robert Kellogg. *The Nature of Narrative*. New York, 1966.

Schön, Donald A. "Generative Metaphor." See ref. Chapter 10.

———. *The Reflective Practitioner: How Professionals Think in Action*. New York, 1983.

Schram, Peninnah. "One Generation Tells Another: The Transmission of Jewish Values through Storytelling." *Literature in Performance* 2 (Apr. 1984): 64–68.

Schreiber, S. M. *An Introduction to Literary Criticism.* See ref. Chapter 2.

Schudson, Michael. *Advertising, the Uneasy Persuasion: Its Dubious Impact on American Society.* New York, 1984.

Schwarz, Daniel R. *The Humanistic Heritage: Critical Theories of the English Novel from James to Hillis Miller.* Philadelphia, 1986.

Scott, Nathan. *Three American Moralists: Mailer, Bellow, Trilling.* Notre Dame, Ind., 1973.

Seabright, Paul. "The Pursuit of Unhappiness: Paradoxical Motivation and the Subversion of Character in Henry James's *Portrait of a Lady.*" In Becker 1988: 313–31.

Seaman, John E. *The Moral Paradox of "Paradise Lost."* The Hague, 1971.

Shahn, Ben. *The Shape of Content.* See ref. Chapter 1.

Shapiro, Barbara J. *Probability and Certainty in Seventeenth-Century England: A Study of the Relationships between Natural Science, Religion, History, Law, and Literature.* Princeton, N.J., 1983.

Sharp, Ronald A. *Friendship and Literature.* See ref. Chapter 6.

Shelley, Percy Bysshe. *A Defense of Poetry.* London, 1821.

Shklar, Judith. "Let Us Not Be Hypocritical." See ref. Chapter 8.

Showalter, Elaine, ed. *The New Feminist Criticism.* See ref. Chapter 12.

Shweder, Richard A. "Storytelling among the Anthropologists." *New York Times Book Review* (Sept. 21, 1986): 1, 38–39.

———. "Post-Nietzschian Anthropology: The Idea of Multiple Objective Worlds." In *Relativism: Confrontation and Interpretation.* Ed. Michael Krausz. Notre Dame, Ind., 1988.

Sidney, Sir Philip. *An Apologie for Poetrie.* See ref. Chapter 8.

Siegle, Robert. *The Politics of Reflexivity.* See ref. Chapter 3.

Simpson, Hilary. *D. H. Lawrence and Feminism.* See ref. Chapter 13.

Singer, Milton. "Personal and Social Identity in Dialogue." In Lee 1982: 129–37.

Sisk, John P. "The Promise of Dirty Words." *American Scholar* 44 (Sum. 1975): 385–404.

Skulsky, Harold. "On Being Moved by Fiction." *Journal of Aesthetics and Art Criticism* 34 (Fall 1980): 5–14.

Slatoff, Walter J. *With Respect to Readers: Dimensions of Literary Response.* Ithaca, N.Y., 1970.

———. *The Look of Distance: Reflections on Suffering and Sympathy in Modern Literature—Auden to Agee, Whitman to Woolf.* Columbus, Ohio, 1985.

Smith, Barbara Herrnstein. "The Ethics of Interpretation." See ref. Chapter 4.

———. "Contingencies of Value." See ref. Chapter 2.

Smith, David L. "Huck, Jim, and American Racial Discourse." See ref. Chapter 13.

Smith, Jonathan Z. *Imagining Religion.* See ref. Chapter 11.

Sollers, Philippe. *Writing and the Experience of Limits.* Ed. David Hayman. Trans. Philip Barnard. New York, 1983.

Sontag, Susan. *Against Interpretation.* New York, 1961.

———. "Pilgrimage." See ref. Chapter 8.

Southern Review. T. S. Eliot. [Anniversary issue] Vol. 21 (Aut. 1985).

Soupault, Philippe. *L'Amitié: Notes et maximes.* See ref. Chapter 6.

Soviet Studies in Literature: A Journal of Translations. See, as a representative of current Soviet ethical and political criticism, the three issues on *Urbanization and Literature: A Discussion* (Fall 1986; Win. 1986–87; Spr. 1987).

Spacks, Patricia M. *Imagining a Self.* Cambridge, Mass., 1976.

Sparshott, Francis. "Truth in Fiction." *Journal of Aesthetics and Art Criticism* 26 (Fall 1967): 3–7.

———. "The Case of the Unreliable Author." See ref. Chapter 5.

Spencer, Herbert. *Philosophy of Style: An Essay* [1852]. New York, 1873.

Spenko, James. "Psychoanalysis, Character, and Fictional Contexts." Ph.D. diss., University of Chicago, 1977.

Springer, Mary Doyle. *A Rhetoric of Literary Character: Some Women of Henry James.* Chicago, 1978.

Sprinker, Michael. "Fiction and Ideology." See ref. Chapter 1.

Starobinski, Jean. *Montaigne in Motion.* See ref. Chapter 8.

Stead, C. K. *The New Poetic: Yeats to Eliot.* London, 1964.

Stein, Walter. *Criticism as Dialogue.* Cambridge, 1969.

Stern, G. B. *Speaking of Jane Austen.* See ref. Chapter 13.

Sternberg, Meir. "The Bible's Art of Persuasion: Ideology, Rhetoric and Poetics in Saul's Fall." *Hebrew Union College Annual* 54 (1983): 45–82.

———. *The Poetics of Biblical Narrative: Ideological Literature and the Drama of Reading.* Bloomington, Ind., 1985.

Stimpson, Catharine R. "Ad/d Feminam: Women, Literature, and Society." In Said 1980: 174–92.

Stoehr, Taylor. "Pornography, Masturbation, and the Novel." *Salmagundi* 2 (1986): 28–56.

Stoyva, Johanna. Review of *The Adrian Mole Diaries,* by Sue Townsend. See ref. Chapter 8.

Strelka, Joseph, ed. *Problems of Literary Evaluation.* See ref. Chapter 2.

Strier, Richard. "Sanctifying the Aristocracy." See ref. Chapter 6.

Stroup, George. *The Promise of Narrative Theology: Recovering the Gospel in the Church.* Atlanta, Ga., 1981.

Strout, Cushing. "The Veracious Imagination." *Partisan Review,* no. 3 (1983): 428–43.

Suleiman, Susan. "Ideological Dissent from Works of Fiction." See ref. Chapter 1.

———. "Reading Robbe-Grillet: Sadism and Text in *Projet pour une revolution à New York." Romantic Review* 68 (Jan. 1977): 43–62.

———. *Authoritarian Fictions.* See ref. Chapter 1.

———. "Writing and Motherhood." In *The (M)other Tongue: Essays in Feminist Psychoanalytic Interpretation.* Ed. Shirley Nelson Garner, et al. Ithaca, N.Y., 1985.

———, ed. *The Female Body in Western Culture.* See ref. Chapter 12.

Suleiman, Susan, and Inge Crossman, eds. *The Reader in the Text.* See ref. Chapter 4.

Sullivan, D. Bradley. "'Education by Poetry' in Robert Frost's Masques." *Papers on Language and Literature* 22 (Sum. 1986): 312–21.

Tate, Allen. "Ezra Pound and the Bollingen Prize." See ref. Introduction to Part 3.

———. "Literature as Knowledge" [1941]. In *Essays of Four Decades*. Chicago, 1968.

Tave, Stuart. *Some Words of Jane Austen*. Chicago, 1973.

Taylor, Charles. "Responsibility for Self." See ref. Chapter 8.

———. *Philosophy and the Human Sciences*. Vol. 2 of *Philosophical Papers*. Cambridge, 1986.

———. Review of *The View from Nowhere*, by Thomas Nagle. *Times Literary Supplement* (Sept. 5, 1986): 962.

Taylor, Lynne, and Barbara Ann Schapiro, eds. *Narcissism and the Text: Studies in Literature and the Psychology of Self*. New York, 1986.

Thayer, Lee, ed. *Communication: Ethical and Moral Issues*. New York, 1973.

———, ed. *Ethics, Morality and the Media: Reflections on American Culture*. New York, 1980.

Theunissen, Michael. *The Other*. See ref. Chapter 3.

Theweleit, Klaus. *Male Fantasies*. See ref. Chapter 12.

Thorpe, James, ed. *The Aims and Methods of Scholarship*. See ref. Chapter 2.

Todorov, Tzvetan. *The Conquest of America*. See ref. Chapter 3.

———. "All against Humanity." See ref. Chapter 12.

———. *Literature and Its Theorists: A Personal View of Twentieth-Century Criticism*. Trans. Catherine Porter. Ithaca, N.Y., 1987. (See esp. pp. 122–68.)

Tolstoy, Leo. *What Is Art?* See ref. Chapter 3.

Tompkins, Jane P., ed. *Reader-Response Criticism*. See ref. Chapter 4.

———. "Sentimental Power: *Uncle Tom's Cabin* and the Politics of Literary History." *Glyph* 8 (1981): 79–102.

Torrey, Bradford. *Friends on the Shelf*. See ref. Chapter 6.

Tovey, Donald Francis. *Beethoven*. See ref. Chapter 1.

———. "The Materials of Beethoven's Language." See ref. Chapter 11.

Tracy, David. *Blessed Rage for Order*. See ref. Chapter 11.

Trilling, Diana, ed. *The Portable D. H. Lawrence*. See ref. Chapter 13.

Trilling, Lionel. *Matthew Arnold*. New York, 1939.

———. *E. M. Forster*. Binghamton, N.Y., 1947.

———. *The Liberal Imagination*. See ref. Chapter 1.

———. "The Fate of Pleasure." In *Beyond Culture*. New York, 1968.

———. "On the Teaching of Modern Literature." See ref. Chapter 3.

———. *Sincerity and Authenticity*. See ref. Chapter 8.

Trollope, Anthony. *An Autobiography*. See ref. Chapter 6.

Trotsky, Leon. *Literature and Revolution* [1923]. Trans. Rose Strunsky. Ann Arbor, Mich., 1966.

———. "Proletarian Culture and Proletarian Art." In Lang and Williams 1972: 60–79.

Trotter, David. *The Making of the Reader: Language and Subjectivity in Modern American, English, and Irish Poetry*. London, 1984.

Tucker, Nicholas, ed. *Suitable for Children? Controversies in Children's Literature*. Berkeley, 1976.

Tuckey, John S., ed. *The Devil's Race-Track*. See ref. Chapter 13.

Tuma, Keith, ed. "Some Things Worth Considering Before Beginning to Think about Poetry and Politics." [Special section] *The Chicago Review* 34 (Spr. 1984): 2–99.

Turnell, Martin. *Modern Literature and Christian Faith*. London, 1961.

Turner, Mark. *Death Is the Mother of Beauty: Mind, Metaphor, Criticism*. Chicago, 1987.

Turner, Victor. "Social Dramas and Stories about Them." In Mitchell 1980.

———. *On the Edge of the Bush: Anthropology as Experience*. Tucson, 1985.

Urmson, J. O. "What Makes a Situation Aesthetic?" *Proceedings of the Aristotelian Society* ([Supp. vol., London] 1957): 75–106.

Vernon, Richard. "*On Liberty,* Liberty and Censorship." *Queen's Quarterly* 94 (Sum. 1987): 267–85.

Vico, Giambattista. *The New Science of Giambattista Vico* [1725, 1730]. Trans. T. G. Bergin and M. H. Fisch. Ithaca, N.Y., 1968.

von Cranach, Mario, and Rom Harré, eds. *The Analysis of Action*. See ref. Chapter 2.

von Hallberg, Robert, ed. *Canons*. See ref. Chapter 2.

———, ed. *Politics and Poetic Value*. [Special issue] *Critical Inquiry* 13 (Spr. 1987). Reprint. Chicago, 1987.

Vygotsky, Lev Semenovich. *Thought and Language*. See ref. Chapter 11.

Waldron, Jeremy. "Judgments of Justice." See ref. Chapter 4.

Walker, Peter. *Moral Choices: Memory, Desire, and Imagination in Nineteenth-Century American Letters*. Baton Rouge, La., 1979.

Wallace, John M. "*Timon of Athens* and the Three Graces." See ref. Chapter 6.

Wallace, Karl R. "An Ethical Basis of Communication." *Speech Teacher* 4 (Jan. 1955): 1–9.

Wallis, N. Hardy. *"The Ethics of Criticism" and Other Essays*. See ref. Chapter 2.

Warren, Robert Penn. "Pure and Impure Poetry" [1943]. *Selected Essays of Robert Penn Warren*. New York, 1958.

Watson, Walter. *The Architectonics of Meaning*. See ref. Chapter 5.

Watts-Dunton, Theodore. *Old Familiar Faces*. See ref. Chapter 6.

Weaver, Richard. *Ideas Have Consequences*. Chicago, 1948.

———. *The Ethics of Rhetoric*. Chicago, 1953.

Weintraub, Karl Joachim. *The Value of the Individual*. See ref. Chapter 8.

Wellek, René. "Criticism as Evaluation." See ref. Chapter 2.

Wenzel, Siegfried. *Preachers, Poets, and the Early English Lyric*. Princeton, N.J., 1986.

Wertsch, James V. *Vygotsky and the Social Formation of Mind*. Cambridge, Mass., 1986.

Weston, Michael. *Morality and the Self*. New York, 1975.

Whateley, Richard. *Historic Doubts Relative to Napoleon Bonaparte*. See ref. Chapter 11.

White, Hayden. *Metahistory*. See ref. Chapter 1.

———. "The Politics of Historical Interpretation: Discipline and De-Sublimation." In Mitchell 1982.

White, James Boyd. *When Words Lose Their Meaning*. See ref. Chapter 11.

"Why the Novel Matters: A Postmodern Perplex." [Conference issue; nineteen pertinent essays] *Novel: A Forum on Fiction* 21 (Win./Spr. 1988): 121–238.

Wieman, Henry N., and Otis M. Walter. "Toward an Analysis of Ethics for Rhetoric." *Quarterly Journal of Speech* 43 (Oct. 1957): 266–70.
Wilde, Oscar. "The Decay of Lying." See ref. Chapter 1.
Williams, Bernard. *Ethics and the Limits of Philosophy.* See ref. Chapter 1.
Williams, Raymond. *Marxism and Literature.* See ref. Chapter 1.
——. *Writing in Society.* London, 1983.
Williams, Tennessee. Preface. *Collected Stories.* See ref. Chapter 5.
Wilson, Edmund. "Marxism and Literature." In *The Triple Thinkers.* New York, 1938.
——. "Why Do People Read Detective Stories?" See ref. Chapter 1.
——. "Who Cares Who Killed Roger Ackroyd?" See ref. Chapter 1.
——. "A Long Talk about Jane Austen." See ref. Chapter 13.
Wilt, Judith. "The Powers of the Instrument." See ref. Chapter 13.
Wimsatt, W. K. "Poetry and Morals: A Relation Reargued." In *The Verbal Icon: Studies in the Meaning of Poetry.* Lexington, Ky., 1954.
Wind, Edgar. *The Eloquence of Symbols.* See ref. Chapter 1.
Winterowd, W. Ross. "The Purification of Literature and Rhetoric." *College English* 49 (Mar. 1987): 257–73.
Winters, Yvor. *In Defense of Reason.* See ref. Chapter 3.
Wittgenstein, Ludwig. *Tractatus Logico-Philosophicus.* See ref. Chapter 11.
——. "A Lecture on Ethics." See ref. Chapter 2.
Wolterstorff, Nicholas. *Works and Worlds of Art.* See ref. Chapter 11.
Woodruff, Paul. "Rousseau, Molière, and the Ethics of Laughter." *Philosophy and Literature* 1 (1976–77): 325–36.
Wordsworth, William. Preface. *Lyrical Ballads* [1800, 1802]. Ed. R. L. Brett and A. R. Jones. 1963. Rev. ed., 1965. Reprint. 1981.
Yeats, William Butler. *Autobiography.* New York, 1953.
Zimmerman, Michael E. *Eclipse of the Self: The Development of Heidegger's Concept of Authenticity* [1981]. Rev. ed. Columbus, Ohio, 1986.

Index of Subjects

Since the indexes of my previous books have sometimes led readers to identify me with views that I reject or question, I offer a friendly warning: many of the ideas indexed here are questioned in the text. The resulting mixture of "mine" and "theirs" may cause some inconvenience for those who read on the run.

(*see also* Conduct; Consequences; Witnesses); diversity of, 67–69, 97–100; ethics of, 9–10, 483–89; freedom of, to withdraw, 141; implied, and flesh-and-blood reader, distinction blurred, 204–5; roles of, 125, 251–60. *See also* Responsibilities, of reader
Reader-response criticism, 83–84, 83n.3
Readers and authors: constituted by stories, 42, 124, 128, 264; as equals, 184–85; as friends (*see* Friendship); inequality of, 100, 185–87
Reading: aloud, 439; constituting selves, 42, 124, 128, 264; as conversation, 157; as interpretation, indeterminate, 80; as meeting of minds, 107; as thinking thoughts of another, 142. *See also* Re-reading
Realism, as standard, 146, 295n.2
Reality: vs. fiction, 14–16; made by stories (*see* Reading: constituting selves); as referred to in stories, 124n; underlying all responsibilities, 133
"Real" world, vs. mythic worlds, 339–40
Reasons: modernist skepticism about, 349; reduced to power games, 384–85; vs. rationalization, 385
Reception, passive, questioned, 295n.3. *See also* Friendship: literary, measures of
Reciprocity of activity, between author and reader, quality of, 179–81, 184–87
Re-creation of stories, wonder of, 138–39
Reflexivity, 40–42, 140
Relativism: refutations of, 82, 346, 348n, 364; as threat, 166, 330, 339
Relativity: of ethical criticism to ethos of readers, 489; total, rejected, 489. *See also* Subjectivism
Religion, 43; "conversation" about in fiction, 453; in Lawrence, 453–54; as tested by philosophy, 358–62
Re-reading, as antidote to superficial ethical criticism, 74–75, 437–39, 443
Reserve, cool, as quality in reader's activity. *See* Intimacy
Responsibilities: defined, 125; distinguished, 42, 126–41
Responsibilities of author: as career author, 129; to implied reader, 127; to

reader's soul, 24, 126–27; to self, 128; to society, 132, chap. 12; to those used as subjects, 130, 130n; to truth, 132–33, 132n; to work of art, 127
Responsibilities of reader: to author, 150; to disagree with implied author, 135, 136, 414; to flesh-and-blood writer, 134; to his or her own soul, 135–36, 164; to implied author, 9–10, 135, 151, 164–65; to other readers, 136; to society, 136–37; to work of art, 135
Responsibility: etymology of, 126n.3; for what we are to become, 483, chap. 9 passim; of writer, to his or her own implied author, 128
Revaluation, 74–75, 110; of canon, 384; as ethical criticism, 105
Rhetoric, fiction as, 13. *See also* Conduct; Consequences; Ethical gifts
Rhetoric, suspicion of, in Locke, 313–14
Rhetorical choice of standards, 70
Rhetorical criticism, 57, 127
Roles: choosing among, 265; playing of, as formation of character, 251–60
Romantic endings, 458–59n.14
Romanticism, 25
Romantic literature, harmful effects of, 425–26
Rules, general, questioned, 51, 151. *See also* Lumping criticism; Universals

Salesmanship, ethics of, 40
Satires, as fictions, 14
Science: dependent on myth, 353–54; metaphoric, 302n.10; "conversation" about in fiction, 455
Scientific myths, attacks on, 351
Second nature, as constituted by literature, 249, 257
Self: inner, vs. "character," chap. 8 passim; as not bounded by skin, 239–40; reader's, duty to, 414–15; social (*see* Social self). *See also* Individual; Individualism
Self-abasement, authors showing, 186
Self-advertisement, macro-metaphor as, 332
Self-cultivation, vs. consequentialism, 166
Self-privileging discourse, 385, 385n
Sexism: in classics (*see* Feminist criticism); in Rabelais, 394–408
Sexual freedom, as banal fixed norm, 441–42

Index of Names and Titles

Mentions of names in the acknowledgments, end-of-chapter references, and bibliography are not included in the index.

Designer: Mark Ong
Compositor: G & S Typesetters, Inc.
Text: 10/13 Sabon
Display: Sabon
Printer: Maple-Vail Book Mfg. Group
Binder: Maple-Vail Book Mfg. Group